T0073945

THERANOSTICS AND PRECISION MEDICINE FOR THE MANAGEMENT OF HEPATOCELLULAR CARCINOMA
VOLUME 3

THERANOSTICS AND PRECISION MEDICINE FOR THE MANAGEMENT OF HEPATOCELLULAR CARCINOMA VOLUME 3

Translational and Clinical Outcomes

Edited by

GANJI PURNACHANDRA NAGARAJU, PhD, DSc, FAACC
*School of Medicine, Division of Hematology and Oncology, University of Alabama,
Birmingham, AL, United States*

SARFRAZ AHMAD, PhD, FAACC, FABAP
*AdventHealth Cancer Institute, Florida State University (FSU) and University of Central Florida (UCF),
Colleges of Medicine, Orlando, FL, United States*

ELSEVIER

ACADEMIC PRESS
An imprint of Elsevier

Academic Press is an imprint of Elsevier
125 London Wall, London EC2Y 5AS, United Kingdom
525 B Street, Suite 1650, San Diego, CA 92101, United States
50 Hampshire Street, 5th Floor, Cambridge, MA 02139, United States
The Boulevard, Langford Lane, Kidlington, Oxford OX5 1GB, United Kingdom

Copyright © 2022 Elsevier Inc. All rights reserved.

No part of this publication may be reproduced or transmitted in any form or by any means, electronic or mechanical, including photocopying, recording, or any information storage and retrieval system, without permission in writing from the publisher. Details on how to seek permission, further information about the Publisher's permissions policies and our arrangements with organizations such as the Copyright Clearance Center and the Copyright Licensing Agency, can be found at our website: www.elsevier.com/permissions.

This book and the individual contributions contained in it are protected under copyright by the Publisher (other than as may be noted herein).

Notices

Knowledge and best practice in this field are constantly changing. As new research and experience broaden our understanding, changes in research methods, professional practices, or medical treatment may become necessary.

Practitioners and researchers must always rely on their own experience and knowledge in evaluating and using any information, methods, compounds, or experiments described herein. In using such information or methods they should be mindful of their own safety and the safety of others, including parties for whom they have a professional responsibility.

To the fullest extent of the law, neither the Publisher nor the authors, contributors, or editors, assume any liability for any injury and/or damage to persons or property as a matter of products liability, negligence or otherwise, or from any use or operation of any methods, products, instructions, or ideas contained in the material herein.

ISBN: 978-0-323-99283-1

For Information on all Academic Press publications
visit our website at https://www.elsevier.com/books-and-journals

Publisher: Stacy Masucci
Acquisitions Editor: Rafael Teixeira
Editorial Project Manager: Tracy Tufaga
Production Project Manager: Sreejith Viswanathan
Cover Designer: Mark Rogers

Typeset by MPS Limited, Chennai, India

Working together
to grow libraries in
developing countries

www.elsevier.com • www.bookaid.org

Dedication

This book is dedicated to our families, teachers, contributors, and friends.

Contents

Contents

26. Epigenetic biomarkers in diagnosis, prognosis, and treatment of hepatocellular carcinoma   415

Eka Kvaratskhelia, Ketevani Kankava, Sandro Surmava and
Elene Abzianidze

List of contributors

Elene Abzianidze Department of Molecular and Medical Genetics, Tbilisi State Medical University, Tbilisi, Georgia

Sarfraz Ahmad AdventHealth Cancer Institute, FSU and UCF Colleges of Medicine, Orlando, FL, United States

Nadia Ahmed Texas College of Osteopathic Medicine, University of North Texas Health Science Center, Fort Worth, TX, United States

Zohaib Ahmed Department of Internal Medicine, AdventHealth, Orlando, FL, United States

Afroz Alam Department of Bioscience and Biotechnology, Banasthali University, Vanasthali, India

Hufsa Ali Texas College of Osteopathic Medicine, University of North Texas Health Science Center, Fort Worth, TX, United States

Sheik Aliya Department of Biological Engineering, NanoBio High-Tech Materials Research Center, Inha University, Incheon, Republic of Korea

Vinit Singh Baghel Department of Biotechnology, Guru Ghasidas Vishwavidyalaya, Bilaspur, India

Obul Reddy Bandapalli Medical Faculty, University of Heidelberg, Heidelberg, Germany; Applied Biology, Indian Institute of Chemical Technology (CSIR-IICT), Hyderabad, India; Hopp Children's Cancer Center (KiTZ), Heidelberg, Germany; Division of Pediatric Neuro Oncology, German Cancer Research Center (DKFZ), German Cancer Consortium (DKTK), Heidelberg, Germany

Riyaz Basha Texas College of Osteopathic Medicine, University of North Texas Health Science Center, Fort Worth, TX, United States

Kevin Benny Texas College of Osteopathic Medicine, University of North Texas Health Science Center, Fort Worth, TX, United States

Ali Ayberk Beşen Başkent Üniversitesi Tıp Fakültesi Tıbbi Onkoloji BD, Adana, Turkey

L.V.K.S. Bhaskar Department of Zoology, Guru Ghasidas Vishwavidyalaya, Bilaspur, India

Produtur Chandramathi Shankar Department of Biotechnology, Yogi Vemana University, Kadapa, India

Amooru G. Damu Department of Chemistry, Biotechnology and Bioinformatics, Yogi Vemana University, Kadapa, India

Said Dermime National Center for Cancer Care and Research, Hamad Medical Corporation, Doha, Qatar; Translational Cancer Research Facility and Clinical Trial Unit, Translational Research Institute, Hamad Medical Corporation, Doha, Qatar

Ashwini Kumar Dixit Department of Botany, Guru Ghasidas Vishwavidyalaya, Bilaspur, India

Vineeta Dixit Department of Zoology, Dr. Bhanvar Singh Porte Govt. College, Pendra, India

Mrigendra Dwivedi Department of Biochemistry, Government Nagarjuna Post Graduate College of Science Raipur, Raipur, India

Sudhakar Dwivedi MDRU, Shyam Shah Medical College, Rewa, India

Aimen Farooq Department of Internal Medicine, AdventHealth, Orlando, FL, United States

Baha Aldeen Bani Fawwaz Department of Internal Medicine, AdventHealth, Orlando, FL, United States

Mohan Krishna Ghanta Department of Pharmacology, MVJ Medical College and Research Hospital, Bangalore, India

Mengni Guo Department of Internal Medicine, AdventHealth, Orlando, FL, United States

Yun Suk Huh Department of Biological Engineering, NanoBio High-Tech Materials Research Center, Inha University, Incheon, Republic of Korea

Mohammad Faiz Hussain Department of General Surgery, Apollo Institute of Medical Sciences and Research, General Hospital, Hyderabad, India

Mohammad Imran Innatura Scientific Pvt. Ltd, Rangareddy, Secunderabad, Telangana, India

Anum Jalil Department of Internal Medicine, AdventHealth, Orlando, FL, United States

Ketevani Kankava Department of Molecular and Medical Genetics, Tbilisi State Medical University, Tbilisi, Georgia

Asmita Karnalkar Department of Anaesthesia, BKL Rural Medical College & Hospital, Ratnagiri, India

Sikandar Khan Department of Internal Medicine, Cleveland Clinic Florida, Weston, FL, United States

Patnala Kiranmayi Department of Biotechnology, Institute of Science Gandhi Institute of Technology and Management, Visakhapatnam, India

Ajay Kumar Department of Zoology, Banaras Hindu University, Varanasi, India

B.D. Ranjitha Kumari Department of Botany, Bharathidasan University, Tiruchirappalli, India

Eka Kvaratskhelia Department of Molecular and Medical Genetics, Tbilisi State Medical University, Tbilisi, Georgia

Dhatri Madduru Department of Biochemistry, Osmania University, Hyderabad, India

Kalisetty Chengaiahgari Maheswari Department of Biotechnology, Sri Venkateswara University, Tirupati, India

Rama Rao Malla Cancer Biology Lab, Department of Biochemistry and Bioinformatics, Institute of Sciences, GITAM (Deemed to be University), Visakhapatnam, India

Devanabanda Mallaiah Department of Biotechnology & Bioinformatics, Yogi Vemana University, Kadapa, India

Nivethitha Manickam School of Life Sciences, Bharathidasan University, Tiruchirappalli, India

Arundhati Mehta Department of Biotechnology, Guru Ghasidas Vishwavidyalaya, Bilaspur, India

Neha Merchant Department of Bioscience and Biotechnology, Banasthali University, Vanasthali, India

Madelyn Miller Burnett School of Biomedical Sciences, College of Medicine, University of Central Florida, Orlando, FL, United States

Rafael Miret Department of Internal Medicine, Cleveland Clinic Florida, Weston, FL, United States

Anil Kumar Moola Department of Biotechnology, Aditya Degree and PG College, Kakinada, India; Department of Entomology, College of Agriculture, Food and Environment, Agriculture Science Center North, University of Kentucky, Lexington, Kentucky, United States

Sirpu Natesh Nagabhishek Cancer Biology Lab, Molecular and Nanomedicine Research Unit, Sathyabama Institute of Science and Technology, Chennai, India

Ganji Purnachandra Nagaraju School of Medicine, Division of Hematology and Medical Oncology, University of Alabama, Birmingham, AL, United States

Venkata Prasuja Nakka Department of Biochemistry, Acharya Nagarjuna University, Nagarjuna Nagar, India

Poojith Nuthalapati PJ Biousys, Irving, TX, United States

Deepika Pamarthy Applied Biology Department, Council of Scientific and Industrial Research-Indian Institute of Chemical Technology, Hyderabad, India

Ramachandra Reddy Pamuru Department of Biochemistry, Yogi Vemana University, Kadapa, India

Sanjay Kumar Pandey MDRU, Shyam Shah Medical College, Rewa, India

Pranathi Pappu BIOCLUES Organization, Hyderabad, India

Kalyani Patil Translational Research Institute, Academic Health System, Hamad Medical Corporation, Doha, Qatar

Sujatha Peela Department of Biotechnology, Dr. B.R. Ambedkar University, Srikakulam, India

Asad Ur Rahman Department of Gastroenterology and Hepatology, Cleveland Clinic Florida, Weston, FL, United States

Ganji Seeta Rama Raju Department of Energy and Materials Engineering, Dongguk University, Seoul, Republic of Korea

Yashwant Kumar Ratre Department of Biotechnology, Guru Ghasidas Vishwavidyalaya, Bilaspur, India

S. Geetha Renuka Department of Obstetrics and Gynecology, Theni Medical College, Theni, India

Amir Riaz Department of Internal Medicine, Cleveland Clinic Florida, Weston, FL, United States

Kallimakula Venkata Reddy Saritha Department of Biotechnology, Sri Venkateswara University, Tirupati, India

Harish Kumar Seenivasan School of Life Sciences, Bharathidasan University, Tiruchirappalli, India

Jeelan Basha Shaik Department of Chemistry, Biotechnology and Bioinformatics, Yogi Vemana University, Kadapa, India

Archana Ashok Sharbidre Department of Zoology, Savitribai Phule Pune University, Pune, India

Sapnita Shinde Department of Biotechnology, Guru Ghasidas Vishwavidyalaya, Bilaspur, India

Dhananjay Shukla Department of Biotechnology, Guru Ghasidas Vishwavidyalaya, Bilaspur, India

Shadab A. Siddiqi Burnett School of Biomedical Sciences, College of Medicine, University of Central Florida, Orlando, FL, United States

Gurdeep Singh Department of Internal Medicine, AdventHealth, Orlando, FL, United States

Mrinalini Singh Experimental Biology Division, Defense Institute of Physiology and Allied Sciences, Timarpur, India

Vibha Sinha Department of Biotechnology, Guru Ghasidas Vishwavidyalaya, Bilaspur, India

Sohail Siraj Texas College of Osteopathic Medicine, University of North Texas Health Science Center, Fort Worth, TX, United States

Vivek Kumar Soni Department of Biotechnology, Guru Ghasidas Vishwavidyalaya, Bilaspur, India

Vishwas Soumya Department of Biotechnology, Institute of Science Gandhi Institute of Technology and Management, Visakhapatnam, India

Gowru Srivani Department of Biosciences and Biotechnology, Banasthali University, Banasthali, India

Ngalah Bidii Stephen Molecular Preventive Medicine, University Medical Center and Faculty of Medicine, University of Freiburg, Freiburg, Germany; Medical Faculty, University of Heidelberg, Heidelberg, Germany

Ahmet Sümbül Taner Başkent Üniversitesi Tıp Fakültesi Tıbbi Onkoloji BD, Adana, Turkey

Ganganapalli Supraja Department of Biotechnology, Sri Venkateswara University, Tirupati, India

Prashanth Suravajhala Department of Biotechnology and Bioinformatics, Birla Institute of Scientific Research (BISR), Jaipur, India

Sandro Surmava Department of Molecular and Medical Genetics, Tbilisi State Medical University, Tbilisi, Georgia

Chandrasekhar Thummala Department of Environmental Science, Yogi Vemana University, Kadapa, India

Atul Kumar Tiwari Department of Zoology, Dr. Bhanvar Singh Porte Govt. College, Pendra, India

Shahab Uddin Translational Research Institute, Academic Health System, Hamad Medical Corporation, Doha, Qatar; Dermatology Institute, Academic Health System, Hamad Medical Corporation, Doha, Qatar; Laboratory Animal Research Center, Qatar University, Doha, Qatar

Ramakrishna Vadde Department of Biotechnology & Bioinformatics, Yogi Vemana University, Kadapa, India

Rahul Kumar Vempati Cancer Biology Lab, Department of Biochemistry and Bioinformatics, Institute of Sciences, GITAM (Deemed to be University), Visakhapatnam, India

Sarojamma Vemula Department of Microbiology, Government Medical College, Anantapur, India

Urvashi Vijay Department of Immunology and Microbiology, SMS Medical College, Jaipur, India

Naveen Kumar Vishvakarma Department of Biotechnology, Guru Ghasidas Vishwavidyalaya, Bilaspur, India

James Wert Department of Internal Medicine, AdventHealth, Orlando, FL, United States

James Yu Department of Internal Medicine, AdventHealth, Orlando, FL, United States

Vadim Zaytsev Department of Internal Medicine, Bridgeport Hospital, Bridgeport, CT, United States

About the editors

Editors: Dr. Ganji Purnachandra Nagaraju, PhD, DSc, FAACC; Dr. Sarfraz Ahmad, PhD, FAACC, FABAP

Dr. Ganji Purnachandra Nagaraju is an assistant professor in the School of Medicine, Division of Hematology and Oncology at University of Alabama, Birmingham, Alabama, United States. Dr. Nagaraju obtained his MSc and his PhD, both in biotechnology, from Sri Venkateswara University in Tirupati, Andhra Pradesh, India. Dr. Nagaraju received his DSc from Berhampur University in Berhampur, Odisha, India. Dr. Nagaraju's research focuses on translational projects related to gastrointestinal malignancies. He has published over 100 research/review papers in highly reputed international journals and has presented more than 50 abstracts at various national and international conferences. He has trained and continues to train many fellows, residents, medical students, and graduate/undergraduate students.

Dr. Nagaraju is an author and an editor of several books published by Springer Nature and Elsevier. He serves as an editorial board member of several internationally recognized academic journals. Dr. Nagaraju has received several international awards, including FAACC. He also holds memberships with the Association of Scientists of Indian Origin in America (ASIOA), the Society for Integrative and Comparative Biology (SICB), the Science Advisory Board, the RNA Society, the American Association for Clinical Chemistry (AACC), American Society for Clinical Pathology (ASCP), and the American Association of Cancer Research (AACR).

Dr. Sarfraz Ahmad is Director of Clinical Research at AdventHealth Medical Group and AdventHealth Cancer Institute (AHCI), Orlando, Florida, United States. He earned his PhD degree in Biochemistry from North-Eastern Hill University, Shillong, India. Before joining AHCI in 2002, he spent 2 years at Indian Institute of Technology, Delhi, India, as researcher, and 10 years in research/teaching at Loyola University of Chicago and University of Illinois at Chicago's Division of Hematology/Oncology, College of Medicine in the United States.

Currently, he is also a professor of Medical Education at University of Central Florida College of Medicine and a professor of Clinical Sciences at Florida State University College of Medicine, Orlando, United States. He has trained numerous fellows, residents, medical students, and graduate/undergraduate students during their scholarly research projects and theses.

Dr. Ahmad's current research focus is on the analyses of clinicopathologic and surgical outcomes of oncology, hematology, and gastroenterology (GI) patients and to better understand the cellular/molecular mechanisms of cancer and related thromboembolic/hematologic disorders. His investigations are also aimed toward the evaluation of novel treatment options (chemo/cellular/immunotherapies) for better management of hemato-oncologic and GI patients. His past research interests focused on the anticoagulant, antithrombin, antiplatelet, and thrombolytic drug development for the management of hematologic and cardiovascular patients. In these various areas of biomedical research and international collaborations, Dr. Ahmad has published over 200 peer-reviewed scholarly research articles and book chapters, and nearly 400 scientific abstracts, which are extensively cited globally. He is a reviewer and has editorial responsibilities for several biomedical journals and books; and has received several competitive research grants and national/international awards for his research contributions/accomplishments. In addition to biomedical science endeavors, Dr. Ahmad is passionate about classical Hindi—Urdu literature and poetry and takes pride with active participation in such forums.

Preface

Hepatocellular carcinoma (HCC) is a major form of primary liver cancer that has emerged as one of the most frequently diagnosed human malignancies worldwide. It predominantly targets individuals with underlying conditions, such as cirrhosis and hepatitis B and hepatitis C infections. Despite the widespread occurrences of HCC, its underlying mechanisms that lead to tumor progression are still unclear. In contrast to various other cancers, systemic therapies for HCC, including chemotherapy and radiotherapy, are not effective enough. Currently, the only viable options for managing advanced HCC are surgical resection and transplantation. Therefore it is crucial to investigate pathways and factors that lead to HCC tumor suppression, thereby advancing novel therapeutic and management options for HCC.

In the current series, we have three different volumes. Volume 1 discusses the biology, pathophysiology, and progression of HCC. Volume 2 discusses multiple signaling and molecular mechanisms/targets associated with HCC progression and metastasis, including renowned and novel biomarkers, as well as diagnostic approaches for advanced HCC. Volume 3 includes a detailed discussion about the translational and clinical outcomes as it relates to the application of nanoparticles, small molecules, phytochemicals, and precision medicine for HCC treatment and management.

Nanoparticles are essential players in contemporary treatment strategies as its diverse application spans from magnetic resonance imaging contrast enhancers to drug delivery agents into the tumor. Chapters 1–3 discuss the elaborate role of nanoparticles and small molecules in HCC theranostic applications. Next, the application of phytochemicals, including curcumin and resveratrol, in liver neoplasm is discussed. Further, nanoparticles formulated from phytochemicals or phyto-nano-formulations and their applicability in HCC treatment are elucidated. Multiple immune checkpoint inhibitors for HCC are outlined.

Further, this volume examines recent developments in the field of immunotherapy for managing HCC with updated clinical trials. It scrutinizes precision medicine approaches in detail applied toward HCC treatment. The expanding role of extracellular vesicles in modulating explicit aspects of HCC advancement, angiogenesis, and metastasis is discussed. The structure, function, tumorigenesis, and prognostic value of cathepsin B are explained briefly. Moreover, recent updates and developments in chemotherapy, which is the most substantial treatment option for advanced HCC, have been evaluated. Finally, recent advances in the medical treatment strategies, perspectives on the therapeutic importance of mRNAs, and pharmacogenomics for HCC are scrutinized.

The aim of this series is to illustrate the biology, pathophysiology, diagnosis, therapeutic targets, and clinical significance of HCC. Understanding these roles could provide important steps forward in evaluating disease progression and potential therapeutic strategies. This series will provide novel ideas to researchers and scholars as well as innovative future perspectives in the field of research and clinical applications.

Ganji Purnachandra Nagaraju
Sarfraz Ahmad

Nanoparticles for diagnosis and treatment of hepatocellular carcinoma

Sheik Aliya and Yun Suk Huh

Department of Biological Engineering, NanoBio High-Tech Materials Research Center,
Inha University, Incheon, Republic of Korea

Abstract

Primary liver cancer universally continues to be one of the leading causes of health problem. Hepatocellular carcinoma (HCC), is a prominent form of primary liver cancer, is also the major cause of cancer-related death worldwide due to lack of proper diagnosis at the early stage of the disease and scarce of appropriate treatment tools. Thus there is high demand for a novel therapeutic approach to treat HCC. Nanotechnology is presently a fast-growing field which offers infinite prospects to design nanoscale products with imaging, diagnosis, and treatment purpose. Forty-five papers were included in the review, most of them contributed latest research related to nanoparticle-based targeted therapy for HCC cancer. Nanoparticles with significant therapeutic potential in clinical trials have been discussed and some of the major limitations are also addressed.

Keywords: Hepatocellular carcinoma; liver cancer; nanoparticles; drug delivery

Abbreviations

ATO	Arsenic trioxide
Au-NPs	Gold NPs
CMCNP-GL	*O*-carboxymethyl chitosan NP modified with glycyrrhizin
CUR	Curcumin
DSN	Diosin
DT	Doxorubicin-Transdrug
FDA	Food and drug administration
GA	Glycyrrhetinic acid
HCC	Hepatocellular carcinoma
MSN	Mesoporous silica nanoparticles

Ganji Purnachandra Nagaraju, Sarfraz Ahmad (eds.)
Theranostics and Precision Medicine for the Management of Hepatocellular Carcinoma, Volume 3
DOI: https://doi.org/10.1016/B978-0-323-99283-1.00023-9

© 2022 Elsevier Inc. All rights reserved.

NPs	Nanoparticles
PEAL-NPs	mPEG-PLGA-PLL copolymer-based NPs
RNAi	RNA interference
SLNs	Solid lipid nanoparticles
SPIONs	Superparamagnetic ironoxide nanoparticles
TiO-NPs	Titanium oxide NPs

Introduction

Hepatocellular carcinoma (HCC), a primary liver cancer, statistically stands in the third position causing major cancer-related death worldwide. Conventional HCC treatment includes curative and palliative care, but it is not effective as the cancer is detected at the advanced stage. Surgical resection is one of the best options considered. While it is limited to patients with metastatic tumors and high chances of recurrent have decreased the survival rate of HCC patient. Chemotherapy is one of the best therapeutic modalities, but the main drawback is the lack of target specificity which leads to damage of the normal cells and concurrent administration leads to the development of drug resistance. Another big challenge with HCC patients is 80%−90% develop liver cirrhosis, which burdens the patient with two diseases [1]. The major reasons for failure in therapy are poor absorption, insolubility of the drug, high fluctuations in blood due to lack of bioavailability, its rapid metabolism and elimination. Thus there is demand for an effective therapeutic strategy to combat advanced or recurrent HCC by developing a drug carrier system.

Cancer Nanotechnology is rapidly growing toward the development of anticancer nanoagents which promises to improve the therapeutic approach against dreadful disease cancer. Nanoparticles (NPs) (nanosize particles of range 1−100 nm) due to their unique properties have wide application promisingly in tumor diagnosis and therapy. Nanosize makes it advantageous as it effectively enters the cell promising it a potential drug delivery system. Peter Speiser, a pioneer who introduced NPs to the world, developed it for vaccination drives, designed to release antigen in a slow pace leading to enhanced immune response than the conventional ones. The group discovered lysosomotropic effect of NPs, the nanocapsules induce drugs into the cells without intracellular accumulation. The properties such as low drug systemic toxicity and targeting specific tumors mark the NPs to have the promising application [2]. Active pharmaceutical ingredients with poor pharmacokinetics and biodistribution are delivered through NPs with low cost, less risk, marginal toxicity, and with high efficiency. With multifunctionality and advanced targeting strategy, NPs are reported to have significant applications in nanomedicine as contrast agents in bioimaging and drug carriers to target tumors [3]. Clinically, to diagnose HCC, ultrasound is the common imaging method applied. However, the sensitivity of this method is limited to 60%−80% only, as it cannot distinguish between normal tissues and lesion ones. Lesions less than 5 mm are not visualized. The imaging modalities include photoacoustic imaging and fluorescence imaging has its own limitation. Recently, photothermal therapy has gained a lot of interest in cancer treatment for its nominal invasiveness. Infrared laser irradiation is used along with photoabsorbers to burn tumor tissue with high specificity. NPs with strong NIR region optical absorbance are currently used in photothermal therapy, they include gold NPs (Au-NPs), carbon nanotubes, Prussian blue NPs, polypyrrole NPs, and copper NPs. Among them, the potential photoacoustic/photothermal imaging agent used for HCC diagnosis and treatment is polypyrrole NPs tagged with SP94 (SFSIIHTPILPL; HCC target peptide). These uniformly tagged NPs exhibit low cytotoxicity, high specificity for HCC cells, high stability, and efficient photothermal conversion proves it to be a potential candidate [4,5]. Normally, NPs injected intravenously are taken up by the liver by opsonization through size-dependent passive targeting process. Studies have been performed on the intracellular transport mechanism of NPs in cells. It has been observed that intracellular trafficking of NPs and its uptake mechanism are different in different cell lines [6]. Active targeting is an effective approach which can be achieved by decorating or glycosylating NPs with a ligand which has high specificity to asialoglycoprotein receptors (highly expressed on hepatoma cells). Notably, HCC patients are reported to exhibit different clinical symptoms mainly because of difference in properties of hepatoma cells [7]. Thus recently a lot of research is done in search of effective NPs to cure HCC. The NPs which are successfully used in the treatment of HCC are represented in Fig. 1.1. Multifunctional NPs are designed or constructed with a combination of drugs to enhance therapeutic effect and a combination of drug with imaging agent to enhance both therapeutic and diagnosis of liver disease [8]. Therefore this review highlights the application of different NPs-based diagnosis and targeted therapy against HCC.

Chitosan nanoparticles

Chitosan, a derivative of chitin (present in the shells of crustaceans and cell wall of fungi), a biodegradable biocompatible polymer, has been approved for drug delivery and tissue engineering (wound dressing) by the US Food and drug administration (US-FDA). Since it is regarded as safe for human consumption, its modified form is exploited in a wide range of potential biomedical applications. NPs derived from chitosan and its derivatives have been used for cancer treatment, heart and lung diseases, drug delivery to

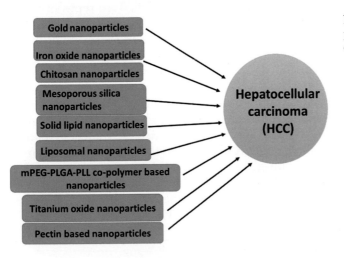

FIGURE 1.1 Different types of nanoparticles used in the treatment of hepatocellular carcinoma.

infected liver, brain, and ocular cells. These NPs carry surface positive charges, mucoadhesive properties and have been reported to be exhibiting low toxicity in both in vitro and in vivo, make it an efficient human drug delivery system [9]. A substantial number of experimental studies have been done to understand the interaction between NPs with different surface charges and the cell membrane. It has been reported that electrostatic interaction during phagocytosis mechanism mainly increased the uptake of charged chitosan NPs by macrophages compared to the neutral particles. While in no-phagocytic normal human liver cell line L02 and hepatoma cell line SMMC-7721, it was observed that positively charged chitosan NPs were taken up in large amounts into the cells compared to the negatively charged ones due to the force (attractive/repulsive) between charged NPs and the negatively charged cancer cell membrane [10]. In another study paclitaxel, a potent anticancer drug loaded in O-carboxymethyl chitosan NP modified with glycyrrhizin (CMCNP-GL) was used to evaluate HCC targeting therapy. The NPs synthesized possessed desired surface charge, small particle size, and high stability facilitated both in vitro and in vivo cellular uptake efficiently. CMCNP-GL was reported to significantly facilitate targeted delivery of paclitaxel into hepatoma carcinoma cells. Accumulation of paclitaxel-enhanced hepatic and systemic toxicity compared to the control makes CMCNP-GL a potential HCC targeting drug carrier [11].

Mesoporous silica nanoparticles

Mesoporous silica nanoparticles (MSNs) have attracted great attention due to remarkable chemical stability, excellent biocompatibility, rigid framework, easily modifiable surface chemistry, large surface area, unique morphological characteristics, high pore volume with well-defined structure, and especially high drug loading capacity [12−14]. Earlier the MSN synthesized had very small pore which limited its application for drug delivery. Recently MSN with large pore and novel structures are developed which improved its efficacy for therapeutic application and also reduced toxicity levels [13]. Two types of mesoporous silica NPs synthesized are short rod and long rod forms. Short less spherical rods tend to accumulate in liver and get easily eliminated through urine and feces whereas the long ones accumulate in spleen with less elimination potential.

The phytochemicals with antiinflammatory, antitumor, antiangiogenesis, and many other pharmacological activities are identified and studied extensively. However, due to water insolubility and low bioavailability limits their clinical efficacy. The above limitations can be addressed by hosting the bioactive phytoconstitutents in the MSN. Pharmacological studies have been done on those constituents which have specific binding sites on the surface of hepatocytes of the rats and HCC cells. Phytochemicals isolated from the roots of *Glycyrrhiza glabra* L. such as with glycyrrhetinic acid (GA) and glycyrrhizin, and curcumin (CUR) derived from *Curcuma longa* were covalently decorated uniformly on MSN surface with high loading capacity. The in vitro experiment showed that MSN-GA-CUR significantly enhanced cellular uptake toward HCC (HepG2) cells through GA receptor-mediated endocytosis mechanism and thus increased cytotoxicity of HCC. The study provides a promising nanoplatform for HCC targeting [12].

Iron oxide nanoparticles

Iron oxide NPs' diameter ranges from 5 nm to 100 nm exhibits highly unique properties which make it feasible for biomedical application. First, they are approved by FDA. Iron oxide NPs have high magnetization value, the so-called superparamagnetic NPs make it an eligible candidate for magnetic resonance imaging (MRI). The paramagnetic property in the presence of magnetic field guides the NPs to the location and drug is released on heated up by magnetic field. Earlier, a magnetic-targeted carrier of size 1–2 μm was designed by a pharmaceutical company to deliver drug (doxorubicin) to cancerous liver cells. The drug-loaded NPs were injected near the liver tumor and powerful magnetic field was applied. This helped in localized targeted retention with extravasation of the NPs into the surrounding tissue [15]. There were no drastic side effects reported because the magnetic field induced drug release from the NPs into the tumor, but when the effect was turned off, the NPs were trapped in the tumor causing very less drug to be circulated throughout the body. Till now phase III clinical trials were done, further study was not done as these NPs increased the survival rate of patients with less curative effect. Further these NPs were later used by labeling them with β-emitters (yttrium-90 and rhenium-188) reported to be very effective against liver tumors [16]. Wilson et al.'s clinical study monitored transcatheter targeted delivery of drug doxorubicin conjugated to magnetic NPs in hepatic cells using intraprocedural MRI. The treated liver tumor volume drastically reduced compared to the normal control ones [17].

The iron NPs advantageous property includes biocompatibility and high conjugation ability with drug biomolecules makes these particles to be used in drug targeting, drug delivery, and local hyperthermia. However, the major limitation is opsonization, which can be overcome by surface modification of iron oxide NPs [18]. Superparamagnetic ironoxide nanoparticles (SPIONs) are synthetic maghemite or magnetite particles of core diameter ranging from 10 nm to 100 nm. Particle size plays a major limitation factor in internalization of NPs in cells. Small size NPs (less than 50 nm) penetrate efficiently than large-size NPs and are easily eliminated through the renal system and Kupffer cells of the liver. Large size evades penetration into cells, increases the blood circulation time period and gradually these particles are prominently taken up by phagocytes (macrophages) in the reticuloendothelial system of liver and other tissues such as bone marrow, spleen, and lymph [19]. SPIONs are coated with polyethylene glycol or any other biocompatible polymers which provide base for therapeutic agents to conjugate and mainly to improve distribution profile of the particles in the blood. SPIONs coated with Pluronics/oleic acid with 193 nm hydrodynamic diameter as observed to be accumulated in the liver of the rat and mainly in the tumors compared to the normal cells [20]. Similar results were reported with experiment using radioactive 59Fe-NPs. In the presence of magnetic field, 114 times more activity of NPs was observed in the tumor region than control without the magnetic field [16]. These particles with magnetic property have opened wide range of horizons as agents of drug delivery and MRI.

Liposomal nanoparticles

Liposomes have been used as drug delivery system for a long period of time owing to their unique properties such as biocompatibility, biodegradability, low cytotoxicity, and immune response, encapsulates both hydrophilic and hydrophobic drugs and even drug combinations. Nanoscale liposomal vesicles are promising candidates for systematic drug delivery systems. The main advantage of liposomal NPs is they encapsulate potential anticancerous natural water insoluble drug and delivers to the targeted site due receptor-specific modification of the surface of the NPs. These NPs have recently emerged as promising nanocarriers to deliver drug combination as evidenced by reports of more clinical trials [21]. The physiochemical properties were evaluated such as size factor, drug release profile, biocompatibility, zeta potential, encapsulation capacity and efficiency, and mainly synchronous release of drug at the targeted site. A comparative study on the effect of dual drug, monodrug, and free drug cocktail on HepG2 cells (in vitro cytotoxicity assay) and HCC xenograft mouse tumor models (in vivo analysis). Curcumin delivered through liposomal NPs neutralize the toxic effect of chemo drug cisplatin. Curcumin proved to regulate the Sp1 and also p-ERK1/2 protein expression through ROS generation which indirectly enhanced the antitumor efficiency of cisplatin. In vivo experiments were done to optimize the synergistic interaction of both the drugs for liver tumors. In another phase III clinical trial on liposomal formulation with drug CPX-351 encapsulated along with two drugs cytarabine and daunorubicin have reported improved therapeutic outcomes compared to the free drug cocktail given. Liposomes have been reported to control the release of drugs and its systemic accumulation in tumor cells without affecting normal cells proves it to be a promising candidate for codelivery of poorly insoluble drugs both in vitro and in vivo [22]. Diosin (DSN), a flavonoid with anticancer potential against colon and HCC did not show effective therapeutic potential due to poor solubility. The authors developed a new liposomal NPs loaded with DSN showed efficient drug dissolution and improved cell permeation into intestine, designating liposomal NPs a potential drug carrier and delivery system [4]. Viroonchatapan et al. designed a core/shell structure, magnetoliposomes, in which iron oxide magnetic core is surrounded by liposome. The core with dextran-iron oxide NPs incorporated into liposomes containing calcein (fluorescent marker) was targeted to mouse liver with the help of an extracorporeal magnet. These structures are very small compared to the albumin microsphere making it a potential drug carrier and targeting the drug delivery with high efficiency [23].

Solid lipid nanoparticles

Solid lipid nanoparticles (SLNs) are made up of biodegradable solid lipids with the mean diameter (photon correlation spectroscopy) ranging from 50 nm to 1000 nm. SLNs of size 120 nm were synthesized at elevated temperature (65°C) at high pressure by homogenization method [24]. SLNs are mainly administered intravenously and are disseminated more in the liver and kidneys [25]. SLNs (medication carriers) was introduced in 1991 as a variable substitute to traditional colloidal carriers (liposomes). They have very remarkable properties which appeal them to be potential particles to enhance drug delivery. The properties are small size, large surface area, and high drug loading capacity. The specific property includes physical stability, exceptional tolerability in any formulations and administration routes whether oral, visual, dermal, rectal or pulmonar, controlled release, the communication of stages at the interface to deliver the drug efficiently and mainly liable degradation with nontoxic byproducts [26]. A new NP prepared with galactosylated dioleoylphosphatidyl ethanolamine abbreviated as tSLN (targeted SLN) with docetaxel-loaded targeted to hepatoma (BEL7402 cell lines) was designed. The NPs exhibited encapsulation efficiency of about more than 90%, low initial burst effect, and nearly 29 days of slow and sustained release of drug. The in vitro cytotoxic activity was greater for tSLN compared to Taxotere and also nontargeted SLN (nSLN). Similar results were also reported in in vivo murine hepatoma model. The effect was mainly due to larger cellular uptake and accumulation of tSLN loaded with drug in tumors. Altogether, tSLN did not show any detrimental effect on normal cells. The results clearly demonstrate that tSLNs loaded with docetaxel are very efficient in the treatment of advanced and metastatic HCC [27]. A lipid NP formulation of small interfering RNA (siRNA), TKM-080301, in preclinical evaluation targeted knocks down of polo-like kinase 1 (PLK1) which are overexpressed in HCC. This resulted in downregulation of RNA induced silencing complex and inhibition of cell proliferation. This proves to be a novel approach to combat solid tumors by targeting PLK1 [28].

Gold nanoparticles

For centuries, gold has been used in medicinal formulations. Now a days Au NPs have been widely designed for biomedicine application such as molecular imaging, target specific drug delivery and cancer treatment. A chemotherapy strategy in which Au-NPs (1 nm in diameter) conjugates with chemo drug has proved to be very efficient to control the proliferation of HCC. The size factor makes the particle more compatible to cross the biological cell membrane and even reaches the nucleus to attach to DNA molecules. A study reported that Au-NPs at low concentration did not show cytotoxic activity against HCC cell lines, HepG2 while high concentration showed remarkable anticancer effect. Engineered NPs have been used as active particles for cancer therapy. Study reported that Au-NPs primarily accumulated in liver. But to target the particles to specific organ or target tumor site, surface modification with appropriate functional moiety is done. In one of the experimental study, Au-NPs were capped with PEG or sodium citrate or dendrimers. These particles exhibited marked cytotoxicity at a very low concentration against HepG2 cells and even toxicity effect by DNA damage was also observed. Altogether, the finding suggests that designing and modification of surface factors enhance the therapeutic potential of Au-NPs against HCC. In future more research should be targeted toward development of NPs with high specificity and reduced toxicity or side effects for efficient liver cancer therapy [29].

Titanium oxide nanoparticles

Titanium oxide nanoparticles (TiO-NPs), metallic NP has attracted researchers' interest for its photodynamic therapy application to kill cancer cells as well as antibiotic resistant bacteria. They have been proved to be excellent nanodrug carriers for targeted drug delivery [30]. Ismail et al. reported that TiO-NPs statistically did not show any cytotoxic activity in HepG2 cell lines due to low cellular accumulation. The authors state that may be due to limited exposure to UV light and unmodified surface results in higher agglomeration [31]. TiO-NPs synthesized by wet chemical method, have been reported to have more biocompatibility and the surface modification with PEG and folic acid ligand, targets the NPs to the surface of cancerous cell. Since TiO-NPs functional efficiency increases when it is complexed or surface modified, $TiO_2-PEG-FA$ complex with paclitaxel drug conjugated was studied for its effect on HepG2, human liver cancer cell lines. Cytotoxic studies proved that the complex showed more cytotoxic effect on the cells reporting the potential use of TiO-NPs as efficient drug nanocarriers [30]. Lee et al. worked on defective TiO-NPs for photocatalytic destruction of HCC using long wavelength visible light. It is to be noted that TiO-NPs increase the strength of nanocomposites, the authors synthesized liposome—TiO-NPs composites. HepG2 cells were subjected to different concentration of TiO-NPs composites, irradiated with 300 W xenon lamp (long-wavelength visible light) for different time interval and singlet oxygen and ROS was monitored. The results report high cytotoxic activity proves the potential application of TiO-NPs for photodynamic cancer treatment [32].

RNA interference (RNAi) has been reported to be a potent and specific regulator of expression of gene by silencing it. Lipid NPs with encapsulated RNAi have been proved to be highly effective to treat liver tumors. Clinical trials of RNAi-lipid NP formulation, ALN-VSP targeting VEGF and kinesin spindle protein were examined (Table 1.1). In tumor biopsies, it was detected that siRNA-mediated targeted cleavage of mRNA in liver, leads to downregulation of specific growth promoting genes and ultimately progression of liver cells to damage reports antitumor activity, and complete liver metastasis regression. The biweekly dose injection of ALN-VSP has been reported to be safe and tolerable. This provides proof that RNAi therapeutics opens new path for development of NPs for treatment of cancer. In future, specific multitargeting and more drugs encapsulated lipid NPs can be designed for better prospects in cancer therapy [33].

Pectin-based nanoparticles

Pectin, a homogalactoronan, a linear biopolymer of α-(1,-4)-linked D-polygalacturonic acid units. The pectin NPs synthesized under mild conditions using aqueous medium containing calcium ions and carbonate ions are extensively studied as they demonstrated potential candidates for drug delivery because of their unique properties. They include subcellular size, thermal stability, redispersibility, drug crystallinity, better intestinal absorption, and dissolution. These polymeric NPs penetrate epithelia very diligently and exhibit sustained release of water insoluble encapsulated drugs very efficiently [34]. Further standardization of increasing the drug loading capacity of these galactose-based NPs to exhibit significant in vivo pharmacokinetics are done. Pectin-based NPs encapsulated with anticancer drug have been used to target HCC (HepG2 cells). The polymeric units without any chemical modification played an efficient targeting headgroup role. 5-FU-loaded pectin-based NPs were fabricated as drug delivery system to HepG2 cells with overexpressed asialoglycoprotein receptor (in vitro cytotoxic studies) and mouse model with hepatic tumor (in vivo studies). Both the studies showed that 5-FU-loaded pectin-based NPs exhibited higher cytotoxic activity and constant drug release profile with better tissue distribution of the drug when compared to free 5-FU delivered. This demonstrates the potential ability of pectin-based NPs as targeted drug delivery system for the treatment of HCC [35].

mPEG-PLGA-PLL copolymer-based nanoparticles

mPEG-PLGA-PLL copolymer-based nanoparticles (PEAL-NPs) are made up of FDA-approved triblock copolymer. They are monomethoxy polyethylene glycol (mPEG) which improves stability and increases half-life of NPs, poly (D,L-lactic-coglycolic acid) (PLGA) which show biocompatible and biodegradable properties and poly(L-lysine) (PLL), a stable cationic molecule which can be modified with many different functional groups [36]. PEAL-NPs conjugated along with lactobionic acid and antibody of vascular endothelial growth factor abbreviated as PEAL-LA/VEGFab-NPs have been used effectively to treat HCC. These NPs offer great advantages over other by showing high stability, less toxicity, cost efficiency, biocompatibility, and targeted delivery of drug. Lactobionic acid is the targeting moiety, which binds specifically to asialoglycoprotein receptor which is overexpressed on HCC cell surface. VEGFab is another moiety which is highly specific for human tumors such as HCC. In HCC, microRNA-99a (miR-99a), a tumor suppressor has been reported to be commonly downregulated. To inhibit HCC progression miR-99a expression should be restored. PEAL-LA/VEGFab-NPs have been efficiently used to deliver miR-99a specifically in both in vitro and in vivo and HCC progression was completely repressed [37]. PEAL and 4-O-beta-D-Galactopyranosyl-D-gluconic acid (Gal)-modified PEAL (PEAL-Gal) are used to investigate cellular uptake mechanism and intracellular trafficking of NPs in different hepatoma cell lines such as HepG2, Huh7, and PLC cells. This study is highly necessary to understand the therapeutic efficiency of NPs [38].

Arsenic, a trace metalloid found in earth's crust exists has highly toxic forms. Arsenic trioxide (ATO) is industrially produced has an exciting application transformation from king of poisons into an anticancer drug. Earlier, ATO has been used in combination of drugs for acute promyelocytic leukemia treatment [39]. PEAL-NPs, a nano drug delivery system, have been successfully used to deliver ATO in the treatment of HCC effects. ATO exhibited antitumor effects by inducing various mechanisms such as initiation of cell cycle arrest at G2/M phase and apoptosis action. ATO induces pyroptosis (cell death mechanism which is triggered by innate immune defense mechanism associated with caspase 1) which activates caspases 3 which cleaves inactive gasdermin D to an active form which is tumor suppressor or pyroptosis executor gasdermin D (molecule induces pore formation). PEAL-NPs conjugated with ATO have been exploited for therapeutic application to treat HCC as it has been proved to induce pyroptosis in HepG2 cells and liver tumors [40].

Nanoparticles in clinical trials to treat hepatocellular carcinoma

Prospective clinical trials and research help in the development and identification of a potential drug that increases our understanding of HCC evaluation and designing strategies

TABLE 1.1 Nanoparticles conjugated with drugs for HCC treatment in clinical trials.

NPs (Drug)	Clinicaltrials.gov identifier (NCT number)	Phase	Objective	Outcome
MRI-SPION radiotherapyIronoxide NPs (Ferumoxytol injection)	NCT04682847	-	MRI cellular imaging of hepatic parenchyma with SPION will be performed for primary and metastatic HCC malignancies to assess treatment response	Study still in process
Doxorubicin-Transdrug	NCT01655693	Phase III	HCC treatment after the failure of Sorafenib treatment	Study completed, results are not posted
Smarticles(Drug: MTL-CEBPA)	NCT02716012	Phase I	To treat advanced HCC patients	Study still in process, results are not posted
Drug: EADM; Ultra-fluid lipoid; Gelatin sponge articles	NCT02630108	Phase III	To treat patients with large and huge HCC	Study completed, results are not posted
Lipid NP(TKM-080301)	NCT02191878	Phase I/II	HCC	Study in extension
DCR-MYC	NCT02314052	Phase I and II	DCR-MYC is a novel synthetic double-stranded RNA in a stable lipid particle suspension that targets the oncogene MYC in HCC	Terminated
ALN-VSP02	NCT01158079NCT00882180	Phase I	Solid liver tumors	Study completed, results are not posted

Note: Data retrieved from https://www.clinicaltrials.gov
HCC, Hepatocellular carcinoma; *NPs*, nanoparticles; *SPION*, superparamagnetic ironoxide nanoparticles.

for diagnosis and treatment. This would result in the decrease mortality and morbidity related with HCC. Clinical trials are summarized in Table 1.1. Doxorubicin-Transdrug (DT) is a nanoparticle formulation of doxorubicin. Both in vitro and in vivo studies (X/myc bi-transgenic MDR murine model of HCC) have shown that DT is effective to overcome multidrug resistance.

Toxicity

NPs are highly advantageous in biomedical application is mainly due to nano size. But this itself reports being the greatest disadvantageous factor. Due to its small size, the particles are able to penetrate the smallest capillaries and get distributed in the whole body, can pass through the membranes affecting the normal physiological function of the cell. While being excreted it is processed in the liver and filtrated through the kidney. If the size is greater than the particles to be filtered through the glomerulus, then they are accumulated in kidney causing renal failure. Some NPs, such as silver NPs have been reported to show doze (5–100 µg/mL) and size (60 nm) dependent toxicity by creating oxidative stress even in germline stem cells, liver, lung and neuroendocrine cells within 24 hours of treatment. While in 28 days, it was reported to alter the blood cholesterol and plasma alkaline phosphatase indicating liver damage probabilities. Liver histopathological studies of rats treated with silver NP have revealed hepatic cytoplasmic vacuolization and focal necrosis [41,42]. In another study, it was reported that mice treated with silica-coated NPs were distributed in most of the organs in 4 weeks of treatment. The liver mainly takes up the NPs and is found to be distributed in other organs such as spleen, lungs, kidney, and heart [43]. Chen et al. have demonstrated greater toxicological effects on ingestion of copper NPs by histological analysis in mice spleen, kidney, and liver [44]. Wang et al. worked on the effect of TiO-NPs (of size 25–80 nm) on female mice. They observed severe biochemical alterations such as changes in lactate dehydrogenase, aspartate amino transferase, and other liver-related enzymes activity. Nephrotoxicity was observed as an increased level of BUN. And pathological effect on liver of mice treated with high dose of TiO-NPs was observed as swelling and degeneration of cells around central vein, hepatocytes with spotty necrosis, and accumulation of NPs. This leads to necrosis not only in kidney and liver but also in spleen and lung tissue [45]. A comparative study on the effect of different NPs (silver, molybdenum oxide aluminum, iron, and TiO-NPs) on rat cell line BRL3A revealed that silver NPs are highly toxic, molybdenum oxide NPs are moderately toxic whereas iron, aluminum, and TiO-NPs displayed low cytotoxicity [42].

Conclusion

HCC, the deadliest disease affecting millions worldwide. Inefficient therapeutic and diagnostic strategies have led to an increase in the death rate. Recent advances in the field of nanomedicine have allowed construction and synthesis of different types of NPs conjugated with drugs exhibiting improved pharmacokinetic properties. Some have been subjected to clinical trials and had been proved to be very effective. But still, some NPs relatively show toxic effects on prolonged and high-dosage administration. Overall, the enhanced controllability, bioavailability, and target specificity of NPs broaden the spectrum in diagnosis and therapeutic application of HCC.

References

[1] Rimassa L. Drugs in development for hepatocellular carcinoma. Gastroenterol Hepatol 2018;14:542.
[2] Azar AT. Modeling and control of drug delivery systems. Elsevier Science; 2021.
[3] Aghebati-Maleki A, Dolati S, Ahmadi M, Baghbanzhadeh A, Asadi M, Fotouhi A, et al. Nanoparticles and cancer therapy: perspectives for application of nanoparticles in the treatment of cancers. J Cell Physiol 2020;235:1962–72.
[4] Freag MS, Elnaggar YS, Abdallah OY. Lyophilized phytosomal nanocarriers as platforms for enhanced diosmin delivery: optimization and ex vivo permeation. Int J Nanomed 2013;8:2385–97.

[5] Jin Y, Yang X, Tian J. Targeted polypyrrole nanoparticles for the identification and treatment of hepatocellular carcinoma. Nanoscale 2018;10:9594−601.

[6] Behzadi S, Serpooshan V, Tao W, Hamaly MA, Alkawareek MY, Dreaden EC, et al. Cellular uptake of nanoparticles: journey inside the cell. Chem Soc Rev 2017;46:4218−44.

[7] Terada T, Iwai M, Kawakami S, Yamashita F, Hashida M. Novel PEG-matrix metalloproteinase-2 cleavable peptide-lipid containing galactosylated liposomes for hepatocellular carcinoma-selective targeting. J Control Release 2006;111:333−42.

[8] Arias JL, Reddy LH, Othman M, Gillet B, Desmaele D, Zouhiri F, et al. Squalene based nanocomposites: a new platform for the design of multifunctional pharmaceutical theragnostics. ACS Nano 2011;5:1513−21.

[9] Mohammed MA, Syeda JTM, Wasan KM, Wasan EK. An overview of Chitosan nanoparticles and its application in non-parenteral drug delivery. Pharmaceutics 2017;9:53.

[10] Arvizo RR, Miranda OR, Thompson MA, Pabelick CM, Bhattacharya R, Robertson JD, et al. Effect of nanoparticle surface charge at the plasma membrane and beyond. Nano Lett 2010;10:2543−8.

[11] Shi L, Tang C, Yin C. Glycyrrhizin-modified O-carboxymethyl chitosan nanoparticles as drug vehicles targeting hepatocellular carcinoma. Biomaterials 2012;33:7594−604.

[12] Lv Y, Li J, Chen H, Bai Y, Zhang L. Glycyrrhetinic acid-functionalized mesoporous silica nanoparticles as hepatocellular carcinoma-targeted drug carrier. Int J Nanomed 2017;12:4361−70.

[13] Knežević NŽ, Durand J-O. Large pore mesoporous silica nanomaterials for application in delivery of biomolecules. Nanoscale 2015;7:2199−209.

[14] Xu C, Lei C, Yu C. Mesoporous silica nanoparticles for protein protection and delivery. Front Chem 2019;7.

[15] Couvreur P. Nanoparticles in drug delivery: past, present and future. Adv Drug Delivery Rev 2013;65:21−3.

[16] Estelrich J, Escribano E, Queralt J, Busquets MA. Iron oxide nanoparticles for magnetically-guided and magnetically-responsive drug delivery. Int J Mol Sci 2015;16:8070−101.

[17] Wilson MW, Kerlan Jr RK, Fidelman NA, Venook AP, LaBerge JM, Koda J, et al. Hepatocellular carcinoma: regional therapy with a magnetic targeted carrier bound to doxorubicin in a dual MR imaging/conventional angiography suite—initial experience with four patients. Radiology 2004;230:287−93.

[18] Mudshinge SR, Deore AB, Patil S, Bhalgat CM. Nanoparticles: emerging carriers for drug delivery. Saudi Pharm J 2011;19:129−41.

[19] Barry SE. Challenges in the development of magnetic particles for therapeutic applications. Int J Hyperth 2008;24:451−66.

[20] Wahajuddin SA. Superparamagnetic iron oxide nanoparticles: magnetic nanoplatforms as drug carriers. Int J Nanomed 2012;7:3445.

[21] Wu C-H, Lan C-H, Wu K-L, Wu YM, Jane W-N, Hsiao M, et al. Hepatocellular carcinoma-targeted nanoparticles for cancer therapy. Int J Oncol 2018;52:389−401.

[22] Zhang X, Guo S, Fan R, Yu M, Li F, Zhu C, et al. Dual-functional liposome for tumor targeting and overcoming multidrug resistance in hepatocellular carcinoma cells. Biomaterials 2012;33:7103−14.

[23] Viroonchatapan E, Sato H, Ueno M, Adachi I, Tazawa K, Horikoshi I. Magnetic targeting of thermosensittve magnetoliposomes to mouse livers in an in situ on-line perfusion system. Life Sci 1996;58:2251−61.

[24] Xu Z, Chen L, Gu W, Gao Y, Lin L, Zhang Z, et al. The performance of docetaxel-loaded solid lipid nanoparticles targeted to hepatocellular carcinoma. Biomaterials 2009;30:226−32.

[25] Mehnert W, Mäder K. Solid lipid nanoparticles: production, characterization and applications. Adv Drug Delivery Rev 2012;64:83−101.

[26] Lingayat VJ, Zarekar NS, Shendge RS. Solid lipid nanoparticles: a review. Nanosci Nanotechnol Res 2017;2:67−72.

[27] Müller RH, Mäder K, Gohla S. Solid lipid nanoparticles (SLN) for controlled drug delivery—a review of the state of the art. Eur J Pharm Biopharm 2000;50:161−77.

[28] Semple SC, Judge AD, Robbins M, Klimuk S, Eisenhardt M, Crosley E, et al. Abstract 2829: preclinical characterization of TKM-080301, a lipid nanoparticle formulation of a small interfering RNA directed against polo-like kinase 1. Cancer Res 2011;71. Avilable from: https://doi.org/10.1158/1538-7445.AM2011-2829.

[29] Paino IMM, Marangoni VS, R.d.C.S. de Oliveira LMG, Antunes V, Zucolotto. Cyto and genotoxicity of gold nanoparticles in human hepatocellular carcinoma and peripheral blood mononuclear cells. Toxicol Lett 2012;215:119−25.

[30] Venkatasubbu GD, Ramasamy S, Reddy GP, Kumar J. In vitro and in vivo anticancer activity of surface modified paclitaxel attached hydroxyapatite and titanium dioxide nanoparticles. Biomed Microdevices 2013;15:711−26.

[31] Ismail AFM, Ali MM, Ismail LFM. Photodynamic therapy mediated antiproliferative activity of some metal-doped ZnO nanoparticles in human liver adenocarcinoma HepG2 cells under UV irradiation. J Photochem Photobiol B 2014;138:99—108.

[32] Lee J, Lee YH, Choi JS, Park KS, Chang KS, Yoon M. Hydrothermal synthesis of defective TiO_2 nanoparticles for long-wavelength visible light-photocatalytic killing of cancer cells. RSC Adv 2015;5:99789—96.

[33] Tabernero J, Shapiro GI, LoRusso PM, Cervantes A, Schwartz GK, Weiss GJ, et al. First-in-humans trial of an RNA interference therapeutic targeting VEGF and KSP in cancer patients with liver involvement. Cancer Discov 2013;3:406—17.

[34] Burapapadh K, Takeuchi H, Sriamornsak P. Development of pectin nanoparticles through mechanical homogenization for dissolution enhancement of itraconazole. Asian J Pharm Sci 2016;11(3):365—75.

[35] Yu C-Y, Wang Y-M, Li N-M, Liu G-S, Yang S, Tang G-T, et al. In vitro and in vivo evaluation of pectin-based nanoparticles for hepatocellular carcinoma drug chemotherapy. Mol Pharm 2014;11:638—44.

[36] He Z, Sun Y, Wang Q, Shen M, Zhu M, Li F, et al. Degradation and bio-safety evaluation of mPEG-PLGA-PLL copolymer-prepared nanoparticles. J Phys Chem C 2015;119:3348—62.

[37] Cai C, Xie Y, Chen X, Liu H, Zhou Y, Zou H, et al. PLGA-based dual targeted nanoparticles enhance miRNA transfection efficiency in hepatic carcinoma. Sci Rep 2017;7:1—12.

[38] Liu P, Sun Y, Wang Q, Sun Y, Li H, Duan Y. Intracellular trafficking and cellular uptake mechanism of mPEG-PLGA-PLL and mPEG-PLGA-PLL-Gal nanoparticles for targeted delivery to hepatomas. Biomaterials 2014;35:760—70.

[39] Hu J, Dong Y, Ding L, Dong Y, Wu Z, Wang W, et al. Local delivery of arsenic trioxide nanoparticles for hepatocellular carcinoma treatment. Signal Transduct Target Ther 2019;4:1—7.

[40] Akhtar A, Wang SX, Ghali L, Bell C, Wen X. Recent advances in arsenic trioxide encapsulated nanoparticles as drug delivery agents to solid cancers. J Biomed Res 2017;31:177.

[41] Ji JH, Jung JH, Kim SS, Yoon J U, Park JD, Choi BS, et al. Twenty eight day inhalation toxicity study of silver nanoparticles in Sprague-Dawley rats. Inhalation Toxicol 2007;19:857—71.

[42] Hussain S, Hess K, Gearhart J, Geiss K, Schlager J. In vitro toxicity of nanoparticles in BRL 3A rat liver cells. Toxicol Vitro 2005;19:975—83.

[43] Schrand AM, Rahman MF, Hussain SM, Schlager JJ, Smith DA, Syed AF. Metal-based nanoparticles and their toxicity assessment. Wiley Interdiscip Rev Nanomed Nanobiotechnol 2010;2:544—68.

[44] Chen Z, Meng H, Xing G, Chen C, Zhao Y, Jia G, et al. Acute toxicological effects of copper nanoparticles in vivo. Toxicol Lett 2006;163:109—20.

[45] Wang J, Zhou G, Chen C, Yu H, Wang T, Ma Y, et al. Acute toxicity and biodistribution of different sized titanium dioxide particles in mice after oral administration. Toxicol Lett 2007;168:176—85.

Theranostics application of nanocarriers in hepatocellular carcinoma

Patnala Kiranmayi[1], Vishwas Soumya[1] and Rama Rao Malla[2]

[1]Department of Biotechnology, Institute of Science Gandhi Institute of Technology and Management, Visakhapatnam, India [2]Cancer Biology Lab, Department of Biochemistry and Bioinformatics, Institute of Sciences, GITAM (Deemed to be University), Visakhapatnam, India

Abstract

Hepatocellular carcinoma (HCC) is the sixth most diagnosed and third most leading cause of death worldwide as per the GLOBOCON 2020. The mortality and incidence rates of HCC are 2–3 times higher in men compared to women in both developed and developing nations. Numerous studies specify that several biological processes like aberrant expression of growth factors, angiogenesis, deregulation of signal transduction mechanisms, and lack of specific drug delivery systems are responsible for increased HCC metastasis and drug resistance. Recent developments in nanotechnology help in finding novel systems for drug delivery to the target sites and negate the vital impediments of resistance to drug and its toxicity. Nanocarriers are nontoxic to the tissues despite staying in the circulation for prolonged periods. Therefore this chapter covers modern breakthrough in the development of organic- and inorganic-based nanocarriers and their applications in HCC treatment. This include organic nanocarriers such as lipid nanocarriers, micelles, dendrimers, chitosan nanoparticles, and liposomes.

Keywords: Hepatocellular carcinoma; organic nanocarriers; inorganic nanocarriers; chemotherapeutics

Abbreviations

HCC	hepatocellular carcinoma
CCA	cholangiocarcinoma
PEG	polyethylene glycol
TPGS-b-PCL	D-tocopherol PEG 1000 succinate polycaprolactone
SFB	sorafenib
CS	chitosan
NP	nanoparticle
PM	polymeric micelles
GA	glycyrrhetinic acid

© 2022 Elsevier Inc. All rights reserved.

HB	hepatoblastoma
BA	butyric acid
PDA	polydopamine
QD	quantum dot
PLGA	polylactic-co-glycolic acid
5-FU	5-fluorouracil
CNTs	carbon nanotubes
SPIONs	superparamagnetic iron-oxide nanoparticles
MRI	magnetic resonance imaging
PAI	photoacoustic imaging
Gd	gadolinium
DTPA	diethylenetriamine pentaacetic acid
NLC	nanostructured lipid carrier
SWNTs	single walled carbon nanotubes

Introduction

Hepatocellular carcinoma (HCC) is a major kind of liver cancer. It is the most recurrent type and reported as a major cause of worldwide cancer deaths with 80% incidence. Numerous studies specify that several biological processes like expression of growth factors, angiogenesis, signal transduction, and cell death play significant roles in cancer metastasis. However, subsequent developments in nanotechnology help in finding novel systems for drug delivery to the target sites and negate the vital impediments of resistance to drug and its toxicity. The system should involve techniques to deliver the drugs with efficacy to the targeted sites for its maximum efficiency without damaging the surrounding healthy tissues. At this stage, approaches based on nanocarriers can be potent in treating HCC effectively. The chapter focusses on the various types of organic and inorganic nanocarriers that acted as encouraging tools for the delivery of drugs to hepatocytes and thereby showing significant change in the tumor microenvironment of HCC.

Therapeutic application of nanocarriers in hepatocellular carcinoma

Nanocarriers are the most robust tools for diagnosis, imaging, and delivery of drug. These nanocarriers have the characteristics of being able to diagnose and image the diseased tissue or detect them at an early stage so that it can be treated simultaneously. This system where the disease is diagnosed and treated simultaneously is aptly known as theranostic nanocarrier system. Of late, various nanocarriers for delivering drug to targeted tumor sites and HCC imaging have been developed. For instance, polymeric micelles-doxorubicin nanocarriers have effectively inhibited HepG2 cell line growth showing greater rate of survival in the mouse xenograft model [1]. This prominent strategy uses a range of nanocarriers like dendrimers, liposomes, micelles, metal oxides, carbon nanotubes, nanogels, and magnetic particles (Fig. 2.1).

The nanocarriers system must possess characters like small size and high surface area. They must be biodegradable with surface-altering properties. These are fast-evolving drug delivery systems exhibiting high efficiency. The highlights of the various theranostic applications of nanocarriers in HCC is depicted in Table 2.1.

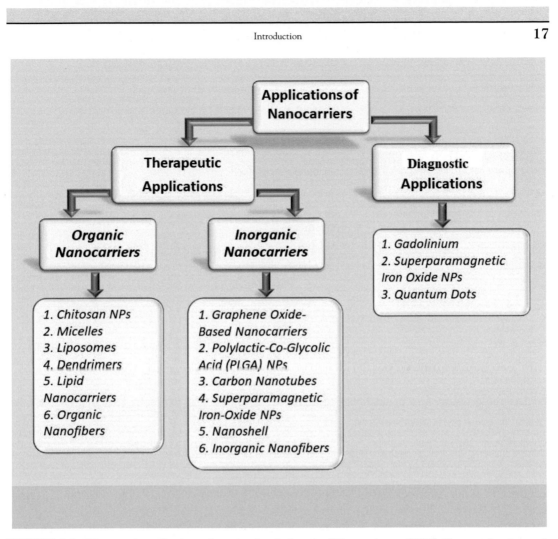

FIGURE 2.1 Theranostic applications of nanocarriers in hepatocellular carcinoma (HCC). The prominent organic nanocarriers used for therapeutic applications include chitosan nanoparticles (NPs), micelles, liposomes, dendrimers, lipid NPs, and organic nanofibers, whereas inorganic nanocarriers include graphene-based nanocarriers, polylactic-co-glycolic acid (PLGA) NPs, carbon nanotubes, supermagnetic iron-oxide NPs, nanoshells, and inorganic nanofibers. The gadolinium-based NPs, supermagnetic iron-oxide NPs, and quantum dots are used in diagnostic purpose.

Organic nanocarriers

Numerous organic-based nanoparticles have been constructed for delivery of drugs. An organic liposome nanocarrier using doxorubicin was the first FDA-approved nanodrug used as an anticancer agent [2]. Polymeric nanocarriers showed promising results when used against HCC in the form of organic nanocarriers [3]. These nanocarriers are nontoxic to the tissues in spite of staying in the circulation for prolonged periods. Moreover, they are biodegradable and biocompatible, accommodating a wide range of cancer drugs that can be conjugated, and encapsulated or adsorbed on to the polymeric nanocarrier surface [4]. While evaluating the antitumor effects in HepG2 cancer cells and in HCC mouse

TABLE 2.1   Theranostic applications of nanocarriers in hepatocellular carcinoma (HCC).

Nano-vehicles	Cargo drug	Implications
Micelles	Sorafenib	Exhibits high antitumor activity
1. Polymeric micelles 2. Polyethylene glycol (PEG)-modified phospholipid micelles		
Gadolinium coloaded liposomes	Sorafenib	Inhibits growth of cells
Dendrimer	Doxorubicin	Exhibits efficiency in inhibiting HCC cell growth
Lipid-polymer hybrid nanoparticles	Sorafenib and doxorubicin	Enhances antitumor activity in HCC
Nanofiber	Doxorubicin	Exhibits efficient tumor-targeting activity
Nanotubes	Doxorubicin	Depresses the growth of HCC cells effectively than free doxorubicin.Exhibits high antitumor activity
1. Chitosan-modified single walled carbon nanotubes (SWNTs) 2. Chitosan-coated multiwall carbon nanotubes		
Nanoshells	Doxorubicin	Exhibits antitumor activityInhibits cell proliferation
1. Superparamagnetic iron-oxide nanoshells 2. Polymer nano-core shell		
Folate-conjugated PEGylated polylactic-co-glycolic acid (PLGA) nanoparticles	Sorafenib	Suppresses tumor cell proliferation
Zinc oxide quantum dots	–	Induces cytotoxicity cell death in HepG2 cancer cells

xenograft using biodegradable D-tocopherol polyethylene glycol (PEG) 1000 succinate polycaprolactone (TPGS-b-PCL) nanoparticles with sorafenib (SFB), it was observed that these nanoparticles were more effectual in suppressing the growth of HepG2 cells compared to free SFB, exhibited delayed growth of tumor in HCC xenograft model. A doxorubicin-loaded nanocarrier galactosylated-polylithocholic-acid was developed by Lee et al., which showed successful results of suppressed HCC metastasis and growth in orthotopic mouse xenograft [5]. Organic nanocarriers include various vehicles like lipid nanocarriers, micelles, dendrimers, chitosan nanoparticles (CS-NPs), and liposomes.

Chitosan nanoparticles

Chitosan (CS) is synthesized by truncated deacetylation of chitin. It is a biologically degradable polymer of cationic polysaccharide. Various therapeutic studies reveal the potency of CS-NPs for delivery of drug in HCC. According to studies conducted by Ye et al., doxorubicin-loaded nanocarrier coated with CS inhibited cell proliferation in HCC [6].

CS-NPs were synthesized by Loutfy et al. for assessment of their in vitro effect on the HepG2 cell model. Based on these studies, they concluded that CS-NPs acted as suitable vehicles for drug delivery, showing good cytotoxic effects toward HCC [7].

Micelles

Polymeric micelles (PM), owing to their small size, core-shell structure, and narrow distribution size, have been utilized for drug delivery in HCC [8]. PMs play an essential role in diagnosis and cancer therapy as they have the ability to solubilize various drugs and imaging agents [9]. They are highly constructive in drug delivery systems while treating HCC. Doxorubicin-loaded glycyrrhetinic acid (GA)-modified PM showed high potential in targeted delivery of drug in HCC [8]. Another novel micelle which was synthesized as galunisertib-loaded hybrid of poly-galacturonic/polyacrylic acid (LY2157299) acted as TGFβ inhibitor in HCC treatment [10]. A PEG derived glycyrrhizic acid-based micelle with loaded doxorubicin was synthesized by Yang et al. for drug delivery in HepG2 cell line [1]. This PM exhibited outstanding efficacy when compared to free doxorubicin. It showed tumor growth inhibition in a HepG2 xenograft.

Liposome

Liposomes are stable biodegradable materials that are used for controlled drug delivery. The inner core of the liposome generally entraps the drugs [11]. Owing to its characteristics like biological compatibility, biodegradability, low toxicity, and ability to accommodate hydrophobic and hydrophilic drugs, it has been used as an effective carrier system for drug delivery [12,13].

In a study by Wang et al., liposomes were coated with polyclonal antibodies of CD147 present in HCC tissues and cell lines. Doxorubicin-loaded new liposome-based carrier loaded was constructed to target CD147. The results exhibited greater cytotoxicity on Huh-7, HepG2, and the HCC3736 model with these nanocarriers [14]. In another study by Persico et al., CS-coated liposomes and butyric acid (BA)-loaded uncoated liposomes were evaluated for their anticancer effects of HepG2 hepatoblastoma (HB) [15]. Results showed that CS-coated liposomes with loaded BA exhibited higher cytotoxicity when compared to uncoated liposomes or free BA [15]. Similar studies conducted by He et al. using SFB-loaded liposomes on Hep3B tumor bearing xenograft nude mice revealed that loaded liposomes were more biocompatible and effective when compared to free SFB [16]. According to several studies, liposomes are considered as novel nanocarriers for advanced stage HCC treatment in future.

Dendrimer

Dendrimers are considered as unique nanocarriers due to their properties like size, structure, solubility, and high drug delivery ability in tumor therapeutics [17]. The external functional groups on dendrimers are responsible for conferring excellent water solubility to these nanocarriers [18]. The core of the dendrimers have the ability to encapsulate drugs that are hydrophobic in nature. They also exhibit efficient renal filtration properties [19]. Based on magnetite nanoparticles (Fe_3O_4) and polydopamine (PDA)-coated multifunctional nanocarriers, a dendrimer was synthesized that proved to be nontoxic and could load chemotherapeutic agents to treat HCC effectively [20]. A PEG conjugated modified multifunctional dendrimer encapsulated with doxorubicin was developed for treating HCC. It was found that the developed dendrimer inhibited the growth of HCC cells [21]. Synthesis of a conjugate of glycyrrhizin-dendrimer and carbon nanotube with loaded doxorubicin lead to exploration of its effectiveness in HCC. The studies on its cytotoxicity, drug-loading capacity, and controlled release determined that dendrimers were effective vehicles for encapsulating ionizable drugs used in HCC therapeutics [22].

Lipid nanocarriers

The lipid nanocarriers are widely used in drug delivery systems for HCC. Bondì et al. synthesized a lipid carrier with loaded SFB drug to check for its anticancer activity by comparing it to free drug. The study suggested that lipid-based nanocarriers acted as good drug delivery agent in HCC therapeutics [23]. In other study conducted by Zhao et al., a lipid carrier was developed for delivery of curcumin and doxorubicin in mice. The study resulted in outstanding inhibition of tumor due to sustained drug release and high encapsulation efficacy [24].

Organic nanofiber

Organic nanofibers are widely used vectors for efficient drug delivery in HCC. The nanofiber with a chemotherapeutic drug can inhibit tumor growth and metastasis in HCC cells. An organic nanofiber loaded with paclitaxel and an incorporated miRNA-145 therapeutic gene was constructed by Ebara et al. in order to analyze the effects of delivered gene as well as drug. There was a significant growth reduction of tumor and metastasis when applied in HCC [25]. Nanofibers in conjugation with doxorubicin were synthesized by Ji et al. and used in cell lines (SMMC7721) of mouse to show that this system exhibited sustained release of drug, thereby inhibiting growth of tumor in mouse [26]. Similarly, nanofiber loaded with doxorubicin was studied as therapeutic system in HCC by Liu et al. The results indicated that the resulting nanofiber exhibited high antitumor efficiency against HCC [27].

Inorganic nanocarriers

Inorganic nanocarriers exhibit various physical properties like magnetic moment (e.g., iron oxides), fluorescence (semiconductor QDs), and optical absorption. They accommodate reactive groups for various biomolecules so that they can attain biological functionality like targeting of specific cells or tissues. Inorganic nanocarriers like silica nanoparticles with modified lipoprotein and loaded drugs like docetaxel and thalidomide when studied, exhibited human HepG2 cell line cytotoxicity with effective inhibition of tumor growth [28].

Graphene oxide-based nanocarriers

Graphene oxide nanocarriers are known to possess an outstanding drug loading capacity due to their high electron transfer capacity from individual graphene sheets. This property makes them good drug carriers in therapeutic applications of HCC [29,30]. Also, owing to their large surface area, these nanocarriers have the capacity to form specific interactions with several molecules of different drugs [31]. The effects of graphene oxide system with drug doxorubicin as well as lactobionic acid, fluoroscein isothiocyanate, and carboxymethyl CS were studied by Yang et al. The use of these nanocarriers resulted in cancer cell death after an incubation period of 24 hours, also showing higher biocompatibility with cell lines of HCC [13]. Another study on graphene nanocomposites incorporating gold nanoparticles, monoclonal antibodies, and folic acid showed enhanced HepG2 cell apoptosis with controlled and targeted drug release [32].

Polylactic-co-glycolic acid nanoparticles

The two monomers, lactic and glycolic acids, copolymerize to form poly(lactic-co-glycolic) acid (PLGA) nanoparticles. The synthetic PLGA polymer is completely biocompatible and is therefore approved by the EMA (European Medicine Agency) and the FDA (US Food and Drug Administration) for use in cancer therapeutics as a drug delivery agent [33]. Many recent studies on HCC revealed that PLGA nanoparticles have good specificity and appreciable drug-loading capacity exhibiting high efficacy in drug delivery. PLGA nanoparticles were formulated by modifying with a CXCR4 antagonist and a lipid coat for SFB drug delivery into HCC. These nanocarriers exhibited increased antiangiogenic effect with delayed progression of tumor. This resulted in increased survival rate in the orthotopic HCC model mice [34]. Lactobionic acid conjugated PLGA nanoparticles with loaded 5-fluorouracil (5-FU) when tested on HepG2 human cancer cell lines exhibited high anticancer efficacy when compared to free 5-FU [35].

Carbon nanotubes

Carbon nanotubes (CNTs) are materials that are shaped like needles and aid in carrying therapeutic drugs to the cellular components [36]. Owing to their small size, strong thermal conductivity, and high mechanical potency, CNTs are regarded as outstanding delivery vehicles for various drugs [37]. They also possess qualities like low toxicity, lesser side effects, good biocompatibility, and high treatment efficiency even at low doses of drug [38]. When tested in Hep2 cell lines, CNTs loaded with doxorubicin showed excellent antitumor activity in HCC model [39]. Ji et al. studied controlled release of doxorubicin loaded in CS and folic acid conjugated single walled CNTs in HCC cell lines. The study showed that these nanocarriers killed HCC cells effectively in nude mice with inhibited growth of HCC when compared to studies conducted with free doxorubicin [40]. Also, SFB-loaded CNTs were designed for increased efficacy against HCC [41].

Superparamagnetic iron-oxide nanoparticles

Superparamagnetic iron-oxide nanoparticles (SPIONs) are excellent agents with high performance in cancer diagnostics and therapeutics. SPIONs with PEG-modified micelles and loaded SFB were synthesized to test the inhibitory effect in HCC. SPIONs could target the specific sites in HCC when influenced by the magnetic field. Also, SPIONs when administered in the HepG2 cells showed high targeting efficacy in an in vitro system with controlled drug loading efficacy and better inhibition effect [42].

Nanoshell

Nanoshells are considered as promising tools in HCC therapies [43]. These are self-assembled polymers forming a core structure. These play a notable role in imaging of HCC [44]. Gold nanoshells are often considered important in the field of cancer therapeutics. Based on the reports of a study conducted by Liu et al., gold nanoshell exhibited excellent targeting ability to BEL-7402 and BEL7404 HCC cells, without attacking the HL-7702 normal cells of liver [45].

Inorganic nanofiber

Inorganic nanofibers, similar to organic nanofibers are considered as excellent agents for drug delivery in HCC. A multilayered polylactide electrospun nanofiber was loaded with cisplatin and used to investigate its effects on HCC in mice. The results showed increased tumor cytotoxicity with prolonged drug release. Also, these nanofibers prevented recurrence of tumor after HCC surgery [46].

Theranostic applications of nanocarriers in hepatocellular carcinoma

The theranostic applications involves carriers that are loaded with diagnostic and therapeutic agents to diagnose and cure cancer. The theranostic nanocarriers play a vital role in diagnosis and treatment of diseases at the cellular and molecular level. Currently, the theranostic delivery systems are being explored for their effective use in HCC treatment. The theranostic nanocarriers incorporate therapeutic agents like peptides, proteins, chemotherapeutic drugs, genetic materials and diagnostic agents like heavy metals, radionuclides, quantum dots (QDs), gadolinium, superparamagnetic iron oxides, and fluorescent dyes, most of which find applications in optical imaging, magnetic resonance imaging (MRI) or nuclear imaging, and computed tomography [47]. For instance, gadolinium-loaded lipid micelles were used as a contrast agents for MRI/photoacoustic imaging (PAI) in HepG2 tumor-bearing mice [29,30].

Gadolinium

Gadolinium is an FDA approved diagnostic agent used for MRI of the liver. It is used for detecting and characterizing the tumor in HCC. Polymeric nanoparticles modified with gadolinium-diethylenetriamine pentaacetic acid (Gd-DTPA) were designed to deliver Gd-DTPA to the targeted tumor. This system aided in early diagnosis of HCC [48]. For liver imaging, Luo et al. synthesized multifunctional MRI probes based on gadolinium that showed powerful influence as MRI contrast agents for detecting tumors in vitro and in vivo [49].

Superparamagnetic iron-oxide nanoparticles

SPIONs are used as a diagnostic agent as well as therapeutic agent in HCC cell line. They have been used in MRI as agents for detecting HCC. They target specific sites under the influence of magnetic field. SPIONs degrade into a soluble form of iron or nontoxic ions inside the body and undergo phagocytosis and lysosomal metabolism for its blood clearance [50]. Ferucarbotran, Ferumoxtran-10, Ferumoxides, Ferropharm, and Ferumoxytol are a few types of SPIONs available in the market which have been clinically tested contrast agents in MRI. Ferumoxide is a dextran-coated SPION and ferucarbotran is a carboxydextran-coated SPION, both of which are approved clinically for imaging HCC [51]. Similarly, ferumoxytol consists of iron-oxide nanoparticles coated with carbohydrate that is also used in imaging [52]. Based on PEG-modified phospholipid micelles, a nanoformulation was designed by incorporating SFB and SPIONs. While investigating the efficacy of this nanoformulation, it was observed that it produced enhanced imaging by magnetic targeting [42].

Iron-oxide nanoparticles, however, showed passive accumulation in organs like lymph nodes, spleen, and liver due to which it has limited clinical use in imaging. Therefore use of iron-oxide nanoparticles such as MRI contrast agents has been discontinued. Other SPIONs like orally administered ferumoxsil and intravenous administered ferumoxide were also discontinued taking into consideration several safety issues [53–56].

Quantum dots

QDs are considered effective diagnostic agents used in theranostic applications of HCC owing to their unique characteristics like photoluminescence. QDs loaded with NLC nanostructured lipid carrier could detect HepG2 cells [57]. QDs when incorporated in imaging systems were found to be suitable for imaging of HCC cells [58]. Similarly, QDs-based liposome carriers were used for imaging tumor during suicide gene therapy [59]. Al-Jamal et al. evinced efficient near-infrared fluorescence imaging in HCC cells of mice using QD fluorescence. Also, nanoscale vesicles formed by encapsulating QDs within liposome bilayers acted as good contrast agent in cancer imaging [60].

Conclusion

Nanocarriers are the most robust tools for diagnosis, imaging, and drug delivery. The nanocarriers have the ability to diagnose and image the diseased tissue or detect them at an early stage. The nanocarriers system possesses small size and high surface area, biodegradable with surface-altering properties, exhibiting high efficiency. Of late, researchers have developed numerous nanocarriers for effective delivery of drugs to HCC sites. The theranostic applications involve carriers loaded with diagnostic and therapeutic agents to diagnose and cure cancer. The theranostic nanocarriers play a vital role in diagnosing and treating cancers at cellular and molecular level. Currently, the theranostic delivery systems are being explored for their effective use in HCC treatment. The theranostic nanocarriers incorporate therapeutic agents like peptides, proteins, chemotherapeutic drugs, genetic materials and diagnostic agents like heavy metals, radionuclides, QDs, gadolinium, superparamagnetic iron oxides, and fluorescent dyes, most of which find applications in nuclear imaging and computed tomography, MRI or optical imaging of HCC.

Acknowledgment

The authors are grateful to the Department of Biotechnology as well as Department of Biochemistry and Bioinformatics, Institute of Science, Gandhi Institute of Technology and Management, Visakhapatnam, Andhra Pradesh, India.

Conflict of interest

The authors declared that there is no conflict of interest.

References

[1] Yang T, Lan Y, Cao M, Xueqin M, Aichen C, Yue S, et al. Glycyrrhetinic acid-conjugated polymeric prodrug micelles co-delivered with doxorubicin as combination therapy treatment for hepatocellular carcinoma. Colloids Surf B 2019;175:106−15. Available from: https://doi.org/10.1016/j.colsurfb.2018.11.082.

[2] Barenholz YC. Doxil®—the first FDA-approved nano-drug: lessons learned. J Controll Rel 2012;160 (2):117−34. Available from: https://doi.org/10.1016/j.jconrel.2012.03.020.

[3] Wang B, Qiao W, Wang Y, Yang L, Zhang Y, Shao P. Cancer therapy based on nanomaterials and nanocarrier systems. J Nanomater 2010;2010. Available from: https://doi.org/10.1155/2010/796303.

[4] Masood F. Polymeric nanoparticles for targeted drug delivery system for cancer therapy. Mater Sci Eng C 2016;60:569−78. Available from: https://doi.org/10.1016/j.msec.2015.11.067.

[5] Bijay S, Yoonjeong J, Sushila M, Hyeon-Jeong K, Ah YL, Sanghwa K, et al. Combination therapy with doxorubicin-loaded galactosylated poly(ethyleneglycol)-lithocholic acid to suppress the tumor growth in an orthotopic mouse model of hepatocellular carcinoma. Biomaterials 2016;116:130−44. Available from: https://doi.org/10.1016/j.biomaterials.2016.11.040.

[6] Ye B-L, Zheng R, Ruan X-J, Zheng Z-H, Cai H-J. Chitosan-coated doxorubicin nano-particles drug delivery system inhibits cell growth of hepatocellular carcinoma via p53/PRC1 pathway. Biochem Biophys Res Commun 2018;495(1):414−20. Available from: https://doi.org/10.1016/j.bbrc.2017.10.156.

[7] Loutfy SA, El-Din HMA, Elberry MH, Allam NG, Hasanin MTM, Abdellah AM. Synthesis, characterization and cytotoxic evaluation of chitosan nanoparticles: in vitro hepatocellular carcinoma model. Adv Nat Sci 2016;7(3):035008.

[8] Huang W, Wang W, Wang P, Tian Q, Zhang C, Wang C, et al. Glycyrrhetinic acid-modified poly(ethylene glycol)-b-poly(γ-benzyl l-glutamate) micelles for liver targeting therapy. Acta Biomater 2010;6(10):3927−35. Available from: https://doi.org/10.1016/j.actbio.2010.04.021.

[9] Blanco E, Kessinger CW, Sumer BD, Gao J. Multifunctional micellar nanomedicine for cancer therapy. Exp Biol Med 2008;234(2):123−31. Available from: https://doi.org/10.3181/0808-mr-250.

[10] Hanafy NAN, Quarta A, Ferraro MM, Dini L, Nobile C, Giorgi MLD, et al. Polymeric nano-micelles as novel cargo-carriers for LY2157299 hepatocellular carcinoma cells delivery. Int J Mol Sci 2018;19(3):748. Available from: https://doi.org/10.3390/ijms19030748.

[11] Immordino ML, Dosio F, Cattel L. Stealth liposomes: review of the basic science, rationale, and clinical applications, existing and potential. Int J Nanomed 2006;1(3):297−315.

[12] Sarfraz M, Afzal A, Raza SM, Bashir S, Madni A, Khan MW, et al. Liposomal co-delivered oleanolic acid attenuates doxorubicin-induced multi-organ toxicity in hepatocellular carcinoma. Oncotarget 2017;8:29. Available from: https://doi.org/10.18632/oncotarget.17559.

[13] Yang G, Yang T, Zhang W, Lu M, Ma X, Xiang G. In vitro and in vivo antitumor effects of folate-targeted ursolic acid stealth liposome. J Agric Food Chem 2014;62(10):2207−15. Available from: https://doi.org/10.1021/jf405675g.

[14] Wang J, Wu Z, Pan G, Ni J, Xie F, Jiang B, et al. Enhanced doxorubicin delivery to hepatocellular carcinoma cells via CD147 antibody-conjugated immunoliposomes. Nanomedicine. 2018;14(6):1949−61. Available from: https://doi.org/10.1016/j.nano.2017.09.012.

[15] Quagliariello V, Masarone M, Armenia E, Giudice A, Barbarisi M, Caraglia M, et al. Chitosan-coated liposomes loaded with butyric acid demonstrate anticancer and anti-inflammatory activity in human hepatoma HepG2 cells. Oncol Rep 2018. Available from: https://doi.org/10.3892/or.2018.6932.

[16] He Q, He X, Deng B, Shi C, Lin L, Liu P, et al. Sorafenib and indocyanine green co-loaded in photothermally sensitive liposomes for diagnosis and treatment of advanced hepatocellular carcinoma. J Mater Chem B 2018;6(36):5823−34. Available from: https://doi.org/10.1039/c8tb01641k.

[17] Noriega-Luna B, Godínez LA, Rodríguez FJ, Rodríguez A, Zaldívar-lelo De Larrea G, Sosa-Ferreyra Bustos E. Applications of dendrimers in drug delivery agents, diagnosis, therapy, and detection. J Nanomater 2014;2014:1−19. Available from: https://doi.org/10.1155/2014/507273.

[18] Sharma AK, Gothwal A, Kesharwani P, Alsaab H, Iyer AK, Gupta U. Dendrimer nanoarchitectures for cancer diagnosis and anticancer drug delivery. Drug Discov Today 2017;22(2):314−26. Available from: https://doi.org/10.1016/j.drudis.2016.09.013.

[19] Peer D, Karp JM, Hong S, Farokhzad OC, Margalit R, Langer R. Nanocarriers as an emerging platform for cancer therapy. Nat Nanotechnol 2007;2(12):751−60. Available from: https://doi.org/10.1038/nnano.2007.387.

[20] Jedrzak A, Grzeskowiak BF, Coy E, Wojnarowicz J, Szutkowski K, Jurga S, et al. Dendrimer based theranostic nanostructures for combined chemo- and photothermal therapy of hepatocellular carcinoma cells in vitro. Colloids Surf B 2018;173:698—708. Available from: https://doi.org/10.1016/j.colsurfb.2018.10.045.

[21] Fu F, Wu Y, Zhu J, Wen S, Shen M, Shi X. Multifunctional lactobionic acid-modified dendrimers for targeted drug delivery to hepatocellular carcinoma cells: investigating the role played by PEG spacer. ACS Appl Mater Interfaces 2014;6(18):16416—25. Available from: https://doi.org/10.1021/am504849x.

[22] Jain NK, Mody N, Tekade RK, Chopdey PK, Mehra NK. Glycyrrhizin conjugated dendrimer and multi-walled carbon nanotubes for liver specific delivery of doxorubicin. J Nanosci Nanotechnol 2014;15 (2):1088—100. Available from: https://doi.org/10.1166/jnn.2015.9039.

[23] Bondì ML, Botto C, Amore E, Emma MR, Augello G, Craparo EF, et al. Lipid nanocarriers containing sorafe-nib inhibit colonies formation in human hepatocarcinoma cells. Int J Pharm 2015;493(1—2):75—85. Available from: https://doi.org/10.1016/j.ijpharm.2015.07.055.

[24] Zhao X, Chen Q, Li Y, Tang H, Liu W, Yang X. Doxorubicin and curcumin co-delivery by lipid nanoparticles for enhanced treatment of diethylnitrosamine-induced hepatocellular carcinoma in mice. Eur J Pharm Biopharm 2015;93:27—36. Available from: https://doi.org/10.1016/j.ejpb.2015.03.003.

[25] Che H-L, Lee HJ, Uto K, Ebara M, Kim WJ, Aoyagi T, et al. Simultaneous drug and gene delivery from the biodegradable poly(-caprolactone) nanofibers for the treatment of hepatocellular carcinoma. J Nanosci Nanotechnol 2015. Available from: https://doi.org/10.1166/jnn.2015.11233.

[26] Ji Y, Xiao Y, Xu L, He J, Qian C, Li W, et al. Drug-bearing supramolecular MMP inhibitor nanofibers for inhibition of metastasis and growth of hepatocellular carcinoma. Adv Sci 2018;5:1700867. Available from: https://doi.org/10.1002/advs.201700867.

[27] Liu S, Wang X, Zhang Z, Zhang Y, Zhou G, Huang Y, et al. Use of asymmetric multilayer polylactide nanofi-ber mats in controlled release of drugs and prevention of liver cancer recurrence after surgery in mice. Nanomedicine. Nanotechnology, Biology and Medicine 2015;11(5):1047—56.

[28] Ao M, Xiao X, Ao Y. Low density lipoprotein modified silica nanoparticles loaded with docetaxel and thalid-omide for effective chemotherapy of hepatocellular carcinoma. Br J Med Biol Res 2018;51. Available from: https://doi.org/10.1590/1414-431x20176650.

[29] Gao P, Liu M, Tian J, Deng F, Wang K, Xu D, et al. Improving the drug delivery characteristics of graphene oxide based polymer nanocomposites through the "one-pot" synthetic approach of single-electrontransfer living radical polymerization. Appl Surf Sci 2016;378:22—9. Available from: https://doi.org/10.1016/j.apsusc.2016.03.207.

[30] Zhang D, Wu M, Zeng Y, Liao N, Cai Z, Liu G, et al. Lipid micelles packaged with semiconducting polymer dots as simultaneous MRI/photoacoustic imaging and photodynamic/photothermal dual-modal therapeutic agents for hepatocellular carcinoma. J Mater Chem B 2016. Available from: https://doi.org/10.1039/c5tb01827g.

[31] Shim G, Kim MG, Park JY, Oh YK. Graphene-based nanosheets for delivery of chemotherapeutics and biological drugs. Adv Drug Deliv Rev 2016;105:205—27. Available from: https://doi.org/10.1016/j.addr.2016.04.004.

[32] Yuan Y, Zhang Y, Liu B, Wu H, Kang Y, Li M, et al. The effects of multifunctional MiR-122-loaded graphene-gold composites on drug-resistant hepatocellular carcinoma. J Nanobiotechnology 2015;13(1). Available from: https://doi.org/10.1186/s12951-015-0070-z.

[33] Danhier F, Ansorena E, Silva JM, Coco R, Le Breton A, Préat V. PLGA-based nanoparticles: an overview of biomedical applications. J Control Rel 2012;161(2):505—22. Available from: https://doi.org/10.1016/j.jconrel.2012.01.043.

[34] Gao DY, Lin TT, Sung YC, Liu YC, Chiang W-H, Chang C-C, et al. CXCR4-targeted lipid-coated PLGA nano-particles deliver sorafenib and overcome acquired drug resistance in hepatocellular carcinoma. Biomaterials 2015;67:194—203. Available from: https://doi.org/10.1016/j.biomaterials.2015.07.035.

[35] Dangi R, Hurkat P, Jain A, Shilpi S, Jain A, Gulbake A, et al. Targeting hepatocellular carcinoma via ASGP receptor using 5-FU-loaded surface-modified PLGA nanoparticles. J Microencapsul 2014;31(5):479—87. Available from: https://doi.org/10.3109/02652048.2013.879929.

[36] Elhissi A, Ahmed W, Hassan IU, Dhanak V, D'Emanuele A. Carbon nanotubes in cancer therapy and drug delivery. J Drug Deliv 2012;2012:1—10. Available from: https://doi.org/10.1155/2012/837327.

[37] He H, Xiao D, Pham-Huy LA, Dramou P, Pham-Huy C. Carbon nanotubes used as nanocarriers in drug and biomolecule delivery. Drug Delivery Approaches Nanosyst 2017;163—212. Available from: https://doi.org/10.1201/9781315225371.

[38] Liu Z, Chen K, Davis C, Sherlock S, Cao Q, Chen X, et al. Drug delivery with carbon nanotubes for in vivo cancer treatment. Cancer Res 2008;68(16):6652–60. Available from: https://doi.org/10.1158/0008-5472.CAN-08-1468.

[39] Qi X, Rui Y, Fan Y, Chen H, Ma N, Wu Z. Galactosylated chitosan-grafted multiwall carbon nanotubes for pH-dependent sustained release and hepatic tumor-targeted delivery of doxorubicin in vivo. Colloids Surf B 2015;133:314–22. Available from: https://doi.org/10.1016/j.colsurfb.2015.06.003.

[40] Ji Z, Lin G, Lu Q, Meng L, Shen X, Dong L, et al. Targeted therapy of SMMC-7721 hepatocellular carcinoma in vitro and in vivo with carbon nanotubes based drug delivery system. J Colloid Interface Sci 2012;365 (1):143–9. Available from: https://doi.org/10.1016/j.jcis.2011.09.013.

[41] Elsayed MM, Mostafa ME, Alaaeldin E, Sarhan HAA, Shaykoon MS, Allam S, et al. Design and characterisation of novel Sorafenib-loaded carbon nanotubes with distinct tumour-suppressive activity in hepatocellular carcinoma. Int J Nanomed 2019;14:8445. Available from: https://doi.org/10.2147/IJN.S223920.

[42] Depalo N, Iacobazzi RM, Valente G, Arduino I, Villa S, Canepa F, et al. Sorafenib delivery nanoplatform based on superparamagnetic iron oxide nanoparticles magnetically targets hepatocellular carcinoma. Nano Res 2017;10(7):2431–48. Available from: https://doi.org/10.1007/s12274-017-1444-3.

[43] Bardhan R, Lal S, Joshi A, Halas NJ. Theranostic nanoshells: from probe design to imaging and treatment of cancer. Acc Chem Res 2011;44(10):936–46. Available from: https://doi.org/10.1021/ar200023x.

[44] Wang Y-XJ, Leung KC-F, Zhu X-M, Wang W, Liang Q, Cheng CHK. In vivo chemoembolization and magnetic resonance imaging of liver tumors by using iron oxide nanoshell/doxorubicin/poly(vinyl alcohol) hybrid composites. Angew Chem Int (Ed.) 2014;53(19):4812–15. Available from: https://doi.org/10.1002/anie.201402144.

[45] Liu SY, Liang ZS, Gao F, Luo SF, Lu GQ. In vitro photothermal study of gold nanoshells functionalized with small targeting peptides to hepatocellular carcinoma cells. J Mater Sci 2010;21(2):665–74. Available from: https://doi.org/10.1007/s10856-009-3895-x.

[46] Zhang Y, Liu S, Wang X, Zhang Z, Jing X, Zhang P, et al. Prevention of local hepatocellular carcinoma recurrence after surgery using multilayered cisplatin-loaded polylactide electrospun nanofibers. Chin J Polym Sci 2014;32(8). Available from: https://doi.org/10.1007/s10118-014-1491-0.

[47] Ye Y. Integrin targeting for tumor optical imaging. Theranostics 2011;1:102. Available from: https://doi.org/10.7150/thno/v01p0102.

[48] Liu Y, Yu D, Zhang N, Lu Z, Liu C, Chen Z. Gadolinium-loaded polymeric nanoparticles modified with Anti-VEGF as multifunctional MRI contrast agents for the diagnosis of hepatocellular carcinoma. Biomaterials 2011;32 (22):5167–76. Available from: https://doi.org/10.1016/j.biomaterials.2011.03.077.

[49] Luo K, Liu G, He B, Wu Y, Gong Q, Song B, et al. Multifunctional gadolinium-based dendritic macromolecules as liver targeting imaging probes. Biomaterials 2011;32(10):2575–85. Available from: https://doi.org/10.1016/j.biomaterials.2010.12.049.

[50] Yu MK, Jeong YY, Park J, Park S, Kim JW, Min JJ, et al. Drug-loaded superparamagnetic iron oxide nanoparticles for combined cancer imaging and therapy in vivo. Angew Chem Int (Ed.) 2008;47(29):5362–5. Available from: https://doi.org/10.1002/anie.200800857.

[51] Arias JL, Reddy LH, Othman M, Gillet B, Desmaele D, Zouhiri F, et al. Squalene based nanocomposites: a new platform for the design of multifunctional pharmaceutical theragnostics. ACS Nano 2011;5(2):1513–21. Available from: https://doi.org/10.1021/nn1034197.

[52] Wang YXJ. Current status of superparamagnetic iron oxide contrast agents for liver magnetic resonance imaging. World J Gastroenterol 2015;21(47):13400–2. Available from: https://doi.org/10.3748/wjg.v21.i47.13400.

[53] Wáng YXJ, Idée JM. A comprehensive literatures update of clinical researches of superparamagnetic resonance iron oxide nanoparticles for magnetic resonance imaging. Quant Imaging Med Surg 2017;7(1):88. Available from: https://doi.org/10.21037/qims.2017.02.09.

[54] Bao Y, Sherwood JA, Sun Z. Magnetic iron oxide nanoparticles as T 1 contrast agents for magnetic resonance imaging. J Mater Chem C 2018;6(6):1280–90. Available from: https://doi.org/10.1039/C7TC05854C.

[55] Azria D, Blanquer S, Verdier JM, Belamie E. Nanoparticles as contrast agents for brain nuclear magnetic resonance imaging in Alzheimer's disease diagnosis. J Mater Chem B 2017;5(35):7216–37. Available from: https://doi.org/10.1039/C7TB01599B.

[56] Wang YXJ. Superparamagnetic iron oxide-based MRI contrast agents: current status of clinical application. Quant Imaging Med Surg 2011;1(1):35.

[57] Olerile LD, Liu Y, Zhang B, Wang T, Mu S, Zhang J, et al. Near-infrared mediated quantum dots and pacli-taxel co-loaded nanostructured lipid carriers for cancer theragnostic. Colloids Surf B 2017;150:121−30. Available from: https://doi.org/10.1016/j.colsurfb.2016.11.032.

[58] Das RK, Mohapatra S. Highly luminescent, heteroatom-doped carbon quantum dots for ultrasensitive sens-ing of glucosamine and targeted imaging of hepatocellular carcinoma cells. J Mater Chem B 2017. Available from: https://doi.org/10.1039/c6tb03141b.

[59] Shao D, Li J, Pan Y, Zhang X, Zheng X, Wang Z, et al. Noninvasive theranostic imaging of HSV-TK/GCV suicide gene therapy in hepatocellular carcinoma by folate-targeted quantum dot-based liposomes. Biomater Sci 2015;3(6):833−41. Available from: https://doi.org/10.1039/C5BM00077G.

[60] Al-Jamal WT, Al-Jamal KT, Cakebread A, Halket JM, Kostarelos K. Blood circulation and tissue biodistribu-tion of lipid-quantum dot (L-QD) hybrid vesicles intravenously administered in mice. Bioconjug Chem 2009;20:1696−702. Available from: https://doi.org/10.1021/bc900047n.

Nanoparticle-based theranostics and their role in hepatocellular carcinoma

Devanabanda Mallaiah[1], Produtur Chandramathi Shankar[2] and Ramakrishna Vadde[1]

[1]Department of Biotechnology & Bioinformatics, Yogi Vemana University, Kadapa, India
[2]Department of Biotechnology, Yogi Vemana University, Kadapa, India

Abstract

Hepatocellular carcinoma (HCC) is the most common cancer of liver and poses significant health challenges. Due to its poor diagnosis, HCC causes high mortality and morbidity around the globe. In addition, toxicity, bioavailability, and drug resistance are the major problems of traditional drugs against liver cancer. So, there is a need to develop advanced theranostics, which can diagnose and treat HCC effectively at the same time. Recently, a new promise has come from nanoparticles (NP) due to their unique physico-chemical properties. Many studies showed nanoparticle-based theranostics improve sensitivity and specificity of HCC management than traditional methods. The present chapter deals about the pathogenesis of HCC and the different types of nanoparticles-based theranostics used in diagnostic imaging and treatment of HCC using both in vitro and in vivo studies. The field of cancer nanotheranostics offers a great promising hope for the future to the development of effective tools for simultaneous therapy and diagnosis of HCC.

Keywords: Hepatocellular carcinoma; nanoparticles; nanotheranostics; diagnosis; therapy

Abbreviations

BHQ1	black hole quencher 1
HCC	hepatocellular carcinoma
MRI	magnetic resonance imaging
NAFLD	nonalcoholic fatty liver disease
NP	nanoparticles
PEG	polyethylene glycol
PLGA	poly(D,L-lactide-*co*-glycolide)

Ganji Purnachandra Nagaraju, Sarfraz Ahmad (eds.)
Theranostics and Precision Medicine for the Management of Hepatocellular Carcinoma, Volume 3
DOI: https://doi.org/10.1016/B978-0-323-99283-1.00019-7

© 2022 Elsevier Inc. All rights reserved.

Introduction

Hepatocellular carcinoma (HCC) is one of the lethal solid cancer and more prevalent in the world. The World Health Organization (WHO) reported that globally among cancer-related deaths, HCC is the fourth most leading cancer [1]. The low survival rates of HCC are mainly due to advanced or terminal stage diagnosis and ineffective therapeutic strategies. Several problems such as less solubility, selectivity, and drug resistance are also associated with conventional strategies. Therefore it is necessary to develop advanced strategies for the management of HCC. The combined early diagnosis and effective therapeutics are important for better clinical results of HCC [2].

The recent developments in nanotechnology will allow advanced nanotheranostics, which are made by individual different types of nanosystems or combined biomaterials. Hybrid nanotheranostic systems made with different organic and inorganic materials increase the complexity and multiple properties. Advanced cancer nanotheranostic platforms display and integrate mainly three features: (1) nano-size; (2) therapeutic agents such as drugs, proteins, nucleic acids, and stimuli-responsive molecules; and (3) diagnostic agents such as fluorescent probes, quantum dots, and metal nanoparticles [3]. Recently, multifunctionality of hybrid nanosystems presents promising strategy in nanotheranostics than hybrid nanoparticles and multifunctional nanoparticles [4].

In addition to control on the size and shape, large surface area, high loading volume, facile functional surfaces, and acceptable biocompatibility are the distinct features endowed with nanoparticles, which allow them to use as advanced theranostics [5]. This chapter deals with pathogenesis of HCC and nanotheranostics for HCC.

Pathogenesis

Different factors are mainly responsible for pathogenesis of HCC (Fig. 3.1). The HCC incidences vary with geographical regions, many cases occur in less developed regions such as Asia and Africa due to etiologic factors (viral hepatitis B and C). Several other environmental factors like alcohol consumption, aflatoxin, and dietary habits also contribute to HCC. It primarily develops from cirrhosis caused by nonalcoholic fatty liver disease (NAFLD) and hepatitis C viral agents [6]. The patients with NAFLD disease associated with obesity, insulin resistance, and hepatic iron-overload which could further prone to advanced fibrosis and cirrhosis and finally HCC. Along with these, male gender, older age, smoking, metabolic syndrome, serum alpha-fetoprotein, and inherited genetic factors are also considered risk

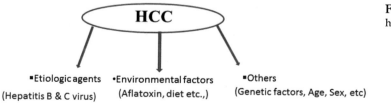

FIGURE 3.1 Pathogenesis of hepatocellular carcinoma.

factors for HCC [7]. Different genomic alterations, genomic instability, and genetic events such as inactivation of p53, β-catenin mutations, methylation of cancer-related genes, overexpresssion of ErbB, and Met receptors are the main causes of HCC [8].

Nanotheranostics in hepatocellular carcinoma

Theranostic approach based on nanoparticles provides simultaneous imaging and therapy of HCC that are presented in Table 3.1 and mechanistic model is depicted in Fig. 3.2. Different nanomaterials have been developed to use as novel theranostics for HCC. Among the nanomaterials, mesoporous nanomaterials based on bismuth loaded with sorafenib, a multikinase inhibitor of HCC, and linked with polyethylene glycol (PEG)-folic acid conjugates, showed that it significantly inhibited proliferation of HCC cells and increased apoptosis by synergistic chemoradiotherapy. Moreover, the nanosystem possessed enhanced contrast efficiency in computed tomography imaging [9]. The nanoparticles based on gadolinium are also used for theranostic magnetic resonance imaging (MRI) and radiation therapy in HCC. The study showed simultaneously by apoptosis imaging and degree of apoptosis, which is observed more in high dose of nanoparticles-mediated radiation therapy [10].

Mesoporous silica nanoparticles supported with lipid bilayer (protocells) were used to prepare theranostics by codelivery with mixtures of diagnostic and therapeutic agents for human HCC [11]. A magnetic OFF-ON state drug delivery system was prepared from iron oxide nanoparticles coated with mesoporous silica and capped DNA hairpin sensor gates, which linked with fluorescence quencher (BHQ1) and 6-carboxyfluorescein. The nanoplatform exhibited high therapeutic as well as diagnostic efficacy in HCC [12]. The upconversion nanoparticles-based micelles designed for both MRI/upconversion luminescence imaging also combined chemo and photodynamic therapy. The theranostic micelles showed remarkable anticancer effect and simultaneously superior imaging of HCC by in vivo model [13]. A melanin-based multifunctional nanoagent was fabricated by conjugating near infrared dye IR820 and encapsulating with PEG. The nanoagent displayed a satisfactory MRI signal as well as high photothermal efficiency in HCC mouse models [14]. A dual sensitive (reduction and pH) micellar nanodrug designed from the copolymer of monomethoxyl PEG and poly(N-(2-aminoethanethiol-co-2-aminoethyldiisopropylamine) aspartamide) incorporated with sorafenib and superparamagnetic iron oxide nanoparticles. The nanodrug showed its potential as promising theranostic by improved significant anticancer effect and facilitated detection, monitoring of HCC by MRI [15].

The importance for chitosan nanoparticles has been growing due to their use in theranostic applications. The biodistribution studies of superparamagnetic iron oxide nanoparticles coated with chitosan showed as good contrast agents for liver diseases. Chitosan derivatives have been also used to prepare drug-loaded nanocarriers and reported interesting results [16]. Redox-responsive theranostic nanoparticles were prepared from poly-(N-ε-carbobenzyloxy-L-lysine)-conjugated hyaluronan copolymers and loaded with doxorubicin and superparamagnetic iron oxide nanoparticles. The nanopolymers showed great potential as nanotheranostics in both in vitro and in vivo studies [17]. Biocompatible and biodegradable nanocarriers were prepared from PEG and poly(D,L-lactide-co-glycolide)

TABLE 3.1 Nanotheranostics used in hepatocellular carcinoma.

Sl. no	Type of nanoparticles	Drug molecule and therapy	Imaging agent and modality	Other targeting molecules	Type of study	References
1	Bismuth-based mesoporous nanomaterial	Sorafenib, bismuth-based nanomaterial and chemoradiotherapy	Bismuth-based nanomaterial and CT	Polyethylene glycol-folic acid conjugate	In vitro-SMCC-7721 and BEL-7402 cell lines and in vivo four-week-old Balb/c nude mice tumor established by SMCC-7721 cell lines	Zhang et al. [9]
2	Gadolinium-based nanoparticles	Gadolinium atoms and radiation therapy	Gadolinium atoms and MRI	EPR effect	In vitro-HepG2 cell lines. In vivo six-week-old male Balb/c mice injected subcutaneously with HepG2 cells in right flank	Hu et al. [10]
3	Nanoporous silica supported lipid bilayer or protocell	Drug cocktail (doxorubicin, Si-RNA, toxin) and chemotherapy	Quantum dots and fluorescence imaging	SP94 peptides	In vitro-Hep3B cell lines	Ashley et al. [11]
4	Mesoporous silica-coated iron oxide nanoparticles	Doxorubicin and chemotherapy	Iron oxide nanoparticles, IR-783, and MRI, in vivo imaging system	Magnetic targeting	In vitro-HepG2 cell linesIn vivo-HepG2-tumor-bearing mice	Liu et al. [12]
5	Upconversion nanoparticles-based micelles	Mitoxantrone and synergistic chemo and photodynamic therapy	Gadolinium ions-MRI, upconversion property-UCL imaging	EPR, anti-EpCAM for active targeting	In vitro-BEL-7404 cellsIn vivo-BEL-7404 tumor-bearing mice	Han et al. [13]
6	Melanin-based nanoparticles	IR 820 and photoacoustic/photothermal therapy	Melanin nanoparticles and photoacoustic/MR imaging	EPR	In vitro-HepG2 cell linesIn vivo-HepG2 subcutaneously injected into mice	Chen et al. [14]

#	Formulation	Therapy	Imaging technique	Targeting	Cell lines/in vivo	Reference
7	Diblock copolymer of monomethoxyl poly(ethylene glycol) and poly(N-(2-aminoethanethiol-co-2-aminoethyldiisopropylamine) aspartamide)	Sorafenib and chemotherapy	Superparamagnetic iron oxide nanoparticles and MRI	Antiglypican-3 antibody	In vitro-HepG2 cell lines In vivo-HepG2-tumor-bearing mice	Cai et al. [15]
8	Chitosan nanoparticles	Doxorubicin, Si-RNA, IP-10 gene, adriamycin etc. and gene therapy, chemotherapy	Superparamagnetic iron oxide nanoparticles and MRI	Modified chitosan nanoparticles	SMCC-7721, HepG2 cell lines	Bonferoni et al. [16]
9	Disulfide bond-linked hyaluronan-g-poly-(N-ε-carbobenzyloxy-L-lysine) grafted copolymers	Doxorubicin	Superparamagnetic iron oxide nanoparticles and MRI	CD44-hyaluronan receptor-ligand interactions	In vitro-HepG2 cell lines In vivo-HepG2-tumor bearing mice	Yang et al. [17]
10	Poly(D,L-lactide-co-glycolide) and polyethylene glycol-poly (D,L-lactide-co-glycolide) copolymers	Sorafenib and chemotherapy	Gd-DTPA complex	–	In vitro- HepG2 cell lines	Feczkó et al. [18]
11	Liposomes	Doxorubicin and chemotherapy, microwave ablation therapy	Doxorbucin/indocyanine green and photoacoustic imaging	EPR effect	In vitro-HepG2 cell lines, in vivo HepG2-tumor-bearing mice	Zhou et al. [19]
12	Magnetic microcapsule	Doxorubicin and chemotherapy	Fe_3O_4 naroparticles and MRI, CT and ultrasound imaging	External EMF	In vitro-HeLa cell lines	Huang et al. [20]
13	TPETS nanodots	TPETS and photodynamic therapy	Nanodots and ex vivo fluorescence imaging	Passive and active targeting- thiolated cRGD	In vitro-HepG2 cell lines In vivo-HepG2-tumor-bearing mice	Gao et al. [21]

(Continued)

TABLE 3.1 (Continued)

Sl. no	Type of nanoparticles	Drug molecule and therapy	Imaging agent and modality	Other targeting molecules	Type of study	References
14	Pd nanosheets	Photothermal and radiotherapy	$Na^{125}I$ or $Na^{131}I$-SPECT/CT imaging	Passive targeting	Nude mice bearing HCC-LM3 human hepatocarcinoma and *Mst1/2* double-knockout hepatoma model	Chen et al. [22]
15	Metal–organic nanoparticles	Photothermal therapy	Fluorescence/photoacoustic/magnetic resonance imaging	Passive targeting	In vitro-HepG2 cell linesIn vivo-HepG2-tumor-bearing mice	Shi et al. [23]
16	Cancer cell membrane-coated magnetic nanoparticles	Ce6 and photodynamic therapy	MR/NIR fluorescence dual-modal imaging	Passive targeting	In vitro-SMMC-7721cell linesIn vivo- SMMC-7721-tumor-bearing mice	Li et al. [24]
17	Oxygen self-sufficient fluorinated polypeptide nanoparticle	BODIPY-Br_2 and photodynamic therapy	NIR imaging	Passive targeting	In vitro-HepG2 cell linesIn vivo-HepG2-tumor-bearing mice	Yuan et al. [25]
18	SP94-modified polypyrrole-BSA-ICG nanoparticles	Polypyrrole and photothermal therapy	Photoacoustic and NIR fluorescence imaging	SP94 targeting	In vitro-Hep 3B cell linesIn vivo-Hep 3B-tumor-bearing mice	Jin et al. [26]
19	Thermally cross-linked superparamagnetic iron oxide nanoparticles and monocrystalline iron oxide nanoparticles	–	MRI	–	In vivo-HepG2-tumor-bearing mice	Li et al. [27]
20	A multifunctional pH-sensitive polymeric nanoparticle	Sorafenib and chemotherapy	Gd ions and MRI	VEGFR antibodies-Active targeting	In vitro-Hep G2 cell linesIn vivo-H22 tumor-tumor bearing mice	Liu et al. [28]

No.	Nanoparticle	Drug/therapy	Imaging/method	Targeting	Model/cell lines	Reference
21	Magnetic nanoparticles	Doxorubicin and chemotherapy	—	SP94 targeting	In situ: Hep G2 cells	Wang et al. [29]
22	Galactose-based nanogels	Iodoazomycinarabinofuranoside and radio- and chemotherapy	—	Asialoglycoprotein receptor-mediated uptake	In vitro-Hep G2 cell lines	Quan et al. [30]
23	Quantum dots	Herpes simplex virus thymidine kinase gene/ganciclovir	NIR fluorescence imaging	EPR	In vitro-HepG2 cell linesIn vivo-HepG2-tumor-bearing mice	Shao et al. [31]
24	Carboxymethyl cellulose modified magnetic nanoparticles	Doxorubicin and chemotherapy	Magnetic nanoparticles and MRI	EpCAM aptamer	In vitro-HepG2.2.15 cell lines	Pilapong et al. [32]
25	Lipid-AuNPs@PDAnanohybrid	Indocyanine green and photothermal therapy	Gadolinium-1,4,7,10-tetraacetic acid and MRI/CT imaging	Lactobionic acid and active targeting	In vitro-HepG2 cell lines	Zeng et al. [33]
26	SPIO-loaded gold nanoparticles	Laser ablation	MRI	Adipose-derived mesenchymal cells	In vitro-HepG2 cell lines	Zhao et al. [34]
27	Mn(HAsO3)@SiO$_2$ nanomaterials	Arsenic trioxide and chemotherapy	Manganese ions and MRI	EPR effect	In vitro-HepG2 cell linesIn vivo-H22 tumor-bearing mice and SMMC-7721 tumor-bearing mice	Zhao et al. [35]
28	Prussian blue nanoparticles	Photothermal therapy	MR imaging	Glypican-3 monoclonal antibody	In vitro-HepG2 cell lines	Li et al. [36]
30	Mesoporous silica nanoparticles	5-Fluorouracil and chemotherapy	Gold nanoparticles and CT imaging	Epithelial cell adhesion molecule	In vitro-HepG2 cell linesIn vivo-HepG2-tumor-bearing mice	Babaei et al. [37]

(Continued)

TABLE 3.1 (Continued)

Sl. no	Type of nanoparticles	Drug molecule and therapy	Imaging agent and modality	Other targeting molecules	Type of study	References
31	Hollow mesoporous Prussian blue nanoparticles	Doxorubicin and synergistic chemo-/thermotherapy	Ultrasound and magnetic resonance imaging	–	–	Wang et al. [38]
32	Mesoporous silica-coated gold nanomaterials	Doxorubicin and chemotherapy	CT imaging	Folic acid and active targeting	In vitro-SMMC-7721 cell lines In vivo- SMMC-7721-tumor-bearing mice	Wang et al. [39]
33	Graphene oxide (GO)-based nanocarrier	Protocatechuic acid	Gadolinium (III) nitrate hexahydrate and magnetic resonance imaging	–	In vitro-HepG2 cell lines	Usman et al. [40]
34	Lipid nanoparticles	10-Hydroxycamptothecin	Ultrasound imaging	Hyaluronic acid	In vitro-SMMC-7721 cell lines In vivo-SMMC-7721-tumor-bearing mice	Zhao et al. [41]
35	Fe@Fe$_3$O$_4$ NP	Active ingredient of Chinese herbs (ginsenoside)	MRI	Auto-targeting ability	In vivo- HCCLM3-tumor-bearing mice	Zhao et al. [42]
36	Polydopamine -coated magnetic nanoparticles	Doxorubicin and chemo/photothermal therapy	MRI	–	In vitro-HepG2 cell lines	Mrówczyński et al. [43]
37	Poly-L-lysine nanoparticle system	Curcumin	Cyanine 5.5 and NIRF imaging	EPR	In vitro-Hep3B cell lines In vivo-Hep3B-tumor-bearing mice	Yang et al. [44]
38	PAMAM dendrimers	Doxorubicin and chemo/photothermal therapy	Magnetite nanoparticles and MRI	EPR	In vitro-HepG2 cell lines	Jędrzak et al. [45]
39	β-Cyclodextrin-based dual-responsive nanosystem	Doxorubicin and curcumin	Fluorescence imaging	Folic acid	In vitro and In vivo studies	Das et al. [46]

MRI, magnetic resonance imaging; NIR, near infrared; VEGFR, vascular endothelial growth factor receptor; EpCAM, epithelial cell adhesion molecule; PAMAM, poly(amidoamine); CT, computed tomography; EPR, enhanced permeability and retention.

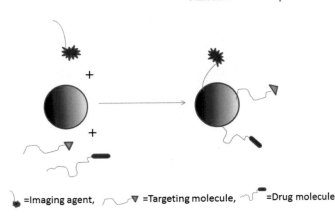

FIGURE 3.2 Theranostic multifunctional hybrid nanoparticles.

=Imaging agent, =Targeting molecule, =Drug molecule

(PLGA) copolymers and loaded with sorafenib and finally attached on their surface with gadolinium complex. The theranostic nanocarrier system exhibited superior anticancer effect and strong MRI signal [18]. The liposomes were encapsulated with doxorubicin and indocyanine green and developed as nanotheranostic platform for HCC. The combination of microwave ablation and doxorbucin-loaded liposomes ablation apparently inhibited HCC and simultaneously doxorbucin-loaded liposomes showed excellent diagnostic abil ity by optoacoustic tomography imaging [19].

The eccentric magnetic microcapsule designed with Fe_3O_4 nanoparticles and polydimethylsiloxane and used to visualize with multimodality imaging and also to achieve local controlled drug release by external electromagnetic field for potential therapy of HCC [20]. The tetraphenylene derivative with typical AIE characteristics (TPETS) organic nanodots were prepared and conjugated with thiolated cRGD. The theranostic nanodots enhanced overall efficacy of image-guided photodynamic therapy of HCC [21]. A pH sensitive multifunctional nanotheranostic platform prepared by Pd nanosheets coordinated their surfaces with radioactive iodide. The combined photothermal and radiotherapy with photoacoustic imaging provided simple and efficient strategy for HCC [22]. Novel self-assembled metal—organic nanoparticles (manganese ions and indocyanine green) developed under the protection of poly(vinylpyrrolidone) and proved multimodal imaging-guided photothermal therapy for HCC [23]. The magnetic nanoparticles were loaded with photosensitizer and coated with cancer cell membrane to improve cellular uptake and biocompatibility. The study showed promising theranostic platform in HCC models by dual-modal MR/NIR imaging with photodynamic therapy [24]. The oxygen self-sufficient fluorinated polypeptide nanoparticles synthesized and loaded with near infrared photosensitizer. The study demonstrated that nanotheranostic platform played a significant role in enhanced photodynamic therapy and near infrared imaging of HCC HepG2 cells [25].

Multifunctional SP94-modified polypyrrole-BSA-ICG nanoparticles synthesized and demonstrated theranostic capability using in vitro and in vivo experiments. The theranostic nanoparticles exhibited dual-modal photoacoustic and near infrared imaging as well as high therapeutic efficiency in HCC [26]. Two thermally cross-linked superparamagnetic and monocrystalline iron oxide nanoparticles synthesized and studied cytotoxicity and imaging capabilities in cultured cells and tumor models. The study suggested that thermally cross-linked nanoparticles may be used as theranostic platform for MRI and monitoring of HCC therapeutic efficiency [27]. Novel multifunctional pH- sensitive polymer nanoparticles developed for both simultaneous MRI and therapy. The novel theranostic platform exhibited good biocompatibility, more resolution, and imaging time in MRI and high anti-HCC therapeutic effect [28]. The theranostic SP94-Fe3-O4-DOX magnetic nanoparticles were designed for effective simultaneous separation and in situ chemotherapy of circulating cancer cells. The nanotheranostic platform showed fast and facile approach in targeted capture and effective therapy for metastasis of HCC [29]. A versatile galactose-based thermosensitive nanogels prepared and encapsulated with iodoazomycinara-binofuranoside and evaluated its hypoxia-selective multimodal theranostic capabilities. The theranostic nanogels demonstrated that they manage solid tumors (HCC) by allowing external beam ration therapy, in situ molecular radiotherapy, and position/single photon emission tomography-based imaging [30]. Quantum dot-based theranostics prepared by covalent linkage between near infrared fluorescent quantum dots and thymidine kinase gene. The quantum dot-based theranostics allowed real-time visualization and tracing of HSV-TK/GCV suicide gene cancer therapy [31]. The development of theranostic nanop-robe by smart magnetic iron oxide nanoparticles and aptamer (DNA-based EpCAM apta-mer) were used simultaneously for targeted imaging and to enhance treatment efficacy of HCC [32]. Multifunctional hybrid nanosystems were synthesized by gold nanoparticles and polydopamine as inner core. The indocyanine green adsorbed electrostatically on polydopamine and finally monolayer lipid self-assembled to form shell. The theranostic nanohybrid system showed dual-modality imaging capability and significant photother-mal therapy of HCC [33]. The superparamagnetic iron oxide-coated gold nanoparticles were loaded in adipose-derived mesenchymal cells and evaluated their theranostic ability toward HCC. The successful transfection of nanotheranostics into mesenchymal stem cells was confirmed by MRI and treated HCC using near infrared laser irradiation [34]. Hollow silica nanopartciles loaded with water soluble manganese arsenite and arsenic trioxide were examined for their theranostic potential. The study proved real-time monitoring and treatment of HCC by smart multifunctional nanodrug delivery system [35].

Glypican-3 monoclonal antibody functionalized Prussian blue nanoparticles are synthe-sized and proved as novel theranostic agents for HCC. The theranostic nanoprobe showed excellent biocompatibility and contrast enhancement by MRI and efficient photothermal therapy of HCC [36]. The PEGylated mesoporous silica nanoparticles hybridized with gold nanoparticles targeted epithelial cell adhesion molecule used as gatekeeper of HCC [37]. Mesoporous composite nanoparticles developed by encapsulation of doxorubicin/perfluorhexane in hollow mesoporous Prussian blue nanoparticles examined their thera-nostic potential. The study observed that nanotheranostic platform used for dual-modality imaging proved efficient combined chemo/thermotherapy against HCC [38].

Multifunctional nanohydrid nanoplatform were prepared by gold-mesoporous silica nanoparticles and modified via folic acid conjugation. The doxorubicin loaded in meso-pores released in a pH responsive manner. The janus gold nanotheranostic platform by synergistic chemoradiotherapy showed excellent anticancer therapy and worked as tar-geted computed tomography imaging agent for HCC [39]. The graphene-based theranostic system synthesized by conjugation of graphene oxide and protocatechuic acid were fol-lowed by surface adsorption of gold nanoparticles. The graphene-based theranostics possessed significant anti-HCC effect and simultaneously acted as MRI contrast agent for

HCC diagnosis [40]. The combination of hyaluronic acid-mediated cell-penetrating peptide-modified 10-hydroxycamptothecin-loaded phase-transformation lipid nanoparticles with low intensity focused ultrasound used as precision theranostics for HCC [41].

A new nanomedicine has been developed by conjugating $Fe@Fe_3O_4$ nanoparticles and Chinese model medicines of ginsenosides and showed theranostic ability for liver cancer [42]. Polydopamine-coated magnetic nanoparticles coated with cyclodextrins loaded with doxorubicin showed both chemo and photothermal therapy of liver cancer in addition as contrast agent of MRI [43]. Poly-L-lysine-based nanoparticle system has been synthesized with pH sensitive release of curcumin and showed promising application in liver cancer theranosis [44]. The poly(amidoamine) (PAMAM) dendrimers functionalized polydopamine-coated magnetite nanoparticles applied successfully in both chemo and photothermal therapy of liver cancer and also exhibited excellent contrast properties [45]. The β-cyclodextrin-based dual-responsive nanoconjugate has been developed with a combination of multiple properties and proved as smart theranostic agent for HCC [46].

Most of the above studies prepared nanoparticles or nanoconjugates from different materials and exploited passive or active targeting strategies. They showed anti-HCC effect of functionalized nanomaterials using simultaneously various imaging methods (MRI, CT, NIR fluorescence, and ultrasound imaging) and therapeutic approaches such as chemotherapy, radiation, and photodynamic therapies.

Conclusions and future perspectives

The growing interest in the field of cancer nanotheranostics offers a promising hope in the development of effective tools for simultaneous diagnosis and therapy of HCC. Different types of nanoparticle-based theranostics have been used in imaging and treatment of HCC using both in vitro and in vivo studies. Among nanotheranostics, multifunctional hybrid nanoparticles-based theranostics have emerged as promising strategies for HCC due to their high therapeutic efficiency and image signal. Although, nanoparticles have limitations owing to composition, morphology, and functional groups, etc., many studies demonstrated the biocompatibility and nontoxicity of nanotheranostics. More studies are still needed to understand the mechanisms of action, long-term effect, and clearance of nanotheranostics before their successful use in clinic.

Conflicts of interest

No potential conflicts of interest.

References

[1] Chen Z, Xie H, Hu M, Huang T, Hu Y, Sang N, et al. Recent progress in treatment of hepatocellular carcinoma. Am J Cancer Res 2020;10(9):2993–3036.
[2] Raoul JL, Kudo M, Finn RS, Edeline J, Reig M, Galle PR. Systemic therapy for intermediate and advanced hepatocellular carcinoma: sorafenib and beyond. Cancer Treat Rev 2018;68:16–24.

[3] Silva CO, Pinho JO, Lopes JM, Almeida AJ, Gaspar MM, Reis C. Current trends in cancer nanotheranostics: metallic, polymeric, and lipid-based systems. Pharmaceutics 2019;11(1):22.

[4] Dykman LA, Khlebtsov NG. Multifunctional gold-based nanocomposites for theranostics. Biomaterials 2016;108:13−34.

[5] Tao Y, Wang J, Xu X. Emerging and innovative theranostic approaches for mesoporous silica nanoparticles in hepatocellular carcinoma: current status and advances. Front BioengBiotechnol 2020;8:184.

[6] Chen Z, Xie H, Hu M, Huang T, Hu Y, Sang N, et al. Recent progress in treatment of hepatocellular carcinoma. Am J Cancer Res 2020;10(9):2993−3036.

[7] Yu Q, Wu L, Ji J, Feng J, Dai W, Li J, et al. Gut microbiota, peroxisome proliferator-activated receptors, and hepatocellular carcinoma. J Hepatocell Carcinoma 2020;7:271−88.

[8] Farazi PA, DePinho RA. Hepatocellular carcinoma pathogenesis: from genes to environment. Nat Rev Cancer 2006;6(9):674−87.

[9] Zhang GC, Liu J, Yu XN, Deng Y, Sun Y, Liu TT, et al. Bismuth-based mesoporous nanoball carrying sorafenib for computed tomography imaging and synergetic chemoradiotherapy of hepatocellular carcinoma. Adv Healthc Mater 2020;9(21):e2000650.

[10] Hu P, Fu Z, Liu G, Tan H, Xiao J, Shi H, et al. Gadolinium-based nanoparticles for theranostic MRI-guided radiosensitization in hepatocellular carcinoma. Front Bioeng Biotechnol 2019;7:368.

[11] Ashley CE, Carnes EC, Phillips GK, Padilla D, Durfee PN, Brown PA, et al. The targeted delivery of multicomponent cargos to cancer cells by nanoporous particle-supported lipid bilayers. Nat Mater 2011;10 (5):389−97.

[12] Liu J, Liu W, Zhang K, Shi J, Zhang Z. A magnetic drug delivery system with "OFF-ON" state via specific molecular recognition and conformational changes for precise tumor therapy. Adv Healthc Mater 2020;9(3): e1901316.

[13] Han Y, An Y, Jia G, Wang X, He C, Ding Y, et al. Theranostic micelles based on upconversion nanoparticles for dual-modality imaging and photodynamic therapy in hepatocellular carcinoma. Nanoscale 2018;10(14):6511−23.

[14] Chen K, Li Q, Zhao X, Zhang J, Ma H, Sun X, et al. Biocompatible melanin based theranostic agent for in vivo detection and ablation of orthotopic micro-hepatocellular carcinoma. Biomater Sci 2020;8 (15):4322−33.

[15] Cai M, Li B, Lin L, Huang J, An Y, Huang W, et al. A reduction and pH dual-sensitive nanodrug for targeted theranostics in hepatocellular carcinoma. Biomater Sci 2020;8(12):3485−99.

[16] Bonferoni MC, Gavini E, Rassu G, Maestri M, Giunchedi P. Chitosan nanoparticles for therapy and theranostics of hepatocellular carcinoma (HCC) and liver-targeting. Nanomaterials 2020;10(5):870.

[17] Yang H, Miao Y, Chen L, Li Z, Yang R, Xu X, et al. Redox-responsive nanoparticles from disulfide bond-linked poly-(N-ε-carbobenzyloxy-L-lysine)-grafted hyaluronan copolymers as theranostic nanoparticles for tumor-targeted MRI and chemotherapy. Int J Biol Macromol 2020;148:483−92.

[18] Feczkó T, Piiper A, Pleli T, Schmithals C, Denk D, Hehlgans S, et al. Theranostic sorafenib-loaded polymeric nanocarriers manufactured by enhanced gadolinium conjugation techniques. Pharmaceutics 2019;11(10):489.

[19] Zhou Q, Wang K, Dou J, Cao F, Liu F, Yuan H, et al. Theranostic liposomes as nanodelivered chemotherapeutics enhanced the microwave ablation of hepatocellular carcinoma. Nanomedicine 2019;14(16):2151−67.

[20] Huang W, Chen Y, Chen L, Zhong J, Johri AM, Zhou J. Multimodality imaging-guided local injection of eccentric magnetic microcapsules with electromagnetically controlled drug release. Cancer Rep (Hoboken) 2019;2(2):e1154.

[21] Gao Y, Zheng QC, Xu S, Yuan Y, Cheng X, Jiang S, et al. Theranostic nanodots with aggregation-induced emission characteristic for targeted and image-guided photodynamic therapy of hepatocellular carcinoma. Theranostics 2019;9(5):1264−79.

[22] Chen M, Guo Z, Chen Q, Wei J, Li J, Shi C, et al. Pdnanosheets with their surface coordinated by radioactive iodide as a high-performance theranosticnanoagent for orthotopic hepatocellular carcinoma imaging and cancer therapy. Chem Sci 2018;9(18):4268−74.

[23] Shi Z, Chu C, Zhang Y, Su Z, Lin H, Pang X, et al. Self-assembled metal-organic nanoparticles for multimodal imaging-guided photothermal therapy of hepatocellular carcinoma. J Biomed Nanotechnol 2018;14(11):1934−43.

[24] Li J, Wang X, Zheng D, Lin X, Wei Z, Zhang D, et al. Cancer cell membrane-coated magnetic nanoparticles for MR/NIR fluorescence dual-modal imaging and photodynamic therapy. Biomater Sci 2018;6(7):1834−45.

[25] Yuan P, Ruan Z, Jiang W, Liu L, Dou J, Li T, et al. Oxygen self-sufficient fluorinated polypeptide nanoparticles for NIR imaging-guided enhanced photodynamic therapy. J Mater Chem B 2018;6(15):2323−31.

[26] Jin Y, Yang X, Tian J. Targeted polypyrrole nanoparticles for the identification and treatment of hepatocellular carcinoma. Nanoscale 2018;10(20):9594−601.

[27] Li M, Kim HS, Tian L, Yu MK, Jon S, Moon WK. Comparison of two ultrasmall superparamagnetic iron oxides on cytotoxicity and MR imaging of tumors. Theranostics 2012;2(1):76−85.

[28] Liu Y, Feng L, Liu T, Zhang L, Yao Y, Yu D, et al. Multifunctional pH-sensitive polymeric nanoparticles for theranostics evaluated experimentally in cancer. Nanoscale 2014;6(6):3231−42.

[29] Wang Y, Jia HZ, Han K, Zhuo RX, Zhang XZ. Theranostic magnetic nanoparticles for efficient capture and in situ chemotherapy of circulating tumor cells. J Mater Chem B 2013;1(27):3344−52.

[30] Quan S, Wang Y, Zhou A, Kumar P, Narain R. Galactose-based thermosensitive nanogels for targeted drug delivery of iodoazomycinarabinofuranoside (IAZA) for theranostic management of hypoxic hepatocellular carcinoma. Biomacromolecules 2015;16(7):1978−86.

[31] Shao D, Li J, Xiao X, Zhang M, Pan Y, Li S, et al. Real-time visualizing and tracing of HSV-TK/GCV suicide gene therapy by near-infrared fluorescent quantum dots. ACS Appl Mater Interfaces 2014;6(14):11082−90.

[32] Pilapong C, Sitthichai S, Thongtem S, Thongtem T. Smart magnetic nanoparticle-aptamer probe for targeted imaging and treatment of hepatocellular carcinoma. Int J Pharm 2014;473(1−2):469−74.

[33] Zeng Y, Zhang D, Wu M, Liu Y, Zhang X, Li L, et al. Lipid-AuNPs@PDAnanohybrid for MRI/CT imaging and photothermal therapy of hepatocellular carcinoma. ACS Appl Mater Interfaces 2014;6(16):14266−77.

[34] Zhao J, Vykoukal J, Abdelsalam M, Recio-Boiles A, Huang Q, Qiao Y, et al. Stem cell-mediated delivery of SPIO-loaded gold nanoparticles for the theranosis of liver injury and hepatocellular carcinoma. Nanotechnology 2014;25(40):405101.

[35] Zhao Z, Wang X, Zhang Z, Zhang H, Liu H, Zhu X, et al. Real-time monitoring of arsenic trioxide release and delivery by activatable T(1) imaging. ACS Nano 2015;9(3):2749−59.

[36] Li Z, Zeng Y, Zhang D, Wu M, Wu L, Huang A, et al. Glypican-3 antibody functionalized Prussian blue nanoparticles for targeted MR imaging and photothermal therapy of hepatocellular carcinoma. J Mater Chem B 2014;2(23):3686−96.

[37] Babaei M, Abnous K, Taghdisi SM, AmelFarzad S, Peivandi MT, Ramezani M, et al. Synthesis of theranostic epithelial cell adhesion molecule targeted mesoporous silica nanoparticle with gold gatekeeper for hepatocellular carcinoma. Nanomedicine 2017;12(11):1261−79.

[38] Zhang N, Wang R, Hao J, Yang Y, Zou H, Wang Z. Mesoporous composite nanoparticles for dual-modality ultrasound/magnetic resonance imaging and synergistic chemo-/thermotherapy against deep tumors. Int J Nanomed 2017;12:7273−89.

[39] Wang Z, Shao D, Chang Z, Lu M, Wang Y, Yue J, et al. Janus gold nanoplatform for synergetic chemoradiotherapy and computed tomography imaging of hepatocellular carcinoma. ACS Nano 2017;11(12):12732−41.

[40] Usman MS, Hussein MZ, Kura AU, Fakurazi S, Masarudin MJ, Ahmad Saad FF. Graphene oxide as a nanocarrier for a theranostics delivery system of protocatechuic acid and gadolinium/gold nanoparticles. Molecules 2018;23(2):500.

[41] Zhao H, Wu M, Zhu L, Tian Y, Wu M, Li Y, et al. Cell-penetrating peptide-modified targeted drug-loaded phase-transformation lipid nanoparticles combined with low-intensity focused ultrasound for precision theranostics against hepatocellular carcinoma. Theranostics 2018;8(7):1892−910.

[42] Zhao X, Wang J, Song Y, Chen X. Synthesis of nanomedicines by nanohybrids conjugating ginsenosides with auto-targeting and enhanced MRI contrast for liver cancer therapy. Drug Dev Ind Pharm 2018;44(8):1307−16.

[43] Mrówczyński R, Jędrzak A, Szutkowski K, Grześkowiak BF, Coy E, Markiewicz R, et al. Cyclodextrin-based magnetic nanoparticles for cancer therapy. Nanomaterials 2018;8(3):170.

[44] Yang DH, Kim HJ, Park K, Kim JK, Chun HJ. Preparation of poly-L-lysine-based nanoparticles with pH-sensitive release of curcumin for targeted imaging and therapy of liver cancer in vitro and in vivo. Drug Deliv 2018;25(1):950−60.

[45] Jędrzak A, Grześkowiak BF, Coy E, Wojnarowicz J, Szutkowski K, Jurga S, et al. Dendrimer based theranostic nanostructures for combined chemo- and photothermal therapy of liver cancer cells in vitro. Colloids Surf B Biointerfaces 2019;173:698−708.

[46] Das M, Solanki A, Joshi A, Devkar R, Seshadri S, Thakore S. β-Cyclodextrin based dual-responsive multifunctional nanotheranostics for cancer cell targeting and dual drug delivery. Carbohydr Polym 2019;206:694−705.

C H A P T E R

4

Therapeutic options for the management of hepatocellular carcinoma

Vibha Sinha[1], Sapnita Shinde[1], Vinit Singh Baghel[1],
Naveen Kumar Vishvakarma[1], Dhananjay Shukla[1],
Atul Kumar Tiwari[2], Ashwini Kumar Dixit[3],
Sanjay Kumar Pandey[4], Sudhakar Dwivedi[4],
Mrinalini Singh[5] and Vineeta Dixit[2]

[1]Department of Biotechnology, Guru Ghasidas Vishwavidyalaya, Bilaspur, India [2]Department of Zoology, Dr. Bhanvar Singh Porte Govt. College, Pendra, India [3]Department of Botany, Guru Ghasidas Vishwavidyalaya, Bilaspur, India [4]MDRU, Shyam Shah Medical College, Rewa, India [5]Experimental Biology Division, Defense Institute of Physiology and Allied Sciences, Timarpur, India

Abstract

Hepatocellular carcinoma (HCC) remains a major global health crisis because its diagnosis at an advanced stage leads to high mortality. The incidence rate and HCC-related death have increased in the past years and the therapeutics available for liver cancer are very limited. The best options available for the treatment of liver cancer are liver resection and the transplantation. The medical treatments include sorafenib, a systemic therapy but it only increases the survival by few months. Other treatment used are immunotherapy and chemotherapy, but new approaches for the treatment are much needed to increase the overall survival rate and limit the adverse effect of chemotherapeutic drugs. Use of nanomedicines and phytochemicals are emerging therapeutic approaches for the treatment of HCC with good results in overall and disease free survival, show less toxicity and very few side effects. Many novel approaches such as the nanomedicines conjugated with different phytochemicals have also been tested and have shown to be of good therapeutic effect. Although various researches have been done to develop the therapeutics for HCC and few of them have reached the clinical trials but their toxicity and adverse side effects still remain major problem. Several other approaches such as adding an adjuvant to decrease the toxicity are also being employed. The present review summarizes the various chemotherapeutic-, immunotherapeutic-, nanomedicine-, and phytochemical-based therapeutics for liver cancer treatment.

Keywords: Hepatocellular carcinoma; immunotherapy; chemotherapy; molecular target therapy; phytochemicals

© 2022 Elsevier Inc. All rights reserved.

Abbreviations

ACT	adoptive cell therapy
AFP	oncofetal protein
ASGPR	asialoglycoprotein receptor
CART	chimeric antigen receptor T cell
CD	cluster of differentiation
CIKs	cytokine-induced killer cells
DCR	diseases control rate
GPC3	glypican
HBV	hepatitis B virus
HCC	hepatocellular carcinoma
HCV	hepatitis C virus
MDR1	multidrug resistance 1
NPs	nanoparticles
OS	overall survival
PDGF-R	platelets-derived growth factor receptor
PFS	progression free survival
SRR	stable response rate
TACE	transarterial chemoembolization
TKI	tyrosine kinase inhibitor
TILs	tumor-infiltrating lymphocytes
VSV	vesicular stomatitis virus

Introduction

Among all cancers, hepatocellular carcinoma (HCC) is the sixth most occurring cancer and have second highest death rate globally [1,2]. It accounted for approximately 8.4 lakhs and 7.8 lakhs, new cases and deaths, respectively in year 2018. The high incidence rate is found in males (596,574 cases) compared to women (244,506 cases) [3,4]. The various factors such as genetic differences and ethnic disparities contribute to the high incidence rate of HCC [5]. The incidence rate of HCC has been found to be the highest in Asian and African continent, a potential cause for it is considered as the high pervasiveness of hepatitis C virus (HCV) and hepatitis B virus (HBV), these viruses lead to development of severe chronic liver diseases leading to liver cirrhosis and ultimately to HCC [6]. Among the two, HBV infection accounts for about 50% incidence rate followed by HCV infection with about 25% incidence rate. The HBV increases the probability for development of HCC to the higher extent as it consists of double-stranded circular DNA which integrates into DNA of hepatic cell and cause genomic instability [1,7]. Other major risk factors contributing to HCC are food contaminated with aflatoxin, heavy alcohol consumption, smoking, diabetes, fatty liver, hypothyroidism, and obesity.

Due to its asymptomatic nature HCC is generally detected in the advanced stages making it nearly impossible to cure [8]. Even though several medical and surgical methods are being used for the treatment of HCC (Fig. 4.1), the survival rate with HCC remains very low even after surgical removal in the initial stages. The higher chances of complication are included with right hepatectomy. To reduce the chance of recurrence and postoperative complication various therapeutic options are available for HCC treatment. Chemotherapeutic drugs which include targeted therapeutic drugs sorafenib, brivanib, sunitinib, etc., and other cytotoxic

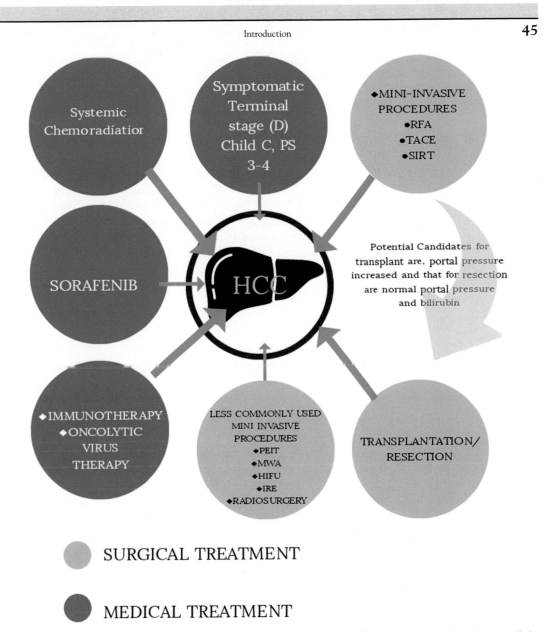

FIGURE 4.1   An overview of the medical and surgical approaches used for the treatment of the hepatocellular carcinoma.

drugs such as doxorubicin, gemcitabine, 5-fluorouracil are used as monotherapy regimens or in combinational therapy. They target various molecules and receptors which are directly or indirectly involved in HCC tumor development and in angiogenesis [4]. Immune system has capacity to destroy cancer cells by the presentation of antigenic peptides of tumor cells by MHC I and II antigen-presenting cells (APCs). Metastatic tumors have developed the capacity to escape this immune clearance mechanism. To combat this immune escaping mechanism of tumor cells targeted therapy is used. Multidrug resistance is one of the obstacles of chemotherapy-based drugs and immunotherapy removes these obstacles by targeting tumor-specific antigen [9]. Immunotherapy can reboot the current immune system and induce new immune responses. It involves various checkpoint inhibitors, vaccine therapies, etc. [10]. Another emerging approach of treatment involves phytochemicals-based therapy and nanomedicine-based therapy. From ancient times phytochemicals have been used to treat various chronic diseases. The progression, prevention, and treatment are directly correlated with diet. Studies suggest that a diet enriched with green vegetables and fresh fruit significantly reduced the risk of the cancers [11]. Different types of bioactive components present in the fruit, vegetable, spices have the capacity to reduce cancer cell proliferation, angiogenesis, and metastasis [12]. The nanomedicine is a rapidly evolving therapeutic treatment which has the potential of overcoming certain limitations with the bioavailability of drug. This review summarizes the various treatment approaches such as chemotherapy, immunotherapy, nanomedicines, and phytochemicals-based therapy and their role in HCC prevention and control.

Chemotherapeutic drugs

Sorafenib

Sorafenib is a chemotherapeutic drug which belongs to the tyrosine kinase inhibitor (TKI) family. It has multiple targets and functions as anti- and antiproliferative agents. Sorafenib targets Raf-1, B-Raf, RAS/MEK/ERK signaling pathway and thus stops proliferation of tumor cells [13]. It also thwarts VEGF-R, platelets-derived growth factors receptor (PDGF-R) and molecules involved in angiogenesis [14]. It increased the OS in treatment group having advanced HCC with median of 28.24 weeks as opposed to just 18.25 weeks in placebo group. The common small side effects associated with sorafenib treatment are diarrhea, nausea, hemorrhage, hand-foot syndrome, and fatigue. It was exciting outcome that these side effects were seen in only about 11% of the population studied [15]. Due to such high success ratio the sorafenib was approved by FDA in 2007 for the advanced cases of HCC.

Brivanib

Brivanib is another drug belonging to TKI family whose main targets are FGF and VEGF and as these two are required for the pathogenesis of HCC, brivanib can effectively inhibit the process. Brivanib alaninate is alanine prodrug of brivanib, and administered orally [16]. In a randomized phase III clinical study, it was found that the overall survival (OS) of patients treated with brivanib was found to be 9 months. In another similar study it was identified that brivanib was not able to increase OS in sorafenib intolerant patients [17].

Sunitinib

Sunitinib is receptor tyrosine kinase inhibitor (RTK) and is administered orally. It has antiangiogenic and antitumor activity. The molecular targets of sunitinib are quite similar to sorafenib. The targets of sunitinib are VEGF receptors (VEGFR-1, 2, and 3), PDGFR (A and B) etc.

Everolimus

Everolimus is a potent inhibitor of the mTOR protein. By targeting VEGF expression in tumors, the mTOR inhibitor also reduces angiogenesis and lowering the risk of recurrence of many cancers [18]. In clinical trials, patients with advanced stage unresectable HCC had a progression free survival (PFS) of around 12 weeks and an overall survival of about 32 weeks [19].

Doxorubicin

Doxorubicin is a transarterial chemoembolization (TACE) drug. Before the sorafenib was approved, it was used for the treatment of HCC [20]. The main pathway of doxorubicin for tumor reduction was binding with DNA. Doxorubicin binds with topoisomerase II and generates reactive oxygen species, which induces death of malignant cells. In phase II clinical study doxorubicin was evaluated in 37 patients the objective response rate was found to be approximately 19% and the median OS of all the patients was 7.3 months. The most common grade 3/4 side effects were also observed [21]. Doxorubicin resistance was also observed in HCC patients because of the expression of multidrug resistance 1 (MDR1) [22].

Gemcitabine

Gemcitabine is nucleotide analog (deoxycytidine) antimetabolite cytotoxic drug. In various preclinical studies gemcitabine has shown antitumor activity against HCC. In phase II study on naive paints with advanced HCC, 18% objective response rate with low side effects was obtained [23]. In another phase II clinical trial, gemcitabine did not show very good results; the OS rate was recorded 0%–5%, these huge differences in the result can be attributed to the different patient population in both the studies [24].

Immunotherapy

The immune system plays an important role in the fight against the malignant tumors. Tumor characteristics such as immune tolerance, immune escape and environment of HCC favor its growth and progression. This immune tolerance of HCC can be credited to several factors such as CTL-associated protein, cluster of differentiation (CD) 279/PD-L1 and LAG-3 [25–27] and are the main targets for immunotherapy. This therapy works on two major principles: the first one is to rejuvenate the immune system and second one is to generate or stimulate new immune responses. Immunotherapy triggers tumor-specific immune responses, improves cellular or humoral immunity and inhibits immune tolerance. Presently, several immunotherapy drugs have shown great potential in the treatment of HCC and hence have been approved by the FDA to treat hematological malignancies, melanomas, and lung cancers. Research on immunotherapy approaches to HCC has recently increased rapidly. Immune-based approach includes checkpoint inhibitors, vaccine therapy, and antigen targeting antibody therapy [28–30].

Checkpoint inhibitors

Immune pathways leading to the activation of the immune responses are controlled by immune checkpoints. These checkpoints perform crucial functions in preventing the autoimmune diseases and maintaining the homeostasis of the immune system. Various cells of the immune systems such as B-lymphocytes, T-lymphocytes, and TAM, etc., are involved in the expression of these checkpoint proteins. These checkpoint proteins are immunosuppressive in nature and keep in check the uncontrolled infection response by the T cells and limits collateral tissue damage [31–33]. In human oncogenic studies LAG-3 protein, CD152, B and T-lymphocyte attenuator protein, CD279 and TIM-3 protein are the most studied checkpoints [31]. Immune checkpoint blockers have the potential to reactivate the T cells having tumor cell specificity [34]. CD152 and CD279 antagonists are very well characterized and FDA approved for the treatment of skin cancer and given their effectiveness they are being considered in the treatment of HCC [35].

CTLA-4 blockers

The main function of CTLA-4 is that it downregulates the immune responses. CTLA-4 becomes upregulated in cancer cells [36]. It is present in $CD4^+$ T cells. When the T-cell receptor gets activated by CD28, CTLA-4 translocates to the cell surface and binds to CD80 and CD86. This binding neutralizes the binding affinity of CD28 and transfers the negative signal to the T cell leading to inhibition of tumor-specific T-lymphocytes (Fig. 4.2). Studies have also shown that CTLA-4 promotes tumor growth and maturation by binding with APCs [25]. CTLA-4 inhibitors prevent binding of CTLA-4 with CD80 (1 and 2) which leads to activation of tumor-specific $CD4^+$ T-lymphocytes. Ipilimumab and tremelimumab are two CTLA-4 inhibitors which were put to test in clinical trials in the year of 2000 after all the promising results obtained in the preclinical investigations. Ipilimumab, a fully humanized mAB was first approved by FDA in the year 2011. Tremelimumab is an anti-CTLA-4 mAB found to be effective against HCV in clinical trials. Study of Kelly et al. has identified that tremelimumab is a safe monotherapy for antitumor and antiviral treatment for HCC [37]. Another ongoing phase III randomized clinical trial on combinational mAB (ipilimumab and nivolumab) will be used to evaluate the efficacy as first-line therapy for HCC.

PD-1/PD-L1 inhibitors

D279 (CD279) is a transmembrane protein present in various cell of immune system. CD279 ligand 1 and 2 are present on somatic cell as well as on immune cells and in some tumor cells. PD-1 suppresses T-cell's activity and downregulates the release of

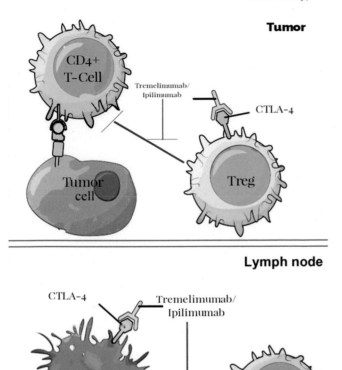

FIGURE 4.2 Blocking action of tremelimumab (and/or) ipilimumab on CTLA-4 leading to the activation and antitumor effect of T cells.

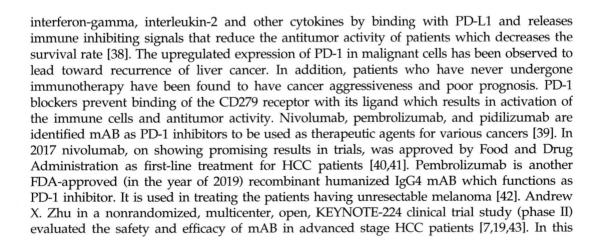

interferon-gamma, interleukin-2 and other cytokines by binding with PD-L1 and releases immune inhibiting signals that reduce the antitumor activity of patients which decreases the survival rate [38]. The upregulated expression of PD-1 in malignant cells has been observed to lead toward recurrence of liver cancer. In addition, patients who have never undergone immunotherapy have been found to have cancer aggressiveness and poor prognosis. PD-1 blockers prevent binding of the CD279 receptor with its ligand which results in activation of the immune cells and antitumor activity. Nivolumab, pembrolizumab, and pidilizumab are identified mAB as PD-1 inhibitors to be used as therapeutic agents for various cancers [39]. In 2017 nivolumab, on showing promising results in trials, was approved by Food and Drug Administration as first-line treatment for HCC patients [40,41]. Pembrolizumab is another FDA-approved (in the year of 2019) recombinant humanized IgG4 mAB which functions as PD-1 inhibitor. It is used in treating the patients having unresectable melanoma [42]. Andrew X. Zhu in a nonrandomized, multicenter, open, KEYNOTE-224 clinical trial study (phase II) evaluated the safety and efficacy of mAB in advanced stage HCC patients [7,19,43]. In this trial a dose of 200 mg of mAB was tested on 200 people who received the dose every 3 weeks for approximately 2 years. This study identified the CRR of 1%, PRR 16%, and stable response rate (SRR) of 44%. Tumor regression rate was 17%, diseases control rates (DCR) were more than 60%, and OS was about 1 year in advanced stage HCC patients and these results were retained for a long stretch of time with tolerable adverse side effects.

Vaccine therapy

In vaccine-based cancer immunotherapy antigenic substances are used for inducing the tumor-specific immune response and these immune responses work on reducing the cancer progression and cancer recurrence. Because of problem in identification of correct tumor antigen there are few clinical trials on tumor vaccines as compare to other immunotherapy for liver cancer and also there is lack of effective tumor vaccine for other types of cancers. If induction of immune response can be achieved by alone or more likely in conjunction with other immune modulators, then it can be proven to be an effective remedy for liver cancer. HCC vaccines incorporate myeloma cells, dendritic cells, antigenic peptides, and deoxyribonucleic acid-based vaccines, some of them successfully reducing tumor relapse and spread.

Hepatocellular carcinoma cells vaccines

HCC cells are used as immunogens for reducing pathogenicity and inducing tumor-specific immune response. HCC cell-based cancer vaccines are mainly of two types, first one is antigen-undefined HCC vaccine and second one antigen-defined HCC cells vaccine [44]. In first type whole tumor cells or lysates are used as tumor antigen, which contain all types of HCC-specific tumor antigens for increasing the immune response DSc are generally used in preparations. On a clinical trial 33 patients were enrolled, in this trial DSc were pulsed with HCC cells and the results were found as; PRR was 12.9%, disease stable rate was 54.8%, disease progression rate was 32.3%, and OS rate was 1 year [42,45,46]. In Another phase I clinical trial bi-sh/RNA granulocytes macrophage colony-stimulating factor was fused with HCC cell lysates, tested on eight patients with advanced stage liver cancer, three of them found good immune response and regular follow-up increased the OS after treatment. It is also identified that because of weak immunogenicity, the HCC cell vaccine efficiency remains indeterminate [47].

Antigen peptide-based vaccine

Peptide-based vaccines are coming into second type, antigen-defined HCC vaccines. This type of vaccination approach targets antigens which are particularly expressed and overexpressed on HCC tumors. From the last few years different types of HCC-associated antigens are identified such as oncofetal protein (AFP) and glypican (GPC3), CT antigens, SSX-2, melanoma antigen gene-A, overexpressed antigen telomerase reverse transcriptase [48,49]. Research identified that GPC3-based vaccines were able to induce peptide-specific killer T cells (CTLs) in advanced stage HCC and these CTLs are responsible for patients' survival [50]. After successful preclinical trials, a phase I trial was conducted. In this trial a total of 33 patients having advanced stage HCC were given GPC3-based vaccines [51]. It was found that, vaccines and their side effects are well tolerable, DCR (partial response + stable diseases) was about 60.7% after 2 months of the treatment start time [52]. Another phase II clinical trial

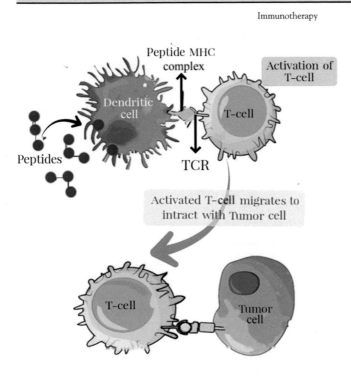

FIGURE 4.3 Activation of the cytotoxic T-lymphocytes with the peptide vaccines, which on activation migrates to the tumor cells and shows antitumor effect.

(single arm and open label) was done on 25 patients who had the initial stage HCC and had undergone surgery and radiofrequency ablation. Chances of recurrence of tumor were reduced in patients who received surgery and vaccination and it indicated the efficacy of GPC3 antigen-based vaccines [53]. Functioning of activation of T-lymphocytes by antigen peptide-based vaccine is depicted in Fig. 4.3.

Dendritic cell vaccines

Dendritic cells (DCs) are the major types of accessory cells also known as APCs of the mammalian immune system that plays an important part in absorption, processing, and in the presentation of antigens. DCs show antitumor effect by activating primary T cells which secrete IFN-gamma that works on the suppression of tumor angiogenesis and induction of memory-based immunity [54]. For the preparation of DCs-based vaccines, DCs are isolated from peripheral blood then treated with GMCSF and TNF-alpha. These modified DCs can recruit effector cells and enhance the release of malignancy-associated antigen and initiate tumor lysis mechanism. A clinical trial of DCs pulsed with hepatocellular-specific antigen, demonstrated that DCs vaccines are well tolerated and work as an effective adjuvant therapy in liver cancer patients. There are only grade 1 and 2 level side effects such as fever and rashes at the site of injection, and very low data of grade 3 level adverse effects [42,45,55].

Adoptive cell therapy

Adoptive cell therapy (ACT) is yet another promising immunotherapy. In this therapy, HCC patient's self-lymphocytes are isolated and then modified by treating them with cytokines or chemokines ex vivo. These modified lymphocytes are then used to eliminate cancer cells by infusing them into patients' blood. ACT for liver carcinoma includes cytokine-induced killer cells (CIKs), tumor-infiltrating lymphocytes (TILs), and chimeric antigen receptor T cells (CARTs).

Cytokine-induced killer cells

CIKs are the major immunologic effector cells which are cytotoxic in nature. They are diverse group of cells which are prepared ex vivo by incubating various cytokines such as interleukin-1, interleukin-2, interferon-gamma, and monoclonal antibodies along with peripheral blood monocytes. After 14–21 days of incubation these modified groups of cells or CIKs are reinfused to HCC patients. These CIKs are MHC independent, $CD3^+$ $CD56^+$, $CD3^-$, $CD56^+$, $CD3^+$, and CD56 population and are capable of the identification of tumor cells. CIKs are used as adjuvant therapy after surgery of HCC [56,57].

Tumor-infiltrating lymphocytes

TILs are group of all lymphocytes that are part of tumor surveillance and are derived from tumor tissue. After isolation they are cultured ex vivo by interleukin-2 and anti-CD-3 antibody and then transfer to the patient. TILs contain tumor-specific immunity and they target tumor-specific antigens [58]. TILs improve diseases prognosis and OS. Although TILs are present rarely in HCC, but research has demonstrated that HCC patients with TILs have better prognosis rate than patients without TILs [59,60]. A phase I study identified that TILs are novel immunotherapy for HCC treatment with lower toxicity value. There are not very much data available because of difficulties in TILs purification and culturing [61].

Chimeric antigen receptor T cell

CARTs are reengineered T-lymphocytes which contain recombinant receptor or monoclonal antibodies for the recognition of tumor-specific antigen. CARTs are MHC-independent cells because they contain recombinant receptors [62].

Oncolytic virus therapy

Oncolytic virus therapy is a novel and rapidly evolving immunotherapy in the treatment of cancer. In this therapy, therapeutic or genetically engineered viruses are inserted into the tumor tissue or in cancer patients. They play a major role in tumor reduction (Fig. 4.4). Oncolytic viruses can replicate in tumors by using their machinery and kill the tumor cell by lysis. They cannot affect normal cells. Commonly used viruses are HSV-1, vesicular stomatitis virus (VSV), poliovirus, reovirus, and vaccinia virus [63]. After so many preclinical trials few have made it successfully to clinical trials [64]. JX594 being one of them, is a modified vaccinia virus with mutated TK gene. Mutation in the TK gene gives the virus ability of tumor cell-specific replication and insertion of (GMCSF) gene kills HCC cells in patients with very few adverse effects. Another clinical trial evaluated safety and efficacy of JX594. The response rate was 62% and OS rate was 6.7 months, survival rate at higher dose was also found to be higher as compared to low dose in advanced stage HCC patients [65,66].

Table 4.1 summarizes various immunotherapy and their clinical trial status.

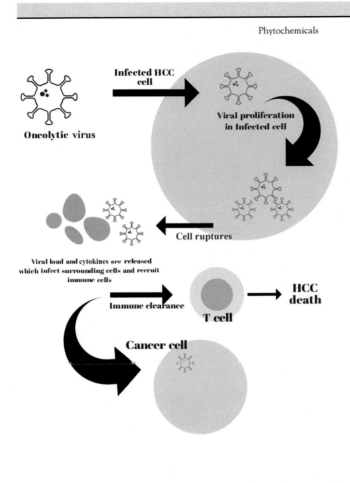

FIGURE 4.4 Mechanism of action of oncolytic virus—HCC-induced oncolytic virus enters the cancerous cells and proliferates leading to cell rupture. Secondary viral particles and cytokines are released due to cell rupture and infects nearby cancerous cells. They also help in recruitment of the immune cells for clearance of the cells.

Phytochemicals

HCC is a terrible form of cancer. The majority of cases of liver cancer spread to other organs. Patients diagnosed with liver cancer, have limited chances for eligibility of treatment rests are mostly susceptible to death either due to severity of the cancer or due to conventional treatment of chemotherapeutic drug making patients nonresponsive to it. Also, these drugs only extend the survival months in patients rather than curing it. The phytochemicals as therapeutic agents hold great promises in treating HCC as they possess least risk and are more tolerable in the body. Some of the phytochemicals studied as therapeutic agents are listed in Table 4.2.

Curcumin

Curcumin is a polyphenolic compound present predominantly in Curcuma *longa* used as spice in cooking, which has established role as antiinflammatory, antioxidant, and anticancerous activity in various cancers [5,67]. It is a highly exploited and widely studied phytochemical giving the result in every perspective by regulating cell cycle, signaling

TABLE 4.1 Various immunotherapies and their clinical trial status.

Immunotherapies

1. Check point inhibitors targets	Drugs	Clinical trial identifier and phase	Result	Status	References
PD1 and PD-L1	(1) Nivolumab	(1) I/II NCT01658878	(1) 15 months' dose escalation	(1) Approved	[39]
	(2) Pembrolizumab	(2) II NCT02702414	(2) 12.9 months	(2) Approved	[40]
	(3) Durvalumab	(3) I/II NCT01693562	(3) 13.2 months	(3) Not approved	
CTLA-4	Tremelimumab	II NCT01008358	8.2 months	Not approved	[17]
PDL-1/ CTLA-4	Durvalumab + Tremelimumab	I/II NCT02519348	Not reported	Not approved	[41]

2. Vaccine therapy

Type	Clinical trial identifier and Phase		Status	References
AFP gene HCC vaccine	I/II NCT00005629	—	Completed	[68]
AFP peptide-pulsed autologous DC	I/II NCT00022334	—	Completed	[42,45]
IMA970A + CV8102 with cyclophosphamide	I/II NCT03203005	—	Under trial	Clinical trial.gov

3. Adoptive cell therapy type	Clinical trial identifier and Phase	—	Status	
CIK	III NCT01749865	—	Completed	[69]
Autologous TILs and IL-2	I NCT01462903	—	Not completed	[61]
Therapeutic allogeneic lymphocytes: irradiated lymphocytes from a donor	I NCT00161187	—	Completed	Clinical trial.gov

TABLE 4.2 Various phytochemicals their source and their anti-HCC activity.

Compound	Plants	Activity in HCC	References
Curcumin	*Curcuma longa*	VEGF, PI3K/AKT	[70]
Resveratrol	Grapes, ground nut, wine	HGF-C-Met	[71]
Quercetin	Onion, citrus fruits,	JNK; cyclinD1	
Triptolide	*Tripterygium wilfordii* Hook F	NF-kB; caspase3	[57]
Betulinic acid	*Betula alba*	PI3K/AKT/mTOR	[29]
Phloretin	Apple tree roots, pears	Upregulates SHP-1; downregulates STAT3	[72]
Capsaicin	Peppers, capsicum	ROS production, TRAIL-induced apoptosis	[73]

pathways, apoptosis induction, inhibition of metastasis, and recently in tumor microenvironment. In HCC curcumin inhibits cancer cell growth by targeting the angiogenesis molecule VEGF [49] which are responsible for providing nourishment to the cancerous cell and PI3K/AKT signaling pathway.

Resveratrol

Resveratrol is an active polyphenolic compound with chemical formula 3,4',5-trihydroxy-trans-stilbene and is present in many dietary sources such as grapes, groundnuts, berries, and red wines. It has the property to reduce the inflammation and its related diseases including neurodegenerative diseases, cardiovascular ailments, and cancers [74]. It shows a chemoprevention property against various cancers including colon, breast, ovarian, lung, and prostate. It targets and inhibits the HGF-c-Met signaling pathway and thus carries a great potential to be used in treatment of HCC [71] which is eventually responsible for the activation of certain other downstream pathways such as RAS/MAPK, PI3K/AKT that are responsible for cell growth, there survivability, motility, and metastasis.

Quercetin

Quercetin (3,3',4',5,7-pentahydroflavone) is a flavonoid present in many various plants such as onion, broccoli, pepper, asparagus, apple, berries, and in citrus fruits. Among the all sources the most bioavailable form of quercetin is glucoside, mainly found in onions. It has shown antioxidant, antiinflammatory activity, and also as a cardioprotectant in animal studies [75]. Quercetin's effective anticancer activity has been studied in various cancers including ovarian, breast, colorectal, gastric, and hepatic cancer. In prostate cancer it has shown to prevent the invasiveness in cells by blocking JNK signaling pathway, whereas in HCC it manages so by downregulating the expression of cyclin D1 [76] which is responsible for transition of cell from G1 phase to S phase. Recently, quercetin has shown inhibitory effective by inactivating JAK2/STAT3 pathway to prevent it further from cell apoptosis, migration, and invasion [77].

Triptolide

Triptolide is a bioactive compound present in *Tripterygium wilfordii* Hook F, which is used frequently for the treatment of inflammation in traditional Chinese medicine [78]. Triptolide is a diterpene triepoxide (lipid) which by downregulating NF-kB signaling prevents invasion, proliferation, and induces apoptosis of HCC cells [6]. The NF-kB signaling plays a crucial role in cancer growth and spread by upregulating MMP-9, it also functions in activating the P53 gene which is a tumor suppressor gene [79,80]. The triptolide not alone has shown a great efficacy, but its combination with sorafenib (an FDA-approved chemotherapeutic drug) has also given a promising treatment for the management of HCC [81]. Also, TP combination with sodium cantharidinate together showed cytotoxic effect on hepatoma cell line 7721 by inhibiting NF-kB and increasing caspase-3 activity. Though, triptolide shows great efficacy in inducing HCC to apoptosis, yet it shows general toxicity in clinical practice. To overcome this the NAD(P)H Quinone oxidoreductase-1 has become a vigorous target in drug development for HCC [82].

HCC shows poor response to conventional chemotherapy and other therapy directed toward blocking its mechanism. A less toxic molecule combined with a vehicle to deliver the medicine in the internalisation of tumor cells, as opposed to in parenchyma, would be the breakthrough treatment for treating such malignancy. By keeping in mind the high lactic acid production by tumor cells, their acidic environment and leaky blood vessels, the natural compound triptolide nanoformulated, coated with folate and pH-sensitive peptide made it efficient to uptake by tumor with limited toxicity and hence, targeting the HCC efficiently [83].

Betulinic acid

Betulinic acid a hydrophobic pentacyclic triterpenoid, mainly found in the bark of *Betula alba*. It shows its anticancer activity by inducing certain factors such as upregulating proapoptotic Bcl-2 proteins such as (Bax, Bad), NF-kB modulation, and inhibiting catalytic activity of topoisomerase I [84]. In HCC betulinic acid targets cancerous cells by suppressing PI3K/AKT/mTOR pathway and further induce apoptosis [32,33]. It also prevents HCC invasion by regulating certain metastasis factors such as MMP-2, MMP-9, and TIMP-2 [85], with minimal toxicity which also makes it a promising drug against HCC.

Phloretin

Phloretin is an odorless flavonoid lipid molecule found in oil-seed camellia, pears, apple tree roots, and muscadine grape. It has shown high safety margin with minimum side effects in several in vitro and in vivo studies such as in noncancerous cells of epithelial breast cells MCF10A [86]. In HCC cells it has shown the upregulation of SHP-1 expression which is mainly a tumor suppressor gene and downregulates STAT3 expression, whose higher expression leads to the poor diagnosis and severe drug resistance when treated with sorafenib [72]. Hence, it could be a potent reagent for targeting HCC.

Capsaicin

Capsaicin is a bioactive vanilloid found in *Capsicum* family, which is responsible for pungency in chili peppers. The anticancer property of capsaicin is controversial where some signifies it as inducer of cancer, while some has studied its anticarcinogenic effects [87]. It reduces the insulin resistance, controls obesity and other cellular metabolism. In several in vivo and in vitro study it has shown inhibition in cellular proliferation, ROS production, inducing apoptosis, and also mediating apoptosis through TRAIL [73].

Nanomedicines

Nanomedicine is an evolving filed in cancer therapeutics, which merges the potentiality of nanoparticles (NPs) by overcoming the limitations of conventional chemotherapeutic drugs or phytochemicals.

Curcumin-conjugated nanoparticles

The low bioavailability and less solubility in water set a major drawback for curcumin in showing the effective result against the disease. To overcome this and target a particular receptor of diseases or highly expressed receptor of different kinds of cancers, a conjugated drug or the effective delivery could be a breakthrough. In HCC the highly expressed asialoglycoprotein receptor (ASGPR) is targeted with galactosylated (specific ligand for ASGPR) BSA nanoparticle loaded with curcumin, which eventually induces apoptosis and prevents cell from migration by inactivating the expression of NF-kB-p65 [88]. Also, curcumin loaded in mesoporous silica NPs has overcome certain other limitation with curcumin such as instability in structure, degradation in UV light, and has shown cytotoxicity effect in HCC 9 [89]. Curcumin also increases the efficiency of other chemotherapeutic drugs such as cisplatin which causes resistance and toxicity after treatment when given alone, whereas when cisplatin is conjugated with curcumin-loaded liposomes it gives higher antitumor activity by increasing ROS level in HCC and eventually improving the treatment [90].

Beta-Sitosterol

Beta-sitosterol is a lipid sterol found in lemon thyme, mixed nuts, conch, and also in *Amorphophallus campanulatus* (Elephant foot yam) whose tuber's methanolic extract suppresses the human hepatoma cell line proliferation [91]. In HepG2 HCC cell line the silver nanoparticle-conjugated beta-sitosterol has shown the morphological apoptosis-related changes by upregulating proapoptotic factors and inducing the ROS and nuclear factor erythroid 2-related factor 2 expression [92], hence preventing the tumor growth and making susceptible to anticancer drugs.

Conclusion

HCC being a regressive tumor still remains a medical concern as no effective drug having good OS effect has been developed. All the therapeutic approaches, be it chemotherapeutic agents, immunotherapy, or any other novel treatment such as oncolytic virus therapy or targeted NPs, either have less effect or are just able to increase the life expectancy just for few months. With only few CKIs such as sorafenib and regorafenib approved for the first-line and second-line treatment, respectively, there is a dire need for the novel drug development. The phyoconstituents are also being explored as a potential candidate for the drug development as they have less side effects and are easily tolerable by the body. Various studies such as done by Shukla et al. (2020) have shown that phytochemicals such as curcumin has great potential to effectively counter metastasis and angiogenesis. More research is yet needed to be done to fill the gap in knowledge for the effective treatment. The various biomarkers for HCC need to be found to effectively study the effect of various treatments.

References

[1] Pinter M, Hucke F, Zielonke N, et al. Epidemiological trends of hepatocellular carcinoma in Austria. Dig Dis 2014;32:664—9.

[2] Torre LA, Bray F, Siegel RL, et al. Global cancer statistics, 2012. CA Cancer J Clin 2015;65:87—108.

[3] Dasgupta P, Henshaw C, Youlden DR, Clark PJ, Aitken JF, Baade PD. Global trends in incidence rates of primary adult liver cancers: a systematic review and *meta*-analysis. Front Oncol 2020;10:171.

[4] Bray F, Ferlay J, Soerjomataram I, Siegel RL, Torre LA, Jemal A. Global cancer statistics 2018: GLOBOCAN estimates of incidence and mortality worldwide for 36 cancers in 185 countries. CA Cancer J Clin 2018;68(6):394—424.

[5] Petrick JL, Florio AA, Znaor A, Ruggieri D, Laversanne M, Alvarez CS, et al. International trends in hepatocellular carcinoma incidence, 1978—2012. Int J Cancer 2020;147(2):317—30.

[6] Venook AP, Papandreou C, Furuse J, de Guevara LL. The incidence and epidemiology of hepatocellular carcinoma: a global and regional perspective. Oncologist 2010; 15 Suppl 4: 5—13 PMID: 21115576 Doi:10.1634/theoncologist.2010-S4-05]

[7] Szabó E, Páska C, Novák PK, Schaff Z, Kiss A. Similarities and differences in hepatitis B and C virus induced hepatocarcinogenesis. Pathol Oncol Res 2004;10(1):5—11.

[8] Finn RS. Emerging targeted strategies in advanced hepatocellular carcinoma. Semin Liver Dis 2013;33: S11—19. Available from: https://doi.org/10.1055/s-0033-1333632.

[9] Pan QZ, Pan K, Wang QJ, Weng DS, Zhao JJ, Zheng HX, et al. Annexin A3 as a potential target for immunotherapy of liver cancer stem-like cells. Stem Cell 2015;33:354—66.

[10] Coffelt SB, de Visser KE. Revving up dendritic cells while braking PD-L1 to jumpstart the cancer-immunity cycle motor. Immunity 2016;44:722—4.

[11] Soerjomataram, Oomen D, Lemmens V, Oenema A, Benetou V, Trichopoulou A, et al. Increased consumption of fruit and vegetables and future cancer incidence in selected European countries. Eur J Cancer 2010;46:2563—80.

[12] Banerjee S, Singh SK, Chowdhury I, Lillard Jr. JW, Singh R. Combinatorial effect of curcumin with docetaxel modulates apoptotic and cell survival molecules in prostate cancer. Front Biosci (Elite Ed) 2017;9:235—45.

[13] Ikeda M, Morizane C, Ueno M, Okusaka T, Ishii H, Furuse J. Chemotherapy for hepatocellular carcinoma: current status and future perspectives. Japanese J Clin Oncol 2018;48(2):103—14. Available from: https://doi.org/10.1093/jjco/hyx180.

[14] Tang W, Chen Z, Zhang W, et al. The mechanisms of sorafenib resistance in hepatocellular carcinoma: theoretical basis and therapeutic aspects. Sig Transduct Target Ther 2020;5:87. Available from: https://doi.org/10.1038/s41392-020-0187-x.

[15] Cheng AL, Kang YK, Chen Z, Tsao CJ, Qin S, Kim JS, et al. Efficacy and safety of sorafenib in patients in the Asia-Pacific region with advanced hepatocellular carcinoma: a phase III randomised, double-blind, placebo-controlled trial. Lancet Oncol 2009; 10:25-34 PMID: 19095497. Available from: https://doi.org/10.1016/S1470-2045(08)70285-7

[16] Finn RS, Kang YK, Mulcahy M, Polite BN, Lim HY, Walters I, et al. Phase II, open-label study of brivanib as second-line therapy in patients with advanced hepatocellular carcinoma. Clin Cancer Res 2012;18(7):2090—8. Available from: https://doi.org/10.1158/1078-0432.CCR-11-1991.

[17] Zhu H, Zhang C, Yang X, Yi C. Treatment with Brivanib alaninate as a second-line monotherapy after Sorafenib failure in hepatocellular carcinoma: a case report. Medicine (Baltimore) 2019;98(10):e14823. Available from: https://doi.org/10.1097/MD.0000000000014823.

[18] Thorat A, Jeng LB, Yang HR, Yeh CC, Hsu SC, Chen TH, et al. Assessing the role of everolimus in reducing hepatocellular carcinoma recurrence after living donor liver transplantation for patients within the UCSF criteria: re-inventing the role of mammalian target of rapamycin inhibitors. Ann Hepatobiliary Pancreatic Surg 2017;21(4):205—11. Available from: https://doi.org/10.14701/ahbps.2017.21.4.205.

[19] Zhu AX, Abrams TA, Miksad R, Blaszkowsky LS, Meyerhardt JA, Zheng H, et al. Phase 1/2 study of everolimus in advanced hepatocellular carcinoma. Cancer 2011;117(22):5094—102. Available from: https://doi.org/10.1002/cncr.26165.

[20] Niessen C, Wiggermann P, Velandia C, Stroszczynski C, Pereira PL. Transarterial chemoembolization - status quo in Germany. Rofo 2013;185(11):1089—94. Available from: https://doi.org/10.1055/s-0033-1335529.

[21] Lee J, Park JO, Kim WS, et al. Phase II study of doxorubicin and cisplatin in patients with metastatic hepatocellular carcinoma. Cancer Chemother Pharmacol 2004;54:385—90. Available from: https://doi.org/10.1007/s00280-004-0837-7.

[22] Buschauer S, Koch A, Wiggermann P, Müller M, Hellerbrand C. Hepatocellular carcinoma cells surviving doxorubicin treatment exhibit increased migratory potential and resistance to doxorubicin re-treatment in vitro. Oncol Lett 2018;15(4):4635–40. Available from: https://doi.org/10.3892/ol.2018.7887.

[23] Alberts SR, Reid JM, Morlan BW, Farr Jr GH, Camoriano JK, Johnson DB, et al. Gemcitabine and docetaxel for hepatocellular carcinoma: a phase II North Central Cancer Treatment Group clinical trial. Am J Clin Oncol 2012;35(5):418–23. Available from: https://doi.org/10.1097/COC.0b013e318219863b.

[24] Fuchs CS, Clark JW, Ryan DP, Kulke MH, Kim H, Earle CC, et al. A phase II trial of gemcitabine in patients with advanced hepatocellular carcinoma. Cancer 2002;94:3186–91. Available from: https://doi.org/10.1002/cncr.10607.

[25] Han Y, Chen Z, Yang Y, Jiang Z, Gu Y, Liu Y, et al. Human CD14$^+$ CTLA-4$^+$ regulatory dendritic cells suppress T-cell response by cytotoxic T-lymphocyte antigen-4-dependent IL-10 and indoleamine-2,3-dioxygenase production in hepatocellular carcinoma. Hepatology 2014;59:567–79. Available from: https://doi.org/10.1002/hep.26694.

[26] Li FJ, Zhang Y, Jin GX, Yao L, Wu DQ. Expression of LAG-3 is coincident with the impaired effector function of HBV-specific CD8(+) Tcell in HCC patients. Immunol Lett 2013;150:116–22. Available from: https://doi.org/10.1016/j.imlet.2012.12.004.

[27] Shi F, Shi M, Zeng Z, Qi RZ, Liu ZW, Zhang JY, et al. PD-1 and PD-L1 upregulation promotes CD8(+) T-cell apoptosis and postoperative recurrence in hepatocellular carcinoma patients. Int J Cancer 2011;128:887–96.

[28] Johnston MP, Khakoo SI. Immunotherapy for hepatocellular carcinoma: current and future. World J Gastroenterol. 2019;25(24):2977–2989. Available from: https://doi.org/10.3748/wjg.v25.i24.2977. PMID: 31293335; PMCID: PMC6603808.

[29] Wen L, Xin B, Wu P, Lin CH, Peng C, Wang G, et al. An efficient combination immunotherapy for primary liver cancer by harmonized activation of innate and adaptive immunity in mice. Hepatology (Baltimore, Md) 2019;69(6):2518–32. Available from: https://doi.org/10.1002/hep.30528.

[30] Zongyi Y, Xiaowu L. Immunotherapy for hepatocellular carcinoma. Cancer Lett 2020;470:8–17. Available from: https://doi.org/10.1016/j.canlet.2019.12.002.

[31] Arias, I.M., Alter, H.J., Boyer, J.L., Cohen, D.E., Shafritz, D.A., Thorgeirsson, S.S (Eds). (2020). The liver: biology and pathobiology. John Wiley & Sons.

[32] Liu W, Li S, Qu Z, Luo Y, Chen R, Wei S, et al. Betulinic acid induces autophagy-mediated apoptosis through suppression of the PI3K/AKT/mTOR signaling pathway and inhibits hepatocellular carcinoma. Am J Transl Res 2019;11(11):6952.

[33] Liu Z, Lin Y, Zhang J, et al. Molecular targeted and immune checkpoint therapy for advanced hepatocellular carcinoma. J Exp Clin Cancer Res 2019;38:447. Available from: https://doi.org/10.1186/s13046-019-1412-8

[34] Haanen JB, Robert C. Immune checkpoint inhibitors. Prog Tumor Res 2015;42:55–66.

[35] Pinato DJ, Guerra N, Fessas P, et al. Immune-based therapies for hepatocellular carcinoma. Oncogene 2020;39:3620–37. Available from: https://doi.org/10.1038/s41388-020-1249-9.

[36] Syn NL, Teng MW, Mok TS, Soo RA. De-novo and acquired resistance to immune checkpoint targeting. Lancet Oncol. 2017, 18 (12): e731–e741. Available from: https://doi.org/10.1016/s1470-2045(17)30607-1. PMID: syn NL29208439

[37] Kelly RJ, Lee J, Bang YJ, Almhanna K, Blum-Murphy M, Catenacci DV, et al. Safety and efficacy of durvalumab and tremelimumab alone or in combination in patients with advanced gastric and gastroesophageal junction adenocarcinoma. Clin Cancer Res 2020;26(4):846–54.

[38] Francisco LM, Salinas VH, Brown KE, Vanguri VK, Freeman GJ, Kuchroo VK, et al. PD-L1 regulates the development, maintenance, and function of induced regulatory T cells. J Exp Med 2009;206(13):3015–29. Available from: https://doi.org/10.1084/jem.20090847.

[39] Eroglu Z, Zaretsky JM, Hu-Lieskovan S, Kim DW, Algazi A, Johnson DB, et al. High response rate to PD-1 blockade in desmoplastic melanomas. Nature 2018;553(7688):347–50. Available from: https://doi.org/10.1038/nature25187.

[40] Elkhoueiry AB, Sangro B, Yau T, Crocenzi TS, Kudo M, Hsu C, et al. Nivolumab in patients with advanced hepatocellular carcinoma (CheckMate 040): an open-label, non-comparative, phase 1/2 dose escalation and expansion trial. Lancet 2017;389(10088):2492.

[41] Yau T, Park JW, Finn RS, Cheng A-L, Mathurin P, Edeline J, et al. LBA38_PRCheckMate 459: a randomized, multi-center phase III study of nivolumab (NIVO) vs sorafenib (SOR) as first-line (1L) treatment in patients (pts) with advanced hepatocellular carcinoma (aHCC). Ann Oncol 2019;30(suppl_5):v851–934.

[42] Finn R, Chan SL, Zhu AX, Knox J, Cheng A, Siegel A, et al. Pembrolizumab vs best supportive care for second-line advanced hepatocellular carcinoma: randomized, phase 3 KEYNOTE-240 study. J Clin Oncol 2016;35(4_suppl):TPS503 503TPS503.

[43] Zhu AX, Finn RS, Edeline J, Cattan S, Ogasawara S, Palmer D, et al. Pembrolizumab in patients with advanced hepatocellular carcinoma previously treated with sorafenib (KEYNOTE-224): a non-randomised, open-label phase 2 trial. Lancet Oncol 2018;19(7):940−52.

[44] Schlom J, Hodge JW, Palena C, Tsang KY, Jochems C, Greiner JW, et al. Therapeutic cancer vaccines. Adv Cancer Res 2014;121:67−124. Available from: https://doi.org/10.1016/B978-0-12-800249-0.00002-0.

[45] Lee W-C, Wang H-C, Hung C-F, Huang P-F, Lia C-R, Chen M-F. Vaccination of advanced hepatocellular carcinoma patients with tumor lysate-pulsed dendritic cells. J Immunother 2005;28:496−504. Available from: https://doi.org/10.1097/01.cji.0000171291.72039.e2.

[46] Palmer DH, Midgley RS, Mirza N, Torr EE, Ahmed F, Steele JC, et al. A phase II study of adoptive immunotherapy using dendritic cells pulsed with tumor lysate in patients with hepatocellular carcinoma. Hepatology 2009;49:124−32. Available from: https://doi.org/10.1002/hep.22626.

[47] Nemunaitis J, Barve M, Orr D, et al. Summary of bi-shRNAfurin/ GM-CSF augmented autologous tumor cell immunotherapy (FANG™) in advanced cancer of the liver. Oncology 2014;87(1):21−9.

[48] Shirakawa H, Suzuki H, Shimomura M, Kojima M, Gotohda N, Takahashi S, et al. Glypican-3 expression is correlated with poor prognosis in hepatocellular carcinoma. Cancer Sci 2009;100:1403−7. Available from: https://doi.org/10.1111/j.1349-7006.2009.01206.x.

[49] Datta S, Misra SK, Saha ML, Lahiri N, Louie J, Pan D, et al. Orthogonal self-assembly of an organoplatinum (II) metallacycle and cucurbit [8] uril that delivers curcumin to cancer cells. Proc Natl Acad Sci 2018;115(32):8087−92.

[50] Zhou F, Shang W, Yu X, Tian J. Glypican-3: a promising biomarker for hepatocellular carcinoma diagnosis and treatment. Med Res Rev 2018;38:741−67. Available from: https://doi.org/10.1002/med.21455.

[51] Yoshikawa T, Nakatsugawa M, Suzuki S, Shirakawa H, Nobuoka D, Sakemura N, et al. HLA-A2-restricted glypican-3 peptide-specific CTL clones induced by peptide vaccine show high avidity and antigen-specific killing activity against tumor cells. Cancer Sci 2011;102:918−25. Available from: https://doi.org/10.1111/j.1349-7006.2011.01896.x.

[52] Nobuoka D, Yoshikawa T, Sawada Y, Fujiwara T, Nakatsura T. Peptide vaccines for hepatocellular carcinoma. Hum Vaccin Immunother 2013;9(1):210−12. Available from: https://doi.org/10.4161/hv.22473.

[53] Sawada Y, Yoshikawa T, Ofuji K, Yoshimura M, Tsuchiya N, Takahashi M, et al. Phase II study of the GPC3-derived peptide vaccine as an adjuvant therapy for hepatocellular carcinoma patients. OncoImmunology 2016;5. Available from: https://doi.org/10.1080/2162402X.2015.1129483.

[54] Shang N, Figini M, Shangguan J, Wang B, Sun C, Pan L, et al. Dendritic cells based immunotherapy. Am J Cancer Res 2017;7(10):2091−102.

[55] Lee J, Lee Y, Lee M, et al. A phase I/IIa study of adjuvant immunotherapy with tumour antigen-pulsed dendritic cells in patients with hepatocellular carcinoma. Br J Cancer 2015;113:1666−76. Available from: https://doi.org/10.1038/bjc.2015.430.

[56] Zhang R, Zhang Z, Liu Z, et al. Adoptive cell transfer therapy for hepatocellular carcinoma. Front Med 2019;13:3−11. Available from: https://doi.org/10.1007/s11684-019-0684-x.

[57] Zhang YQ, Shen Y, Liao MM, Mao X, Mi GJ, You C, et al. Galactosylated chitosan triptolide nanoparticles for overcoming hepatocellular carcinoma: enhanced therapeutic efficacy, low toxicity, and validated network regulatory mechanisms. Nanomedicine 2019;15(1):86−97.

[58] Shirabe K, Motomura T, Muto J, Toshima T, Matono R, Mano Y, et al. Tumor-infiltrating lymphocytes and hepatocellular carcinoma: pathology and clinical management. Int J Clin Oncol 2010;15:552−8. Available from: https://doi.org/10.1007/s10147-010-0131-0.

[59] Ding W, Xu X, Qian Y, Xue W, Wang Y, Du J, et al. Prognostic value of tumor-infiltrating lymphocytes in hepatocellular carcinoma: a *meta*-analysis. Medicine 2018;97(50):e13301. Available from: https://doi.org/10.1097/MD.0000000000013301.

[60] Tian M, Liu W, Wang H, et al. Tissue-infiltrating lymphocytes signature predicts survival in patients with early/intermediate stage hepatocellular carcinoma. BMC Med 2019;17:106. Available from: https://doi.org/10.1186/s12916-019-1341-6.

[61] Jiang SS, Tang Y, Zhang YJ, Weng DS, Zhou ZG, Pan K, et al. A phase I clinical trial utilizing autologous tumor-infiltrating lymphocytes in patients with primary hepatocellular carcinoma. Oncotarget 2015;6 (38):41339−49. Available from: https://doi.org/10.18632/oncotarget.5463.

[62] Mizukoshi E, Kaneko S. Immune cell therapy for hepatocellular carcinoma. J Hematol Oncol 2019;12(1):52. Available from: https://doi.org/10.1186/s13045-019-0742-5.

[63] Sun W, Shi Q, Zhang H, Yang K, Ke Y, Wang Y, et al. Advances in the techniques and methodologies of cancer gene therapy. Discov Med. 2019;27(146):45-55. PMID: 30721651.

[64] Chang JF, Chen PJ, Sze DY, Reid T, Bartlett D, Kirn DH, et al. Oncolytic virotherapy for advanced liver tumours. J Cell Mol Med 2009;13(7):1238–47. Available from: https://doi.org/10.1111/j.1582-4934.2008.00563.x.

[65] Heo J, Reid T, Ruo L, Breitbach CJ, Rose S, Bloomston M, et al. Randomized dose-finding clinical trial of oncolytic immunotherapeutic vaccinia JX-594 in liver cancer. Nat Med 2013;19(3):329–36. Available from: https://doi.org/10.1038/nm.3089.

[66] Yoo SY, Badrinath N, Woo HY, Heo J. Oncolytic virus-based immunotherapies for hepatocellular carcinoma. Mediators Inflamm 2017;2017:5198798. Available from: https://doi.org/10.1155/2017/5198798.

[67] Soni VK, Shukla D, Kumar A, Vishvakarma NK. Curcumin circumvent lactate-induced chemoresistance in hepatic cancer cells through modulation of hydroxycarboxylic acid receptor-1. Int J Biochem Cell Biol 2020;123:105752. Available from: https://doi.org/10.1016/j.biocel.2020.105752.

[68] Pardee AD, Shi J, Butterfield LH. Tumor-derived α-fetoprotein impairs the differentiation and T cell stimulatory activity of human dendritic cells. J Immunol 2014;193(11):5723–32. Available from: https://doi.org/10.4049/jimmunol.1400725.

[69] Guo Y, Han W. Cytokine-induced killer (CIK) cells: from basic research to clinical translation. Chin J Cancer 2015;34(3):99–107. Available from: https://doi.org/10.1186/s40880-015-0002-1.

[70] Pan Z, Zhuang J, Ji C, Cai Z, Liao W, Huang Z. Curcumin inhibits hepatocellular carcinoma growth by targeting VEGF expression. Oncol Lett 2018;15(4):4821–6.

[71] Gao F, Deng G, Liu W, Zhou K, Li M. Resveratrol suppresses human hepatocellular carcinoma via targeting HGF-c-Met signaling pathway. Oncol Rep 2017;37(2):1203–11.

[72] Saraswati S, Alhaider A, Abdelgadir AM, Tanwer P, Korashy HM. Phloretin attenuates STAT-3 activity and overcomes sorafenib resistance targeting SHP-1—mediated inhibition of STAT3 and Akt/VEGFR2 pathway in hepatocellular carcinoma. Cell Commun Signal 2019;17(1):1–18.

[73] Scheau C, Badarau IA, Caruntu C, Mihai GL, Didilescu AC, Constantin C, et al. Capsaicin: effects on the pathogenesis of hepatocellular carcinoma. Molecules 2019;24(13):2350.

[74] Bishayee A, Politis T, Darvesh AS. Resveratrol in the chemoprevention and treatment of hepatocellular carcinoma. Cancer Treat Rev 2010;36(1):43–53.

[75] Dabeek WM, Marra MV. Dietary quercetin and kaempferol: Bioavailability and potential cardiovascular-related bioactivity in humans. Nutrients 2019;11(10):2288.

[76] Wu L, Zhang Q, Mo W, Feng J, Li S, Li J, et al. Quercetin prevents hepatic fibrosis by inhibiting hepatic stellate cell activation and reducing autophagy via the TGF-β1/Smads and PI3K/Akt pathways. Sci Rep 2017;7(1):1–13.

[77] Wu L, Li J, Liu T, Li S, Feng J, Yu Q, et al. Quercetin shows anti-tumor effect in hepatocellular carcinoma LM3 cells by abrogating JAK2/STAT3 signaling pathway. Cancer Med 2019;8(10):4806–20.

[78] Yi JM, Huan XJ, Song SS, Zhou H, Wang YQ, Miao ZH. Triptolide induces cell killing in multidrug-resistant tumor cells via CDK7/RPB1 rather than XPB or p44. Mol Cancer Ther 2016;15(7):1495–503.

[79] Sun YY, Xiao L, Wang D, Ji YC, Yang YP, Ma R, et al. Triptolide inhibits viability and induces apoptosis in liver cancer cells through activation of the tumor suppressor gene p53. Int J Oncol 2017;50(3):847–52.

[80] Wang H, Ma D, Wang C, Zhao S, Liu C. Triptolide inhibits invasion and tumorigenesis of hepatocellular carcinoma MHCC-97H cells through NF-κB signaling. Med Sci Monit 2016;22:1827–36.

[81] Alsaied OA, Sangwan V, Banerjee S, Krosch TC, Chugh R, Saluja A, et al. Sorafenib and triptolide as combination therapy for hepatocellular carcinoma. Surgery 2014;156(2):270–9.

[82] Zhang K, Chen D, Ma K, Wu X, Hao H, Jiang S. NAD (P) H: quinone oxidoreductase 1 (NQO1) as a therapeutic and diagnostic target in cancer. J Med Chem 2018;61(16):6983–7003.

[83] Ling D, Xia H, Park W, Hackett MJ, Song C, Na K, et al. pH-sensitive nanoformulated triptolide as a targeted therapeutic strategy for hepatocellular carcinoma. ACS Nano 2014;8(8):8027–39.

[84] Fulda S. Betulinic acid for cancer treatment and prevention. Int J Mol Sci 2008;9(6):1096–107.

[85] Wang W, Wang Y, Liu M, Zhang Y, Yang T, Li D, et al. Betulinic acid induces apoptosis and suppresses metastasis in hepatocellular carcinoma cell lines in vitro and in vivo. J Cell Mol Med 2019;23(1):586–95.

[86] Wu CH, Ho YS, Tsai CY, Wang YJ, Tseng H, Wei PL, et al. In vitro and in vivo study of phloretin-induced apoptosis in human liver cancer cells involving inhibition of type II glucose transporter. Int J Cancer 2009;124(9):2210–19.

[87] Georgescu SR, Sârbu MI, Matei C, Ilie MA, Caruntu C, Constantin C, et al. Capsaicin: friend or foe in skin cancer and other related malignancies? Nutrients 2017;9(12):1365.

[88] Huang Y, Hu L, Huang S, Xu W, Wan J, Wang D, et al. Curcumin-loaded galactosylated BSA nanoparticles as targeted drug delivery carriers inhibit hepatocellular carcinoma cell proliferation and migration. Int J Nanomed 2018;13:8309.

[89] Kong ZL, Kuo HP, Johnson A, Wu LC, Chang KLB. Curcumin-loaded mesoporous silica nanoparticles markedly enhanced cytotoxicity in hepatocellular carcinoma cells. Int J Mol Sci 2019;20(12):2918.

[90] Cheng Y, Zhao P, Wu S, Yang T, Chen Y, Zhang X, et al. Cisplatin and curcumin co-loaded nano-liposomes for the treatment of hepatocellular carcinoma. Int J Pharm 2018;545(1-2):261—73.

[91] Bin Sayeed MS, Ameen SS. Beta-sitosterol: a promising but orphan nutraceutical to fight against cancer. Nutr Cancer 2015;67(8):1216—22.

[92] Raj RK. β-Sitosterol-assisted silver nanoparticles activates Nrf2 and triggers mitochondrial apoptosis via oxidative stress in human hepatocellular cancer cell line. J Biomed Mater Res Part A 2020;108(9):1899—908.

Targeting hepatocellular carcinoma by small-molecule inhibitors

Rahul Kumar Vempati and Rama Rao Malla

Cancer Biology Lab, Department of Biochemistry and Bioinformatics, Institute of Sciences, GITAM (Deemed to be University), Visakhapatnam, India

Abstract

Hepatocellular carcinoma (HCC) and cholangiocarcinoma are the main liver cancer subtypes. The major etiological factors involved in the occurrence of HCC comprise hepatitis B and C virus infection, alcohol abuse, smoking, obesity, genetic factors, environmental carcinogens, and microbial toxins. HCC can be cured if diagnosed at an early stage. Several small-molecule inhibitors have been developed specifically against disease-related therapeutic targets. In this chapter, a concise overview is provided on the status and therapeutic importance of small-molecule inhibitors specific to HCC.

Keywords: Drug resistance; hepatocellular carcinoma; long noncoding RNAs; small molecules; therapeutic targets

Abbreviations

CD	cluster of differentiation
DK4/6	cyclin-dependent kinases 4/6
cKIT	tyrosine protein kinase KIT
c-MET	hepatocyte growth factor receptor/tyrosine protein kinase MET
COX2	cyclooxygenase 2
CSC	cancer stem cells
CREB	cAMP response element binding protein
ERK	extracellular signal regulated kinase
FGFR	fibroblast growth factor receptor
FLT3	FMS-like tyrosine kinase 3
GLUT-1	glucose transporter-1
GAS6	growth-arrest-specific protein-6 precursor
HBV	hepatitis B virus
HCC	hepatocellular carcinoma
HCV	hepatitis C virus

Ganji Purnachandra Nagaraju, Sarfraz Ahmad (eds.)
Theranostics and Precision Medicine for the Management of Hepatocellular Carcinoma, Volume 3
DOI: https://doi.org/10.1016/B978-0-323-99283-1.00012-4

© 2022 Elsevier Inc. All rights reserved.

HGF	hepatocyte growth factor
HIF-2α	hypoxia inducing factor-2 alpha
HK2	hexokinase 2
IGF	insulin-like growth factor
MAPK	mitogen-activated protein kinase
MCL-1	myeloid cell leukemia 1
MCT4	monocarboxylate transporter 4
MEK	mitogen-activated protein kinase
PD-1	programmed cell death protein 1
PDGFR	platelet-derived growth factor receptor
PD-L1	programmed death ligand 1
PFKP	phosphofructokinase
PI3K	phosphoinositide 3 kinase
PKM2	pyruvate kinase isozyme M2
PPARα	peroxisome-proliferator-activated receptor-alpha
PTEN	phosphatase and tensin homolog
RET	proto oncogene tyrosine protein kinase receptor RET
RTK	receptor tyrosine kinases
ROS	reactive oxygen species
SCID	severe combined immunodeficiency
SMAD7	mothers against decapentaplegic homolog 7
T53INP	tumor protein p53-inducible nuclear protein 1
TGF-β	transforming growth factor-beta
TIE2	tyrosine protein kinase receptor
Tie-2	precursor
VEGF	vascular endothelial growth factor

Introduction

Liver cancer (LC) is a complicated and debilitating disease and can often be fatal if it is not detected at an early stage. It is the sixth most reported cancer and stands in second place in causing death from cancer around the world. According to recent statistics, the fatality rate of LC cancer was found to be higher in men than women. Particularly, men in the age group of 45—60 are highly susceptible to LC than the other age groups. The incidence rate of LC is very high in the population of East Asia and comparatively low in South Asia [1]. The most common risk factors involved in the occurrence of LC are chronic viral infections, cirrhosis, alcohol abuse, smoking, obesity, genetic abnormalities, anabolic steroids, environmental carcinogens, and fungal toxins (e.g., aflatoxin) [2—9]. Apart from these factors, the risk of LC can be enhanced by a few rare metabolic diseases [10—14]. Primary LCs that often occur in human beings are hepatocellular carcinoma (HCC), cholangiocarcinoma (CCA), and hepatoblastoma (HB).

HCC is the most prevalent form of LC, and it is largely due to Hepatitis B and C (HBV and HCV) viral infections [15]. Chronic infection by HBV and HCV induces severe inflammatory responses in the liver, causing cirrhosis, which ultimately leads to HCC [16]. Abnormal release of inflammatory cytokines and hyperactivation of signaling pathways were found to be the major cause for an acute inflammatory response in HBV- and HCV-induced HCC [17]. Very recently, HCV core protein was reported to modulate several signaling pathways causing hepatic oncogenesis [18]. Mainly, signaling pathways like TGFβ, p53, MAPK, COX2, VEGF, Wnt, and PPARα are affected in HCC induced by HBV and HCV. Aberrant Notch signaling was also identified as a causative factor of HCC in the absence of viral infection [19,20]. In patients suffering from viral hepatitis, consumption of alcohol and aflatoxin were found to seriously aggravate the chances of hepatic cancer [21]. Early-stage disease diagnosis is very much essential for enhancing the patient's survival in the case of HCC due to its poor prognosis [22]. Most of the patients suffering from HCC die early because of the progression of the disease at a meteoric speed. Resection and transplantation of the liver is the only option to save the patient at an advanced stage of HCC [23,24]. Several frontline drugs like cabozantinib, sorafenib, lenvatinib, and regorafenib are frequently used in the treatment of HCC [25]. Recently, research has been mainly focused on developing and screening small-molecule inhibitors (SMIs) for HCC specific targets. In this chapter, we intend to discuss novel small molecules that have been recognized recently for targeting HCC.

Small-molecule inhibitors and their relevance in cancer

SMIs are organic compounds with low molecular weight and are easily penetrable into a cell without difficulty. SMIs are capable of affecting the cellular function by binding to their specific targets [26]. Macromolecules such as proteins, nucleic acids, and lipids generally act as cellular targets for SMIs [27–30]. Extracellular glycoproteins, cell surface receptors, cytoskeletal proteins, antiapoptotic proteins, heat shock proteins, proteasomes, and matrix metalloproteinases are successfully used as targets for SMIs in various primary and metastatic cancers [31–37]. SMIs like Imatinib, Gefitinib, Erlotinib, Sunitinib, Lapatinib, Bortezomib, Batimastat, Ganetespib, and Obatoclax, which are developed against different molecular targets, are now considered as the most promising drugs for various primary cancers.

Current small-molecule inhibitors used in HCC

Chemotherapy is often considered as an important option for HCC treatment in cases where surgery fails. Drugs like 5-fluorouracil (5-FU), cisplatin (CIS), doxorubicin (DOXO), oxaliplatin (OX), and capecitabine are the most common drugs used for HCC treatment [38–41]. For patients, where the disease is in the worst condition, a combination of two or three of these drugs is recommended to reduce the chances of fatality. For example, 5-FU, OX, and leucovorin are used as a combination for patients who are at the advanced stage of HCC [42]. Recent investigations have shown that small-molecule multiple kinase inhibitors have significant potential for the treatment of HCC at advanced stages and can be used as frontline therapeutic drugs.

Sorafenib

Sorafenib, a multiple kinase inhibitor, is mostly used to treat metastatic HCC [43]. It mainly exerts its action by inhibiting kinases involved in proliferation, metastasis, and angiogenesis. Some of its targets include Raf kinases, VEGFR1, VEGFR2, VEGFR3, PDGFRβ, and FLT3 [44]. Sorafenib was shown to have very few limitations in clinical trials (stage I and II) and was very effective in disease stabilization [45]. Liu et al. have shown that sorafenib can efficiently reduce proliferation and induce programmed cell death in

HCC cells by inhibiting the phosphorylation of MEK, ERK, and eIF4E [46]. They have also identified that sorafenib reduces Cyclin D1 levels and downregulates Mcl-1, an antiapoptotic protein, in a manner independent of the MEK/ERK pathway. Sorafenib, in combination with pravastatin, a statin with antitumor activity, prolonged time to disease progression without any major side effects. But, pravastatin and sorafenib were not able to extend the overall survival of HCC patients [47,48]. Parthenolide is a sesquiterpene lactone and it is an important bioactive component of *Tanacetum parthenium*. It has antiinflammatory and anticancer activity on various cancer cell lines [49]. Very recently, Liang et al. demonstrated that sorafenib in combination with parthenolide nanocrystals has a superior therapeutic effect on the HCC cell line, HepG2 [50]. In combination, they showed high inhibitory activity on cell proliferation and migration. Similarly, sorafenib in combination with ellagic acid showed a significant synergistic antitumor effect on the HCC rat model [51]. Together, they increased ROS production and mitochondrial membrane potential with discharge of cytochrome C in HCC hepatocytes. Also, in combination, they enhanced the activity of caspase 3 and reduced the HCC hepatocyte viability. In a case study on a 68-year-old man diagnosed with advanced HCC, preclinical experiments on combined therapy using sorafenib as well as panobinostat showed significant results [52]. Together, they were able to hamper the cell growth and induce apoptosis, and were capable of inhibiting angiogenesis.

Regorafenib

Regorafenib (Stivarga) is also a multikinase inhibitor and a structural analog of Sorafenib. It is used as a second-line drug to treat metastatic HCC cases that have progressed on sorafenib [53]. The biological targets of regorafenib include angiogenesis, components of stroma, and oncogenic receptor tyrosine kinases (RTKs) [54]. It targets cell surface receptors, VEGFR2 and TIE2, and shows a potent antiangiogenic activity. Regorafenib was also found to be more efficacious together with other SMIs in HCC when compared to its individual effect [55]. Simultaneous combination of regorafenib and CDK4/6 inhibitor, palbociclib, has a superior antitumor effect on HCC cells [56]. Together, they suppressed cell proliferation, induced cell death, reduced the spheroid cell growth, and decreased metastasis. Moreover, a combination of both drugs impaired uptake of glucose and its utilization, downregulated the expression of hypoxia specific factors HIF-1alpha, HIF-2alpha, GLUT-1, and MCT4, and activated HK2, PFKP, aldolase A, and PKM2 expression. A sequential administration of sorafenib and regorafenib also showed positive results with minimal side effects in an advanced stage HCC [57]. They increased the progression-free survival of the HCC patients and enhanced the disease stability.

Lenvatinib

Lenvatinib (lenvima) is also a multiple kinase inhibitor, and it is used for advanced and unresectable HCC treatment [58]. The targets of this SMI include VEGFR 1−3, PDGFRα, FGFR 1−4, RET, and KIT. Because of its dual action on both VEGFR and FGFR, it acts as a strong inhibitor of tumor angiogenesis and proliferation [59]. Very recently, Deng et al. reported that VEGFR and FGFR expression are high in advanced HCC and treating the patients in these cases with lenvatinib not only downregulates tumor progression but also elicits antitumor immunity [60]. Simultaneous administration of lenvatinib and PD-1 monoclonal antibodies synergistically activated anticancer immune response and suppressed tumor angiogenesis [61]. Lenvatinib was also shown to inhibit CD44 and CD133 positive HCC stem cells by specifically inhibiting FGFR1—3 signaling [62].

Cabozantinib

Cabozantinib (Cometriq, Cabometyx) is a second-line multikinase inhibitor with broad target specificity [63]. Some of its targets include c-MET, VEGFR, GAS6 receptor (AXL), KIT, and FLT3. Cabozanitib was shown to have a considerable capacity to increase the HCC patients' median survival with prior sorafenib treatment, indicating sequential administration of both the drugs can have a significant therapeutic effect on advanced HCC patients [64]. According to a recent observation by Yang et al., patients with postsurgery bone metastasis due to amplification of oncogenic RET, high tumor mutational burden, as well as overexpression of PD-L1, treatment using cabozantinib and anti-PD-L1 antibody combination increased survival by more than 2 years [65].

Viral proteins as therapeutic targets for small-molecule inhibitors in HCC

HBV- and HCV-dependent infections are often persistent in chronic hepatitis. Hepatitis virus adopts multiple strategies for its survival within the host [66]. The entry, existence, and multiplication of viruses within the host are determined by virus-encoded proteins. HCV envelope protein, E2 glycoprotein, is essential for virus entry into hepatocytes. It interacts with hepatocyte surface protein CD81 and other coreceptors and initiates downstream signaling that favors virus entry [67]. E2 glycoprotein was specifically found to interact with the CD81 large extracellular loop [68]. Olaby et al. have done a detailed analysis on the structure of E2 glycoprotein, and after screening several SMIs, they identified a compound 281816 as a potential inhibitor of E2-CD81 interaction [69]. NS3, a nonstructural HCV protein, is critical for polyprotein processing [70]. Considering its importance in viral replication, NS3 is regarded as a potential antiviral target. SMIs, ellagitannins (punicalagin, punicalin, and ellagic acid), extracted from pomegranate fruit peel, were shown to efficiently inhibit the protease activity of HCV NS3 [71]. HBx is a polyfunctional protein and it is essential for the viral life cycle [72]. It has a great significance on the risk of HCC [73]. It is known to control both viral and cellular gene expression [72,74]. An SMI, dicoumarol, which is known to inhibit NADPH: quinone oxidoreductase, significantly reduced the expression of HBx [75].

Signaling pathway components as small-molecule targets in HCC

Recent reports have shown that altered cellular signaling mechanisms are linked to HCC development [76]. Targeting the components of these pathways can help to either completely prevent or delay the progression of the tumor [77]. In HCC, several growth factor receptors, including VEGFR, EGFR, IGFR, and C-MET have notable effects on the development and progression of tumors [78]. VEGF and VEGFR are vital angiogenic factors, and they play crucial roles in tumor growth and invasion [79]. Studies have shown that the expression levels of both VEGF and VEGFR isoforms are elevated in HCC patients and they act as prognostic markers [78,80,81]. The core protein of HCV is known to enhance VEGF expression as well as angiopoietin in HCC [18]. Regulated expression of HCV core protein in hepatoma cell lines evokes the activation of E2F1, p38, apoptosis signal-regulating kinase 1, JNK, ERK, CREB, activating transcription factor 2 (ATF2), specificity protein 1 (SP1), and HIF-1alpha [82]. JNK, p38, and ERK pathways regulate core protein-mediated induction of TGF-beta 2 and VEGF. The core protein of HCV was also shown to modulate other multiple signaling pathways like TGF-beta, Wnt/Catenin, PPAR-alpha, and Cox2, which are associated with HCC development [83−86]. Targeting these pathways could also limit HCC progression. Hepatitis Bx antigen (HBx-ag) was recently shown to be associated with the upregulation of VEGFR3, an important factor involved in angiogenesis [87]. High VEGF expression is positively correlated with tumor grade, poor prognosis, vascular invasion, as well as disease recurrence in HCC; hence, it could be the most druggable target [88]. EGF/EGFR signaling was shown to enhance cell proliferation as well as angiogenesis in HCC via PI3K/AKT/mTOR and RAF/MEK/ERK signaling pathways [89].

EGFR is overexpressed in HCC and it is a possible target in sorafenib-resistant HCC cells [90,91]. EGFR inhibitors were able to enhance the efficacy of sorafenib in drug-resistant cells. Insulin-like growth factor (IGF) signaling is related to cell growth, evasion of apoptosis, as well as cell motility. Dysregulation of the IGF signaling pathway is often observed in HCC [92]. Overexpression of IGF-2 is the major reason for hyperactive IGF signaling in HCC [93]. Hepatocyte growth factor (HGF) is mainly involved in the invasion of malignant tumors. It interacts with its high-affinity membrane receptor c-Met, which is a tyrosine kinase [94]. Inappropriate c-Met activation leads to cell proliferation and metastasis in HCC [95]. HCC patients with abnormal expression of c-Met have a very poor chance of survival [96]. HGF/C-Met signaling determines the tumor aggressiveness and it is a promising diagnostic as well as a prognostic biomarker for HCC [97]. C-Met is also closely associated with drug resistance in HCC [98]. β-catenin, a central mediator of the Wnt pathway, acts as a vital factor during the early events of hepatic carcinogenesis. Abnormal activity of the Wnt pathway in HCC was found to be due to mutations in β-catenin gene 1 (CTNBB1) [99]. TGF-β crosstalk with Wnt pathway has been noticed in HCC [100]. Recently, PKF115-854 and CGP04909 were found to be efficient in antagonizing the β-catenin-dependent cellular effects [101].

Drug resistance in HCC: a major concern for the development of new SMIs

Drug resistance is a big setback in the treatment of cancers and it still remains as the major cause of tumor relapse. Recently, cases showing resistance to the drugs used in the treatment of HCC were reported. Continuous efforts are being made to understand the molecular basis of drug resistance in HCC. Li et al. reported that HCC stem cells isolated from the sorafenib-resistant PLC/PRF/5-R culture are also resistant to sorafenib and they are more tumorigenic than normal cancer stem cells (CSCs). They identified that the IL-6/STAT3 pathway plays a significant role in imparting drug resistance. Downregulation of IL-6 by shRNA-mediated knockdown improved the sensitivity of HCC stem cells to sorafenib [102]. Torrin2, a SMI of mTOR, exhibits a significant cytotoxic effect on sorafenib-resistant HCC cell lines by suppressing the oncogenic mTORC2-AKT-BAD pathway [103]. CD24 is a membrane-bound sialoglycoprotein and its expression levels correlate with resistance to sorafenib and disease progression in HCC. CD24 mediated activation of protein phosphatase 2A (PP2A) and subsequent inactivation of the mTOR/Akt pathway was found to be the major reason behind autophagy-induced sorafenib resistance in HCC [104]. mTOR mediated Phosphorylation of ATG13 suppresses autophagy. Phosphorylated ATG13 is the direct target of PP2A and its dephosphorylation activates autophagy. **Tumor Necrosis Factor Alpha Induced Protein 8 (TNFAIP8)** is a prooncogenic protein and it belongs to the TIPE (Tumor Necrosis Induced Protein 8 like) family of proteins. It is associated with various cancers like prostate, lung, breast, colon, esophagus, ovary, cervix, pancreas, and liver. TNFAIP8 protein levels are exorbitantly high in HCC cells. It promotes cell proliferation, metastasis, and autophagy. It plays an antiapoptotic role and renders the hepatic cancer cells resistant to drugs, sorafenib, and regorafenib. TNFAIP8 induces autophagy by blocking the mTOR/Akt pathway and by directly interacting with ATG3-ATG7 proteins in HCC cells [105]. ULK1, an autophagy activating kinase, was found to exert a key tumor-promoting role in HCC. Defusing the ULK1 activity by Gene Knockout/Gene knockdown decreased the cell proliferation as well as metastasis of HCC cells. Sorafenib was able to show a considerable effect on ULK1 ablated HCC cells. XST14, a SMI of ULK1, enhanced the potency of sorafenib in HCC cells, indicating that, downregulation of autophagy/autophagy-related proteins could help target drug resistance in HCC cells (Fig. 5.1) [106].

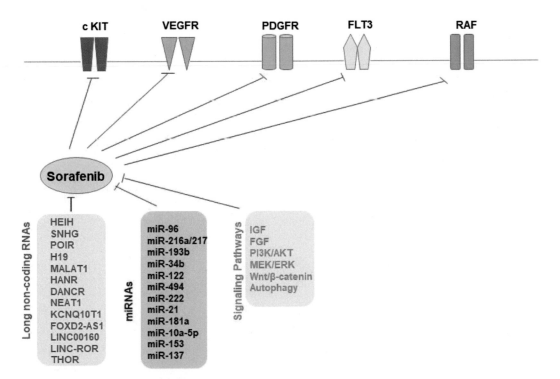

FIGURE 5.1 Sorafenib is a frontline small-molecule inhibitor that inhibits hepatocellular carcinoma by targeting receptor tyrosine kinases (VEGFR, PDGFR, cKIT, FLT3, and RAF). It is negatively regulated by ncRNAs (lncRNAs and miRNAs) and signaling pathways to induce the resistance.

Noncoding RNAs induced drug resistance in HCC

Noncoding RNAs (ncRNAs) are functional RNAs and they lack the capability of being translated into proteins [107]. There are mainly two different types of noncoding RNAs: (1) long noncoding RNAs (lncRNA) and (2) short noncoding RNAs [108]. Short regulatory noncoding RNAs include miRNA, siRNA, snRNA, snoRNA, and piwi RNA. Noncoding RNAs which promote cancer are oncogenic ncRNAs and which suppress cancer are tumor suppressor ncRNAs. Oncogenic ncRNAs assist cell proliferation, EMT, invasion, metastasis, as well as drug resistance (Table 5.1) [124,125]. Recently, many studies have pointed out the upcoming roles of ncRNAs in the drug resistance of HCC [126]. Specifically, LncRNAs were shown to induce chemoresistance by sponging (binding to complementary sites in the seed region of miRs) tumor suppressor miRNAs in HCC cells [126]. Shen et al. have proven that expression of LncRNA HEIH is elevated in sorafenib-resistant HCC cells and it enhances resistance to sorafenib via PI3K/Akt pathway by sponging miR-98-5P. HEIH silencing was able to sensitize and stimulate HCC cells to the cytostatic and cell-death-inducing effect of sorafenib [109]. Similarly, lncRNA SNHG was also shown to enhance resistance to sorafenib by activating the AKT-mediated pathway in HCC cell lines. It has also been observed that miR-21, which is

TABLE 5.1 List of LncRNAs involved in Sorafenib drug resistance.

LncRNA	Expression status	miRNA/pathway regulated	References
HEIH	Overexpressed	miR-98-5p/PI3K/AKT	[109]
SNHG	Overexpressed	AKT	[110]
POIR	Overexpressed	miR-182-5p	[111]
H19	Overexpressed	miR-675	[112]
MALAT-1	Overexpressed	miR-140-5p/Aurora A	[113]
HANR	Overexpressed	miR-29b	[114]
DANCR	Overexpressed	IL-6/STAT3	[115]
NEAT1	Overexpressed	miR-149-5p/AKT	[116]
KCNQ1OT1	Overexpressed	PD-L1	[117]
FOXD2-AS1	Downregulated	miR-150-5p/TMEM9	[118]
LINC00160	Overexpressed	PIK3R3	[119]
LINC-ROR	Overexpressed	FOXM1	[120]
THOR	Overexpressed	β-Catenin	[121]
TUC338	Overexpressed	RASAL1	[122]
VLDLR	Overexpressed	ABCG2	[123]

overexpressed in HCC cells, promotes the expression of lncRNA SNHG after translocation to the nucleus [110]. Very recently, Chen et al. experimentally proved that lncRNA-POIR is upregulated in HCC cells and promotes resistance to sorafenib by supporting EMT via sponging miR-182-5p [111]. LncRNA H19, a highly upregulated lncRNA in HCC, was shown to elevate sorafenib resistance by upregulating the miR-675. Knockdown of lncRNA H19 was able to inhibit sorafenib resistance in HCC. MALAT-1 is a prooncogenic lncRNA and acts as a prognostic biomarker in HCC. HCC cells, which are resistant to sorafenib, show very high levels of MALAT-1 and its upregulation is associated with the decreased expression of tumor suppressor miRNA, miR-140-5p, and increased expression of tumor-promoting Aurora A kinase [112]. Silencing MALAT-1 increases sorafenib sensitivity in HCC cells. LncRNA-HANR, a wellknown tumorigenic lncRNA, is profoundly expressed in HCC [113]. Its overexpression is directly correlated with sorafenib resistance in HCC. HANR induces sorafenib resistance by facilitating autophagy. ATG 9A, an autophagy-related protein, which is involved in phagophore assembly is a direct effector of miR-29b. HANR suppresses miR-29b and facilitates autophagy-mediated drug resistance in HCC cells [114]. Other lncRNAs such as DANCR, NEAT1, TUC338, VLDLR, LINC00160, FOXD2-AS1, LINC-ROR, THOR, and TUC338 were known to trigger resistance to sorafenib in HCC [115−123].

CSCs contribute to the recurrence, progression, and chemoresistance in HCC [127]. miRNAs regulate stem-cell-mediated tumorigenesis of HCC. Contemporary studies have also broadly emphasized the prominence of miRNAs in CSCs mediated drug resistance in HCC. miR-96 is an oncogenic miRNA, and it is upregulated in CSCs. miR-96 targets 3′UTR of TP53INP1mRNA and downregulates its expression in CSCs. Simultaneously, upregulation of miR-96 was also correlated with sorafenib resistance in CSCs [127]. miR-216a/217 is a cancerogenic miRNA and it is frequently overexpressed in HCC cells. It activates oncogenic PI3k/AKT and TGF-beta pathways by aiming at PTEN and SMAD7, respectively [128]. Activation of these two pathways correlates with escalated resistance to sorafenib in HCC cells. miR-193b is a tumor suppressor and its expression is reduced in sorafenib-resistant HCC [129]. Downregulation of miR-193b results in the overexpression of antiapoptotic protein MCL-1. Transfecting miR-193b into sorafenib-resistant cells suppresses MCL-1 and induces apoptosis. Downregulation of tumor suppressor miRNA, miR-34a, and upregulation of its target, BCL-2, was detected in sorafenib-resistant cell lines. Ectopically expressed miR-34a suppresses BCL-2 expression and activates apoptosis in HCC cells with sorafenib resistance [130]. miR-122 is a liver-specific miRNA and it is downregulated in sorafenib-resistant HCC cells. Insulin-like growth factor 1 receptor (IGF 1R) is the direct target of miR-122. IGF 1/IGF II-mediated IGF 1R signaling in miR-122 downregulated HCC cells inhibit sorafenib-induced apoptosis and confers resistance. IGF 1R signaling in miR-122 downregulated HCC cells also activates the RAS/RAF/ERK signaling pathway that promotes drug resistance. Sorafenib, in combination with IGF 1R inhibitor PPP or NVP-AEW541, significantly induces apoptosis in sorafenib tolerating HCC cells (Fig. 5.2) [131].

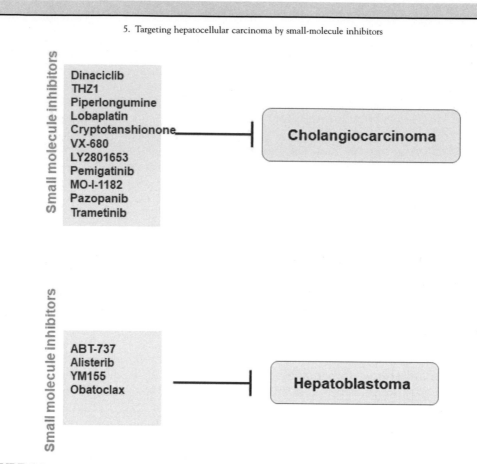

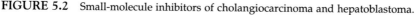

FIGURE 5.2   Small-molecule inhibitors of cholangiocarcinoma and hepatoblastoma.

Conclusion

HCC is one of the LCs caused by risk factors, hepatitis B and C viral infections. Several SMIs targeting various molecular targets have been developed to combat HCC. The front-line multikinase SMIs like sorafenib, regorafenib, lenvatinib, and cabozantinib are potentially used in the cases where HCC is refractory to surgery and other anticancer drugs like CIS, DOXO, and 5-FU. Sorafenib, regorafenib, lenvatinib, and cabozantinib showed great potency as proliferation, migration, invasion inhibitors, and apoptosis inducers when treated individually or in combination with other drugs. SMIs, developed recently, for treating CCA and HB, have also shown great promise in suppressing the diseases. The major disappointment in the treatment of HCC is resistance development to the frontline drugs. Some of the important factors which help in the development of resistance to frontline drugs used in HCC have been identified, and the molecular details involved in the resistance mechanism have been elucidated. Strategies for developing more specific and effective SMIs are highly recommended to overcome the limitations involved in the treatment of HCC.

Acknowledgment

The authors are grateful to the Institute of Science, Gandhi Institute of Technology and Management, Visakhapatnam, Andhra Pradesh, India.

Conflict of interest

The authors declared that there is no conflict of interest.

Funding

This project is supported by CSIR, New Delhi, India (File No: 37(1683)/17/EMR-II), dated on 05.05.2017.

References

[1] Ghouri YA, Mian I, Rowe JH. Review of hepatocellular carcinoma: epidemiology, etiology, and carcinogenesis. J Carcinog 2017;16:1. Available from: https://doi.org/10.4103/jcar.JCar_9_16.

[2] Matsushita H, Takaki A. Alcohol and hepatocellular carcinoma. BMJ Open Gastroenterol 2019;6(1).e000260. Available from: https://doi.org/10.1136/bmjgast-2018-000260.

[3] Sidharthan S, Kottilil S. Mechanisms of alcohol-induced hepatocellular carcinoma. Hepatol Int 2014;8 (2):452−7. Available from: https://doi.org/10.1007/s12072-013-9494-4.

[4] Tanaka K, Tsuji I, Wakai K, Nagata C, Mizoue T, Inoue M, et al.Research Group for the Development and Evaluation of Cancer Prevention Strategies in Japan Cigarette smoking and liver cancer risk: an evaluation based on a systematic review of epidemiologic evidence among Japanese Jpn J Clin Oncol 2006;36(7):445−56 Epub 2006 Jun 16. PMID: 16782973. Available from: https://doi.org/10.1093/jjco/hyl040.

[5] Su CH, Lin Y, Cai L. Genetic factors, viral infection, other factors and liver cancer: an update on current progress. Asian Pac J Cancer Prev 2013;14(9):4953−60. Available from: https://doi.org/10.7314/apjcp.2013.14.9.4953.

[6] Woodward C, Smith J, Acreman D, Kumar N. Hepatocellular carcinoma in body builders; an emerging rare but serious complication of androgenic anabolic steroid use. Ann Hepatobiliary Pancreat Surg 2019;23 (2):174−7. Available from: https://doi.org/10.14701/ahbps.2019.23.2.174.

[7] Niedfeldt MW. Anabolic steroid effect on the liver. Curr Sports Med Rep 2018;17(3):97−102. Available from: https://doi.org/10.1249/JSR.0000000000000467.

[8] Hamid AS, Tesfamariam IG, Zhang Y, Zhang ZG. Aflatoxin B1-induced hepatocellular carcinoma in developing countries: geographical distribution, mechanism of action and prevention. Oncol Lett 2013;5(4):1087−92. Available from: https://doi.org/10.3892/ol.2013.1169.

[9] Santella RM, Wu HC. Environmental exposures and hepatocellular carcinoma. J Clin Transl Hepatol 2013;1 (2):138−43. Available from: https://doi.org/10.14218/JCTH.2013.008XX.

[10] van Ginkel WG, Pennings JP, van Spronsen FJ. Liver cancer in tyrosinemia type 1. Adv Exp Med Biol 2017;959:101−9. Available from: https://doi.org/10.1007/978-3-319-55780-9_9.

[11] Antoury C, Lopez R, Zein N, Stoller JK, Alkhouri N. Alpha-1 antitrypsin deficiency and the risk of hepatocellular carcinoma in end-stage liver disease. World J Hepatol 2015;7(10):1427−32. Available from: https://doi.org/10.4254/wjh.v7.i10.1427.

[12] Baravelli CM, Sandberg S, Aarsand AK, Tollånes MC. Porphyria cutanea tarda increases risk of hepatocellular carcinoma and premature death: a nationwide cohort study Orphanet J Rare Dis 2019;14(1):77. PMID: 30944007; PMCID: PMC6448269. Available from: https://doi.org/10.1186/s13023-019-1051-3.

[13] Demo E, Frush D, Gottfried M, Koepke J, Boney A, Bali D, et al. Glycogen storage disease type III-hepatocellular carcinoma a long-term complication? J Hepatol 2007;46(3):492−8. Epub 2006 Nov 9. PMID: 17196294; PMCID: PMC2683272. Available from: https://doi.org/10.1016/j.jhep.2006.09.022.

[14] Xu R, Hajdu CH. Wilson disease and hepatocellular carcinoma. Gastroenterol Hepatol (N Y) 2008;4(6):438–9 PMID: 21904522; PMCID: PMC3093704.

[15] El-Serag HB. Epidemiology of viral hepatitis and hepatocellular carcinoma Gastroenterology 2012;142(6):1264–73. PMID: 22537432; PMCID: PMC3338949. Available from: https://doi.org/10.1053/j.gastro.2011.12.061.

[16] Zakaria MK, Sankhyan A, Ali A, Fatima K, Azhar E, et al. HBV/HCV infection and inflammation. J GenetSyndr Gene Ther 2014;5:241. Available from: https://doi.org/10.4172/2157-7412.1000241.

[17] Budhu A, Wang XW. The role of cytokines in hepatocellular carcinoma J Leukoc Biol 2006;80(6):1197–213. Epub 2006 Aug 31. PMID: 16946019. Available from: https://doi.org/10.1189/jlb.0506297.

[18] Mahmoudvand S, Shokri S, Taherkhani R, Farshadpour F. Hepatitis C virus core protein modulates several signaling pathways involved in hepatocellular carcinoma World J Gastroenterol 2019;25(1):42–58. PMID: 30643357; PMCID: PMC6328967. Available from: https://doi.org/10.3748/wjg.v25.i1.42.

[19] Huang Q, Li J, Zheng J, Wei A. The carcinogenic role of the Notch signaling pathway in the development of hepatocellular carcinoma. J Cancer 2019;10(6):1570–9. Available from: https://doi.org/10.7150/jca.26847.

[20] Villanueva A, Alsinet C, Yanger K, Hoshida Y, Zong Y, Toffanin S, et al. Notch signaling is activated in human hepatocellular carcinoma and induces tumor formation in mice Gastroenterology 2012;143(6):1660–9. e7. Available from: https://doi.org/10.1053/j.gastro.2012.09.002.

[21] Chu YJ, Yang HI, Wu HC, et al. Aflatoxin B1 exposure increases the risk of hepatocellular carcinoma associated with hepatitis C virus infection or alcohol consumption. Eur J Cancer 2018;94:37–46. Available from: https://doi.org/10.1016/j.ejca.2018.02.010.

[22] Kudo M. Early detection and curative treatment of early-stage hepatocellular carcinoma Clin Gastroenterol Hepatol 2005;3(10 Suppl 2):S144–8. PMID: 16234064. Available from: https://doi.org/10.1016/s1542-3565(05)00712-3.

[23] Shimada M, Takenaka K, Kawahara N, Kajiyama K, Yamamoto K, Shirabe K, et al. Surgical treatment strategy for patients with stage IV hepatocellular carcinoma Surgery 1996;119(5):517–22. PMID: 8619206. Available from: https://doi.org/10.1016/s0039-6060(96)80260-1.

[24] Lee HW, Suh KS. Liver transplantation for advanced hepatocellular carcinoma. Clin Mol Hepatol 2016;22 (3):309–18. Available from: https://doi.org/10.3350/cmh.2016.0042.

[25] Huang A, Yang XR, Chung WY, Dennison AR, Zhou J. Targeted therapy for hepatocellular carcinoma Signal Transduct Target Ther 2020;5(1):146. PMID: 32782275; PMCID: PMC7419547. Available from: https://doi.org/10.1038/s41392-020-00264-x.

[26] Khera N, Rajput S. Therapeutic potential of small molecule inhibitors J Cell Biochem 2017;118(5):959–61. Epub 2017 Jan 10. PMID: 27813176. Available from: https://doi.org/10.1002/jcb.25782.

[27] Lomenick B, Olsen RW, Huang J. Identification of direct protein targets of small molecules. ACS Chem Biol 2011;6(1):34–46. Available from: https://doi.org/10.1021/cb100294v.

[28] Litovchick A, Tian X, Monteiro MI, et al. Novel nucleic acid binding small molecules discovered using DNA-encoded chemistry. Molecules 2019;24(10):2026. Available from: https://doi.org/10.3390/molecules24102026.

[29] Sudhahar CG, Haney RM, Xue Y, Stahelin RV. Cellular membranes and lipid-binding domains as attractive targets for drug development. Curr Drug Targets 2008;9(8):603–13. Available from: https://doi.org/10.2174/138945008785132420.

[30] Evans JF, Hutchinson JH. Seeing the future of bioactive lipid drug targets. Nat Chem Biol 2010;6(7):476–9. Available from: https://doi.org/10.1038/nchembio.394.

[31] Costa AF, Campos D, Reis CA, Gomes C. Targeting glycosylation: a new road for cancer drug discovery Trends Cancer 2020;6(9):757–66. Epub 2020 May 4. PMID: 32381431. Available from: https://doi.org/10.1016/j.trecan.2020.04.002.

[32] Peterson JR, Mitchison TJ. Small molecules, big impact: a history of chemical inhibitors and the cytoskeleton. Chem Biol 2002;9(12):1275–85. Available from: https://doi.org/10.1016/s1074-5521(02)00284-3.

[33] Derakhshan A, Chen Z, Van Waes C. Therapeutic small molecules target inhibitor of apoptosis proteins in cancers with deregulation of extrinsic and intrinsic cell death pathways Clin Cancer Res 2017;23(6):1379–87. Epub 2016 Dec 30. PMID: 28039268; PMCID: PMC5354945. Available from: https://doi.org/10.1158/1078-0432.CCR-16-2172.

[34] Kang MH, Reynolds CP. Bcl-2 inhibitors: targeting mitochondrial apoptotic pathways in cancer therapy. Clin Cancer Res 2009;15(4):1126–32. Available from: https://doi.org/10.1158/1078-0432.CCR-08-0144.

[35] Jego G, Hazoumé A, Seigneuric R, Garrido C. Targeting heat shock proteins in cancer Cancer Lett 2013;332 (2):275–85. Epub 2010 Nov 13. PMID: 21078542. Available from: https://doi.org/10.1016/j.canlet.2010.10.014.

[36] Ao N, Chen Q, Liu G. The small molecules targeting ubiquitin-proteasome system for cancer therapy. Comb Chem High Throughput Screen 2017;20(5):403—13. Available from: https://doi.org/10.2174/1386207320666170710124746.

[37] Cathcart J, Pulkoski-Gross A, Cao J. Targeting matrix metalloproteinases in cancer: bringing new life to old ideas. Genes Dis 2015;2(1):26—34. Available from: https://doi.org/10.1016/j.gendis.2014.12.002.

[38] Link JS, Bateman JR, Paroly WS, Durkin WJ, Peters RL. 5-Flourouracil in hepatocellular carcinoma: report of twenty-one cases. Cancer 1977;39(5):1936—9. PMID: 192441. Available from: https://doi.org/10.1002/1097-0142(197705)39:5 < 1936::aid-cncr2820390504 > 3.0.co;2-n.

[39] Ma MC, Chen YY, Li SH, Cheng YF, Wang CC, Chiu TJ, et al. Intra-arterial chemotherapy with doxorubicin and cisplatin is effective for advanced hepatocellular cell carcinoma ScientificWorldJournal 2014;2014:160138. Epub 2014 May 22. PMID: 24967421; PMCID: PMC4055608. Available from: https://doi.org/10.1155/2014/160138.

[40] Petrelli F, Coinu A, Borgonovo K, Cabiddu M, Ghilardi M, Lonati V, et al. Oxaliplatin-based chemotherapy: a new option in advanced hepatocellular carcinoma. A systematic review and pooled analysis Clin Oncol (R Coll Radiol) 2014;26(8):488—96. Epub 2014 May 21. PMID: 24856442. Available from: https://doi.org/10.1016/j.clon.2014.04.031.

[41] Pelizzaro F, Sammarco A, Dadduzio V, Pastorelli D, Giovanis P, Soldà C, et al. Capecitabine in advanced hepatocellular carcinoma: a multicenter experience Dig Liver Dis 2019;51(12):1713—19. Epub 2019 Jul 16. PMID: 31320302. Available from: https://doi.org/10.1016/j.dld.2019.06.015.

[42] Qin S, Bai Y, Lim HY, Thongprasert S, Chao Y, Fan J, et al. Randomized, multicenter, open-label study of oxaliplatin plus fluorouracil/leucovorin vs doxorubicin as palliative chemotherapy in patients with advanced hepatocellular carcinoma from Asia J Clin Oncol 2013;31(28):3501—8. Epub 2013 Aug 26. PMID: 23980077. Available from: https://doi.org/10.1200/JCO.2012.44.5643.

[43] Wilhelm S, Carter C, Lynch M, Lowinger T, Dumas J, Smith RA, et al. Discovery and development of sorafenib: a multikinase inhibitor for treating cancer Nat Rev Drug Discov 2006;5(10):835—44. Erratum in: Nat Rev Drug Discov. 2007 Feb;6(2):126. PMID: 17016424. Available from: https://doi.org/10.1038/nrd2130.

[44] Furuse J. Sorafenib for the treatment of unresectable hepatocellular carcinoma. Biologics. 2008;2(4):779—88. Available from: https://doi.org/10.2147/btt.s3410.

[45] Almhanna K, Philip PA. Safety and efficacy of sorafenib in the treatment of hepatocellular carcinoma. Onco Targets Ther 2009;2:261—7. Available from: https://doi.org/10.2147/ott.s5548.

[46] Liu L, Cao Y, Chen C, Zhang X, McNabola A, Wilkie D, et al. Sorafenib blocks the RAF/MEK/ERK pathway, inhibits tumor angiogenesis, and induces tumor cell apoptosis in hepatocellular carcinoma model PLC/PRF/5. Cancer Res 2006;66(24):11851—8. Available from: https://doi.org/10.1158/0008-5472.CAN-06-1377.

[47] Riaño I, Martín L, Varela M, Serrano T, Núñez O, Mínguez B, et al. Efficacy and safety of the combination of pravastatin and sorafenib for the treatment of advanced hepatocellular carcinoma (ESTAHEP clinical trial) Cancers (Basel) 2020;12(7):1900. PMID: 32674461; PMCID: PMC7409102. Available from: https://doi.org/10.3390/cancers12071900.

[48] Jouve JL, Lecomte T, Bouché O, Barbier E, Khemissa Akouz F, Riachi G, et al. PRODIGE-11 investigators/collaborators. Pravastatin combination with sorafenib does not improve survival in advanced hepatocellular carcinoma J Hepatol 2019;71(3):516—22. Epub 2019 May 22. PMID: 31125576. Available from: https://doi.org/10.1016/j.jhep.2019.04.021.

[49] Mathema VB, Koh YS, Thakuri BC, Sillanpää M. Parthenolide, a sesquiterpene lactone, expresses multiple anti-cancer and anti-inflammatory activities Inflammation 2012;35(2):560—5. PMID: 21603970. Available from: https://doi.org/10.1007/s10753-011-9346-0.

[50] Liang P, Wu H, Zhang Z, Jiang S, Lv H. Preparation and characterization of parthenolide nanocrystals for enhancing therapeutic effects of sorafenib against advanced hepatocellular carcinoma. Int J Pharm 2020;583:119375. Available from: https://doi.org/10.1016/j.ijpharm.2020.119375.

[51] Salimi A, Saboji M, Seydi E. Synergistic effects of ellagic acid and sorafenib on hepatocytes and mitochondria isolated from a hepatocellular carcinoma rat model Nutr Cancer 2020;1—9. Oct. Available from: https://doi.org/10.1080/01635581.2020.1829653.

[52] Knieling F, Waldner MJ, Goertz RS, Strobel D. Quantification of dynamic contrast-enhanced ultrasound in HCC: prediction of response to a new combination therapy of sorafenib and panobinostat in advanced hepatocellular carcinoma BMJ Case Rep 2012. Dec 17;2012:bcr2012007576. Available from: https://doi.org/10.1136/bcr-2012-007576.

[53] Shlomai A, Leshno M, Goldstein DA. Regorafenib treatment for patients with hepatocellular carcinoma who progressed on sorafenib—a cost-effectiveness analysis. PLoS One 2018;13(11):e0207132. Available from: https://doi.org/10.1371/journal.pone.0207132.

[54] Wilhelm SM, Dumas J, Adnane L, Lynch M, Carter CA, Schütz G, et al. Regorafenib (BAY 73—4506): a new oral multikinase inhibitor of angiogenic, stromal and oncogenic receptor tyrosine kinases with potent preclinical antitumor activity Int J Cancer 2011;129(1):245—55. Epub 2011 Apr 22. PMID: 21170960. Available from: https://doi.org/10.1002/ijc.25864.

[55] Fondevila F, Méndez-Blanco C, Fernández-Palanca P, González-Gallego J, Mauriz JL. Anti-tumoral activity of single and combined regorafenib treatments in preclinical models of liver and gastrointestinal cancers Exp Mol Med 2019;51(9):1—15. PMID: 31551425; PMCID: PMC6802659. Available from: https://doi.org/10.1038/s12276-019-0308-1.

[56] Digiacomo G, Fumarola C, La Monica S, Bonelli MA, Cretella D, Alfieri R, et al. Simultaneous combination of the cdk4/6 inhibitor palbociclib with regorafenib induces enhanced anti-tumor effects in hepatocarcinoma cell lines. Front Oncol 2020;10:563249. Available from: https://doi.org/10.3389/fonc.2020.563249.

[57] Ogasawara S, Ooka Y, Itokawa N, Inoue M, Okabe S, Seki A, et al. Sequential therapy with sorafenib and regorafenib for advanced hepatocellular carcinoma: a multicenter retrospective study in Japan Invest N Drugs 2020;38(1):172—80. Epub 2019 Jun 6. PMID: 31172442. Available from: https://doi.org/10.1007/s10637-019-00801-8.

[58] Iwamoto H, Suzuki H, Shimose S, et al. Weekends-off lenvatinib for unresectable hepatocellular carcinoma improves therapeutic response and tolerability toward adverse events. Cancers (Basel) 2020;12(4):1010. Available from: https://doi.org/10.3390/cancers12041010.

[59] Matsuki M, Hoshi T, Yamamoto Y, et al. Lenvatinib inhibits angiogenesis and tumor fibroblast growth factor signaling pathways in human hepatocellular carcinoma models. Cancer Med 2018;7(6):2641—53. Available from: https://doi.org/10.1002/cam4.1517.

[60] Deng H, Kan A, Lyu N, Mu L, Han Y, Liu L, et al. Dual vascular endothelial growth factor receptor and fibroblast growth factor receptor inhibition elicits antitumor immunity and enhances programmed cell death-1 checkpoint blockade in hepatocellular carcinoma Liver Cancer 2020;9(3):338—57. Epub 2020 Feb 25. PMID: 32647635; PMCID: PMC7325120. Available from: https://doi.org/10.1159/000505695.

[61] Finn RS, Ikeda M, Zhu AX, Sung MW, Baron AD, Kudo M, et al. Phase Ib study of lenvatinib plus pembrolizumab in patients with unresectable hepatocellular carcinoma J Clin Oncol 2020;38(26):2960—70. Epub 2020 Jul 27. PMID: 32716739; PMCID: PMC7479760. Available from: https://doi.org/10.1200/JCO.20.00808.

[62] Shigesawa T, Maehara O, Suda G, Natsuizaka M, Kimura M, Shimazaki T, et al. Lenvatinib suppresses cancer stem-like cells in HCC by inhibiting FGFR 1—3 signaling, but not FGFR4 signaling. Carcinogenesis. 2021;42(1):58—69. Available from: https://doi.org/10.1093/carcin/bgaa049 May.

[63] Abou-Alfa GK, Meyer T, Cheng AL, El-Khoueiry AB, Rimassa L, Ryoo BY, et al. Cabozantinib in patients with advanced and progressing hepatocellular carcinoma N Engl J Med 2018;379(1):54—63. PMID: 29972759; PMCID: PMC7523244. Available from: https://doi.org/10.1056/NEJMoa1717002.

[64] Kelley RK, Ryoo BY, Merle P, Park JW, Bolondi L, Chan SL, et al. Second-line cabozantinib after sorafenib treatment for advanced hepatocellular carcinoma: a subgroup analysis of the phase 3 CELESTIAL trial ESMO Open 2020;5(4):e000714. PMID: 32847838; PMCID: PMC7451459. Available from: https://doi.org/10.1136/esmoopen-2020-000714.

[65] Yang X, Shi J, Chen X, Jiang Y, Zhao H. Efficacy of cabozantinib and nivolumab in treating hepatocellular carcinoma with ret amplification, high tumor mutational burden, and pd-l1 expression Oncologist 2020;25(6):470—4. Epub 2020 Feb 26. PMID: 32100934; PMCID: PMC7288626. Available from: https://doi.org/10.1634/theoncologist.2019-0563.

[66] Dandri M, Petersen J. Mechanism of hepatitis b virus persistence in hepatocytes and its carcinogenic potential Clin Infect Dis 2016;62(Suppl 4):S281—8. PMID: 27190317; PMCID: PMC4889895. Available from: https://doi.org/10.1093/cid/ciw023.

[67] Falkowska E, Kajumo F, Garcia E, Reinus J, Dragic T. Hepatitis C virus envelope glycoprotein E2 glycans modulate entry, CD81 binding, and neutralization J Virol 2007;81(15):8072—9. Epub 2007 May 16. PMID: 17507469; PMCID: PMC1951298. Available from: https://doi.org/10.1128/JVI.00459-07.

[68] Tian ZF, Shen H, Fu XH, Chen YC, Blum HE, Baumert TF, et al. Interaction of hepatitis C virus envelope glycoprotein E2 with the large extracellular loop of tupaia CD81 World J Gastroenterol 2009;15(2):240−4. PMID: 19132776; PMCID: PMC2653318. Available from: https://doi.org/10.3748/wjg.15.240.

[69] Al Olaby RR, Cocquerel L, Zemla A, et al. Identification of a novel drug lead that inhibits HCV infection and cell-to-cell transmission by targeting the HCV E2 glycoprotein. PLoS One 2014;9(10):e111333. Available from: https://doi.org/10.1371/journal.pone.0111333.

[70] Tomei L, Failla C, Santolini E, De Francesco R, La Monica N. NS3 is a serine protease required for processing of hepatitis C virus polyprotein. J Virol 1993;67(7):4017−26. Available from: https://doi.org/10.1128/JVI.67.7.4017-4026.1993.

[71] Reddy BU, Mullick R, Kumar A, Sudha G, Srinivasan N, Das S. Small molecule inhibitors of HCV replication from pomegranate. Sci Rep 2014;4:5411. Available from: https://doi.org/10.1038/srep05411.

[72] Slagle BL, Bouchard MJ. Hepatitis B virus x and regulation of viral gene expression. Cold Spring Harb Perspect Med 2016;6(3):a021402. Available from: https://doi.org/10.1101/cshperspect.a021402.

[73] Geng M, Xin X, Bi LQ, Zhou LT, Liu XH. Molecular mechanism of hepatitis B virus X protein function in hepatocarcinogenesis. World J Gastroenterol 2015;21(38):10732−8. Available from: https://doi.org/10.3748/wjg.v21.i38.10732.

[74] Guerrieri F, Belloni L, D'Andrea D, Pediconi N, Le Pera L, Testoni B, et al. Genome-wide identification of direct HBx genomic targets BMC Genomics 2017;18(1):184. PMID: 28212627; PMCID: PMC5316204. Available from: https://doi.org/10.1186/s12864-017-3561-5.

[75] Cheng ST, Hu JL, Ren JH, Yu HB, Zhong S, Wai Wong VK, et al. Dicoumarol, an NQO1 inhibitor, blocks cccDNA transcription by promoting degradation of HBx J Hepatol 2020. Sep:S0168-8278(20)33661-8. Available from: https://doi.org/10.1016/j.jhep.2020.09.019.

[76] Kitisin K, Pishvaian MJ, Johnson LB, Mishra L. Liver stem cells and molecular signaling pathways in hepatocellular carcinoma. Gastrointest Cancer Res 2007;1(4 Suppl 2):S13−21.

[77] Dhml M, Satyanarayana A. Molecular signaling pathways and therapeutic targets in hepatocellular carcinoma. Cancers (Basel) 2020;12(2):491. Available from: https://doi.org/10.3390/cancers12020491.

[78] Chu JS, Ge FJ, Zhang B, Wang Y, Silvestris N, Liu LJ, et al. Expression and prognostic value of VEGFR-2, PDGFR-β, and c-Met in advanced hepatocellular carcinoma J Exp Clin Cancer Res 2013;32(1):16. PMID: 23552472; PMCID: PMC3623756. Available from: https://doi.org/10.1186/1756-9966-32-16.

[79] Ceci C, Atzori MG, Lacal PM, Graziani G. Role of VEGFs/VEGFR-1 signaling and its inhibition in modulating tumor invasion: experimental evidence in different metastatic cancer models. Int J Mol Sci 2020;21(4):1388. Available from: https://doi.org/10.3390/ijms21041388.

[80] Yamaguchi R, Yano H, Iemura A, Ogasawara S, Haramaki M, Kojiro M. Expression of vascular endothelial growth factor in human hepatocellular carcinoma. Hepatology. 1998;28(1):68−77. Available from: https://doi.org/10.1002/hep.510280111.

[81] Schoenleber SJ, Kurtz DM, Talwalkar JA, Roberts LR, Gores GJ. Prognostic role of vascular endothelial growth factor in hepatocellular carcinoma: systematic review and meta-analysis Br J Cancer 2009;100(9):1385−92. PMID: 19401698; PMCID: PMC2694418. Available from: https://doi.org/10.1038/sj.bjc.6605017.

[82] Hassan M, Selimovic D, Ghozlan H, Abdel-kader O. Hepatitis C virus core protein triggers hepatic angiogenesis by a mechanism including multiple pathways. Hepatology. 2009;49(5):1469−82. Available from: https://doi.org/10.1002/hep.22849.

[83] Taniguchi H, Kato N, Otsuka M, Goto T, Yoshida H, Shiratori Y, et al. Hepatitis C virus core protein upregulates transforming growth factor-beta 1 transcription. J Med Virol 2004;72(1):52−9. Available from: https://doi.org/10.1002/jmv.10545.

[84] Liu J, Ding X, Tang J, Cao Y, Hu P, Zhou F, et al. Enhancement of canonical Wnt/β-catenin signaling activity by HCV core protein promotes cell growth of hepatocellular carcinoma cells PLoS One 2011;6(11):e27496. Epub 2011 Nov 15. PMID: 22110662; PMCID: PMC3216985. Available from: https://doi.org/10.1371/journal.pone.0027496.

[85] Tanaka N, Moriya K, Kiyosawa K, Koike K, Aoyama T. Hepatitis C virus core protein induces spontaneous and persistent activation of peroxisome proliferator-activated receptor alpha in transgenic mice: implications for HCV-associated hepatocarcinogenesis. Int J Cancer 2008;122(1):124−31. Available from: https://doi.org/10.1002/ijc.23056.

[86] Joo M, Hahn YS, Kwon M, Sadikot RT, Blackwell TS, Christman JW. Hepatitis C virus core protein suppresses NF-kappaB activation and cyclooxygenase-2 expression by direct interaction with IkappaB kinase beta J Virol 2005;79(12):7648−57. PMID: 15919917; PMCID: PMC1143634. Available from: https://doi.org/10.1128/JVI.79.12.7648-7657.2005.

[87] Lian Z, Liu J, Wu M, Wang HY, Arbuthnot P, Kew M, et al. Hepatitis B x antigen up-regulates vascular endothelial growth factor receptor 3 in hepatocarcinogenesis. Hepatology. 2007;45(6):1390—9. Available from: https://doi.org/10.1002/hep.21610.

[88] Choi SB, Han HJ, Kim WB, Song TJ, Choi SY. VEGF overexpression predicts poor survival in hepatocellular carcinoma. Open Med (Wars) 2017;12:430—9. Available from: https://doi.org/10.1515/med-2017-0061.

[89] Huang P, Xu X, Wang L, Zhu B, Wang X, Xia J. The role of EGF-EGFR signalling pathway in hepatocellular carcinoma inflammatory microenvironment J Cell Mol Med 2014;18(2):218—30. Epub 2013 Nov 25. PMID: 24268047; PMCID: PMC3930409. Available from: https://doi.org/10.1111/jcmm.12153.

[90] Buckley AF, Burgart LJ, Sahai V, Kakar S. Epidermal growth factor receptor expression and gene copy number in conventional hepatocellular carcinoma. Am J Clin Pathol 2008;129(2):245—51. Available from: https://doi.org/10.1309/WF10QAAED3PP93BH.

[91] Ezzoukhry Z, Louandre C, Trécherel E, Godin C, Chauffert B, Dupont S, et al. EGFR activation is a potential determinant of primary resistance of hepatocellular carcinoma cells to sorafenib Int J Cancer 2012;131 (12):2961—9. Epub 2012 Apr 30. PMID: 22514082. Available from: https://doi.org/10.1002/ijc.27604.

[92] Breuhahn K, Longerich T, Schirmacher P. Dysregulation of growth factor signaling in human hepatocellular carcinoma. Oncogene. 2006;25(27):3787—800. Available from: https://doi.org/10.1038/sj.onc.1209556.

[93] Martinez-Quetglas I, Pinyol R, Dauch D, Torrecilla S, Tovar V, Moeini A, et al. IGF2 is up-regulated by epigenetic mechanisms in hepatocellular carcinomas and is an actionable oncogene product in experimental models Gastroenterology 2016;151(6):1192—205. Epub 2016 Sep 7. PMID: 27614046. Available from: https://doi.org/10.1053/j.gastro.2016.09.001.

[94] Xiang C, Chen J, Fu P. HGF/Met signaling in cancer invasion: the impact on cytoskeleton remodeling. Cancers (Basel) 2017;9(5):44. Available from: https://doi.org/10.3390/cancers9050044.

[95] Suzuki K, Hayashi N, Yamada Y, Yoshihara H, Miyamoto Y, Ito Y, et al. Expression of the c-met protooncogene in human hepatocellular carcinoma. Hepatology. 1994;20(5):1231—6.

[96] Kim JH, Kim HS, Kim BJ, Jang HJ, Lee J. Prognostic value of c-Met overexpression in hepatocellular carcinoma: a *meta*-analysis and review. Oncotarget 2017;8(52):90351—7. Available from: https://doi.org/10.18632/oncotarget.20087.

[97] Wang H, Rao B, Lou J, et al. The function of the HGF/c-Met axis in hepatocellular carcinoma. Front Cell Dev Biol 2020;8:55. Available from: https://doi.org/10.3389/fcell.2020.00055.

[98] Xiang QF, Zhan MX, Li Y, Liang H, Hu C, Huang YM, et al. Activation of MET promotes resistance to sorafenib in hepatocellular carcinoma cells via the AKT/ERK1/2-EGR1 pathway. Artif Cell Nanomed Biotechnol 2019;47(1):83—9. Available from: https://doi.org/10.1080/21691401.2018.1543195.

[99] Javanmard D, Najafi M, Babaei MR, et al. Investigation of *CTNNB1* gene mutations and expression in hepatocellular carcinoma and cirrhosis in association with hepatitis B virus infection. Infect Agent Cancer 2020;15:37. Available from: https://doi.org/10.1186/s13027-020-00297-5.

[100] Steinway SN, Zañudo JG, Ding W, Rountree CB, Feith DJ, Loughran Jr TP, et al. Network modeling of TGFβ signaling in hepatocellular carcinoma epithelial-to-mesenchymal transition reveals joint sonic hedgehog and Wnt pathway activation. Cancer Res 2014;74(21):5963—77. Available from: https://doi.org/10.1158/0008-5472.CAN-14-0225.

[101] Vilchez V, Turcios L, Marti F, Gedaly R. Targeting Wnt/β-catenin pathway in hepatocellular carcinoma treatment. World J Gastroenterol 2016;22(2):823—32. Available from: https://doi.org/10.3748/wjg.v22.i2.823.

[102] Li Y, Chen G, Han Z, Cheng H, Qiao L, Li Y. IL-6/STAT3 signaling contributes to sorafenib resistance in hepatocellular carcinoma through targeting cancer stem cells. Onco Targets Ther 2020;13:9721—30. Available from: https://doi.org/10.2147/OTT.S262089.

[103] Hu YT, Shu ZY, Jiang JH, Xie QF, Zheng SS. Torin2 overcomes sorafenib resistance via suppressing mTORC2-AKT-BAD pathway in hepatocellular carcinoma cells Hepatobiliary Pancreat Dis Int 2020. Sep 28: S1499-3872(20)30207-1. Available from: https://doi.org/10.1016/j.hbpd.2020.09.010.

[104] Lu S, Yao Y, Xu G, Zhou C, Zhang Y, Sun J, et al. CD24 regulates sorafenib resistance via activating autophagy in hepatocellular carcinoma Cell Death Dis 2018;9(6):646. PMID: 29844385; PMCID: PMC5974417. Available from: https://doi.org/10.1038/s41419-018-0681-z.

[105] Niture S, Gyamfi MA, Lin M, Chimeh U, Dong X, Zheng W, et al. TNFAIP8 regulates autophagy, cell steatosis, and promotes hepatocellular carcinoma cell proliferation Cell Death Dis 2020;11(3):178. PMID: 32152268; PMCID: PMC7062894. Available from: https://doi.org/10.1038/s41419-020-2369-4.

[106] Xue ST, Li K, Gao Y, Zhao LY, Gao Y, Yi H, et al. The role of the key autophagy kinase ULK1 in hepatocellular carcinoma and its validation as a treatment target. Autophagy 2020;16(10):1823−37. Available from: https://doi.org/10.1080/15548627.2019.1709762.

[107] Beermann J, Piccoli MT, Viereck J, Thum T. Non-coding RNAs in development and disease: background, mechanisms, and therapeutic approaches. Physiol Rev 2016;96(4):1297−325. Available from: https://doi.org/10.1152/physrev.00041.2015.

[108] Brosnan CA, Voinnet O. The long and the short of noncoding RNAs. Curr Opin Cell Biol 2009;21(3):416−25. Available from: https://doi.org/10.1016/j.ceb.2009.04.001.

[109] Shen Q, Jiang S, Wu M, Zhang L, Su X, Zhao D. LncRNA HEIH confers cell sorafenib resistance in hepatocellular carcinoma by regulating miR-98-5p/PI3K/AKT pathway. Cancer Manag Res 2020;12:6585−95. Available from: https://doi.org/10.2147/CMAR.S241383.

[110] Li W, Dong X, He C, Tan G, Li Z, Zhai B, et al. LncRNA SNHG1 contributes to sorafenib resistance by activating the Akt pathway and is positively regulated by miR-21 in hepatocellular carcinoma cells J Exp Clin Cancer Res 2019;38(1):183. PMID: 31053148; PMCID: PMC6499991. Available from: https://doi.org/10.1186/s13046-019-1177-0.

[111] Chen BW, Zhou Y, Wei T, Wen L, Zhang YB, Shen SC, et al. lncRNA-POIR promotes epithelial-mesenchymal transition and suppresses sorafenib sensitivity simultaneously in hepatocellular carcinoma by sponging miR-182-5p. J Cell Biochem 2020. Available from: https://doi.org/10.1002/jcb.29844 Sep.

[112] Xu Y, Liu Y, Li Z, Li H, Li X, Yan L, et al. Long noncoding RNA H19 is involved in sorafenib resistance in hepatocellular carcinoma by upregulating miR-675 Oncol Rep 2020;44(1):165−73. Epub 2020 May 8. PMID: 32627034; PMCID: PMC7251775. Available from: https://doi.org/10.3892/or.2020.7608.

[113] Fan L, Huang X, Chen J, Zhang K, Gu YH, Sun J, et al. Long noncoding RNA MALAT1 contributes to sorafenib resistance by targeting miR 140 5p/Aurora A signaling in hepatocellular carcinoma Mol Cancer Ther 2020;19(5):1197−209. Epub 2020 Mar 27. PMID: 32220970. Available from: https://doi.org/10.1158/1535-7163.MCT-19-0203.

[114] Shi Y, Yang X, Xue X, Sun D, Cai P, Song Q, et al. HANR enhances autophagy-associated sorafenib resistance through miR-29b/ATG9A axis in hepatocellular carcinoma Onco Targets Ther 2020;13:2127−37. PMID: 32210579; PMCID: PMC7069583. Available from: https://doi.org/10.2147/OTT.S229913.

[115] Liu Y, Chen L, Yuan H, Guo S, Wu G. LncRNA DANCR promotes sorafenib resistance via activation of IL-6/STAT3 signaling in hepatocellular carcinoma cells Onco Targets Ther 2020;13:1145−57. PMID: 32103983; PMCID: PMC7008197. Available from: https://doi.org/10.2147/OTT.S229957.

[116] Niu Y, Tang G, Wu X, Wu C. LncRNA NEAT1 modulates sorafenib resistance in hepatocellular carcinoma through regulating the miR-149-5p/AKT1 axis Saudi J Gastroenterol 2020;26(4):194−203. Epub ahead of print. PMID: 32461380; PMCID: PMC7580733. Available from: https://doi.org/10.4103/sjg.SJG_4_20.

[117] Zhang J, Zhao X, Ma X, Yuan Z, Hu M. KCNQ1OT1 contributes to sorafenib resistance and programmed death-ligand-1-mediated immune escape via sponging miR-506 in hepatocellular carcinoma cells Int J Mol Med 2020;46(5):1794−804. Epub 2020 Aug 25. PMID: 33000204; PMCID: PMC7521583. Available from: https://doi.org/10.3892/ijmm.2020.4710.

[118] Sui C, Dong Z, Yang C, Zhang M, Dai B, Geng L, et al. LncRNA FOXD2-AS1 as a competitive endogenous RNA against miR-150-5p reverses resistance to sorafenib in hepatocellular carcinoma. J Cell Mol Med 2019;23(9):6024−33. Available from: https://doi.org/10.1111/jcmm.14465.

[119] Zhang W, Liu Y, Fu Y, Han W, Xu H, Wen L, et al. Long noncoding RNA LINC00160 functions as a decoy of microRNA-132 to mediate autophagy and drug resistance in hepatocellular carcinoma via inhibition of PIK3R3 Cancer Lett 2020;478:22−33. Epub 2020 Feb 14. PMID: 32067991. Available from: https://doi.org/10.1016/j.canlet.2020.02.014.

[120] Zhi Y, Abudoureyimu M, Zhou H, Wang T, Feng B, Wang R, et al. FOXM1-mediated LINC-ROR regulates the proliferation and sensitivity to sorafenib in hepatocellular carcinoma Mol Ther Nucleic Acids 2019;16:576−88. Epub 2019 Apr 17. PMID: 31082791; PMCID: PMC6514537. Available from: https://doi.org/10.1016/j.omtn.2019.04.008.

[121] Cheng Z, Lei Z, Yang P, Si A, Xiang D, Zhou J, et al. Long noncoding RNA THOR promotes liver cancer stem cells expansion via β-catenin pathway Gene 2019;684:95−103. Epub 2018 Oct 22. PMID: 30359743. Available from: https://doi.org/10.1016/j.gene.2018.10.051.

[122] Jin W, Chen L, Cai X, Zhang Y, Zhang J, Ma D, et al. Long noncoding RNA TUC338 is functionally involved in sorafenib-sensitized hepatocarcinoma cells by targeting RASAL1 Oncol Rep 2017;37(1):273–80. Epub 2016 Nov 15. PMID: 27878301. Available from: https://doi.org/10.3892/or.2016.5248.

[123] Takahashi K, Yan IK, Wood J, Haga H, Patel T. Involvement of extracellular vesicle long noncoding RNA (linc-VLDLR) in tumor cell responses to chemotherapy Mol Cancer Res 2014;12(10):1377–87. Epub 2014 May 29. PMID: 24874432; PMCID: PMC4201956. Available from: https://doi.org/10.1158/1541-7786.MCR-13-0636.

[124] Do H, Kim W. Roles of oncogenic long non-coding rnas in cancer development. Genomics Inf 2018;16(4): e18. Available from: https://doi.org/10.5808/GI.2018.16.4.e18.

[125] Wang WT, Han C, Sun YM, Chen TQ, Chen YQ. Noncoding RNAs in cancer therapy resistance and targeted drug development J Hematol Oncol 2019;12(1):55. PMID: 31174564; PMCID: PMC6556047. Available from: https://doi.org/10.1186/s13045-019-0748-z.

[126] Wang M, Yu F, Chen X, Li P, Wang K. The underlying mechanisms of noncoding RNAs in the chemoresistance of hepatocellular carcinoma. Mol Ther Nucleic Acids 2020;21:13–27. Available from: https://doi.org/10.1016/j.omtn.2020.05.011.

[127] Sukowati CH, Rosso N, Crocè LS, Tiribelli C. Hepatic cancer stem cells and drug resistance: relevance in targeted therapies for hepatocellular carcinoma. World J Hepatol 2010;2(3):114–26. Available from: https://doi.org/10.4254/wjh.v2.i3.114.

[128] Xia H, Ooi LL, Hui KM. MicroRNA-216a/217-induced epithelial-mesenchymal transition targets PTEN and SMAD7 to promote drug resistance and recurrence of liver cancer Hepatology 2013;58(2):629–41. Epub 2013 Jun 25. PMID: 23471579. Available from: https://doi.org/10.1002/hep.26369.

[129] Mao K, Zhang J, He C, Xu K, Liu J, Sun J, et al. Restoration of miR-193b sensitizes Hepatitis B virus-associated hepatocellular carcinoma to sorafenib Cancer Lett 2014;352(2):245–52. Epub 2014 Jul 14. PMID: 25034398. Available from: https://doi.org/10.1016/j.canlet.2014.07.004.

[130] Yang F, Li QJ, Gong ZB, Zhou L, You N, Wang S, et al. MicroRNA-34a targets Bcl-2 and sensitizes human hepatocellular carcinoma cells to sorafenib treatment Technol Cancer Res Treat 2014;13(1):77–86. Epub 2013 Jul 11. PMID: 23862748. Available from: https://doi.org/10.7785/tcrt.2012.500364.

[131] Xu Y, Huang J, Ma L, Shan J, Shen J, Yang Z, et al. MicroRNA-122 confers sorafenib resistance to hepatocellular carcinoma cells by targeting IGF-1R to regulate RAS/RAF/ERK signaling pathways Cancer Lett 2016;371(2):171–81. Epub 2015 Dec 3. PMID: 26655273. Available from: https://doi.org/10.1016/j.canlet.2015.11.034.

Curing of liver cancer: an update on the efficacy of bioactive compounds

Anil Kumar Moola[1,6,*], S. Geetha Renuka[2],
Harish Kumar Seenivasan[3,*], Nivethitha Manickam[3],
Sujatha Peela[4] and B.D. Ranjitha Kumari[5]

[1]Department of Biotechnology, Aditya Degree and PG College, Kakinada, India [2]Department of Obstetrics and Gynecology, Theni Medical College, Theni, India [3]School of Life Sciences, Bharathidasan University, Tiruchirappalli, India [4]Department of Biotechnology, Dr. B.R. Ambedkar University, Srikakulam, India [5]Department of Botany, Bharathidasan University, Tiruchirappalli, India [6]Department of Entomology, College of Agriculture, Food and Environment, Agriculture Science Center North, University of Kentucky, Lexington, Kentucky, United States

Abstract

Liver cell pathology involves increased hepatocyte and bile duct cell proliferation. Liver cancer (LC) is among the deadliest of all cancers with a fatality rate of approximately 60%−70%, and a recurrence rate of about 60%−70%. LC is the most common type of LC. Many cases of LC are due to infection with hepatitis and excessive drinking. Liver fat, aflatoxin, and obesity are other possible causes. Even with an improved understanding of LC pathology, therapies have been quite limited in treating patients' symptoms. Currently, a partial hepatectomy, radiation, and chemotherapy are being used to treat the disease. Liver carcinogenesis and disease progression can be controlled and even eliminated using bioactive compounds. Compounds found in plants, microorganisms, and algae that act as antimicrobials or healing agents are commonly referred to as bioactive. Recently, different bioactive compounds and nanoparticles have been shown to slow down the growth and spread of cancer effectively.

Keywords: Liver cancer; bioactive compounds; plants; algae; microorganisms

* Authors Anil Kumar Moola and Harish Kumar Seenivasan contributed equally to this chapter.

Abbreviations

AKT	AKT serine/threonine kinase
BA	bile acid
BAX	BCL2-associated X, apoptosis regulator
Bcl-2	B-cell lymphoma 2
CCA	cholangiocarcinoma
CSC	cancer stem cells
DKK1	dickkopf Wnt signaling pathway inhibitor 1
DNA	deoxyribonucleic acid
EGCG	epigallocatechin gallate
ER	endoplasmic reticulum
ERK	extracellular regulated kinase
FDA	Food and Drug Administration
Fgf15	fibroblast growth factor 15 precursor
FLT3	Fms-like tyrosine kinase 3
FXR	farnesoid X receptor
HCC	hepatocellular carcinoma
HMG-CoA	β-hydroxy β-methylglutaryl-CoA
IBABP	ileal bile acid-binding protein
JNK	c-Jun N-terminal kinases
LAPC3	Los Angeles Prostate Cancer-3
LC	liver cancer
MAPK	mitogen-activated protein kinases
MSC	mesenchymal stem cells
NAFLD	nonalcoholic fatty liver disease
NASH	nonalcoholic steatohepatitis
PARP	poly(ADP-ribose) polymerase
PDGFR-β	platelet-derived growth factor receptor-β
PKC	protein kinase C
p53	tumor suppressor protein 53
TAA	thioacetamide
VEGFR	vascular endothelial growth factor receptor

Background study of liver cancer

The liver is a critical organ of the human body, especially in maintaining homeostasis [1]. It has been reported that in the 20th century, liver cancer (LC) is more common in developing countries [2]. LC is a severe disease with an unfavorable prognosis due to the cancer stem cells present in all the cells of the body [(cancer stem cells (CSCs)]. The type of liver tumor varies, with cholangiocarcinoma, intrahepatic cholangiocarcinoma, pediatric neoplasm hepatoblastoma, and liver carcinoma all included [3,4]. The hepatic stem cell is generally responsible for generating tumor types in the liver [5]. Liver CSCs are the major source of hepatocellular cancer and responsible for tumorigenesis, metastasis, recurrence, and chemoresistance [6]. Although the causes of LC differ depending on the characteristics of viral infections, climatic factors, and lifestyle, the factors associated with viral infections, climatic factors, and lifestyle are all associated with LC. A wide range of treatment options are available for different stages of LC. LC that has progressed into more advanced stages of disease might benefit from treatment strategies that include chemotherapy, immunotherapy, oncolytic therapy, and targeted therapies [7].

In the early stages of LC, the options for treatment included surgery, chemotherapy, and nonsurgical approaches. The HepG2 and MHCC97-L cell lines are treated with Berberine in the laboratory, where the cells are treated in vitro and exposed to a variety of different effects, such as Bax activation, the release of cytochrome C to the cytosol, downregulation of Akt activity, and upregulation of P38 MAPK signaling, caspases 3 and 9 activations, and Beclin-1 [8]. Sorafenib is an FDA-approved medication that is useful for treating hepatocellular carcinoma, and it is also known by several brand names, including Nexavar and BAY43−9006. Raf kinases, VEGFR-2/3, PDGFR-β, Flt3, and c-Kit are targeted by sorafenib, inhibiting their tyrosine kinase receptors [9]. Stem cell therapy using mesenchymal stem cells (MSCs) is also popular. These MSCs possess migratory pathotropic properties that can fight against tumor cells by secreting Dkk-1 during stem cell therapy to inhibit the expression of factors involved in the Wnt signaling pathway (bcl-2, c-Myc, β-catenin, and survivin). Inhibition of the Wnt signaling pathway is consequently accomplished, leading to inhibition of proliferation and induction of cell apoptosis in HepG2 cells [10].

Introduction

LC is one of the most common causes of death. It affects both men and women, and it ranks eighth on the list of most frequent diseases. LC is very prevalent in East Asia, the Middle East, and Africa west of the Sahara. In the countries listed above, the likelihood of developing lung cancer is low. The population range of LAPC3 in the United States is 500,000 to 1,000,000. It is more common in men to have this condition [11,12]. The LC mortality rates were increased fourfold among men and twofold among women [13]. In 2018, a mortality rate of 8.5 per 100,000 individuals is reported [14]. The primary forms of LC are HCC and iCCA, which are commonly caused by liver fibrosis, liver cirrhosis, nonalcoholic liver disease, and chronic liver damage [15]. Endoplasmic Reticulum (ER) stress-induced carcinogenesis results from accumulation of unfolded proteins leading to apoptotis [16]. The primary preference for LC is generally chemotherapy and immunotherapy for more than 90% of the cases [17]. Biocompounds and advances in nanotechnology are being found and developed daily in the present era. The main components of garlic are allicin, alliin, diallyl sulfide, diallyl disulfide, diallyl trisulfide, ajoene, and S-allyl-cysteine (*Allium sativum* L.) [18]. The bioactive compounds are also extracted from bacteria, fungi, and algae. Am2-M, At2-M, Ga-C, Ga-M, Ph3-M, and Pr3-M, extracted from marine microalgae species, are reported to induce cell death in the in vitro models of human LC. Additionally, β-carotene, fucoxanthin, and astaxanthin are extracted from algae.

Role of bioactive compounds in liver cancer

Plants and their parts were eaten and used in folk medicine until recently (Table 6.1). Nowadays, plants are used to extract nanoparticles and treat several diseases. Researchers used nanotechnology to improve cancer treatment. In the example, epigallocatechin-3-gallate (EGCG) from green tea is shown to reduce cancer growth in animal models in vivo [54]. The FDA has

TABLE 6.1   Source of bioactive compounds from various sources, that is, plant, algae and microorganism.

Bioactive compounds	Species	Source	References
N,N-dimethylglycine methyl ester, (9,12,15-) octadecatrienoic acid, N,N-dimethylglycine, and n-hexadecanoic acid	*Saueda monoica* Forssk	Plant	[19]
Lunasin	*Glycine max*	Plant	[20]
Glu−Gln−Arg−Pro−Arg	*Oryza sativa* (Rice bran)	Plant	[21]
Phenolic acids, flavonoids, isothiocyanates, tannins and saponins	*Moringa oleifera*	Plant	[22]
Curcumin	*Curcuma longa*	Plant	[23]
Quercetin	*Capparis spinosa, Piper genus*	Plant	[24]
Gambogic acid (gamboge)	*Garcinia hanburryi* Hook	Plant	[25]
Atractylenolide	*Atractylodis macrocephalae*	Plant	[26]
Silibinin	*Silybum marianum* (L.) Gaertn	Plant	[27]
Psoralidin	*Psoralea corylifolia* L.	Plant	[28]
Gossypol	*Gossypium genus*	Plant	[29]
Alkaloid: boldine	*Peumus boldus* Molina	Plant	[30]
Piperine	*Piper nigrum* L.	Plant	[31]
Resveratrol	*Vitis vinifera* Linnaeus	Plant	[32]
β-Carotene	*Haematococcus* species, *Dunaliella salina*	Microalgae	[33]
Astaxanthin	*Chlorella zofigiensis, Haematococcus pluvialis, Chlorococcum* species	Microalgae	[34,35]
Lutein	*Chlorella sorokiniana, Dunaliella salina, Chlorella prothecoides*	Microalgae	[36−38]
Violaxanthin	*Chlorella ellipsoidea, Dunaliella tertiolecta*	Microalgae	[39]
Zeaxanthin	*Synechocystis* species, *Chlorella saccharophila*	Microalgae	[40]
Fucoxanthin	*Phaeodactylum tricornutum, Isochrysis* species	Microalgae	[41,42]
MGDG (Monogalactosyldiacylglycerol)	*Gymnodinium mikimotoi, Stephanodiscus* species, *Pavlova lutheri, Stephanodiscus* species	Microalgae	[43]
DGDG (Digalactosyldiacylglycerol)	*Stephanodiscus* species	Microalgae	[44]
SQAG (Sulfo-quinovosyl-acyl-glycerol)	*Stephanodiscus* species	Microalgae	[45]
Sulfated polysaccharide β-(1,3)-glucan	*Chlorophyte, Chlorella vulgaris, Chlorella stigmatophora*	Microalgae	[46]

(Continued)

TABLE 6.1 (Continued)

Bioactive compounds	Species	Source	References
Sulfated polysaccharide	*Isochrysis galbana, Haptophyte*	Microalgae	[47]
Sulfated polysaccharide	*Porphydium* species, *Rhodophyte*	Microalgae	[48]
Sulfated polysaccharide	*Gyrodinium impudicum, Dinoflagellate*	Microalgae	[49]
Extracellular polysaccharide s-Spirulan	*Arthrospira platensis* Cyanobacteria	Microalgae	[50]
Amides	*Lyngbya majuscule*	Microalgae	[51]
Quinones	*Calothrix* species	Microalgae	[52]
Phenolic compounds	*Chlorella ellipsoidea, Spirulina maxima, Nannochloropsis* species	Microalgae	[53]

approved natural bioactive compounds that contain anticancer drugs. Recent news reports claim that fruits and vegetables with phytochemical concentrations may help lower cancer risk. Hydrolyzable tannins (ellagitannins and gallotannins), condensed tannins (proanthocyanidins), anthocyanins, antioxidants, and antiproliferative and flavonoids are all widely present in biological activity. Pomegranate extracts, which reduce the risk of skin cancer, are currently being studied to see if they can also treat other cancers, such as breast, prostate, lung, and colon cancers [55]. Marine animals, crops, herbs, algae, bacteria, and other microorganisms all contain biologically active compounds. Catechin, coumaric acid, and ascorbic acid are 3 of the 16 chemicals found in chlorogenic acid. Additionally, sea cucumber extracts have been found to affect liver enzyme activity (mainly the superoxide dismutase, glutathione peroxidase, serum direct bilirubin, alanine and aspartate aminotransferases, and hepatic malondialdehyde) [56].

Bioactive compounds from plants for curing liver cancer

Plants provide a significant source of bioactive compounds because they also produce many secondary metabolites and other crucial metabolic products. Piper species, like Piperales, are abundant in the reservoir and contain various alkaloids, tannins, flavonoids, glycosides, saponins, terpenoids, steroids, terpenes, and chalcones [57]. EGCG impairs the growth of HepG2, HuH-7, Hep3B, and HLE cell lines. Onions, apples, berries, black tea, and red wine contain a polyphenolic compound known as quercetin, which inhibits the in vitro growth of HepG2 cell lines by inhibiting the activity of protein signaling pathways such as AKT, ERK, protein kinase C (PKC-alpha), and c-Jun N-terminal kinases (JNK). Flavonoids, found in celery, clover, thyme, dandelion, thyme, perilla, chamomile tea, carrots, green peppers, olive oil, mint, rosemary, navel oranges, and oregano, are also present in celery, chamomile tea, carrots, green peppers, olive oil, mint, rosemary, navel oranges, and oregano. In hepatoma cell lines including SK-Hep-1, PLC/PRF/5, HepG2, Hep3B, and HA22T/VGH, Luteolin and Silibinin promote G0/G1 cell cycle arrest and hepatoma cell apoptosis through Bax/Bcl-XL and caspase-3 activation [58–61]. Black locust (*Robinia pseudoacacia*) contains the compound acacetin (5,7-dihydroxy-4'-methoxy flavone), which

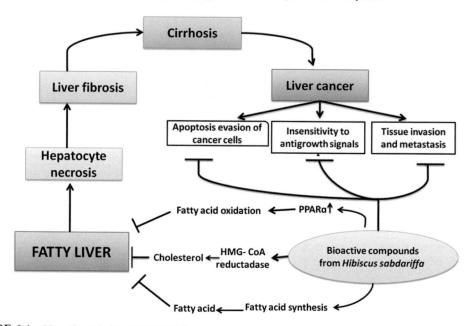

FIGURE 6.1   Hypothesis behind CURING liver cancer by using bioactive compounds.

inhibits the growth of the HepG2 cell line slowing down the cell cycle phase G1. Additionally, it induces apoptosis by activating the p53 pathway and downstream pro-apoptotic targets, p21/WAFI and Bax proteins [62]. Favas, soybeans, kudzu, lupin, and psoralea are among many plants containing genistein, an isoflavone. HepG2 cells are p53-dependent, cycline-dependent kinase 2 (Cdk2) is blocked, and G2/M cell cycle arrest occurs as a result of genistein [63]. Daidzein, a soybean-present isoflavone, inhibits hepatoma cell growth activity of HepG2, Hep3B, Huh7, PLC, and HA22T cell lines by promoting apoptosis through caspase-3 activation and poly (ADP-ribose) Polymerase cleavage [64]. Stilbenes, a bioactive chemical compound, is found in many pathogens, including bacteria and fungi, in the compound trans-resveratrol (3',4',5-trihydroxy-trans-stilbene). HepG2, Hep3B, and H22 cell lines are reported to be inhibited by trans-resveratrol, which may help prevent the growth of HCC (hepatocellular carcinoma) [65–67]. Curcumin is an economically valuable compound that inhibits cell growth by inducing apoptosis and increasing p53 protein accumulation [68]. Caffeic acid is found in many plants and foods, such as coffee beans, strawberries, and oats. Caffeic acid activates cell growth arrest and apoptosis in cancer cells [69]. In addition to ellagic acid, an array of phenolic acid plant foods are utilized to make ellagitannins, most notably blackberries, strawberries, raspberries, cranberries, walnuts, pecans, pomegranates, and wolfberries. The antimutagenic effect of ellagic acid in *Salmonella* strains TA98 and TA100 inhibits the spread of genetic mutations [70]. Proprietary components, such as resins, wood gums, flavone and anthocyanin pigments, and other aromatic compounds contain protocatechuic acid, which interferes with cell growth by increasing JNK and p38 protein activity [71]. Capsaicin is another bioactive compound that promotes apoptosis in HepG2 cells [72–75]. A plant called *Hibiscus sabdariffa* Linne is a traditional Chinese medicine. It is a treatment for various diseases that affect the liver, including preventing cancer cell evasion, interfering with cell growth, spreading into and infiltrating tissue, and progressing to and fostering metastasis. In addition, it promotes enzyme production, such as fatty acid synthase and HMG-CoA reductase, which enables the repair of the fatty liver (Fig. 6.1) [76]. Also, high amounts of fruit-containing polyphenols including grapes, black currant, plum, grenade, and apples, induce antioxidant activity and decrease the LC risk factor [77].

Bioactive compounds from microalgae for curing liver cancer

The microalgae are eukaryotic, or eukaryotic, eukaryotic microorganisms capable of producing as much as 40% of global foodstuffs. Additionally, these microbes take 5−8 hours to double in number after starting from just one microalga [78]. Like higher plants, microalgae use sunlight to create their food. In addition to the major metabolic byproducts, they produce several secondary metabolites to help protect against external factors, such as pathogenic organisms. *Navicula incerta* is the source of the compound stigmasterol, which induces cell death in human HepG2 liver cells [79]. Astaxanthin is a keto-carotenoid found in various microalgal species such as *Haematococcus pluvialis*, *Chlorella zofingiensis*, *Chlorococcum* sp., *Phaffia rhodozyma*, and *Agrobacterium aurantiacum*. It protects hepatocytes from potentially harmful chemicals such as carbon tetrachloride [34]. HePG2, MCF7, HCT116, and A549 cell growth in vitro are inhibited by microalgal species, including *H. pluvialis* and *Dunaliella salina*, which produce carotenoids that target and inhibit cancer cell growth [80]. However, *D. salina* has low bioavailability of β-carotene, which reduces solubility and absorption of the nutrient. It has been reported that lowering liver function enzymes, collagen-1, alpha-smooth muscle actin, interleukin-6 serum, tumor necrosis factor-alpha, transforming growth factor-beta, and elevated matrix metalloproteinase-9 can cure TAA-induced fibrosis [81].

Bioactive compounds from bacteria and another microbial source for curing liver cancer

Microorganisms produce numerous metabolites to counteract other organisms, fungi, and pathogenic organisms. The bacteria is specifically adapted to thrive in a wide range of environmental conditions, exhibiting thermophilic, archaeal, and other extremophile characteristics. Of particular note, marine bacteria produce a diverse range of metabolites [82]. Liver diseases, including nonalcoholic fatty liver disease and nonalcoholic steatohepatitis, may be greatly curtailed by the intestinal microbiota, which consists of groups of bacteria known as Proteobacteria, Enterobacteria, and Bacteroides (nonalcoholic steatohepatitis) [83]. Farnesoid X receptor (FXR) activation and ileal bile acid (BA)-binding protein (IBABP) upregulation (8.4-fold) in addition to the regulation of α organic solute transporter (3.1-fold) is achieved by the common intestinal bacterial strains, such as *Bacteroides dorei* and *Eubacterium limosum* (OST) [84]. Through downregulation of the FXR-FGF15 gut−liver axis, probiotics (*Lactobacillus casei*, *L. plantarum*, *L. acidophilus*, and *L. delbrueckii* subsp.) increase ileal BA deconjugation, fecal BA excretion, and induce hepatic BA neosynthesis [85]. Probiotics are said to be a good source of bioactive compounds, particularly polysaccharides. *Agaricus blazei* is an edible form of macrofungi used to treat liver disease. It has also been reported to improve many pathological conditions in the liver by producing -glucan, which protects benzo(a)pyrene-induced DNA damage in HepG2 cells and reduces the formation of abnormal collagen fiber in HCC cells [77]. Spirulina and Dunaliella microalgae extracts were given to mice with mouth tumors. Harvard University published two reports on tumor treatment using rodent mouths. Thirty percent of the animals with a complete tumor regression had complete tumor regression, while the other 70% had some tumor regression. In a subsequent experiment, it was discovered that Spirulina and Dunaliella extracts had no effect on rodent tumor growth [86].

Conclusion and future perspectives

Many disease conditions can be effectively treated or managed using plant extracts, microorganisms, and algae extracts (Fig. 6.1). According to research, curcumin, one of the standard treatment options for numerous cancers, such as LC and its progression, is successful. Myricetin exhibits antitumorigenic activity against in vitro human cancer cells. The effects of Vitamin E tocotrienols on LC cells are similar to that of myricetin. In addition, there are numerous bioactive compounds, some of which are known to be effective in combatting various cancers, present in multiple bioactive compounds. Future research may deal with LC and metastasis, and it is necessary to examine and update treatment approaches for these cancers and metastases.

Conflict of interest

Authors declare that there is no conflict of interest.

References

[1] Tanimizu N, Miyajima A. Molecular mechanism of liver development and regeneration. Int Rev Cytol 2007;259:48.
[2] McGlynn KA, Tsao L, Hsing AW, Devesa SS, Fraumeni Jr JF. International trends and patterns of primary liver cancer. Int J Cancer 2001;94(2):290−6.
[3] Yang ZF, Ho DW, Ng MN, Lau CK, Yu WC, Ngai P, et al. Significance of CD90 + cancer stem cells in human liver cancer. Cancer Cell 2008;13(2):153−66.
[4] Anthony PP. Precursor lesions for liver cancer in humans. Cancer Res 1976;36(7 Part 2):2579−83.
[5] Sia D, Villanueva A, Friedman SL, Llovet JM. Liver cancer cell of origin, molecular class, and effects on patient prognosis. Gastroenterology 2017;152(4):745−61.
[6] Cheng Z, Li X, Ding J. Characteristics of liver cancer stem cells and clinical correlations. Cancer Lett 2016;379 (2):230−8.
[7] Liu CY, Chen KF, Chen PJ. Treatment of liver cancer. Cold Spring Harb Perspect Med 2015;5(9):a021535.
[8] Wang N, Feng Y, Zhu M, Tsang CM, Man K, Tong Y, et al. Berberine induces autophagic cell death and mitochondrial apoptosis in liver cancer cells: the cellular mechanism. J Cell Biochem 2010;111(6):1426−36.
[9] Cervello M, Bachvarov D, Lampiasi N, Cusimano A, Azzolina A, McCubrey JA, et al. Molecular mechanisms of sorafenib action in liver cancer cells. Cell Cycle 2012;11(15):2843−55.

[10] Hou L, Wang X, Zhou Y, Ma H, Wang Z, He J, et al. Inhibitory effect and mechanism of mesenchymal stem cells on liver cancer cells. Tumor Biol 2014;35(2):1239–50.

[11] Bosch FX, Ribes J, Borràs J. Epidemiology of primary liver cancer. Semliver Dis 1999;19(03):271–85.

[12] Bosch FX, Ribes J, Díaz M, Cléries R. Primary liver cancer: worldwide incidence and trends. Gastroenterology 2004;127(5):S5–16.

[13] Deuffic S, Poynard T, Buffat L, Valleron AJ. Trends in primary liver cancer. Lancet 1998;351(9097):214–15.

[14] Shi JF, Cao M, Wang Y, Bai FZ, Lei L, Peng J, et al. Is it possible to halve the incidence of liver cancer in China by 2050? Int J Cancer 2020;148:1051–65.

[15] Castelli G, Pelosi E, Testa U. Liver cancer: molecular characterization, clonal evolution and cancer stem cells. Cancers 2017;9(9):127.

[16] Kim C, Kim B. Anti-cancer natural products and their bioactive compounds inducing ER stress-mediated apoptosis: a review. Nutrients 2018;10(8):1021.

[17] Anwanwan D, Singh SK, Singh S, Saikam V, Singh R. Challenges in liver cancer and possible treatment approaches. Biochim Biophysica Acta-Rev Cancer 2020;1873(1):188314.

[18] Shang A, Cao SY, Xu XY, Gan RY, Tang GY, Corke H, et al. Bioactive compounds and biological functions of garlic (*Allium sativum* L.). Foods 2019;8(7):246.

[19] Al-Shawi AA, Hameed MF, Ali NH, Hussein KA. Investigations of phytoconstituents, antioxidant and anti-liver cancer activities of *Saueda monoica* Forssk extracted by microwave-assisted extraction. Asian Pac J Cancer Prev 2020;21(8):2349–55.

[20] Hsieh CC, Hernández-Ledesma B, De Lumen BO. Soybean peptide lunasin suppresses in vitro and in vivo 7, 12-dimethylbenz [a] anthracene-induced tumorigenesis. J Food Sci 2010;75(9):H311–16.

[21] Kannan A, Hettiarachchy NS, Lay JO, Liyanage R. Human cancer cell proliferation inhibition by a pentapeptide isolated and characterized from rice bran. Peptides 2010;31(9):1629–34.

[22] Vergara-Jimenez M, Almatrafi MM, Fernandez ML. Bioactive components in *Moringa oleifera* leaves protect against chronic disease. Antioxidants 2017;6(4):91.

[23] Bao W, Li K, Rong S, Yao P, Hao L, Ying C, et al. Curcumin alleviates ethanol-induced hepatocytes oxidative damage involving heme oxygenase-1 induction. J Ethnopharmacol 2010;128(2):549–53.

[24] Kalantari H, Foruozandeh H, Khodayar MJ, Siahpoosh A, Saki N, Kheradmand P. Antioxidant and hepatoprotective effects of *Capparis spinosa* L. fractions and quercetin on tert-butyl hydroperoxide-induced acute liver damage in mice. J Traditional Complementary Med 2018;8(1):120–7.

[25] Yihebali CI II, Zhan XK, Hao YU, Xie GR, Wang ZZ, Wei XIAO, et al. An open-labeled, randomized, multicenter phase IIa study of gambogic acid injection for advanced malignant tumors. Chin Med J 2013;126(9):1642–6.

[26] Ma L, Mao R, Shen K, Zheng Y, Li Y, Liu J, et al. Atractylenolide I-mediated Notch pathway inhibition attenuates gastric cancer stem cell traits. Biochemical Biophysical Res Commun 2014;450(1):353–9.

[27] Wesołowska O, Łania-Pietrzak B, Kuźdżał M, Stańczak K, Mosiądz D, Dobryszycki P, et al. Influence of silybin on biophysical properties of phospholipid bilayers 1. Acta Pharmacol Sin 2007;28(2):296–306.

[28] Chopra B, Dhingra AK, Dhar KL. *Psoralea corylifolia* L. (Buguchi)—folklore to modern evidence. Fitoterapia 2013;90:44–56.

[29] Wang HM, Chiu CC, Wu PF, Chen CY. Subamolide E from *Cinnamomum subavenium* induces sub-G1 cell-cycle arrest and caspase-dependent apoptosis and reduces the migration ability of human melanoma cells. J Agric Food Chem 2011;59(15):8187–92.

[30] Paydar M, Kamalidehghan B, Wong YL, Wong WF, Looi CY, Mustafa MR. Evaluation of cytotoxic and chemotherapeutic properties of boldine in breast cancer using in vitro and in vivo models. Drug Design, Dev Ther 2014;8:719.

[31] Derosa G, Maffioli P, Sahebkar A. Ellagic acid and its role in chronic diseases. Anti-inflammatory nutraceuticals and chronic diseases. Cham: Springer; 2016. p. 473–9.

[32] Al-Alawi RA, Al-Mashiqri JH, Al-Nadabi JS, Al-Shihi BI, Baqi Y. Date palm tree (*Phoenix dactylifera* L.): natural products and therapeutic options. Front Plant Sci 2017;8:845.

[33] Markou G, Iconomou D, Sotiroudis T, Israilides C, Muylaert K. Exploration of using stripped ammonia and ash from poultry litter for the cultivation of the cyanobacterium *Arthrospira platensis* and the green microalga *Chlorella vulgaris*. Bioresour Technol 2015;196:459–68.

[34] Yuan JP, Peng J, Yin K, Wang JH. Potential health-promoting effects of astaxanthin: a high-value carotenoid mostly from microalgae. Mol Nutr Food Res 2011;55(1):150–65.

[35] Liu J, Sun Z, Gerken H, Liu Z, Jiang Y, Chen F. Chlorella zofingiensis as an alternative microalgal producer of astaxanthin: biology and industrial potential. Mar Drugs 2014;12(6):3487–515.

[36] Fu W, Guðmundsson Ó, Paglia G, Herjólfsson G, Andrésson ÓS, Palsson BØ, et al. Enhancement of carotenoid biosynthesis in the green microalga Dunaliella salina with light-emitting diodes and adaptive laboratory evolution. Appl Microbiol Biotechnol 2013;97(6):2395–403.

[37] Cordero BF, Obraztsova I, Couso I, Leon R, Vargas MA, Rodriguez H. Enhancement of lutein production in Chlorella sorokiniana (Chorophyta) by improvement of culture conditions and random mutagenesis. Mar Drugs 2011;9(9):1607–24.

[38] Shi XM, Chen F. High-yield production of lutein by the green microalga Chlorella protothecoides in heterotrophic fed-batch culture. Biotechnol Prog 2002;18(4):723–7.

[39] Pasquet V, Morisset P, Ihammouine S, Chepied A, Aumailley L, Berard JB, et al. Antiproliferative activity of violaxanthin isolated from bioguided fractionation of Dunaliella tertiolecta extracts. Mar Drugs 2011;9(5):819–31.

[40] Lagarde D, Beuf L, Vermaas W. Increased production of zeaxanthin and other pigments by application of genetic engineering techniques to Synechocystis sp. strain PCC 6803. Appl Environ Microbiol 2000;66(1):64–72.

[41] Kim Y, Seo JH, Kim H. β-Carotene and lutein inhibit hydrogen peroxide-induced activation of NF-κB and IL-8 expression in gastric epithelial AGS cells. J Nutr Sci Vitaminol 2011;57(3):216–23.

[42] Crupi P, Toci AT, Mangini S, Wrubl F, Rodolfi L, Tredici MR, et al. Determination of fucoxanthin isomers in microalgae (Isochrysis sp.) by high-performance liquid chromatography coupled with diode-array detector multistage mass spectrometry coupled with positive electrospray ionization. Rapid Commun Mass Spectrometry 2013;27(9):1027–35.

[43] Mizushina Y, Hada T, Yoshida H. In vivo antitumor effect of liposomes with sialyl Lewis X including monogalactosyl diacylglycerol, a replicative DNA polymerase inhibitor, from spinach. Oncol Rep 2012;28(3):821–8.

[44] Hossain Z, Kurihara H, Hosokawa M, Takahashi K. Growth inhibition and induction of differentiation and apoptosis mediated by sodium butyrate in Caco-2 cells with algal glycolipids. Vitro Cell Develop Biology-Animal 2005;41(5–6):154–9.

[45] Maeda N, Kokai Y, Hada T, Yoshida H, Mizushina Y. Oral administration of monogalactosyl diacylglycerol from spinach inhibits colon tumor growth in mice. Exp Ther Med 2013;5(1):17–22.

[46] Guzman S, Gato A, Lamela M, Freire-Garabal M, Calleja JM. Anti-inflammatory and immunomodulatory activities of polysaccharide from Chlorella stigmatophora and Phaeodactylum tricornutum. Phytotherapy Res 2003;17(6):665–70.

[47] Sadovskaya I, Souissi A, Souissi S, Grard T, Lencel P, Greene CM, et al. Chemical structure and biological activity of a highly branched (1→ 3, 1→ 6)-β-d-glucan from Isochrysis galbana. Carbohydr Polym 2014;111:139–48.

[48] Matsui MS, Muizzuddin N, Arad S, Marenus K. Sulfated polysaccharides from red microalgae have antiinflammatory properties in vitro and in vivo. Appl Biochem Biotechnol 2003;104(1):13–22.

[49] Bae SY, Yim JH, Lee HK, Pyo S. Activation of murine peritoneal macrophages by sulfated exopolysaccharide from marine microalga Gyrodinium impudicum (strain KG03): Involvement of the NF-κB and JNK pathway. Int Immunopharmacol 2006;6(3):473–84.

[50] Challouf R, Trabelsi L, Ben Dhieb R, El Abed O, Yahia A, Ghozzi K, et al. Evaluation of cytotoxicity and biological activities in extracellular polysaccharides released by cyanobacterium Arthrospira platensis. Braz Arch Biol Technol 2011;54(4):831–8.

[51] Kwan JC, Teplitski M, Gunasekera SP, Paul VJ, Luesch H. Isolation and biological evaluation of 8-epi-malyngamide C from the Floridian marine cyanobacterium Lyngbya majuscula. J Nat Products 2010;73(3):463–6.

[52] Hatae N, Satoh R, Chiba H, Osaki T, Nishiyama T, Ishikura M, et al. N-substituted calothrixin B derivatives inhibited the proliferation of HL-60 promyelocytic leukemia cells. Med Chem Res 2014;23(11):4956–61.

[53] Abd El-Baky HH, El-Baz FK, El Baroty GS. Enhancing antioxidant availability in wheat grains from plants grown under seawater stress in response to microalgae extract treatments. J Sci Food Agric 2010;90(2):299–303.

[54] Nobili S, Lippi D, Witort E, Donnini M, Bausi L, Mini E, et al. Natural compounds for cancer treatment and prevention. Pharmacol Res 2009;59(6):365–78.

[55] Sharma P, McClees SF, Afaq F. Pomegranate for prevention and treatment of cancer: an update. Molecules 2017;22(1):177.

[56] Esmat AY, Said MM, Soliman AA, El-Masry KS, Badiea EA. Bioactive compounds, antioxidant potential, and hepatoprotective activity of sea cucumber (*Holothuria atra*) against thioacetamide intoxication in rats. Nutrition 2013;29(1):258−67.

[57] Mgbeahuruike EE, Yrjönen T, Vuorela H, Holm Y. Bioactive compounds from medicinal plants: focus on Piper species. South Afr J Botany 2017;112:54−69.

[58] Chang J, Hsu Y, Kuo P, Kuo Y, Chiang L, Lin C. Increase of Bax/Bcl-XL ratio and arrest of cell cycle by luteolin in immortalized human hepatoma cell line. Life Sci 2005;76(16):1883−93.

[59] Ramakrishnan G, Lo Muzio LORENZO, Elinos-Báez CM, Jagan S, Augustine TA, Kamaraj S, et al. Silymarin inhibited proliferation and induced apoptosis in hepatic cancer cells. Cell Prolif 2009;42(2):229−40.

[60] Chen CH, Huang TS, Wong CH, Hong CL, Tsai YH, Liang CC, et al. Synergistic anti-cancer effect of baicalein and silymarin on human hepatoma HepG2 Cells. Food Chem Toxicol 2009;47(3):638−44.

[61] Varghese L, Agarwal C, Tyagi A, Singh RP, Agarwal R. Silibinin efficacy against human hepatocellular carcinoma. Clin cancer Res 2005;11(23):8441−8.

[62] Hsu YL, Kuo PL, Lin CC. Acacetin inhibits the proliferation of Hep G2 by blocking cell cycle progression and inducing apoptosis. Biochem Pharmacol 2004;67(5):823−9.

[63] Park JH, Oh EJ, Choi YH, Kang CD, Kang HS, Kim DK, et al. Synergistic effects of dexamethasone and genistein on the expression of Cdk inhibitor p21WAF1/CIP1 in human hepatocellular and colorectal carcinoma cells. Int J Oncol 2001;18(5):997−1002.

[64] Su SJ, Chow NH, Kung ML, Hung TC, Chang KL. Effects of soy isoflavones on apoptosis induction and G2-M arrest in human hepatoma cells involvement of caspase-3 activation, Bcl-2 and Bcl-XL downregulation, and Cdc2 kinase activity. Nutr Cancer 2003;45(1):113−23.

[65] Kuo PL, Chiang LC, Lin CC. Resveratrol-induced apoptosis is mediated by p53-dependent pathway in Hep G2 cells. Life Sci 2002;72(1):23−34.

[66] Stervbo U, Vang O, Bonnesen C. Time-and concentration-dependent effects of resveratrol in HL-60 and HepG2 cells. Cell Prolif 2006;39(6):479−93.

[67] Sun ZJ, Pan CE, Liu HS, Wang GJ. Anti-hepatoma activity of resveratrol in vitro. World J Gastroenterol 2002;8(1):79.

[68] Jiang MC, Yang-Yen HF, Lin JK, Yen JJ. Differential regulation of p53, c-Myc, Bcl-2 and Bax protein expression during apoptosis induced by widely divergent stimuli in human hepatoblastoma cells. Oncogene 1996;13(3):609−16.

[69] Lee YS. Role of NADPH oxidase-mediated generation of reactive oxygen species in the mechanism of apoptosis induced by phenolic acids in HepG2 human hepatoma cells. Arch Pharmacal Res 2005;28 (10):1183−9.

[70] Soni KB, Lahiri M, Chackradeo P, Bhide SV, Kuttan R. Protective effect of food additives on aflatoxin-induced mutagenicity and hepatocarcinogenicity. Cancer Lett 1997;115(2):129−33.

[71] Yip ECH, Chan ASL, Pang H, Tam YK, Wong YH. Protocatechuic acid induces cell death in HepG2 hepatocellular carcinoma cells through a c-Jun N-terminal kinase-dependent mechanism. Cell Biol Toxicol 2006;22 (4):293−302.

[72] Huang SP, Chen JC, Wu CC, Chen CT, Tang NY, Ho YT, et al. Capsaicin-induced apoptosis in human hepatoma HepG2 cells. Anticancer Res 2009;29(1):165−74.

[73] Baek YM, Hwang HJ, Kim SW, Hwang HS, Lee SH, Kim JA, et al. A comparative proteomic analysis for capsaicin-induced apoptosis between human hepatocarcinoma (HepG2) and human neuroblastoma (SK-N-SH) cells. Proteomics 2008;8(22):4748−67.

[74] Joung EJ, Li MH, Lee HG, Somparn N, Jung YS, Na HK, et al. Capsaicin induces heme oxygenase-1 expression in HepG2 cells via activation of PI3K-Nrf2 signaling: NAD (P) H: quinone oxidoreductase as a potential target. Antioxid Redox Signal 2007;9(12):2087−98.

[75] Lee YS, Kang YS, Lee JS, Nicolova S, Kim JA. Involvement of NADPH oxidase-mediated generation of reactive oxygen species in the apototic cell death by capsaicin in HepG2 human hepatoma cells. Free Radic Res 2004;38(4):405−12.

[76] Lin HH, Chen JH, Wang CJ. Chemopreventive properties and molecular mechanisms of the bioactive compounds in *Hibiscus sabdariffa* Linne. Curr Med Chem 2011;18(8):1245−54.

[77] Zhou Y, Li Y, Zhou T, Zheng J, Li S, Li HB. Dietary natural products for prevention and treatment of liver cancer. Nutrients 2016;8(3):156.

[78] Martínez Andrade KA, Lauritano C, Romano G, Ianora A. Marine microalgae with anti-cancer properties. Mar Drugs 2018;16(5):165.

[79] Kim YS, Li XF, Kang KH, Ryu B, Kim SK. Stigmasterol isolated from marine microalgae *Navicula incerta* induces apoptosis in human hepatoma HepG2 cells. BMB Rep 2014;47(8):433.

[80] El-Baz FK, Hussein RA, Mahmoud K, Abdo SM. Cytotoxic activity of carotenoid rich fractions from *Haematococcus pluvialis* and *Dunaliella salina* microalgae and the identification of the phytoconstituents using LC-DAD/ESI-MS. Phytotherapy Res 2018;32(2):298–304.

[81] El-Baz FK, Ali SI, Basha M, Kassem AA, Shamma RN, Elgohary R, et al. Design and evaluation of bioenhanced oral tablets of *Dunaliella salina* microalgae for treatment of liver fibrosis. J Drug Deliv Sci Technol 2020;59:101845.

[82] Debbab A, Aly AH, Lin WH, Proksch P. Bioactive compounds from marine bacteria and fungi. Microb Biotechnol 2010;3(5):544–63.

[83] Ni Y, Ni L, Zhuge F, Fu Z. The gut microbiota and its metabolites, novel targets for treating and preventing non-alcoholic fatty liver disease. Mol Nutr Food Res 2020;64(17):2000375.

[84] Zhang X, Osaka T, Tsuneda S. Bacterial metabolites directly modulate farnesoid X receptor activity. Nutr Metab 2015;12(1):1–14.

[85] Degirolamo C, Rainaldi S, Bovenga F, Murzilli S, Moschetta A. Microbiota modification with probiotics induces hepatic bile acid synthesis via downregulation of the Fxr-Fgf15 axis in mice. Cell Rep 2014;7(1):12–18.

[86] Capelli B, Cysewski GR. Potential health benefits of spirulina microalgae. Nutrafoods 2010;9(2):19–26.

Plant therapeutics for hepatocellular carcinoma

Chandrasekhar Thummala[1] and
Ramachandra Reddy Pamuru[2]

[1]Department of Environmental Science, Yogi Vemana University, Kadapa, India
[2]Department of Biochemistry, Yogi Vemana University, Kadapa, India

Abstract

Liver is an important organ of human body involved in the regulation of several physiological processes including lipolysis, glycogenolysis, drug detoxification, emulsification of food, and urea formation. Liver diseases including cancer, reduce its functional rate and damage tissue completely. It is found that liver cancer (hepatocellular carcinoma) is a second leading disease causing death worldwide. Carcinoma develops in the hepatocytes of liver or due to migration of cancer cells from other tissue tumors at metastatic stage. These malignant hepatic cells are dangerous and grow faster. The uncontrollable large tumors in liver cause inflammation, cirrhosis, and finally failure of liver functions. Methods in curing cancer often show side effects besides deteriorating the health. Various types of treatments using different nature medicine are in use against hepatocellular carcinoma. Among all, plant-based anticancer pharmaceuticals hold great importance in treating or preventing lung cancer without or less side effects. The present review emphasizes the basics of liver cancer and available natural compounds from plants and their role in antihepatocellular carcinoma.

Keywords: Hepatocellular carcinoma; cirrhosis; plant-based drugs; anticancer

Abbreviations

HepG2 cells	hepatocellular carcinoma cells
MRI	magnetic resonance imaging
ROS	reactive oxygen species
SMMC-7721	human hepatocellular carcinoma cell lines
SREBP1	sterol regulatory element-binding protein 1
WHO	World Health Organization

© 2022 Elsevier Inc. All rights reserved.

Introduction

The most common disease causing death in the world is cancer. According to World Health Organization (WHO), the estimated deaths are 9.6 million in the year 2018 with 18.1 million new cases globally. The common tumors identified in men are liver, colorectal, stomach, prostate and lung cancers whereas in woman lung, colorectal, cervical, thyroid, and breast cancers. Among all, hepatocellular carcinoma is one of the most leading cancers which occupies fifth place in case of men and ninth place in women [1,2]. More than 8.4 million liver cancer cases were reported worldwide in 2018. Occurrence of liver cancer is often evidenced with consumption of alcohol, aflatoxin containing foods, and high fatness in the body [3]. Contrast to this it was found that there is a decrease in the risk of liver cancer with coffee and fish consumption. As per WHO in 2018, highest liver cancer age-standardized rate was found in Mongolia (93.7), followed by Egypt (32.2), Gambia (23.9), Vietnam (23.2), Laos (22.4), Cambodia (21.8), Guinea (21.8), Thailand (21), China (18.3), South Korea (17.3), North Korea (16.5), etc., per million people (Fig. 7.1). It is reported that Mongolia had highest rate of age-standardized liver cancer risk in both men (117) and women (74.1) per million population. Liver cancer is the second most common death-causing cancer among men than in women. The occurrence of this cancer is most common over the age of 75 years. People who are living in the underdeveloped and developing countries are showing highest incidences of liver cancer (83%). Africa and Asian countries are most affected whereas Latin America, Caribbean, and European countries are lowest affected ones. The death rate of liver cancer is highly increasing due to asymptomatic condition at the early stages and is diagnosed only at the advanced stage and moreover very poor survival rate is reported after diagnosis.

Surgery, chemotherapy, and radiation are the predominant methods of cancer treatment including liver cancer. These methods are executed lonely or in blend with one to other.

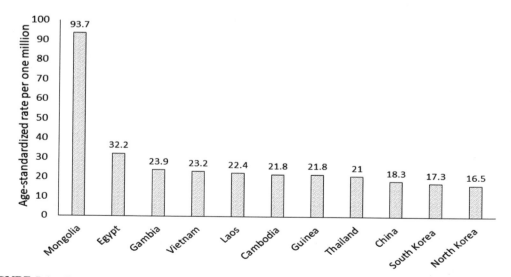

FIGURE 7.1   Occurrence of liver cancer age-standardized rate per million population in various countries.

The chemotherapeutics of cancer are not so effective many times and cause different side effects and damage various parts of the body. Surgery is possible only in certain cancers and many times this may not successfully eliminate the cancer totally. Radiation therapy is also not successive in many cases. However, these methods are killing normal cells and sometimes they may affect other organs. Due to the adverse effects of these methods, there is a dire need to focus on methods which can treat cancer with high efficacy and with almost no or less side effects. An array of research is being done to find the natural compounds from plant species in the treatment of liver cancer [4,5]. Finding various natural compounds to decrease the risk of liver cancer is desirable at this point of time.

The secondary metabolites of plants play an important role in treating various ailments in humans and animals. It is under practice to use plant-based medicine in most of the Asian countries such as India, China, Pakistan, Bangladesh, Vietnam, Sri Lanka, Nepal, and Bhutan. Ayurveda, Yunani, Homeopathy, and Folk medicine are predominant plant-based prehistoric era medicinal studies still in use in many areas of India, China, and some other Asian countries. Many plant species used in traditional medicine are found with its individual components through advanced research. Later, laboratories are in focus to isolate plant-based compounds from various plant species having anticancer activity [6,7]. The present chapter deals with basics of liver cancer and various phytomedicine identified against hepatocellular carcinoma.

Biology of liver

As the largest organ in the body, liver occupies 2% of total human body weight. It is located in the upper right part of the abdomen and is a bilobed (large left lobe and short left lobe) reddish brown organ. Gallbladder situated on liver collects bile juice and releases to small intestine through bile ducts for emulsification of fats during digestion. Functional roles of liver are energy metabolism, immunity, nutrition, reproduction, growth, detoxification, gluconeogenesis, lipolysis, etc. It is also known that liver is involved in more than 500 metabolic functions of an individual, but no function is specifically performed by liver alone. Due to various physiological roles of liver and no specified physiological function, it is named as "jack of all trades but master on none." However, it is the only organ having regeneration capacity in the human body. The major roles of liver include filtration of digestive tract blood, metabolization and detoxification of drugs and chemicals, synthesize blood clotting factors and release of bile salts for digestion of food in intestine. Different diseases are attributed to liver. They are inflammation, cirrhosis, hepatitis, failure, cancer, gallstones, ascites, primary sclerosing cholangitis, hemochromatosis, primary biliary cirrhosis, etc.

Histopathology of liver

The small structural unit of liver is hepatic lobules, which are formed in the dividing sheets of connective tissue into parenchyma. Liver as septa forms with tissue capsules branches connected and extended. Liver tissue is consisting of lymphatic vessels, bile

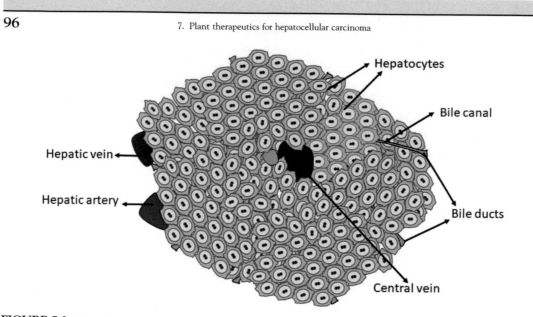

FIGURE 7.2 Histological appearance of liver.

ducts and afferent blood vessels. Liver cells generally named as hepatocytes. These are arranged toward portal tracts from central vein and are $25-30\,\mu$ in size and polygonal in shape. One to other hepatocytes are attached to biliary and lateral surfaces of tract. These cells are identical each other and bearing, ovular nuclei locate in the middle, eosinophilic cytosol, and granules with full of scattered glycogen, lipofuscin, and fat vacuoles. The hepatocyte nuclei is pleomorphic in nature. It is found that at birth nuclei of hepatocytes are mononuclear, at age 8 (10%), 15 (15%), and adult (25%) binuclear in shape. In every $50-300$ days, near portal space of liver new hepatocytes constantly rejuvenated and death of these cells occurs near central vein. Bile ducts, Kupffer cells, central canal, hepatic sinusoids, hepatic portal vein, and hepatic artery appear in the transverse section of liver (Fig. 7.2).

Liver cancer risk factors and diagnosis

Liver cancer begins in hepatocytes commonly called hepatocellular carcinoma. Hepatoblastoma and intrahepatic cholangiocarcinoma are the other types of liver cancers which are not common. Liver cancers mostly triggered by other cancers which are at metastatic stage. Colon cancer is the one that can easily spread to liver. In liver cancer, abnormal cell growth occurs in hepatocytes and begin to form tumor. Benign and malignant type liver tumors are often identified. Benign tumors may not reach to metastatic stage and do not spread to other parts of the body. In contrast, malignant tumors divide rapidly and reach to metastatic stage and spread to other parts of the body. The cells of blood vessels, bile duct, and liver are the source for liver cancer.

Many risk factors were identified as causatives of liver cancer. The primary risk factors include hepatitis C virus, hepatitis B virus, alcoholic consumption, diabetes, cirrhosis, aflatoxin exposure, fatty liver disease, and inherited liver diseases (Table 7.1). Long-term usage of high dose of oral contraceptives (estrogen and progesterone) also increases the risk of liver cancer. Liver cirrhosis patients have high risk for developing liver carcinoma (90%—95%). It is a known fact that chemical or viral cirrhosis increases liver carcinoma risk and cirrhosis increases the metastasis liver cancer from other organs. Moreover, sequential changes that occur in mature liver cells may finally lead in the formation of dysplastic nodules. The tumor cells undergo genetic modification frequently and lead to cellular proliferation. Hepatitis C virus shows indirect effects along with cirrhosis whereas hepatitis B virus causes more genetic variations.

Usually, liver cancer is asymptomatic but yellowing of eyes and skin can be diagnosed at the chronic condition. At the chronic state, patients of liver cancer often suffer with weakness, weight loss, swelling of abdomen, fever, and right upper abdominal pain [9,24]. Serum α-fetoprotein levels correlate with liver carcinoma growth but is not easy to identify if its amounts are low. About 20% of patients are diagnosed with hepatocellular carcinoma at more than 400 ng/mL serum levels of α-fetoprotein [9]. Recent technology developed noninvasive imaging methods to identify various types of disorders in humans. The magnetic resonance imaging (MRI), multiphasic multidetector-row CT, ultrasound, and CT scan are

TABLE 7.1 Various risk factors of liver cancer.

Sl. no.	Risk factor	Effects	References
1	Aflatoxin contaminated food	Increases liver cancer risk	[8–10]
2	Obesity or fatty body and diabetes		[11–13]
3	Alcohol consumption		[8,12,14]
4	Hepatitis B and C virus		[8]
5	Nonalcoholic fatty liver disease		[8]
6	Wilson's disease	Less common risk factor for hepatocellular carcinoma	[14–18]
7	Hereditary hemochromatosis		
8	Deficiency of α1-antitrypsin		
9	Autoimmune hepatitis		
10	Primary biliary cirrhosis		
11	Oral contraceptives	Increases risk of liver cancer	[19]
12	Drinking coffee	Decreases liver cancer risk	[20]
13	Eating fish	May decrease risk of liver cancer	[21]
14	Proper physical activity		[22,23]
15	Low physical activity	May increase risk of liver cancer	[22]

some of the noninvasive imaging methods [25–27]. Using these methods 60%–80% of 1 cm diameter tumors and 80%–95% of 3–5 cm diameter tumors can be detected [16,28].

Natural compounds on liver cancer

The role of liver in the maintenance of normal physiology of an individual is well described. A few diseases attributed to liver at different conditions were studied. Out of all methods curing liver diseases (including tumors), the best one found is plant-based drugs which are free from side effects, more effective and less toxic. Different plant species are identified with antiliver disease functions. *Andrographis paniculata, Coccinia grandis, Phyllanthus emblica, Chamomile capitula, Lepidium sativum, Garcinia mangostana, Silybum marianum, Flacourtia indica, Aegle marmelos, Azadirachta indica, Prosthechea michuacana, Jatropha curcas, Solanum nigrum, Orthosiphon stamineus, Trigonella foenumgraecum, Foeniculum vulgare, Swertia chirata, Eclipta alba, Annona squamosa, Picrorhiza kurroa, Curcuma longa, Ficus carica, Cassia roxburghii, Wedelia calendulacea,* and *Sargassum polycystum* are some of the plants used to cure liver diseases [29]. Several compounds were isolated from the plants which act against hepatocellular carcinoma. Some of the plant-based compounds and their hepatoprotective and antiliver cancer activity were discussed in the following section.

Curcumin

C. longa (Turmeric) belongs to family Zingiberaceae and mostly grow in the tropical regions of Asia and Africa. Rhizome of turmeric is harvested, dried, and powdered and is used as spice in Asian cuisine, especially in India (National Toxicology Programme). Turmeric is water-insoluble lipophilic polyphenol stable at acidic pH [30]. Chemically turmeric is comprised of diferuloylmethane (Curcumin), bisdemethoxycurcumin, demethoxycurcumin, and volatile oils such as tumerone, zingiberone, and atlantone along with sugars, resins, and proteins. Turmeric is known for the treatment of host of liver diseases such as hepatitis, jaundice, and cirrhosis [31]. The predominant compound isolated from *C. longa* is curcumin (Fig. 7.3), which decreases reactive oxygen species (ROS), increases P21 (CIP1/WAF1) protein and ion potential of mitochondrial membrane. Potentially curcumin inhibits proliferation, P21 (RAS), factor NF-k, PCNA, MMP-9 secretion, P34 (CDC2), cyclin E, and histone deacylase thereby induces apoptosis in carcinoma tissue [32–43].

Silibinin/silymarin

S. marianum (milk thistle) belongs to family Asteraceae and is a biennial or annual plant which produces purple color flowers. Silybum is a herb that grows upright up to 200 cm with conical shape. This plant is native of Southern Europe and Asia. At present it can be found all over the world. It is a known plant for traditional treatment of hepatocellular diseases. Silibinin (silymarin) a major constituent of silymarin is a flavonolignan isolated from *S. marianum* and has great potentiality in the treatment of liver cancer. Silymarin is also a chemosensitizing and chemopreventive agent for various cancers (Fig. 7.4).

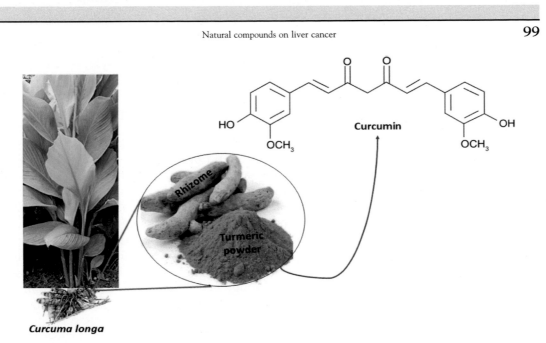

FIGURE 7.3 *Curcuma longa* plant, rhizome and its powder, and structure of curcumin.

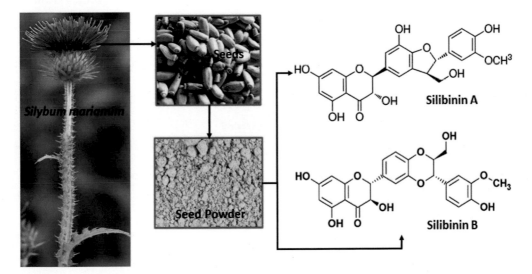

FIGURE 7.4 *Silybum marianum* plant, seeds and powder and major seed components (Silibinin A and B).

Resveratrol

Chemically resveratrol is a polyphenol found in skins of red grapes, red wine, mulberries, grape (purple) juice, and in lower amounts in many other plant sources. Resveratrol is a potential medicine used to treat many diseases. Most commonly resveratrol controls high cholesterol and cardiac diseases. Resveratrol and its conjugates play important role in the treatment of hepatocellular carcinoma (Fig. 7.5).

Many studies were conducted to test the role of resveratrol and its conjugates on hepatocellular carcinoma in vitro. Delmas et al. [44] demonstrated the resveratrol-mediated inhibition of FAO and HepG2 cell growth through lowering the mitosis process and increasing the S, G2, and M phases of the cancer cells. However, the postreceptor mechanism of HepG2 lowered the growth and invasion tested by De Lédinghen et al. [45]. The decreased hepatic carcinoma cells AH109A growth and invasion with the treatment of resveratrol through reduced oxidative stress is also demonstrated [46,47]. Resveratrol lowers the levels of HIF-1α and VEGF, stops cell G1 phase, elevates p53, p51, and bax, thereby increased the attack of HepG2 cells toward apoptosis [48,49]. Cytotoxicity of resveratrol was tested in HepG2 and H4IIE cell lines in vitro. The most common function of resveratrol against liver cancer is inducing apoptosis in the proliferated cell mass, besides elevating levels of caspase (2, 3, 8, or 10), DNA fragmentation, iNOS, eNOS, NO, and cell cycle regulation through arrest of G1, G2, or M phases in carcinoma cells [50−55]. Yu et al. [56] tested the resveratrol-induced HepG2 cell apoptosis by lowering MMP-9, NF-κβ, and TNF-α in vitro. CAV1 elevated expression by resveratrol in HepG2 decreased the cancer cell growth and apoptosis through cell cycle regulation, p38MAPK activity and caspase-3 by resveratrol was tested [57]. Better killing efficacy of HepG2 cells through elevating NADPH and increasing detoxifying enzymes with incubation of resveratrol was tested by Colin et al. [58]. Observed elevation in the

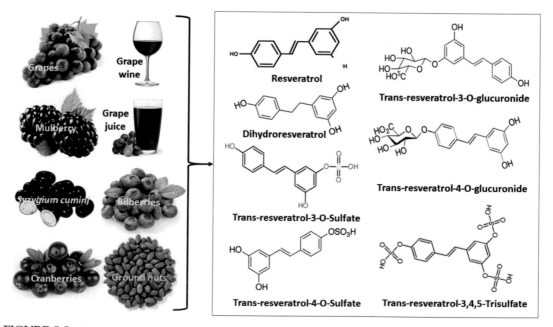

FIGURE 7.5   Various sources for resveratrol, structure, and its conjugates.

TABLE 7.2 In vivo role of resveratrol on hepatocellular carcinoma.

Animal model	References	Specific action	Impacts of resveratrol
Sprague-Dawley rats	[60]	Reduced cell proliferation and Bcl-2; elevated Bax and apoptosis	Initiated the formation of phenobarbital promoted heterocyte nodule; initiated diethylnitrosamine (DENA) suppression
	[61]	Reduced lipid peroxidation and fatty acid synthase in males	Instigated glutathione S transferase (placental) " + ve" hepatic preneoplastic foci; initiated DENA suppression
	[62]	In females, initiated formation of polychlorinated biphenyl-77 mediated liver cancer	—
BALB/c mice treated with H22 liver cancer cells	[63]	Pauses S-phase of cell cycle in males	Used for cancer treatment with 5-fluorouracil
	[64]	Elevated caspase-3 and apoptosis, and reduced cell growth	Lowered HepG2 growth with low CAVI-expression
	[64]	Inhibits cyclin B1 and p34cdc2	Reduction in size of tumors
	[65]	Shows immunomodulatory functions	Reduced liver cancer tumors
Wistar rats implanted with AH-130 liver cancer cells	[66]	Increased apoptosis and G2 or M phase cells	Hepatocellular carcinoma arrest
Donryu rats implanted with AH109A liver cancer cells	[67]	Reduced very-density lipoprotein, low-density lipoprotein, serum triglycerides, and lipid peroxidation	Reduced tumor proliferation and metastasis

levels of LDH, TG, ALP, and G1 or S phase of cell cycle reduced growth of SK-CHA I cells incubated with resveratrol [59]. Many reports also revealed the inhibitory activity of hepatocellular carcinoma by resveratrol in vivo (Table 7.2).

Tanshinone IIA

Salvia miltiorrhiza (Danshen) is Chinese oriental traditional medicinal plant. It is a herb which grows up to 1200 m in the forests, stream banks, and hillsides. Tanshinone IIA is isolated from *S. miltiorrhiza* (Fig. 7.6). This compound is a well-known herbal Chinese medicine used for treating hepatocellular carcinoma. Tanshinone IIA well proved as a drug for liver cancer treatment. It induces malignant cell apoptosis through downregulation of c-myc and Bcl-2 and upregulation of p53, fas, and bax. *Salvia* arrests the cell cycle at G1 or G0 stage thereby induces apoptosis of

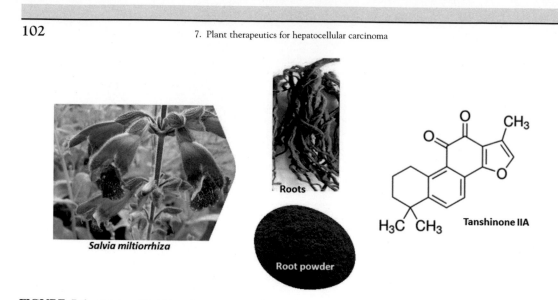

FIGURE 7.6 *Salvia miltiorrhiza* plant, roots and powder and structure of major root compound Tanshinone IIA.

hepatocellular carcinoma. DNA synthesis inhibition was reported in liver tumor cells after treatment with tanshinone IIA.

Emodin

Reynoutria multiflora is a climbing perennial plant which grows from underground tubers (Fig. 7.7). This plant grows in China, Japan and East Asia. In China, *R. multiflora* is harvested from cultivated lands, wild and home gardens. Leaves and seeds are consumed raw or as cooked food and acts as medicine. Emodin isolated from *R. multiflora* has been used in Chinese herbal medicine since many years to treat various ailments including hepatocellular carcinoma. Sterol regulatory element-binding protein 1 (SREBP1) dependent and independent apoptotic pathway in liver cancer cells is mediated by emodin (Fig. 7.7). Recently Yang et al. [68] demonstrated the growth inhibition of hepatocellular carcinoma by emodin through inhibiting dependent and independent SREBP1 cell proliferation thereby induction of intrinsic caspase dependent and independent apoptosis. They concluded that emodin has great potential in controlling hepatocellular carcinoma by targeting SREBP1.

Polyphyllin D

Paris polyphylla belongs to family Melanthiaceae and found in India, China, and Taiwan. This plant is perennial shrub grows up to 3 feet with 30 cm radial growth. An anticancerous agent polyphyllin D (a saponin) is isolated from *P. polyphylla*. Polyphyllin D induces hepatocellular carcinoma cells (HepG2 cells) DNA fragmentation. It is proved that polyphyllin D induces mitochondrial membrane potential depolarization, releases hydrogen peroxide, generates cytochrome C, and apoptosis inducing factor thereby elicit programmed cell death in cancer tissue [69] (Fig. 7.8).

FIGURE 7.7 *Reynoutria multiflora* plant, roots and powder and structure of major root compound emodin.

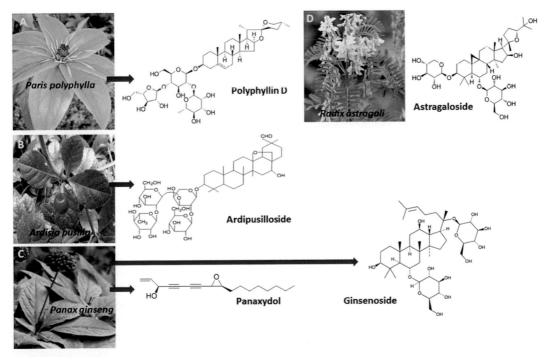

FIGURE 7.8 Antihepatocellular carcinoma compounds from selected plant species.

Ardipusilloside I

Ardisia pusilla (Coralberry/Marlberry) belongs to family Myrsinaceae. This medicinal plant is distributed in tropic regions of the United States, Australia, Pacific Island, and Asia. It is a stoloniferous shrub showing pale green leaves, creamy/white flowers, and red berries. Triterpene saponin ardipusilloside I isolated from *A. pusilla* is a potential antiliver carcinoma agent. This compound suppresses the tumor cell proliferation through lowering the metalloprotenase 2 and 9 expression and elevating Rac1 levels. Ardipusilloside I inhibits invasion and metastasis of hepatocellular carcinoma [70] (Fig. 7.8).

Panaxydol and ginsenoside

Panax ginseng and *Withania somnifera* (Ginseng and Ashwagandha) are small woody shrub belongs to family Araliaceae and Solanaceae distributed in Asian (China, India, Korea, Japan, etc.), American and African continents. Bioactive panaxydol is extracted from the roots of *P. ginseng/W. somnifera* common drug for hemostatic and blood disorders. Apart from this, panaxydol found to induce cell differentiation in human hepatocellular carcinoma cell lines (SMMC-7721) [71]. Another compound extracted from *Ginseng* is ginsenosides which inhibits the growth of liver cancer cells (SMMC-7721). Gensinoside-Rh2 treatment (10 mg/mL) decreased the γ-GT, heat-resistant ALP and AFP expression significantly [72] (Fig. 7.8).

Astragaloside

Radix astragali, a Chinese herb which belongs to family Fabaceae is a renewed traditional medicine. Astragaloside prepared from *R. astragali* is a potential medicine for treating cancer. Astragaloside regulates the hepatic cancer cell (Bel-7402) expression of p-glycoprotein (improves the efficiency of drug during chemotherapy to suppress tumor) and resistance of 5-FU during chemotherapy [73].

Piper betel leaves

One of the traditional plants used in every customary occasion in Indian culture is leaves of *Piper betel* which belongs to family Piperaceae. The leaves of this plant are enriched with medicinal and antioxidant properties. It has the capacity to restrict mutations in genes. In HepG2 cells, *Piper* leaves inhibit the glutathion S-transferase and increase the hepatocellular carcinoma cell sensitivity during chemotherapy [74].

Green tea

Camellia sinensis, a wide cultivar in India, China, Indonesia, and Japan is used in the preparation of green, black, and oolong tea which belongs to family Theaceae. This plant is a bush with evergreen leaves which are used in preparing green tea in these countries. Polyphenols (30%−40%) are the major components of green tea and a cup of green tea consists 50−150 mg of polyphenols [75]. Khan et al. [76], Cao et al. [77], and Yang et al.

[78] tested the hepatoprotective function of green tea through its catechins which improves the antioxidant function of the patients and maintains the protein thiols at intracellular level. Most interestingly in rodents, green tea found to inhibit or prevent the liver cancer development by lowering growth of hepatic neoplasm [79].

Conclusion and future outlook

The traditional medicine is one of the vital treatment available for hepatocellular carcinoma. Traditional medicine is the major source of primary healthcare for over 65% of the world population. There are many plants in usage as traditional medicine. In Peru, commonly used herbal medicines are originated from Europe and Asia [80]. Besides India, China has developed lot of traditional medicine and methods for treating various ailments [81]. Some of the traditional medicinal plants used for the treatment of hepatocellular carcinoma are mentioned in this chapter. Based on this knowledge, plant-based compounds can be used to develop antihepatocellular carcinoma pharmaceutical drugs with no side effects. Many studies in the direction for generating plant-based pharmaceutical drugs in treating liver cancer should needs focus in near future. Molecular mechanism of the plant-based antihepatocellular carcinoma drugs is another area to be focused and elucidated in future.

Acknowledgments

Authors are thankful to their institutions and concerned departments for the provision of facility and constant encouragement in writing the book chapter. Authors are highly thankful to the unknown authors for the plant pictures and compound structures uploaded to Google.

Conflict of interest

Authors have no difference of opinion on this chapter and declare no conflict of interest.

References

[1] El-Serag HB. Hepatocellular Carcinoma. N Engl J Med 2011;365:1118−27.
[2] World Health Organization (WHO). Latest global cancer data: cancer burden rises to 18.1 million new cases and 9.6 million cancer deaths in 2018; 2018.
[3] Bray F, et al. Global cancer statistics 2018: GLOBOCAN estimates of incidence and mortality worldwide for 36 cancers in 185 countries. CA Cancer J Clin 2018;68(6):394−424.
[4] Cragg GM, Newman DJ. Plants as a source of anti-cancer agents. J Ethnopharmacol 2005;100(1−2):72−9.
[5] Cragg GM, et al. Anticancer agents from natural products. CRC Press; 2011.
[6] Rajaratnam M, et al. Herbal medicine for treatment and prevention of liver diseases. J Pre-Clin Clin Res 2014;8 (2):55−60.
[7] Anchala IK, et al. Medicinal plants commonly used against cancer in traditional medicine formulae in Sri Lanka. Saudi Pharma J 2019;27:565−73.

[8] El-Serag HB, Rudolph KL. Hepatocellular carcinoma: epidemiology and molecular carcinogenesis. Gastroenterol 2007;132:2557–76.

[9] Raphael SW, et al. Hepatocellular carcinoma: focus on different aspects of management ISRN. Oncology. 2012;2012:421673.

[10] Bressac B, et al. Selective G to T mutations of p53 gene in hepatocellular carcinoma from southern Africa. Nature 1991;350(6317):429–31.

[11] Polesel J, et al. The impact of obesity and diabetes mellitus on the risk of hepatocellular carcinoma. Ann Oncol 2009;20:353–7.

[12] Ascha MS, et al. The incidence and risk factors of hepatocellular carcinoma in patients with nonalcoholic steatohepatitis. Hepatology 2010;51(6):1972–8.

[13] El-Serag HB, et al. The association between diabetes and hepatocellular carcinoma: a systematic review of epidemiologic evidence. Clin Gastroenterol Hepatol 2006;4:369–80.

[14] Donato F, et al. Alcohol and hepatocellular carcinoma: the effect of lifetime intake and hepatitis virus infections in men and women. Am J Epidemiol 2002;155:323–31.

[15] Heidelbaugh JJ, Bruderly M. Cirrhosis and chronic liver failure: part I. Diagnosis and evaluation. Am Fam Physician 2006;74:756–62.

[16] Sanyal AJ, et al. The etiology of hepatocellular carcinoma and consequences for treatment. Oncologist 2010;15(4):14–22.

[17] Alan D, et al. Risk factors for hepatocellular carcinoma. Clin Liver Dis 2012;1(6):180–2.

[18] Ferenci P, et al. World gastroenterology organisation guideline. Hepatocellular carcinoma (HCC): a global perspective. J Gastrointestin Liver Dis 2010;19:311–17.

[19] Ning An MB. Oral contraceptives use and liver cancer risk: a dose–response meta-analysis of observational studies. Medicine (Baltim) 2015;94(43):e1619.

[20] Takashi T, et al. Coffee consumption and liver cancer risk in Japan: a meta-analysis of six prospective cohort studies. Nagoya J Med Sci 2019;81(1):143–50.

[21] Lemonica K. Dietary factors can protect against liver cancer development. World J Hepatol 2017;9(3):119–25.

[22] Tracey GS, et al. Physical activity compared to adiposity and risk of liver-related mortality: results from two prospective, nationwide cohorts. J Hepatol 2020;72(6):P1062–9.

[23] Lin Z-Z, et al. Physical activity and liver cancer risk: a systematic review and meta-analyses. Clin J Sport Med 2021;31(1):86–90.

[24] El-Serag HB, et al. Diagnosis and treatment of hepatocellular carcinoma. Gastroenterol 2008;134(6):1752–63.

[25] Marrero JA, et al. Improving the prediction of hepatocellular carcinoma in cirrhotic patients with an arterially-enhancing liver mass. Liver Transpl 2005;11:281–9.

[26] Cabrera R, Nelson DR. Review article: the management of hepatocellular carcinoma. Aliment Pharmacol Ther 2010;31(4):461–76.

[27] Bolog N, et al. CT and MR imaging of hepatocellular carcinoma. J Gastrointes Liver Dis 2011;20(2):181–9.

[28] Ryder SD. Guidelines for the diagnosis and treatment of hepatocellular carcinoma (HCC) in adults. Gut 2003;52(3):iii1–8.

[29] Handa SS, Sharma A, Chakraborti KK. Natural products and plants as liver protecting drugs. Fitoterapia. 1986;57(5):307–52.

[30] Aggarwal BB, et al. Anticancer potential of curcumin: preclinical and clinical studies. Anticancer Res 2003;23(1A):363–98.

[31] Moken Y, et al. Studies on the chemical constituents of common turmeric (Curcuma longa). Zhongcoayoa 1984;15:197–8.

[32] Lin L-I, et al. Curcumin inhibits SK-Hep-1 hepatocellular carcinoma cell invasion in vitro and suppresses matrix metalloproteinase-9 secretion. Oncology 1998;55(4):349–53.

[33] Chuang S-E, et al. Inhibition by curcumin of diethylnitrosamine-induced hepatic hyperplasia, inflammation, cellular gene products and cellcycle-related proteins in rats. Food Chem Toxicol 2000;38(11):991–5.

[34] Ohashi Y, et al. Prevention of intrahepatic metastasis by curcumin in an orthotopic implantation model. Oncol 2003;65(3):250–8.

[35] Fang J-Y, et al. Efficacy and irritancy of enhancers on the in-vitro and in-vivo percutaneous absorption of curcumin. J Pharma Pharmacol 2003;55(5):593–601.

[36] Chan W-H, et al. Curcumin inhibits ROS formation and apoptosis in methylglyoxal treated human hepatoma G2 cells. Ann N Y Acad Sci 2005;1042:372–8.

[37] Yoysungnoen P, et al. Antiangiogenic activity of curcumin in hepatocellular carcinoma cells implanted nude mice. Clin Hemorheol Microcirc 2005;33(2):127–35.

[38] Yoysungnoen P, et al. Effects of curcumin on tumor angiogenesis and biomarkers, COX-2 and VEGF, in hepatocellular carcinoma cell-implanted nude mice. Clin Hemorheol Microcirc 2006;34(1–2):109–15.

[39] Yoysungnoen P, et al. Anti-cancer and anti-angiogenic effects of curcumin and tetrahydrocurcumin on implanted hepatocellular carcinoma in nude mice. World J Gastroenterol 2008;14:2003–9.

[40] Cao J, et al. Mitochondrial and nuclear DNA damage induced by curcumin in human hepatoma G2 cells. Toxicol Sci 2006;91(2):476–83.

[41] Cao J, et al. Curcumin induces apoptosis through mitochondrial hyperpolarization and mtDNA damage in human hepatoma G2 cells. Free Radic Biol Med 2007;43:968–75.

[42] Lv BH, et al. Inhibition of curcumin on histone deacetylase and expression promotion of P21 (WAF1/CIP1) in HepG2 cells. Zhongguo Zhong Yao Za Zhi 2007;32:2051–5.

[43] López-Lázaro M. Anticancer and carcinogenic properties of curcumin: considerations for its clinical development as a cancer chemopreventive and chemotherapeutic agent. Mol Nutr Food Res 2008;52(1):S103–27.

[44] Delmas D, et al. Inhibitor effect of resveratrol on the proliferation of human and rat hepatic derived cell lines. Oncol Rep 2000;7:847–52.

[45] De Lédinghen V, et al. Trans-resveratrol, a grape vine derived polyphenol, blocks hepatocyte growth factor-induced invasion of hepatocellular carcinoma cells. Int J Oncol 2001;19:83–8.

[46] Kozuki Y, et al. Resveratrol suppresses hepatoma cell invasion independently of its anti-proliferative action. Cancer Lett 2001;167:151–6.

[47] Miura D, et al. Resveratrol inhibits hepatoma cell invasion by suppressing gene expression on hepatocyte growth factor via its reactive oxygen species-scavenging property. Clin Exp Metas 2004;25:445–51.

[48] Kuo P, et al. Resveratrol-induced apoptosis is mediated by p53-dependent pathway in Hep G2 cells. Life Sci 2002;72:23–34.

[49] Zhang Q, et al. Resveratrol inhibits hypoxia-induced accumulation of hypoxia-inducible factor-1a and VEGF expression in human tongue squamous cell carcinoma and hepatoma cells. Mol Cancer Ther 2005;10:1465–74.

[50] Kim HJ, et al. Cytotoxic and antimutagenic stilbenes from seeds of Paeonia lactiflora. Arch Pharm Res 2002;3:293–9.

[51] Sun Z, et al. Anti-hepatoma activity of resveratrol in vitro. World J Gastroenterol 2002;8:79–81.

[52] Kocsis Z, et al. Chemopreventive properties of trans resveratrol against the cytotoxicity of chloroacetanilide herbicides in vitro. Int J Hyg Environ Health 2005;208:211–18.

[53] Michels G, et al. Resveratrol induces apoptotic cell death in rat H4IIE hepatoma cells but necrosis in C6 glioma cells. Toxicol 2006;225:173–82.

[54] Stervbo U, et al. Time- and concentration-dependent effects of resveratrol in HL-60 and HepG2 cells. Cell Prolif 2006;39:479–93.

[55] Notas G, et al. Resveratrol exerts its antiproliferative effect on HepG2 hepatocellular carcinoma cells, by inducing cell cycle arrest, and NOS activation. Biochem Biophys Acta 2006;1760:1657–66.

[56] Yu H, et al. Resveratrol inhibits tumor necrosis factor-a-mediated matrix metalloproteinase-9 expression and invasion of human hepatocellular carcinoma cells. Biomed Pharmacother 2008;62:366–72.

[57] Yang H-l, et al. Caveolin-I enhances resveratrol-mediated cytotoxicity and transport in a hepatocellular carcinoma model. J Transl Med 2009;7:22.

[58] Colin D, et al. Antiproliferative activities of resveratrol and related compounds in human hepatocyte derived HepG2 cells are associated with biochemical cell disturbance revealed by fluorescence analyses. Biochimie 2008;90:1674–84.

[59] Roncoroni L, Elli L, Dolfini E, et al. Resveratrol inhibits cell growth in a human cholangiocarcinoma cell line. Liver Int 2008;28:1426–36.

[60] Bishayee A, Dhir N. Resveratrol-mediated chemoprevention of diethylnitrosamine-initiated hepatocarcinogenesis: inhibition of cell proliferation and induction of apoptosis. Chem Biol Interact 2009;179:131–44.

[61] Kweon S, Kim Y, Choi H. Grape extracts suppress the formation of preneoplastic foci and activity of fatty acid synthase in rat liver. Exp Mol Med 2003;35:371–8.

[62] Tharappel JC, Lehmler H-J, Srinivasan C, Robertson LW, Spear BT, Glauert HP. Effect of antioxidant phyto-chemicals on the hepatic tumor promoting activity of 3,30,4,40-tetrachlorobiphenyl (PCB-77). Food Chem Toxicol 2008;46:3467—74.

[63] Wu S-L, Sun Z-J, Yu L, Meng K-W, Qin X-L, Pan C. Effect of resveratrol and in combination with 5-FU on murine liver cancer. World J Gastroenterol 2004;10:3048—52.

[64] Yu L, Sun Z-J, Wu SL, Pan C-E. Effect of resveratrol on cell cycle proteins in murine transplantable liver can-cer. World J Gastroenterol 2003;9:2341—3.

[65] Liu H-S, Pan C-E, Yang W, Liu X-M. Antitumor and immunomodulatory activity of resveratrol on experi-mentally implanted tumor of H22 in Balb/c mice. World J Gastroenterol 2003;9:1474—6.

[66] Carbo N, Costelli P, Baccino FM, Lopez-Soriano FJ, Argiles JM. Resveratrol, a natural product present in wine, decreases tumour growth in a rat tumour model. Biochem Biophys Res Commun 1999;254:739—43.

[67] Miura D, Miura Y, Yagasaki K. Hypolipidemic action of dietary resveratrol, a phytoalexin in grapes and red wine, in hepatoma-bearing rats. Life Sci 2003;73:1393—400.

[68] Yang N, et al. Emodin induced SREBP1-dependent and SREBP1-independent apoptosis in hepatocellular car-cinoma cells. Front Pharmacol 2019;10:709.

[69] Cheung JY, et al. Polyphyllin D is a potent apoptosis inducer in drug-resistant HepG2 cells. Cancer Lett 2005;217(2):203—11.

[70] Lou L, et al. Ardipusilloside inhibits survival, invasion and metastasis of human hepatocellular carcinoma cells. Phytomedicine 2012;19:603—8.

[71] Wang ZJ, et al. Induction of differentiation by panaxydol in human hepatocarcinoma smmc-7721 cells via camp and map kinase dependent mechanism. Yakugaku Zasshi 2011;131:993—1000.

[72] Zeng XL, Tu ZG. Induction of differentiation by ginsenoside rh2 in hepatocarcinoma cell smmc-7721. Ai Zheng 2004;23(8):879—84.

[73] Wang PP, et al. Astragaloside reduces the expression level of p-glycoprotein in multidrug-resistant human hepatic cancer cell lines. Mol Med Rep 2014;9:2131—7.

[74] Young SC, et al. Increased sensitivity of hep g2 cells toward the cytotoxicity of cisplatin by the treatment of piper betel leaf extract. Arch Toxicol 2006;80:319—27.

[75] Miyagawa C, et al. Protective effect of green tea extract and tea polyphenols against the cytotoxicity of 1,4-naphthoquinone in isolated rat hepatocytes. Biosci Biotechnol Biochem 1997;61:1901—5.

[76] Khan SG, et al. Enhancement of antioxidant and phase II enzymes by oral feeding of green tea polyphenols in drinking water to SKH-1 hairless mice: possible role in cancer chemoprevention. Cancer Res 1992;52:4050—2.

[77] Cao J, et al. Chemopreventive effects of green and black tea on pulmonary and hepatic carcinogenesis. Fundam Appl Toxicol 1996;29:244—50.

[78] Yang CS, et al. Blood and urine levels of tea catechins after ingestion of different amounts of green tea by human volunteers. Cancer Epidemiol Biomarkers Prev 1998;7(4):351—4.

[79] Hirose M, et al. Inhibitory effects of 1-ohexyl-2,3,5- trimethylhydroquinone (HTHQ), green tea catechins and other antioxidants on 2-amino-6- methyldipyrido[1,2-a:3′,2′-d] imidazole (Glu-P-1)-induced rat hepatocarci-nogenesis and dose dependent inhibition by HTHQ of lesion induction by Glu-P-1 or 2-amino-3,8-dimethyli-midazo[4,5-f]quinoxaline (MeIQx). Carcinogenesis 1995;16:3049—55.

[80] Roskov Y, et al. Species 2000 & ITIS catalogue of life. < http://www.catalogueoflife.org/col >. 2016.

[81] Xia Liao, et al. Traditional Chinese medicine as supportive care for the management of liver cancer: past, present, and future. Gen Dis 2020;7(3):370—9.

Phytochemicals for hepatocellular carcinoma therapy: from in vitro to clinic

Ganganapalli Supraja[1], Kalisetty Chengaiahgari Maheswari[1], Deepika Pamarthy[2] and Kallimakula Venkata Reddy Saritha[1]

[1]Department of Biotechnology, Sri Venkateswara University, Tirupati, India
[2]Applied Biology Department, Council of Scientific and Industrial Research-Indian Institute of Chemical Technology, Hyderabad, India

Abstract

Hepatocellular carcinoma (HCC) or liver cancer ranks first among four leading cancers in the world according to Cancer Statistics 2021. It has gained place in the field of oncology due to the various paths of origin and alterations of genes at molecular level. These include mutations, epigenetic modifications of various genes associated with cell cycle regulation, tumor suppressor genes, and oncogenes. Different types of liver cancers include HCC, intrahepatic cholangiocarcinoma, angiosarcoma, and hepatoblastoma. HCC occurs widely in the liver. Early-stage detection is difficult due to unavailability of biological markers. In recent years, the methods to treat cancer have evolved greatly, involving reduced side effects. The current review signifies the role of medicinal herbs and secondary metabolites which are gaining important roles as anticancer therapies. We discuss herein research updates on plants and their medicinal properties, and role of herbs, and metabolites available, as targeted treatments for HCC, briefing upon their molecular expression patterns. This compendium of phytochemicals and natural products can be used to develop potential therapeutics for treatment of hepatocellular carcinoma.

Keywords: Herbs; secondary metabolites; gene expression patterns; hepatocellular carcinoma

Abbreviations

AKT	seronine/threonine protein kinase
APC	adenomatous polyposis coli protein
BIRC5	baculoviral inhibitor of apoptosis repeat containing 5

© 2022 Elsevier Inc. All rights reserved.

EGFR   epidermal growth factor receptor
HCC   hepatocellular Carcinoma
MYC   master regulator of cell cycle entry and proliferative metabolism
p16   cyclin-dependent kinase inhibitors (CDKN2A)
p21   cyclin-dependent kinase inhibitors (CDKN1A)
p27   cyclin-dependent kinase inhibitors (CDKN1B)
p53   Tumor protein 53
TGFA   transforming growth factor alpha
VEGF   vascular endothelial growth factor
YAP   yes-associated protein 1

Introduction

Liver is the largest vital organ in the human body and has the greatest regenerative power, with primary function being detoxification which is mandatory to maintain good health [1]. Damage to liver leads to disease or illness and also increases the risk of liver cancer. Birth defects, alcohol abuse, infection with hepatitis B and C viruses, genetic diseases such as hemochromatosis, and cirrhosis cause liver damage which ultimately lead to liver cancer [2]. Liver cancer is the sixth frequently diagnosed and third leading cause for mortality, globally. It frequently occurs in men compared to women [3]. Liver cancer is also linked to obesity, fatty liver disease, and diabetes. Substances such as herbicides, heavy metals, vinyl chloride, and aflatoxins may also cause liver cancer [4].

Liver cancer is usually categorized into primary and secondary. Primary liver cancer arises inside the liver whereas secondary liver cancer is caused due to spreading of cancer cells from other organs. There are various kinds of primary liver cancer comprising hepatocellular carcinoma (HCC), fibrolamellar HCC, cholangiocarcinoma, angiosarcoma, and hepatoblastoma [5]. HCC, the commonest type of cancer develops in hepatocytes and is also referred to as hepatoma, accounting for 75% of all liver cancers. Fibrolamellar HCC, a histological variant of HCC occurs in young adults and is characterized by the presence of fibrous layers between tumor cells. Unlike HCC, it has different demographics and risk factors. Cholangiocarcinoma, more commonly referred to as common bile duct cancer develops in bile ducts within the liver. In addition, angiosarcoma, a rare sort of cancer grows in blood vessels of the liver. Finally, hepatoblastoma occurs in children and caused by a genetic alteration. HCC is the most common type of liver cancer among all [6].

Genes associated with hepatocellular carcinoma

The expression pattern of tumor suppressor and oncogenes are altered in HCC. Genes associated with HCC include tumor suppressor genes such as p53, p21, p27, p16, VEGF, and EGFR. p53 gene plays a role in repair mechanism of DNA, apoptosis, angiogenesis, and cell cycle control. It was reported that p53 involves only in the progression of HCC, not in initiation. p53 mutations and methylation of CpG islands cause tumorigenesis by blocking cell cycle check points [7]. On the other hand, the function of p21 is to activate caspases involved in apoptosis. Downregulation of p21 is noticed in HCC, followed by active proliferation of cells and blockage of apoptosis mechanism [7]. The role of p27 gene is to promote

G1 to S phase transition in cell cycle. In HCC decreased expression of p27 is observed in some case studies. Single nucleotide polymorphism of p27 and p21 increases the risk of HCC. Hypermethylation of p27 promoter leads to downregulation of p27 expression and is reported in HCC [8,9]. Normal function of p16 is to regulate cell cycle by binding to cyclin-dependent kinase 4 and prevents its interaction with cyclin D1. Posttranscriptional regulation of p16 is detected in initial stages of HCC [10,11].

Genes involved in WNT- and TGF-β-signaling cascade

Beta-catenin, E-cadherin, Axin1, Axin2, genes involved in WNT signaling cascade were also found to be involved in HCC. Epigenetic alterations of E-cadherin promoter prevents its binding to beta-catenin, enhancing cell invasiveness and metastasis to surrounding tissues, observed in HCC [11]. Normal role of Axin is to act as an antagonist to Wnt β-signaling cascade. Transformation of virus to HCC cells restores the Axin1 mutation and enhances tumor suppressor activity [12]. Adenomatous polyposis coli protein (APC) acts as negative regulator and is involved in WNT signaling. Hypermethylation of adenomatous polyposis promoter inactivates its gene expression in HCC [13,14]. Insulin-like growth factor II, a tumor suppressor gene involves in growth, migration, and differentiation of cells via the WNT signaling cascade. In HCC, either loss or mutation of insulin-like growth factor II gene is reported in patients in Japan and United States [15,16]. In comparison to HCC and non tumour liver tissues mutation observed in smad4 and smad2 genes. In smad4 T →C transition took place leading to Cys 401 Arg conversion. Similarly A→G transition observed at codon 407 in smad2 leading to Gln 407 Arg. conversion [17]. Next-generation sequencing technology revealed mutations in cell cycle-associated genes, PI3K/MTOR cascade genes, WNT signaling genes, RAS/MAPK cascade genes, and chromatin remodeling complexes, JAK/STAT signaling gene [18]. Oncogenes associated with HCC include MYC gene (master regulator of cell cycle entry and proliferative metabolism), EGF gene (epidermal growth factor), TGFA gene (transforming growth factor alpha), CNNTB1 gene, AKT and RAS genes [19]. Bioinformatics approach revealed genes associated with HCC, including YAP gene, associated with Hippo Pathway, and cIAP1 gene (BIRC2) associated with cell death pathway, and various genes yet to be validated by in vivo experiments. Metabolic pathways associated with amino acid, carbohydrate, glycan biosynthesis genes show dysfunctional roles more predominantly in female patients of HCC than in males. Transcriptional factors GATA3 and TAL1 show their action on ALDH1A2 gene involved in amino acid and carbohydrate metabolism. In HCC, disruption of ALDH1A2 was observed by in silico approach [20] (Fig. 8.1).

Herbs and their secondary metabolites

Traditionally, herbs and their secondary metabolites are used as formulations for treatment of diseases globally. The current review includes the details of herbs and their secondary metabolites as strategy for the treatment of HCC. HCC is treated by radio therapy, chemotherapy, and transplantation of liver depending on the stage associated with HCC progression. Formulations include herbs and secondary metabolites. The list of herbs and their metabolites used in treatment of HCC are given in Table 8.1.

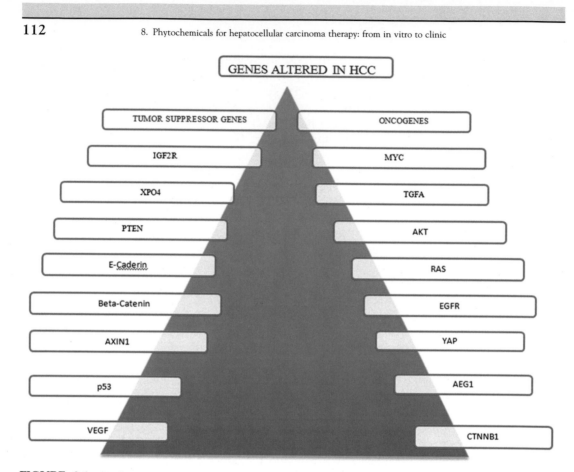

FIGURE 8.1   **Various tumor suppressor genes and oncogenes involved in HCC.** *HCC,* hepatocellular carcinoma.

Baliospermum montanum

Baliospermum montanum, commonly known as Red physic nut belongs to Euphorbiaceae. Its root and leaves contain secondary metabolites such as montanin, baliospermin, 12-deoxyphorbol-13-palmitate, 12-deoxy-5β-hydroxyphorbol-β-myristate, and 12-deoxy-16-hydroxyphorbol-13-palmitate, β-sitosterol, β-D-glucoside, and hexacosanol [21]. Axillarenic acid, alkaloids, 12-deoxy-5β-hydroxyphorbol-13-myristate, anthroquinone, cardiac glycosides, 13-palmitate, 12 deoxyphorbol-13-palmitate, saponin, terpenoids, montanin, tannins are metabolites from *B. montanum* [22]. Ethanolic extract from leaf of *B. montanum* showed antiinflammatory, antiallergic, cytotoxic activity in HepG2 and KKU-M156 cell lines [23]. Methanolic extract of leaf and elicitor treated callus showed cell cycle arrest at G0/G1 phase and S, and G2/M transitions with enhanced apoptosis upon treatment of Hep-2 and Pc-3 cell lines [22]. Benja-ummarit extract from *B. montanum* showed antiangiogenic and antiproliferative effects in diethylnitrosamine (DENA)-induced HCC in Wistar rats and human HCC cell lines [24] (Fig. 8.2).

TABLE 8.1 Role of secondary metabolites and their anti cancer properties.

Sl. No	Name of the plant	Secondary metabolites	Biological effects	Anticancer effects
1	*Solanum nigrum*	• Polyphenols • Anthocyanidin • Luteolin • Kaempferol • Dillapiole • Limonene • Uttroside B	Antipyretic, diuretic, hepatoprotective, and antiinflammation	Antiproliferative, cell cycle arrest, apoptosis, hepatoprotective, and shows cytotoxicity
2	*Tripterygium wilfordii*	• Triptolide • Triterpenoid • Celastrol • Diterpene triepoxide • Tripfordines	Antiinflammatory, immune modulation, antiproliferative, proapoptotic activity, antiobesity, antidiabetic, and prevents cardiovascular diseases	Promote apoptosis, cell cycle arrest, hepatoprotective, antiproliferative, and shows cytotoxicity
3	*Mangifera indica*	• Gallotannins • Terpenoids • Xanthones • Phenolics • Flavonoids • Anthraquinone • Saponins	Antibacterial, antioxidant, and antitumor	Cell cycle arrest, promotes apoptosis, cytotoxicity, reduced tumor, and hepatotoxicity
4	*Woodfordia fruticose*	• Phenolics • Tanins • Flavonoids • Teroids hecogenin • Meso-inositol • Triterpenoids • Bergenin • Quercetin glycosides	Antifungal, antibacterial, antimicrobial, and antitumor	Cell cycle arrest at S phase, antiproliferative and cytotoxicity. Prevents metastasis and promotes apoptosis
5	*Allium sativum*	• Organosulfur derivatives • Inulin • Allithiamine • Sallylcysteine • Allicin • Ajoene • N-feruloyltyramine • Diallyl sulfide	Antidiabetic, cancer bacterial, viral, helminthic, and cell cycle arrest	Promotes apoptosis, cell cycle arrest, and inhibits proliferation
6	*Zingiber officinale*	• Phenols—gingerols, shogaol • Terpenes • Polysaccharides • Organic acid	Antiobesity, diabetic, inflammatory cancer, microbial, nausea, emetic	Promotes apoptosis, cell cycle arrest, and inhibit proliferation
7	*Calotropis procera*	• Norditerpenic esters • Cysteine protease-procerain • Alkaloids • Flavonoids • Sterol • Cardenolides • Saponins	Anticoagulant, diarrheal, ulcer, analgesic, inflammatory, antioxidant	Induces apoptosis, antiproliferative, and arrest cell cycle

(Continued)

TABLE 8.1 (Continued)

Sl. No	Name of the plant	Secondary metabolites	Biological effects	Anticancer effects
8	*Cassia fistula*	• Rhein • Triterpenes • Flavonoids • Tanins • Glycosides	Antioxidant, inflammatory, diabetic microbial fertility, and tumor	Enhances apoptosis, antiproliferative, and cell cycle arrest
9	*Baliospermum montanum*	• Alkaloids • Anthroquinones • Phenols • Saponins • Terpenoids • Coumarins • Cardiac glycosides	Antibacterial, inflammatory, fungal, and allergy	Enhances apoptosis, arrest cell cycle, antiproliferative, and antiangiogenesis
10	*Azadirachta indica*	• Terpenoids • Azadirachtin • Gedunin • Meliacarpin • Nimbin • Salannin • Vilasinin	Antibacterial, fungal, inflammatory, pyretic gastric, and hypoglycemic	Promotes apoptosis antiproliferative, and arrest cell cycle
11	*Artemisia absinthium*	• Sesquiterpene lactones • Flavonoids • Phenolic compounds • Tannins • Glucosides • Essential oil	Antiinflammatory, hepatoprotective, helminthic, depressant, and bacterial	Promotes apoptosis, arrest the cell cycle, and generation of reactive oxygen radicals
12	*Aloe barbadensis* Miller	• Polysaccharide • Phenols • Anthraquinones • Aromatic quinines	Antibacterial, tumor, arthritic, rheumatic, diabetic, and inflammatory	Promotes apoptosis shows cytotoxicity, antiangiogenesis, and antiinflammatory
13	*Apium graveolens*	• Flavonoids • Alkaloids • Steroids • Glycosides • Phenols • Furocoumarins	Cardiovascular prevention, lowering blood glucose level, blood pressure; antibacterial, fungal oxidant	Antiproliferative, promotes apoptosis and induces autophagy
14	*Amaranthus spinosus*	• Flavonoids • Alkaloids • Saponins • Tanins • Terpenoids • Cardiac glycosides • Anthroquinones • Steroids	Antimicrobial, inflammatory, malarial, androgenic, hyperlipidemic, cancer, oxidant pyretic activity	Promote apoptosis, prevents cell proliferation, and antiinflammation
15	*Asparagus racemosus*	• Phenols • Coumarin • Lignans • Monoterpenes • Carotinoids • Glycosides	Hepatoprotective, ulcer, diarrheal, diabetic, dyspepsia, bacterial, and tumor	Promotes apoptosis, prevents cell proliferation, and prevents metastasis

(Continued)

TABLE 8.1 (Continued)

Sl. No	Name of the plant	Secondary metabolites	Biological effects	Anticancer effects
		• Flavonoids • Alkaloids • Xanthines		
16	*Arachniodes exilis*	• Flavonoids • Phenols • Saponins • Phloroglucinol derivatives	Antibacterial, antiinflammatory, sedative activities, anticancer, antioxidant	Promotes apoptosis and prevents angiogenesis
17	*Astragalus membranaceus*	• Triterpene • Saponins • Flavonoids • Coumarin	Immunomodulation, antioxidative, antiinflammatory	Antiangiogenesis, inhibits proliferate
18	*Annona reticulata*	• Tannins • Flavonoids • Steroids • Alkaloids • Phenols • Glycosides	Anthelmintic, antipyretic, antiinflammatory, analgesic	Antitumor hepatoprotective, antineoplastic, and induce apoptotic
19	*Brassica nigra*	• Flavonoids • Essential oils • Alkaloids • Phenols	Antiviral, antitumor	Shows cytotoxicity, antioxidant, antiangiogenic, cell cycle arrest
20	*Carica papaya*	• Colletrotrichum gloesporiodes • Lycopine • Danielone−phytoalexin • Papain • Chymopapain	• Antioxidant • Antihypertensive • Antiinflammatory • Antifungal • Antifertility • Antitumor • Immunomodulatory activity • Antimicrobial	Hepatoprotective, inhibits the growth and antioxidant
21	*Citrus lemon*	• Phenols • Flavonoids • Tocopherol • Rosmarinic acid • Hesperetin • Proanthocyanidins	• Antiinflammatory • Antibacterial • Anticancerous	Apoptosis, cell cycle arrest, antioxidant and hepatoprotective
22	*Vitis vinifera*	• Resveratrol oligomers • Polyphenols • Flavonoids • Anthocyanins • Stilbenes • Procyanidines	• Antibacterial • Antifungal • Antiinflammative	Antiproliferative, cell cycle arrest, and antioxidant
23	*Lawsonia inermis*	• Lawsone • Phenols • Flavonoids • Saponins • Terpenoids • Quinones • Coumarins	• Antibacterial • Antifungal • Hepatoprotective • Antidiabetic • Antidiarrhea • Diuretic • Molluscidal	Apoptotic, cell cycle arrest and antioxidant

(Continued)

TABLE 8.1   (Continued)

Sl. No	Name of the plant	Secondary metabolites	Biological effects	Anticancer effects
24	*Moringa oleifera*	• Xanthones • Tannins • Proanthocyanidin • Niazirin • Niazirinin • Flavonoids • Beta-sitosterol • Kaempferol • Octacosanol	• Hyperlipidemic • Antidiabetic • Antiulcer • Prevents nephrotoxicity • Retinoprotective	Apoptosis, cell cycle arrest, antioxidant, and hepatoprotective.
25	*Sesamum indicum*	• Sesamol flavonoid • Essential oil	• Antioxidant, antihepatotoxicity • Antiinflammatory • Antiaging • Antiinflammatory • Antimutagenic	Apoptosis, cell cycle arrest, antioxidant, and antiproliferative
26	*Phoenix dactylifer*	• β-D-Glucan • Alkaloids • Flavonoids	Antioxidative	Apoptosis, antiproliferative, and cell cycle arrest

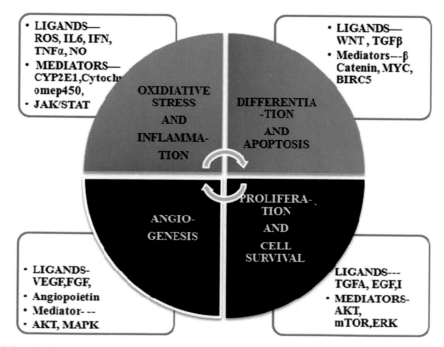

FIGURE 8.2   Mechanisms involved in origin of hepatocellular carcinoma.

Azadirachta indica

Neem is the common name given to *Azadirachta indica*, an Indian medicinal herb. Nimbin, nimbic acid, nimbidinin, and tetranortriterpenoid 13, 14-desepoxyazadirachintin-A, etc. are metabolites from its leaves. Terpenoids of *A. indica* showed downregulation of Akt mRNA, resulting in prevention of cell division, cell growth, and activation of proapoptotic factors leading to apoptosis [25]. Aqueous extract from *A. indica* showed significant reduction in tumor incidence, tumor multiplicity, enhanced survival rate, decreased level of alpha-fetoprotein, elevated the levels of glutathione-S-transferase and glutathione peroxidase when given to *N*-nitrosodiethylamine (NDEA)-induced hepatocarcinogenic male Balb/c mice [26,27]. Hydroethanolic extracts of *A. indica* showed decreased expression of VEGF/FGF2/CD166 indicating antiangiogenesis and reduction of tumor size [28].

Artemisia absinthium

Wormwood is the common name given to *Artemisia absinthium* and belongs to Asteraceae. It possesses anticancer, antibacterial, and antiinflammatory properties. Absintin, arabsin, artabin, santonin are metabolites obtained from *A. absinthium* which are sesquiterpene lactones, phenolic compounds and glucosides in nature [29,30]. Ethanol extract from *A. absinthium* exhibited apoptosis, induction of cell cycle arrest through endoplasmic reticulum stress, mitochondrial-dependent cascade, elevated levels of reactive oxygen species (ROS) and C/EBP—homologous protein (CHOP), induced the cleavage of caspase 3 and 9, poly (ADP-ribose) polymerase in H22 cells and BEL-7404 cell lines [31,32].

Astragalus membranaceus

Astragalus membranaceus, is a Chinese medicinal herb belongs to Leguminosae, used in cancer therapeutics. Flavonoids, saponins, triterpene, polysaccharides, and phytosterols are chemical components of metabolites from *A. membranaceus* [20]. Saponin extract from *A. membranaceus* showed cell cycle arrest and promoted apoptosis. Polysaccharides also promote apoptosis by downregulation of Notch1 expression, Bcl-2, Bax, and procaspases 3 and 8 genes in H22 cell lines. [33,34]. A study revealed that H22-bearing carcinoma cells in mice showed elevated levels of interleukin 2, 6, and tumor necrosis factor alpha in serum resulting in antitumor properties when treated with *Astragalus* polysaccharides [34,35]. A saponin from *A. membranaceus* showed apoptosis in HepG2 cells through ERK-independent NF-κB signaling pathway by downregulation of alpha-fetoprotein marker for HCC [36,37]. Metabolites from *A. membranaceus* were used as therapeutics for ovarian cancer, breast cancer, and cervical cancer, therefore it is a potential anticancer agent [38].

Solanum nigrum

Solanum nigrum is known as European black night shade belongs to Solanaceae. It is known that Uttroside B, a secondary metabolite obtained from leaves of *S. nigrum* acts as a potent antitumor drug exhibits apoptosis and cytotoxicity in HepG2 cell lines by lower expression of genes associated with MAPK, and mTOR signaling cascade [39]. A metabolite

12-o-tetradecanoylphorbol-13-acetate obtained from aqueous and phenolic extracts of *S. nigrum* has role in inhibition of protein kinase C and dephosphorylation of p38 and ERK was found by immunoblotting assays upon treatment of HepG2 cell lines [40]. Solasonine, solasodine, and solamargine are glycoalkaloids obtained from *S. nigrum* and they act through antitumor properties by preventing cell cycle progression at S phase and promoting apoptosis in HepG2 cell lines [41]. Together with aqueous extract of *S. nigrum*, cisplatin, doxorubicin upon treatment of Hep3B and HepJ5 cell lines revealed antitumor properties by promoting apoptosis via break down of caspase 7 protein and microtubule-associated protein 1 and 3A [42]. Methanolic extract from fruit peels of *S. melongena* proved to have antitumor and hepatoprotectant properties in HepG2 cell lines and carbon tetrachloride-induced HCC due to low expression of alpha-fetoprotein, AST, and ALT serum levels [43,44]. Solamargine, a glycoside obtained from *S. nigrum* prevents metastasis and invasiveness of tumor cells by promoting low expression of MMP-2,9 proteins in HepG2 cell lines, which upon further investigation showed therapeutic activity in HCC [45]. Solamargine treatment in SMMC-7721 cell line showed apoptosis via increased expression of caspase 3 and arrest of cell cycle at G2/M phase [46]. A polyphenolic extract from *S. nigrum* showed anticancer effects by arresting cell cycle at G2/M phase, reduced expression of CDC25 protein and elevated levels of caspases 3, 8, 9 expression in HepG2 cell lines and mouse in vivo model of HCC [47]. Astrocytes treated with methanolic extract from leaf of *S. nigrum* showed restoration of oxidative levels, therefore this acted as potent antioxidant [48]. Oral administration of *S. nigrum* extract together with hydroxyproline in thioacetamide induced liver fibrosis in mice showed low expression of transforming growth factor at transcription and translational levels and restores normal function of liver [49].

Tripterygium wilfordii

Tripterygium wilfordii belongs to celastraceae used in Chinese traditional medicine. It is known as thunder god vine. Triptolide, celastrol, diterpene triepoxide, tripfordines are the metabolites obtained from *T. wilfordii*. It is reported that triptolide and celastrol have pharmacological properties that prevent neuronal damage, cardiovascular associated diseases, act as antitumor and antidiabetic agents [50]. Celastrol, a metabolite obtained from roots of *T. wilfordii* act as antitumor agent by promoting apoptosis, cell cycle arrest at G0 phase of cell cycle, prevents tumor cell migration by limiting CXCR4, PI3K and IL-6. Phosphorylated Akt expression levels are evidenced from HepG2 and Hepa3B cell lines and Black mouse [51]. Celastrol acts as antiapoptotic agent through downregulation of Bcl-2 expression and elevated levels of Bax, cytochrome c, and caspases 3,9 indicating activation of mitochondrial-mediated apoptosis signaling cascades [52]. Celastrol given to HCC-induced rats by DENA shows decrease in alanine aminotransferase, alpha-fetoprotein, alkaline phosphatase, MDM2 (murine double minute), p53, cytochrome C, Bcl-x, Bax, and caspases expression levels indicating promotion of apoptosis [53,54]. Studies reported that celastrol elevates sorafenib-mediated antitumor effects by elevating expression of genes associated with AKT and VEGF signaling cascades in Hepa-16 cell lines [55]. Celastrol induces apoptosis by downregulation of E2F1 expression in HepG2 cell lines [56]. Triptolide, a metabolite upon treatment of SMMC-7721 cell lines showed apoptosis and promoted DNA fragmentation, resulting in growth inhibition in HCC [53].

Mangifera indica

Mangifera indica belongs to Anacardiaceae, originated from Eastern India, Burma, and Assam. Secondary metabolites from *M. indica* constitute flavonoids, phenolics, xanthones, terpenoids, gallotannins, saponins [57,58]. Mangiferin, a metabolite from *M. indica* shows low expression of LEF1, AKT1, WNT1, BID, BIRC5, CND1, MYC, CCND1, and AXIN2 genes in MHCC97L and HLF carcinoma cell lines. Study reports showed inhibition of growth, progression, and invasiveness of tumor cells in carcinoma-implanted mice treated with mangiferin [59]. *N*-Nitrosodiethylamine-induced carcinoma in mice showed reduced AST, ALP, LDH, and ALT levels with histological sections revealing normal architecture of liver treated with mangiferin [60]. Ethanolic extract from bark of *M. indica* and leaf of *Psidium guajava* upon treatment of HepG2 and CCD45-SK cell lines showed reduced cell proliferation [61]. Aqueous extract from *Mangifera*, carrot, and wheat in combination showed decreased lipid profile, malondialdehyde, and oxidative stress in carbon tetrachloride-induced HCC in albino mice [62]. Pyrogallol, a phenolic metabolite from *M. indica* shows cell cycle arrest at S phase, cytotoxicity, low expression of cyclin D, E, A, and phosphorylated AKT-PI3K genes in Hep3B and Huh 7 cell lines [63]. This provides insights of cell inhibition through PI3K/AKT pathways.

Woodfordia fruticosa Kurz

Woodfordia fruticosa is known as Fire flame bush belongs to Lythraceae. Phenols, flavonoids, tannins, octacosanol, β-sitosterol, hecogenin, betulin, oleanolic acid, ursolic acid, gallic acid, ellagic acid, norbergenin, napthaquinone, and ellagic acid are the chemical components of metabolites from *W. fruticosa* [64]. Extracts from flowers of *W. fruticosa* Kurz showed reduced alanine aminotransferase, glutathione peroxidase, and alkaline phosphate levels in diclofenac sodium-induced liver toxicity in rats, therefore it shows hepatoprotective properties [65]. Withaferin A, a metabolite obtained from *W. fruticosa* prevented growth, metastasis of tumor, causes high expression of Bax/p53, VEGF genes and inhibits intrahepatic metastasis in carcinoma cell lines [66]. Aqueous extract from *W. fruticosa* showed elevated Fas and procapases 3, 8, 9 and TNF-alpha levels which signify antiproliferative, and induction of apoptosis in carcinoma cell lines. It showed cell cycle arrest in MCF-7, HCT-116, and HepH2 cell lines [67].

Allium sativum

Allium sativum is of Indian origin and commonly known as garlic belongs to Amaryllidaceae. Garlic plays a role in inhibition of tumor growth, prevention of DNA damage, and regulation of detoxification by its available allyl derivatives [68]. Allithiamine, sallylcysteine, allicin, ajoene are sulfur derivatives from *A. sativum*. When garlic oil and cinamonic oil are pretreated with DENA, 2-acetylaminofluorene-(2-AAF)-induced HCC rats showed significant reduction in glutathione (GSH), and superoxide dismutase levels, indicating reduction in cytotoxicity and reversion of p53 mutation. *N*-feruloyltyramine, a metabolite from Laba garlic plays a role in inhibition of tumor progression with cytotoxic and antioxidative properties in HepG2 and L02 cell lines [69]. Studies on aflatoxin B1 pretreated

HepG2 cell lines showed less genotoxicity when treated with organosulfur derivatives of *A. sativum* [70]. Diallyl sulfide derivatives from garlic when treated to J5 liver tumor cell lines showed cell cycle arrest at G2/M phase, affected cell viability, caused low and elevated expression of Cdk7 and Cyclin B1, respectively [71]. Crude extract from garlic showed inhibition of cell cycle progression, and elevated expression of caspases indicating apoptosis [72]. *N*-trans-feruloyloctopamine, a metabolite obtained from garlic skin shows downregulation of phosphorylation of Akt and p38 MAPK, and upregulation of E-cadherin, resulting in inhibition of cell proliferation and invasion of cells, following MAPK and PI3K/Akt cascades [73]. Quantitative studies showed upregulation of Bax and FasL mRNA transcripts when nude mice were treated with allicin [74].

Zingiber officinale

Ginger is the common name of *Zingiber officinale*. Shogaol, 6-gingerol, 8-gingerol, Quercetin, zingerone, zingiberene, beta-sesquiphellandrene are active metabolites from *Z. officinale*. Gingerol and Paradol from root extract of ginger showed cytotoxicity and inactivation of NF-κB expression in HepG2 and MCF-7 cell lines [75]. Methanolic leaf extract from *Z. officinale* played a role in inhibition of cell proliferation, activation of caspase 3, resulting in promotion of apoptosis and cell cycle arrest at S and G2/M phase, inhibition of free radical generation through superoxide dismutase and glutathione peroxidase activity in HepG2 cell lines [76,77]. Upregulation of p53 expression and activating proapoptotic factors resulting in apoptosis are observed in nude mouse treated with juice from ginger [78,79].

Calotropis procera

Calotropis procera is a medicinal plant from India, commonly termed as Arka. Cardenolides, calotropin, frugoside, calotropagenin, calotoxin, uscharin, amyrin, rutin, polyphenols, cyaindin-3-rhamnoglucoside, riterpene calotropenyl acetate, benzolisoleneolone are metabolites which are glycosides and flavonoids in nature [80]. Latex extract from *C. procera* shows decreased vascular endothelial growth factor in serum, cytotoxicity is noticed upon treatment of -myc transgenic mouse and Huh7, and COS-1 cell lines [81]. Cardenolide, a metabolic extract of leaf from *C. procera* showed cytotoxicity and death of cells in A549, HCT-116, and HepG2 cell lines [82]. Root extract from *C. procera* showed elevated levels of p53 gene and alteration of Bax, Bcl-2 genes resulting in induction of apoptosis in HepG2 and MCF-7 cell lines [83].

Cassia fistula

Golden shower is the name given to *Cassia fistula* from South Asia. Lupeol, beta-sitosterol, oleic, stearic acid, rhein, chrysophanol, oxyanthraquinones, chrysophanol, galactomannan, sennosides A and B are the metabolites from *C. fistula* and contribute to its role in medicinal therapeutics [84,85]. Cassine, spectaline are alkaloids from *C. fistula* and upon treatment of HepG2 cell lines showed low expression of cyclin D1 resulting in arrest of cell cycle at G1/S phase, and inhibition of ERK expression levels [86]. Amentoflavione, a biflavonoid metabolite obtained from leaves of *C. fistula*, in HepG2 cell lines showed cytotoxicity from spectroscopic studies [87]. Ethanolic extract from leaf of *C. fistula* showed low expression of liver disease-associated markers AST, ALT, ALP, LDH, and bilirubin. Its treatment to DENA-induced carcinoma Wistar rats elicits hepatoprotection [88]. Oil from *C. fistula* has sulfurous acid and cyclohexyl-methyl octadecyl ester, upon treatment of HepG2 cell lines, showed inhibition of cell growth [89]. Rhein, a metabolite treated to MCF-7 and HepG2 cell lines showed elevated expression of p53, Casp-3 and -9 genes and decreased expression of Bcl-2 levels, therefore results in apoptosis [90].

Aloe barbadensis Miller

A. barbadensis Miller is known as Aloe Vera. Anthraquinones, aromatic quinines, polysaccharides, malolyl glucans, emodin, and chrysophanol are metabolites from *A. barbadensis* Miller which are anthraquinone derivatives [91]. Anthracene and anthraquinone derivatives have antiproliferative effects. Extract from Aloe Vera and *Calligonum comosum* induced apoptosis through upregulation of p53 and downregulation of Bcl-2 gene expression in Hep-2 cells [92,93].

Apium graveolens

Apium graveolens is a medicinal herb, native to Europe. Mass spectroscopic studies revealed furocoumarins, steroids, alkaloids, glycosides are chemical nature of metabolites from *A. graveolens* [94]. The seed oil showed decreased proliferative cell nuclear antigen expression, AST, ALT, and γ-GGT serum levels and elevated caspase 3, upon treatment of diethyl nitrosamine-induced HCC in rats [95]. Sedanolide, a metabolite from seed oil showed downregulation of phosphoinositide 3-kinase, mTOR, and Akt levels, and upregulation of Beclin-1, LC3-II expression, inducing autophagy by regulating PI3K, p53, and NF-κB signaling cascades in J5 cell lines [96]. Methanolic extract from seeds of *A. graveolens* shows hepatoprotective activity when given to di-(2-ethylhexyl) phthalate (DEHP)-induced mice [97].

Amaranthus spinosus

Amaranthus spinosus, a medicinal herb belongs to Amaranthaceae. Flavonoids, alkaloids, saponins, tanins, terpenoids, cardiac glycosides, anthroquinones, steroids are the chemical nature of metabolites from *A. spinosus*. Quercetins, Kaempferol, isoamaranthine, hydroxycinnamates, amaranthine are metabolites from *A. spinosus* [98]. Fatty acid (14E, 18E, 22E, 26E) together with methyl nonacosa 14, 18, 22, 26 tetraenoate from *A. spinosus* shows antitumor, antiproliferative, decreased expression of cyclin B1, Bcl-2 genes and elevated levels of Bcl-2 genes and cell cycle arrest at G2/M phase in HepG2 cell lines. Ethanolic extract from leaf of *A. spinosus* showed low viable count and prolonged the life of tumor-treated

Swiss albino mice [58]. Methanolic extract from leaf of *A. spinosus* showed reduction in size of tumor and decreased cell count, and viability in HepG2 cells [99].

Asparagus racemosus

Asparagus racemosus is commonly known as Shatavari, a medicinal plant. Asparanin A, Asparanin B, Asparanin C, Asparanin G, Asparanin H, Sarsasapogenin, diosgenin, racemofuran are metabolites from *A. racemosus*. It acts as antiulcer, antidiarrheal, antidiabetic, antidyspepsia, antibacterial, and has antitumor effects [100]. Polysaccharides from *Asparagus* when treated to SK-Hep1 and Hep3B cell lines showed apoptosis, downregulation of phosphorylated AKT, mTOR, and ERK expression levels and suppressed the migration, invasion, and angiogenesis by HIF-1 alpha/VEGF signaling pathway [101]. The aqueous extract of *A. racemosus* and cyclophosphamide together act as adjuvant in BALB/c mice and showed tumor suppressive activity [102]. Ursane, a glycoside metabolite from roots of *A. racemosus*, together with oleanane, lupine upon treatment of HepG2 cell lines showed antitumor effects [102,103].

Arachniodes exilis

Arachniodes exilis belongs to Dryopteridaceae family and has potential anticancer properties. Phenols, flavonoids, and phloroglucinols are chemical nature of metabolites from *A. exilis*. The role of metabolites includes cytotoxicity. Flavonoids from *A. exilis* cause inhibition of tumor growth, induction of apoptosis, elevated levels of reactive oxygen radicals and activation of caspases 3 and 9 in HepG2 cell lines through MAPK pathway [78]. Flavonoids from *A. exilis* showed inhibition of tumor and angiogenesis of tumor cells by expression of proapoptotic proteins Bax and caspase 3 while HIF-1α and VEGF were suppressed [104]. Ethanolic extract from *A. exilis* acts as hepatoprotective due its antioxidative properties in liver [105].

Annona reticulata

Bullock's heart is the common given name for *Annona reticulata*. Phenols, flavonoids, glycosides, tannins, dopamine, salsolinol, anonaine, and germacrene are chemical nature of metabolites which have anticancer, antiulcer, and antihelminthic potential, obtained from *A. reticulata* [106]. Aqueous extract from dried peel of *A. reticulata* together with SnO_2 nano particles treated to HepG2 cell lines resulted in restoration of normal morphology of cells and caused inhibition of cell proliferation [107]. Alkaloid extract from *A. reticulata* treated to HCC-induced mice showed decreased biochemical markers including glutamyl oxaloacetate transaminase, alkaline phosphatase, aid phosphatase and showed hepatoprotective effect [99]. Phenolic compounds from *Annona* and *Catunaregam nilotica* upon treatment of A549, Pc-3, MCF-7, and HepG2 cell lines showed antioxidant properties [108]. Reports showed that leaves of *Annona* show antioxidant, antibacterial and anticancer, cytological effects on various cancerous cells [109].

Brassica nigra

Brassica nigra is known as Black Mustard. Kaempferol, a flavonoid metabolite from *B. nigra* when treated to HepG2, HeLa, HCT, MCF-7, and Hep-2 cell lines showed cytotoxicity [110]. Isorhamnetin 3-*O*-β-D-glucopyranoside, a metabolite present in methanolic extract from leaf of *B. nigra* treated to cell lines showed increase in metabolizing enzymes and microsomal activity [68]. Hydromethanolic extract from seed of *B. nigra* treated to acetaminophen-induced toxicity in HepG2 cell line, showed prevention of ROS, thereby acting as antihepatotoxic [111]. Oleanolic acid, ursolic acid, maslinic acid are triterpenic acids from *B. nigra* and showed antiangiogenic properties by downregulation of hypoxia-inducible factor-1R, VEGF, IL-8, ROS, and NO expression levels in Hep3B, Huh7, HA22T cell lines [112].

Citrus limon

Citrus limon belongs to Rutaceae. Ethanolic extract from leaves of lemon upon treatment of HepG2, KB, and TSGH.9201 cell lines showed antioxidant, antiproliferative, cycloxygenase-2 inhibitory activities. Trolox, phenols, phenolic acids, flavonoids, rosmarinic acid are phytochemical metabolites from *C. limon* [113]. *Citrus* induces cytotoxicity in HepG2 and A549 human lung adenocarcinoma cell lines in time dependent manner and with increase in maturity stages of leaf. It arrests the cell cycle at G1 phase, causes DNA fragmentation, and finally cell death, implicating apoptosis and increased expression level of nitric oxide [114]. Diosmetin, a flavonoid obtained from *C. limon* treatment of HepG2 cell lines helped in evaluating the expression of p53 gene, resulting in apoptosis-dependent pathway and downregulation of NF-κB, and Notch3, thereby enhancing cell death [115]. Hesperidin obtained from citrus fruits, upon treatment of HepG2 cell lines showed induction of apoptosis by procaspases 3 and upregulation of Bax protein expression, and reduction of mitochondrial membrane potential, which ultimately showed inhibitory effects on CAMKIV (calcium/calmodulin-dependent protein kinase IV) [116]. Mutated citrus fruits irradiated by gamma irradiation show apoptosis and inhibit the growth of HepG2, HCT-116, MCF-7, and HeLa cell lines and is confirmed by trypan blue exclusion assay [117]. Eriocitrin a flavonoid isolated from lemon acts as antioxidant agent, inhibits the cell growth by arresting cell cycle at S phase and increased expression of p53, cyclin A, cyclin D3, and CDK6 are seen in HCC cell lines [118].

Vitis vinifera

Resveratrol, a metabolite from *Vitis vinifera* when treated to HepG2 cell lines showed cytotoxicity, cell cycle arrest at G2/M phase, generation of ROS, elevated procapases 3 and Bax/Bcl-2 protein ratios signifying induction of apoptosis [119]. Stilbenes from callus culture of *V. vinifera* upon treatment of HepG2 and MRC 5 human fibroblast cell lines showed antiproliferative activity and cell cycle arrest, thereby acting as potent anticancer agent [120,121]. In Brazil, grape pomace extract containing phenols treated to HepG2 cell lines shows antioxidant activity, cytotoxicity, increased mitochondrial respiration, and decreased glycolytic metabolism and cells die of necrosis, these are not toxic to human noncancer fibroblast cell lines [122]. Pterostilbene, a natural analog of resveratrol prevents cell growth in HCC cells by stress and autophagy-dependent manner in endoplasmic reticulum through factor elF2 alpha. It acts as potent agent of dephosphorylation of elF2 alpha thereby causing cell death [123]. A stilbene obtained from *V. vinifera* prevented cell growth by arresting cell cycle at G1 and G2/M phase of cell cycle, and decreased ROS in HCC cells [124].

Lawsonia inermis

Lawsonia inermis is commonly known as henna. It has antifungal, antibacterial, hepatoprotective activities. In male Wistar rats treated with 2-acetylaminofluorene (2-AAF), damage is induced in hepatic cells, which can be detected by elevated levels of SGOT, ALP, and SGPT. When these rats are fed with But-L l, a metabolite from *L. inermis*, they demonstrate normal levels of markers in liver and restoration of normal architecture of liver [125]. Lawsone isolated from *L. inermis* extract treated to A549, DLD1, HepG2 cell lines, which signifies apoptosis by measuring the ROS-generated and decreased mitochondria membrane potential [126]. Daltons lymphoma ascites bearing mice when given ethanolic root extract showed increased WBC, platelets, and decreased RBC, monocytes, hemoglobin, and histopathological studies showed normal liver and kidney sections [127]. Cytotoxic effect of two plants of henna and *Strobilanthes crispus* on Caco-2, HepG2, MCF-7 cell lines showed cytotoxicity by measuring the c-myc expression pattern and downregulation of c-myc expression [128]. Methanolic and ethyl acetate extract of leaf has its apoptosis and antioxidant properties, and cell cycle arrest at G0/G1 in HepG2 cell lines [129].

Moringa oleifera

Moringa oleifera is of Indian origin, commonly known as drum stick. Quercetin-3—0-glucoside, sitosterol, lutein, and 4-(β-D-glucopyranosyl-1 → 4-α-L-rhamnopyranosyloxy)-benzyl isothiocyanate are metabolites obtained from crude extracts of *M. oleifera*, upon treatment of HCC (HepG2), Caco-2, HEK293 cell lines show cytotoxicity and induced apoptosis [130]. Vicenin-2, a flavonoid metabolite obtained from *Ocimum sanctum* and *M. oleifera* treated to HepG2, C3A, and SNU-387 cell lines and hepatocellular nude mice showed downregulation of STAT-3 expression along with JAK1, JAK2, and AKT gene expression. It is also observed that increased caspase 3 and decreased expression of VEGF, Bcl-2, Bclxl, suggest that vicenin-2 act as a STAT-3 inhibitor [131]. Naphthalene, a metabolic compound obtained from *M. oleifera* oil has role in free radical and hydrogen peroxide scavenging, antioxidant properties. Oil from seeds of *M. oleifera* treated to MCF-7, HCT-116, HepG2, Hep-2 cell lines showed antioxidant properties [132]. Seed oil from *M. oleifera* in free MO and nano formulations induced apoptosis mediated by mitochondria in cell lines including HepG2 resulting in a potent anticancer target activity [133]. The crude aqueous extract of *M. oleifera* resulted in increased lipid peroxidation, DNA damage, low expression of c-myc, Bcl-2, and Hsp-70 protein expression with increase in Bax, PARP-1 cleavage showed apoptosis in HepG2 cell lines [134].

Sesamum indicum

Benne is common name for *Sesamum indicum*, and is native to Africa and India. Sesamol is a metabolite from seed whose phenolic extract treated to cell lines and animal models showed its role in prevention of oxidative stress through its ability for free radical scavenging and lipid peroxidation, regulating apoptosis and causing the arrest of the cell cycle. A study reports that sesamol showed antiproliferative effects by downregulating mitochondrial autophagy, Bcl-2 gene expression along with downregulation of p38, PARP, p53, Bax, AKT, Bcl-x, LOX-1, TGF-Beta1, COX-2, and upregulation of IL-10, Nrf-2 genes, signifying apoptosis and cell cycle arrest in cell lines and animal models [135–137].

Phoenix dactylifer

Phoenix dactylifer is commonly known as dates. Ethanolic extract of Ajwa date pulp when treated to HepG2 cell lines showed presence of β-D-Glucan and showed apoptosis under phase contrast microscopy by suppressing CHEK2, ATM, TP53 genes, and MTT assay showed inhibition of growth in time and dosage-dependent manner in HepG2 cell lines, decreased mitochondrial membrane potential, and increased reactive oxygen free radicals. It showed elevation of S and G2/M phase of cell cycle [138]. In DENA-induced liver cancer in rats, when treated with aqueous extract of Ajwa dates showed reversion to normal liver architecture in tissue sections of liver [139].

Carica papaya

Carica papaya is one of the cultivated fruits in the tropical regions of the world and is considered as power house of nutrients. It has antioxidant, antitumor, antimicrobial, antifertility, antiamoebic activity, antifungal activity [140]. Dry extracts of seed from ripe and unripe fruit show its antioxidant properties by reducing the stress levels in human preadipocytes (SW872) and HCC cells (HepG2) cell lines by inducing hydrogen peroxide [141]. A study reports that diclofenac sodium-induced liver damage in rats when treated with aqueous extract of dry *Carica papaya* leaf and cocoa mistletoes shows increased aspartate amino transaminase, alanine aminotransferase, alkaline phosphatase, and ROS production which indicates normal functioning of the liver [142]. Ethanol extract of flowers and petioles of male *Carica papaya* constitutes stigmast-4-ene-3-one, sitosterol, and palmitic acid, and inhibited growth in MCF-7, HepG2, Hela, NCl-H460 cell lines [143]. Hepatotoxicity induced with CCl4 in rats showed increased levels of serum alkaline phosphatase, aspartate aminotransferase, and bilirubin when treated with hydroethanol extract of *A. sativum* and *C. papaya* brings the serum marker levels to normal [144].

Conclusion

HCC is recognized as one of the most aggressive and fatal malignancies worldwide. HCC is primarily caused due to chronic infections such as hepatitis B and hepatitis

C viruses, excessive alcohol consumption, fatty liver disease, birth defects, obesity, and exposure to toxic contaminants such as aflatoxin B1. Current treatment options for HCC management include surgically removing part of the liver containing the tumor, transplantation, radiation, liver ablation, and the use of anticancer drugs. Diagnosing the disease at an early stage is the key to successful management of HCC as the 5-year survival is approximately 31% if diagnosed at initial stage of tumor development. However, the 5-year survival is below 11% if the tumor is detected at a later stage. There is a desperate need to investigate innovative approaches for early tumor detection that can possibly lead to improved HCC management. In this review, the effect of herbal compounds and their role against HCC is discussed with a major emphasis on the fundamental conception of phytochemicals. The aim of this review is to provide a better understanding in the prevention and treatment of HCC by discussing current research updates and the role of available metabolites and herbs as targeted treatment option against HCC (Table 8.1).

Conflict of interest

The authors declare no conflict of interest.

References

[1] Michalopoulos GK. Liver regeneration. J Cell Physiol 2007;213:286—300.
[2] Böhm F, Köhler UA, Speicher T, Werner S. Regulation of liver regeneration by growth factors and cytokines. EMBO Mol Med 2010;2:294—305.
[3] Sung H, Ferlay J, Siegel RL, Laversanne M, Soerjomataram I, Jemal A, et al. Global cancer statistics 2020: GLOBOCAN estimates of incidence and mortality worldwide for 36 cancers in 185 countries. CA Cancer J Clin 2021;71:209—49.
[4] VoPham T. Environmental risk factors for liver cancer and nonalcoholic fatty liver disease. Curr Epidemiol Rep 2019;6:50—66.
[5] Ananthakrishnan A, Gogineni V, Saeian K. Epidemiology of primary and secondary liver cancers. Semin Intervent Radiol 2006;23(1):47—63.
[6] Sia D, Villanueva A, Friedman SL, Llovet JM. Liver cancer cell of origin, molecular class, and effects on patient prognosis. Gastroenterology 2017;152:745—61.
[7] Martin J, Dufour J-F. Tumor suppressor and hepatocellular carcinoma. World J Gastroenterol 2008;14:1720.
[8] Ohkoshi S, Yano M, Matsuda Y. Oncogenic role of p21 in hepatocarcinogenesis suggests a new treatment strategy. World J Gastroenterol 2015;21:12150.
[9] Liu F, Wei YG, Luo LM, Wang WT, Yan LN, Wen TF, et al. Genetic variants of p21 and p27 and hepatocellular cancer risk in a Chinese Han population: a case-control study. Int J Cancer 2013;132:2056—64.
[10] Zang J-J, Xie F, Xu J-F, Qin Y-Y, Shen R-X, Yang J-M, et al. P16 gene hypermethylation and hepatocellular carcinoma: a systematic review and meta-analysis. World J Gastroenterol 2011;17:3043.
[11] Matsuda Y. Molecular mechanism underlying the functional loss of cyclindependent kinase inhibitors p16 and p27 in hepatocellular carcinoma. World J Gastroenterol 2008;14:1734.
[12] Satoh S, Daigo Y, Furukawa Y, Kato T, Miwa N, Nishiwaki T, et al. AXIN1 mutations in hepatocellular carcinomas, and growth suppression in cancer cells by virus-mediated transfer of AXIN1. Nat Genet 2000;24:245—50.
[13] Hankey W, Frankel WL, Groden J. Functions of the APC tumor suppressor protein dependent and independent of canonical WNT signaling: implications for therapeutic targeting. Cancer Metastasis Rev 2018;37:159—72.
[14] Csepregi A, Röcken C, Hoffmann J, Gu P, Saliger S, Müller O, et al. APC promoter methylation and protein expression in hepatocellular carcinoma. J Cancer Res Clin Oncol 2008;134:579—89.

[15] Ou J-M, Lian W-S, Qiu M-K, Dai Y-X, Dong Q, Shen J, et al. Knockdown of IGF2R suppresses proliferation and induces apoptosis in hemangioma cells in vitro and in vivo. Int J Oncol 2014;45:1241−9.

[16] Oka Y, Waterland RA, Killian JK, Nolan CM, Jang HS, Tohara K, et al. M6P/IGF2R tumor suppressor gene mutated in hepatocellular carcinomas in Japan. Hepatology 2002;35:1153−63.

[17] Yakicier M, Irmak A, Romano A, Kew M, Ozturk M. Smad2 and Smad4 gene mutations in hepatocellular carcinoma. Oncogene 1999;18:4879−83.

[18] Schulze K, Nault J-C, Villanueva A. Genetic profiling of hepatocellular carcinoma using next-generation sequencing. J Hepatol 2016;65:1031−42.

[19] Zender L, Villanueva A, Tovar V, Sia D, Chiang DY, Llovet JM. Cancer gene discovery in hepatocellular carcinoma. J Hepatol 2010;52:921−9.

[20] Auyeung KK, Han Q-B, Ko JK. Astragalus membranaceus: a review of its protection against inflammation and gastrointestinal cancers. Am J Chin Med 2016;44:1−22.

[21] Johnson M, Wesely E, Hussain MZ, Selvan N. In vivo and in vitro phytochemical and antibacterial efficacy of *Baliospermum montanum* (Willd.) Muell. Arg. Asian Pac J Tropical Med 2010;3:894−7.

[22] Sushma B, Raveesha H. Effect of elicitors treated callus of *Baliospermum montanum* (Willd.) Muell. Arg. on cell cycle arrest and apoptosis in HEP-2 and PC-3 cells. Res J Pharm Technol 2020;13:5443−50.

[23] Pipatrattanaseree W, Itharat A, Mukkasombut N, Saesiw U. Potential in vitro anti-allergic, anti-inflammatory and cytotoxic activities of ethanolic extract of *Baliospermum montanum* root, its major components and a validated HPLC method. BMC Complement Altern Med 2019;19:1−12.

[24] Kaewnoonual N, Itharat A, Pongsawat S, Nilbu-Nga C, Kerdput V, Pradidarcheep W. Anti-angiogenic and anti-proliferative effects of Benja-ummarit extract in rats with hepatocellular carcinoma. Biomed Rep 2020;12:109−20.

[25] Akinloye OA, Akinloye DI, Lawal MA, Shittu MT, Metibemu DS. Terpenoids from *Azadirachta indica* are potent inhibitors of Akt: validation of the anticancer potentials in hepatocellular carcinoma in male Wistar rats. J Food Biochem 2021;45:e13559.

[26] Bharati S, Rishi P, Koul A. *Azadirachta indica* exhibits chemopreventive action against hepatic cancer: studies on associated histopathological and ultrastructural changes. Microsc Res Tech 2012;75:586−95.

[27] He Z, Jiang C, Zhang J, Yin Z, Yin Z, Zhu Y, et al. Neem tree (*Azadirachta indica*) extract specifically suppresses the growth of tumors in H22-bearing Kunming mice. Z Naturforschung C 2016;71:201−8.

[28] Raissa R, Riawan W, Safitri A, Beltran MAG, Aulanni'am Aa. Anti-cancer effects of *Azadirachta indica* in diethylnitrosamine-induced hepatocellular carcinoma in Wistar rats. IJITEE 2020;9:304−7.

[29] Hashimi A, Siraj MB, Ahmed Y, Siddiqui MA, Jahangir U. One for all-*Artemisia absinthium* (Afsanteen). CELLMED 2019;9:5.1−9.

[30] Kumar S, Kumari R. Artemisia: a medicinally important genus. J Complement Med Alt Healthc 2018;7.

[31] Wei X, Xia L, Ziyayiding D, Chen Q, Liu R, Xu X, et al. The extracts of *Artemisia absinthium* L. suppress the growth of hepatocellular carcinoma cells through induction of apoptosis via endoplasmic reticulum stress and mitochondrial-dependent pathway. Molecules 2019;24:913.

[32] Batiha GE-S, Olatunde A, El-Mleeh A, Hetta HF, Al-Rejaie S, Alghamdi S, et al. Bioactive compounds, pharmacological actions, and pharmacokinetics of wormwood (*Artemisia absinthium*). Antibiotics 2020;9:353.

[33] Huang W-H, Liao W-R, Sun R-X. Astragalus polysaccharide induces the apoptosis of human hepatocellular carcinoma cells by decreasing the expression of Notch1. Int J Mol Med 2016;38:551−7.

[34] Yejin W, Yanqun W. Inhibition of *Astragalus membranaceus* polysaccharides against liver cancer cell HepG2. African J Microbiology Res 2010;4:2181−3.

[35] Lai X, Xia W, Wei J, Ding X. Therapeutic effect of Astragalus polysaccharides on hepatocellular carcinoma H22-bearing mice. Dose Response 2017;15 1559325816685182.

[36] Auyeung KK-W, Law P-C, Ko JK-S. *Astragalus saponins* induce apoptosis via an ERK-independent NF-κB signaling pathway in the human hepatocellular HepG2 cell line. Int J Mol Med 2009;23:189−96.

[37] Zang W, Bian H, Huang X, Yin G, Zhang C, Han L, et al. Traditional Chinese medicine (TCM) *Astragalus membranaceus* and *Curcuma wenyujin* promote vascular normalization in tumor-derived endothelial cells of human hepatocellular carcinoma. Anticancer Res 2019;39:2739−47.

[38] Miraj S, Kiani S. Astragalus membranaceus: a review study of its anti-carcinoma activities. Der Pharmacia Lett 2016;8:59−65.

[39] Nath LR, Gorantla JN, Thulasidasan AKT, Vijayakurup V, Shah S, Anwer S, et al. Evaluation of uttroside B, a saponin from *Solanum nigrum* Linn, as a promising chemotherapeutic agent against hepatocellular carcinoma. Sci Rep 2016;6:1−13.

[40] Yang M-Y, Hsu L-S, Peng C-H, Shi Y-S, Wu C-H, Wang C-J. Polyphenol-rich extracts from *Solanum nigrum* attenuated PKC α-mediated migration and invasion of hepatocellular carcinoma cells. J Agric Food Chem 2010;58:5806–14.

[41] Fekry MI, Ezzat SM, Salama MM, Alshehri OY, Al-Abd AM. Bioactive glycoalkaloides isolated from *Solanum melongena* fruit peels with potential anticancer properties against hepatocellular carcinoma cells. Sci Rep 2019;9:1–11.

[42] Wang C-K, Lin Y-F, Tai C-J, Wang C-W, Chang Y-J, Choong C-Y, et al. Integrated treatment of aqueous extract of *Solanum nigrum*-potentiated cisplatin-and doxorubicin-induced cytotoxicity in human hepatocellular carcinoma cells. Evid Based Complement Alternat Med 2015;(2015).

[43] Salama M, Ezzat SM. In vitro and in vivo anticancer activity of the fruit peels of *Solanum melongena* L. against hepatocellular carcinoma. J Carcinogen Mutagen 2013;4.

[44] Lin H-M, Tseng H-C, Wang C-J, Lin J-J, Lo C-W, Chou F-P. Hepatoprotective effects of *Solanum nigrum* Linn extract against CCl4-iduced oxidative damage in rats. Chem Biol Interact 2008;171:283–93.

[45] Sani IK, Marashi SH, Kalalinia F. Solamargine inhibits migration and invasion of human hepatocellular carcinoma cells through down-regulation of matrix metalloproteinases 2 and 9 expression and activity. Toxicol Vitro 2015;29:893–900.

[46] Ding X, Zhu F-S, Li M, Gao S-G. Induction of apoptosis in human hepatoma SMMC-7721 cells by solamargine from *Solanum nigrum* L. J Ethnopharmacol 2012;139:599–604.

[47] Wang HC, Chung PJ, Wu CH, Lan KP, Yang MY, Wang CJ. *Solanum nigrum* L. polyphenolic extract inhibits hepatocarcinoma cell growth by inducing G2/M phase arrest and apoptosis. J Sci Food Agric 2011;91:178–85.

[48] Campisi A, Acquaviva R, Raciti G, Duro A, Rizzo M, Santagati NA. Antioxidant activities of *Solanum nigrum* L. leaf extracts determined in in vitro cellular models. Foods 2019;8:63.

[49] Hsieh C-C, Fang H-L, Lina W-C. Inhibitory effect of *Solanum nigrum* on thioacetamide-induced liver fibrosis in mice. J Ethnopharmacol 2008;119:117–21.

[50] Chen S-R, Dai Y, Zhao J, Lin L, Wang Y, Wang Y. A mechanistic overview of triptolide and celastrol, natural products from *Tripterygium wilfordii* Hook F. Front Pharmacol 2018;9:104.

[51] Kun-Ming C, Chih-Hsien C, Chen-Fang L, Ting-Jung W, Hong-Shiue C, Wei-Chen L. Potential anticancer effect of celastrol on hepatocellular carcinoma by suppressing CXCR4-related signal and impeding tumor growth in vivo. Arch Med Res 2020;51:297–302.

[52] Li P-P, He W, Yuan P-F, Song S-S, Lu J-T, Wei W. Celastrol induces mitochondria-mediated apoptosis in hepatocellular carcinoma Bel-7402 cells. Am J Chin Med 2015;43:137–48.

[53] Chan EW-C, Cheng SC-S, Sin FW-Y, Xie Y. Triptolide induced cytotoxic effects on human promyelocytic leukemia, T cell lymphoma and human hepatocellular carcinoma cell lines. Toxicol Lett 2001;122:81–7.

[54] Chang W, He W, Li P-P, Song S-S, Yuan P-F, Lu J-T, et al. Protective effects of Celastrol on diethylnitrosamine-induced hepatocellular carcinoma in rats and its mechanisms. Eur J Pharmacol 2016;784:173–80.

[55] Zhang R, Chen Z, Wu S-S, Xu J, Kong L-C, Wei P. Celastrol enhances the anti-liver cancer activity of sorafenib. Med Sci Monit 2019;25:4068.

[56] Ma L, Peng L, Fang S, He B, Liu Z. Celastrol downregulates E2F1 to induce growth inhibitory effects in hepatocellular carcinoma HepG2 cells. Oncol Rep 2017;38:2951–8.

[57] Jhaumeer Laulloo S, Bhowon M, Soyfoo S, Chua L. Nutritional and biological evaluation of leaves of Mangifera indica from Mauritius. J Chem 2018;(2018).

[58] Maldonado-Celis ME, Yahia EM, Bedoya R, Landázuri P, Loango N, Aguillón J, et al. Ospina, chemical composition of mango (*Mangifera indica* L.) fruit: nutritional and phytochemical compounds. Front Plant Sci 2019;10:1073.

[59] Tan H-Y, Wang N, Li S, Hong M, Guo W, Man K, et al. Repression of WT1-mediated LEF1 transcription by mangiferin governs β-catenin-independent Wnt signalling inactivation in hepatocellular carcinoma. Cell Physiol Biochem 2018;47:1819–34.

[60] Hong D, Henary H, Falchook G, Naing A, Fu S, Moulder S, et al. First-in-human study of pbi-05204, an oleander-derived inhibitor of akt, fgf-2, nf-κβ and p70s6k, in patients with advanced solid tumors. Invest New Drugs 2014;32:1204–12.

[61] Kemegne GA, Bettache N, Nyegue MA, Etoa F-X, Menut C. Cytotoxic activities of *Psidium guajava* and *Mangifera indica* plant extracts on human healthy skin fibroblasts and human hepatocellular carcinoma. Issues Biol Sci Pharm Res 2020;8:58–64.

[62] Ebeid H, Gibriel AA, Al-Sayed H, Elbehairy S, Motawe E. Hepatoprotective and antioxidant effects of wheat, carrot, and mango as nutraceutical agents against CCl4-induced hepatocellular toxicity. J Am Coll Nutr 2015;34:228–31.

[63] Ahn H, Im E, Lee DY, Lee H-J, Jung JH, Kim S-H. Antitumor effect of Pyrogallol via miR-134 mediated S phase arrest and inhibition of PI3K/AKT/Skp2/cMyc signaling in hepatocellular carcinoma. Int J Mol Sci 2019;20:3985.

[64] Kumar D, Sharma M, Sorout A, Saroha K, Verma S. *Woodfordia fruticosa* Kurz.: a review on its botany, chemistry and biological activities. J Pharmacogn Phytochem 2016;5:293.

[65] Baravalia Y, Vaghasiya Y, Chanda S. Hepatoprotective effect of Woodfordia fruticosa Kurz flowers on diclofenac sodium induced liver toxicity in rats. Asian Pac J Trop Med 2011;4:342−6.

[66] Wang Y-X, Ding W-B, Dong C-W. Withaferin A suppresses liver tumor growth in a nude mouse model by downregulation of cell signaling pathway leading to invasion and angiogenesis. Trop J Pharm Res 2015;14:1005−11.

[67] Ahmed W, Mofed D, Zekri A-R, El-Sayed N, Rahouma M, Sabet S. Antioxidant activity and apoptotic induction as mechanisms of action of *Withania somnifera* (Ashwagandha) against a hepatocellular carcinoma cell line. J Int Med Res 2018;46:1358−69.

[68] Omar S, Al-Wabel N. Organosulfur compounds and possible mechanism of garlic in cancer. Saudi Pharm J 2010;18:51−8.

[69] Gao X, Wang C, Chen Z, Chen Y, Santhanam RK, Xue Z, et al. Effects of N-trans-feruloyltyramine isolated from laba garlic on antioxidant, cytotoxic activities and H_2O_2-induced oxidative damage in HepG2 and L02 cells. Food Chem Toxicol 2019;130:130−41.

[70] Belloir C, Singh V, Daurat C, Siess MH, Le A-M. Bon, protective effects of garlic sulfur compounds against DNA damage induced by direct-and indirect-acting genotoxic agents in HepG2 cells. Food Chem Toxicol 2006;44:827−34.

[71] Wu C-C, Chung J-G, Tsai S-J, Yang J, Sheen L. Differential effects of allyl sulfides from garlic essential oil on cell cycle regulation in human liver tumor cells. Food Chem Toxicol 2004;42:1937−47.

[72] Bagul M, Kakumanu S, Wilson TA. Crude garlic extract inhibits cell proliferation and induces cell cycle arrest and apoptosis of cancer cells in vitro. J Med Food 2015;18:731−7.

[73] Bai Z-T, Wu Z-R, Xi L-L, Li X, Chen P, Wang F-Q, et al. Inhibition of invasion by N-trans-feruloyloctopamine via AKT, p38MAPK and EMT related signals in hepatocellular carcinoma cells. Bioorg Med Chem Lett 2017;27:989−93.

[74] Zhang Z-m, Zhong N, Gao H-q, Zhang S-z, Yuan W, Hua X, et al. Inducing apoptosis and upregulation of Bax and Fas ligand expression by allicin in hepatocellular carcinoma in Balb/c nude mice. Chin Med J 2006;119:422−6.

[75] El-Sayeh NE, Elsaadany S, Elmassry R, Hefnawy H. Cytotoxic effect of ginger root (*Zingiber officinale*) on liver and breast cancer. Zagazig J Agric Res 2018;45:995−1001.

[76] Nair SV, Hettihewa M, Rupasinghe H. Apoptotic and inhibitory effects on cell proliferation of hepatocellular carcinoma HepG2 cells by methanol leaf extract of *Costus speciosus*. BioMed Res Int 2014;(2014).

[77] Ahmad N, Sulaiman S, Mukti NA, Murad NA, Abd Hamid NA, Yusof YAM. Effects of ginger extract (*Zingiber officinale* Roscoe) on antioxidant status of hepatocarcinoma induced rats. Malays J Biochem Mol Biol 2006;14:7−12.

[78] Li H, Chen J, Xiong C, Wei H, Yin C, Ruan J. Apoptosis induction by the total flavonoids from *Arachniodes exilis* in HepG2 cells through reactive oxygen species-mediated mitochondrial dysfunction involving MAPK activation. Evid Based Complement Alternat Med 2014;(2014).

[79] Li C-L, Ou C-M, Huang C-C, Wu W-C, Chen Y-P, Lin T-E, et al. Carbon dots prepared from ginger exhibiting efficient inhibition of human hepatocellular carcinoma cells. J Mater Chem B 2014;2:4564−71.

[80] Parihar G, Balekar N. *Calotropis procera*: a phytochemical and pharmacological review. Thai J Pharm Sci 2016;40.

[81] Choedon T, Mathan G, Arya S, Kumar VL, Kumar V. Anticancer and cytotoxic properties of the latex of *Calotropis procera* in a transgenic mouse model of hepatocellular carcinoma. World J Gastroenterol 2006;12:2517.

[82] Jacinto SD, Chun EAC, Montuno AS, Shen C-C, Espineli DL, Ragasa CY. Cytotoxic cardenolide and sterols from *Calotropis gigantea*. Nat Product Commun 2011;6 1934578X1100600614.

[83] Priya V, Jain P, Vanathi BM, Raj PV, Kamath BV, Rao JV, et al. Methanolic root extract of *Calotropis gigantea* induces apoptosis in human hepatocellular carcinoma by altering Bax/Bcl-2 expression. Am J Pharmacol Sci 2015;3:13−17.

[84] Rahmani AH. *Cassia fistula* Linn: potential candidate in the health management. Pharmacognosy Res 2015;7:217.

[85] Danish M, Singh P, Mishra G, Srivastava S, Jha K, Khosa R. *Cassia fistula* Linn. (Amulthus)—an important medicinal plant: a review of its traditional uses, phytochemistry and pharmacological properties. J Nat Prod Plant Resour 2011;1:101−18.

[86] Pereira RM, Ferreira-Silva GA, Pivatto M, de Ávila Santos L, da Silva Bolzani V, de Paula DAC, et al. Alkaloids derived from flowers of Senna spectabilis, (−)-cassine and (−)-spectaline, have antiproliferative activity on HepG2 cells for inducing cell cycle arrest in G1/S transition through ERK inactivation and downregulation of cyclin D1 expression. Toxicol Vitro 2016;31:86−92.

[87] Srividhya M, Hridya H, Shanthi V, Ramanathan K. Bioactive Amento flavone isolated from Cassia fistula L. leaves exhibits therapeutic efficacy. 3 Biotech 2017;7:33.

[88] Pradeep K, Raj Mohan CV, Gobianand K, Karthikeyan S. Protective effect of Cassia fistula Linn. on diethylnitrosamine induced hepatocellular damage and oxidative stress in ethanol pretreated rats. Biol Res 2010;43:113−25.

[89] Safwat G, Hamed M, Moatamed S. Studies of the biological activity of Cassia fistula. Pharmacol Online 2018;1:75−85.

[90] Al-Fatlawi AA, Al-fatlawi AA, Zafaryab M, Irshad M, Ahmad I, Kazim Z, et al. Rhein induced cell death and apoptosis through caspase dependent and associated with modulation of p53, bcl-2/bax ratio in human cell lines. Int J Pharm Pharm Sci 2014;6:215219.

[91] Radha MH, Laxmipriya NP. Evaluation of biological properties and clinical effectiveness of Aloe vera: a systematic review. J Tradit Complement Med 2015;5:21−6.

[92] Shalabi M, Khilo K, Zakaria MM, Elsebaei MG, Abdo W, Awadin W. Anticancer activity of Aloe vera and Calligonum comosum extracts separately on hepatocellular carcinoma cells. Asian Pac J Trop Biomed 2015;5:375−81.

[93] Chinchilla N, Carrera C, Durán AG, Macías M, Torres A, Macías FA. Aloe barbadensis: how a miraculous plant becomes reality. Phytochem Rev 2013;12:581−602.

[94] Kooti W, Ali-Akbari S, Asadi-Samani M, Ghadery H, Ashtary-Larky D. A review on medicinal plant of Apium graveolens. Adv Herb Med 2015;1:48−59.

[95] Ahmedy O. Study of the anticancer potential of celery seed oil against chemically induced hepatocellular carcinoma in rats: a mechanistic approach. Al-Azhar J Pharm Sci 2016;53:14−28.

[96] Hsieh S-L, Chen C-T, Wang J-J, Kuo Y-H, Li C-C, Hsieh L-C, et al. Sedanolide induces autophagy through the PI3K, p53 and NF-κB signaling pathways in human liver cancer cells. Int J Oncol 2015;47:2240−6.

[97] Jain G, Pareek H, Khajja B, Jain K, Jhalani S, Agarwal S, et al. Modulation of di-(2-ethylhexyl) phthalate induced hepatic toxicity by Apium graveolens L. seeds extract in rats. Afr J Biochem Res 2009;3:222−5.

[98] Peter K, Gandhi P. Rediscovering the therapeutic potential of Amaranthus species: a review. Egypt J Basic Appl Sci 2017;4:196−205.

[99] Rajasekaran S, Dinesh M, Kansrajh C, Baig FHA. Amaranthus spinosus leaf extracts and its anti-inflamatory effects on cancer. Indian J Res Pharm Biotechnol 2014;2:1058.

[100] Alok S, Jain SK, Verma A, Kumar M, Mahor A, Sabharwal M. Plant profile, phytochemistry and pharmacology of Asparagus racemosus (Shatavari): a review. Asian Pac J Trop Dis 2013;3:242−51.

[101] Cheng W, Cheng Z, Xing D, Zhang M. Asparagus polysaccharide suppresses the migration, invasion, and angiogenesis of hepatocellular carcinoma cells partly by targeting the HIF-1α/VEGF signalling pathway in vitro. Evid Based Complement Alternat Med 2019;(2019).

[102] Siddiqui NA, Ali M, Ahmad A, Khan TH, Ahmad A. New ursane glycoside from the roots of Asparagus racemosus. Asian J Chem 2013;25:8557−60.

[103] Yang H, Kim HW, Kim YC, Sung SH. Cytotoxic activities of naturally occurring oleanane-, ursane-, and lupane-type triterpenes on HepG2 and AGS cells. Pharmacogn Mag 2017;13:118.

[104] Li H, Jiang D, Zhang L, Wu J. Inhibition of tumor growth of human hepatocellular carcinoma HepG2 cells in a nude mouse xenograft model by the total flavonoids from Arachniodes exilis. Evid Based Complement Alternat Med 2017;(2017).

[105] Zhou D, Ruan J, Cai Y, Xiong Z, Fu W, Wei A. Antioxidant and hepatoprotective activity of ethanol extract of Arachniodes exilis (Hance) Ching. J Ethnopharmacol 2010;129:232−7.

[106] Jamkhande PG, Wattamwar AS. Annona reticulata Linn. (Bullock's heart): plant profile, phytochemistry and pharmacological properties. J Tradit Complement Med 2015;5:144−52.

[107] Roopan SM, Kumar SHS, Madhumitha G, Suthindhiran K. Biogenic-production of SnO2 nanoparticles and its cytotoxic effect against hepatocellular carcinoma cell line (HepG2). Appl Biochem Biotechnol 2015;175:1567−75.

[108] Mariod AA, Abdelwahab SI, Elkheir S, Ahmed YM, Fauzi PNM, Chuen CS. Antioxidant activity of different parts from Annona squamosa, and Catunaregam nilotica methanolic extract. Acta Scientiarum Polonorum Technologia Alimentaria 2012;11:249−58.

[109] Balderrama-Carmona AP, Silva-Beltrán NP, Gálvez-Ruiz J-C, Ruíz-Cruz S, Chaidez-Quiroz C, Morán-Palacio EF. Antiviral, antioxidant, and antihemolytic effect of *Annona muricata* L. Leaves extracts. Plants 2020;9:1650.

[110] Ahmed SA, Kamel EM. Chemical constituents, cytotoxic and antibacterial activities of the aerial parts of *Brassica nigra*. Int J Bioassays 2013;2:1134–8.

[111] Parikh H, Pandita N, Khanna A. Phytoextract of Indian mustard seeds acts by suppressing the generation of ROS against acetaminophen-induced hepatotoxicity in HepG2 cells. Pharm Biol 2015;53:975–84.

[112] Lin C-C, Huang C-Y, Mong M-C, Chan C-Y, Yin M-C. Antiangiogenic potential of three triterpenic acids in human liver cancer cells. J Agric Food Chem 2011;59:755–62.

[113] Lin J-T, Chen Y-C, Lee Y-C, Hou C-WR, Chen F-L, Yang D-J. Antioxidant, anti-proliferative and cyclooxygenase-2 inhibitory activities of ethanolic extracts from lemon balm (*Melissa officinalis* L.) leaves. LWT 2012;49:1–7.

[114] Kim JH, Kim MY. Apoptotic properties of *Citrus sudachi* Hort, ex Shirai (Rutaceae) extract on human A549 and HepG2 cancer cells. Trop J Pharm Res 2016;15:1167–74.

[115] Qiao J, Liu J, Jia K, Li N, Liu B, Zhang Q, et al. Diosmetin triggers cell apoptosis by activation of the p53/Bcl-2 pathway and inactivation of the Notch3/NF-κB pathway in HepG2 cells. Oncol Lett 2016;12:5122–8.

[116] Naz H, Tarique M, Ahamad S, Alajmi MF, Hussain A, Rehman MT, et al. Hesperidin-CAMKIV interaction and its impact on cell proliferation and apoptosis in the human hepatic carcinoma and neuroblastoma cells. J Cell Biochem 2019;120:15119–30.

[117] Kim JH, Kim MY. Anticancer effect of citrus fruit prepared by gamma irradiation of budsticks. J Life Sci 2015;25:1051–8.

[118] Wang Z, Zhang H, Zhou J, Zhang X, Chen L, Chen K, et al. Eriocitrin from lemon suppresses the proliferation of human hepatocellular carcinoma cells through inducing apoptosis and arresting cell cycle. Cancer Chemother Pharmacol 2016;78:1143–50.

[119] Aja I, Ruiz-Larrea MB, Courtois A, Krisa S, Richard T, Ruiz-Sanz J-I. Screening of natural stilbene oligomers from *Vitis vinifera* for anticancer activity on human hepatocellular carcinoma cells. Antioxidants 2020;9:469.

[120] Giovannelli L, Innocenti M, Santamaria A, Bigagli E, Pasqua G, Mulinacci N. Antitumoural activity of viniferin-enriched extracts from *Vitis vinifera* L. cell cultures. Nat Product Res 2014;28:2006–16.

[121] Mihai R, Cristina S, Helepciuc F, Brezeanu A, Stoian G. Biotic and abiotic elicitors induce biosynthesis and accumulation of resveratrol with antitumoral activity in the long-term *Vitis vinifera* L. callus cultures. Rom Biotechnol Lett 2011;16.

[122] De Sales NF, Silva da Costa L, Carneiro TI, Minuzzo DA, Oliveira FL, Cabral L, et al. Anthocyanin-rich grape pomace extract (*Vitis vinifera* L.) from wine industry affects mitochondrial bioenergetics and glucose metabolism in human hepatocarcinoma HepG2 cells. Molecules 2018;23:611.

[123] Yu C-L, Yang S-F, Hung T-W, Lin C-L, Hsieh Y-H, Chiou H-L. Inhibition of eIF2α dephosphorylation accelerates pterostilbene-induced cell death in human hepatocellular carcinoma cells in an ER stress and autophagy-dependent manner. Cell Death Dis 2019;10:1–15.

[124] Notas G, Nifli A-P, Kampa M, Vercauteren J, Kouroumalis E, Castanas E. Resveratrol exerts its antiproliferative effect on HepG2 hepatocellular carcinoma cells, by inducing cell cycle arrest, and NOS activation. Biochim Biophys Acta 2006;1760:1657–66.

[125] Al-Snafi A. A review on *Lawsonia inermis*: a potential medicinal plant. Int J Curr Pharm Res 2019;11:1–13.

[126] Ishteyaque S, Mishra A, Mohapatra S, Singh A, Bhatta RS, Tadigoppula N, et al. In vitro: cytotoxicity, apoptosis and ameliorative potential of *Lawsonia inermis* extract in human lung, colon and liver cancer cell line. Cancer Investig 2020;38:476–85.

[127] Priya R, Ilavenil S, Kaleeswaran B, Srigopalram S, Ravikumar S. Effect of Lawsonia inermis on tumor expression induced by Dalton's lymphoma ascites in Swiss albino mice. Saudi J Biol Sci 2011;18:353–9.

[128] Endrini S, Rahmat A, Ismail P, Taufiq-Yap Y. Comparing of the cytotoxicity properties and mechanism of *Lawsonia inermis* and *Strobilanthes crispus* extract against several cancer cell lines. J Med Sci 2007;7:1098–102.

[129] Dutta S, Deba N, Pattnaik AK, Bersa SE. Apoptosis-inducing potential of *Lawsonia alba* lam. Leaves on hepatocellular carcinoma (hep-g2) cells along with its anti-oxidant property. Int J Pharm Pharm Sci 2016;8:156–62.

[130] Maiyo FC, Moodley R, Singh M. Cytotoxicity, antioxidant and apoptosis studies of quercetin-3-O glucoside and 4-(β-D-glucopyranosyl-1→ 4-α-L-rhamnopyranosyloxy)-benzyl isothiocyanate from *Moringa oleifera*. Antcancer Agents Med Chem 2016;16:648–56.

[131] Huang G, Li S, Zhang Y, Zhou X, Chen W. Vicenin-2 is a novel inhibitor of STAT3 signaling pathway in human hepatocellular carcinoma. J Funct Foods 2020;69:103921.

[132] Hussein MA, Gobba NA, El Bishbishy MH. Composition, in vitro antioxidant and antitumor properties of essential oil from the seeds of *Moringa oleifera*. Int J Pharm Scien 2014;4:532—40.

[133] Abd-Rabou AA, Zoheir KM, Kishta MS, Shalby AB, Ezzo MI. Nano-micelle of *Moringa oleifera* seed oil triggers mitochondrial cancer cell apoptosis. Asian Pac J Cancer Prevent 2016;17:4929.

[134] Tiloke C, Phulukdaree A, Gengan RM, Chuturgoon AA. *Moringa oleifera* aqueous leaf extract induces cell-cycle arrest and apoptosis in human liver hepatocellular carcinoma cells. Nutr Cancer 2019;71:1165—74.

[135] Majdalawieh AF, Mansour ZR. Sesamol, a major lignan in sesame seeds (*Sesamum indicum*): anti-cancer properties and mechanisms of action. Eur J Pharmacol 2019;855:75—89.

[136] Xu P, Cai F, Liu X, Guo L. Sesamin inhibits lipopolysaccharide-induced proliferation and invasion through the p38-MAPK and NF-κB signaling pathways in prostate cancer cells. Oncol Rep 2015;33:3117—23.

[137] Liu Z, Ren B, Wang Y, Zou C, Qiao Q, Diao Z, et al. Sesamol induces human hepatocellular carcinoma cells apoptosis by impairing mitochondrial function and suppressing autophagy. Sci Rep 2017;7:1—12.

[138] Khan F, Khan TJ, Kalamegam G, Pushparaj PN, Chaudhary A, Abuzenadah A, et al. Anti-cancer effects of Ajwa dates (*Phoenix dactylifera* L.) in diethylnitrosamine induced hepatocellular carcinoma in Wistar rats. BMC Complement Alternat Med 2017;17:1—10.

[139] Siddiqui S, Ahmad R, Khan MA, Upadhyay S, Husain I, Srivastava AN. Cytostatic and anti-tumor potential of Ajwa date pulp against human hepatocellular carcinoma HepG2 cells. Sci Rep 2019;9:1—12.

[140] Vij T, Prashar Y. A review on medicinal properties of *Carica papaya* Linn. Asian Pac J Trop Dis 2015;5:1—6.

[141] Somanah J, Bourdon E, Bahorun T. Extracts of Mauritian *Carica papaya* (var. solo) protect SW872 and HepG2 cells against hydrogen peroxide induced oxidative stress. J Food Sci Technol 2017;54:1917—27.

[142] Oseni O, Odesani E, Oloyede O, Adebayo O, Ogundare M. Antioxidant and hepatoprotective activities of *Carica papaya* (Papaw Leaf) and *Loranthus bengwensis* (cocoa mistletoes) against diclofenac induced hepatotoxicity in rats. Int J Life Sci Scienti Res 2018;4:1974—82.

[143] Nga VT, Trang NTH, Tuyet NTA, Phung NKP, Duong NTT, Thu NTH. Ethanol extract of male *Carica papaya* flowers demonstrated non-toxic against MCF-7, HEP-G2, HELA, NCI-H460 cancer cell lines. Vietnam J Chem 2020;58:86—91.

[144] Pure NJ. Hepatoprotective effect of hydroethanol extracts of *Allium sativum* and *Carica papaya* on CCl4-induced liver damage in rats. Nig J Pure Appl Sci 2020;33:3639—49.

Resveratrol for hepatocellular carcinoma therapy

Kalisetty Chengaiahgari Maheswari, Ganganapalli Supraja and Kallimakula Venkata Reddy Saritha

Department of Biotechnology, Sri Venkateswara University, Tirupati, India

Abstract

Since time of evolution of medicine, plants and plant derivatives were treasured for their therapeutic properties. Phytochemicals including phytoalexins, natural phenols, and other secondary metabolites are under constant research for their antimicrobial, antipyretic, antioxidant, antiinflammatory, antihistonic and antitumorigenic properties. Resveratrol is one of the phytoderivatives under constant research for its promising effects in the treatment of cancer. Numerous investigations were reported pointing the antitumorigenic action of resveratrol. In the current study, role of this stilbenoid against hepatocellular carcinoma is conferred through various observations.

Keywords: Resveratrol; stilbenoid; hepatocellular carcinoma; liver; cancer; tumor; apoptosis; antioxidant

Abbreviations

AH	ascites hepatoma
Bax	B-cell-associated X protein
Bcl-2	B-cell lymphoma-2
BW	Body weight
COX	cyclo-oxygenase
2,4-D	2,4-Dichlorophenoxy acetic acid
DDT	dichlorodiphenyltrichloroethane
DENA	diethylnitrosamine
DNA	deoxyribonucleic acid
HCC	hepatocellular carcinoma
H₂O₂	hydrogen peroxide
ISR	induced systemic resistance
NFE2	nuclear factor erythroid 2
NF-kB	nuclear factor kappa B cells

Ganji Purnachandra Nagaraju, Sarfraz Ahmad (eds.)
Theranostics and Precision Medicine for the Management of Hepatocellular Carcinoma, Volume 3
DOI: https://doi.org/10.1016/B978-0-323-99283-1.00011-2

© 2022 Elsevier Inc. All rights reserved.

Nrf2   NFE-related factor-2
OH*   hydroxyl ion
PCNA   proliferating cell nuclear antigen
ROS   reactive oxygen species
SAR   systemic acquired resistance
2,4,5-т 2,4,5-Trichlorophenoxy acetic acid
UV   ultraviolet

Introduction

Resveratrol is a natural phenol and phytoalexin synthesized as a secondary metabolic molecule during defense mechanism within the plants against biotic and abiotic annoyance. Because of its antioxidant and antitumorigenic activity, resveratrol is gaining attention of the researchers to combat cancer and multiple diseases.

Structure

Resveratrol (3,4′,5-trihydoxy trans stilbene) is a stilbenoid. It possesses two phenolic rings which are connected by a double bond. Resveratrol is synthesized by the reaction between 4-coumaroyl Co-A and malonyl Co-A by the enzyme stilbene synthase. Thus it takes chalconoid structure. It belongs to the family of phenyl propanoids. Resveratrol occurs in cis and *trans* isomeric forms. Of both, *trans* form is stable and biologically active including the induction of cellular responses, viz., arresting cell cycle, differentiation, apoptosis, and enhancing antiproliferation of cancer cells [1—3]. Photoisomerization of *trans* form to the *cis-* form occurs under ultraviolet (UV) irradiation [4]. *Cis*-resveratrol upon UV irradiation results in "Resveratrone," which has fluorescence nature [5]. *Trans*-resveratrol is stable in its solid state at 40°C and 75% humidity in air [6]. It can also be stabilized by transport proteins [7]. Fermented grapes and pomace peel possess stable resveratrol which can be stowed for long intervals [8].

Source

Resveratrol is a phytochemical most abundantly available in grape peels. It is also produced in peanuts, knotweeds and pine trees, cocoa bushes and berries [8,9]. Its composition varies in the plants and within the plants too depending upon their geographical and seasonal occurrences. Peanuts show one-fourth percent of resveratrol as that of found in red wine. Based on the cultivar type, sprouting peanuts possess similar amount of resveratrol as that of grapes [9]. The skin of mulberries contains 50 μg of resveratrol per gram dry weight [10]. The amount of resveratrol in various food components is shown in Table 9.1.

Chemical synthesis

Resveratrol was first isolated by Michio Takaoka from grandiflorum variety, *Veratrum album* in 1939 [11,12] and later from Japanese knotweed roots in 1963 [13]. The initial

TABLE 9.1 Amount of resveratrol in various food sources.

Source	Weight (g)	Total resveratrol (mg)
Peanuts (raw)	146	0.01−0.26
Peanut butter	258	0.04−0.13
Red grapes	160	0.24−1.25
Cocoa powder	200	0.28−0.46

product of Sirtris pharmaceuticals was resveratrol formulation which was cofounded by the Professor of Harvard University, David Sinclair [14].

Functions of resveratrol

Resveratrol shows antimicrobial, antioxidant, antihistamine, and antitumor activities.

Resveratrol as a phytoalexin

Phytoalexins are natural secondary metabolites synthesized and accumulated within the plant cells after disclosure to pathogens. As a phytoalexin, resveratrol is produced in the plants as a part of induced systemic resistance (ISR) and systemic acquired resistance (SAR) during biotic and abiotic stress conditions. ISR, a short-term hypersensitive response deploys ROS (reactive oxygen species) such as super oxides and hydrogen peroxides to kill invading pathogen. It also triggers apoptosis of cells (programmed cell death) that were present surrounding the cells under biotic stress thus preventing the spreading of the pathogen to the rest of the plant. Whereas in case of SAR, certain hormones were released by the communication between pathogen-infected tissue with the rest of the plant. They trigger expression of certain defense genes which produce certain phytoalexins which kill pathogens. Yet the underlying mechanism of antiproliferative activity is under studies [15].

Resveratrol as a natural phenol

Natural phenols are the phenolic group containing phytochemicals that were produced as secondary metabolites against pathogen attack or environmental stress. They have anti-fungal and antigermicidal properties. But recently, their significant endogenous and exog-enous role on cell growth, cell multiplication, and apoptosis reflects cancer prevention. The chalconoid structure is influencing different molecules involved in the regulation of cell cycle. Their role in sensitizing the neoplastic cells for chemotherapy is additional importance in cancer treatment [16]. Resveratrol, a nonflavonoid polyphenol is undergoing in vivo trials for human cancer research for its natural apoptotic and cell cycle-regulating activity [17].

Resveratrol as a natural antioxidant

Antioxidants are molecules which prevent oxidation of other compounds or molecules. These are the reducing agents which donate free electrons to free radicals thus protecting the cells from oxidation. Thus antioxidants are also called as natural scavengers of free radicals or ROS. Oxidation of cells results in oxidative stress, which leads to various adverse effects such as cell aging, apoptosis, and organ dysfunction. Excessive amount of free radicals is also observed to be triggering tumor initiation and proliferation by suppressing the expression of antitumor genes. Its antioxidant effect is dependent on the arrangement of functional group on nuclear structure. Resveratrol being naturally occurring food derivative, numerous studies confirmed it as a potential natural antioxidant [18]. But its low bioavailability is restricting its application in therapeutic usage. Hence numerous derivatives were synthesized through esterification which showed good antioxidant properties such as inhibition of DNA scission and copper ion-induced low-density lipoprotein oxidation [19].

Resveratrol as anticarcinogenic agent

Antitumor activity of resveratrol was demonstrated by numerous studies facilitating its implementation in chemotherapeutic usage in treating various cancer types [20,21]. Numerous in vitro and in vivo studies confirmed the inhibition of tumorigenesis stages such as initiation, formation, and progression of tumor cells by the application of resveratrol [22−24]. Chemotherapeutic usage of resveratrol due to its antihistamine, antioxidant, proapoptosis, and antimultiplicative actions were also noticed [23,25]. Resveratrol is alleged to target intracellular signaling pathway molecules by modulation of numerous transcription factors, upstream kinases, and their regulators [26].

Reactive oxygen species

ROS are extremely reactive molecules that are formed during the aerobic metabolism due to electron acceptance of O_2. Most of these exist as free radicals, that is, having one or more unpaired electrons such as superoxide, peroxyl, hydroxyl, and alkoxyl radicals, singlet oxygen, and alpha-oxygen or as nonradicals that don't contain unpaired electrons such as hydrogen peroxide, hypochlorous acid, peroxynitrile, and ozone. In living organisms, ROS are produced as a natural byproduct during normal aerobic metabolism of oxygen which possess significant play in signaling and homeostasis of the cell [27,28]. ROS are inherent for cell functioning and occur in little and static levels in normal cells. These are present in normal metabolic processes such as photoprotection and stress tolerance

[29]. Excessive production of ROS results in oxidative stress showing harmful effects such as irreversible DNA damage, abnormal functionality of cells. This in turn results in the initiation and proliferation of cancer cells [28].

Role of resveratrol on hepatocellular carcinoma (liver cancer)

Hepatocellular carcinoma (HCC) or liver cancer is evolving as the dreadful forms of tumor as observed by its global cumulative incidence. Major threat aspects of HCC are hepatitis, alcoholism, and obesity [30,31]. The effect of resveratrol was investigated on liver cancer using animal models of different sex and age groups. Tumor initiation and proliferation was initiated through transplantation of liver tumor cells to the host models.

Intravenous administration of resveratrol since Day 1 of the implantation in adult male Wistar rats gave a jab with AH-130 Yoshida ascites resulted in the decrease in number of cancer cells compared to the control rats. But still no change in tumor volume was noticed even after a week [32]. Numerous in vivo studies inducing HCC through diethylnitrosamine (DENA) injection following phenobarbital for tumor promotion in rats were reported. Among them, Bishayee and Dhir [33] provided resveratrol to female Sprague–Dawley rats for 4 weeks prior tumor initiation which then continued for 16 weeks. Resveratrol dosage at 100 and 300 mg/kg BW decreased the advent and proliferation of hepatocyte lumps compared to only DENA-injected animals without resveratrol treatment. In addition to that 300 mg/kg BW resveratrol administration improved cellular building of liver tissue. All the three doses of resveratrol treatment, decreased the proliferation of hepatic cells as signposted by decreased expression of PCNA. The resveratrol (100 and 300 mg/kg BW)-treated rats showed raised Bax expression and fall in Bcl-2 expression in liver cells indicating the aiding of apoptosis.

Furthermore, higher doses of resveratrol in rats reduced peroxidation of the lipids and carbonyl content of protein in livers in comparison to only DENA-injected rats, representing its role in free radical scavenging and decreasing the occurrence of tumor [34]. Resveratrol treatment enhanced Nrf2; Bishayee et al. [34] pointed out its antioxidant effect. Decrease in the expression of HSP70 and COX-2, as well as reduction of DENA triggers relocation of NF-kB to the nucleus, signifies the antihistamine activity of resveratrol [35]. In another research, they observed the decrease in tumor proliferation by resveratrol treatment (in a dose-dependent manner) post 14 weeks of cancer injection. Their study strengthens that even least dosage of resveratrol (50 mg/kg BW) showed significant reduction of the lump multiplicity [36]. Rajasekaran et al. [37] reported that daily oral administration of resveratrol (20 mg/kg BW) for 15 days from the start and post-DENA injection facilitates the inhibition of HCC in 6- to 8-week-old male rats. They have observed that resveratrol administration upregulated apoptotic markers expression and downregulated antiapoptotic markers expression. It also decreased cell clustering and change in cellular architecture unlike in control rats injected with DENA.

Lin et al. [38] assessed the potency of resveratrol therapy on the pretumorous phase of liver tumorigenesis in male HBx transgenic mice, which would instinctively indulge HCC at later ages. Daily resveratrol intake (0.024%) through diet for 4 months resulted in the fall of HCC occurrence by 5.3-fold and decreased the expression of cancer development. The outcomes of liver tumor models have been constantly optimistic, specifying a potential significance of resveratrol in HCC inhibition and/or treatment. Salado et al. [39] cast-off B16 melanoma (B16M) cells to investigate the curative role of resveratrol on hepatic metastasis occurrence, enormously due to over accumulation of proinflammatory cytokines.

Conclusions and future perspectives

Resveratrol is reported to having antitumorigenic property against various cancerous cells. But the less bioavailability of resveratrol is minimizing the studies of beneficiary effect of resveratrol as anticarcinogenic compound. Hence, there is a great need of isolating the bioavailability form of resveratrol. Even though numerous in vitro and in vivo studies were done to assess the bio- and chemotherapeutic activity of resveratrol, extensive research has to be done through clinical trials to confirm its potential for further therapeutic usage.

Conflict of interest

The authors declare no conflict of interest.

References

[1] Akinwumi BC, et al. Biological activities of stilbenoids. Int J Mol Sci 2018;19(3):792.
[2] Anisimova NY, et al. Trans-, cis-, and dihydro-resveratrol: a comparative study. Chem Cent J 2011;5(1):1−6.
[3] Orallo F. Comparative studies of the antioxidant effects of cis-and trans-resveratrol. Curr Med Chem 2006;13 (1):87−98.
[4] Bernard E, et al. Resveratrol photoisomerization: an integrative guided-inquiry experiment. J Chem Educ 2007;84(7):1159.
[5] Yang I, et al. Photochemical generation of a new, highly fluorescent compound from non-fluorescent resveratrol. Chem Commun 2012;48(32):3839−41.
[6] Prokop J, et al. Resveratrol and its glycon piceid are stable polyphenols. J Med Food 2006;9(1):11−14.
[7] Pantusa M, et al. Stability of trans-resveratrol associated with transport proteins. J Agric Food Chem 2014;62 (19):4384−91.
[8] Jasiński M, et al. Resveratrol in prostate diseases−a short review. Cent European J Urol 2013;66(2):144.
[9] Koushki M, et al. Effect of resveratrol supplementation on inflammatory markers: a systematic review and *meta*-analysis of randomized controlled trials. Clin Ther 2018;40(7):1180−92 e1185.
[10] Stewart JR, et al. Resveratrol: a candidate nutritional substance for prostate cancer prevention. J Nutr 2003;133(7):2440S−3S.
[11] Bertelli A, et al. Stability of resveratrol over time and in the various stages of grape transformation. Drugs Exp Clin Res 1998;24(4):207−11.
[12] Takaoka M. Resveratrol, a new phenolic compound, from Veratrum grandiflorum. Nippon Kagaku Kaishi 1939;60:1090−100.
[13] Takaoka M. The phenolic substances of white hellebore (*Veratrum grandiflorum* Loes. Fill). V. Nippon Kagaku Kaishi 1940;61(10):1067−9.
[14] Nonomura S, Kanagawa H, Makimoto A. Chemical constituents of polygonaceous plants. I. Studies on the components of Ko-J O-Kon. (*Polygonum cuspidatum* Sieb. Et Zucc.). Yakugaku Zasshi 1963;83:988−90.
[15] Weintraub A. Resveratrol: the hard sell on anti-aging. New York: Bloomberg Businessweek; 2009.
[16] Chripkova M, et al. Antiproliferative effect of indole phytoalexins. Molecules 2016;21(12):1626.

[17] Carocho M, Ferreira ICFR. The role of phenolic compounds in the fight against cancer—a review. Anticancer Agents Med Chem 2013;13(8):1236–58.

[18] Carter LG, et al. Resveratrol and cancer: focus on in vivo evidence. Endocr Relat Cancer 2014;21(3):R209–25.

[19] Malhotra A, et al. An organ system approach to explore the antioxidative, anti-inflammatory, and cytoprotective actions of resveratrol. Oxid Med and Cell Longev 2015;803–971.

[20] Yang T, et al. Properties and molecular mechanisms of resveratrol: a review. Pharmazie 2015;70(8):501–6.

[21] Kuršvietienė L, et al. Multiplicity of effects and health benefits of resveratrol. Medicina 2016;52(3):148–55.

[22] Bishayee A. Cancer prevention and treatment with resveratrol: from rodent studies to clinical trials. Cancer Prev Res (Phila) 2009;2(5):409–18.

[23] Zykova TA, et al. Resveratrol directly targets COX-2 to inhibit carcinogenesis. Mol Carcinog 2008;47(10):797–805.

[24] Varoni EM, et al. Anticancer molecular mechanisms of resveratrol. Front Nutr 2016;3:8.

[25] Pezzuto JM. Resveratrol as an inhibitor of carcinogenesis. Pharm Biol 2008;46(7–8):443–573.

[26] Van Ginkel PR, et al. Resveratrol inhibits tumor growth of human neuroblastoma and mediates apoptosis by directly targeting mitochondria. Clin Cancer Res 2007;13(17):5162–9.

[27] Kundu JK, Surh Y-J. Cancer chemopreventive and therapeutic potential of resveratrol: mechanistic perspectives. Cancer Lett 2008;269(2):243–61.

[28] Devasagayam T, et al. Free radicals and antioxidants in human health: current status and future prospects. J Assoc Physicians India 2004;52(794804):4.

[29] Edreva A. Generation and scavenging of reactive oxygen species in chloroplasts: a submolecular approach. Agric Ecosyst Environ 2005;106(2–3):119–33.

[30] Grant JJ, Loake GJ. Role of reactive oxygen intermediates and cognate redox signaling in disease resistance. Plant Physiol 2000;124(1):21–30.

[31] El Serag HB, Rudolph KL. Hepatocellular carcinoma: epidemiology and molecular carcinogenesis. Gastroenterology 2007;132(7):2557–76.

[32] Alter MJ. Epidemiology of hepatitis C virus infection. World J Gastroenterol 2007;13(17):2436.

[33] Bishayee A, Dhir N. Resveratrol-mediated chemoprevention of diethylnitrosamine-initiated hepatocarcinogenesis: inhibition of cell proliferation and induction of apoptosis. Chem Biol Interact 2009;179(2–3):131–44.

[34] Bishayee A, et al. Resveratrol suppresses oxidative stress and inflammatory response in diethylnitrosamine-initiated rat hepatocarcinogenesis. Cancer Prev Res (Phila) 2010;3(6):753–63.

[35] Bishayee A, et al. Suppression of the inflammatory cascade is implicated in resveratrol chemoprevention of experimental hepatocarcinogenesis. Pharm Res 2010;27(6):1080–91.

[36] Luther DJ, et al. Chemopreventive doses of resveratrol do not produce cardiotoxicity in a rodent model of hepatocellular carcinoma. Invest New Drugs 2011;29(2):380–91.

[37] Rajasekaran D, et al. Resveratrol interferes with N-nitrosodiethylamine-induced hepatocellular carcinoma at early and advanced stages in male Wistar rats. Mol Med Rep 2011;4(6):1211–17.

[38] Lin H-C, et al. Resveratrol helps recovery from fatty liver and protects against hepatocellular carcinoma induced by hepatitis B virus X protein in a mouse model. Cancer Prev Res (Phila) 2012;5(7):952–62.

[39] Salado C, et al. Resveratrol prevents inflammation-dependent hepatic melanoma metastasis by inhibiting the secretion and effects of interleukin-18. J Transl Med 2011;9(1):1–11.

Curcumin: a spice pigment against hepatic cancer

Vivek Kumar Soni[1],*, Yashwant Kumar Ratre[1],*, Arundhati Mehta[1], Ashwini Kumar Dixit[2], Mrigendra Dwivedi[3], Dhananjay Shukla[1], Ajay Kumar[4] and Naveen Kumar Vishwakarma[1]

[1]Department of Biotechnology, Guru Ghasidas Vishwavidyalaya, Bilaspur, India
[2]Department of Botany, Guru Ghasidas Vishwavidyalaya, Bilaspur, India
[3]Department of Biochemistry, Government Nagarjuna Post Graduate College of Science Raipur, Raipur, India [4]Department of Zoology, Banaras Hindu University, Varanasi, India

Abstract

Hepatic cancer is one of the most deadly malignancies owing to the pivotal role of liver in physiological homeostasis. Various strategies are being implemented to combat the onset and progression of liver cancer that has achieved promising success. However, conventional therapeutic approaches have their own limitations, particularly nonspecific toxicity and the onset of the chemoresistance. Therefore alternative approaches, including bioactive components of natural origins are being explored for their antineoplastic activity. Curcumin, the yellow pigment of turmeric spice, has shown effective cytotoxic activity against numerous malignant cells, including hepatic cancer. The abilities of curcumin such as its antioxidant nature, antiinflammatory effects, immunostimulatory activity, and protective behavior against organ damage make this phytochemical as a better choice of therapeutic agent in various medical ailments including malignancies of hepatic origin. Mechanistic explorations on curcumin have identified various molecular targets for its therapeutic effects against liver cancer. Moreover, curcumin is devoid of any specific adverse effects and safe for consumption. Curcumin also exhibits chemosensitizing ability and makes liver cancer cells more susceptible to conventional chemotherapeutic drugs. Although few concerns, including bioavailability and its metabolism limit the optimal clinical exploitation of curcumin, its derivatives is found to

---

* Authors Vivek Kumar Soni and Yashwant Kumar Ratre contributed equally to this chapter as first authors.

Ganji Purnachandra Nagaraju, Sarfraz Ahmad (eds.)
Theranostics and Precision Medicine for the Management of Hepatocellular Carcinoma, Volume 3
DOI: https://doi.org/10.1016/B978-0-323-99283-1.00007-0

© 2022 Elsevier Inc. All rights reserved.

overcome such obstacles. Collectively curcumin stands high in prospective therapeutic molecules against liver cancers with evident success in preclinical as well clinical investigations.

Keywords: Curcumin; liver cancer; chemosensitization; immunomodulation; analogs

Abbreviations

AFP	α-Fetoprotein
AIDS	Acquired immunodeficiency syndrome
ALT	alanine aminotransferase
AP1	activator protein 1
ASK1	signal-regulating kinase 1
AST	aspartate aminotransferase
ATF2	activating transcription factor 2
BDMC	bisdemethoxycurcumin
CD$^+$	cluster of differentiation
CDKN1A	cyclin-dependent kinase inhibitor 1A
CDKs	cyclin-dependent kinases
Chk1	checkpoint kinase 1
COX-2	cycloxygenase-2
CTGF	connective tissue growth factor
CUR3d	diarylheptanoids
CVDs	cardiovascular diseases
DAMP	damage-associated molecular pattern
DRs	death receptors
EF24	diphenyldifluoroketone
EMT	epithelial-mesenchymal transition
FDA	US Food and Drug Administration
GATA4	GATA-binding protein 4
GL63	(1E,4E)-1,5-bis(2-bromophenyl)penta-1,4-dien-3-one
GLUT4	glucose transporter type 4
GRAS	generally Recognized As Safe
H$_2$O$_2$	hydrogen peroxide
HBV	hepatitis B virus
HCAR1	hydroxycarboxylic acid receptor 1
HCC	hepatocellular carcinoma
HCV	hepatitis C virus
HDAC	histone deacetylases
HDV	hepatitis D virus
HIF	hypoxia inducible factor
HSPs	heat shock proteins
HZC	hydrazinocurcumin
IFN-γ	interferon gamma
IGF	insulin-like growth factor
IL	interleukin
iNOS	inducible nitric oxide synthase
JNK	c-Jun N-terminal kinase
LC3	microtubule-associated protein 1A/1B-light chain 3
LCSCs	liver cancer stem cells
LDHs	lactate dehydrogenases
MAPK	mitogen-activated protein kinase
MCT	monocarboxylate transporter

MDM2	mouse double minute 2 homolog
MDR	multiple drug resistance
MMP-9	matrix metalloproteinase-9
mTOR	mammalian target of rapamycin
NADPH	reduced nicotinamide adenine dinucleotide phosphate
NF-κB	nuclear factor kappa light chain enhancer of activated B cells
NK	natural killer cells
NOS	nitric oxide synthase
OHC	octahydrocurcumin
PARP1	poly [ADP-ribose] polymerase 1
PI3K	phosphoinositide 3-kinases
PKM2	pyruvate kinase M2
PLKs	polo-like kinases
RNS	reactive nitrogen species
ROS	reactive oxygen species
SDF-1	stromal cell-derived factor 1
SOD	superoxide dismutase
SQSTM1	sequestosome-1
STAT3	signal transducer and activator of transcription 3
TGFβ	transforming growth factor beta
TGF-β1	transforming growth factor beta 1
THC	tetrahydrocurcumin
TLR4	toll-like receptor
TME	tumor microenvironment
TNF-α	tumor necrosis factor alfa
TP53	tumor protein 53
UNC119	uncoordinated119
VEGF	vascular endothelial growth factor

Introduction

Liver cancer is one of the most common lethal type of cancers which accounts for the fifth position to the occurrence and third position in mortality rate worldwide killing 50,000 people per year in both male and female. Hepatocellular carcinoma (HCC) accounts for about 90% of liver cancer [1]. The major cause of HCC is a viral infection such as hepatitis B virus (HBV), hepatitis C virus (HCV), and hepatitis D virus (HDV). Hence, various antiviral drugs are being used to minimize the viral load in order to prevent the spread of infection and live cancer development [2–4]. Further, a lot of steps are also being taken to prevent the progression of liver cancers such as chemotechniques, surgically liver resections, liver transplantation, radiotherapy, and many more [5,6]. However, the higher mortality rate of liver cancer is due to delay diagnosis, very low objective response rate, and reoccurrence [7]. So, the liver cancer patient's overall 5-year survival rate is still remains less than 18% [8]. Therefore preventing the loss and side effects caused by the HCC has been a major step toward the future for improving the efficacy of established therapy as well as development of safe and effective therapeutic agents.

Curcumin is a spice bioactive component from turmeric that has received a great deal of attention from both the medicinal science realm and the culinary worlds. The medicinal properties of turmeric, the source of curcumin, have been well established since from thousands of years back; however, the ability to determine the precise mechanism of action and the bioactive components has only recently been investigated. Curcumin is a major active polyphenolic compound of turmeric also known as diferuloylmethane and its IUPAC name is (1E,6E)-1,7-bis(4-hydroxy-3-methoxyphenyl)-1,6-heptadiene-3,5-dione. Curcumin is yellow in color and isolated from the rhizome and root of *Curcuma longa* and *Curcuma domestica* [9–11].

Curcumin has been reported to inhibit the spread of different forms of cancer, including HCC. Curcumin exerts effective anticancer properties primarily by affecting a variety of signaling pathways and molecular targets, such as PI3K/Akt, Wnt/β-catenin, TGF-β1/smad3, insulin-like growth factor (IGF), and vascular endothelial growth factor (VEGF) [12–15]. While a variety of mechanisms have been proposed for antitumor activity of curcumin, but the precise mechanistic pathways of cytotoxic action of curcumin against HCC is not fully known. However, various investigations have contributed to a better understanding of its antineoplastic activity against malignancies, including those of hepatocellular origin. Moreover, these investigations along with clinical trials pave the path for its application in clinical settings to prevent as well as cure neoplastic disorders.

Curcumin: the golden spice component

Curcumin, a polyphenol exhibits multiple health assets by targeting multiple signaling molecules/pathways [16]. Curcumin has shown effective therapeutic benefits against inflammatory circumstances [16], metabolic syndrome [18], pain [19], and also aid in the cure of inflammatory and degenerative eye conditions [20,21]. Also, it has been shown that curcumin has an advantageous stand in ailments associated with kidneys [22]. While there seem to be various therapeutic benefits of curcumin supplementation, most of these benefits are speculated due to its antioxidant and antiinflammatory effects. Given its reported benefits through modulating the inflammatory and antioxidant pathways, one of the major problems with the ingestion of curcumin is its low bioavailability, which appears to be mainly due to poor absorption, rapid metabolism, and rapid consumption [23,24]. Several agents have been examined to improve curcumin bioavailability by addressing these various concerns through diverse mechanisms. Most of them have been developed to block the metabolic pathway of curcumin to increase its bioavailability. For example, piperine, a known bioavailability enhancer, is the major active component of black pepper [25] and is linked with an increase of 2000% in the bioavailability of curcumin [26]. Therefore the issue of poor bioavailability can be resolved by mingle agents such as piperine that enhances curcumin bioavailability. This can be achieved through the formation of curcumin conjugate complex.

The multidimensional uses of curcumin have been seen according to different cultures, places, weather, etc. For example, in India it's widely used in curries and as an antiseptic whereas in Japan turmeric is used in tea. In Korea, it is served in the drink. US Food and Drug Administration (FDA) approved curcumin as "Generally Recognized As Safe" (GRAS) [16] and strong resistance and Protection profiles have been observed in clinical trials even consumed daily between 4000 and 12,000 mg/day [27,28].

Biological activity of curcumin

Curcumin has been shown to offer tremendous activities under the various geographical regions of biology. Curcumin regulates different pathways through modulation of corresponding signaling molecules' activity or expression and equilibrates the homeostatic nature. Curcumin has the ability to module a range of physiological parameters and alter the pathological consequences associated with diverse circumstances [13,17,29,30]. Moreover, this golden spice component is credited with abilities to counter the neuropsychiatric ailments [31]. Antioxidant and antiinflammatory activities of curcumin are mainly sought as underlying force in its therapeutic as well preventive abilities [17,30,32].

Antioxidant activity

Antioxidant and antiinflammatory, these two properties, are majorly counted under the biological activities and these mechanistically underlay to primarily regulate and affect various pathways. In oxidative stress, curcumin has been shown to boost structural markers [32]. It is proved that like superoxide dismutase (SOD), curcumin can elevate the serum activity of antioxidants [18]. Recent systemic reviews and *meta*-analysis on oxidative stress and curcumin indicate that this yellow spice component significantly exhibits antioxidant activity. The antioxidant activity of curcumin is assessed through analysis of various parameters such as plasma activity of SOD and catalase, and serum activity of GSH and lipid peroxidase [32]. Curcumin exerts its antioxidant activity by scavenging the free radicals of reactive oxygen species (ROS) and reactive nitrogen species (RNS) [33]. Curcumin modulates the mechanism of GSH, catalase, and SOD enzyme activity and neutralizes the free radicals of ROS and RNS [34,35]. The role of curcumin in the attenuation of ROS-activating enzymes including lipoxygenase/cyclooxygenase and xanthine hydrogenase/oxidase has also been reported [34].

Antiinflammatory activity

Curcumin displays efficient antiinflammatory activity by modulating expression/activity of inflammation regulatory molecules [17,36]. Neurodegenerative, autoimmune, endocrine, cardiovascular, and neoplastic diseases are a few examples of chronic illnesses that are developed by inflammatory cascade [37,38]. Alzheimer's disease, Parkinson's disease, epilepsy, cerebral injury, allergy, asthma, bronchitis, colitis, arthritis, multiple sclerosis, AIDS, depression, fatigue, psoriasis, diabetes, obesity, cardiovascular disease, metabolic syndrome, and cancer are examples of chronic diseases [18]. Curcumin can attenuate the signaling of NF-kB and TNF-α production, which regulates the inflammatory cascade. In this context, curcumin downregulates TNF-α production by the inhibition of p300/CREB-specific acetyl transferase which prevents the acetylation of histone and nonhistone proteins, their regulation, and ultimately inhibits the transcription process [39]. Curcumin also exerts its antiinflammatory activity through the modulation of some other molecules that are directly or indirectly involved in the inflammation process. Further, the inflammation regulatory action of curcumin also depends on its ability to modulate inflammatory cytokines including interleukins (IL-1 and IL-6), and chemokines, inducible nitric oxide synthase (iNOS), cycloxygenase-2 (COX-2), and cyclin D1 [40,41].

Cardioprotective activity

To note, curcumin shows its tremendous effect on cardiomyocyte injuries, chronic heart failure, cardiac hypertrophy, and cholesterol absorption (Soni et al., 2020). Cardiovascular diseases (CVDs) are also counted as the foremost threatening disease worldwide. Therapeutic value of curcumin in CVDs like diseases is also well proven [42,43]. Curcumin acts as a good cardio protectant, attenuates the induced hypertrophic tension, and helps in the maintenance of cardiomyocyte population. Curcumin also prevents collagen accumulation, and extracellular matrix remodeling. Moreover, curcumin downregulates the activity of gelatinase B and gelatinolytic in cardiomyocytes [44]. Further, curcumin is helpful in the inhibition of norepinephrine-induced apoptosis and keeps a balanced physiological status [45]. In cardiomyoblasts, curcumin treatment protected them from hydrogen peroxide (H_2O_2)-induced apoptosis by increasing the activity of HO-1 protein, Bcl-2/Bax ratio, and decreasing caspase-3 activation [46]. In addition, curcumin suppresses NADPH-mediated ROS stress by inhibiting PI3K/Akt-signaling pathway, and increasing Na^+/Ca^+ exchanger expression [43,47]. Curcumin is also demonstrated as helpful in the inhibition of hypertrophic response via inhibition of zinc finger transcription factor, GATA4, and functional proteins, including intrinsic histone acetyltransferase and p300 [48]. Moreover, curcumin exerts cardioprotective action against chronic heart failure by elevating the expression of Dickkopf-related protein-3, JNK, p38, MAPK, and apoptosis signal-regulating kinase 1 (ASK1) [49].

Immune regulatory activity

In the current scenario of unprecedented COVID-19 pandemic, there is a necessity to boost immunity and maintain a strong and active immune system. Curcumin has an astounding activity to modulate immune regulatory molecules and cells such as T-lymphocytes, B-lymphocytes, macrophages, dendritic subsets, and NK cells. Curcumin also acts as an immune booster to boost up immunity and prevent immunological diseases [13,15,50−52]. Curcumin treatment significantly reduces neutrophils and eosinophils count and elevates lymphocyte count [53]. It was seen that curcumin boosts immunity even at low lymphocyte count. Curcumin administration significantly reduces the proinflammatory molecule (TNF-α, IFN-γ, and IL-1β) produced from Th1 cells and increases the production of antiinflammatory molecules (TGF-β, IL-4, and IL-10) [54,55]. In myasthenia gravis, curcumin lowers T cells population and increases NKR-P1 cell number along with B-cell differentiation [52]. Moreover, curcumin modulates the macrophage population for their phenotypic polarization which creates an immunized microenvironment [13,15,55]. Physical components of tumor microenvironment (TME) (such as tumor acidosis) can modulate the macrophage polarization in tumor-bearing host [56] which can be targeted for therapeutic interventions. Nevertheless, curcumin was shown to modulate the physical constituents of TME (oxygen level, pH level, etc.) [14]. Furthermore, an in silico study with CD4 and CD8 receptors has predicted a strong binding affinity of curcumin with these immune receptors which can be suggested for its strong antioxidant activity. Moreover, curcumin also suppresses the deltamethrin-regulated thymic apoptosis [57]. In addition, curcumin also enhances phagocytic activity via increase the level of IgG and IgM [51].

Antidiabetic activity

Many developing as well as developed countries suffer from diabetes as the most prominent problem. Many of the research groups are continually working on developing effective antidiabetic drugs with minimum side effects. Numerous studies suggest that curcumin has the activity of promising antidiabetic agent which also reduces the anomalies of development of type 2 diabetes mellitus in prediabetic individuals [58]. In addition, curcumin can be of great privilege to cure complications of diabetic retinopathy [59]. Curcumin suppresses the activity of α-amylase and α-glucosidase and regulates the activity of insulin in hyperglycemic patients [60]. Noteworthy, curcumin also accelerates Akt phosphorylation and level of glucose transporter type 4 (GLUT 4) in skeletal muscles [60]. Curcumin administration in the diabetic rats for 12 weeks, improved the pancreatic islets by increasing the number of small islets of Langerhans around the pancreas with no lymphocytes infiltration [61].

Antineoplastic activity

Curcumin has been proven for its potent antineoplastic activity in different types of cancer. Curcumin exerts apoptotic activity against a wide variety of cancer cells by modulating the mitochondrial membrane potential and suppressing the level of antiapoptotic proteins such as Bcl xL [62]. In several cancer cell lines, curcumin has shown an ability to decrease the survivability via increasing the activities of Death receptors (Dr4 and Dr5) [63,64]. The level of expression of Dr on tumor cells is positively correlated with the induction of apoptosis through activation of tumor necrosis factor (TNF) and consequent signaling cascade. Moreover, curcumin can influence the activity and/or expression of many of the intracellular molecular moieties including activator protein-1 (AP-1), cyclooxygenase II (COX-2), matrix metalloproteinase-9 (MMP-9), nitric oxide synthase (NOS), (signal transducer and activator of transcription 3) STAT3, and transcription factors such as NF-κB [13,14,29,65,66]. Various reports confirm and contribute to tolling evidences favoring anticancer potential of this magical spice component. A recent report on chemosensitizing activity of curcumin has demonstrated that this yellow pigment of turmeric has anti-Warburg effect on HepG2 cells [29]. Curcumin decreases the glucose consumption and lactate production by modulating glucose transporter (GLUT), monocarboxylate transporter (MCT; also known as lactate transporter), lactate dehydrogenases (LDHs), HIF1α, and PKM2 [13,29,66]. Various preclinical and clinical studies have identified many other targets of curcumin that are directly or indirectly involved in its antineoplastic activity.

Curcumin and liver cancer

Primary liver cancer remains one of the foremost common malignant tumors in the alimentary tract, despite the numerous progresses toward diagnosis and cure. Curcumin plays a crucial role in suppressing the growth and progression of HCC through modulating various signaling pathways. Moreover, this bioactive component of turmeric has shown potential to act as an adjuvant in strengthening the antineoplatic activity of chemotherapeutic drugs. Nevertheless, curcumin also has utilities in managing the malignancy-associated ill effects in patients.

Curcumin and prevention of hepatic cancer

Over the past several years, a number of in vitro and in vivo studies have demonstrated the antineoplastic action of curcumin and its analogs against hepatic cancer. Various in vitro and in vivo studies indicate the apoptosis-inducing ability of curcumin induces against liver cancer cells. Curcumin significantly induces ROS production, lipid peroxidation, and diminishes the mitochondrial membrane potential in HCC cell lines [24]. Curcumin triggers apoptosis cascade by downregulating expression of antiapoptotic such as Bcl-2 and upregulating proapoptotic-like molecules including caspase-3, caspase-9, and Bax [67].

The PI3K/Akt-signaling pathway is closely associated with malignancy and proliferation and is a potential target of various chemotherapeutic agents. The altered regulation of cell cycle, autophagy, invasion, epithelial-mesenchymal transition (EMT), and angiogenesis in cancer has also been associated with hyperactivated PI3K/Akt-signaling pathway. It was reported that in the liver cancer cell lines including hepatoma cell lines such as Huh7, Hep3B, HepG2, SK-Hep-1, and QGY-7703, curcumin treatment blocks the progression via arresting the cell cycle in S phase [68] and G2/M phase. Curcumin also inhibits the expression of checkpoint kinase 1(Chk1) [69]. Wang and his team have shown that curcumin significantly inhibits the activation of PI3K/Akt/mTOR signaling pathway in liver cancer stem cells (LCSCs); thus inhibits growth as well as metastasis [67]. PI3K/Akt-signaling pathway is also reported in the regulation of cyclin-dependent kinase inhibitor 1A (CDKN1A; also known asp21 or WAF1), a crucial regulator of cell cycle. CDKN1A expression was found higher on curcumin treatment along with inhibition of hepatocellular tumorigenesis [70].

ERK1/2 and JNK MAPK pathways are the central pathways and their deregulated activation induces the activator protein 1 (AP1) activation. AP1 activation is responsible for carcinoma onset. It was seen that curcumin significantly reduces the activation of AP1/MAPK pathway in liver tissue and prevents HCC [71].

Curcumin modulates angiogenic regulatory molecules: CTGF, SDF-1, VEGF, and IL-6, these are some molecules that confirm a pleiotropic role on hepatic cancer progression. CTGF, SDF-1, VEGF, and IL-6 cooperate with HIF-1α expression that suggests a potent marker for cancer prevention. The liver cancer cell treated with curcumin revealed that this golden bioactive component of turmeric can significantly suppress the expression of IL-6, SDF-1, and VEGF. It was also seen that curcumin shows no effect on VEGF, IL-6 expression, or ROS production when HIF-1α was knocked down in HSCs [72]. This suggests that curcumin acts through modulating the HIF-1α for its antiangiogenic consequences. Unique TME also favors the stabilization of HIF-1 [73,74]. Curcumin was found to alter the biophysical constitution of TME in animal model of lymphoma [14].

Curcumin has been registered for their apoptotic activity by participating in the active autophagy process. Microtubule-associated protein light chain 3 (LC3), sequestosome-1 (SQSTM1), Bcl-2 are some molecules that identify with the process of autophagy [75]. Curcumin treated liver cancer cells show higher expression of LC3 II and along with a decline in the expression of SQSTM1. This indicates autophagy-inducing ability of curcumin. Moreover, curcumin administration also protects from liver fibrosis by significantly attenuating in the level of alanine aminotransferase (ALT), aspartate aminotransferase (AST), and α-fetoprotein (AFP) and increasing serum albumin level [76]. Amino acid metabolism, especially metabolic trails of glutamine, is also linked with phenotypic aggressiveness of malignant cells. Amino acid levels also regulate the pathophysiological consequences in malignant, physiological as well as psychiatric disorders [77,78]. Owing to diverse metabolic targets and modulatory potential, curcumin is also expected to modulate amino acid metabolism in tumor cells of hepatic origin.

NF-kB signaling plays a major role in maintaining the microenvironment of most of the malignancy including carcinomas of hepatocellular origins [79]. MYC, cyclin D1, JNK, and STAT3 are prooncogenic molecules that regulate NF-kB signaling and control the chemoresistance phenotype in diverse forms of cancers. Convincing studies suggest that curcumin-mediated tumorigenic inhibition also depends on the inhibition of NF-kB signaling as well as expression of NF-kB signaling regulatory molecules, such as MYC, cyclin D1, JNK, and STAT3 [80]. Furthermore, curcumin also modulates the lactate-induced chemoresistance in the HepG2 cell line (Soni et al., 2020). A report suggests the role of suppressed expression of GLUT, STAT-3, MDR, HCAR1, and LDH in curcumin inhibited survival of HepG2 cells [29].

In hepatic carcinoma patients, the high expression of damage-associated molecular pattern (DAMP) molecules HSP-70 and TLR-4 is detected. It was seen that curcumin exerts apoptotic ability against HepG2 cells by significantly reducing the expression of HSP-70 and TLR-4 [68]. miR-21 has been reported as in the malignant properties of HCC and linked with a TIMP3/TGF-β1/smad3-signalling pathway. Curcumin attenuates miR-21 expression and inhibits TIMP3/TGF-β1/smad3-signaling pathway in HCC [12].

It is documented that UNC119 showed a higher expression in HCC cells and tissue. In vitro and in vivo studies suggest that UNC119 helps in tumor growth proliferation and their metastasis via the Wnt/β-catenin signal pathway and TGF-β/EMT pathway. Interestingly, curcumin has reported in the inhibition of proliferation and progression of hepatic cancer by reducing the expression of UNC119 [81,82].

Curcumin analog against liver cancer

Curcumin has a potent anticancer activity but its poor solubility, bioavailability, pharmacokinetics, and pharmacodynamics prevent it from becoming a promising and effective anticancer therapeutic candidate [5]. Curcumin analogs or derivatives overcomes these limitations and therefore emerged as the best therapeutic options for the treatment of liver cancer.

Recently, Wang and his team reported inhibition of hepatic cancer cell survival by a novel curcumin analog WZ35 via inhibiting YAP-mediated autophagy. They also reported induction of ROS-mediated cell death and inhibition of metastasis in liver cancer by WZ35 [83]. Liu and collogues synthesized 3,3′-hydroxy curcumin (1b), and tested its cytotoxic activity. The findings of their study suggest high cytotoxic ability of 1b against HepG2 cells than curcumin due to improved stability and massive uptake. More so, they showed the implication of ROS-mediated pathway in 1b-mediated apoptosis [24]. CA, a monocarbonyl analog of curcumin, has exhibited its antitumor activity in HEp-2 cells. Chen and coworkers reported that in HEp-2 hepatic cancer cell line, CA15 significantly inhibited the NF-kB signaling and showed a low unwanted toxic effect than parental curcumin [84].

Diphenyldifluoroketone (EF24), an artificially designed structural analog of curcumin, has also shown potent antineoplastic activity. In HepG2 cells, EF24 is observed in the attenuation of cancer progression by inhibition of invasion and migration through preventing the phosphorylation of Src [85]. Liu et al. reported G2/M phase cell cycle arrest, and apoptosis induction in Hepa1–6 and H22 murine liver cancer cell lines as well as in an in vivo model by Ef24. In addition, they showed antiangiogenic activity of EF24. In their study, they documented inhibition of phosphorylation of ERK1/2 and Akt, declined expression of VEGF, and increased cleaved caspase-3 level and Bax/Bcl-2 ratio after the treatment with ER24. Moreover, they also detected upregulated expression of pp53, p53, and p21 and decreased cyclin B1 and Cdc2 levels in EF24 treated groups [86]. Nanoparticle formulation of curcumin (NFC) has shown a strong tumor growth inhibitory ability. NFC resolves the poor solubility problem and has shown to reverse the multidrug resistance property in liver cancer. In a study, NFC in combination with sorafenib has significantly triggered apoptosis and cell cycle arrest in hepatocellular carcinoma cells. Further, this study also reports suppression of MMP9 expression by NFC via NF-κB/p65-signaling pathway. In addition, NFC also reduced the number of CD133-positive populations (cancer initiating cells) of HCC cells [87]. Bisdemethoxycurcumin (BDMC), a natural derivative of curcumin has shown apoptosis stimulating activity in activated hepatic stellate cells [88]. BDMC triggers the apoptosis cascade via lowering Bcl-2HO-1 levels, and augmenting ROS production through cannabinoid receptor (CBR) 2 [88]. Huang and colleagues studied on a novel curcumin analog C66 and demonstrated its protective effect on CCl4-induced liver fibrosis via altering the expression cannabinoid receptors [89]. C66 was found more potent than conventional curcumin. In their study, C66 upregulated the hepatic expression of CB2 receptor via attenuating JNK/NF-kB-mediated signaling pathway [89].

A curcumin analog hydrazinocurcumin (HZC) also has the potency to decrease the growth and proliferation of different types of cancers, including liver cancer. HZC inhibits STAT-3 activity by preventing the phosphorylation of STAT-3 in the HepG2 cells. In vivo studies in the DEN-induced rat also support the anti-HCC activity of HZC. Due to two methoxy groups, HZC shows higher anti-COX-2 activity than curcumin [90]. Liu et al. tested a new curcumin analog FLLL32, which has a potent anticancer activity. FLLL32 can significantly inhibit IL-6-induced STAT3 activation in vitro and in vivo [91]. FLLL32 inhibits JAK2 activity in human hepatocellular cancer [91].

Tetrahydrocurcumin (THC) is reported as a metabolite of curcumin and has tremendous biological activity. In the H22 cell line, THC significantly increased p53 protein level, and decreased MDM2 level culminating in an increased apoptotic activity. THC also reduced Bcl-2 activity and induced Bax activity, which was speculated for elevated cytochrome C release from mitochondria and subsequent onset of apoptotic cell death in the H22 cells [92].

Xiao and colleagues identified a new analog of curcumin (1E,4E)-1,5-bis(2-bromophenyl)penta-1,4-dien-3-one (GL63) which has exhibited more cytotoxicity and stable pharmacokinetics in the HepG2 cancer cell line and primary hepatocyte cells of rat as compared to curcumin. GL63 was found to activate caspase-3 and -9 and induced the apoptotic death of HepG2 cells. Further, they reported that GL63 induces apoptosis via triggering ER stress in HCC cells [93]. Bhullar et al. synthesized a curcumin analog diarylheptanoids (CUR3d), structurally similar to curcumin. They reported that CUR3d has multiple targets including HSP 90, Rho A and B genes, cyclins and CDKs, PLKs, topoisomerase, ATF2, PARP1, HIF-1α, Wnt/β-catenin signaling,

TP53, MDM2, HDACs, cathepsin, thioredoxin, Cox-2, glutathione s-transferaseP1−1, and many more to induce the apoptosis in HepG2 hepatic cancer cells. CUR3d activates caspase-3 whereas downregulates Bcl-2 and BIRC5 in HepG2 cells. CUR3d strongly impairs DNA integrity. In the HepG2 cells, CUR3d downregulates mTOR, and Akt expression and inhibits PI3K/Akt pathway. Besides, CUR3d also downregulates MAPK pathway via attenuating the protein kinase c activity [94]. Zhou and colleagues revealed the antihepatocarcinoma activity of double glutathione conjugate 3,5-bis(2-hydroxybenzylidene)tetrahydro-4Hpyran-4-one (EF25-(GSH)$_2$) curcumin analog. They explored the antiproliferative and autophagy-inducing nature of EF25-(GSH)2 in HepG2 cells. EF25-(GSH)2 arrested the cell cycle in the G2/M phase and induced cell death via both caspase-dependent and caspase-independent apoptotic mechanisms [95].

Zhang and his team explore the anticancer activity of hydrogenated metabolite of curcumin—octahydrocurcumin (OHC) in the H22-induced ascites tumor mice model. As compared to curcumin, OHC potentially activated p53 expression and downregulated MDM2 expression. They also observed OHC treatment induced proapoptotic Bax and Bad proteins while inhibited expression of antiapoptotic Bcl-2 and Bcl-xL proteins. Further, treatment of OHC significantly elevated the expression of cytochrome C, caspase-9, caspase-3, and cleaved PARP [96].

Collectively, a large number of analogs of curcumin with vivid variations were tested for effectiveness against liver cancer in laboratory and clinical investigations. Most of these analogs have shown promising success in overcoming the limitations associated with parental curcumin molecule or effectively augmented their antineoplatic activity against cancer cells of hepatic origin. Many of such analogs of curcumin are listed in Table 10.1 along with their cell type/model in which they were evaluated along with their mechanism of action.

Limitations and prospects

Despite demonstrated multifunctional ability, the health benefit of curcumin is limited. Curcumin is nonpolar in nature so that it has a poor bioavailability which might be inherent in its absorption, high metabolism ability, and rapid systemic elimination from the body [23,24]. After oral administration of 12 g of curcumin, only 0.051 μg/mL concentration of curcumin has been detected in the human plasma [28]. The solubility of curcumin in the water is very low (about 11 ng/mL) and is sensitive to deterioration particularly in alkaline conditions while in acidic conditions, a slow rate of destruction has been reported [97]. Only a small portion of orally administered curcumin is absorbed in the intestine and the major fraction is excreted out from the body in the feces. The absorbed part of curcumin rapidly metabolizes in the liver and plasma [98]. A lot of strategies are being implemented to enhance the poor bioavailability of curcumin. Use of conjugation therapy, nanoparticle technology, analogs of curcumin, phosphatidylcholine, and cyclodextrin complexes, as well as synthetic liposomal formulations, are some measures to improve/enhance the bioavailability of curcumin [5].

For the past several years, a lot of clinical trials have been conducted or are ongoing to check the chemopreventive and therapeutic ability of curcumin against cancers of different origins such as colon, liver, lungs, lymphoma, and neuronal. Although clinical trial results are very encouraging, there is a need for systematic review and critical evaluation of the clinical effect of curcumin and its analog.

TABLE 10.1 Various curcumin analogs found effective against liver cancer along with their mechanism of action.

Curcumin analogs	Cell line/system	Mechanism of action	Reference
(1E,4E)-1,5-bis(2-bromophenyl) penta-1,4-dien-3-one (GL63)	HepG2 cell line and rat primary hepatocyte cells	More cytotoxicity and stable pharmacokinetics, activates caspase-3 and -9 and induces apoptosis, triggers ER stress.	[93]
3,3'-hydroxy curcumin (1b)	HepG2 cell	Inhibits the cell survival, induces the ROS-mediated apoptosis.	[24]
Bisdemethoxycurcumin (BDMC)	HSC-T6 cell line	Induces the apoptosis, inhibiting the expression of Bcl-2, reduces the HO-1 level, increases the ROS production and CBR2-dependent formation of DISC.	[88]
CA15	HEp-2 cells	Inhibits cancer proliferation, inhibits the NF-kB signaling.	[84]
C66	CCl4-induced liver fibrosis	Increases cytotoxicity, C66 upregulating the hepatic CB2 receptor expression via JNK phosphorylation and NF-kB attenuation.	[89]
Diarylheptanoids (CUR3d)	HepG2	Multiple targets modulation such as HSP 90, Rho A and B gene, cycline and CDKs, PLKs, topoisomerase, ATF2, PARP1, HIF-1α, Wnt/β-catenin signaling, TP53, MDM2, HDACs, cathepsin, thioredoxin, Cox-2, glutathione s-transferaseP1−1, activates caspase-3, downregulates the Bcl-2 and BIRC5, disturbs the DNA integrity, downregulates the mTor and Akt expression, and modulates the PI3K/Akt pathway. Downregulates the MAPK pathway.	[94]
Diphenyldifluoroketone (EF24)	HepG2 cell	Decreases the metastasis of cancer, prevents the phosphorylation of Src-signaling pathway.	[85]
EF24	Hepa1-6 and H22 and in vivo	Suppresses growth of liver cancer, G2/M phase cell cycle arrest, inhibits the ERK1/2, upregulates caspase-3 and Bax/Bcl-2 and Bax/Bcl-xL ratio, overexpresses the pp53, p53, and p21, decreases the cyclin B1 and Cdc2, downregulates VEGF, Cox-2.	[86]
FLLL32	Hep3B and SNU-398 cells and in vivo study	Anticancer activity, inhibits IL-6-induced STAT3 activation, inhibits the JAK2 activity.	[91]

(Continued)

TABLE 10.1 (Continued)

Curcumin analogs	Cell line/system	Mechanism of action	Reference
Glutathione conjugate 3,5-bis(2-hydroxybenzylidene)tetrahydro-4Hpyran-4-one (EF25-(GSH)$_2$)	HepG2, SMMC-7721, BEL-7402 and immortalized human liver cell line (HL-7702)	Arrests the cell cycle on G2/M phase, and induces the cell death via both caspase-dependent and caspase-independent apoptotic mechanism.	[95]
Hydrazinocurcumin (HZC)	HepG2 cell line and in vivo	Decreases the growth and proliferation, inhibits the STAT-3 activity by preventing the phosphorylation, anti-COX-2 activity.	[90]
NFC a polymeric nanoparticle	In vitro, in vivo study	Increases solubility, reverses the multidrug resistance property. Reduces the number of CD133 positive population.	[87]
Octahydrocurcumin (OHC)	H22-induced ascites tumor mice model	Activates p53 expression and downregulates MDM2 expression, induces the proapoptotic Bax and Bad proteins, inhibits expressions of antiapoptotic Bcl-2 and Bcl-xL proteins, increases level of cytochrome C, caspase-9, caspase-3, increases the cleavage of PARP.	[96]
Tetrahydrocurcumin (THC)	H22 cell line	Activates apoptosis by increasing the p53 protein level, decreases the MDM2 level, reduces the Bcl-2 activity, induces the Bax activity, and increases cytochrome release.	[92]
WZ35	HCCLM3 cells	Antiproliferative activity, YAP-mediated autophagy, activates ROS, and prevents liver cancer metastasis.	[83]

Conclusion

In HCC, the therapeutic and chemo preventive ability of curcumin majorly depends on its antioxidant and antiinflammatory activities, signaling cascade modulation, pharmacodynamic, and pharmacokinetic nature. Several in vitro and in vivo studies suggest that curcumin has strong potency of antineoplastic activity against several types of cancers, including liver cancer. However, a substantial amount of work and significant efforts is required before regular clinical use of curcumin in the therapeutic management of HCC patients. The bioavailability of curcumin is a major roadblock in its preventive and therapeutic utilization [5]. The low therapeutic concentration of curcumin in humans is quite cited for the want of successful clinical tests. The epidemiological study conducted in South Asia, where part of turmeric, provides significant indications of its possible effects against liver cancer. Although curcumin is a regular dietary component in various regions of the globe and is considered safe and nontoxic as a pigment of spice turmeric, its single usage and long-term effects needs to be critically evaluated. The high doses remain a source of medically administered anxiety and a safe dosage rule needs to be established.

Acknowledgments

Financial support in the form of UGC-SRF (to Vivek Kumar Soni) GGU-VRET-Fellowship (to Yashwant Kumar Ratre and Arundhati Mehta) are acknowledged. Assistance and support received from respective institutes and organizations of authors are also duly acknowledged. Authors are also thankful to the UGC-Special Assistance Program (UGC-SAP) at the Department of Biotechnology (Guru Ghasidas Vishwavidyalaya) for necessary facilities in preparation of the manuscript. Dr Lalita Sharma (New Delhi) is also thankfully acknowledged for critical suggestions in the improvement of this chapter.

Declarations of interest

Authors declare no conflict of interest.

Funding

No specific grant from funding agencies in the public, commercial, or not-for-profit sectors was received for preparation of this manuscript.

References

[1] EASL (European Association for the Study of the Liver). EASL Clinical Practice Guidelines: management of hepatocellular carcinoma. J Hepatol 2018;69(1):182–236. Available from: https://doi.org/10.1016/j.jhep.2018.03.019.

[2] Abbas Z, Abbas M, Abbas S, Shazi L. Hepatitis D and hepatocellular carcinoma. World J Hepatol 2015;7 (5):777–86. Available from: https://doi.org/10.4254/wjh.v7.i5.777.

[3] Bai PS, Xia N, Sun H, Kong Y. Pleiotrophin, a target of miR-384, promotes proliferation, metastasis and lipogenesis in HBV-related hepatocellular carcinoma. J Cell Mol Med 2017;21(11):3023–43. Available from: https://doi.org/10.1111/jcmm.13213.

[4] Harouaka D, Engle RE, Wollenberg K, Diaz G, Tice AB, Zamboni F, et al. Diminished viral replication and compartmentalization of hepatitis C virus in hepatocellular carcinoma tissue. Proc Natl Acad Sci U S A 2016;113(5):1375–80. Available from: https://doi.org/10.1073/pnas.1516879113.

[5] Mehta A, Soni VK, Shukla D, Vishvakarma NK. (2020) Cyanobacteria: a potential source of anticancer drugs. In: Advances in cyanobacterial biology. Elsevier, Academic Press, London, pp 369–384. <https://doi.org/10.1016/B978-0-12-819311-2.00024-3>.

[6] Forner A, Reig ME, de Lope CR, Bruix J. Current strategy for staging and treatment: the BCLC update and future prospects. Semliver Dis 2010;30(1):61–74. Available from: https://doi.org/10.1055/s-0030-1247133.

[7] Peters GJ, Honeywell RJ. Drug transport and metabolism of novel anticancer drugs. Expert Opin Drug Metab Toxicol 2015;11(5):661–3. Available from: https://doi.org/10.1517/17425255.2015.1041255.

[8] Kulik LM, Chokechanachaisakul A. Evaluation and management of hepatocellular carcinoma. Clliver Dis 2015;19(1):23–43. Available from: https://doi.org/10.1016/j.cld.2014.09.002.

[9] Abrahams S, Haylett WL, Johnson G, Carr JA, Bardien S. Antioxidant effects of curcumin in models of neurodegeneration, ageing, oxidative and NITROSATIVE stress: a review. Neuroscience. 2019. Available from: https://doi.org/10.1016/j.neuroscience.2019.02.

[10] Rastegar R, Akbari Javar H, Khoobi M, et al. Evaluation of a novel biocompatible magnetic nanomedicine based on beta-cyclodextrin, loaded doxorubicin-curcumin for overcoming chemoresistance in breast cancer. Artif Cell Nanomed Biotechnol 2018;46:207—16. Available from: https://doi.org/10.1080/21691401.2018.1453829.

[11] Aggarwal BB, Kumar A, Bharti AC. Anticancer potential of curcumin: preclinical and clinical studies. Anticancer Res 2003;23(1A):363—98.

[12] Li J, Wei H, Liu Y, Li Q, Guo H, Guo Y, et al. Curcumin inhibits hepatocellular carcinoma via regulating miR-21/TIMP3 axis. Evid Based Complement Alternat Med 2020;2020:2892917. Available from: https://doi.org/10.1155/2020/2892917.

[13] Vishvakarma NK. Novel antitumor mechanisms of curcumin: implication of altered tumor metabolism, reconstituted tumor microenvironment and augmented myelopoiesis. Phytochem Rev 2014;13(3):717—24. Available from: https://doi.org/10.1007/s11101-014-9364-2.

[14] Vishvakarma NK, Kumar A, Singh SM. Role of curcumin-dependent modulation of tumor microenvironment of a murine T cell lymphoma in altered regulation of tumor cell survival. Toxicol Appl Pharmacol 2011;252 (3):298—306. Available from: https://doi.org/10.1016/j.taap.2011.03.002.

[15] Vishvakarma NK, Kumar A, Kumar A, Kant S, Bharti AC, Singh SM. Myelopotentiating effect of curcumin in tumor-bearing host: role of bone marrow resident macrophages. Toxicol Appl Pharmacol 2012;263 (1):111—21. Available from: https://doi.org/10.1016/j.taap.2012.06.004.

[16] Gupta SC, Patchva S, Aggarwal BB. Therapeutic roles of curcumin: lessons learned from clinical trials. AAPS J 2013;15(1):195—218. Available from: https://doi.org/10.1208/s12248-012-9432-8.

[17] Aggarwal BB, Harikumar KB. Potential therapeutic effects of curcumin, the anti-inflammatory agent, against neurodegenerative, cardiovascular, pulmonary, metabolic, autoimmune and neoplastic diseases. Int J Biochem Cell Biol 2009;41(1):40—59. Available from: https://doi.org/10.1016/j.biocel.2008.06.010.

[18] Panahi Y, Hosseini MS, Khalili N, Naimi E, Simental-Mendía LE, Majeed M, et al. Effects of curcumin on serum cytokine concentrations in subjects with metabolic syndrome: a post-hoc analysis of a randomized controlled trial. Biomed Pharmacother 2016;82:578—82. Available from: https://doi.org/10.1016/j.biopha.2016.05.037.

[19] Kuptniratsaikul V, Dajpratham P, Taechaarpornkul W, Buntragulpoontawee M, Lukkanapichonchut P, Chootip C, et al. Efficacy and safety of Curcuma domestica extracts compared with ibuprofen in patients with knee osteoarthritis: a multicenter study. Clin Interv Aging 2014;9:451—8. Available from: https://doi.org/10.2147/CIA.S58535.

[20] Mazzolani F, Togni S. Oral administration of a curcumin-phospholipid delivery system for the treatment of central serous chorioretinopathy: a 12-month follow-up study. Clin Ophthalmol 2013;7:939—45. Available from: https://doi.org/10.2147/OPTH.S45820.

[21] Allegri P, Mastromarino A, Neri P. Management of chronic anterior uveitis relapses: efficacy of oral phospholipidic curcumin treatment. Long-term follow-up. Clin Ophthalmol 2010;4:1201—6. Available from: https://doi.org/10.2147/OPTH.S13271.

[22] Trujillo J, Chirino YI, Molina-Jijón E, Andérica-Romero AC, Tapia E, Pedraza-Chaverrí J. Renoprotective effect of the antioxidant curcumin: recent findings. Redox Biol 2013;1(1):448—56. Available from: https://doi.org/10.1016/j.redox.2013.09.003.

[23] Liu W, Zhai Y, Heng X, Che FY, Chen W, Sun D, et al. Oral bioavailability of curcumin: problems and advancements. J Drug Target 2016;24(8):694—702. Available from: https://doi.org/10.3109/1061186x.2016.1157883.

[24] Liu G-Y, Sun Y-Z, Zhou N, Du X-M, Yang J, Guo S-J. 3,3′-OH curcumin causes apoptosis in HepG2 cells through ROS-mediated pathway. Eur J Med Chem 2016;112:157—63. Available from: https://doi.org/10.1016/j.ejmech.2016.02.019.

[25] Han HK. The effects of black pepper on the intestinal absorption and hepatic metabolism of drugs. Expert Opin Drug Metab Toxicol 2011;7(6):721—9. Available from: https://doi.org/10.1517/17425255.2011.570332.

[26] Shoba G, Joy D, Joseph T, Majeed M, Rajendran R, Srinivas PS. Influence of piperine on the pharmacokinetics of curcumin in animals and human volunteers. Plantamedica 1998;64(4):353—6. Available from: https://doi.org/10.1055/s-2006-957450.

[27] Basnet P, Skalko-Basnet N. Curcumin: an anti-inflammatory molecule from a curry spice on the path to cancer treatment. Molecules 2011;16(6):4567—98. Available from: https://doi.org/10.3390/molecules16064567.

[28] Lao CD, Ruffin 4th MT, Normolle D, Heath DD, Murray SI, Bailey JM, et al. Dose escalation of a curcuminoid formulation. BMC Complement Altern Med 2006;6:10. Available from: https://doi.org/10.1186/1472-6882-6-10.

[29] Soni VK, Shukla D, Kumar A, Vishvakarma NK. Curcumin circumvent lactate-induced chemoresistance in hepatic cancer cells through modulation of hydroxycarboxylic acid receptor-1. Int J Biochem Cell Biol 2020;123:105752. Available from: https://doi.org/10.1016/j.biocel.2020.105752 Epub 2020 Apr 20. PMID: 32325281.

[30] Soni VK, Mehta A, Ratre YK, Tiwari AK, Amit A, Singh RP, et al. Curcumin, a traditional spice component, can hold the promise against COVID-19? Eur J Pharmacol 2020;886:173551. Available from: https://doi.org/10.1016/j.ejphar.2020.173551 Epub 2020 Sep 12. PMID: 32931783.

[31] Soni VK, Mehta A, Shukla D, Kumar S, Vishvakarma NK. Fight COVID-19 depression with immunity booster: curcumin for psychoneuroimmunomodulation. Asian J Psychiatr 2020;53:102378. Available from: https://doi.org/10.1016/j.ajp.2020.102378 Epub 2020 Sep 1. PMID: 32916441; PMCID: PMC7462590.

[32] Sahebkar A, Serbanc MC, Ursoniuc S, Banach M. Effect of curcuminoids on oxidative stress: a systematicreview and *meta*-analysis of randomized controlled trials. J Funct Foods 2015;18:898–909.

[33] Menon VP, Sudheer AR. Antioxidant and anti-inflammatory properties of curcumin. Adv Exp Med Biol 2007;595:105–25. Available from: https://doi.org/10.1007/978-0-387-46401-5_3.

[34] Lin YG, Kunnumakkara AB, Nair A, Merritt WM, Han LY, Armaiz-Pena GN, et al. Curcumin inhibits tumor growth and angiogenesis in ovarian carcinoma by targeting the nuclear factor-kappaB pathway. Clin Cancer Res 2007;13(11):3423–30. Available from: https://doi.org/10.1158/1078-0432.CCR-06-3072.

[35] Marchiani A, Rozzo C, Fadda A, Delogu G, Ruzza P. Curcumin and curcumin-like molecules: from spice to drugs. Curr Med Chem 2014;21(2):204–22. Available from: https://doi.org/10.2174/092986732102131206115810.

[36] Recio MC, Andujar I, Rios JL. Anti-inflammatory agents from plants: progress and potential. Curr Med Chem 2012;19(14):2088–103. Available from: https://doi.org/10.2174/092986712800229069.

[37] Aggarwal BB, Shishodia S, Sandur SK, Pandey MK, Sethi G. Inflammation and cancer: how hot is the link? Biochem Pharmacol 2006;72(11):1605–21. Available from: https://doi.org/10.1016/j.bcp.2006.06.029.

[38] Amor S, Peferoen LA, Vogel DY, Breur M, van der Valk P, Baker D, et al. Inflammation in neurodegenerative diseases—an update. Immunology 2014;142(2):151–66. Available from: https://doi.org/10.1111/imm.12233.

[39] Gupta SC, Tyagi AK, Deshmukh-Taskar P, Hinojosa M, Prasad S, Aggarwal BB. Downregulation of tumor necrosis factor and other proinflammatory biomarkers by polyphenols. Arch Biochem Biophys 2014;559:91–9. Available from: https://doi.org/10.1016/j.abb.2014.06.006.

[40] Cho JW, Lee KS, Kim CW. Curcumin attenuates the expression of IL-1beta, IL-6, and TNF-alpha as well as cyclin E in TNF-alpha-treated HaCaT cells; NF-kappaB and MAPKs as potential upstream targets. Int J Mol Med 2007;19(3):469–74.

[41] Crețu E, Trifan A, Vasincu A, Miron A. Plant-derived anticancer agents - curcumin in cancer prevention and treatment. Rev Med Chir Soc Med Nat Iasi 2012;116(4):1223–9.

[42] Hernández M, Wicz S, Corral RS. Cardioprotective actions of curcumin on the pathogenic NFAT/COX-2/prostaglandin E2 pathway induced during *Trypanosoma cruzi* infection. Phytomedicine 2016;23(12):1392–400. Available from: https://doi.org/10.1016/j.phymed.2016.06.017.

[43] Yu W, Zha W, Ke Z, Min Q, Li C, Sun H, et al. Curcumin protects neonatal rat cardiomyocytes against high glucose-induced apoptosis via PI3K/Akt signalling pathway. J Diabetes Res 2016;2016:4158591. Available from: https://doi.org/10.1155/2016/4158591.

[44] Kohli S, Chhabra A, Jaiswal A, Rustagi Y, Sharma M, Rani V. Curcumin suppresses gelatinase B mediated norepinephrine induced stress in H9c2 cardiomyocytes. PLoS One 2013;8(10):e76519. Available from: https://doi.org/10.1371/journal.pone.0076519.

[45] Manghani C, Gupta A, Tripathi V, Rani V. Cardioprotective potential of curcumin against norepinephrine-induced cell death: a microscopic study. J Microsc 2017;265(2):232–44. Available from: https://doi.org/10.1111/jmi.12492.

[46] Yang X, Jiang H, Shi Y. Upregulation of heme oxygenase-1 expression by curcumin conferring protection from hydrogen peroxide-induced apoptosis in H9c2 cardiomyoblasts. Cell Biosci 2017;7:20. Available from: https://doi.org/10.1186/s13578-017-0146-6.

[47] Bai XJ, Hao JT, Wang J, Zhang WF, Yan CP, Zhao JH, et al. Curcumin inhibits cardiac hypertrophy and improves cardiovascular function via enhanced Na^+/Ca^{2+} exchanger expression after transverse abdominal aortic constriction in rats. Pharmacol Rep 2018;70(1):60–8. Available from: https://doi.org/10.1016/j.pharep.2017.07.014.

[48] Katanasaka Y, Sunagawa Y, Hasegawa K, Morimoto T. Application of curcumin to heart failure therapy by targeting transcriptional pathway in cardiomyocytes. Biol Pharm Bull 2013;36(1):13–17. Available from: https://doi.org/10.1248/bpb.b212022.

[49] Cao Q, Zhang J, Gao L, Zhang Y, Dai M, Bao M. Dickkopf-3 upregulation mediates the cardioprotective effects of curcumin on chronic heart failure. Mol Med Rep 2018;17(5):7249—57. Available from: https://doi.org/10.3892/mmr.2018.8783.

[50] Abdollahi E, Momtazi AA, Johnston TP, Sahebkar A. Therapeutic effects of curcumin in inflammatory and immune-mediated diseases: a nature-made jack-of-all-trades? J Cell Physiol 2018;233(2):830—48. Available from: https://doi.org/10.1002/jcp.25778.

[51] Mahmoud HK, Al-Sagheer AA, Reda FM, Mahgoub SA, Ayyat MS. Dietary curcumin supplement influence on growth, immunity, antioxidant status, and resistance to aeromonashydrophila in oreochromisniloticus. Aquaculture 2017;475:16—23.

[52] Wang S, Li H, Zhang M, Yue LT, Wang CC, Zhang P, et al. Curcumin ameliorates experimental autoimmune myasthenia gravis by diverse immune cells. Neurosci Lett 2016;626:25—34. Available from: https://doi.org/10.1016/j.neulet.2016.05.020.

[53] Shakeri F, Boskabady MH. Anti-inflammatory, antioxidant, and immunomodulatory effects of curcumin in ovalbumin-sensitized rat. Biofactors 2017;43(4):567—76. Available from: https://doi.org/10.1002/biof.1364.

[54] Afia M, Alshehri M, Alfaifi M, Shakor ABA. Repressive effect of curcumin against 2-amino3-methylimidazo 4,5-f quinoline induced hepato- and immunotoxicity in mice. Indian J Exp Biol 2017;55:365—71.

[55] Yang Z, He C, He J, Chu J, Liu H, Deng X. Curcumin-mediated bone marrow mesenchymal stem cell sheets create a favorable immune microenvironment for adult full-thickness cutaneous wound healing. Stem Cell Res Ther 2018;9(1):21. Available from: https://doi.org/10.1186/s13287-018-0768-6.

[56] Vishvakarma NK, Singh SM. Immunopotentiating effect of proton pump inhibitor pantoprazole in a lymphoma-bearing murine host: Implication in antitumor activation of tumor-associated macrophages. Immunol Lett 2010;134(1):83—92. Available from: https://doi.org/10.1016/j.imlet.2010.09.002.

[57] Kumar A, Sasmal D, Jadav SS, Sharma N. Mechanism of immunoprotective effects of curcumin in DLM-induced thymic apoptosis and altered immune function. an In silico and In vitro study. Immunopharmacol Immunotoxicol 2015;37(6):488—98. Available from: https://doi.org/10.3109/08923973.2015.1091004.

[58] Chuengsamarn S, Rattanamongkolgul S, Luechapudiporn R, Phisalaphong C, Jirawatnotai S. Curcumin extract for prevention of type 2 diabetes. Diabetes Care 2012;35(11):2121—7. Available from: https://doi.org/10.2337/dc12-0116.

[59] Li J, Wang P, Ying J, Chen Z, Yu S. Curcumin attenuates retinal vascular leakage by inhibiting calcium/calmodulin-dependent protein kinase II activity in streptozotocin-induced diabetes. Cell Physiol Biochem 2016;39(3):1196—208. Available from: https://doi.org/10.1159/000447826.

[60] Wojcik M, Krawczyk M, Wojcik P, Cypryk K, Wozniak LA. Molecular mechanisms underlying curcumin-mediated therapeutic effects in type 2 diabetes and cancer. Oxid Med Cell Longev 2018;2018:9698258. Available from: https://doi.org/10.1155/2018/9698258.

[61] Chanpoo M, Petchpiboonthai H, Panyarachun B, Anupunpisit V. Effect of curcumin in the amelioration of pancreatic islets in streptozotocin-induced diabetic mice. J Med Assoc Thai 2010;93(Suppl 6):S152—9.

[62] Balasubramanian S, Eckert RL. Curcumin suppresses AP1 transcription factor-dependent differentiation and activates apoptosis in human epidermal keratinocytes. J Biol Chem 2007;282(9):6707—15. Available from: https://doi.org/10.1074/jbc.M606003200.

[63] Ashour AA, Abdel-Aziz AA, Mansour AM, Alpay SN, Huo L, Ozpolat B. Targeting elongation factor-2 kinase (eEF-2K) induces apoptosis in human pancreatic cancer cells. Apoptosis 2014;19(1):241—58. Available from: https://doi.org/10.1007/s10495-013-0927-2.

[64] Lee HP, Li TM, Tsao JY, Fong YC, Tang CH. Curcumin induces cell apoptosis in human chondrosarcoma through extrinsic death receptor pathway. Int Immunopharmacol 2012;13(2):163—9. Available from: https://doi.org/10.1016/j.intimp.2012.04.002.

[65] Hahn YI, Kim SJ, Choi BY, Cho KC, Bandu R, Kim KP, et al. Curcumin interacts directly with the Cysteine 259 residue of STAT3 and induces apoptosis in H-Ras transformed human mammary epithelial cells. Sci Rep 2018;8(1):6409. Available from: https://doi.org/10.1038/s41598-018-23840-2.

[66] Siddiqui FA, Prakasam G, Chattopadhyay S, Rehman AU, Padder RA, Ansari MA, et al. Curcumin decreases Warburg effect in cancer cells by down-regulating pyruvate kinase M2 via mTOR-HIF1α inhibition. Sci Rep 2018;8(1):8323. Available from: https://doi.org/10.1038/s41598-018-25524-3.

[67] Wang J, Wang C, Bu G. Curcumin inhibits the growth of liver cancer stem cells through the phosphatidylinositol 3-kinase/protein kinase B/mammalian target of rapamycin signaling pathway. Exp Ther Med 2018;15(4):3650—8. Available from: https://doi.org/10.3892/etm.2018.5805.

[68] Ren B, Luo S, Tian X, Jiang Z, Zou G, Xu F, et al. Curcumin inhibits liver cancer by inhibiting DAMP molecule HSP70 and TLR4 signaling. Oncol Rep 2018;40(2):895–901. Available from: https://doi.org/10.3892/or.2018.6485.

[69] Wang WZ, Cheng J, Luo J, Zhuang SM. Abrogation of G2/M arrest sensitizes curcumin-resistant hepatoma cells to apoptosis. FEBS Lett 2008;582(18):2689–95. Available from: https://doi.org/10.1016/j.febslet.2008.06.048.

[70] Zeng Y, Shen Z, Gu W, Wu M. Inhibition of hepatocellular carcinoma tumorigenesis by curcumin may be associated with CDKN1A and CTGF. Gene 2018;651:183–93. Available from: https://doi.org/10.1016/j.gene.2018.01.083.

[71] Liang Z, Wu R, Xie W, Xie C, Wu J, Geng S, et al. Effects of curcumin on tobacco smoke-induced hepatic MAPK pathway activation and epithelial-mesenchymal transition in vivo. Phytother Res 2017;31(8):1230–9. Available from: https://doi.org/10.1002/ptr.5844.

[72] Shao S, Duan W, Xu Q, Li X, Han L, Li W, et al. Curcumin suppresses hepatic stellate cell-induced hepatocarcinoma angiogenesis and invasion through downregulating CTGF. Oxid Med Cell Longev 2019;2019:8148510. Available from: https://doi.org/10.1155/2019/8148510.

[73] Vishvakarma NK, Singh SM. Mechanisms of tumor growth retardation by modulation of pH regulation in the tumor-microenvironment of a murine T cell lymphoma. Biomed Pharmacother 2011;65(1):27–39. Available from: https://doi.org/10.1016/j.biopha.2010.06.012.

[74] Vishvakarma NK, Singh SM. Augmentation of myelopoiesis in a murine host bearing a T cell lymphoma following in vivo administration of proton pump inhibitor pantoprazole. Biochimie 2011;93(10):1786–96. Available from: https://doi.org/10.1016/j.biochi.2011.06.022.

[75] Lee YJ, Kim NY, Suh YA, Lee C. Involvement of ROS in curcumin-induced autophagic cell death. Korean J Physiol Pharmacol 2011;15(1):1–7. Available from: https://doi.org/10.4196/kjpp.2011.15.1.1.

[76] Elmansi AM, El-Karef AA, Shishtawy M, Eissa LA. Hepatoprotective effect of curcumin on hepatocellular carcinoma through autophagic and apoptic pathways. Ann Hepatol 2017;16(4):607–18. Available from: https://doi.org/10.5604/01.3001.0010.0307.

[77] Mehta A, Soni VK, Sharma K, Ratre YK, Shukla D, Singh AK, et al. Finding Horcrux of psychiatric symptoms in COVID-19: deficiencies of amino acids and vitamin D. Asian J Psychiatr 2021;55:102523. Available from: https://doi.org/10.1016/j.ajp.2020.102523.

[78] Soni VK, Sharma K, Mehta A, Ratre YK, Kumar S, Shukla D, et al. A physiological link for psychiatric symptoms in COVID-19: role of amino acid (2020d) deficiency. Asian J Psychiatr 2020;53:102426. Available from: https://doi.org/10.1016/j.ajp.2020.102426 Epub 2020 Sep 25. PMID: 33264844; PMCID: PMC7518799.

[79] Luedde T, Schwabe RF. NF-κB in the liver—linking injury, fibrosis and hepatocellular carcinoma. Nat Rev Gastroenterol Hepatol 2011;8(2):108–18. Available from: https://doi.org/10.1038/nrgastro.2010.213.

[80] Marquardt JU, Gomez-Quiroz L, Arreguin Camacho LO, Pinna F, Lee YH, Kitade M, et al. Curcumin effectively inhibits oncogenic NF-κBsignaling and restrains stemness features in liver cancer. J Hepatol 2015;63(3):661–9. Available from: https://doi.org/10.1016/j.jhep.2015.04.018.

[81] Liu ZH, Zhang YF, Xu ZD, Z H L, Y F Z, Z D X. UNC119 promoted cell growth and migration by Wnt/β-catenin signal and TGF-β/EMT signal pathway in hepatocellular carcinoma. J BUON 2018;23(6):1717–24.

[82] Zhao Z, Malhotra A, Seng WY. Curcumin modulates hepatocellular carcinoma by reducing UNC119 expression. J Environ Pathol Toxicol Oncol 2019;38(3):195–203. Available from: https://doi.org/10.1615/JEnvironPatholToxicolOncol.2019029549.

[83] Wang L, Zhu Z, Han L, Zhao L, Weng J, Yang H, et al. A curcumin derivative, WZ35, suppresses hepatocellular cancer cell growth via downregulating YAP-mediated autophagy. Food Funct 2019;10(6):3748–57. Available from: https://doi.org/10.1039/c8fo02448k.

[84] Chen J, Zhang L, Shu Y, Chen L, Zhu M, Yao S, et al. Curcumin analogue CA15 exhibits anticancer effects on HEp-2 cells via targeting NF-κB. BioMed Res Int 2017;2017:4751260. Available from: https://doi.org/10.1155/2017/4751260.

[85] Zhao R, Tin L, Zhang Y, Wu Y, Jin Y, Jin X, et al. EF24 suppresses invasion and migration of hepatocellular carcinoma cells in vitro via inhibiting the phosphorylation of Src. BioMed Res Int 2016;2016:8569684. Available from: https://doi.org/10.1155/2016/8569684.

[86] Liu H, Liang Y, Wang L, Tian L, Song R, Han T, et al. In vivo and in vitro suppression of hepatocellular carcinoma by EF24, a curcumin analog. PLoS One 2012;7(10):e48075. Available from: https://doi.org/10.1371/journal.pone.0048075.

[87] Hu B, Sun D, Sun C, Sun YF, Sun HX, Zhu QF, et al. A polymeric nanoparticle formulation of curcumin in combination with sorafenib synergistically inhibits tumor growth and metastasis in an orthotopic model of human hepatocellular carcinoma. Biochem Biophys Res Commun 2015;468(4):525–32. Available from: https://doi.org/10.1016/j.bbrc.2015.10.031.

[88] Lee PJ, Woo SJ, Jee JG, Sung SH, Kim HP. Bisdemethoxycurcumin Induces apoptosis in activated hepatic stellate cells via cannabinoid receptor 2. Molecules 2015;20(1):1277—92. Available from: https://doi.org/10.3390/molecules20011277.

[89] Huang SS, Chen DZ, Wu H, Chen RC, Du SJ, Dong JJ, et al. Cannabinoid receptors are involved in the protective effect of a novel curcumin derivative C66 against CCl4-induced liver fibrosis. Eur J Pharmacol 2016;779:22—30. Available from: https://doi.org/10.1016/j.ejphar.2016.02.067.

[90] Zhao JA, Peng L, Geng CZ, Liu YP, Wang X, Yang HC, et al. Preventive effect of hydrazinocurcumin on carcinogenesis of diethylnitrosamine-induced hepatocarcinoma in male SD rats. Asian Pac J Cancer Prev 2014;15(5):2115—21. Available from: https://doi.org/10.7314/apjcp.2014.15.5.2115.

[91] Liu Y, Fuchs J, Li C, Lin J. IL-6, a risk factor for hepatocellular carcinoma: FLLL32 inhibits IL-6-induced STAT3 phosphorylation in human hepatocellular cancer cells. Cell Cycle 2010;9(17):3423—7. Available from: https://doi.org/10.4161/cc.9.17.12946.

[92] Liu W, Zhang Z, Lin G, Luo D, Chen H, Yang H, et al. Tetrahydrocurcumin is more effective than curcumin in inducing the apoptosis of H22 cells via regulation of a mitochondrial apoptosis pathway in ascites tumor-bearing mice. Food Funct 2017;8(9):3120—9. Available from: https://doi.org/10.1039/c7fo00484b.

[93] Xiao J, Chu Y, Hu K, Wan J, Huang Y, Jiang C, et al. Synthesis and biological analysis of a new curcumin analogue for enhanced anti-tumor activity in HepG 2 cells. Oncol Rep 2010;23(5):1435—41. Available from: https://doi.org/10.3892/or_00000781.

[94] Bhullar KS, Jha A, Rupasinghe HP. Novel carbocyclic curcumin analog CUR3d modulates genes involved in multiple apoptosis pathways in human hepatocellular carcinoma cells. Chem Biol Interact 2015;242:107—22. Available from: https://doi.org/10.1016/j.cbi.2015.09.020.

[95] Zhou T, Ye L, Bai Y, Sun A, Cox B, Liu D, et al. Autophagy and apoptosis in hepatocellular carcinoma induced by EF25-(GSH)2: a novel curcumin analog. PLoS One 2014;9(9):e107876. Available from: https://doi.org/10.1371/journal.pone.0107876.

[96] Zhang Z, Luo D, Xie J, Lin G, Zhou J, Liu W, et al. Octahydrocurcumin, a final hydrogenated metabolite of curcumin, possesses superior anti-tumor activity through induction of cellular apoptosis. Food Funct 2018;9 (4):2005—14. Available from: https://doi.org/10.1039/c7fo02048a.

[97] Tønnesen HH, Karlsen J. Studies on curcumin and curcuminoids. VI. Kinetics of curcumin degradation in aqueous solution. Z Lebensm Unters Forsch 1985;180(5):402—4. Available from: https://doi.org/10.1007/BF01027775.

[98] Hoehle SI, Pfeiffer E, Sólyom AM, Metzler M. Metabolism of curcuminoids in tissue slices and subcellular fractions from rat liver. J Agric Food Chem 2006;54(3):756—64. Available from: https://doi.org/10.1021/jf058146a.

Curcumin formulated nanoparticles for hepatocellular carcinoma

Neha Merchant[1], Sujatha Peela[2], Afroz Alam[1] and Ganji Purnachandra Nagaraju[3]

[1]Department of Bioscience and Biotechnology, Banasthali University, Vanasthali, India
[2]Department of Biotechnology, Dr. B.R. Ambedkar University, Srikakulam, India
[3]School of Medicine, Division of Hematology and Oncology, University of Alabama, Birmingham, AL, United States

Abstract

Curcumin is a vital spice of Asia and a therapeutic plant with multiple biological properties such as antiinflammatory, antimicrobial, antioxidant, antiviral, and so on. It is a hydrophobic bioactive compound that has drawn attention for its various pharmacological actions. Despite numerous advantages, curcumin exhibits low bioavailability, rapid metabolism, and poor water solubility, making it unsuitable for effective therapeutic applications. Investigators are constantly attempting to improve the pharmacological as well as biological properties of curcumin to render its weaknesses by developing enhanced drug delivery mechanisms, predominantly nanoformulations. Hepatocellular carcinoma (HCC) is a complex disease as it poses a substantial health challenge globally because of the absence of treatment options except liver transplantation and resection surgery. Research efforts and facts from current literature have revealed reasonable competency of curcumin nanoformulations as it elevates all the pharmacological properties of curcumin and can prove to be a potential system for targeted HCC therapy. In this chapter, we discuss various curcumin nanoformulations, their therapeutic implications, and the antitumor activity of curcumin-mediated nanoformulations for managing HCC.

Keywords: Curcumin; hepatocellular carcinoma; nanoformulations; targeted treatment; nanotechnology

Abbreviations

AuNPs	Gold nanoparticles
CD	Cyclodextrins
CLNP	Curcumin-loaded liposomes nanoparticles
CYP 2E1	Cytochrome isoform 2E1

Ganji Purnachandra Nagaraju, Sarfraz Ahmad (eds.)
Theranostics and Precision Medicine for the Management of Hepatocellular Carcinoma, Volume 3
DOI: https://doi.org/10.1016/B978-0-323-99283-1.00025-2

© 2022 Elsevier Inc. All rights reserved.

DEN	Diethyl nitrosamine
EGFR	Epidermal growth factor receptors
EPR	Enhanced permeability and retention
HCC	Hepatocellular carcinoma
IL	Interleukin
LAC-NPs	Lactosylated nanoparticles
LPS	Lipopolysaccharide
MPEG-PCL	Monomethoxy poly(ethylene glycol)-poly(3-caprolactone)
NF-kB	Nuclear factor kappa-b
NIPAAM	N-isopropylacrylamide
NO	Nitric oxide
PGE2	Prostaglandin E2
PVA	Polyvinyl alcohol
SHH	Sonic hedgehog
Sp	Specificity protein
STAT	Signal transducers and activators of transcription

Introduction

Curcumin ($C_{21}H_{20}O_6$) or diferuloylmethane or 1,7-bis(4-hydroxy-3-methoxy phenyl)-1,6-heptadiene-3,5-dione, extracted from the rootstalk of turmeric or *Curcuma longa* is the most exemplified polyphenol because of its biological effects viz; as antiinflammatory, antimicrobial, antioxidant, antiviral, and so on [1]. Curcumin's anticancer properties is the most investigated and remain understand constant scrutiny in modern-day research [2]. Curcumin was initially segregated by Vogel and Pelletier at Harvard College Laboratory in 1815 [3]. Curcumin's pharmacological properties have been linked with several chronic ailments like arthritis, obesity, inflammation, metabolic syndrome, neurodegenerative ailments, and cancer [4].

Curcumin is known to regulate multiple signaling pathways at molecular levels depending on the cellular background and the target, triggering upregulation or downregulation [5]. Therefore, it acts upon numerous cellular signaling targets making it competent to fulfill various actions. Curcumin inhibits metastasis and cell proliferation at molecular levels as well as induces apoptosis through regulating various pro-inflammatory factors, growth factors, receptors, transcription factors, and protein kinases [6]. The antitumor properties of curcumin have been widely examined and shown to play a vital role as a preventative and a therapeutic agent for many cancers [7], including breast, gastrointestinal, head and neck, genitourinary, lung, melanoma, hematological, sarcoma, neurological, and hepatocellular carcinoma (HCC).

HCC is one of the most predominant classes of primary liver cancer, the sixth most prevalent malignancy, and a key cause of tumor-associated mortalities globally [8]. HCC is dominant in people with chronic liver ailments like cirrhosis caused due to viral hepatitis infection, chronic alcohol consumption, exposure to carcinogens such as nitrosamines and aflatoxin B1 [9]. Approximately 10% of HCC cases are existent in noncirrhotic liver [10]. The advancement of HCC is a slow-growing nodule that can remain dormant for several years [11]. Clinical properties of HCC depend on the proportions of the tumor mass or masses; larger tumors lead to upper abdominal discomfort, malaise, weight loss, pressure effects, and fatigue [12]. Common duct bile compression causes jaundice or hepatic decompensation [13]. Moreover, ascites imply coexistence of cirrhosis or advanced disease stage [14]. Other indications of HCC include paraneoplastic syndrome, gastrointestinal/esophageal variceal bleeding, hormonal imbalance, fever-induced due to tumor-necrosis, and hypercalcemia [15–16].

Chemotherapy, liver transplantation, and surgical resection are extensively used for the treatment of HCC but provide limited applicability [17]. A treatment of choice for managing advanced HCC is chemotherapy; however, low specificity and elevated toxicity of chemopreventive agents leads to complete toxicity as well as multiple side effects [18]. The primary prognostic factors for surgery are the tumor size and liver function [19]. Secondary treatment option: liver transplant is also limited since it is successful only during the initial stages of tumor progression and there is a scarcity of organ donors around the world [20]. Additionally, there is a strong likelihood of tumor recurrence in the transplanted liver [21].

Numerous alternative therapeutic approaches to manage HCC have been analyzed and are still under investigation, such as microwave coagulation, radiofrequency ablation, microspheres, intra-tumor ethanol injection, arterial chemoembolization, nanoformulations, and so on [18]. Targeted drug delivery using nanoformulations can provide high drug efficacy and negligible side effects [22]. Curcumin nanoformulations are known to exhibit superior therapeutic advantages compared to the free curcumin with increased solubility, high drug encapsulation efficiency, increased cellular uptake, improved bioavailability, and so on [23]. Moreover, through enhanced permeability and retention (EPR) property, it can also preferentially gather at the tumor site aiming to minimize toxicity on healthy cells while retaining antitumor efficacy [24].

In human beings, the efficiency of curcumin and its biological potency depends on its bioavailability [25]. Curcumin consists of binary aryl rings that contain ortho-methoxy phenolic OH groups that are proportionally connected with a β-diketone moiety [26]. Curcumin consists of binary para hydroxyl, keto, methoxy clusters, and an active methylene cluster [27]. Curcumin is polyphenolic and a hydrophobic compound, which makes it water insoluble in neutral and acidic environments while soluble in acetone, methanol, dimethylsulfoxide, and ethanol [28]. Despite multidisciplinary therapeutic benefits, curcumin has been associated with severe drawbacks, viz., poor bioavailability, absorption, aqueous solubility, increased metabolism, and rapid excretion [29]. These factors limit the practical applications of curcumin and obstruct its applicability as a commercial therapeutic compound.

To overcome these challenges, several innovative approaches have been commenced, such as using adjuvant compounds (piperine), formulating liposomal curcumin, phospholipid complexes, curcumin nanoparticles, and developing structural curcumin analogs [30]. Multiple attempts have been made to not only enhance the bioavailability of the innovative formulations but also improve drug targeting at the diseased location with the help of aptamer, peptide mediation, and antibody [31]. Effective curcumin drug delivery using nanotechnology overcomes many barriers like solubility, degradation, stability, and rapid metabolism, in addition to minimizing the unintentional toxicity in the surrounding tumor environment [32]. Despite the extensive research that aims to prevail the barriers of curcumin applicability, the emergence of nanoformulations act as a breakthrough that reasonably incorporates a definitive transition to managing an array of chronic ailments using nanocurcumin via a successful drug delivery process.

Chemicals involved in hepatocellular carcinoma

Multiple chemicals induce experimental HCC, including diethyl nitrosamine (DEN), anabolic steroids, aflatoxin B1, thioacetamide, alcohol, and carbon-tetrachloride [33]. DEN is a prominent hepatocarcinogenic substance, which can be obtained from various medical products, agricultural substances, ground water, cosmetics, alcohol, tobacco smoke, and some fried meals [34–35]. Rat models induced with DEN are extensively employed as experimental models for investigating hepatocarcinogenesis [36]. DEN administered into animal models causes liver malignancy with a low incidence rate in other tissues [37] [38]. Whereas nitrosamine is known to be metabolized by the human liver, which is triggered by cytochrome isoform 2E1 (CYP 2E1) followed by oxidative stress force, and cell damage because of augmented production of reactive oxygen species [39].

Traditional HCC management techniques like ablation, radiotherapy, chemotherapy, and surgical resection warrant very little hope for complete therapeutic restoration due to poor prognosis and severe toxic effects associated with these treatment options. Consequently, synthesizing efficient and reliable antitumor drugs such as natural polyphenols is warranted for the inhibition of HCC progression and metastasis. The application of nanoformulations as drug delivery agents in various biological fields, including cancer research, has improved the efficacy of drug delivery, bioavailability, sustainability, absorption, stability, and solubility [40]. Additionally, it has also enhanced the therapeutic efficiency of various antitumor drugs [41]. Moreover, the emergence of nanotechnology-assisted imaging techniques in cancer research has shown to be a significant breakthrough for cancer detection [42]. Nanoformulations encapsulating antitumor drugs hold the potential to enhance drug concentration into HCC tissues and act at molecular levels, thereby augmenting the antitumor efficacy.

Curcumin nanoformulations in hepatocellular carcinoma

In recent years, several curcumin nanoformulations are being synthesized with a primary focus on enhancing the bioavailability and solubility of curcumin [3]. Few nanoformulations target longtime circulations and body retention, while others focus on intracellular release mechanisms and cellular drug delivery [43]. Numerous curcumin nanoformulations have been known to impact the pharmaceutical applications and have shown to exhibit significant effects in the diagnosis of severe ailments such as HCC.

Nanoparticles

Approximately 1 to 100 nm in size (diameter), nanoparticles retain unique biological, physical, and chemical properties, which can exhibit significant benefits in drug delivery [44]. These particles are 1000 times more condensed in comparison to a typical human cell and are made up of materials that are designed at molecular levels [45]. Nanoparticles are capable of targeted as well as controlled drug delivery systems [46]. Drugs encapsulated within nanoparticles can improve their solubility and pharmacokinetics, provide controlled drug release and targeted delivery of drugs [47]. Until now, the following nanoparticles have been widely used to boost the medicinal properties of curcumin; albumin-based, solid lipid, polymer, magnetic, and gold nanoparticles (AuNPs) [48].

Colloidal submicron nanoparticles formed by synthetic or natural phospholipids by diffusing them in water or aqueous agents are known as solid lipid nanoparticles [49]. These categories of curcumin nanoparticles are extremely stable, biocompatible, and scalable, making them a very favorable drug delivery system [50]. The drug to lipid ratio of these particles is also very high, thereby exhibiting enhanced solubility of poorly soluble agents. Lipid curcumin nanoparticles exhibit improved solubility in comparison to the indigenous curcumin and diminish the activities of lipopolysaccharide (LPS)-induced pro-inflammatory mediators such as interleukin (IL)-6, NO, and PGE2, via obstruction of NF-kB activation [51]. Polymeric nanoparticles are biocompatible and tiny, which allows them to circulate for longer durations within the blood stream [52]. Various natural, as well as synthetic polymers, are developed and identified to synthesize curcumin nanoparticles such as hydrophobically altered starch, silk fibroin, chitosan, N-isopropylacrylamide (NIPAAM), Nvinyl-2-pyrrolidone, polyvinyl alcohol (PVA), polyethylene glycol monoacrylate [NIPAAM (VP/PEG A)], and poly(lactic-co-glycolic acid) (PLGA) [53]. Magnetic nanoparticles contain a metal or metal oxide core, which can be operationalized inside an inorganic or polymer-metal coating that confirms the magnetic nanoparticles stability and biocompatibility [54]. These nanoparticles are biopolymeric, have distinctive physical properties, and are inexpensive [55−56]. Albumin is a protein carrier of choice for drug delivery due to various properties such as binding capacity, nontoxic, and biodegradable [57]. Another novel material of choice is AuNPs that have optical as well as catalytic properties, which are biocompatibility and nontoxicity [58]. AuNPs that are developed using plant extracts are widely employed in therapeutic areas [59].

Liposomes

Liposomes are sphere-shaped sacs that consist of phospholipid bilayers encircling aqueous units resembling very close to the skeleton of a cell membrane [60]. Liposomes are an ideal mode of delivery for biologically active agents in vivo as well as in vitro conditions [61]. Liposomes are a preferred choice of drug delivery system due to their many advantages: easy preparation, flexibility, enhanced solubility, very low toxicity, increased biocompatibility as well as biodegradability [62]. The liposome size range is around 25−2.5 mm [63]. Vesicle proportion is a vital aspect to determine the liposome circulation period. The size, as well as bilayers, influence the amount of drug encapsulated within the liposome [64]. Several investigations reveal that curcumin is solubilized by liposomes inside the phospholipid bilayer [65]. Additionally, liposomes allow curcumin distribution over the aqueous medium while also enhancing its therapeutic efficiency [66]. Liposomal drugs are primarily accumulated in the lungs, bone marrow, spleen, liver, and other vital organs, improving the therapeutic index of the drug while reducing its toxic effects [67]. Extensive research has been conducted revealing that liposomal curcumin is the most efficient drug delivery system for managing various cancers, including HCC.

Conjugates and cyclodextrins

Conjugates are complexes formed by adjoining diverse molecules through covalent bonds [68]. Curcumin conjugation along with hydrophilic polymers as well as small molecules are known to enhance drug solubility as well as bioavailability [69]. A study reported that curcumin union with hyaluronic acid diminishes the properties of AuNPs [70]. Cyclodextrins (CD) or a-, b-, g-cyclodextrins are a multicomponent hybrid drug transport components that carry noncovalently bound drugs [71]. These oligosaccharides are bucket shaped that consist of either six (a-), seven (b-), or eight (g-) D-glucopyranose elements connected by a 1,4-glycosidic bond to produce macrocycles [72]. CDs are known to improve drug stability and solubility while assisting drug delivery in its active form to the tumor cell [73]. b-CD and g-CD, along with their derivatives, are potent options for drug delivery due to their adaptability, easy synthesis, and low cost [74].

Micelles, nanospheres, and microcapsules

Micelles are a cluster of amphiphilic surface-active agents, which spontaneously accumulate in a spherical vesicle in an aqueous solution [75]. Water-insoluble drugs like curcumin are widely used to be delivered through micelles [76]. Nanospheres, also called solid matrix particles, are polymeric nanoparticles with solid mass consisting of sphere-shaped polymeric mediums [77]. The primary active drug is distributed through the entire polymeric core, while the active element is released through the process of diffusion into the environment [78]. Microcapsules contain the major active drug, while a polymeric shell forms the outer coating [79].

Miscellaneous nanoformulations

Various other nanoformulations of curcumin have been developed in addition to those listed above; metallo-complexes, nanogels, yeast cells, and nanodisks with a common aim of enhancing the biological properties of curcumin. Nanogels are composed of chemical or physical cross-linking polymer synthesized hydrogel under controlled settings [80]. Nanogels offer an extremely powerful drug storage and release system due to their cross-linked structure [81]. Nanodisks, on the other hand, are discoidal lipid bilayers that are apolipoprotein-stabilized and soluble in aqueous mediums by two circling amphipathic helical protein belts known as membrane scaffold proteins [82].

Synthesis of nanoformulations

An array of multiple techniques is developed to synthesize nanaocurcumin, including nanoprecipitation, coacervation technique, spray drying, solid dispersion, single emulsion, emulsion, solvent evaporation, ionic gelation, microemulsion, Fessi method, antisolvent precipitation, thin-film hydration, wet milling, ultra-sonication, and emulsion polymerization [83−84]. Many researchers have reviewed the advantages and characteristics of each of these synthesis techniques. Out of all the techniques listed above, the most efficient are antisolvent precipitation and ionic gelation since they reveal improved solubility and stability compared to all other methods. The ability of polymers to cross link in order to make nanoparticles with the coexistence of counter ions is known as ionic gelation [85]. This technique has been employed to prepare natural polymers such as chitosan that are biodegradable, nontoxic, and biocompatible. Based on ionic gelation, various investigation has outlined the potential of using natural polymer nanoparticles for oral administration of curcumin [86]. Another extensively used technique for the synthesis of curcumin nanoparticles is antisolvent precipitation [87]. The efficiency of this technique relies on the stirring speed, time interval, and temperature. Solid dispersion is a nanoformulation synthesis process in which the molecular dispersion of distinct complexes takes place, typically a hydrophobic agent like curcumin dispersed in a solid hydrophilic medium [88]. The drug is released by dissolving solid dispersions as tiny colloidal units of aqueous media [89]. The constituent part size is reduced to nanorange with enhanced wettability, thereby improving drug bioavailability and pharmacokinetic properties [90]. Various methods are used to produce solid dispersions like solvent-based methods, fusion-melt methods, or hybrid techniques that include the combination of solvent and fusion [91]. The stability and solubility of curcumin water were enhanced by a solution mixing technique to prepare curcumin-Eudragit PO by a study led by Li et al. [92]. Additionally, curcumin-Gelucire50/13 solid dispersion, which was synthesized by spray drying, exhibited improved water solubility as compared to the native curcumin [93]. Various investigations have revealed the efficacy of this nanoformulation synthesis technique as being cost effective and promising for future advancements while providing enhanced solubility and stability to curcumin nanoparticles [94].

Anticancer properties of curcumin facilitated nanoformulations

The emergence of nanotechnology has brought several opportunities for enhancing the therapeutic efficacy of curcumin, such as improved bioavailability, cell uptake, and aqueous dispersion [95]. Being an extremely pleiotropic molecule, curcumin exhibits efficient properties as an anticancer drug against several cancers, including HCC [96]. Various molecular mechanisms are involved that mediate the apoptotic, antimetastatic, and antiinvasive properties of curcumin on tumor cells [97]. Members of sonic hedgehog (SHH)/ GLIs, epidermal growth factor receptors (EGFR), and Wnt/β-catenin are involved in inhibiting the oncogenic pathways by curcumin [98]. Moreover, the downstream signaling transcription factors such as signal transducers and activators of transcription (STATs), Akt, and nuclear factor-kappa B (NF-κB) mediate the inhibition of tumorigenesis by curcumin [99]. Curcumin's therapeutic efficiency is restricted because of its metabolic instability and extremely poor bioavailability [100]. Consequently, delivering analogs and nanoformulations of curcumin to malignant cells alone or codelivered with other antitumor agents can potentially improve curcumin's therapeutic effectiveness against HCC progression [101]. Novel curcumin nanoformulations are known to overcome drug resistance, enrich antitumorigenic efficacy, and completely eradicate tumor mass in patients.

Widespread investigations in human HCC cells lines, as well as animal models, have revealed enhanced cellular uptakes of curcumin nanoformulations compared to native curcumin because of chemokine inhibition and metastasis and subsequently delaying proliferation [102]. The permissive chemotherapy, as well as chemopreventive properties, are mediated via various mechanisms involved in apoptosis (caspase-8, -3, and -9), cell proliferation (Cyclin D1, c-Myc), and cell survival (Bcl-2, Bcl-xL) for selectively targeting proliferating tumor cells over normal tissues [103–104]. The anticancer properties of curcumin at the molecular level underline the mechanism of inhibiting specificity protein (Sp) transcriptions factors – Sp1, Sp3, and Sp4 [105]. Malignant HCC tumor suppression by curcumin is associated with upregulating pro-apoptotic proteins like Noxa, Bax, Bim, Bak, and Puma, downregulating antiapoptotic proteins viz; Bcl-xL, XIAP, and Bcl-2, growth factors viz; HER2 and EGFR, and inhibiting the activation of c-Jun N terminal kinase, protein serine/threonine kinases, and protein tyrosine kinases that diminish the metastatic properties [106].

The anticancer properties of curcumin nanoparticles have been studied in various cancers. Gou et al. reported through an in vivo investigation that encapsulation of curcumin within monomethoxy poly(ethylene glycol)-poly(3-caprolactone) (MPEG-PCL) micelles inhibited colon cancer cell line proliferation [107]. Another study reported that curcumin-loaded liposomes nanoparticles (CLNP) inhibited the proliferative activities of melanoma cell lines as a result of improved drug delivery [108]. The same nanoparticles were also reported to inhibit skin cancer cell lines [108]. A study concerning HCC reported that the codelivery of curcumin and sorafenib using pH-sensitive lactosylated nanoparticles (LAC-NPs) significantly inhibited HCC tumor activity with very low toxicity [109]. Most of these investigations show enhanced tumor-targeted efficacy as compared to indigenous curcumin. In a polarized environment, curcumin nanoparticles exhibit an excellent capacity to perforate inside the cell and a superior electron transfer rate to cross the plasma membrane [110]. Therefore, nanoformulation particle size reveals to have enhanced solubility, improved therapeutic efficacy, and robust anticancer activity against multiple malignancies, particularly HCC.

Conclusion

Curcumin is a widely available, inexpensive polyphenol that exhibits numerous anticancers, antioxidant, antiinflammatory properties [111]. Multiple preclinical and clinical studies have revealed the significance of curcumin in inhibiting cancer proliferation and metastasis as a key bioactive and therapeutic agent [95]. HCC is an extremely abrasive malignancy that shows a low response rate towards most traditional therapies [112]. Low cellular uptake of antitumor drugs and insufficient targeting efficacy is the primary obstacle to achieving satisfactory results; therefore, multifunctional nanoformulations that are being developed consist of antitumor drugs (natural and synthetic) along with specialized antibodies [113]. These multifunctional nanoformulations are used for prognosis, treatment, and further exploration of HCC.

Nanoformulations have attracted much attention because of their capacity to tackle numerous signaling pathways involved in HCC [114–115]. Several curcumin nanoformulations discussed in this chapter can enhance the bioavailability of curcumin with minimum toxic effects. Multiple preclinical and clinical trials have established that curcumin nanoformulations improve the bioavailability and exhibit reduced toxicity as compared to

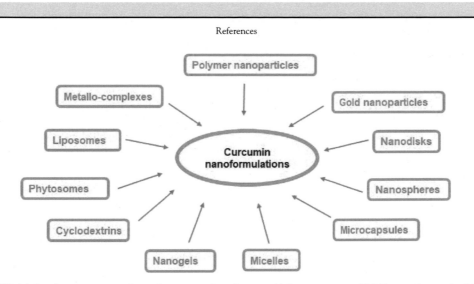

FIGURE 11.1 Curcumin nanoformulations used in hepatocellular carcinoma (HCC) to enhance its bioavailability and solubility. Arrows indicate curcumin nanoformulations developed from various nanomaterials.

native curcumin [116−118]. Additionally, implementing curcumin nanoformulations as a combination drug is efficient in diminishing the dose of the primary drug, thereby improving the overall therapeutic effectiveness of the drug and reducing toxic effects [119]. Therefore, the emergence of nanoformulations is a breakthrough that integrates a conclusive transition to control an array of serious ailments such as HCC using nanocurcumin as a drug delivery agent (Fig. 11.1).

Funding

None to declare

Conflict of interest

None to disclose

References

[1] Giordano A, Tommonaro G. Curcumin and cancer. Nutrients 2019;11(10):2376.
[2] Perrone D, Ardito F, Giannatempo G, Dioguard M, Troiano G, Lo Russo L, et al. Biological and therapeutic activities, and anticancer properties of curcumin. Exp Ther Med 2015;10(5):1615−23.
[3] Adahoun MA, Al-Akhras M-AH, Jaafar MS, Bououdina M. Enhanced anti-cancer and antimicrobial activities of curcumin nanoparticles. Artif Cells Nanomed Biotechnol 2017;45(1):98−107.
[4] Hewlings SJ, Kalman DS. Curcumin: a review of its effects on human health. Foods 2017;6(10):92.
[5] Kunnumakkara AB, Bordoloi D, Harsha C, Banik K, Gupta SC, Aggarwal BB. Curcumin mediates anticancer effects by modulating multiple cell signaling pathways. Clin Sci 2017;131(15):1781−99.
[6] Qadir MI, Naqvi STQ, Muhammad SA, Qadir M, Naqvi ST. Curcumin: a polyphenol with molecular targets for cancer control. Asian Pac J Cancer Prev 2016;17(6):2735−9.

[7] Todoric J, Antonucci L, Karin M. Targeting inflammation in cancer prevention and therapy. Cancer Prev Res 2016;9(12):895−905.

[8] Ma C, Zhang Q, Greten TF. Nonalcoholic fatty liver disease promotes hepatocellular carcinoma through direct and indirect effects on hepatocytes. FEBS J 2018;285(4):752−62.

[9] Desai A, Sandhu S, Lai J-P, Sandhu DS. Hepatocellular carcinoma in non-cirrhotic liver: a comprehensive review. World J Hepatol 2019;11(1):1.

[10] Ding Z, Lin K, Fu J, Huang Q, Fang G, Tang Y, et al. An MR-based radiomics model for differentiation between hepatocellular carcinoma and focal nodular hyperplasia in non-cirrhotic liver. World J Surg Oncol 2021;19(1):1−10.

[11] Attwa MH, El-Etreby SA. Guide for diagnosis and treatment of hepatocellular carcinoma. World J Hepatol 2015;7(12):1632.

[12] Lee YR, Kim G, Tak WY, Jang SY, Kweon YO, Park JG, et al. Circulating exosomal noncoding RNAs as prognostic biomarkers in human hepatocellular carcinoma. Int J Cancer 2019;144(6):1444−52.

[13] Fargo MV, Grogan SP, Saguil A. Evaluation of jaundice in adults. Am Fam Physician 2017;95(3):164−8.

[14] Bernardi M, Ricci CS, Santi L. Hyponatremia in patients with cirrhosis of the liver. J Clin Med 2015;4(1):85−101.

[15] Kuchay MS, Mishra SK, Farooqui KJ, Bansal B, Wasir JS, Mithal A. Hypercalcemia of advanced chronic liver disease: a forgotten clinical entity!. Clin Cases Miner Bone Metab 2016;13(1):15.

[16] Suzuki E, Ooka Y, Chiba T, Kobayashi K, Kanogawa N, Motoyama T, et al. Incidental tumor necrosis caused by the interventional alteration of hepatic arterial flow in patients with advanced hepatocellular carcinoma. Clin J Gastroenterol 2015;8(1):41−6.

[17] Lurje I, Czigany Z, Bednarsch J, Roderburg C, Isfort P, Neumann UP, et al. Treatment strategies for hepatocellular carcinoma—a multidisciplinary approach. I J Mol Sci 2019;20(6):1465.

[18] Lin J, Wu L, Bai X, Xie Y, Wang A, Zhang H, et al. Combination treatment including targeted therapy for advanced hepatocellular carcinoma. Oncotarget 2016;7(43):71036.

[19] Goh BK, Teo JY, Chan CY, Lee SY, Jeyaraj P, Cheow PC. Importance of tumor size as a prognostic factor after partial liver resection for solitary hepatocellular carcinoma: implications on the current AJCC staging system. J Surg Oncol 2016;113(1):89−93.

[20] Carvalho A, Rocha A, Lobato L. Liver transplantation in transthyretin amyloidosis: issues and challenges. Liver Transpl 2015;21(3):282−92.

[21] Sapisochin G, Bruix J. Liver transplantation for hepatocellular carcinoma: outcomes and novel surgical approaches. Nat Rev Gastroenterol Hepatol 2017;14(4):203−17.

[22] Rostami E. Progresses in targeted drug delivery systems using chitosan nanoparticles in cancer therapy: a mini-review. J Drug Deliv Sci Technol 2020;58:101813.

[23] Deljoo S, Rabiee N, Rabiee M. Curcumin-hybrid nanoparticles in drug delivery system. Asian J Nanosci Mater 2019;2(1):66−91.

[24] Kalyane D, Raval N, Maheshwari R, Tambe V, Kalia K, Tekade RK. Employment of enhanced permeability and retention effect (EPR): nanoparticle-based precision tools for targeting of therapeutic and diagnostic agent in cancer. Mater Sci Eng C 2019;98:1252−76.

[25] Zhao JA, Sang MX, Geng CZ, Wang SJ, Shan BE. A novel curcumin analogue is a potent chemotherapy candidate for human hepatocellular carcinoma. Oncol Lett 2016;12(5):4252−62.

[26] Jha NS, Mishra S, Jha SK, Surolia A. Antioxidant activity and electrochemical elucidation of the enigmatic redox behavior of curcumin and its structurally modified analogues. Electrochim Acta 2015;151:574−83.

[27] Nakai R, Fukuda S, Kawase M, Yamashita Y, Ashida H. Curcumin and its derivatives inhibit 2, 3, 7, 8,-tetra-chloro-dibenzo-p-dioxin-induced expression of drug metabolizing enzymes through aryl hydrocarbon receptor-mediated pathway. Biosci Biotechnol Biochem 2018;82(4):616−28.

[28] Stanić Z. Curcumin, a compound from natural sources, a true scientific challenge—a review. Plant Foods Hum Nutr 2017;72(1):1−12.

[29] Kakkar V, Saini K, Saini M, Kumar M, Narula P, Duggal I. Comparison of therapeutic efficacy of nanoformulations of curcumin vs tetrahydrocurcumin in various disorders. Nanoformulations in human health. Springer; 2020. p. 377−401.

[30] Tomeh MA, Hadianamrei R, Zhao X. A review of curcumin and its derivatives as anticancer agents. I J Mol Sci 2019;20(5):1033.

[31] Karthikeyan A, Senthil N, Min T. Nanocurcumin: a promising candidate for therapeutic applications. Front Pharmacol 2020;11:487.

[32] Tibbitt MW, Dahlman JE, Langer R. Emerging frontiers in drug delivery. J Am Chem Soc 2016;138(3):704−17.

[33] Usmani A, Mishra A, Ahmad M. Nanomedicines: a theranostic approach for hepatocellular carcinoma. Artif Cells Nanomed Biotechnol 2018;46(4):680−90.

[34] Lee BK, Yun YH, Park K. Etiology of hepatocellular carcinoma and treatment through medicinal plants: a comprehensive review. Orient Pharm Exp Med 2018;18(3):187−97.

[35] Bhatia S. Natural history of untreated hepatocellular carcinoma in a US cohort and the role of cancer surveillance. Clin Gastroenterol Hepatol 2017;15(2):273−81.

[36] Prasad R, Pandey R, Varma A, Barman I. Evaluation of Antioxidant properties of Quercetin in DEN-induced Hepatocellular Carcinoma in BALB/c mice. NEHU J 2019;94.

[37] Santos NP, Colaco AA, Oliveira PA. Animal models as a tool in hepatocellular carcinoma research: a Review. Tumor Biol 2017;39(3) 1010428317695923.

[38] Lau JKC, Zhang X, Yu J. Animal models of non-alcoholic fatty liver disease: current perspectives and recent advances. J Pathol 2017;241(1):36−44.

[39] Mohi-Ud-Din R, Mir RH, Sawhney G, Dar MA, Bhat ZA. Possible pathways of hepatotoxicity caused by chemical agents. Curr Drug Metab 2019;20(11):867−79.

[40] Baig B, Halim SA, Farrukh A, Greish Y, Amin A. Current status of nanomaterial-based treatment for hepatocellular carcinoma. Biomed Pharmacother 2019;116:108852.

[41] Bhatia S. Natural polymer drug delivery systems: nanoparticles, plants, and algae. Springer; 2016.

[42] Wang C, Fan W, Zhang Z, Wen Y, Xiong L, Chen X. Advanced nanotechnology leading the way to multimodal imaging-guided precision surgical therapy. Adv Mater 2019;31(49):1904329.

[43] Lopalco A, Denora N. Nanoformulations for drug delivery: safety, toxicity, and efficacy. Computational toxicology. Springer; 2018. p. 347−65.

[44] Lee BK, Yun YH, Park K. Smart nanoparticles for drug delivery: boundaries and opportunities. Chem Eng Sci 2015;125:158−64.

[45] Bhatia S. Nanoparticles types, classification, characterization, fabrication methods and drug delivery applications. Natural polymer drug delivery systems. Springer; 2016. p. 33−93.

[46] Prasad R, Pandey R, Varma R, Barman I. Polymer based nanoparticles for drug delivery systems and cancer therapeutics. Natural polymers for drug delivery. Oxfordshire; 2016. p. 53−70.

[47] Xu X, Ho W, Zhang X, Bertrand N, Farokhzad O. Cancer nanomedicine: from targeted delivery to combination therapy. Trends Mol Med 2015;21(4):223−32.

[48] Esim O, Hascicek C. Albumin-based nanoparticles as promising drug delivery systems for cancer treatment. Curr Pharm Anal 2021;17(3):346−59.

[49] Sarangi MK, Padhi S. Solid lipid nanoparticles−a review. Drugs 2016;5:7.

[50] Scioli Montoto S, Muraca G, Ruiz ME. Solid lipid nanoparticles for drug delivery: pharmacological and biopharmaceutical aspects. Front Mol Biosci 2020;7:319.

[51] Aggarwal BB, Deb L, Prasad S. Curcumin differs from tetrahydrocurcumin for molecular targets, signaling pathways and cellular responses. Molecules 2015;20(1):185−205.

[52] Banik BL, Fattahi P, Brown JL. Polymeric nanoparticles: the future of nanomedicine. Wiley Interdiscipl Rev Nanomed Nanobiotechnol 2016;8(2):271−99.

[53] Sharma S, Parmar A, Kori S, Sandhir R. PLGA-based nanoparticles: a new paradigm in biomedical applications. TrAC Trends Anal Chem 2016;80:30−40.

[54] Cardoso VF, Francesko A, Ribeiro C, Bañobre-López M, Martins P, Lanceros-Mendez S. Advances in magnetic nanoparticles for biomedical applications. Adv Healthcare Mater 2018;7(5):1700845.

[55] Shabatina TI, Vernaya OI, Shabatin VP, Melnikov MY. Magnetic nanoparticles for biomedical purposes: modern trends and prospects. Magnetochemistry 2020;6(3):30.

[56] Chivere VT, Kondiah PP, Choonara YE, Pillay V. Nanotechnology-based biopolymeric oral delivery platforms for advanced cancer treatment. Cancers 2020;12(2):522.

[57] Jain A, Singh SK, Arya SK, Kundu SC, Kapoor S. Protein nanoparticles: promising platforms for drug delivery applications. ACS Biomater Sci Eng 2018;4(12):3939−61.

[58] Wang Y, Feng L, Wang S. Gold nanoparticles applications: from artificial enzyme till drug delivery. Artif Cells Nanomed Biotechnol 2018;46(2):250−4.

[59] Noruzi M. Biosynthesis of gold nanoparticles using plant extracts. Bioprocess Biosyst Eng 2015;38(1):1–14.

[60] Manju S, Sreenivasan K. Composition design and medical application of liposomes. Eur J Med Chem 2019;164:640–53.

[61] Daraee H, Etemadi A, Kouhi M, Alimirzalu S, Akbarzadeh A. Application of liposomes in medicine and drug delivery. Artif Cells Nanomed Biotechnol 2016;44(1):381–91.

[62] Bozzuto G, Molinari A. Liposomes as nanomedical devices. Int J Nanomed 2015;10:975.

[63] Shelley H, Babu RJ. Self-assembly of size-controlled liposomes on DNA nanotemplates. Nat Chem 2016;8 (5):476–83.

[64] Maritim S, Boulas P, Lin Y. Comprehensive analysis of liposome formulation parameters and their influence on encapsulation, stability and drug release in glibenclamide liposomes. Int J Pharm 2021;592:120051.

[65] Chang M, Wu M, Li H. Antitumor activities of novel glycyrrhetinic acid-modified curcumin-loaded cationic liposomes in vitro and in H22 tumor-bearing mice. Drug Deliv 2018;25(1):1984–95.

[66] Sun DD, Lee PI. Chitosan and hyaluronan coated liposomes for pulmonary administration of curcumin. Int J Pharm 2017;525(1):203–10.

[67] Feng T, Wei Y, Lee RJ, Zhao L. Liposomal curcumin and its application in cancer. Int J Nanomed 2017;12:6027.

[68] Wang Y, Feng L, Wang S. Conjugated polymer nanoparticles for imaging, cell activity regulation, and therapy. Adv Funct Mater 2019;29(5):1806818.

[69] Moballegh Nasery M, et al. Curcumin delivery mediated by bio-based nanoparticles: a review. Molecules 2020;25(3):689.

[70] Manju S, Sreenivasan K. Conjugation of curcumin onto hyaluronic acid enhances its aqueous solubility and stability. J Colloid Interface Sci 2011;359(1):318–25.

[71] Enoch IV, Ramasamy S, Mohiyuddin S, Gopinath P, Manoharan R. Cyclodextrin–PEG conjugate-wrapped magnetic ferrite nanoparticles for enhanced drug loading and release. Appl Nanosci 2018;8(3):273–84.

[72] Hagl S, Kocher A, Schiborr C, Kolesova N, Frank J, Eckert GP. Potential role of curcumin and its nanoformulations to treat various types of cancers. Biomolecules 2021;11:392 2021, s Note: MDPI stays neutral with regard to jurisdictional claims in published.

[73] Shelley H, Babu RJ. Role of cyclodextrins in nanoparticle-based drug delivery systems. J Pharm Sci 2018;107 (7):1741–53.

[74] Son GH, Lee JB, Cho WC. β-Cyclodextrin coated and folic acid conjugated magnetic halloysite nanotubes for targeting and isolating of cancer cells. Colloids Surf B Biointerfaces 2019;181:379–88.

[75] Hanafy NA, El-Kemary M, Leporatti S. Micelles structure development as a strategy to improve smart cancer therapy. Cancers 2018;10(7):238.

[76] Hagl S, Kocher A, Schiborr C, Kolesova N, Frank J, Eckert GP. Curcumin micelles improve mitochondrial function in neuronal PC12 cells and brains of NMRI mice—Impact on bioavailability. Neurochem Int 2015;89:234–42.

[77] Huo X, Zhang Y, Jin X, Jin Y, Zhang L. A novel synthesis of selenium nanoparticles encapsulated PLGA nanospheres with curcumin molecules for the inhibition of amyloid β aggregation in Alzheimer's disease. J Photochem Photobiol B Biol 2019;190:98–102.

[78] Son G-H, Lee B-J, Cho C-W. Mechanisms of drug release from advanced drug formulations such as polymeric-based drug-delivery systems and lipid nanoparticles. J Pharm Invest 2017;47(4):287–96.

[79] Juni K, Nakano M. Clinical uses of microcapsules and microspheres, in microcapsules and nanoparticles. Medicine and pharmacy. CRC Press; 2020. p. 257–64.

[80] Li X-M, Wu Z-Z, Zhang B, Pan Y, Meng R, Chen H-Q. Fabrication of chitosan hydrochloride and carboxymethyl starch complex nanogels as potential delivery vehicles for curcumin. Food Chem 2019;293:197–203.

[81] Seok H-Y, Rejinold NS, Lekshmi KM, Cherukula K, Park I-K, Kim Y-C. CD44 targeting biocompatible and biodegradable hyaluronic acid cross-linked zein nanogels for curcumin delivery to cancer cells: in vitro and in vivo evaluation. J Controlled Release 2018;280:20–30.

[82] Subramani PA, Panati K, Narala VR. Curcumin nanotechnologies and its anticancer activity. Nutr Cancer 2017;69(3):381–93.

[83] Kumar A, Dixit CK. Methods for characterization of nanoparticles. Advances in nanomedicine for the delivery of therapeutic nucleic acids. Elsevier; 2017. p. 43–58.

[84] Pham BT, Such CH, Hawkett BS. Synthesis of polymeric janus nanoparticles and their application in surfactant-free emulsion polymerizations. Polym Chem 2015;6(3):426–35.

[85] Esquivel R, Juárez J, Almada M, Ibarra J, Valdez MA. Synthesis and characterization of new thiolated chitosan nanoparticles obtained by ionic gelation method. Int J Polym Sci 2015;2015.

[86] JB VK, Madhusudhan B. Synthesis, characterization and hemocompatibility evaluation of curcumin encapsulated chitosan nanoparticles for oral delivery. Int J Adv Res 2015;3(4):604−11.

[87] Riewe J, Erfle P, Melzig S, Kwade A, Dietzel A, Bunjes H. Antisolvent precipitation of lipid nanoparticles in microfluidic systems—a comparative study. Int J Pharm 2020;579:119167.

[88] Kurmi R, Mishra DK, Jain DK. Solid dispersion: a novel means of solubility enhancement. J Crit Rev 2016;3(1):1−8.

[89] Sun DD, Lee PI. Probing the mechanisms of drug release from amorphous solid dispersions in medium-soluble and medium-insoluble carriers. J Controlled Release 2015;211:85−93.

[90] Alshora DH, Ibrahim MA, Alanazi FK. Nanotechnology from particle size reduction to enhancing aqueous solubility. Surface chemistry of nanobiomaterials. Elsevier; 2016. p. 163−91.

[91] Jadav N, Paradkar A. Solid dispersions: technologies used and future outlook. Nanopharmaceuticals. Elsevier; 2020. p. 91−120.

[92] Li J, Lee IW, Shin GH, Chen X, Park HJ. Curcumin-Eudragit® E PO solid dispersion: a simple and potent method to solve the problems of curcumin. Eur J Pharm Biopharm 2015;94:322−32.

[93] Mendonça LM, Machado CdS, Teixeira CCC, Freitas LAPd, Bianchi MLP, Antunes LMG. Comparative study of curcumin and curcumin formulated in a solid dispersion: evaluation of their antigenotoxic effects. Genet Mol Biol 2015;38:490−8.

[94] Kuang Y-Y, Zhang Z-B, Xie M-L, Wang J-X, Le Y, Chen J-F. Large-scale preparation of amorphous cefixime nanoparticles by antisolvent precipitation in a high-gravity rotating packed bed. Ind Eng Chem Res 2015;54(33):8157−65.

[95] Yallapu MM, Nagesh PKB, Jaggi M, Chauhan SC. Therapeutic applications of curcumin nanoformulations. AAPS J 2015;17(6):1341−56.

[96] Cheng Y, Zhao P, Wu S, Yang T, Chen Y, Zhang X, et al. Cisplatin and curcumin co-loaded nano-liposomes for the treatment of hepatocellular carcinoma. Int J Pharm 2018;545(1−2):261−73.

[97] Elmansi AM, El-Karef AA, El-Shishtawy MM, Eissa LA. Hepatoprotective effect of curcumin on hepatocellular carcinoma through autophagic and apoptic pathways. Ann Hepatol 2017;16(4):607−18.

[98] Patel SS, Acharya A, Ray R, Agrawal R, Raghuwanshi R, Jain P. Cellular and molecular mechanisms of curcumin in prevention and treatment of disease. Crit Rev Food Sci Nutr 2020;60(6):887−939.

[99] Panahi Y, Darvishi B, Ghanei M, Jowzi N, Beiraghdar F, Varnamkhasti BS. Molecular mechanisms of curcumins suppressing effects on tumorigenesis, angiogenesis and metastasis, focusing on NF-κB pathway. Cytokine Growth Factor Rev 2016;28:21−9.

[100] Zamani M, Sadeghizadeh M, Behmanesh M, Najafi F. Dendrosomal curcumin increases expression of the long non-coding RNA gene MEG3 via up-regulation of epi-miRs in hepatocellular cancer. Phytomedicine 2015;22(10):961−7.

[101] Kong Z-L, Kuo H-P, Johnson A, Wu L-C, Chang KLB. H.-P, Johnson A, Wu L-C, Chang KLB. Curcumin-loaded mesoporous silica nanoparticles markedly enhanced cytotoxicity in hepatocellular carcinoma cells. Int J Mol Sci 2019;20(12):2918.

[102] Hu Z, Chen J, Zhou S, Yang N, Duan S, Zhang Z, et al. Mouse IP-10 gene delivered by folate-modified chitosan nanoparticles and dendritic/tumor cells fusion vaccine effectively inhibit the growth of hepatocellular carcinoma in mice. Theranostics 2017;7(7):1942.

[103] Xue H-Y, Liu Y, Liao J-Z, Lin J-S, Li B, Yuan W-G, et al. Gold nanoparticles delivered miR-375 for treatment of hepatocellular carcinoma. Oncotarget 2016;7(52):86675.

[104] Bhattacharya S, Mondal L, Mukherjee B, Dutta L, Ehsan I, Debnath CM, et al. Apigenin loaded nanoparticle delayed development of hepatocellular carcinoma in rats. Nanomed Nanotechnol Biol Med 2018;14(6):1905−17.

[105] Alhalmi A, Beg S, Kohli K, Waris M, Singh T. Nanotechnology based approach for hepatocellular carcinoma targeting. Curr Drug Targets 2021;22(7):779−92.

[106] NavaneethaKrishnan S, Rosales JL, Lee K-Y. ROS-mediated cancer cell killing through dietary phytochemicals. Oxidative Med Cellular Longevity 2019;2019.

[107] Gou M, Men K, Shi H, Xiang M, Zhang J, Song J, et al. Curcumin-loaded biodegradable polymeric micelles for colon cancer therapy in vitro and in vivo. Nanoscale 2011;3(4):1558−67.

[108] Chen Y, Wu Q, Zhang Z, Yuan L, Liu X, Zhou L. Preparation of curcumin-loaded liposomes and evaluation of their skin permeation and pharmacodynamics. Molecules 2012;17(5):5972–87.

[109] Bian Y, Guo D. Targeted therapy for hepatocellular carcinoma: co-delivery of sorafenib and curcumin using lactosylated pH-responsive nanoparticles. Drug Design Dev Ther 2020;14:647.

[110] Zhu J, Hou J, Zhang Y, Tian M. Polymeric antimicrobial membranes enabled by nanomaterials for water treatment. J Memb Sci 2018;550:173–97.

[111] Batra H, Pawar S, Bahl D. Curcumin in combination with anti-cancer drugs: a nanomedicine review. Pharmacol Res 2019;139:91–105.

[112] Khemlina G, Ikeda S, Kurzrock R. The biology of Hepatocellular carcinoma: implications for genomic and immune therapies. Mol Cancer 2017;16(1):1–10.

[113] Kumar V, Rahman M, Gahtori P, Al-Abbasi F, Anwar F, Kim HS. Current status and future directions of hepatocellular carcinoma-targeted nanoparticles and nanomedicine. Expert Opin Drug Deliv 2020;1–22.

[114] Liu L, Dai H, Wu Y, Li B, Yi J, Xu C, et al. In vitro and in vivo mechanism of hepatocellular carcinoma inhibition by β-TCP nanoparticles. Int J Nanomed 2019;14:3491.

[115] Kadry MO, Abdel-Megeed RM, El-Meliegy E, Abdel-Hamid A-HZ. Crosstalk between GSK-3, c-Fos, NFκB and TNF-α signaling pathways play an ambitious role in Chitosan Nanoparticles Cancer Therapy. Toxicol Rep 2018;5:723–7.

[116] Elkeiy MM, Khamis AA, El-Gamal MM, Gazia MMA, Zalat ZA, El-Magd MA. Chitosan nanoparticles from artemia salina inhibit progression of hepatocellular carcinoma in vitro and in vivo. Environ Sci Pollut Res 2020;27(16):19016–28.

[117] Varshosaz J, Farzan M. Nanoparticles for targeted delivery of therapeutics and small interfering RNAs in hepatocellular carcinoma. World J Gastroenterol 2015;21(42):12022.

[118] Zatsepin TS, Kotelevtsev YV, Koteliansky V. Lipid nanoparticles for targeted siRNA delivery—going from bench to bedside. Int J Nanomed 2016;11:3077.

[119] Mignani S, Bryszewska M, Klajnert-Maculewicz B, Zablocka M, Majoral J-P. Advances in combination therapies based on nanoparticles for efficacious cancer treatment: an analytical report. Biomacromolecules 2015;16(1):1–27.

Role of phytoconstituents in the hepatocellular carcinoma management: current perspective, challenges, and future perspectives

Archana Ashok Sharbidre

Department of Zoology, Savitribai Phule Pune University, Pune, India

Abstract

Hepatocellular carcinoma (HCC) is considered the most prevalent type of liver cancer globally amidst various primary liver cancers. Current treatment measures caused inconstant success rates with a poor prognosis owing to drug resistance and toxicity in liver cancer patients. Plant-based natural products are now attaining appreciable attention due to their minor side effects concomitant with their use. Thus, chemoprevention of cancer via dietary supplements and other phytochemicals has engrossed consideration recently. Moreover, scientific evidence signifies that these phytoconstituents use multiple intracellular signals selectively interfering with angiogenesis and metastasis during HCC management, consequently lessening the risk in contradiction of HCC. Various clinical trials were also completed using these phytoconstituents. Still, numerous phytoconstituents are under investigation and lack the scientific information to sustenance their anticancer properties and the plausible molecular mechanism behind them. It is also very essential to check their availability and probable toxicity. The current book chapter gives a comprehensive summary of the dietary agents. Potent phytoconstituents tried in the prevention and management of HCC emphasize various mechanisms accountable for their effects during the preliminary phases of carcinogenesis. It also apprises the phytoconstituents currently under clinical trials, an endeavor to cast light on its importance in HCC management.

Keywords: Hepatocellular carcinoma; phytoconstituents; HCC signaling pathways; clinical trials; drug development

Abbreviations

AC-H3	Acetylation of histone H3
AC-H4	Acetylation of histone H4

© 2022 Elsevier Inc. All rights reserved.

Akt	Serine/threonine-specific protein kinase
AP-1	Activator protein 1
ATP	Adenosine triphosphate
Bax	bcl-2-like protein 4
Bcl-2	B-cell lymphoma 2
Bcl-xL	B-cell lymphoma-extra large
CAM	Complementary and alternative medicine
cdc2	Cyclin-dependent kinase 1
cdc25c	Cell division cycle 25C
Chk1	Checkpoint kinase 1
COX	Cyclooxygenase
CREB	cAMP response element-binding protein
CSC	Stem-like cells
DMBA	7,12-dimethylbenz (a)anthracene
DNMT	DNA Methyltransferases
EECG	Epigallocatechin-3-gallate
EHHM	E-[6′-(5′-hydroxypentyl) tricosyl]-4-hydroxy-3-methoxycinnamate
EMT	Epithelial-mesenchymal transition
ER	Endoplasmic reticulum
ERK	Extracellular-signal-regulated kinase
GST	Glutathione S-transferases
HCC	Hepatocellular carcinoma
Hgf	Hepatocyte growth factor
HIF-1	Hypoxia-inducible factor-1
IGF	Insulin-like growth factor
IGFBP1	Insulin-like growth factor-binding protein 1 precursor
IL-6	Interleukin 6
iNOS	Inducible nitric oxide
JNK	c-Jun N-terminal kinase
Keap1	Kelch ECH associating protein 1
LC3	Microtubule-associated protein 1A/1B-light chain 3
MAPK	Mitogen-activated protein kinase
MMP	Matrix metallopeptidase
mTOR	Mammalian target of *rapamycin*
NF-κB	Nuclear factor kappa light chain enhancer of activated B cells
NLRP3	NLR family pyrin domain containing 3
Nrf2	Nuclear factor erythroid 2-related factor 2
PEITC	Phenethyl Isothiocyanate
PI3K	Phosphoinositide 3-kinase
PKC	Protein kinase C
PLK1	Serine/threonine-protein kinase
PPAR-γ	Peroxisome proliferator-activated receptor gamma
PTEN	Phosphatase and tensin homolog
ROS	Reactive oxygen species
STAT3	Signal transducer and activator of transcription 3
TGF	Transforming growth factor
TGF-α	Transforming growth factor-α
TIMP1	Tissue inhibitor matrix metalloproteinase 1
TRAIL	TNF-related apoptosis-inducing ligand
VEGF	Vascular endothelial growth factor
YAP	Yes-associated protein

Introduction

The liver is considered the most critical organ as it plays essential tasks of maintaining our body's normal physiological functions [1] and thus is also venerable to damage. Keeping the liver fit is very vital and necessary for complete health and welfare. But certain behaviors and conditions like alcohol consumption, obesity, long-term infection of hepatitis B virus or hepatitis C virus, cirrhosis, diabetes, and intake of aflatoxin-contaminated food might increase the threat of liver cancer [2]. Liver cancer comprises primarily of hepatocellular carcinoma (HCC) besides cholangiocarcinoma, a bile duct cancer. Compared to both, HCC is the most common, more fatal, and critical to treat [3].

Liver cancer is typically common in Southeast Asian countries and Sub-Saharan Africa as compared to the US. Above 800,000 people are spotted with this cancer per annum all over the globe. Liver cancer is a chief reason for worldwide cancer deaths, leading to about 700,000 deaths yearly [4,5]. Since 1980 toll incidences of liver cancer have tripled with doubled death rates [6]. Among the HCC medicare patients, the nonalcoholic fatty liver disease became the communal etiology and root of impermanence [7,8].

Ever since the HCC events in patients with chronic viral hepatitis cirrhosis have been notorious, it could be appreciated to discover an alternative and operative method for its preclusion and effective handling. VEGF angiogenesis stands paramount amongst several signaling pathways involved in HCC progression [9]. The diets enriched with vegetables and fruits are recommended as they can condense the peril of various types of cancer because the phytoconstituents present in them are accountable for declining the risk [10].

Hepatocellular carcinoma management with dietary natural products and combination therapy

In cancer treatment, generally, chemotherapy, along with radiotherapy, is used. But these medications have limited clinical effectiveness due to their toxic adversative effects and incidences of drug resistance. Numerous cancer cells have acquired apoptosis resistance, causing a common attribute and obstacle in traditional anticancer treatments.

Due to their active components, the dietary natural foodstuffs possibly improve efficiency, decline dose, and amend anticancer drugs' toxic effects. Dietary broccoli can reduce fatty liver and liver cancer development in mice treated with Diethyl nitrosamine and fed on a western or control diet [11]. Grape seeds extract showed a positive effect on chemically encouraged in vivo and in vitro liver cancer [12], and muscadine grape extract helped in the reduction of liver and lung metastasis with treble negative breast cancer developed in mice mutually by gut microbiome fluctuations (P05−017−19) [13]. A Thai traditional medicine called Benja-ummarit (BU) ('Phaetsat Songkhro'), composed of eight herbs, showed antiangiogenic and antiproliferative effects in rats suffering from HCC [14]. Gambogic acid, the gamboge resin element, constrained the proliferation of HepG2 as well as several other kinds of cancerous cells in "in vitro" studies [15].

Combining these dietary products and anticancer treatments might be a unique approach in HCC treatment. Many cancer cells have acquired a conjoint attribute of resistance towards apoptosis, causing a significant impediment in traditional anticancer therapies. Epidemiological indications bring to light that a diet abundant in natural phytoconstituents contained in fruits and vegetables could subordinate liver cancer risk [16]. Diet enriched with Olive oil repressed HCC tumor growth by modulating focal adhesion pathway [17]. Genistein is an isoflavone phytoestrogen obtained from soy and possesses antineoplastic activity. Genistein and Trichostatin A can significantly hinder the HCC cell growth by reactivating the ERα gene and thus show a considerable role in the apoptosis process [18], induce apoptosis and reestablish revival of DNMT1, DNMT3a, and DNMT3b genes in HCC [19].

In chemotherapy, NF-κB normalizes cell endurance, and its instigation subsidizes resistance to the drug through proapoptosis inhibition. Anticancer activities are augmented by a combination of intracellular drug accumulation and dietary supplements [20,21]. *Hericium erinaceu* and *Agaricus blazei* sensitized doxorubicin-generated apoptosis by hindering NF-κB provocation [22,23]. Cancer cells attain drug resistance by altering the PI3K/AKT pathway, and *Pleurotus pulmonarius* mediated inactivation of this pathway pointedly heightened the sensitivity of HCC cells towards cisplatin [24]. Asparagus polysaccharide suppressed the proliferation, promoted HCC cell apoptosis observed in "in vivo" and "in vitro" models [25], and inhibited invasion and migration, besides angiogenesis of HCC cells moderately by using signaling pathway of HIF-1α/VEGF [26].

Integrating radiotherapy and DMBA-induced liver damage and carcinogenesis in rats, apricot attenuated oxidative stress by modulating expressions of CREB, Bcl-2, caspases, Bax, NFκ-B, and AP-1 [27]. S-allylcysteine (SAC), obtained from garlic, was found to surmount MHCC97L cell spread and metastasis of HCC by induced apoptosis and necrosis. This process occurs by repressing Bcl-2 and Bcl-xL in addition to triggering caspase-3 and caspase-9 [28]. Additionally, SAC might suggestively influence arrest in the MHCC97L cell at the S phase along with cdc25c, cdc2, and cyclin B1 downregulation [28]. Combining these dietary products and anticancer treatments might be a unique approach in HCC treatment (Table 12.1).

Potent phytoconstituents having hepatocellular carcinoma activity

Green tea phytoconstituents exhibited chemopreventive and therapeutic potential against HCC [29] and, in mice model, averted toxin-generated hepatotoxicity by decreasing iNOS consequential prooxidants [30]. EECG present in green tea suppressed preneoplastic abrasions in liver established in an innovative rat model with nonalcoholic steatohepatitis [31] and persuaded HCC cell apoptosis by aerobic glycolytic pathway via impeding of phosphofructokinase activity [32]. *Alpinia officinarum* has conspired as a gold colliery of impending therapeutics [33], and Diarylheptanoids isolated from its rhizomes showed potent anticancer activity [34]. Aqueous extracts of *Andrographis paniculata* also showed promising results on liver tumors [35] and is considered for CAM as a convincing immunoregulatory target (a potent immunoregulatory target) [36].

Glycyrrhizin, a bioactive compound of *Glycyrrhiza glabra,* is found to be very effective in chronic hepatitis B and C [37—39] as it modulated liver carcinogen metabolizing enzymes

TABLE 12.1 Various dietary natural products with antihepatocellular carcinoma (anti-HCC) potential.

Dietary	Bioactive constituent	Cancer model (cell line/animal)	Mode of action	Reference
Olive oil	Oleocanthal ligstroside aglycone Hydroxytyrosol	HepG2, Huh7, Hep3B, and PLC/PRF/5	Increased intracellular ROS, inhibited COX-1 and COX-2 suppress the TGF-α-induced migration, modulation of autophagy	[121–124]
Soy	Genistein	HepG2, Bel-7402, and SMMC-7721 Hepa1–6	Metastasis inhibition by retrogressive EMT proliferation, induces apoptosis	[125,126]
Apple polyphenol	Phloretin	Albino rats	Chemopreventive effect against Diethylnitrosamine-induced HCC	[127]
Tamarillo (*Cyphomandra betacea*)		HepG2	Antiproliferative	[128]
Parsley, dandelion, thyme, celery, green pepper, and others	Luteolin	HepG2	Induces apoptosis ROS-mediated pathway	[129]
Passiflora caerulea	Chrysin	QGY7701 and HepG2	Diminish motility and proliferation of cells, encourages apoptosis	[130]
Citrus fruits	Hesperidin, Eriocitrin, Naringenin	HepG2, Huh 7, and HA22T Xenograft tumors	Increases intracellular ROS, induces apoptosis, arrests cell cycle	[131–134]
Grapes, delphinium	Proanthocyanidin Resveratrol	HepG2 and Huh7 H22 mice	Autophagy-mediated cell death, inhibits expression of VEGF via a NF-κB-targeted mechanism	[135,136]
Mango	Isoquercitrin	Liver cancerous cells; nude mice bearing tumor	Persuade apoptosis and constrain tumor growth by amending signaling pathways of PKC and MAPK	[137]
Cucumbers, persimmons, onions, apples, and strawberries	Fisetin	Cells of liver cancer	Brings apoptosis via Nrf2-Keap1-arbitrated oxidative stress	[138]
Sesame seeds, sesame oil	Sesamol	HepG2; xenograft model using nude mice	Constrains proliferation with apoptosis	[139]
Eggplants, peaches, prunes, leaves of *Hibiscus sabdariffa*	Chlorogenic acid	HepG2; xenograft model	Hinders proliferation and the xenograft advancement	[140]

(Continued)

TABLE 12.1   (Continued)

Dietary	Bioactive constituent	Cancer model (cell line/animal)	Mode of action	Reference
Pomegranate		HCC rat model	Suppressed cell proliferation and induced apoptosis	[141,142]
Garlic (*Allium sativum*)	Organosulfur compounds, diallyl sulfide, s-allyl cysteine, flavanols	MHCC97L in vivo xenograft liver tumor model	Augmented levels of Caspase-3 & -9; upregulated p53, E-cadherin, and tumor suppressor and downregulated VEGF, Bcl-xL expressions, and Bcl-2; suppressed proteins of cell cycle (cyclin B1), hindered the migration and invasion, inhibited progression and metastasis of HCC tumor	[28]
Ginger (*Zingiber officinale*)	Shogaols, gingerols, geraniol, 6-shogaol	HepG2 Hep3B Huh7 rats	Arrested G2/M-phase of cell cycle, antiinvasive by MMP-9 and TIMP-1 modulation; 6-shogaol controlled urokinase-type plasminogen activity	[143—145]
Citrus fruits	Limonin	HepG2, Huh7, and normal hepatic cell line L02	Triggering PI3K/Akt signaling	[146]
Cruciferous vegetable	Oltipraz	HepG2	Hepatitis B virus replication inhibition in Dose- proportional manner	[147]
Red fruits and vegetables	Lycopene	mice	Stalled the onset of experimentally induced HCC	[148,149]
Asparagus	Polysaccharide	HepG2, Hep-3B, and Sk-Hep1	Suppressed the migration, invasion, and angiogenesis; HIF-1α/VEGF signaling pathway	[25,26,150,151]

in the rat HCC model [40,41]. *Nigella sativa* possesses a potent anticancer activity [42,43] and protected against diethylnitrosamine-induced hepatocarcinogenesis [44]. A pentacyclic terpenoid called ursolic acid (UA), is abundantly present in fruit peel and in many herbs like lavender (*Lavandula augustifolia*), peppermint leaves (*Mentha piperita* L.), thyme (*Thymus vulgaris* L.), catnip (*Nepeta sibthorpii*), and holy basil (*Ocimum sanctum* L.). [45,46]. UA suppressed the biosynthesis of cholesterol and exerted anti-HCC effects [47]. UA repressed HCC cell growth over p38 MAPK-governed expression of FOXO3a and IGFBP1 [48] and by inhibiting the STAT3 phosphorylation signaling pathway. It is suggested that it could be a conceivable health care invention and might be used every day for cancer prevention, besides a promising contender for liver cancer chemotherapy [49]. Sorafenib's anticancer effect was enhanced by sensitizing HCC cells by a Chinese herb constituent, Emodin, by suppressing cholesterol metabolism [50]. A traditional Chinese herbal medicine containing Oridonin, a core bioactive component of *Rabdosia rubescens*, can be used in

TABLE 12.2 Potent phytoconstituents with antihepatocellular carcinoma (anti-HCC) activity concerning their source and contrivance of action.

Phytoconstituents	Plant source	Contrivance of action	Reference
Lycium polysaccharide portion	*Lycium barbarum*	Apoptosis & inflammation	[152,153]
EECG	*Camellia sinensis*	Subdued ERK phosphorylation, IGF-1R, Akt; triggered liver AMP-activated kinase protein	[154–156]
Diarylheptanoids, flavonoids	*Alpinia officinarum*	Downregulated cytokines of proinflammation & TNF-α; constraining alpha-fetoprotein levels and amended hepatic functions	[157–159]
Andrographolide	*Andrographis paniculata*	Arrested cell cycle, activated ROS-dependent JNK and caspase cascade	[160–162]
Glycyrrhizin	*Glycyrrhiza glabra*	Increased phosphorylation of MMP-9, ERK1/2, and JNK1/2	[163,164]
Thymoquinone	*Nigella sativa*	Regulated p53, iNOS, and caspases signaling pathways; cell death & inhibited proliferation	[165,166]
Phenylpropanoids, essential oils, sesquiterpenoids, lignans	*Illicium verum*	Apoptosis; diminished oxidative stress & tumor metastasis inhibition; Modifying expressions of p53 and Bax; GST enzymes upregulation	[167,168]
Matrine	*Sophora flavescens Ait*	Attenuated phosphorylation of PI3K P110a (a subunit of PI3K) in Hep3B, Huh7, and hepatic CSC	[169]
D-limonene	Citrus fruit peels	Chemoprevention of AKR mice hepatocarcinogenesis	[170–172]

hepatoma treatment by pointing the Akt Pathway in HCC and HepG2 cell lines [51]. Collusive anticancer activity between Sorafenib and 20(S)-Ginsenoside Rg3 was found in "in vitro" and "in vivo" HCC cell lines (HepG2 and Huh7) by moderating the signaling pathway of PTEN/Akt [52]. D-Limonene found in citrus fruits is satisfactorily endured in patients suffering from progressive cancer [53]. The other potent phytoconstituents having HCC activity are enlisted in Table 12.2.

Polyphenols in hepatocellular carcinoma treatment

Polyphenols are secondary metabolites developed in plants normally intricated in ultra-violet radiation defense or pathogens aggression [54]. Polyphenols are recognized to diminish HCC invasion [55,56]. They also showed notable efficient apoptosis and suppressed liver cancer cell proliferation by targeting various pathways (Fig. 12.1) [57–59]. Polyphenols are having potent in vivo and in vitro anti-HCC activity abridged in Table 12.3. The majority of these polyphenols have encouraged apoptosis and repressed the proliferation in diverse HCC cell lines studied. It overlapped approaches such as caspase-dependent and caspase-independent signaling pathways of apoptotis, ROS pathway, mTOR pathway, and JNK pathways [110,111]. Other strategies used were ER stress induction and regulation of mitochondrial-mediated pathways [112,113].

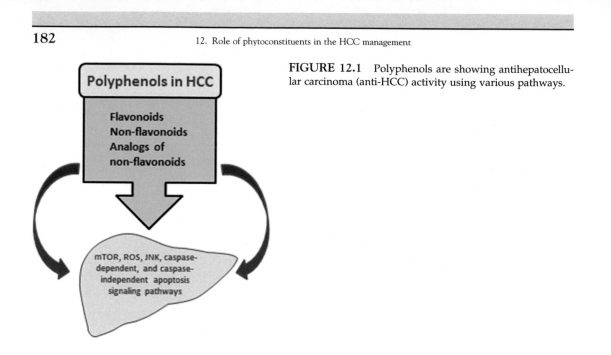

FIGURE 12.1 Polyphenols are showing antihepatocellular carcinoma (anti-HCC) activity using various pathways.

TABLE 12.3 Polyphenols having antihepatocellular carcinoma (anti-HCC) activity about their source and contrivance of action.

Polyphenols	Compounds	Cancer model (cell line/animal)	Contrivance of action	Reference
Flavonoids	Hesperidin	HepG2	Apoptosis	[60]
	Tricetin	Hep G2 and PLC/PRF/5	Apoptosis by the ROS/c-Jun NH2-terminal kinase pathway	[61]
	Isoorientin (*Gypsophila elegans*)	HepG2	Arrested cell cycle at G1phase, elevated ROS and apoptosis	[57]
	Pinocembrin (*Elytranthe parasitica*)	HepG2	Apoptotic and MAPK cellular signaling	[62]
	Apigenin	Huh-7, HepG2, HCC Rats	TRAIL-induced apoptosis by ERK-dependent Dr5 upregulation	[63–65]
	Oroxylin A	HepG2	Proapoptotic activity, Beclin 1-mediated autophagy via suppressing signaling of PI3K-PTEN-Akt-mTOR	[66,67]
	Kushenol H, kushenol N, kurarinone, kurarinol, norkurarinol (*Sophora flavescens*)	HepG2, Bel-7402, HL-7702, Huh-7, H22 Mouse	STAT3	[68]

(Continued)

TABLE 12.3 (Continued)

Polyphenols	Compounds	Cancer model (cell line/animal)	Contrivance of action	Reference
	Avicularin	Huh7	PPAR-γ, NF-κB (p65), COX-2 events.	[69]
	Morusin (*Morus alba*)	HepG2 and Hep3B BALB/C-nu/nu	Increased active caspase-3 and ratio of Bax/Bcl-2 expression, IL-6-induced STAT3 phosphorylation	[55]
	Liquiritigenin (*Glycyrrhiza radix*)	PLC/PRF/5, HepG2, Nude Mice/BALB/cA/	MAPKs- mediated pathway	[70]
	Dihydromyricetin (DHM) (*Hovenia dulcis*)	HepG2, HL7702, L02, SMMC-7721, Primary cells: 4401, 4403, 1204 Nude mice/BALB/cA	P53-activation-dependent mechanism	[71]
	Luteoloside (*Gentiana macrophylla*)	SMMC-7721, SNU-449, MHCCLM3, Hep3B, Huh-7, Mice/BALB/cA MHCC97-H	Proliferation suppression by inhibiting NLRP3 inflammasome	[72]
	Proanthocyanidins (GPC)	HepG2	Apoptosis induction	[73]
	Silybin (SIL) (*Silybum marianun*)	HepG2 mice/athymic nude	RBP-Jκ, Bcl2, BAX, survivin, Notch1, Hes1, cyclin D1, β-actin	[74]
	2',4'-dihydroxychalcone (*Oxytropis falcata*)	Mice/ICR, SMMC-7721	Antiproliferative and proapoptotic	[75]
	(+)-Cyanidan-3-ol (*Acacia catechu*)	HepG2 Balb/c mice	Increased expression levels of bcl-2, caspase, and suppressed NF-κB and AP-1	[76]
	Silibinin	HuH7 mice/nude	Induced AC-H4, caspase-3, caspase-9, CDK4, p-ERK, p21, p27, Ki-67, p-survivin, E2F1, AC-H3, p-Rb, PTEN, Plk1, p-AKT, Chk1	[77,78]
	Isorhamnetin	BEL-7402	Induced apoptosis	[79]
Flavonone	Naringenin	HepG2	Induced cell cycle, arrest apoptosis and growth inhibition	[80]
	Naringin	HepG2	Induced apoptosis	[81]
Flavones	Baicalein	SMMC-7721	Induced autophagy by ER stress	[82]

(Continued)

TABLE 12.3   (Continued)

Polyphenols	Compounds	Cancer model (cell line/animal)	Contrivance of action	Reference
	Tangeretin	HepG2	Targeted JNK/Bcl-2/Beclin-1	[83]
	Combination of Wogonin and Sorafenib	HepG2, Hep3B, SMMC-7721Bel-7402	Apoptosis potentiation and autophagy retardation	[84]
	Isoorientin	HepG2 mice	Persuaded autophagy and ROS	[85]
	Luteolin	SMMC-7721	Augmented expression of LC3B-II alteration and Beclin-1	[86]
Flavonols	Galangin	Hep3B, HepG2	Hindered signaling pathways of p53 and TGF-receptor/Smad	[87,88]
	Kaempferol	HepG2, SK-HEP-1 and Huh 7	Augmented autophagy	[89,90]
	Quercetin	LM3, LM6, Mice	Repealing JAK2/STAT3 signaling Attenuation of AKT signaling pathway	[91–93]
	Myricetin	HepG2	downregulating expression of YAP	[94]
Flavanols	EGCG	HepG2	Amplified Beclin1, Atg5, p62 autophagic substrate, endorsed LC3-II synthesis	[95]
	Combination of EGCG and Doxorubicin	Hep3B	Autophagy inhibition	[96]
Anthocyanidins	Delphinidin	SMMC-7721	Induced necrosis	[97]
Chalcones	Xanthohumol (*Humulus lupulus*)	Huh7 and HepG2	Stifled migration and proliferation, expression of TNF induced NF-κB activity and interleukin-8	[98]
	2,3,4′-trimethoxy-2′-hydroxy-chalcone (CH1) and 3′-bromo-3,4-dimethoxy-chalcone (CH2)	HepG2 and Huh-7	Caspase-dependent pathway, ROS.	[99]
	Butein (*Rhus vericiflua*)	HepG2, Hep3B, LO2, Huh7, Bel-7402, and HCC-LM3	Aurora B inhibition	[100]
	Cardamonin (CADMN) Cardamom and Greater Galangal (*Alpinia species*)	HepG2	Involvement of ROS, inhibiting NF-κB pathway by enhancing the apoptosis	[101]

(Continued)

TABLE 12.3   (Continued)

Polyphenols	Compounds	Cancer model (cell line/animal)	Contrivance of action	Reference
Nonflavonoids				
Stilbenes	Resveratrol	MHCC-97H, Huh 7	Subdued PI3K/Akt with augmented autophagy	[102,103]
Hydroxycinnamates	EHHM	HepG2	Elevated expression of Atg5, Beclin-1, and LC3-II	[104]
Assorted nonflavonoids	Curcumin	HepG2, Huh 7	Induced autophagy and cell death with diminished SQSTM1 expression	[105,106]
	Curcumin with Adriamycin (Doxorubicin)	HepG2	Apoptosis and autophagy	[107]
Nonflavonoid analogs	EF25-(GSH)2	HL-7702	Persuaded autophagy and apoptosis	[108]
	WZ35	HCCLM3	Suppress cell growth and inhibit autophagy inhibition	[109]

Phytoconstituents evaluated in clinical trials of hepatocellular carcinoma

Due to poor prognosis, recurrence, and metastasis, HCC patients allegedly suffered a lessened survival period ensuing surgery. Currently, effectual therapies are unavailable for the late phase of HCC patients with the least survival rates due to inadequate chemotherapeutics. To sustain liver equilibrium, autophagy performs manifold purposes [114]. To date, Sorafenib is the lone molecular-based cure that is FDA approved for initial or progressive HCC and dealt prolonged endurance for fewer than three months in a phase III trial piloted in patients of the Asia-Pacific region [115].

Following are the clinical trials done on phytoconstituents against various stages of HCC displayed in Table 12.4. This data was collected from the ClinicalTrials.gov website.

Conclusions and future perspectives

HCC is painstaking, a quiet assassin disease that causes approximately one million deceases comprehensively per annum. Compared to women, it is found to anguish men more frequently [116]. At present, no approved chemotherapy is available for HCC management. Conventional chemotherapy has been unsuccessful in effectively reducing mortality rates and thus a risky prerequisite for novel therapeutic methodologies. Practicing CAM for cancer treatment is widely accepted. Still, it is strongly assumed that herbs can ensure miracles. The phytoconstituents have dual roles. They can provide nourishment to the entire body as supportive to the vital organs, including the liver, and at the same time, show anticancer properties making them more approachable striking [117].

TABLE 12.4   List of phytoconstituents currently in the clinical trial on hepatocellular carcinoma (HCC).

Phytoconstituents	Source	Assessment	Stage of HCC targeted	Phase	Status (CT.govID)
Diammonium glycyrrhizinate + Ulinastatin drug	*Glycyrrhiza glabra*	Safety and efficacy in prevention of postoperative relapse	Stage I	Not applicable	Completed NCT01643447
Ginsenoside Rg3 capsule + drug: placebo	*Panax sp.* (ginseng)	Conservative therapy to assess the efficiency and safety of ginsenoside Rg3 (20 mg BID) and placebo in anticipation and treatment of postoperative recurrence of liver cancer, respectively	Stage I and II	Not applicable	Completed NCT01717066
Yang Yin Fu Zheng therapy	*Radix codonopsis* and *Radix astragali*	To perceive the efficiency of routine medical care collectively with Yang Yin Fu Zheng remedy	HBV- HCC IIb, IIIa, IIIb	Early Phase 1	Completed NCT02927626
Colchicine	*Colchicum autumnale*	Effect of Colchicine for the palliative management of HCC patients with distant metastasis or large vessel invasion	HCC metastasis invasion	Phase 2	Recruiting NCT01935700
Silybin	*Silybum marianum*	To evaluate efficacy in reducing liver function tests in advanced HCC	Advanced HCC	Phase 1	Completed NCT01129570

*Designates reference from http://www.clinicaltrials.gov with corresponding identifier code (NCT).

Phytoconstituents can be a significant economic treatment choice for HCC patients. They are proven to inhibit, control, or block the signals by which normal cells are converted to cancerous cells. Moreover, they are extensively explored to check their prospective in cancer treatment, and several of them have exhibited reassuring results in effective cancer preemption and treatment. The results of various clinical trial phases are accompanied by inspiring preclinical significances to specify the approaches to use these phytoconstituents in realistic conditions. Still, we have to accept specific confines of practice using them as therapeutic agents to combat HCC, which is essential to resolve.

For example, most reported phytoconstituents are still in the preclinical stage lacking proper molecular communications with various signaling targets and pathways, need to study using in silico tactics such as molecular docking. There are limited studies regarding this issue [118,119]. This book chapter will surely put the limelight on phytoconstituents' interactions with different signaling pathways and can be supplemented by quite a few in vitro and in vivo models (Fig. 12.2). Further, its necessities to be observed for their safety in long-term use.

Thus, extensive and conscientious clinical trials are sought to authenticate their safeties, potency, adversative effects, before clinching them as anticancer treatments. Besides general levels of standardizations for the effectiveness of phytoconstituents, the other factors like their bio-obtainability, security, eminence, bio-composition, invention processes, supervisory, and endorsement practices are also responsible for encompassing the

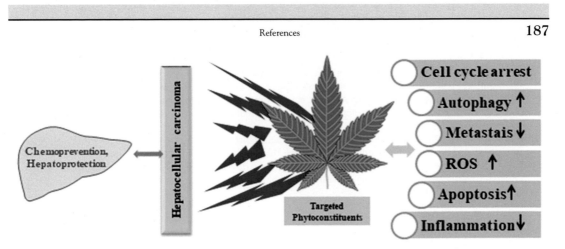

FIGURE 12.2   Phytoconstituents showing hepatoprotection and antihepatocellular carcinoma (anti-HCC) activity by targeting various pathways.

international standard. Ironically, the pharmaceutical industry is well equipped with enormous information and capability in drug improvement. Consequently, an amalgamation between traditional and modern drugs could be a more favorable attitude to divulge novel plant-derived molecules to the arcade. In HCC management, synergistic effects of combinations of agents with chemotherapeutic potential and phytoconstituents would be more acceptable with fewer side effects. Recently, oncology researchers were attracted to phytoconstituents for their anticancer and chemo-preventive properties as they can damage only cancer cells without affecting normal cells [120].

Efforts taken in this book chapter will convey a database of phytoconstituents used for in vitro, in vivo, and clinical studies of HCC. It is hoped that this data will be tremendously expedient in identifying a sequence of other plant-procured drugs to manage HCC with the least aftereffects.

Conflict of interest

None

References

[1] Subramoniam A, Pushpangadan P. Development of phytomedicines for liver disease. Indian J Pharmacol 1999;31(3):166.
[2] https://www.cdc.gov/cancer/liver/index.htm.
[3] https://www.cancer.gov/types/liver.
[4] Bosch FX, Ribes J, Díaz M, Cléries R. Primary liver cancer: worldwide incidence and trends. Gastroenterology 2004;127(5):S5—16.
[5] https://www.cancer.org/cancer/liver-cancer.
[6] El-Serag HB. Hepatocellular carcinoma: recent trends in the United States. Gastroenterology 2004;127(5): S27—34.
[7] Forner A, Reig M, Bruix J. Hepatocellular carcinoma. Lancet 2018;391(10127):1301—14.

[8] Hester D, Golabi P, Paik J, Younossi I, Mishra A, Younossi ZM. Among medicare patients with hepatocellular carcinoma, non-alcoholic fatty liver disease is the most common etiology and cause of mortality. J Clin Gastroenterol 2020;54(5):459–67. Available from: https://doi.org/10.1097/mcg.0000000000001172.

[9] Li T, Zhu Y, Qin CY, Yang Z, Fang A, Xu S, et al. Expression and prognostic significance of vascular endothelial growth factor receptor 1 in hepatocellular carcinoma. J Clin Pathol 2012;65(9):808–14. Available from: https://doi.org/10.1136/jclinpath-2012-200721.

[10] Nishino H, Murakoshi M, Tokuda H, Satomi Y. Cancer prevention by carotenoids. Arch Biochem Biophys 2009;483(2):165–8. Available from: https://doi.org/10.1016/j.abb.2008.09.011.

[11] Chen YJ, Wallig MA, Jeffery EH. Dietary broccoli lessens development of fatty liver and liver cancer in mice given diethylnitrosamine and fed a western or control diet. J Nutr 2016;146(3):542–50. Available from: https://doi.org/10.3945/jn.115.228148.

[12] Hamza AA, Heeba GH, Elwy HM, Murali C, El-Awady R, Amin A. Molecular characterization of the grape seeds extract's effect against chemically induced liver cancer: *in vivo* and *in vitro* analyses. Sci Rep 2018;8 (1):1270. Available from: https://doi.org/10.1038/s41598-018-19492-x.

[13] Collard M, Austin N, Tallant A, Gallagher P. Muscadine grape extract reduces lung and liver metastasis in mice with triple-negative breast cancer in association with changes in the gut microbiome (P05-017-19). Curr Dev Nutr 2019;3(Supplement_1):nzz030–05. Available from: https://doi.org/10.1093/cdn/nzz030. P05-017-19.

[14] Kaewnoonual N, Itharat A, Pongsawat S, Nilbu-Nga C, Kerdput V, Pradidarcheep W. Antiangiogenic and anti-proliferative effects of Benja-ummarit extract in rats with hepatocellular carcinoma. Biomed Rep 2020;12 (3):109–20. Available from: https://doi.org/10.3892/br.2020.1272.

[15] Yan F, Wang M, Li J, Cheng H, Su J, Wang X, et al. Gambogenic acid induced mitochondrial-dependent apoptosis and referred to phospho-Erk1/2 and phospho-p38 MAPK in human hepatoma HepG2 cells. Environ Toxicol Pharmacol 2012;33(2):181–90. Available from: https://doi.org/10.1016/j.etap.2011.12.006.

[16] Kensler TW, Qian GS, Chen JG, Groopman JD. Translational strategies for cancer prevention in liver. Nat Rev Cancer 2003;3(5):321–9. Available from: https://doi.org/10.1038/nrc1076.

[17] Lee C, Fan ST, Sit WH, Jor IW, Wong LL, Man K, et al. Olive oil enriched diet suppresses hepatocellular carcinoma (HCC) tumor growth via focal adhesion pathway. Cancer Res 2007; 67(9 Suppl.), LB-60.

[18] Sanaei M, Kavoosi F, Salehi H. Genistein and Trichostatin A induction of estrogen receptor alpha gene expression, apoptosis and cell growth inhibition in hepatocellular carcinoma HepG 2 cells. Asian Pac J Cancer Prev 2017;18(12):3445–50. Available from: https://doi.org/10.22034/APJCP.2017.18.12.3445.

[19] Sanaei M, Kavoosi F, Roustazadeh A, Golestan F. Effect of Genistein in comparison with trichostatin a on reactivation of DNMTs genes in hepatocellular carcinoma. J Clin Transl Hepatol 2018;6(2):141–6. Available from: https://doi.org/10.14218/JCTH.2018.00002.

[20] Zhang XY, Bai DC, Wu YJ, Li WG, Liu NF. Proanthocyanidin from grape seeds enhances antitumor effect of doxorubicin both *in vitro* and *in vivo*. Pharmazie 2005;60:533–8.

[21] Liang G, Tang A, Lin X, Li L, Zhang S, Huang Z, et al. Green tea catechins augment the antitumor activity of doxorubicin in an *in vivo* mouse model for chemoresistant liver cancer. Int J Oncol 2010;37:111–23.

[22] Lee JS, Hong EK. *Agaricus blazei* Murill enhances doxorubicin-induced apoptosis in human hepatocellular carcinoma cells by NFκB-mediated increase of intracellular doxorubicin accumulation. Int J Oncol 2011;38:401–8. Available from: https://doi.org/10.3892/ijo.2010.852.

[23] Lee JS, Hong EK. *Hericium erinaceus* enhances doxorubicin-induced apoptosis in human hepatocellular carcinoma cells. Cancer Lett 2010;297:144–54. Available from: https://doi.org/10.1016/j.canlet.2010.05.006.

[24] Xu W, Huang JJ, Cheung PC. Extract of *Pleurotus pulmonarius* suppresses liver cancer development and progression through inhibition of VEGF-induced PI3K/AKT signaling pathway. PLoS One 2012;7:e34406. Available from: https://doi.org/10.1371/journal.pone.0034406.

[25] Xiang J, Xiang Y, Lin S, Xin D, Liu X, Weng L, et al. Anticancer effects of deproteinized asparagus polysaccharide on hepatocellular carcinoma *in vitro* and *in vivo*. Tumour Biol 2014;35(4):3517–24. Available from: https://doi.org/10.1007/s13277-013-1464-x.

[26] Cheng W, Cheng Z, Xing D, Zhang M. Asparagus polysaccharide suppresses the migration, invasion, and angiogenesis of hepatocellular carcinoma cells partly by targeting the HIF-1α/VEGF signalling pathway in vitro. Evid Based Complement Alternat Med eCAM 2019;3769879. Available from: https://doi.org/10.1155/2019/3769879.

[27] Karabulut AB, Karadag N, Gurocak S, Kiran T, Tuzcu M, Sahin K. Apricot attenuates oxidative stress and modulates of Bax, Bcl-2, caspases, NFκ-B, AP-1, CREB expression of rats bearing DMBA-induced liver damage and treated with a combination of radiotherapy. Food Chem Toxicol 2014;70:128−33.

[28] Ng KTP, Guo DY, Cheng Q, Geng W, Ling CC, Li CX. A garlic derivative, S-allylcysteine (SAC), suppresses proliferation and metastasis of hepatocellular carcinoma. PLoS One 2012;7(2):e31655. Available from: https://doi.org/10.1371/journal.pone.0031655.

[29] Darvesh AS, Bishayee A. Chemopreventive and therapeutic potential of tea polyphenols in hepatocellular cancer. Nutr Cancer 2013;65(3):329−44. Available from: https://doi.org/10.1080/01635581.2013.767367.

[30] Chen JH, Tipoe GL, Liong EC, So HS, Leung KM, Tom WM, et al. Green tea polyphenols prevent toxin-induced hepatotoxicity in mice by down-regulating inducible nitric oxide-derived prooxidants. Am J Clin Nutr 2004;80(3):742−51. Available from: https://doi.org/10.1093/ajcn/80.3.742.

[31] Sumi T, Shirakami Y, Shimizu M, Kochi T, Ohno T, Kubota M, et al. (-)-Epigallocatechin-3-gallate suppresses hepatic preneoplastic lesions developed in a novel rat model of non-alcoholic steatohepatitis. Springerplus 2013;2:690. Available from: https://doi.org/10.1186/2193-1801-2-690.

[32] Li S, Wu L, Feng J, Li J, Liu T, Zhang R, et al. *In vitro* and *in vivo* study of epigallocatechin-3-gallate-induced apoptosis in aerobic glycolytic hepatocellular carcinoma cells involving inhibition of phosphofructokinase activity. Sci Rep 2016;6:28479. Available from: https://doi.org/10.1038/srep28479.

[33] Ghosh S, Rangan L. *Alpinia*: the gold mine of future therapeutics. 3 Biotech 2013;3(3):173−85. Available from: https://doi.org/10.1007/s13205-012-0089-x.

[34] An N, Zou ZM, Tian Z, Luo XZ, Yang SL, Xu LZ. Diarylheptanoids from the rhizomes of *Alpinia officinarum* and their anticancer activity. Fitoterapia 2008;79(1):27−31. Available from: https://doi.org/10.1016/j.fitote.2007.07.001.

[35] Neha T, Rawal UM. Effect of aqueous extract of *Andrographis paniculata* on liver tumor. Indian J Pharmacol 1998;30(5):318.

[36] Vojdani A, Erde J. Regulatory T cells, a potent immunoregulatory target for CAM researchers: modulating tumor immunity, autoimmunity and alloreactive immunity (III). Evid Based Complement Alternat Med 2006;3(3):309−16. Available from: https://doi.org/10.1093/ecam/nel047.

[37] Sato H, Goto W, Yamamura J, Kurokawa M, Kageyama S, Takahara T, et al. Therapeutic basis of glycyrrhizin on chronic hepatitis B. Antiviral Res 1996;30(2−3):171−7. Available from: https://doi.org/10.1016/0166-3542(96)00942-4.

[38] Arase Y, Ikeda K, Murashima N, Chayama K, Tsubota A, Koida I, et al. The long term efficacy of glycyrrhizin in chronic hepatitis C patients. Cancer 1997;79(8):1494−500. Available from: https://doi.org/10.1002/(SICI)1097-0142(19970415)79:83.0.CO;2-B.

[39] Shiota G, Harada K-I, Ishida M, Tomie Y, Okubo M, Katayama S, et al. Inhibition of hepatocellular carcinoma by glycyrrhizin in diethylnitrosamine-treated mice. Carcinogenesis 1999;20(1):59−63. Available from: https://doi.org/10.1093/carcin/20.1.59.

[40] Paolini M, Barillari J, Broccoli M, Pozzetti L, Perocco P, Cantelli-Forti G. Effect of liquorice and glycyrrhizin on rat liver carcinogen metabolizing enzymes. Cancer Lett 1999;145(1−2):35−42. Available from: https://doi.org/10.1016/s0304-3835(99)00225-6.

[41] Shi L, Tang C, Yin C. Glycyrrhizin-modified O-carboxymethyl chitosan nanoparticles as drug vehicles targeting hepatocellular carcinoma. Biomaterials 2012;33(30):7594−604. Available from: https://doi.org/10.1016/j.biomaterials.2012.06.072.

[42] Randhawa MA, Alghamdi MS. Anticancer activity of *Nigella sativa* (black seed)-a review. Am J Chin Med 2011;39(6):1075−91. Available from: https://doi.org/10.1142/S0192415X1100941X.

[43] Majdalawieh AF, Fayyad MW. Recent advances on the anti-cancer properties of *Nigella sativa*, a widely used food additive. J Ayurveda Integr Med 2016;7(3):173−80. Available from: https://doi.org/10.1016/j.jaim.2016.07.004.

[44] Iddamaldeniya SS, Wickramasinghe N, Thabrew I, Ratnatunge N, Thammitiyagodage MG. Protection against diethylnitrosoamine-induced hepatocarcinogenesis by an indigenous medicine comprised of *Nigella sativa*, *Hemidesmus indicus* and *Smilax glabra*: a preliminary study. J Carcinog 2003;2(1):6. Available from: https://doi.org/10.1186/1477-3163-2-6.

[45] Woźniak Ł, Skąpska S, Marszałek K. Ursolic acid—a pentacyclic triterpenoid with a wide spectrum of pharmacological activities. Molecules 2015;20(11):20614−41. Available from: https://doi.org/10.3390/molecules201119721.

[46] Yadav VR, Prasad S, Sung B, Kannappan R, Aggarwal BB. Targeting inflammatory pathways by triterpenoids for prevention and treatment of cancer. Toxins (Basel) 2010;2(10):2428−66. Available from: https://doi.org/10.3390/toxins2102428.

[47] Kim GH, Kan SY, Kang H, Lee S, Ko HM, Kim JH, et al. Ursolic acid suppresses cholesterol biosynthesis and exerts anti-cancer effects in hepatocellular carcinoma cells. Int J Mol Sci 2019;20(19):4767. Available from: https://doi.org/10.3390/ijms20194767.

[48] Yang LJ, Tang Q, Wu J, Chen Y, Zheng F, Dai Z, et al. Inter-regulation of IGFBP1 and FOXO3a unveils novel mechanism in ursolic acid-inhibited growth of hepatocellular carcinoma cells. J Exp Clin Cancer Res 2016;35:59. Available from: https://doi.org/10.1186/s13046-016-0330-2 Erratum in: J Exp Clin Cancer Res 2016;35:81.

[49] Liu T, Ma H, Shi W, Duan J, Wang Y, Zhang C, et al. Inhibition of STAT3 signaling pathway by ursolic acid suppresses growth of hepatocellular carcinoma. Int J Oncol 2017;51(2):555−62. Available from: https://doi.org/10.3892/ijo.2017.4035.

[50] Kim YS, Lee YM, Oh TI, Shin DH, Kim GH, Kan SY, et al. Emodin sensitizes hepatocellular carcinoma cells to the anti-cancer effect of sorafenib through suppression of cholesterol metabolism. Int J Mol Sci 2018;19 (10):3127. Available from: https://doi.org/10.3390/ijms19103127.

[51] Li X, Chen W, Liu K, Zhang S, Yang R, Liu K, et al. Oridonin sensitizes hepatocellular carcinoma to the anti-cancer effect of sorafenib by targeting the Akt pathway. Cancer Manag Res 2020;12:8081−91. Available from: https://doi.org/10.2147/CMAR.S257482.

[52] Lu M, Fei Z, Zhang G. Synergistic anticancer activity of 20(S)-Ginsenoside Rg3 and Sorafenib in hepatocellular carcinoma by modulating PTEN/Akt signaling pathway. Biomed Pharmacother 2018;97:1282−8. Available from: https://doi.org/10.1016/j.biopha.2017.11.006.

[53] Vigushin DM, Poon GK, Boddy A. Phase I and pharmacokinetic study of D-limonene in patients with advanced cancer. Cancer Research Campaign Phase I/II Clinical Trials Committee. Cancer Chemother Pharmacol 1998;42:111−17.

[54] Pandey KB, Rizvi SI. Plant polyphenols as dietary antioxidants in human health and disease. Oxid Med Cell Longev 2009;2(5):270−8. Available from: https://doi.org/10.4161/oxim.2.5.9498.

[55] Gao L, Wang L, Sun Z, Li H, Wang Q, Yi C, et al. Morusin shows potent antitumor activity for human hepatocellular carcinoma in vitro and in vivo through apoptosis induction and angiogenesis inhibition. Drug Des Devel Ther 2017;11:1789−802. Available from: https://doi.org/10.2147/DDDT.S138320.

[56] Zhang HH, Zhang Y, Cheng YN, Gong FL, Cao ZQ, Yu LG, et al. Metformin incombination with curcumin inhibits the growth, metastasis, and angiogenesis of hepatocellular carcinoma in vitro and in vivo. Mol Carcinog 2018;57:44−56. Available from: https://doi.org/10.1002/mc.22718.

[57] Lin X, Wei J, Chen Y, He P, Lin J, Tan S, et al. Isoorientin from Gypsophila elegans induces apoptosis in liver cancer cells via mitochondrial-mediated pathway. J Ethnopharmacol 2016;187:187−94. Available from: https://doi.org/10.1016/j.jep.2016.04.050.

[58] Zhang Y, Duan W, Owusu L, Wu D, Xin Y. Epigallocatechin-3-gallate induces the apoptosis of hepatocellular carcinoma LM6 cells but not non-cancerous liver cells. Int J Mol Med 2015;35(1):117−24. Available from: https://doi.org/10.3892/ijmm.2014.1988.

[59] Ali H, Dixit S, Ali D, Alkahtane AA, Alarifi S, Ali BA, et al. Isolation and evaluation of biological efficacy of quercetol in human hepatic carcinoma cells. Drug Des Devel Ther 2016;10:155−62. Available from: https://doi.org/10.2147/DDDT.S95275.

[60] Banjerdpongchai R, Wudtiwai B, Khaw-On P, Rachakhom W, Duangnil N, Kongtawelert P. Hesperidin from citrus seed induces human hepatocellular carcinoma HepG2 cell apoptosis via both mitochondrial and death receptor pathways. Tumour Biol 2016;37(1):227−37. Available from: https://doi.org/10.1007/s13277-015-3774-7.

[61] Hsu YL, Hou MF, Tsai EM, Kuo PL. Tricetin, a dietary flavonoid, induces apoptosis through the reactive oxygen species/c-Jun NH2-terminal kinase pathway in human liver cancer cells. J Agric Food Chem 2010;23:12547−56. Available from: https://doi.org/10.1021/jf103159r.

[62] Kumar N, Shrungeswara AH, Mallik SB, Biswas S, Mathew J, Nandakumar K, et al. Pinocembrin-enriched fractions of Elytranthe parasitica (L.) Danser modulates apoptotic and MAPK cellular signaling in HepG2 Cells. Anticancer Agents Med Chem 2018;18(11):1563−72. Available from: https://doi.org/10.2174/1871520618666180911112127.

[63] Kim EY, Kim AK. Apigenin sensitizes Huh-7 human hepatocellular carcinoma cells to TRAIL-induced apoptosis. Biomol Ther (Seoul) 2012;20(1):62−7. Available from: https://doi.org/10.4062/biomolther.2012.20.1.062.

[64] Kim EY, Yu JS, Yang M, Kim AK. Sub-toxic dose of apigenin sensitizes HepG2 cells to TRAIL through ERK-dependent up-regulation of TRAIL receptor DR5. Mol Cells 2013;35(1):32−40. Available from: https://doi.org/10.1007/s10059-013-2175-2.

[65] Bhattacharya S, Mondal L, Mukherjee B, Dutta L, Ehsan I, Debnath MC, et al. Apigenin loaded nanoparticle delayed development of hepatocellular carcinoma in rats. Nanomedicine 2018;14(6):1905−17. Available from: https://doi.org/10.1016/j.nano.2018.05.011.

[66] Hu Y, Yang Y, You QD, Liu W, Gu HY, Zhao L, et al. Oroxylin A induced apoptosis of human hepatocellular carcinoma cell line HepG2 was involved in its antitumor activity. Biochem Biophys Res Commun 2006;351 (2):521−7. Available from: https://doi.org/10.1016/j.bbrc.2006.10.064.

[67] Zou M, Lu N, Hu C, Liu W, Sun Y, Wang X, et al. Beclin 1-mediated autophagy in hepatocellular carcinoma cells: Implication in anticancer efficiency of oroxylin A via inhibition of mTOR signaling. Cell Signal 2012;24:1722−32.

[68] Sun M, Cao H, Sun L, Dong S, Bian Y, Han J, et al. Antitumor activities of kushen: literature review. Evid Based Complement Alternat Med 2012;373219. Available from: https://doi.org/10.1155/2012/373219.

[69] Wang Z, Li F, Quan Y, Shen J. Avicularin ameliorates human hepatocellular carcinoma via the regulation of NF-κB/COX-2/PPAR-γ activities. Mol Med Rep 2019;19(6):5417−23. Available from: https://doi.org/10.3892/mmr.2019.10198.

[70] Wang D, Lu J, Liu Y, Meng Q, Xie J, Wang Z, et al. Liquiritigenin induces tumor cell death through mitogen-activated protein kinase- (MPAKs-) mediated pathway in hepatocellular carcinoma cells. Biomed Res Int 2014;2014:965316. Available from: https://doi.org/10.1155/2014/965316.

[71] Zhang Q, Liu J, Liu B, Xia J, Chen N, Chen X, et al. Dihydromyricetin promotes hepatocellular carcinoma regression via a p53 activation-dependent mechanism. Sci Rep 2014;14:4628. Available from: https://doi.org/10.1038/srep04628.

[72] Fan SH, Wang YY, Lu J, Zheng YL, Wu DM, Li MQ, et al. Luteoloside suppresses proliferation and metastasis of hepatocellular carcinoma cells by inhibition of NLRP3 inflammasome. PLoS One 2014;9(2):e89961. Available from: https://doi.org/10.1371/journal.pone.0089961.

[73] Upanan S, Yodkeeree S, Thippraphan P, Punfa W, Wongpoomchai R, Limtrakul Dejkriengkraikul P. The Proanthocyanidin-rich fraction obtained from red rice germ and bran extract induces HepG2 hepatocellular carcinoma cell apoptosis. Molecules (Basel, Switzerland) 2019;24(4):813. Available from: https://doi.org/10.3390/molecules24040813.

[74] Mastron JK, Siveen KS, Sethi G, Bishayee A. Silymarin and hepatocellular carcinoma: a systematic, comprehensive, and critical review. Anticancer Drugs 2015;26(5):475−86. Available from: https://doi.org/10.1097/CAD.0000000000000211.

[75] Guo C, Li Y, Zhang H, Wang Z, Jin M, Zhang L, et al. Enhancement of antiproliferative and proapoptotic effects of cadmium chloride combined with hSmac in hepatocellular carcinoma cells. Chemotherapy 2011;57:27−34. Available from: https://doi.org/10.1159/000321031.

[76] Monga J, Pandit S, Chauhan RS, Chauhan CS, Chauhan SS, Sharma M. Growth inhibition and apoptosis induction by (+)-cyanidan-3-ol in hepatocellular carcinoma. PLoS One 2013;8(7):e68710. Available from: https://doi.org/10.1371/journal.pone.0068710.

[77] Varghese L, Agarwal C, Tyagi A, Singh RP, Agarwal R. Silibinin efficacy against human hepatocellular carcinoma. Clin Cancer Res 2005;11(23):8441−8. Available from: https://doi.org/10.1158/1078-0432.CCR-05-1646. PMID 16322307.

[78] Chhabra N, Buzarbaruah S, Singh R, Kaur J. Silibinin: a promising anti-neoplastic agent for the future? A critical reappraisal. Int J Nutr Pharmacol Neurol Dis 2013;3(3):206.

[79] Teng BS, Lu YH, Wang ZT, Tao XY, Wei DZ. In vitro anti-tumor activity of isorhamnetin isolated from Hippophae rhamnoides L. against BEL-7402 cells. Pharmacol Res 2006;54(3):186−94. Available from: https://doi.org/10.1016/j.phrs.2006.04.007.

[80] Arul D, Subramanian P. Naringenin (citrus flavonone) induces growth inhibition, cell cycle arrest and apoptosis in human hepatocellular carcinoma cells. Pathol Oncol Res 2013;19(4):763−70. Available from: https://doi.org/10.1007/s12253-013-9641-1.

[81] Banjerdpongchai R, Wudtiwai B, Khawon P. Induction of human hepatocellular carcinoma HepG2 cell apoptosis by naringin. Asian Pac J Cancer Prev 2016;17(7):3289−94.

[82] Wang Z, Jiang C, Chen W, Zhang G, Luo D, Cao Y, et al. Baicalein induces apoptosis and autophagy via endoplasmic reticulum stress in hepatocellular carcinoma cells. Biomed Res Int 2014;2014:732516. Available from: https://doi.org/10.1155/2014/732516.

[83] Zheng J, Shao Y, Jiang Y, Chen F, Liu S, Yu N, et al. Tangeretin inhibits hepatocellular carcinoma proliferation and migration by promoting autophagy-related BECLIN1. Cancer Manag Res 2019;11:5231−42. Available from: https://doi.org/10.2147/CMAR.S200974.

[84] Rong LW, Wang RX, Zheng XL, Feng XQ, Zhang L, Zhang L, et al. Combination of wogonin and sorafenib effectively kills human hepatocellular carcinoma cells through apoptosis potentiation and autophagy inhibition. Oncol Lett 2017;13(6):5028−34. Available from: https://doi.org/10.3892/ol.2017.6059.

[85] Yuan L, Wei S, Wang J, Liu X. Isoorientin induces apoptosis and autophagy simultaneously by reactive oxygen species (ROS)-related p53, PI3K/Akt, JNK, and p38 signaling pathways in HepG2 cancer cells. J Agric Food Chem 2014;62(23):5390−400. Available from: https://doi.org/10.1021/jf500903g.

[86] Cao Z, Zhang H, Cai X, Fang W, Chai D, Wen Y, et al. Luteolin promotes cell apoptosis by inducing autophagy in hepatocellular carcinoma. Cell Physiol Biochem 2017;43(5):1803−12. Available from: https://doi.org/10.1159/000484066.

[87] Wen M, Wu J, Luo H, Zhang H. Galangin induces autophagy through upregulation of p53 in HepG2 cells. Pharmacology 2012;89(5−6):247−55. Available from: https://doi.org/10.1159/000337041.

[88] Wang Y, Wu J, Lin B, Li X, Zhang H, Ding H, et al. Galangin suppresses HepG2 cell proliferation by activating the TGF-β receptor/Smad pathway. Toxicology 2014;326:9−17. Available from: https://doi.org/10.1016/j.tox.2014.09.010.

[89] Huang WW, Tsai SC, Peng SF, Lin MW, Chiang JH, Chiu YJ, et al. Kaempferol induces autophagy through AMPK and AKT signaling molecules and causes G2/M arrest via downregulation of CDK1/cyclin B in SK-HEP-1 human hepatic cancer cells. Int J Oncol 2013;42(6):2069−77. Available from: https://doi.org/10.3892/ijo.2013.1909.

[90] Guo H, Lin W, Zhang X, Zhang X, Hu Z, Li L, et al. Kaempferol induces hepatocellular carcinoma cell death via endoplasmic reticulum stress-CHOP-autophagy signaling pathway. Oncotarget 2017;8(47):82207−16. Available from: https://doi.org/10.18632/oncotarget.19200.

[91] Wu L, Li J, Liu T, Li S, Feng J, Yu Q, et al. Quercetin shows anti-tumor effect in hepatocellular carcinoma LM3 cells by abrogating JAK2/STAT3 signaling pathway. Cancer Med 2019;8(10):4806−20. Available from: https://doi.org/10.1002/cam4.2388.

[92] Ji Y, Li L, Ma YX, Li WT, Li L, Zhu HZ, et al. Quercetin inhibits growth of hepatocellular carcinoma by apoptosis induction in part via autophagy stimulation in mice. J Nutr Biochem 2019;69:108−19. Available from: https://doi.org/10.1016/j.jnutbio.2019.03.018.

[93] Yamada N, Matsushima-Nishiwaki R, Kozawa O. Quercetin suppresses the migration of hepatocellular carcinoma cells stimulated by hepatocyte growth factor or transforming growth factor-α: attenuation of AKT signaling pathway. Arch Biochem Biophys 2020;682:108296. Available from: https://doi.org/10.1016/j.abb.2020.108296.

[94] Li M, Chen J, Yu X, Xu S, Li D, Zheng Q, et al. Myricetin suppresses the propagation of hepatocellular carcinoma via down-regulating expression of YAP. Cells 2019;8(4):358. Available from: https://doi.org/10.3390/cells8040358.

[95] Bimonte S, Albino V, Piccirillo M, Nasto A, Molino C, Palaia R, et al. Epigallocatechin-3-gallate in the prevention and treatment of hepatocellular carcinoma: experimental findings and translational perspectives. Drug Des Devel Ther 2019;13:611−21. Available from: https://doi.org/10.2147/DDDT.S180079.

[96] Chen L, Ye HL, Zhang G, Yao WM, Chen XZ, Zhang FC, et al. Autophagy inhibition contributes to the synergistic interaction between EGCG and doxorubicin to kill the hepatoma Hep3B cells. PLoS One 2014;9(1): e85771. Available from: https://doi.org/10.1371/journal.pone.0085771.

[97] Feng R, Wang SY, Shi YH, Fan J, Yin XM. Delphinidin induces necrosis in hepatocellular carcinoma cells in the presence of 3-methyladenine, an autophagy inhibitor. J Agric Food Chem 2010;58(7):3957−64. Available from: https://doi.org/10.1021/jf9025458.

[98] Dorn C, Weiss TS, Heilmann J, Hellerbrand C. Xanthohumol, a prenylated chalcone derived from hops, inhibits proliferation, migration and interleukin-8 expression of hepatocellular carcinoma cells. Int J Oncol 2010;36(2):435−41.

[99] Ramirez-Tagle R, Escobar CA, Romero V, Montorfano I, Armisén R, Borgna V, et al. Chalcone-induced apoptosis through caspase-dependent intrinsic pathways in human hepatocellular carcinoma cells. Int J Mol Sci 2016;17(2):260. Available from: https://doi.org/10.3390/ijms17020260.

[100] Zhou Y, Li M, Yu X, Liu T, Li T, Zhou L, et al. Butein suppresses hepatocellular carcinoma growth via modulating Aurora B kinase activity. Int J Biol Sci 2018;14(11):1521–34. Available from: https://doi.org/10.7150/ijbs.25334.

[101] Badroon NA, Abdul Majid N, Alshawsh MA. Antiproliferative and apoptotic effects of cardamonin against hepatocellular carcinoma HepG2 Cells. Nutrients 2020;12(6):1757. Available from: https://doi.org/10.3390/nu12061757.

[102] Liao PC, Ng LT, Lin LT, Richardson CD, Wang GH, Lin CC. Resveratrol arrests cell cycle and induces apoptosis in human hepatocellular carcinoma Huh-7 cells. J Med Food 2010;13(6):1415–23. Available from: https://doi.org/10.1089/jmf.2010.1126.

[103] Zhang B, Yin X, Sui S. Resveratrol inhibited the progression of human hepatocellular carcinoma by inducing autophagy via regulating p53 and the phosphoinositide 3-kinase/protein kinase B pathway. Oncol Rep 2018;40(5):2758–65. Available from: https://doi.org/10.3892/or.2018.6648.

[104] Cheng X, Zhong F, He K, Sun S, Chen H, Zhou J. EHHM, a novel phenolic natural product from *Livistona chinensis*, induces autophagy-related apoptosis in hepatocellular carcinoma cells. Oncol Lett 2016;12 (5):3739–48. Available from: https://doi.org/10.3892/ol.2016.5178.

[105] Rainey N, Motte L, Aggarwal BB, Petit PX. Curcumin hormesis mediates a cross-talk between autophagy and cell death. Cell Death Dis 2015;6(12):e2003. Available from: https://doi.org/10.1038/cddis.2015.343.

[106] Elmansi AM, El-Karef AA, Shishtawy MMEl, Eissa LA. Hepatoprotective effect of curcumin on hepatocellular carcinoma through autophagic and apoptic pathways. Ann Hepatol 2017;16(4):607–18. Available from: https://doi.org/10.5604/01.3001.0010.0307.

[107] Qian H, Yang Y, Wang X. Curcumin enhanced adriamycin-induced human liver-derived Hepatoma G2 cell death through activation of mitochondria-mediated apoptosis and autophagy. Eur J Pharm Sci 2011;43 (3):125–31. Available from: https://doi.org/10.1016/j.ejps.2011.04.002.

[108] Zhou T, Ye L, Bai Y, Sun A, Cox B, Liu D, et al. Autophagy and apoptosis in hepatocellular carcinoma induced by EF25-(GSH)2; a novel curcumin analog. PLoS One 2014;9(9):e107876. Available from: https://doi.org/10.1371/journal.pone.0107876.

[109] Wang L, Zhu Z, Han L, Zhao L, Weng J, Yang H, et al. A curcumin derivative, WZ35, suppresses hepatocellular cancer cell growth via downregulating YAP-mediated autophagy. Food Funct 2019;10(6):3748–57. Available from: https://doi.org/10.1039/c8fo02448k.

[110] Jiang K, Wang W, Jin X, Wang Z, Ji Z, Meng G. Silibinin, a natural flavonoid, induces autophagy via ROS-dependent mitochondrial dysfunction and loss of ATP involving BNIP3 in human MCF7 breast cancer cells. Oncol Rep 2015;33:2711–18.

[111] Yang J, Pi C, Wang G. Inhibition of PI3K/Akt/mTOR pathway by apigenin induces apoptosis and autophagy in hepatocellular carcinoma cells. Biomed Pharm103 2018;699–707.

[112] Maclean KH, Dorsey FC, Cleveland JL, Kastan MB. Targeting lysosomal degradation induces p53-dependent cell death and prevents cancer in mouse models of lymphomagenesis. J Clin Investig 2008;118:79–88.

[113] Zhang J, Lai WJ, Li Q, Jin J, Xiao BD, Guo W, et al. Inhibition of hepatocellular stem cells by oncolytic virus targeting Wnt signaling pathway. Prog Biochem Biophys 2017;44:326–37.

[114] Kiruthiga C, Devi KP, Nabavi SM, Bishayee A. Autophagy: a potential therapeutic target of polyphenols in hepatocellular carcinoma. Cancers (Basel) 2020;12(3):562. Available from: https://doi.org/10.3390/cancers12030562.

[115] Cheng AL, Kang YK, Chen Z, Tsao CJ, Qin S, Kim JS, et al. Efficacy and safety of Sorafenib in patients in the Asia-Pacific region with advanced hepatocellular carcinoma: a phase III randomised, double-blind, placebo-controlled trial. Lancet Oncol 2009;10(1):25–34. Available from: https://doi.org/10.1016/S1470-2045(08)70285-7.

[116] Jemal A, Murray T, Ward E, Samuels A, Tiwari RC, Ghafoor A, et al. Cancer statistics. CA Cancer J Clin 2005;55(1):10–30. Available from: https://doi.org/10.3322/canjclin.55.1.10 Erratum in: CA Cancer J Clin 2005;55(4):259.

[117] Mishra LC. Scientific basis for ayurvedic therapies. CRC Press; 2004. p. 231–54.

[118] Thavamani BS, Mathew M, Dhanabal SP. *Cocculus hirsutus*: molecular docking to identify suitable targets for hepatocellular carcinoma by *in silico* technique. Pharmacogn Mag 2016;12(Suppl 3):S350–2. Available from: https://doi.org/10.4103/0973-1296.185769.

[119] Tabassum H, Ahmad IZ. Molecular docking and dynamics simulation analysis of Thymoquinone and Thymol compounds from *Nigella sativa* L. that Inhibits P38 Protein: probable remedies for hepatocellular carcinoma. Med Chem 2020;6(3):350–7. Available from: https://doi.org/10.2174/1573406415666190416165732.

[120] Lee WL, Huang JY, Shyur LF. Phytoagents for cancer management: regulation of nucleic acid oxidation, ROS, and related mechanisms. Oxid Med Cell Longev 2013;925804. Available from: https://doi.org/10.1155/2013/925804.

[121] Zhao B, Ma Y, Xu Z. Hydroxytyrosol, a natural molecule from olive oil, suppresses the growth of human hepatocellular carcinoma cells via inactivating AKT and nuclear factor-kappa B pathways. Cancer Lett 2014;347(1):79—87. Available from: https://doi.org/10.1016/j.canlet.2014.01.028.

[122] Cusimano A, Balasus D, Azzolina A, Augello G, Emma MR, Di Sano C, et al. Oleocanthal exerts antitumor effects on human liver and colon cancer cells through ROS generation. Int J Oncol 2017;51(2):533—44. Available from: https://doi.org/10.3892/ijo.2017.4049.

[123] Yamada N, Matsushima-Nishiwaki R, Masue A, Taguchi K, Kozawa O. Olive oil polyphenols suppress the TGF-α-induced migration of hepatocellular carcinoma cells. Biomed Rep 2019;1:1—5. Available from: https://doi.org/10.3892/br.2019.1215.

[124] De Stefanis D, Scimè S, Accomazzo S, Catti A, Occhipinti A, Bertea CM, et al. Anti-proliferative effects of an extra-virgin olive oil extract enriched in ligstroside aglycone and oleocanthal on human liver cancer cell lines. Cancers 2019;11:1640. Available from: https://doi.org/10.3390/cancers11111640.

[125] Dai W, Wang F, He L, Lin C, Wu S, Chen P, et al. Genistein inhibits hepatocellular carcinoma cell migration by reversing the epithelial-mesenchymal transition: partial mediation by the transcription factor NFAT1. Mol Carcinog 2015;54(4):301—11. Available from: https://doi.org/10.1002/mc.22100.

[126] Sanaei M, Kavoosi F, Valiani A, Ghobadifar MA. Effect of genistein on apoptosis and proliferation of hepatocellular carcinoma hepa1—6 cell line. Int J Prev Med 2018;9:12. Available from: https://doi.org/10.4103/ijpvm.IJPVM_249_16.

[127] Alansari WS, Eskandrani AA. The anticarcinogenic effect of the apple polyphenol Phloretin in an experimental rat model of hepatocellular carcinoma. Arab J Sci Eng 2020;45:4589—97. Available from: https://doi.org/10.1007/s13369-020-04478-7.

[128] Mutalib MA, Ali F, Othman F, Ramasamy R, Rahmat A. Phenolics profile and anti-proliferative activity of *Cyphomandra Betacea* fruit in breast and liver cancer cells. Springerplus 2016;5(1):2105. Available from: https://doi.org/10.1186/s40064-016-3777-x.

[129] Chen C, Wang L, Wang R, Luo X, Li Y, Li J, et al. Phenolic contents, cellular antioxidant activity and anti-proliferative capacity of different varieties of oats. Food Chem 2018;239:260—7. Available from: https://doi.org/10.1016/j.foodchem.2017.06.104.

[130] Huang C, Wei YX, Shen MC, Tu YH, Wang CC, Huang HC. Chrysin, abundant in *Morinda citrifolia* fruit water-EtOAc extracts, combined with Apigenin synergistically induced apoptosis and inhibited migration in human breast and liver cancer cells. J Agric Food Chem 2016;64(21):4235—45. Available from: https://doi.org/10.1021/acs.jafc.6b00766.

[131] Zhang J, Song J, Wu D, Wang J, Dong W. Hesperetin induces the apoptosis of hepatocellular carcinoma cells via mitochondrial pathway mediated by the increased intracellular reactive oxygen species, ATP and calcium. Med Oncol 2015;32(4):101. Available from: https://doi.org/10.1007/s12032-015-0516-z.

[132] Wang Z, Zhang H, Zhou J, Zhang X, Chen L, Chen K, et al. Eriocitrin from lemon suppresses the proliferation of human hepatocellular carcinoma cells through inducing apoptosis and arresting cell cycle. Cancer Chemother Pharmacol 2016;78(6):1143—50. Available from: https://doi.org/10.1007/s00280-016-3171-y.

[133] Yeh MH, Kao ST, Hung CM, Liu CJ, Lee KH, Yeh CC. Hesperidin inhibited acetaldehyde-induced matrix metalloproteinase-9 gene expression in human hepatocellular carcinoma cells. Toxicol Lett 2009;184 (3):204—10. Available from: https://doi.org/10.1016/j.toxlet.2008.11.018.

[134] Yen HR, Liu CJ, Yeh CC. Naringenin suppresses TPA-induced tumor invasion by suppressing multiple signal transduction pathways in human hepatocellular carcinoma cells. Chem Biol Interact 2015;235:1—9. Available from: https://doi.org/10.1016/j.cbi.2015.04.003.

[135] Feng LL, Liu BX, Zhong JY, Sun LB, Yu HS. Effect of grape procyanidins on tumor angiogenesis in liver cancer xenograft models. Asian Pac J Cancer Prev 2014;5(2):737—41. Available from: https://doi.org/10.7314/apjcp.2014.15.2.737.

[136] Yu HB, Zhang HF, Zhang X, Li DY, Xue HZ, Pan CE, et al. Resveratrol inhibits VEGF expression of human hepatocellular carcinoma cells through a NF-kappa B-mediated mechanism. Hepatogastroenterology 2010;57(102—103):1241—6.

[137] Huang G, Tang B, Tang K, Dong X, Deng J, Liao L et al. Isoquercitrin inhibits the progression of liver cancer *in vivo* and *in vitro* via the MAPK signaling pathway. Oncol RepAvailable from: https://doi.org/10.3892/or.2014.3099.

[138] Youns M, Abdel Halim Hegazy W. The natural flavonoid Fisetin inhibits cellular proliferation of hepatic, colorectal, and pancreatic cancer cells through modulation of multiple signaling pathways. PLoS One 2017;12(1):e0169335. Available from: https://doi.org/10.1371/journal.pone.0169335.

[139] Liu Z, Ren B, Wang Y, Zou C, Qiao Q, Diao Z, et al. Sesamol induces human hepatocellular carcinoma cells apoptosis by impairing mitochondrial function and suppressing autophagy. Sci Rep 2017;7:45728. Available from: https://doi.org/10.1038/srep45728.

[140] Yan Y, Liu N, Hou N, Dong L, Li J. Chlorogenic acid inhibits hepatocellular carcinoma *in vitro* and *in vivo*. J Nutr Biochem 2017;46:68—73. Available from: https://doi.org/10.1016/j.jnutbio.2017.04.007.

[141] Bhatia D, Thoppil RJ, Mandal A, Samtani KA, Darvesh AS, Bishayee A. Pomegranate bioactive constituents suppress cell proliferation and induce apoptosis in an experimental model of hepatocellular carcinoma: role of Wnt/ β -Catenin signaling pathway. Evid Based Complement Alternat Med 2013;2013:371813. Available from: https://doi.org/10.1155/2013/371813.

[142] Bishayee A, Thoppil RJ, Darvesh AS, Ohanyan V, Meszaros JG, Bhatia D. Pomegranate phytoconstituents blunt the inflammatory cascade in a chemically induced rodent model of hepatocellular carcinogenesis. J Nutr Biochem 2013;24(1):178—87. Available from: https://doi.org/10.1016/j.jnutbio.2012.04.009.

[143] Weng CJ, Chou CP, Ho CT, Yen GC. Molecular mechanism inhibiting human hepatocarcinoma cell invasion by 6-shogaol and 6-gingerol. Mol Nutr Food Res 2012;56(8):1304—14. Available from: https://doi.org/10.1002/mnfr.201200173.

[144] Al-Abbasi FA, Alghamdi EA, Baghdadi MA, Alamoudi AJ, El-Halawany AM, El-Bassossy HM, et al. Gingerol synergizes the cytotoxic effects of Doxorubicin against liver cancer cells and protects from its vascular toxicity. Molecules 2016;21(7):886. Available from: https://doi.org/10.3390/molecules21070886.

[145] Sawada S, Okano J, Imamoto R, Yasunaka Y, Abe R, Koda M, et al. Preventive effect of Geraniol on Diethylnitrosamine-induced hepatocarcinogenesis in rats. Yonago Acta Med 2016;59(1):37—43.

[146] Tang Z, Tang Y, Li L, Liu T, Yang J. Limonin provokes hepatocellular carcinoma cells with stemness entry into cycle via activating PI3K/Akt signaling. Biomed Pharmacother 2019;117:109051. Available from: https://doi.org/10.1016/j.biopha.2019.109051.

[147] Chi WJ, Doong SL, Lin Shiau SY, Boone CW, Kelloff GJ, Lin JK. Oltipraz, a novel inhibitor of hepatitis B virus transcription through elevation of p53 protein. Carcinogenesis 1998;19(12):2133—8. Available from: https://doi.org/10.1093/carcin/19.12.2133.

[148] Bhatia N, Singh B, Koul A. Lycopene treatment stalls the onset of experimentally induced hepatocellular carcinoma: a radioisotopic, physiological and biochemical analysis. Hepatoma Res 2018;4(9).

[149] Ip BC, Liu C, Ausman LM, von Lintig J, Wang XD. Lycopene attenuated hepatic tumorigenesis via differential mechanisms depending on carotenoid cleavage enzyme in mice. Cancer Prev Res (Phila) 2014;7 (12):1219—27. Available from: https://doi.org/10.1158/1940-6207.CAPR-14-0154.

[150] Zhang MG, Chen G, Liu L. The extraction of asparagus polysaccharide and its effect on the growth of human hepatic cancer SMMC-7721 cells in vitro. J Interv Radiol 2011;20(6):465—9.

[151] Ding JY, Wang X, Weng LL. Effects of Asparagus polysaccharides on growth, invasion and migration of human hepatocellular carcinoma cells under hypoxia. Shandong Medical Journal 2017;57(14):23—6.

[152] Zhang Q, Lv X, Wu T, Ma Q, Teng A, Zhang Y, et al. Composition of *Lycium barbarum* polysaccharides and their apoptosis-inducing effect on human hepatoma SMMC-7721 cells. Food Nutr Res 2015;59:28696. Available from: https://doi.org/10.3402/fnr.v59.28696.

[153] Ceccarini MR, Vannini S, Cataldi S, Moretti M, Villarini M, Fioretti B, et al. *In vitro* protective effects of *Lycium barbarum* berries 16 D. S. MANDLIK AND S. K. MANDLIK cultivated in Umbria (Italy) on human hepatocellular carcinoma cells. Bio Med Res Int 2016;2016:7529521.

[154] Kuo PL, Lin CC. Green tea constituent (-)-epigallocatechin-3-gallate inhibits Hep G2 cell proliferation and induces apoptosis through p53-dependent and Fas-mediated pathways. J Biomed Sci 2003;10(2):219—27. Available from: https://doi.org/10.1007/BF02256057.

[155] Shimizu M, Shirakami Y, Sakai H, Tatebe H, Nakagawa T, Hara Y, et al. EGCG inhibits activation of the insulin-like growth factor (IGF)/IGF-1 receptor axis in human hepatocellular carcinoma cells. Cancer Lett 2008;262(1):10—18. Available from: https://doi.org/10.1016/j.canlet.2007.11.026.

[156] Chen C, Yu R, Owuor ED, Kong AN. Activation of antioxidant-response element (ARE), mitogen-activated protein kinases (MAPKs) and caspases by major green tea polyphenol components during cell survival and death. Arch Pharmacal Res 2000;23(6):605−12. Available from: https://doi.org/10.1007/BF02975249.

[157] Zhang HT, Wu J, Wen M, Su LJ, Luo H. Galangin induces apoptosis in hepatocellular carcinoma cells through the caspase 8/t-Bid mitochondrial pathway. J Asian Nat Prod Res 2012;14(7):626−33. Available from: https://doi.org/10.1080/10286020.2012.682152.

[158] Elgazar AA, Selim NM, Abdel-Hamid NM, El-Magd MA, El Hefnawy HM. Isolates from *Alpinia officinarum* Hance attenuate LPS-induced inflammation in HepG2: evidence from *in silico* and *in vitro* studies. Phytother Res 2018;32(7):1273−88. Available from: https://doi.org/10.1002/ptr.6056.

[159] Abass SA, Abdel-Hamid NM, Abouzed TK, ElShishtawy MM. Chemosensitizing effect of *Alpinia officinarum* rhizome extract in cisplatin-treated rats with hepatocellular carcinoma. Biomed Pharmacother 2018;101:710−18. Available from: https://doi.org/10.1016/j.biopha.2018.02.128.

[160] Geethangili M, Rao YK, Fang SH, Tzeng YM. Cytotoxic constituents from *Andrographis paniculata* induce cell cycle arrest in jurkat cells. Phytother Res 2008;22(10):1336−41. Available from: https://doi.org/10.1002/ptr.2493.

[161] Shi M-D, Lin H-H, Lee Y-C, Chao J-K, Lin R-A, Chen J-H. Inhibition of cell-cycle progression in human colorectal carcinoma Lovo cells by andrographolide. Chem Biol Interact 2008;174(3):201−10. Available from: https://doi.org/10.1016/j.cbi.2008.06.006.

[162] Zhou J, Zhang S, Choon-Nam O, Shen HM. Critical role of pro-apoptotic Bcl-2 family members in andrographolide-induced apoptosis in human cancer cells. Biochem Pharmacol 2006;72(2):132−44. Available from: https://doi.org/10.1016/j.bcp.2006.04.019.

[163] Hemieda F, Serag H, El-Baz E, Ramadan S, Faried AE, Hemieda S. Therapeutic efficacy of licorice and/ or cisplatin against diethylnitrosamine and carbon tetrachloride-induced hepatocellular carcinoma in rats. J Am Sci 2016;12:10−19.

[164] Zhang Y, Yan C, Li Y, Mao X, Tao W, Tang Y, et al. Therapeutic effects of *Euphorbia pekinensis* and *Glycyrrhiza glabra* on hepatocellular carcinoma ascites partially via regulating the Frk-Arhgdib-Inpp5d-Avpr2-Aqp4 signal axis. Sci Rep 2017;7:41925. Available from: https://doi.org/10.1038/srep41925.

[165] Abdel-Hamid NM, Abdel-Ghany MI, Nazmy MH, Amgad SW. Can methanolic extract of Nigella sativa seed affect glyco-regulatory enzymes in experimental hepatocellular carcinoma? Environ Health Prev Med 2013;18(1):49−56. Available from: https://doi.org/10.1007/s12199-012-0292-8.

[166] Khan F, Kalamegam G, Gari M, Abuzenadah A, Chaudhary A, Al Qahtani M, et al. Evaluation of the effect of *Nigella sativa* extract on human hepatocellular adenocarcinoma cell line (HepG2) in vitro. BMC Genomics 2014;15(Suppl 2):P63. Available from: https://doi.org/10.1186/1471-2164-15-S2-P63.

[167] Lombardi VR, Carrera I, Cacabelos R. *In vitro* screening for cytotoxic activity of herbal extracts. Evid Complement Alternat Med 2017;2017:2675631. Available from: https://doi.org/10.1155/2017/2675631.

[168] Yadav AS, Bhatnagar D. Chemo-preventive effect of Star anise in N-nitrosodiethylamine initiated and phenobarbital promoted hepato-carcinogenesis. Chem Biol Interact 2007;169(3):207−14. Available from: https://doi.org/10.1016/j.cbi.2007.06.032.

[169] Liu J, Zhang L, Ren Y, Gao YL, Kang L, Lu SP. Matrine inhibits the expression of adhesion molecules in activated vascular smooth muscle cells. Mol Med Rep 2016;13:2313. Available from: https://doi.org/10.3892/mmr.2016.4767.

[170] Giri RK, Parija T, Das BR. d-limonene chemoprevention of hepatocarcinogenesis in AKR mice: inhibition of c-jun and c-myc. Oncol Rep 1999;6:1123−7.

[171] Kaji I, Tatsuta M, Iishi H. Inhibition by d-limonene of experimental hepatocarcinogenesis in Sprague−Dawley rats does not involve p21 (ras) plasma membrane association. Int J Cancer 2001;93:441−4.

[172] Parija T, Das BR. Involvement of YY1 and its correlation with c-myc in NDEA induced hepatocarcinogenesis, its prevention by d-limonene. Mol Biol Rep 2003;30(1):41−6. Available from: https://doi.org/10.1023/a:1022207630482.

Phytonanoformulations for hepatocellular carcinoma therapy

Mohammad Imran[1], Gowru Srivani[2] and Ganji Seeta Rama Raju[3]

[1]Innatura Scientific Pvt. Ltd, Rangareddy, Secunderabad, Telangana, India
[2]Department of Biosciences and Biotechnology, Banasthali University, Banasthali, India
[3]Department of Energy and Materials Engineering, Dongguk University, Seoul, Republic of Korea

Abstract

Hepatocellular carcinoma (HCC) is the second common type of cancer and the leading cause of cancer-related mortalities around the world. However, clinical stage of therapeutics, diagnosis, and level of treatment options are still limited, which warrants an immediate need to develop novel drugs to improve therapeutic effects and survival rate of HCC. This leads to the generation of nanomedicine. Moreover, phytonanomedicine is the fast-growing formulations in nanotechnology field that offers countless possibilities to design drugs at nanoscale with its unique properties. Phytonanomedicine allows scientists to prepare different methods of drug delivery that are used in multiple ways such as diagnosis, imaging, and treatment. This chapter covers the characteristic of HCC, role of nanomedicine in HCC treatment including nanoparticle (NP) properties, and the importance of nanocarriers in drug delivery. It also highlights the role of phytochemicals with NPs therapy in HCC.

Keywords: Hepatocellular carcinoma; nanomedicine; nanoparticles; nanocarriers

Abbreviations

AgNPs	silver nanoparticles
ALL	acute lymphoma leukemia
AuNPs	gold nanoparticles
BRAF-B	Raf murine sarcoma viral oncogene gene
CDKN2	cyclic-dependent kinase 2A inhibitor
CE	cinnamon extract
CNND1	cyclin D1 protein

Ganji Purnachandra Nagaraju, Sarfraz Ahmad (eds.)
Theranostics and Precision Medicine for the Management of Hepatocellular Carcinoma, Volume 3

197

DOI: https://doi.org/10.1016/B978-0-323-99283-1.00026-4
© 2022 Elsevier Inc. All rights reserved.

CTNNB1	catenin beta-1
DAD	diallyl disulfide
DAPI-4′,6	diamidino-2-phenylindole
DAS	diallyl sulfide
DAT	diallyl trisulfide
EACG	ethanolic extract of *Antrodia cinnamonea* with ginger
EGCG	epigallocatechin gallate
FGF19	fibroblast growth factor 19
Ftub-4	fosbretabulin A4
IT-141-	intezyme technologies
KHOS	Ewing osteosarcoma cell line-312H
MAPK	mitogen-activated protein kinase
2-MCA	2-methoxy cinnamaldehyde
NF-kB	nuclear factor kappa-activated B cells
NLC	nanostructured lipid carriers
NT8e	head and neck cancer cell lines
P21	protein in cancer
PBCA	polybutylcyanoacrylate
PDGFR	platelet-derived growth receptor family
PIHCA	polyisohexyl cyanoacrylate
PLGA	poly(D,L-lactide-*co*-glycolide) (PLGA)
PLK1	polo-like kinase 1
ROS	reactive oxygen species
SAMC	S-allylmercaptocysteine
STAT3	signal transducer and activator of transcription-3
TACE	transarterial chemoembolization
TGF-β	transforming growth factor-β
VEGF-A	vascular endothelial growth factor A
VEGFR	vascular endothelial growth receptor family

Introduction

Among various dreadful diseases affecting globally, hepatocellular carcinoma (HCC) [1] is the prevalent one and stands second position of in mortality [2]. HCC is prevalent in man and ranks fifth in terms of malignance [3]. Ninety percent malignancy of liver is seen in patients having a history of liver disorders such as hepatitis B and C, alcohol addiction, liver cirrhosis, chemical-induced toxicity such as aflotoxins, smoking, oxidative stress, diabetes, nonalcoholic fatty liver (NAFL), hemochromatosis—a hereditary disorder, autoimmune hepatitis, and immune-related disorders such as primary biliary cirrhosis [4,5]. By early detection of HCC, survival rate of diseased patient can be enhanced [6] but unfortunately due to unclear and overlapping of other disease symptoms, it is difficult to identify HCC in its early stages. Nearly 25%−30% of diagnosis have been noticed in early stages of HCC [7]. Moreover, using tumor-specific markers and other serological hepatic characteristics might serve as a prognostic factor in the treatment of HCC [8]. Symptoms observed in HCC patients are jaundice, upper quadrant abdominal pain, anorexia, weight loss, liver enlargement, diarrhea, hemobilia. Some patients experience more severe symptoms such as abdominal pain, hepatic portal vein invasion, peritoneal bleeding due to HCC rupture, thrombosis, and hepatic vein occlusion leading to Budd−Chiari syndrome [9].

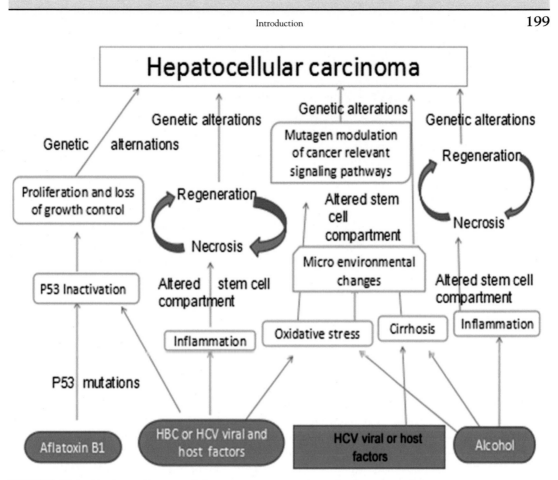

FIGURE 13.1 Etiology of hepatocellular carcinoma representing the diverse risk factors.

Currently, various treatments are available for managing HCC such as surgery resection, liver transplantation, ablation, trans arterial chemoembolization (TACE), radiotherapy, chemotherapy, combination therapy [9]. However, the treatment of choice depends on patient condition and the stage of HCC. Surgical resection is one of the best way to treat HCC in its early stages [10]. In addition, liver transplantation is another option to increase the life span of the patients. However, unfortunately liver transplant cannot eradicate the tumor completely and chances of recurrence are high due to invasion of microscopic vascular cancer existence (Fig. 13.1).

In 2007 USFDA approved the administration of tyrosine multikinase drug, sorafenib (Nexavir) to HCC patients as a first-line therapeutic drug. Chemotherapy exhibits positive results by suppression of Raf serine/threonine kinases [11] (BRAF), platelet-derived growth factor receptor family (PDGFR-β), and vascular endothelial growth factor receptor family (VEGFR-1,2,3). This results in tumor growth inhibition by suppressing cell proliferation and angiogenesis [12]. However, this chemotherapeutic agent exhibited poor pharmacokinetics and adverse effects such as high blood pressure, hand-foot skin reactions alopecia, nausea, mucositis, toxicity, and diarrhea [13].

Current therapies such as radiotherapy, chemotherapy, and locoregional therapy are limited due to nonspecific biodistribution, toxic side effects, and multidrug resistance. To overcome these issues, phytochemicals are introduced to treat HCC, such as curcumin, resveratrol, genistein, ferulic acid, cinnamon, saffron, coffee, garlic, ginger, and other cruciferous vegetables [14]. Endocarp fruit extracts of nephelium lappaceum are commonly known as rambutan fruit that is available in south-east Asian countries. The methanolic extract of endocarp fruits contains polyphenolic compounds such as phenols, flavonoids [15] that exhibit apoptotic and cytotoxic effect on HepG2 cell lines (human HCC cells). The present therapeutic strategies remain limited due to its damaging effect on healthy cells. Hence, recent developments in nanomedicines provide effective therapeutic options for HCC by improving efficiency of target-specific drug delivery to reduce poor stability and solubility with minimal toxicity. In addition, it also reduces drug resistance by high degree of drug distribution, and inhibits proteases activity to prevent drug degradation [15]. This chapter covers various nanomedicines including nanoparticle (NP) characteristics, nanocarriers, nanophytochemicals, and their effects on the clinical usage for effective HCC therapy.

Nanomedicine

Nanomedicine is an emergent field, which refers to natural, supplementary material composed of NPs, either bound or unbound state with external dimensions. NPs exhibit both passive and active delivery of cancer drugs. These NPs include liposomes, magnetic NPs, polymeric NPs, dendimers, nanoshells [16–19], carbon nanotubes [20], and quantum dots [21]. Nanovehicles are drug loadable NPs and depending on the functionlization, the NPs exhibit different functional groups on the surface of NPs. The functionlized NPs are able to target the specific cells in the tumor. These nanovehicles are clinically accepted in various therapeutic platforms against different cancers such as ovarian, prostate, breast, and liver cancers. For example, NPs with polymer-based mitoxantrone-loaded poly-isohexyl-cyanoacrylate (PIHCA) have been shown to exhibit 88.9% potency rate in Phase II clinical trials and entered in Phase III trials in HCC [22]. Another study showed NP (100–200 nm) loaded chemotherapeutic drug named fosbretabulin-A4 (Ftub-4) encapsulated in pegylated polymer poly(D,L-lactide-co-glycolide) (PLGA) is helpful in the suppression of micro tubulin in HCC [23]. Currently undergoing clinical trials that are waiting for the clinical approval in nanotechnology applications are tabulated in Tables 13.1–13.3.

Properties of nanoparticles

Nanotechnology is the fastest growing field and has attracted many biomedical researchers due to its robust therapeutic effects and unique characteristics of NPs such as size, shape, surface charge, high specific surface area, drug loading capacity, targeting of tumor site without damaging the surrounding tissue cells with less side effects, and ability to improve the patient's quality of life. Before designing nanomedicine, various characteristics of NPs must be considered such as size, shape, surface area, surface charge, toxicity, cellular uptake mechanism, and the interaction of NPs with biological system [43,44] (Fig. 13.2).

TABLE 13.1 Current clinically approved nanoparticles therapies and diagnostics, grouped by their broad indication.

Brand name	Type of particle	Investigations	Clinical trial identification no.	Clinical phase updates
ThermoDox [24] (Celsion)	Lysothermosensitive Liposomal doxorubicin releases the drug under heat conditions	Temperature triggered Doxorubicin release:Breast cancer recurrence at chest wall (microwave) HCC (radiofrequency ablation) Liver tumors (mild hypothermia)	NCT02536183 (Phase I) recruiting NCT00826085 (Phase I/II) completed NCT02112656 (Phase III) completed NCT02181075 Phase I completed 2019 additions NCT03749850 (Phase I) not yet recruiting	3 trials completed.Published results show ThermoDox in combination with extremely induced-mild hyperthermia increase—intratumoral concentration of dox-3.7 times as compared to Thermodox without hyperthermia induction.
Liposomes (gene therapy: cancer) TKM-08031 (Arbutus Biopharma)	Lipid-particle targeting polo-like kinase-1 (PLK1) for delivery of SiRNA	HCC	NCT02191878 (Phase I/II) completed 2016	0 new trails1-trail completed
MTL-CEBPA (mini alpha)	Double-stranded RNA formulated into SMARTICLES amphoteric liposomes	Advanced liver cancer	NCT02716012 (Phase I) Recruiting	
IT-141 (Intezyme Technologies) Micelles (cancer)	Micelle formulation of SN-38	Advanced cancer	NCT03096340 (Phase I) Recruiting	
Doxil Caelyx [25] (Janssen)	Liposomal doxorubicin (PEGlyated)	Ovariancancer (secondary to platinum-based therapies) HIV-associatedKaposi sarcoma (secondary to chemotherapy multiple-myeloma)FDA (1995)EMA (1996)	Various cancer including solidmalignancies,breast cancer, ovarian, leukemialymphomas, prostate,metastatic or liver caner	2016, Doxil: 166Caelyx: 90,2019; Doxil: 182
Abraxane [26]	Albumin particle-bound Paclitaxel	Advanced nonsmall cell lung cancer (surgery or radiation) is not an option, metastatic breast cancer (secondary) Metastatic-pancreatic cancer (primary) FDA (2005)EMA (2008)	Various cancer including solid-malignancies; breast, lymphomas	Abraxane: 295, 2019; Abraxane: 432.

TABLE 13.2 List of liposomal formulations which have been approved and entered in clinical trials.

Sl. no.	Drug name	Type of particle	Investigations	Clinical trial identifier no.	Clinical phase
1	Lipoplatin	Cisplatin	Breast cancer Gastric cancer and nonsmall cell lung cancer	NCT02702700	Phase III
2	Thermodox Liposomal Doxorubicin	Doxorubicin	Liver metastases Colorectal cancer Primary HCC Breast cancer	NCT02112656 NCT00617981	Phase III
3	TL1	Topotecan	Small cell lung cancer,solid tumor, ovarian cancer	NCT00765973	Phase I
4	L-BLP25	Tecemotide	Nonsmall-cell lung neoplasms, carcinoma	NCT00157196	Phase II
5	Rexin-G	Cyclin G1 Gene	All solid tumorsSoft tissue sarcoma,osteosarcoma and breast cancer	NCT00505271	Phase I, II. approved in Philippines
6	OSI-211	Lurtotecan	SCLC carcinoma, small cell	NCT00046787	Phase II

TABLE 13.3 List of nanoformulation drugs which have been approved and entered in clinical trials.

Sl. no.	Product name and type of NPs	Type of particle	Investigations	Clinical trial identifier no.	Clinical phase
1	Aurimmune (CYT-6091) metallic NPs	TNF-α loaded with Gold NPs	Various types of cancers such as breast, ovarian, lung, pancreatic, colorectal, Gastrointestinal, kidney, adrenocortical cancer, sarcoma, and melanoma	NCT00436410	Early Phase I
2	Zinostatin Stimalamer Conjugate (Polymeric conjugates)	Zinostatin	HCC,primary unresectable	Resource	Approved in Japan 1993
3	CRLX101, a cyclodextrin Olaparib (polymeric conjugates)	Olaparib	NSCLC, SCLC Urothelial and Prostate Cancer	NCT02769962	Phase I Phase II
4	XMT1001 (Fleximertm) (polymeric conjugates)	Camptothec-in	Small cell lung cancer, Nonsmall cell lung cancer	NCT00455052	Phase I
5	Genexol-PMTM (polymeric micelles)	Paclitaxel	Breast cancer, nonsmall cell lung cancer	Resource	Approved in South Korea in 2006
6	Oncoprex (polymeric micelles)	FUS1(TUSC2) encapsulated liposomes	Lung cancer	NCT01455389	Phase I, Phase II
7	Lipusu	Paclitaxel Liposome Gemcitabine	Lung squamous cell carcinoma	NCT01994031	Phase IV

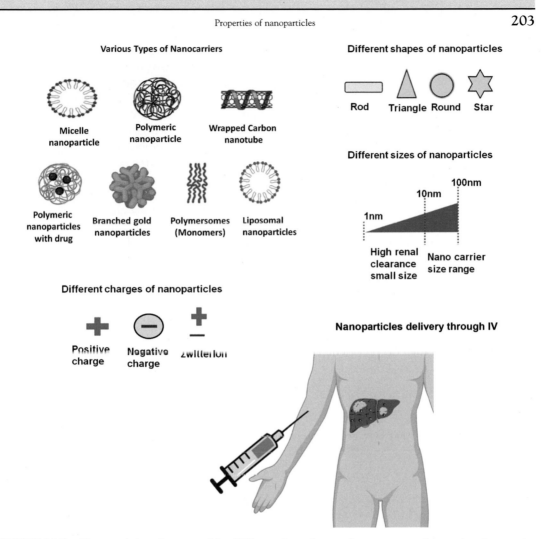

Various Types of Nanocarriers

Micelle nanoparticle

Polymeric nanoparticle

Wrapped Carbon nanotube

Polymeric nanoparticles with drug

Branched gold nanoparticles

Polymersomes (Monomers)

Liposomal nanoparticles

Different charges of nanoparticles

Positive charge

Negative charge

Zwitterion

Different shapes of nanoparticles

Rod   Triangle   Round   Star

Different sizes of nanoparticles

100nm

10nm

1nm

High renal clearance small size

Nano carrier size range

Nanoparticles delivery through IV

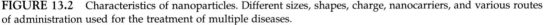

FIGURE 13.2   Characteristics of nanoparticles. Different sizes, shapes, charge, nanocarriers, and various routes of administration used for the treatment of multiple diseases.

Size

Size of NPs plays a crucial role in administration and elimination of drug. Smaller NP size leads to increased cellular uptake, renal clearance, and in vivo removal. Larger NP size leads to poor cellular uptake due to enhanced permeability retention (EPR) effect. Larger NP size is also associated with limited diffusion into extracellular spaces, leading to failure in reaching the targeted tumor sites and lower renal clearance [45–47].

Shape and charge

Shape of NPs plays a vital role in affecting the integration and drug pharmacokinetic properties [48]. Various shapes and structures of NPs such as rod, spherical, triangle, star, tubes, fibers, and planes influence their endocytosis process, biodistribution, integration, and elimination. Spherical-shaped AuNPs of same size exhibits greater affinity toward cellular uptake in HeLa cells as compared to rod-shaped AuNPs [49]. In mouse leukemic monocyte macrophage cells (RAW264-7 cells) triangular-shaped AuNPs showed higher affinity of cellular uptake as compared to rod- and star-shaped. In triangular-shaped NPs, surface to volume ratio is greater as compared to spherical-shaped NPs according to Nambara and their coworkers [50]. The mechanism of cellular uptake involves the attachment of NP to cell membrane with help of energy-dependent pathways. Triangular-shaped NPs show larger contact area with flat surface exhibiting greater adhesion area and higher cellular uptake mechanism. The magnitude and nature of surface charge force [51] depends on the stability, biodistribution, solubility, cellular uptake mechanisms, and carcinogenic properties of NPs. Among the various charged NPs, positively charged NPs exhibit increase rate of cellular uptake in culture medium and high binding capacity to cell membrane. Upon comparison between (polyethylene glycol (PEG)-functionalized particles and positively charged functionalized silica NPs in physiological media, the cellular uptake mechanism shows greater affinity toward positively charged particles. Positive surface charge is observed when encapsulation of NPs is done to achieve greater integration and increased circulation time. The cell membrane consists of bilayer phospholipid composition that is negatively charged and is highly susceptible to cationic charged particles. Therefore highly positive charged NPs exhibit potent carcinogenic effect as they penetrate directly into cell membrane, breakdown membrane, followed by cell death [52,53].

Nanocarriers

Increasing the evidences of development of drug delivery methods to its specific target location for therapy of HCC. However, nanocarriers increase the therapeutic efficacy of phytotherapy and chemotherapy drugs by preventing protease degradation, protection from intolerant environment, increasing the half-life, retaining time in circulation, and controlled drug release. Moreover, nanocarriers facilitate enhanced absorption through epithelium and target-specific delivery to improved access for intracellular targets [54,55]. Various nanocarriers use, and materials are illustrated in Table 13.4 and Fig. 13.3.

Nanophytochemicals used in cancer treatment

Apart from the traditional cancer treatment options such as chemotherapy, radiotherapy, and surgery, inhibition of tumor growth cells has been prevalent. Phytochemicals are extracted for various purposes, most importantly for the management of severe diseases such as cancers [56]. Phytochemicals exhibit promising inhibitory effects on tumor growth and focus on various cellular pathways of tumor cells, while exhibiting no serious side effects on normal cells [57−59]. For example, *Nephelium lappaceum*, commonly named as rambutan fruit endocarp extracts show potential effect on liver cancer (HepG2 cells).

TABLE 13.4 List of the nanocarriers and their applications.

Sl. no	Nanooarticles and size	Composition	Therapeutic uses	References
1	Liposomes (size 0.2—3.5 um)	Phospholipids or lipoproteins	Drug/gene delivery, cosmetics, Solid tumors	[27,28]
2	Niosomes	Double layer of nonionic surfactant	Drug/gene delivery, cosmetics	
3	Micelles (size 5—100 nm)	Assembly of polymer, phospholipid surfactant	Lung, ovary, breast cancer Cell lines. Surface cleaning, cosmetics, Drug/gene delivery, surface cleaning, cosmetics.	[29,30]
4.	Nanoemulsions (size 10—200 nm)	Lipid + surfactant	Drug/gene therapy, cosmetics, Multiple-actinic-keratosis (NCT01893203) and actinic keratosis	[31,32]
5	Microemulsions (5—200 nm)	Lipid + surfactant + cosurfactant	Drug/gene delivery,cosmetics, oncaspar approved by EMA used for Acute lymphoma leukemia (ALL).	[33]
6	Lipid Nanoparticles (a) Solid lipid NPs (b) (SLN) (50—100 nm) (c) Nanostructured lipid carriers (NLC)	Solid lipid + stabilizer, Solid lipid + liquid, Lipid + stabilizer	Drug/gene delivery, SLN used in treatment of breast cancer and NLC used in colon cancer treatment.	[34,35]
7	Dendimers	Branched polymers forms like a tree	Drug/gene therapy Advanced solid tumors, Immunotherapy of prostate cancer	[36]
8	Polymericnanoparticles	Prepared by different types of polymers	Drug/gene therapy. Used in the treatment of metastatic pancreatic cancer, Advanced solid tumors	[37]
9	Nanocrystals	100% drug molecules incorporated and they are of nanosize.	High-dose drug delivery. Used in the treatment of metastatic cancer, eradication of cancer ouscells from bone marrow transplants in non-Hodgkin's lymphoma.	[38]
10.	Quantum dots (size of 2—10 nm)	Semiconductor nanocrystals (Cdse, Zns, Inas, Pbs, Gan)	Used in imaging and early diagnosis of tumor cells.	[39]
11	Fullerenes (size about 1 nm)	Cylindrical fullerenes are called as carbon nanotubes or "bucky tubes"	Used in treatment of Lung cancer.	[40]
12	Metallic nanoparticles	Colloidal drug delivery systems, gold NPs (AuNPs), silver NPs (AgNPs). Iron oxide, copper, platinum	AuNPs—Imaging, early detection of tumors. AgNPs—antimicrobial and antioxidant properties.	[41]
13	PEGlyation	PEG chains attached to the surface of the particle by chemical bonding or physical interactions	Used in the treatment of melanoma, hepatobiliary tumors, Solid tumors, lung cancer.	[42]

Obtained from J Pharm Sci 2020;23:132—57. http://www.cspsCanada.org.

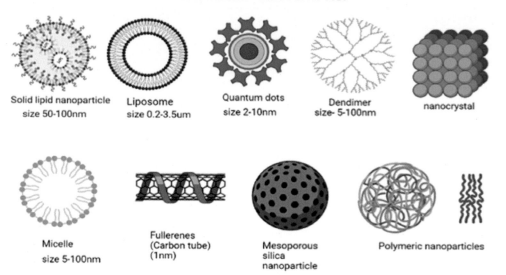

LIST OF NANOCARRIERS - THERAPEUTIC USES

FIGURE 13.3 Characteristics of nanocarriers. Various types of nanocarriers such as solid lipid nanoparticle (NP), liposome, quantum dots, dendimer, nanocrystal, micelle, fullerenes, mesoporous silica NP, and polymeric NPs used for targeted drug delivery.

The following flowchart represents the role of phytochemical constituents extracted from different medicinal plants that are used in various cancer treatments.

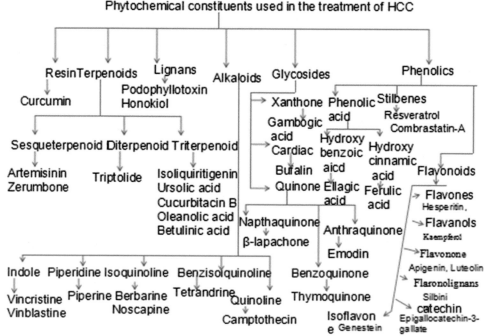

Phytochemical-based nanomedicines have been used with chemotherapeutic drugs to reduce the adverse side effects, administer the maximal therapeutic dose, and to reduce the anticancer drug resistance.

For example, coencapsulated epigallocatechin gallate (EGCG) with PLGA casein NPs combined with paclitaxel (PTX) minimized the adverse effects of paclitaxel [56]. Wang et al. revealed that the combination of doxorubicin (DOX) and encapsulation of curcumin (CUR) with lipid-coated PLGA NPs (DOX-CUR-LNPs) were prepared to study the cytotoxicity effects against osteosarcoma. They compared the cytotoxicity effect of DOX-LNPs (59.6%) and CUR-LNPs (70.7%) and revealed that the synergistic effects of DOX-CUR-LNPs (81%) result in higher cytotoxicity. In addition, it was also shown that there was a fivefold IC50 value reduction against KHOS osteosarcoma cells as compared to DOX-LNPs and CUR-LNPs [60]. Similarly PTX-TQ-PLGA exhibits greater cytotoxicity against MCF-7 breast cancer as compared to regular effect as demonstrated by Soni and group [61]. Similarly, Mohan et al. explained the synergistic effect of DOX-trans resveratrol-PEG liposomes and revealed the in vitro cytotoxic effect on NT8e head and neck cancer by inhibiting the cell cycle and mechanisms such as downstream apoptosis through the involvement of caspase-3 like protein [62].

Phytochemicals used in the treatment of hepatocellular carcinoma

1. *Ginger*: Ginger is a common dietary supplement that constitutes extract such as zingerone, 6-gingerol, 6-shagoal, and ginger oleoresin, which exhibit potent anticancer activity [63,64]. Combination of ethanolic extract of *Antrodia cinnamonea* with ginger (EACG) is involved in various signaling pathways such as mitogen-activated protein kinase MAPK that is helpful in cell apoptosis. Ginger exhibits hepatoprotective activity against acetaminophen-induced hepatotoxicity and nephrotoxicity in rats. Ginger is loaded with exosomes such as NPs (GENPs) exhibiting potent efficacy on acetaminophen-induced HCC [65].

2. *Cinnamon*: Obtained from the bark of *Cinnamomum verum* plant, cinnamon is used across the world due to its flavor nature. Cinnamon consists of two bioactive compounds, namely 2-methoxy cinnamaldehyde and cuminaldehyde. The bark extract of cinnamon cassia exhibit promising effect on HCC by reducing ALT, AST, and ASP levels in liver. Cinnamon extract (CE) dose of about 100−150 mg/kg loaded with TiO_2 nanoparticles (CE-TiO_2 NPs) show potent efficacy on HCC [66]. 2-MCA is used for the treatment of HCC SK-Hep-1 cells both in vitro and in vivo cells. Cuminaldehyde is used for inhibiting the growth of liver cells by inhibiting the mitochondrial membrane potential, caspase-3, and caspase-9 activation [67].

3. *Garlic*: Garlic or *Allium sativum* is widely used in cooking as a flavoring agent. It shows various medicinal benefits such as antibacterial, scavenging of ROS species, antiangiogenesis, inhibition of inflammation, proliferation, encouraging DNA repair, immunomodulator [68], and anticancer. Many phytochemicals have been extracted like organosulfur compounds that show lipid soluble property namely diallyl sulfide (DAS), diallyl trisulfide (DAT), and diallyl disulfide (DAD). Other extracts namely S-allylmercaptocysteine (SAMC) and S-allyl cysteine (SAC) exhibit water-soluble nature. Rich source of SAMC is present in aged garlic, which is helpful in hepatoprotection.

Recent studies reveal that SAMC is involved in the interaction between TGF-β and MAPK, resulting in HepG2 cells inhibition by apoptosis [69]. In other studies, SAC exhibits anticancer properties by apoptosis, inhibition of S-phase in cell cycle of HCC, and inhibition of invasion and migration of HCC cells [70]. Among these phytochemical constituents, DAT is loaded with polybutylcyanoacrylate (PBCA) NPs (DAT-PBCA-NPs) that show suppressive effect on nude mice, which have undergone orthotopic transplantation of BALB/c (BALB/c-Albino nude mice inbred starin), HepG2 cell lines of HCC [71].

4. *Saffron*: Saffron is found in the flowers of *Crocus sativus* [72] and is used as a spice. It contains phytochemicals such as anthocyanin, carotene, lycopene, and crocin. Saffron exhibits anticancer property by undergoing the apoptosis, decreasing the telomerase activity of cancer cells such as QGY-7703, increasing the expression of P21, and enhancing Bax/Bcl-2 cells. Saffron contains carotenoids, which are helpful in the treatment of HCC by inhibiting STAT3 (signal transducer and activator of transcription-3), which is mainly involved in the growth of cancer cells, invasion, formation of new blood vessels that leads to metastasis of Hep3B and HepG2 cells [73]. Crocin also exhibits promising antineoplastic, antiproliferative [74], antiinflammatory, and proapoptotic properties. Crocin helps in the prevention of early dysplasia [75] of liver cells by inhibiting mechanisms such as cell cycle arrest in S-phase and G2/M phase, NF-kB cells and antitelomerase enzyme activity in HepG2 cells, leading cancer cell death. Crocin loaded with chitosan-alginate polymers exhibit promising effect against HCC [76].

5. *Coffee*: Coffee is a common beverage consumed around the world. Chlorogenic acid, caffeine, and diterpenes are the bioactive components of coffee. Various studies reveal that coffee exhibits antiproliferative, antioxidant, antiinflammatory, antifibrotic properties [77]. According to the World cancer Research Fund (WCRF) and International Agency for Research on Cancer(IARC), coffee helps in the prevention of HCC [78]. According to the research conducted among two million participants, 35% of risk is reduced in HCC by consuming two cups of coffee every day. Coffee NPs loaded with water-soluble AgNPs show a positive effect against HCC in HepG2 cell lines [79].

6. *Curcumin*: Curcumin is the bioactive component of turmeric, which exhibits various therapeutic properties such as antiinflammatory, anticancer activity, angiogenesis reduction, sensitize in chemotherapy resistance, [80] and tumor invasion. Curcumin is a cancer cell marker in cells such as HepG2 by reducing the concentration of SQSTM1 in "in vitro" condition [25]. It is also responsible for altering various signaling pathways such as growth factors, signaling of cytokine receptors, adhesion molecules, protein kinases, and inhibition of proteins caspase-3, caspase-9, and Bcl-2 to cancer cell leading to apoptosis in HCC cells. Curcumin loaded with nanostructures exhibits increased efficacy for anticancer drugs as compared to individual drug. For example, curcumin loaded with lipid nanocarriers (Cur-NLC) shows greater apoptosis effect on HepG2 cells and antiproliferative effect as compared to curcumin alone [26]. Curcumin inhibits NF-kB activity in HCC and induced cell death [24]. Curcumin helps in the protection of organs such as heart, kidney, oral mucosa, and liver from being toxicity induced by chemotherapy and radiation as well as helps in antiaging by free radical scavenging in HCC [24].

7. *Resveratrol*: Resveratrol is a polyphenol that is obtained naturally from plants such as peanuts, grapes, berries, and possess multiple therapeutic properties such as antiinflammatory [81], antiaging [82], antioxidant [83], and anticancer [84,85] activities. When resveratrol is used as a drug in free form its efficacy and therapeutic dose is reduced as compared to the NPs such as PLGA loading drug (PLGA-RES), which exhibits a potent therapeutic dose and drug protection to reach the target site without undergoing any degradation. Recently, inhalable nanocarriers have been developed to increase the therapeutic efficacy of resveratrol against HCC [86–88].

8. *Genistein*: Genistein is an isoflavone that is primarily obtained from soybean products which show promising therapeutic effects, mainly when genistein is loaded with star-shaped NP copolymer mannitol PLGA-TGPS, which exhibits potent therapeutic effect against liver cancer [89].

Conclusion

An increase in HCC cases have been observed over the past two decades. However, early HCC tumor detection is extremely challenging and therapeutic options are not up to mark. The interest has grown toward low toxicity with high efficiency therapeutics, which has resulted in the development of nanomedicines. Thus nanomedicines offer promising hope in providing effective nanoformulations for HCC. Phytonanomedicines are receiving great attention from scientists because of its multiple properties. Natural phytochemicals exhibit potential anticancer properties. Phytochemicals combination with NPs enhance the therapeutic efficacy and offer new strategy to treat HCC. Resveratrol, curcumin, garlic, genistein, and other phytochemicals combined with NPs are useful to treat HCC. Additional research is required to understand the exact mechanism associated with NPs and their long-term effect. In spite of various limitations such as poor bioavailability, composition, low solubility, research on phytonanomedicine is increasing day by day. This leads to the development of nanoanticancer agents, which are focused on the treatment of HCC. Moreover, clinical trials are required to reduce the possibilities of adverse reactions, immune toxicities. Altogether, phytochemical combined NP drug delivery has great potential for the effective treatment of HCC.

References

[1] Hartke J, Johnson M, Ghabril M. The diagnosis and treatment of hepatocellular carcinoma. Semin Diagn Pathol 2017;34:153–9.

[2] Kalyan A, Nimeiri H, Kulik L. Systemic therapy of hepatocellular carcinoma: current and promising. Clliver Dis 2015;19:421–32.

[3] Hemalatha G, Sivakumari K, Rajesh S, Shyamala Devi K. , Phytochemical profiling, anticancer and apoptotic activity of graviola (*Annona muricata*) fruit extract against human hepatocellular carcinoma (HepG-2) cells. Int J Zool Appl Biosci 2020;5:32–47.

[4] Li L-M, Hu Z-B, Zhou Z-X, Chen X, Liu F-Y, Zhang J-F, et al. Serum microRNA profiles serve as novel biomarkers for HBV infection and diagnosis of HBV-positive hepatocarcinoma. Cancer Res 2010;70:9798–807.

[5] Yang N, Ekanem NR, Sakyi CA, Ray SD. Hepatocellular carcinoma and microRNA: new perspectives on therapeutics and diagnostics. Adv Drug Deliv Rev 2015;81:62—74.

[6] Kakushadze Z, Raghubanshi R, Yu W. Estimating cost savings from early cancer diagnosis. Data 2017;2:30.

[7] Iranshahy M, Rezaee R, Karimi G. Hepatoprotective activity of metformin: a new mission for an old drug? Eur J Pharmacol 2019;850:1—7.

[8] Li C, Zhang W, Yang H, Xiang J, Wang X, Wang J. Integrative analysis of dysregulated lncRNA-associated ceRNA network reveals potential lncRNA biomarkers for human hepatocellular carcinoma. PeerJ 2020;8:e8758.

[9] Dimitroulis D, Damaskos C, Valsami S, Davakis S, Garmpis N, Spartalis E, et al. From diagnosis to treatment of hepatocellular carcinoma: an epidemic problem for both developed and developing world. World J Gastroenterol 2017;23:5282.

[10] Singh AK, Kumar R, Pandey AK. Hepatocellular carcinoma: causes, mechanism of progression and biomarkers. Curr Chem Genom Transl Med 2018;12:9—26.

[11] Wilhelm SM, Adnane L, Newell P, Villanueva A, Llovet JM, Lynch M. Preclinical overview of sorafenib, a multikinase inhibitor that targets both Raf and VEGF and PDGF receptor tyrosine kinase signaling. Mol Cancer Ther 2008;7:3129—40.

[12] Liu L, Cao Y, Chen C, Zhang X, McNabola A, Wilkie D, et al. Sorafenib blocks the RAF/MEK/ERK pathway, inhibits tumor angiogenesis, and induces tumor cell apoptosis in hepatocellular carcinoma model PLC/PRF/5. Cancer Res 2006;66:11851—8.

[13] Wu S, Chen JJ, Kudelka A, Lu J, Zhu X. Incidence and risk of hypertension with sorafenib in patients with cancer: a systematic review and meta-analysis. Lancet Oncol 2008;9:117—23.

[14] Rizwanullah M, Amin S, Mir SR, Fakhri KU, Rizvi MMA. Phytochemical based nanomedicines against cancer: current status and future prospects. J Drug Target 2018;26:731—52.

[15] Chowdhury A, Kunjiappan S, Panneerselvam T, Somasundaram B, Bhattacharjee C. Nanotechnology and nanocarrier-based approaches on treatment of degenerative diseases. Int Nano Lett 2017;7:91—122.

[16] Perumal A, AlSalhi MS, Kanakarajan S, Devanesan S, Selvaraj R, Tamizhazhagan V. Phytochemical evaluation and anticancer activity of rambutan (Nephelium lappaceum) fruit endocarp extracts against human hepatocellular carcinoma (HepG-2) cells. Saudi J Biol Sci 2021;28:1816—25.

[17] Campbell RB. Tumor physiology and delivery of nanopharmaceuticals. Anticancer Agents Med Chem 2006;6:503—12.

[18] Dong X, Mumper RJ. Nanomedicinal strategies to treat multidrug-resistant tumors: current progress. Nanomed (Lond) 2010;5:597—615.

[19] El-Readi MZ, Althubiti MA. Cancer nanomedicine: a new era of successful targeted therapy. J Nanomater 2019;2019:4927312.

[20] Schroeder A, Heller DA, Winslow MM, Dahlman JE, Pratt GW, Langer R, et al. Treating metastatic cancer with nanotechnology. Nat Rev Cancer 2011;12:39—50.

[21] Fischer HC, Liu L, Pang KS, Chan WCW. Pharmacokinetics of nanoscale quantum dots: in vivo distribution, sequestration, and clearance in the rat. Adv Funct Mater 2006;16:1299—305.

[22] Alidori S, Bowman RL, Yarilin D, Romin Y, Barlas A, Mulvey JJ, et al. Deconvoluting hepatic processing of carbon nanotubes. Nat Commun 2016;7:12343.

[23] Mohamed NK, Hamad MA, Hafez MZ, Wooley KL, Elsabahy M. Nanomedicine in management of hepatocellular carcinoma: challenges and opportunities. Int J Cancer 2017;140:1475—84.

[24] Chen S-Y, Lee Y-R, Hsieh M-C, Omar HA, Teng Y-N, Lin C-Y, et al. Enhancing the anticancer activity of antrodia cinnamomea in hepatocellular carcinoma cells via cocultivation with ginger: the impact on cancer cell survival pathways. Front Pharmacol 2018;9:780.

[25] Aly SM, Fetaih HA, Hassanin AA, Abomughaid MM, Ismail AA. Protective effects of garlic and cinnamon oils on hepatocellular carcinoma in albino rats. Anal Cell Pathol 2019;2019.

[26] Ng KT, Guo DY, Cheng Q, Geng W, Ling CC, Li CX, et al. A garlic derivative, S-allylcysteine (SAC), suppresses proliferation and metastasis of hepatocellular carcinoma. PLoS One 2012;7:e31655.

[27] Akbarzadeh A, Rezaei-Sadabady R, Davaran S, Joo S, Zarghami N, Hanifehpour Y, et al. Liposomes: classification, preparation and applications. Nanoscale Res Lett 2013;8(1):102.

[28] Allen TM, Cullis PR. Liposomal drug delivery systems: from concept to clinical applications. Adv Drug Deliv Rev 2013;65:36—48.

[29] Bahadori F, Topçu G, Eroğlu MS, Önyüksel H. A new lipid-based nano formulation of vinorelbine. AAPS PharmSciTech 2014;15:1138–48.

[30] Torchilin VP. Micellar nanocarriers: pharmaceutical perspectives. Pharm Res 2007;24:1–16.

[31] Azeem A, Rizwan M, Ahmad FJ, Iqbal Z, Khar RK, Aqil M, et al. Nanoemulsion components screening and selection: a technical note. AAPS PharmSciTech 2009;10:69–76.

[32] Tadros T, Izquierdo P, Esquena J, Solans C. Formation and stability of nano-emulsions. Adv Colloid Interface Sci 2004;108–109:303–18.

[33] He CX, He ZG, Gao JQ. Microemulsions as drug delivery systems to improve the solubility and the bioavailability of poorly water-soluble drugs. Expert Opin Drug Deliv 2010;7:445–60.

[34] Pardeike J, Hommoss A, Müller RH. Lipid nanoparticles (SLN, NLC) in cosmetic and pharmaceutical dermal products. Int J Pharm 2009;366:170–84.

[35] Zhao Y, Huang L. Lipid nanoparticles for gene delivery. Adv Genet 2014;88:13–36.

[36] Caster JM, Patel AN, Zhang T, Wang A. Investigational nanomedicines in 2016: a review of nanotherapeutics currently undergoing clinical trials. Wiley Interdiscip Rev Nanomed Nanobiotechnol 2017;9.

[37] Guarneri V, Dieci MV, Conte P. Enhancing intracellular taxane delivery: current role and perspectives of nanoparticle albumin-bound paclitaxel in the treatment of advanced breast cancer. Expert Opin Pharmacother 2012;13:395–406.

[38] Junghanns JU, Müller RH. Nanocrystal technology, drug delivery and clinical applications. Int J Nanomed 2008;3:295–309.

[39] Walling MA, Novak JA, Shepard JRE. Quantum dots for live cell and in vivo imaging. Int J Mol Sci 2009;10:441–91.

[40] Hilder TA, Hill JM. Carbon nanotubes as drug delivery nanocapsules. Curr Appl Phys 2008;8:258–61.

[41] Shao J, Griffin RJ, Galanzha EI, Kim JW, Koonce N, Webber J, et al. Photothermal nanodrugs: potential of TNF-gold nanospheres for cancer theranostics. Sci Rep 2013;3:1293.

[42] Kurmi BD, Gajbhiye V, Kayat J, Jain NK. Lactoferrin-conjugated dendritic nanoconstructs for lung targeting of methotrexate. J Pharm Sci 2011;100:2311–20.

[43] Jeevanandam J, Barhoum A, Chan YS, Dufresne A, Danquah MK. Review on nanoparticles and nanostructured materials: history, sources, toxicity and regulations. Beilstein J Nanotechnol 2018;9:1050–74.

[44] Cardoso VMdO, Moreira BJ, Comparetti EJ, Sampaio I, Ferreira LMB, Lins PMP, et al. Is nanotechnology helping in the fight against COVID-19? Front Nanotechnol 2020;2.

[45] Poojari R, Srivastava R, Panda D. Nanomechanics of Fosbretabulin A4 polymeric nanoparticles in liver cancer cells. In: Proceedings of the IEEE fifteeth international conference on nanotechnology (IEEE-NANO). Rome, Italy; 2015. p. 1406–9.

[46] Owens 3rd DE, Peppas NA. Opsonization, biodistribution, and pharmacokinetics of polymeric nanoparticles. Int J Pharm 2006;307:93–102.

[47] Petros RA, DeSimone JM. Strategies in the design of nanoparticles for therapeutic applications. Nat Rev Drug Discov 2010;9:615–27.

[48] Chen LT, Weiss L. The role of the sinus wall in the passage of erythrocytes through the spleen. Blood 1973;41:529–37.

[49] Rampersaud S, Fang J, Wei Z, Fabijanic K, Silver S, Jaikaran T, et al. The effect of cage shape on nanoparticle-based drug carriers: anticancer drug release and efficacy via receptor blockade using dextran-coated iron oxide nanocages. Nano Lett 2016;16:7357–63.

[50] Chithrani BD, Chan WC. Elucidating the mechanism of cellular uptake and removal of protein-coated gold nanoparticles of different sizes and shapes. Nano Lett 2007;7:1542–50.

[51] Nambara K, Niikura K, Mitomo H, Ninomiya T, Takeuchi C, Wei J, et al. Reverse size dependences of the cellular uptake of triangular and spherical gold nanoparticles. Langmuir 2016;32:12559–67.

[52] Peng Y, Lu B, Wang N, Li L, Chen S. Impacts of interfacial charge transfer on nanoparticle electrocatalytic activity towards oxygen reduction. Phys Chem Chem Phys 2017;19:9336–48.

[53] Hühn D, Kantner K, Geidel C, Brandholt S, De Cock I, Soenen SJ, et al. Polymer-coated nanoparticles interacting with proteins and cells: focusing on the sign of the net charge. ACS Nano 2013;7:3253–63.

[54] Din FU, Aman W, Ullah I, Qureshi OS, Mustapha O, Shafique S, et al. Effective use of nanocarriers as drug delivery systems for the treatment of selected tumors. Int J Nanomed 2017;12:7291–309.

[55] Barua S, Mitragotri S. Challenges associated with penetration of nanoparticles across cell and tissue barriers: a review of current status and future prospects. Nano Today 2014;9:223−43.

[56] Surh Y-J. Cancer chemoprevention with dietary phytochemicals. Nat Rev Cancer 2003;3:768−80.

[57] Shao J, Fang Y, Zhao R, Chen F, Yang M, Jiang J, et al. Evolution from small molecule to nano-drug delivery systems: an emerging approach for cancer therapy of ursolic acid. Asian J Pharm Sci 2020;15:685−700.

[58] Park JH, Lee S, Kim J-H, Park K, Kim K, Kwon IC. Polymeric nanomedicine for cancer therapy. Prog Polym Sci 2008;33:113−37.

[59] Liang X-J, Chen C, Zhao Y, Wang PC. Circumventing tumor resistance to chemotherapy by nanotechnology, In Multi-drug resistance in cancer, Springer 2010, pp. 467−488.

[60] Basnet P, Skalko-Basnet N. Curcumin: an anti-inflammatory molecule from a curry spice on the path to cancer treatment. Molecules 2011;16:4567−98.

[61] Narayanan S, Mony U, Vijaykumar DK, Koyakutty M, Paul-Prasanth B, Menon D. Sequential release of epigallocatechin gallate and paclitaxel from PLGA-casein core/shell nanoparticles sensitizes drug-resistant breast cancer cells. Nanomedicine 2015;11:1399−406.

[62] Soni P, Kaur J, Tikoo K. Dual drug-loaded paclitaxel−thymoquinone nanoparticles for effective breast cancer therapy. J Nanopart Res 2015;17:1−12.

[63] Wang L, Wang W, Rui Z, Zhou D. The effective combination therapy against human osteosarcoma: doxorubicin plus curcumin co-encapsulated lipid-coated polymeric nanoparticulate drug delivery system. Drug Deliv 2016;23:3200−8.

[64] Mohan A, Narayanan S, Balasubramanian G, Sethuraman S, Krishnan UM. Dual drug loaded nanoliposomal chemotherapy: a promising strategy for treatment of head and neck squamous cell carcinoma. Eur J Pharm Biopharm 2016;99:73−83.

[65] Zhuang X, Deng Z-B, Mu J, Zhang L, Yan J, Miller D, et al. Ginger-derived nanoparticles protect against alcohol-induced liver damage. J Extracell Vesicles 2015;4:28713.

[66] Shakeel M, Jabeen F, Iqbal R, Chaudhry AS, Zafar S, Ali M, et al. Assessment of titanium dioxide nanoparticles (TiO2-NPs) induced hepatotoxicity and ameliorative effects of Cinnamomum cassia in Sprague-Dawley rats. Biol Trace Elem Res 2018;182:57−69.

[67] Goel A, Aggarwal BB. Curcumin, the golden spice from Indian saffron, is a chemosensitizer and radiosensitizer for tumors and chemoprotector and radioprotector for normal organs. Nutr Cancer 2010;62:919−30.

[68] Rawat D, Shrivastava S, Ahmad R, Chhonker S, Mehrotra A, Koiri RK. An overview of natural plant products in the treatment of hepatocellular carcinoma. Anticancer Agents Med Chem 2018;18:1838−59.

[69] Wang F, Ye X, Zhai D, Dai W, Wu Y, Chen J, et al. Curcumin-loaded nanostructured lipid carrier induced apoptosis in human HepG2 cells through activation of the DR5/caspase-mediated extrinsic apoptosis pathway. Acta Pharm 2020;70:227−37.

[70] Marquardt JU, Gomez-Quiroz L, Arreguin Camacho LO, Pinna F, Lee YH, Kitade M, et al. Curcumin effectively inhibits oncogenic NF-κB signaling and restrains stemness features in liver cancer. J Hepatol 2015;63:661−9.

[71] Zhang Z-m, Yang X-y, Deng S-h, Wei X, Gao H-q. Anti-tumor effects of polybutylcyanoacrylate nanoparticles of diallyl trisulfide on orthotopic transplantation tumor model of hepatocellular carcinoma in BALB/c nude mice. Chin Med J 2007;120:1336−42.

[72] Tian N, Shangguan W, Zhou Z, Yao Y, Fan C, Cai L. Lin28b is involved in curcumin-reversed paclitaxel chemoresistance and associated with poor prognosis in hepatocellular carcinoma. J Cancer 2019;10:6074−87.

[73] Elmansi AM, El-Karef AA, El-Shishtawy MM, Eissa LA. Hepatoprotective effect of curcumin on hepatocellular carcinoma through autophagic and apoptic pathways. Ann Hepatol 2017;16:607−18.

[74] Kennedy OJ, Roderick P, Buchanan R, Fallowfield JA, Hayes PC, Parkes J. Coffee, including caffeinated and decaffeinated coffee, and the risk of hepatocellular carcinoma: a systematic review and dose−response meta-analysis. BMJ Open 2017;7:e013739.

[75] Liu T, Tian L, Fu X, Wei L, Li J, Wang T. Saffron inhibits the proliferation of hepatocellular carcinoma via inducing cell apoptosis. Panminerva Med 2019;62:7−12.

[76] EL-Maraghy SA, Rizk SM, El-Sawalhi MM. Hepatoprotective potential of crocin and curcumin against iron overload-induced biochemical alterations in rat. Afr J Biochem Res 2009;3:215−21.

[77] Amin A, Hamza AA, Daoud S, Khazanehdari K, Al Hrout A, Baig B, et al. Saffron-based crocin prevents early lesions of liver cancer: in vivo, in vitro and network analyses. Recent Pat Anticancer Drug Discov 2016;11:121−33.

[78] Noureini SK, Wink M. Antiproliferative effects of crocin in HepG2 cells by telomerase inhibition and hTERT down-regulation. Asian Pac J Cancer Prev 2012;13:2305—9.

[79] Chunyan W, Valiyaveettil S. Correlation of biocapping agents with cytotoxic effects of silver nanoparticles on human tumor cells. RSC Adv 2013;3:14329—38.

[80] Bolhassani A, Khavari A, Bathaie SZ. Saffron and natural carotenoids: biochemical activities and anti-tumor effects. Biochim Biophys Acta (BBA)-Rev Cancer 2014;1845:20—30.

[81] Yousef M, Vlachogiannis IA, Tsiani E. Effects of resveratrol against lung cancer: in vitro and in vivo studies. Nutrients 2017;9:1231.

[82] Ko J-H, Sethi G, Um J-Y, Shanmugam MK, Arfuso F, Kumar AP, et al. The role of resveratrol in cancer therapy. Int J Mol Sci 2017;18:2589.

[83] Sun L, Chen B, Jiang R, Li J, Wang B. Resveratrol inhibits lung cancer growth by suppressing M2-like polarization of tumor associated macrophages. Cell Immunol 2017;311:86—93.

[84] Wright C, Iyer AKV, Yakisich JS, Azad N. Anti-tumorigenic effects of resveratrol in lung cancer cells through modulation of c-FLIP. Curr Cancer Drug Targets 2017;17:669—80.

[85] Srivani G, Behera SK, Dariya B, Aliya S, Alam A, Nagaraju GP. Resveratrol binds and inhibits transcription factor HIF-1α in pancreatic cancer. Exp Cell Res 2020;394:112126.

[86] Shukla SK, Kulkarni NS, Farrales P, Kanabar DD, Parvathaneni V, Kunda NK, et al. Sorafenib loaded inhalable polymeric nanocarriers against non-small cell lung cancer. Pharm Res 2020;67.

[87] Vaidya B, Kulkarni NS, Shukla SK, Parvathaneni V, Chauhan G, Damon JK, et al. Development of inhalable quinacrine loaded bovine serum albumin modified cationic nanoparticles: repurposing quinacrine for lung cancer therapeutics. Int J Pharm 2020;577:118995.

[88] Parvathaneni V, Kulkarni NS, Shukla SK, Farrales PT, Kunda NK, Muth A, et al. Systematic development and optimization of inhalable pirfenidone liposomes for non-small cell lung cancer treatment. Pharmaceutics 2020;12:206.

[89] Wu B, Liang Y, Tan Y, Xie C, Shen J, Zhang M, et al. Genistein-loaded nanoparticles of star-shaped diblock copolymer mannitol-core PLGA—TPGS for the treatment of liver cancer. Mater Sci Eng C Mater Biol Appl 2016;59:792—800.

CHAPTER

14

Immune checkpoint inhibitors for hepatocellular carcinoma

Venkata Prasuja Nakka

Department of Biochemistry, Acharya Nagarjuna University, Nagarjuna Nagar, India

Abstract

Hepatocellular carcinoma (HCC), the most prevalent liver cancer world over, with a high mortality rate associated with cancer. Chemotherapy has disadvantages such as toxicity, resistance to chemicals, and the need for adjunctive therapy. Immune checkpoint inhibitors seem promising therapeutic strategies aiming at various cancers. Sorafenib inhibits kinases, only a single drug approved for treating advanced-stage HCC, however, with a limitation of poor clinical outcome. Recent studies suggest immunotherapy as a feasible approach for patients suffering from HCC via inhibiting the activity of immune checkpoint markers such as programmed cell death receptor-1 (PD-1) and cytotoxic T-lymphocyte associated protein-4 (CTLA-4) using specific monoclonal antibodies. This chapter discusses the recent developments in immunotherapy and combination therapy for HCC in clinical settings. Further, the immunology of the liver will also highlight in the context of hepatocarcinogenesis. Thus it would provide a better insight to understand the novel therapeutic strategies and potential biomarkers pertinent to the immunotherapy for HCC.

Keywords: Hepatocellular carcinoma; monoclonal antibodies; immunotherapy; PD-1 receptor; PD-L1/ligand to PD-1; CTLA-4; combination immunotherapy

Abbreviations

ACT	Adoptive cell transfer
APCs	Antigen presenting cells
CARs	Chimeric antigen receptors
CTLA-4	Cytotoxic T-lymphocyte associated protein-4
CTLs	Cytotoxic T-lymphocytes
DCs	Dendritic cells
ECs	Endothelial cells
FDA	Food and Drug Administration (United States)
HBV/HCV	Hepatitis B virus/hepatitis C virus
HCC	Hepatocellular carcinoma
INF-γ	Interferon-γ

Ganji Purnachandra Nagaraju, Sarfraz Ahmad (eds.)
Theranostics and Precision Medicine for the Management of Hepatocellular Carcinoma, Volume 3

215

LTβR	Lymphotoxin (LT) α and β and their receptor
MHC	Major Histocompatibility complex
MAbs/Mab	Monoclonal antibodies/monoclonal antibody
NK cells	Natural killer cells
NK-T cells	Natural killer T cells
NAFLD	Nonalcoholic fatty liver disease
PD-1	Programmed cell death receptor-1
PD-L1	Programmed cell death receptor-1 ligand
ROS	Reactive oxygen species
Tregs	Regulatory T cells
TGF-β	Transforming growth factor-beta
TAAs	Tumor-associated antigens
TILs	Tumor-infiltrating lymphocytes
TNF-α	Tumor necrosis factor-α
VEGF	Vascular endothelial growth factor

Introduction

HCC stands second foremost reason of cancer-associated deaths the world over [1]. The predominant risk factors for HCC include viral infections such as hepatitis B and C, consumption of alcohol, cirrhosis, and NAFLD [2,3]. Small tumors of HCC are curable, yet patients will experience a reoccurrence of HCC over time [4]. The clinical outcome of HCC is relatively more heterogeneous than the other malignancies, due to which the prognosis of the disease makes it difficult [5]. The recent breakthroughs in immunotherapy have tremendously changed the face of cancer treatment. However, successful immunotherapy in HCC patients would be challenging because of the inherent immunosuppressive function of the liver [6]. A fine balance between immune tolerance and immunity seems to be critical for a proper functioning of the liver [7]. Thus it necessitates an in-depth understanding of how immune cells function in the liver pathophysiology. Liver cirrhosis potentially leads to the dysfunction of immune surveillance; reduces the synthesis of proteins critical for regulating innate immunity and phagocytosis [8]. Increased inflammation also leads to the damage of liver tissue that eventually switches to immunodeficiency and cancer [7].

The strategy of immunotherapy seems effective for HCC patients through better safety and efficacy. Preventing tumor escape from immune surveillance would be a rate-limiting step for successful immunotherapy. MAbs effectively regulate immune checkpoint markers, for instance, PD-1, PD-L1, and CTLA-4 responsible for tumor escape . Thus MAbs selectively promote the T-cell-specific antitumor activity by blocking immune checkpoint markers. Indeed, nivolumab (anti-PD-1 MAb) showed better efficacy in clinical trials for HCC therapy, which got approval as the second line of treatment, with sorafenib being the first line [9]. The efficacy of novel agents aiming at HCC is under evaluation in many preclinical and clinical studies. TAAs seem very useful in the development of therapeutic vaccines for HCC [10]. Another variety of tumor-suppressive strategies includes ACT, in which immune cells from the patient blood are subjected to genetic engineering to express tumor-specific antigens called CARs [11]. This chapter summarizes the currently existing or approved immunotherapy, critical points of ongoing clinical trials, and potential combination therapy strategies for HCC.

TABLE 14.1 Immune cells and their role in HCC.

Immune cell type	Mechanism of action	Possible role in HCC
NK cells	Cytokine release; eliminate HBV and HCV-infected cells; Fas/Fas-L and perforin/granzyme-mediated apoptotic cell death	Dysregulation of NK cell function results in tumor progression [14]
NK-T cells	Cytokines secretion (IL-4 and IFN-γ); leads to liver inflammation and fibrosis	Proliferation and transformation of hepatocytes [15]
DCs	Act as an APC; form as periportal lymphoid structures upon inflammation, which facilitate liver-infiltrating T cells	Depletion in DCs exacerbates liver damage, inflammation, and favors fibrosis development [12]
CTLs	Kill the target cells via perforin, granzyme-A&B and in association with Fas/Fas-L signaling	Metabolic activation of CTLs triggers liver injury and hepatocarcinogenesis [16]
LTβR cytokines	Upregulate in HBV/HCV infections and HCC	Sustained LT expression leads to HCC. Pharmacological inhibition of LTβR signaling prevents liver damage and promotes liver regeneration [17]
Tregs and CD4$^+$ T cells	CD4$^+$ T cells arbitrate responses of antisenescence in collaboration with monocytes	Increased Tregs correlate with poor survival and highly recurrent HCC in clinical settings [18] TILs express exhaustion markers such as PD-1, CTLA-4, etc., in HCC
Regulatory B cells	Regulate B cells; secrete antiinflammatory IL-10	Curtail TNF-α release thus acting as an antiinflammatory that favors tumor progression [15]

The immunology of hepatocellular carcinoma

The liver is rich in the immune cell population, such as NK cells (innate immunity), T cells, B cells (adaptive immunity), Kupffer cells (resident liver macrophages), etc., vital for immunoregulation. NK cells account for about 30%—50% population of the total lymphocytes present in the liver. NK cells seem to mediate immunity against viral hepatitis and modulate liver fibrosis. NK-T cells, a unique subset of T cells enriched in the liver and regulate immune responses of acute liver inflammation, cancer, autoimmunity, viral infections, etc. [12,13] (Table 14.1).

The liver has an exclusive blood supply system called liver sinusoids, which maintain the blood flow at a slow rate that paves the liver to carry out vital immunological functions. This slow blood supply through liver sinusoids enables the exchange of nontoxic dietary and circulating environmental antigens and endotoxins from the gut-derived microflora [12,15]. Inflammation seems beneficial in the healthy liver to carry on functions of metabolic and tissue remodeling. This physiologically relevant inflammation plus exposure to the dietary or microbial products in the liver leads to the surge of the immune response. The liver has a unique self-repairing feature against acute liver injuries due to the reentry of differentiated hepatocytes into the cell cycle. Predominantly, HCCs occur under conditions such as liver fibrosis, chronic inflammation, and cirrhosis. [19]. Apoptosis or programmed cell death of hepatocytes plays dual roles as follows: (1) hepatoprotective by removing damaged liver cells and (2) if persistent leads to harmful effects. The caspase-8, which is known to execute hepatocyte apoptosis, also has opposite roles, such as DNA response to damage. Caspase-8 seems to protect hepatocytes against increased cell proliferation-associated genomic instability, and thus early hepatocarcinogenesis [20].

Activated adaptive immunity provoke inflammatory responses that eventually lead to cellular stresses such as the generation of ROS, dysfunction of subcellular organelles such as mitochondria, DNA damage, etc., in hepatocytes [15]. The liver inflammation maintains the tissue homeostasis in physiological conditions; however, dysregulation of inflammation leads to pathological events associated with chronic infection, autoimmunity, and tumorigenesis. Various mechanisms involved in liver homeostasis often immunosuppressive, thus ensuing tolerance.

Immune responses of the liver that promotes tumor cell proliferation

The liver has a constant circulation of NK cells, NK-T cells, and monocytes, which actively interact with hepatic ECs, Kupffer cells, hepatocytes, and DCs. A small number of gut-derived endotoxins that pass through the liver sinusoids ensues tolerance via inducing the expression of PD-L1, interleukin-10, and prostaglandin-E2 by APCs such as Kupffer cells and DCs [12]. The cell-surface receptors (PD-L1 and CTLA-4) on APCs mediate immunosuppression, a key for promoting tumor cell proliferation.

A defective antiviral response of liver resident T cells causes exhaustion of immune cells. Thus hepatocytes fail to stimulate a subset of T cells (CD4$^+$) but can still trigger CTLs (CD8$^+$). The condition sustains liver inflammation, development of liver fibrosis, and exhaustion of CTLs mediated by PD-1 (reviewed in Ref. [12]). Thus immune cells exhaustion accompanied by immune tolerance compromise the abilities of T-lymphocytes to immune surveillance, recognition, and removal of malignant cells.

CD4 + play a dual task in HCC described as follows. For example, TILs express exhaustion markers PD-1, CTLA-4, etc., that increase expression of IL-10, TGF-β, and CCL20 (chemokine ligand 20). Infiltrating CD8$^+$ cells activate PD-L1 via IFN-γ [21]. Counteracting exhaustion markers using MAbs against PD-1, PD-L1, and CTLA-4 would be a promising therapeutic strategy for HCC. Targeting NK cells is another feasible therapeutic approach, which comprises ACT of NK cells (allogeneic), genetic manipulation, and NK cell-specific chemotherapy [14].

Chronic inflammation, fibrosis development, and cirrhosis are the major factors that contribute to liver cancer. Thus therapeutic strategies should be optimally aimed toward chronic inflammation without impairing immune surveillance functions of innate or adaptive immunity. The role of TILs seems critical to the outcome of HCC. The surge of T- and B-lymphocytes infiltrating tumor cell population correlates with the increased expression of granzyme-B, IFN-γ, and diminished tumor survival [22]. Increase in Tregs number linked to poor survival in HCC victims. Of note, the inhibitory effect of Tregs seems a foremost hindrance to provoke an efficient antitumor immunity in HCC. Tregs are of two different types based on the secretion of cytokines (IL-10 and TGF-β), which initiate signaling pathways via chemokine receptors such as

CCL20 and CCR6 [22]. Thus a balance of Tregs function appears as an attractive therapeutic strategy to reinstate antitumor potential in HCC patient's immunity.

Immune checkpoint inhibitors and hepatocellular carcinoma

Immune checkpoint inhibitors PD-1 and PD -L1 are transmembrane proteins critical to tumor escape from immune surveillance [23]. PD-1 protein belongs to CD28 superfamily predominantly expressed on activated CTLs (CD8$^+$ T cells) and Tregs. PD-L1 upregulates on the activated T cells and APCs such as DCs, and macrophages. The PD-1/PD-L1 pathway plays a role in peripheral immune tolerance. In brief, PD-1 relays a coinhibitory signal in association with TCR upon binding to its ligand PD-L1. This particular machinery favors the tumor microenvironment to escape from T-cell-mediated immune surveillance. Thus blocking the interaction between PD-1, PD-L1, and CTLA-4, B-7 has proven efficacy in HCC patients (Fig. 14.1).

The anti-PD-1 MAb, called pembrolizumab approved by the FDA after the clinical trial (KEYNOTE-224) to treat the patients suffering from HCC. Of note, the pembrolizumab was recommended to those who received the sorafenib as first-line therapy [24]. FDA also approved another anti-PD-1 MAb nivolumab based on the CHECKMATE-040 clinical trial, which showed a durable objective response and safety in HCC patients [9].

The combination of MAbs approved by the FDA for HCC treatment includes atezolizumab and durvalumab, which block PD-L1. The clinical trial (IMbrave150) atezolizumab plus bevacizumab combination showed better efficacy in patients with unresectable HCC. Of note, the combination seems to have an advantage over sorafenib in terms of progression-free survival outcomes [25].

MAbs durvalumab and tremelimumab target PD-L1 and CTLA-4, respectively, both received an orphan drug designation for the treatment of HCC. A global Phase III clinical trial HIMALAYA under progress in evaluating the efficacy of MAbs durvalumab as monoimmunotherapy, durvalumab and tremelimumab as a combination therapy versus sorafenib in patients with advanced HCC (https://clinicaltrials.gov/ct2/show/NCT03298451). The currently approved immune checkpoint inhibitors are summarized in Table 14.2.

Combination immunotherapy: potential treatment of the future?

Regardless of the promising outcome from clinical trials aiming at immune checkpoint inhibitors as monotherapy for HCC victims, only a limited patient population has benefitted [26–28]. Targeting either PD-1 (receptor) or PD-L1 (ligand) alone seems for CD8$^+$ T cells to curtail immune suppression in the tumor microenvironment. Thus targeting multiple mechanisms might help to develop potential therapeutic strategies for HCC patients.

Combinations of CTLA-4 and PD-1/PD-L1 inhibitors subjected to clinical evaluation for efficacy testing in HCC patients. The combination of nivolumab plus ipilimumab blocking PD-1 and CTLA-4 got FDA approval after the clinical trial (CHECKMATE-040). The clinical trial carried out in HCC patients who already received sorafenib treatment as the first-line (refer to Table 14.3). HCC tumors appear extremely vascularized with prominent arterial blood flow [26]. Thus it is worth considering angiogenesis inhibitors as adjunctive

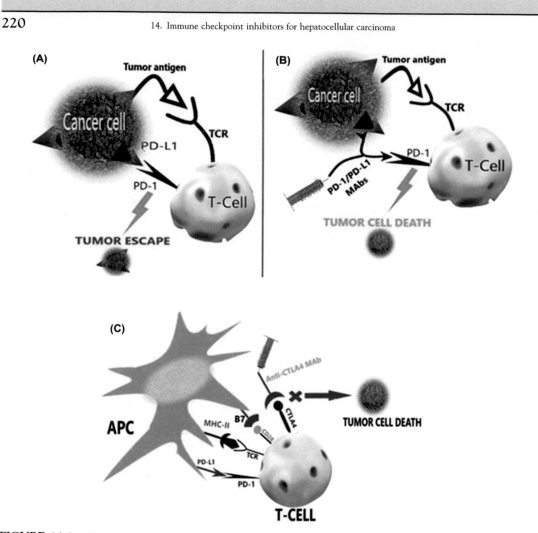

FIGURE 14.1 Depicts the machinery of how tumor escapes from immune surveillance, also immunotherapy strategy for hepatocellular carcinoma (HCC) by inhibiting PD-1/PD-L1 interactive pathway. (A) The interactive pathway linking PD-L1 (a tumor cell transmembrane protein) and PD-1 expressed on T cells (tumor specific) regulates the immune system negatively. Specific communication between PD-1/PD-L1 downregulates the proliferation, activation of T cells. Cytokine secretion further favors tumor escape from immune surveillance. (B) MAbs against PD-1(receptor) and PD-L1 (ligand) promote the T-cell antitumor activity and elimination of tumor. (C) The CTLA-4 antibodies prevent binding of CTLA-4 to B-7, thus allowing the binding of CD28 to B-7 and concomitant cytotoxic T cells (CD8$^+$) activation in the lymph node. Prevention of CTLA-4 expressed on the Tregs seems critical to promote antitumorigenic activity of T cell.

therapy to immune checkpoint inhibitors. A combination of atezolizumab with bevacizumab inhibits PD-L1 VEGF, respectively. Indeed, FDA approved this for treating unresectable HCC. Overall survival rate observed with atezolizumab plus bevacizumab being 67.2% and with the sorafenib 54.6% [25]. Table 14.3 summarizes potential combination therapies with approved trade names and relevant references to clinical data.

TABLE 14.2   Approved MAbs that inhibit immune checkpoint markers for the management of HCC.

Drug target molecule	Name and class of the drug	Mode of action	Approved trademark
PD-1	Nivolumab (human IgG4 class MAb)	Binds to PD-1 of T-cell	OPDIVO (Bristol-Myers Squibb)
	Pembrolizumab (humanized IgG4 class MAb)	Binds to PD-1 of T cell. Recommended after sorafenib treatment as adjunctive therapy (second line) for patients suffering from HCC	Keytruda (Merck)
PD-L1	Atezolizumab (human IgG1 class MAb)	Binds to PD-L1 of tumor cells; curtails interaction between PD-L1 with PD-1	Tecentriq (Genentech)
	Durvalumab (humanized IgG1 class MAb)		Imfinzi (AstraZeneca)
CTLA-4	Tremelimumab (humanized IgG2 class MAb)	Blocks CTLA-4 activity; promotes T-cell-mediated antitumor immune response	Imfinzi (AstraZeneca)
	Ipilimumab		Yervoy (Bristol Myers Squibb)

TABLE 14.3   Current status of important combination therapies using immune checkpoint inhibitors.

Drug targets	Drug combination	Approved trade names
PD-1 + CTLA-4	Nivolumab + ipilimumab	OPDIVO + Yervoy (Bristol-Myers Squibb)
PD-1 + Multikinase	Nivolumab + sorafenib	OPDIVO + Nexavar (Bayer and Onyx)
PD-L1 + VEGF Inhibitor	Atezolizumab + bevacizumab	Tecentriq + AVASTIN (Genentech and Roche)

Conclusion and future perspective

HCC stands high in cancer-related deaths the world over. The pathway of the PD-1/PD-L1 axis and CTLA-4 (potential markers of immune checkpoints) is critical to tumor escape from immune surveillance. Thus preventing tumor escape would be a rate-limiting step for successful immunotherapy. Consistent with the role of immune check point markers, blocking their activity using specific MAbs reinstates the antitumorigenic ability in the tumor microenvironment. Combination immunotherapy targets multiple mechanisms thus appears an effective therapeutic strategy for treating HCC patients. Combination therapy induces a better antitumor T-cell immune response and generates adequate cytotoxic T cells specific to the tumor. Most of the immunotherapies approved as the second-line treatment to those with HCC and had already the first-line sorafenib treatment or intolerant to it.

Of note, inducing an antitumor response without eliciting autoimmunity would be more beneficial for HCC patients. The tumor antigen-specific vaccine strategies such as DC cell, peptide, and ACT vaccines are underway to address the same. CAR immunotherapy also seems like one of the potential approaches for HCC. A recent study suggests that T cells and NK cells transduced by CARs can effectively destroy HCC cancer cells by recognizing CD147, also known as Basigin [29]. Overall, identifying newer biomarkers and understanding their mechanism of action underlying the tumor progression would provide better insights to develop potential immunotherapeutic for HCC patients.

Acknowledgments

The author acknowledges financial assistance from the University Grants Commission Faculty Recharge Program (UGC-FRP) start-up grant and Science and Engineering Research Board (EEQ/2017/000804), Government of India.

References

[1] Wallace MC, Preen D, Jeffrey GP, Adams LA. The evolving epidemiology of hepatocellular carcinoma: a global perspective. Expert Rev Gastroenterol Hepatol 2015;9:765−79.

[2] Janevska D, Chaloska-Ivanova V, Janevski V. Hepatocellular carcinoma: risk factors, diagnosis and treatment. Open Access Maced J Med Sci 2015;3:732−6.

[3] Ramakrishna G, Rastogi A, Trehanpati N, Sen B, Khosla R, Sarin SK. From cirrhosis to hepatocellular carcinoma: new molecular insights on inflammation and cellular senescence. Liver Cancer 2013;2:367−83.

[4] El Dika I, Khalil DN, Abou-Alfa GK. Immune checkpoint inhibitors for hepatocellular carcinoma. Cancer 2019;125:3312−19.

[5] Fransvea E, Paradiso A, Antonaci S, Giannelli G. HCC heterogeneity: molecular pathogenesis and clinical implications. Cell Oncol 2009;31:227−33.

[6] Obeid JM, Kunk PR, Zaydfudim VM, Bullock TN, Slingluff Jr CL, Rahma OE. Immunotherapy for hepatocellular carcinoma patients: is it ready for prime time? Cancer Immunol Immunother 2018;67:161−74.

[7] Kubes P, Jenne C. Immune responses in the liver. Rev Annu Rev Immunol 2018;36:247−77.

[8] Albillos A, Lario M, Álvarez-Mon M. Cirrhosis-associated immune dysfunction: distinctive features and clinical relevance. J Hepatol 2014;61:1385−96.

[9] Khoueiry AB, Sangro B, Yau T, et al. Nivolumab in patients with advanced hepatocellular carcinoma (CheckMate 040): an open-label, non-comparative, phase 1/2 dose escalation and expansion trial. Lancet 2017;389:2492−502.

[10] Lu L, Jiang J, Zhan M, Zhang H, Wang QT, Sun SN, et al. Targeting tumor-associated antigens in hepatocellular carcinoma for immunotherapy: past pitfalls and future strategies. Hepatology 2021;73:821−32. Available from: https://doi.org/10.1002/hep.31502.

[11] Akce M, Zaidi MY, Waller EK, El-Rayes BF, Lesinski GB. The potential of CAR T cell therapy in pancreatic cancer. Front Immunol 2018;9:2166.

[12] Heymann F, Tacke F. Immunology in the liver−from homeostasis to disease. Nat Rev Gastroenterol Hepatol 2016;13:88−110.

[13] Krämer B, et al. Natural killer p46High expression defines a natural killer cell subset that is potentially involved in control of hepatitis C virus replication and modulation of liver fibrosis. Hepatology 2012;56:1201−13.

[14] Juengpanich S, Shi L, Iranmanesh Y, Chen J, Cheng Z, Khoo AK, et al. The role of natural killer cells in hepatocellular carcinoma development and treatment: a narrative review. Transl Oncol 2019;12:1092−107.

[15] Ringelhan M, Pfister D, O'Connor T, Pikarsky E, Heikenwalder M. The immunology of hepatocellular carcinoma. Nat Immunol 2018;19:222−32.

[16] Wolf MJ, et al. Metabolic activation of intrahepatic CD8$^+$ T cells and NKT cells causes non-alcoholic steatohepatitis and liver cancer via cross-talk with hepatocytes. Cancer Cell 2014;26:549−64.

[17] Haybaeck J, et al. A lymphotoxin-driven pathway to hepatocellular carcinoma. Cancer Cell 2009;16:295—308.

[18] Fu J, et al. Impairment of CD4$^+$ cytotoxic T cells predicts poor survival and high recurrence rates in patients with hepatocellular carcinoma. Hepatology 2013;58:139—49.

[19] Llovet JM, Zucman-Rossi J, Pikarsky E, Sangro B, Schwartz M, Sherman M, et al. Hepatocellular carcinoma. Nat Rev Dis Primers 2016;2:16018. Available from: https://doi.org/10.1038/nrdp.2016.18.

[20] Boege Y, et al. A dual role of caspase-8 in triggering and sensing proliferation-associated DNA damage, a key determinant of liver cancer development. Cancer Cell 2017;3:342—59.

[21] Xie QK, Zhao YJ, Pan T, Lyu N, Mu LW, Li SL, et al. Programmed death ligand 1 as an indicator of pre-existing adaptive immune responses in human hepatocellular carcinoma. Oncoimmunology 2016;5:e1181252. Available from: https://doi.org/10.1080/2162402X.2016.1181252.

[22] Garnelo M, et al. Interaction between tumour-infiltrating B cells and T cells controls the progression of hepatocellular carcinoma. Gut 2017;66:342—51.

[23] Zeng Z, Yang B, Liao ZY. Current progress and prospect of immune checkpoint inhibitors in hepatocellular carcinoma. Oncol Lett 2020;20:45.

[24] Zhu AX, Finn RS, Edeline J, Cattan S, Ogasawara S, Palmer D, et al. Pembrolizumab in patients with advanced hepatocellular carcinoma previously treated with sorafenib (KEYNOTE-224): A non-randomised, open-label phase 2 trial. Lancet Oncol 2018;19:940—52.

[25] Finn RS, Qin S, Ikeda M, Galle PR, Ducreux M, Kim TY, et al.IMbrave150 Investigators Atezolizumab plus bevacizumab in unresectable hepatocellular carcinoma. N Engl J Med 2020;382:1894—905.

[26] Lee YH, Tai D, Yip C, Choo SP, Chew V. Combinational immunotherapy for hepatocellular carcinoma: radiotherapy, immune checkpoint blockade and beyond. Front Immunol 2020;11:568759.

[27] Tai D, Choo SP, Chew V. Rationale of immunotherapy in hepatocellular carcinoma and its potential biomarkers. Cancers (Basel), 11. 2019. p. 1926.

[28] Zhongqi F, Xiaodong S, Yuguo C, Guoyue L. Can combined therapy benefit immune checkpoint blockade response in hepatocellular carcinoma? Anticancer Agents Med Chem 2019;19:222—8.

[29] Tseng HC, Xiong W, Badeti S, et al. Efficacy of anti-CD147 chimeric antigen receptors targeting hepatocellular carcinoma. Nat Commun 2020;11:4810.

Recent advancements in immunotherapy interventions for the management of liver cancer

Dhatri Madduru[1], Ngalah Bidii Stephen[2,3], Urvashi Vijay[4], Pranathi Pappu[5], Prashanth Suravajhala[6] and Obul Reddy Bandapalli[3,7,8,9]

[1]Department of Biochemistry, Osmania University, Hyderabad, India [2]Molecular Preventive Medicine, University Medical Center and Faculty of Medicine, University of Freiburg, Freiburg, Germany [3]Medical Faculty, University of Heidelberg, Heidelberg, Germany [4]Department of Immunology and Microbiology, SMS Medical College, Jaipur, India [5]BIOCLUES Organization, Hyderabad, India [6]Department of Biotechnology and Bioinformatics, Birla Institute of Scientific Research (BISR), Jaipur, India [7]Applied Biology, Indian Institute of Chemical Technology (CSIR-IICT), Hyderabad, India [8]Hopp Children's Cancer Center (KiTZ), Heidelberg, Germany [9]Division of Pediatric Neuro Oncology, German Cancer Research Center (DKFZ), German Cancer Consortium (DKTK), Heidelberg, Germany

Abstract

Immunotherapy is one of the leading-edge cancer treatments in recent times and it has proven to be a promising biological approach with the potential to boost one's own immune system to combat a broad spectrum of cancers. Immunotherapy can be performed by employing diverse methods such as T-cell transfer therapy, treatment with vaccines, immune checkpoint inhibitors, immune system modulators, and monoclonal antibodies. Various immunotherapeutic agents have been explored to awaken immune response to combat liver cancer. Around the globe, liver cancer occupies the fourth position among all the contributors of cancer associated mortality, with the most common subtype being hepatocellular carcinoma (HCC). Though immunotherapy exhibits many prospective results, yet there are some side effects such as autoimmune and infusion reactions associated with it, which need to be addressed to develop a holistic, more compelling therapeutic approach for prognosis and better management of liver cancer. The review

Ganji Purnachandra Nagaraju, Sarfraz Ahmad (eds.)
Theranostics and Precision Medicine for the Management of Hepatocellular Carcinoma, Volume 3

225

aims to bridge this gap and we focus on the advancements immunotherapy has seen over the last few years in the management of liver cancer.

Keywords: Immunotherapy; hepatocellular carcinoma; cell-based therapies; immune checkpoint inhibitors; vaccines; monoclonal antibodies

Abbreviations

ADCC	Antibody-dependent cell-mediated cytotoxicity
AFP	Alpha fetoprotein
APC	Antigen-presenting cells
Bcl-xL	B-cell lymphoma-extra large
BTLA	B and T lymphocyte attenuator
CAR	Chimeric antigen receptor
CD	Cluster of differentiation
CTL	Cytotoxic T lymphocyte
CRCL	Chaperone-rich cell lysate
CRISPR-Cas9	Clustered regularly interspaced short palindromic repeats-Cas9
CTLA-4	Cytotoxic T-lymphocyte associated antigen 4
DAMP	Damage-associated molecular pattern
DC	Dendritic cell
DNA	Deoxyribonucleic acid
DNAJB1-PRKACA	DnaJ heat shock protein family member B1- protein kinase cAMP activated catalytic subunit alpha
EpCAM	Epithelial cell adhesion molecule
FDA	Food and Drug Administration
GLYCAR	Glypican 3-specific chimeric antigen receptor
GM-CSF	Granulocyte macrophage colony stimulating factor
GPC3	Glypican-3
GPI	Glycosyl phosphatidyl inositol
HCC	Hepatocellular carcinoma
HCV	Hepatitis C virus
HBV	Hepatitis B virus
HLA	Human leukocyte antigen
HER2	Human epidermal growth factor receptor 2
hTERT	Human telomerase reverse transcriptase
IDO	Indoleamine 2,3-dioxygenase
IFNγ	Interferon gamma
IL	Interleukin
iPS	Induced pluripotent stem cells
LAG3	Lymphocyte activation gene 3
mAb	Monoclonal antibody
MAGE-A	Melanoma-associated antigen
MAMP	Microbe-associated molecular pattern
MDSC	Myeloid-derived suppressor cells
MET	Mesenchymal epithelial transition factor
MHC	Major histocompatibility complex
MRP3	Multidrug resistance-associated protein 3
MUC1	Mucin1
NK	Natural killer
NKG2DL	Natural killer group 2D ligand
NY-ESO-1	New York esophageal squamous cell carcinoma-1

PD1	Programmed cell death protein 1
PD-L1	Programmed death ligand 1
PD-L2	Programmed death ligand 2
poly-ICLC	polyinosinic-polycytidylic acid-poly-l-lysine carboxymethylcellulose
SSX-2	Synovial sarcoma X-2
SKP2	S-phase kinase associated proetin 2
TAA	Tumor-associated antigen
TAI	Transcatheter arterial infusion
TCR	T cell receptors
TEM1	Tumor endothelial marker 1
TGF-β	Transforming growth factor beta
Th cells	Helper T cells
TIL	Tumor-infiltrating lymphocyte
TIM3	T cell immunoglobulin and mucin domain containing 3
TNF	Tumor necrosis factor
Treg	Regulatory T cells
VEGF	Vascular endothelial growth factor
VEGFR	Vascular endothelial growth factor receptor

Introduction

Among the global health concerns, liver cancer occupies the fourth position in contribution towards cancer associated deaths. The most common and second lethal form of liver cancer is hepatocellular carcinoma (HCC) constituting approximately 90% and arises due to multiple factors. The major factors contributing towards the risk of HCC comprise liver cirrhosis, chronic viral infections including hepatitis C virus (HCV) and hepatitis B virus (HBV), exposure to environmental agents, heavy alcohol intake, genetic, metabolic, dietary toxins (e.g., aflatoxin B1), and other conditions associated with liver damage. The liver functions primarily by identifying molecular patterns associated with microbes such as microbe-associated molecular patterns (MAMPs) and damage-associated molecular patterns (DAMPs) followed by their clearance. Hence, the cellular components of innate and adaptive immunity involving natural killer (NK) cells, Cluster of differentiation 4 + (CD4 +) T lymphocytes, Kupffer cells, CD8 + T lymphocytes, and other cell types prevailing in the liver for instance hepatocytes, endothelial cells, liver sinusoidal, and hepatic stellate cells participate in pathogen detection, antigen presentation, and cytokine production. HCC commences with dysregulation of immunological networks to generate immunosuppressive tumor microenvironment [1,2].

The HCC is a challenging disease and many trials to develop effective drugs have failed during the past decade. Although conventional therapies such as surgery, radiotherapy, and chemotherapy are employed for the treatment of HCC due to their limited application, cancer immunotherapy has come into existence in recent years [3]. Immunotherapy is believed as a fourth pillar in cancer therapy along with other treatments [4]. It is based on the strategy to awaken an immune response to mount against cancer [5]. This therapy targets various immune system components such as T cells, dendritic cells, antibodies, immune checkpoint regulators, etc. (Fig. 15.1). Some of the immune checkpoint inhibitor drugs which were shown encouraging outcomes against HCC are Atezolizumab (Tecentriq) [inhibitor of Programmed death-ligand 1 (PD-L1) protein], Nivolumab

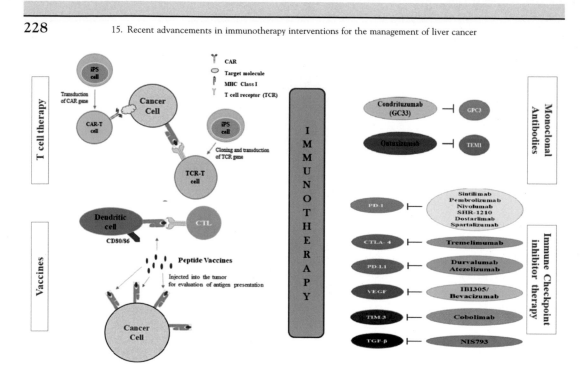

FIGURE 15.1 Diagrammatic representation of various immunotherapeutic strategies to combat hepatocellular carcinoma.

(Opdivo), Pembrolizumab (Keytruda), and Ipilimumab (Yervoy) [inhibitor of cytotoxic T-lymphocyte-associated antigen 4 (CTLA-4)]. Recently, the United States Food and Drug Administration (FDA) gave approval for Nivolumab (2017), Pembrolizumab (2018), Nivolumab with Ipilimumab (2020), and Atezolizumab with Bevacizumab (2020) for their therapeutic application in HCC. In addition to these, many other drugs either individually or in a combinatorial method are still under clinical trials for evaluation of safety and efficacy.

We detail the developments and advancements of immunotherapy towards HCC treatment.

Types of immunotherapy

T-cell therapy

Tumor development critically depends on the regulation and activity of T lymphocytes specifically CD8 + T lymphocytes as they are competent in the eradication of cancer cells. This activity is maximized by regulatory T (Treg) cells, CD4 + T lymphocytes, interleukins for instance interleukin-2 (IL-2) as well as cytokines to overcome immunosuppressive tumor microenvironment [6]. T cell or tumor-infiltrating lymphocyte (TIL) therapy is performed by isolating lymphocytes from resected tumors and culturing ex vivo to further administer these cells into cancer patients. Although this therapy is applied in certain types of cancers, so far it is not employed in HCC [4].

Genetically modified T cell therapy

Genetically modified T cell therapy employs genetically engineered T cells specific to particular cancer possessing T cell receptors (TCRs) with enhanced recognition towards tumor antigens and epitopes [7,8]. This can be performed in two ways: first, utilizing TCR specific to tumor antigen derived from T cells of tumor or their clones, and, second, using chimeric antigen receptor (CAR). An antigen recognition receptor encompassing a single chain having both heavy chain variable and light chain variable regions of monoclonal antibody (mAb) displaying specificity towards surface antigen of tumor is represented as an extracellular portion of CAR while the intracellular portion of TCR upon binding with costimulatory molecules forms the intracellular domain of CAR [4].

Chimeric antigen receptor T cell therapy

Chimeric antigen receptor (CAR) T cell therapy includes modified T cells expressed by viral vectors and consisting of monoclonal antibodies recognizing tumor-specific antigens [4]. This includes T lymphocyte isolation for the patient's blood, stimulation, and expansion, followed by reinfusion of T lymphocytes specific for antigen back into the patient. Wu et al. conducted a clinical trial (NCT02395250) of combined therapy using Sorafenib, a multikinase inhibitor, and glypican-3 (GPC3)-targeted CAR-T cell therapy on the HCC mouse model and found upregulated apoptosis in tumors. They proposed a therapeutic potential for this combined treatment [9]. Currently, around 14 clinical trials are active and 1 has been completed to evaluate the usefulness of this therapy against HCC (Table 15.1). Predominantly anti- GPC3 agents are under consideration. GPC3 is a 580 amino acid heparan sulfate chain proteoglycan bound to the membrane with a glycosylphosphatidylinositol (GPI) anchor. This protein has a molecular weight of 65 KDa that is encoded by the gene localized on the X chromosome (Xq26) and is primarily expressed in kidney, lung, and liver tissues. In addition, its presence in the placenta of the fetus facilitates embryonic cell proliferation and differentiation by binding to factors like Wnt, insulin-like growth factor, and fibroblast growth factor. Around $\geq 80\%$ of HCC patients expressed GPC3 and are involved in neoplastic transformation of HCC therefore is a perfect target for immunotherapy [10].

TCR-engineered T (TCR-T) cell therapy

This treatment employs T lymphocytes with modified gene encoding TCR specific for many surface antigen peptides expressed on tumor and major histocompatibility complex (MHC) and is effective against tumors expressing target antigen epitopes. However, human leukocyte antien (HLA) restrictions need to be considered [4].

Vaccines

Tumors escape immune surveillance mechanisms of the host by reducing antigen presentation, and expression of HLA-class I. Tumor vaccines work by boosting immune responses towards tumor-specific antigens. However, previously, it was a challenge to identify a particular tumor antigen, but this problem is successfully addressed by parallel deoxyribonucleic acid (DNA) sequencing facilitating the use of vaccines in individual or

TABLE 15.1 Summary of completed and ongoing clinical trials (including FDA approved) of immunotherapy against liver cancer/hepatocellular carcinoma (HCC).

Trail identifier	Targets	Drugs/biological	Other treatment	Patients	Status	Phase of trail	Estimated date of completion
T cell therapy, CAR-T cell therapy and TCR-T cell therapy							
NCT03146234	GPC3	CAR-GPC3 T cells	–	GPC3 + refractory HCC patients	Completed	–	Completed
NCT02587689	Mucin1 (MUC1)	anti-MUC1 CAR-T cells	–	MUC1 + Advanced Refractory tumors	Recruiting	Phase 1 Phase 2	October 2018
NCT02715362 Gene-modified patient T cells	GPC3	(Transcatheter arterial infusion) TAI-GPC3-CAR-T cells	4-1BB costimulator	GPC3 + advanced HCC patients	Recruiting	Phase 1 Phase 2	March 2019
NCT03672305	c-mesenchymal epithelial transition factor (c-Met)/ programmed cell death ligand 1 (PD-L1)	Injection of CAR-T cells	–	Primary HCC	No recruitment yet	Early Phase 1	October 2019
NCT02729493	Epithelial cell adhesion molecule (EPCAM)	EPCAM-targeted CAR-T cells	–	Liver cancer	Recruiting	NA	November 2019
NCT03084380	GPC3	Retroviral vector-mediated transduced autologous T cells with anti-GPC3 CARs	Cyclophosphamide Fludarabine	GPC3 + advanced HCC patients	No recruitment yet	Phase 1 Phase 2	May 2020
NCT03013712	EpCAM	CAR-T cells	–	EpCAM positive HCC patients	Recruiting	Phase 1 Phase 2	December 2020

NCT Number	Target	Intervention	Condition	Status	Phase	Date
NCT04121273	GPC3	CAR-T cells	–	GPC3 + advanced HCC patients	Recruiting	Phase 1	November 2021
NCT03993743	CD-147	CD147-CART	–	Advanced HCC patients	Recruiting	Phase 1	May 2022
NCT03980288	Glypican-3	CAR-GPC3 T cells infusion	Fludarabine cyclophosphamide	GPC3 + advanced HCC patients	Recruiting	Phase 1	June 2022
NCT04506983	GPC3	GPC3-CAR-T cells	–	HCC patients	No recruitment yet	Phase 1	November 2022
NCT04550663	Natural killer group 2D ligand (NKG2DLs)	NKG2D (KD-025) CAR-T cells	–	Relapsed/Refractory NKG2DL + Tumors	No recruitment yet	Phase 1	March 2023
NCT03302403	GPC3	CAR-GPC3 T cell	Fludarabine cyclophosphamide	HCC patients	Active, No recruitment yet	NA	December 2023
NCT03884751	Glypican-3	CAR-GPC3 T cells injection		GPC3 + advanced HCC patients	Recruiting	Phase 1	May 2024
NCT0319854	GPC3 and/or transforming growth factor beta (TGFβ)	CAR-T cells	–	GPC3 + HCC Patients	Recruiting	Phase 1	August 2024
NCT02905188	GPC3	Glypican 3-specific chimeric antigen receptor (GLYCAR) T cells	Cytoxan Fludarabine	HCC patients	Recruiting	Phase 1	October 2036
Vaccines						
NCT02409524	–	Individualized anticancer vaccine chaperone rich cell lysate (CRCL)-AlloVax) AlloStim followed by CRCL	–	Advanced HCC	Completed	Phase 2	Completed
NCT01974661	–	Allogenic dendritic cell-based therapeutic vaccine COMBIG-DC (Ilixadencel)	–	HCC	Completed	Phase 1	Completed
NCT03203005	–	IMA970A (Vaccine) plus CV8102 (adjuvant)	Cyclophosphamide	Early and intermediate stage HCC	Completed	Phase 1 Phase 2	Completed

(*Continued*)

TABLE 15.1 (Continued)

Trial identifier	Targets	Drugs/biological	Other treatment	Patients	Status	Phase of trial	Estimated date of completion
NCT01147380	–	Adoptive transfer of activated natural killer (NK) cells extracted from Liver NK cell inoculation/cadaveric donor liver graft	–	Liver transplant recipients with HCC	Completed	Phase 1	Completed
NCT00322361	–	RECOMBIVAX HB Modified process hepatitis B vaccine	–	HCC Patients	Completed	Phase 2	Completed
NCT00005629	–	Alpha fetoprotein (AFP) gene hepatocellular carcinoma vaccine	–	Liver Cancer	Completed	Phase 1 Phase 2	Completed
NCT02089919	–	Cancer stem cell vaccine	–	HCC Patients	Completed	Phase 1 Phase 2	Completed
NCT00022334	–	Dendritic cells (DCs) pulsed with four AFP peptides	–	Liver Cancer	Completed	Phase 1 Phase 2	Completed
NCT01018381	–	Dietary supplement Arabinoxylan rice bran (MGN-3/Biobran)	Entecavir	HCC	Completed	NA	Completed
NCT01522820	–	DEC-205/New York esophageal squamous cell carcinoma-1 (NY-ESO-1) fusion protein CDX-1401	Sirolimus	Recurrent HCC	Completed	Phase 1	Completed
NCT01749865	–	Cytokine-induced killer cells	–	HCC	Completed	Phase 3	Completed
NCT00028496	–	Recombinant fowlpox-CEA(6D)/TRICOM vaccine Sargramostim recombinant fowlpox granulocyte macrophage colony stimulating factor (GM-CSF) vaccine adjuvant	–	Primary HCC	Completed	Phase 1	Completed
NCT00019331	–	Aldesleukin ras peptide cancer vaccine Sargramostim	DetoxPC	HCC	Completed	Phase 2	Completed
NCT00027534	–	TRICOM-CEA(6D) DCs loaded with TRICOM-CEA(6D)	–	Advanced or metastatic HCC	Completed	Phase 1	Completed
NCT00222664	–	Hep-V Vax	–	Liver cancer	Completed	Phase 4	Completed
NCT00004604	–	CEA RNA-pulsed DC cancer vaccine	–	Metastatic HCC	Completed	Phase 1	Completed

NCT Number		Intervention	Combination	Condition	Status	Phase	Completed
NCT0016187	–	Therapeutic allogeneic lymphocytes	–	HCC	Completed	Phase 1	June 2006
NCT00327496	–	Tumor lysate-pulsed dendritic cells	–	Advanced HCC	No recruitment yet	NA	March 2013
NCT01266707	–	Angiogenic peptide vaccine therapy in treating patients with human leukocyte antigen- A (HLA-A*2402) restriction /vaccine specific for VEGFR1 and VEGFR2 epitope	–	Advanced HCC	Recruiting	Phase 1	July 2014
NCT00553683	–	Cyclophosphamide polyinosinic-polycytidylic acid-poly-l-lysine carboxymethylcellulose (poly-ICLC)	3-Dimensional conformal radiation therapy	Unresectable, recurrent, primary, or metastatic liver cancer	No recruitment yet	Phase 1 Phase 2	December 2019
NCT02256514	–	Oral immunotherapy hepcortespenlisimut-L (V5)	–	Advanced HCC	Enrolling by invitation	Phase 2	December 2019
NCT02232490	–	Placebo-controlled hepcortespenlisimut-L (Hepko-V5)	–	Advanced HCC	Recruiting	Phase 3	February 2020
NCT02432963	–	p53 expressing modified vaccinia virus Ankara vaccine	Pembrolizumab	HCC	No recruitment yet	Phase 1	December 2020
NCT03674073	–	Personalized neoantigen-based dendritic cell (DC) vaccine	Microwave Ablation procedure	HCC	Recruiting	Phase 1	
NCT04251117	–	Personalized neoantigen DNA vaccine (GNOS-PV02), plasmid encoded IL-12 (INO-9012)	Pembrolizumab (MK-3475)	Advanced HCC	Recruiting	Phase 1 Phase 2	February 2022
NCT04317248	–	Multiple signals loaded dendritic cells vaccine	Cyclophosphamide	Hepatitis B related HCC	Recruiting	Phase 2	April 2022
NCT03942328	–	Pneumococcal 13-valent conjugate vaccine/therapeutic autologous dendritic cells	External beam radiation therapy	Liver cancer	Recruiting	Early phase 1	May 2022

(Continued)

TABLE 15.1 (Continued)

Trail identifier	Targets	Drugs/biological	Other treatment	Patients	Status	Phase of trail	Estimated date of completion
NCT04147078	–	DC vaccine subcutaneous administration	–	HCC	Recruiting	Phase 1	June 2023
NCT03311334	–	DSP-7888 Dosing emulsion	Nivolumab, Pembrolizumab	HCC	Recruiting	Phase 1 Phase 2	February 2024
NCT04248569	DnaJ heat shock protein family member B1- protein kinase cAMP activated catalytic subunit alpha (DNAJB1-PRKACA) fusion kinase	Peptide vaccine	Nivolumab, Ipilimumab	Metastatic fibrolamellar HCC	Recruiting	Phase 1	March 2024
NCT04246671	–	TAEK-VAC-HerBy	Human epidermal growth factor receptor 2 (HER2) and PD-1/PD-L1 antibodies	Advanced HER2 expressing HCC	Recruiting	Phase 1 Phase 2	December 2024
NCT04634357	–	ET140203 T cells	–	AFP-positive/HLA-A2-positive HCC patients	No recruitment yet	Phase 1 Phase 2	February 2025
Monoclonal antibodies							
NCT00746317	GPC3	Condrituzumab/GC33	–	Advanced or metastasis liver cancer (HCC)	Completed	Phase 1	Completed
NCT01507168	GPC3	GC33 (RO5137382)	Placebo	Advanced or metastasis liver cancer (HCC)	Completed	Phase 2	Completed

NCT number	Target	Agent	Comparator	Condition	Status	Phase	Completion
NCT00976170	GPC3	GC33(RO5137382)	Sorafenib	Advanced or metastasis liver cancer (HCC)	Completed	Phase 1	Completed
NCT00847054	Tumor endothelial marker 1 (TEM1)	Ontuxizumab (MORAb-004)	–	Liver Cancer	Completed	Phase 1	Completed
NCT01773434	TEM1	Ontuxizumab (MORAb-004)	–	HCC	Completed	Phase 1	Completed
Immune checkpoint inhibitor therapy							
NCT02947165	TGF-β programmed cell death protein 1 (PD-1)	NIS793 PDR001 (Spartalizumab)	–	Advanced HCC	No recruitment yet	Phase 1	April 2021
NCT02702401	PD-1	Pembrolizumab	Placebo	HCC	No recruitment yet	Phase 3	June 2021
NCT02576509	PD-1	Nivolumab	Sorafenib	Advanced HCC	No recruitment yet	Phase 3	December 2021
NCT03062358	PD-1	Pembrolizumab	Placebo	Advanced HCC	No recruitment yet	Phase 3	January 2022
NCT03298451	PD-L1 Cytotoxic T-lymphocyte associated antigen 4 (CTLA-4)	Durvalumab Tremelimumab	Sorafenib	Advanced HCC	Recruiting	Phase 3	April 2022
NCT03713593	Vascular endothelial growth factor receptor (VEGFR)-1-3 PD-1	Lenvatinib Pembrolizumab	Saline placebo	Advanced HCC	No recruitment yet	Phase 3	May 2022
NCT03764293	PD-1	SHR-1210	Apatinib Sorafenib	Advanced HCC	Recruiting	Phase 3	June 2022

(Continued)

TABLE 15.1 (Continued)

Trail identifier	Targets	Drugs/biological	Other treatment	Patients	Status	Phase of trail	Estimated date of completion
NCT03434379	PD-L1 VEGF	Atezolizumab Bevacizumab	Sorafenib	Advanced HCC	No recruitment yet	Phase 3	June 2022
NCT03794440	PD-1 VEGF	Sintilimab IBI305	Sorafenib	Advanced HCC	Recruiting	Phase 2 Phase 3	December 2022
NCT03847428	PD-L1 VEGF	Durvalumab Bevacizumab	Placebo	Recurrent HCC	Recruiting	Phase 3	September 2023
NCT03680508	T cell immunoglobulin and mucin domain containing 3 (TIM-3) PD-1	TSR-022 (Cobolimab) TSR-042 (Dostarlimab)	—	Liver cancer	Recruiting	Phase 2	October 2023
NCT03755739	PD-1	Pembrolizumab	—	Advanced HCC	Recruiting	Phase 2 Phase 3	November 2033
FDA approved							
NCT01658878	PD-1	Nivolumab	Sorafenib Ipilimumab Cabozantinib	Advanced Liver cancer	No recruitment yet	Phase 1 Phase 2	April 2022
NCT03434379	PD-L1 Vascular endothelial growth factor (VEGF)	Atezolizumab Bevacizumab	Sorafenib	Advanced or metastatic HCC	No recruitment yet	Phase 3	June 2022

Data collection from https://clinicaltrials.gov/; https://www.fda.gov/.

combination with immune modulators as a prospective therapeutic strategy towards HCC [5]. A clinical trial (phase I) was conducted by Sawada et al. on the generation of GPC-3 reactive cytotoxic T lymphocytes (CTLs) [11]. A plethora of tumor-associated antigens (TAAs) have been predicted including human telomerase reverse transcriptase (hTERT), synovial sarcoma X-2 (SSX-2), melanoma-associated antigen (MAGE-A), and New York esophageal squamous cell carcinoma-1 (NY-ESO-1); however, GPC-3, alpha fetoprotein (AFP), and multidrug resistance-associated protein 3 (MRP3) were found to be efficient against HCC [5,12]. Additionally, researchers have identified that HLA-A24 (60% of Japanese population) and HLA-A2 (40% Japanese, Major Europeans, and North Americans) restricted GPC3-derived peptide-specific CTLs elicited antitumor effects against HCC [13,14]. Nobuoka et al. developed an intratumoral injection method to enhance antitumor action of vaccines [10,15].

Monoclonal antibodies

Many TAAs have been recognized in HCC, including glypican-3, epithelial cell adhesion molecule (EpCAM), and tumor endothelial marker 1 (TEM1). In HCC, upregulation of EpCAM, a transmembrane glycoprotein (type I), was observed. Physiologically, it is a part of intricate cell signaling, migration, proliferation, metabolism, adhesion, regeneration, organogenesis of the liver, and metastasis. TEM1 (CD248/endosialin) is a transmembrane glycoprotein (type C) rich in sialic acid belonging to a family of lectin receptors detected in HCC at both transcripts as well as protein levels, whereas in healthy individuals, it is expressed in mesenchymal stem cell surfaces, endothelial progenitor cells, and fibroblasts involved in local invasion, vascular adhesion, and migration as well as metastasis in tumors. Various humanized monoclonal antibodies have been studied for their use to treat HCC. Ishiguro et al. developed a completely humanized recombinant IgG2 mAb Condrituzumab (GC33) targeting the C-terminal region of GPC3 and induces antibody-dependent cell-mediated cytotoxicity (ADCC) to dampen liver cancer growth [16]. The application of Condrituzumab was determined by phase I (NCT00746317) [17] and phase II and III (NCT01507168 and NCT00976170) [18,19] clinical trials. Similarly, in the United States, phase I clinical trials were conducted with advanced HCC patients and found that patients expressing high GPC3 were responding well towards GC33 antitumor activity [17]. In Japan, Ikeda et al. also observed similar results during phase I clinical trials on GC33 [20]. Another phase I study on ERY974, T-cell redirecting bi-specific GPC3/CD3 antibody confirms the antitumor activity on GPC3 positive cancer cells [10,21]. Other mAbs directing GPC3 include YP7 [22,23] against C-terminal, NH3, an antibody with the variable domain of heavy chain against the GPC3 core epitope [24]. Another humanized IgG1/K mAb, Ontuxizumab aiming TEM1 studied in phase I clinical trials (NCT00847054) [25] and (NCT01773434) [26] in HCC patients showed promising results [2].

Immune checkpoint inhibitors

Immune checkpoints can be defined as subsets of molecules expressed on membranes and are involved in immune response modulation. Various immune cells express these immune checkpoints which include natural killer (NK) cells, monocytes, myeloid-derived suppressor cells (MDSC), macrophages associated with tumors, B cells, and T cells. These checkpoints primarily function through the prevention of uncontrolled constant stimulation of responses exerted by T cells upon infection. The widely studied checkpoints involved in liver cancer are lymphocyte activation gene 3 protein (LAG-3), B and T lymphocyte attenuator (BTLA), programmed cell death protein 1 (PD-1), T cell immunoglobulin, and mucin-domain containing (TIM-3), and cytotoxic T lymphocyte protein 4 (CTLA-4) [3].

Programmed cell death protein 1

Programmed cell death protein 1 (PD-1) is a crucial player in the effector response of immune activation. This receptor protein is expressed by diverse immune cells such as activated B cells, CD8 + T lymphocytes, CD4 + T lymphocytes, Natural killer (NK) cells, Treg cells, dendritic cells (DCs), monocytes, and MDSC. PD-1 can be activated by two ligands namely programmed death-ligand 1 (PD-L1) and programmed death-ligand 2 (PD-L2). PD-L1, expressed on a variety of tumor cells, epithelial, endothelial, parenchymal, and hematopoietic cells including MDSC and antigen-presenting cells (APCs) is upregulated by cytokines especially interferon gamma (IFN-γ) as well as by the action of oncogenes. In a tumor hypoxic microenvironment, upon chronic exposure to the antigen, TAAs-specific T cells produce IFN-γ, which upregulates PD-L1 whose expression was further persuaded by APCs in reactive T lymphocytes. This interaction of PD-1 with PD-L1 results in the blockade of T cell receptor (TCR) signaling through feedback inhibition for downregulation of antiapoptotic molecule expression such as B-cell lymphoma extra large (Bcl-xL) and proinflammatory factors eventually suppressing the proliferation of T cells and cytotoxic mediators secretion by exhaustion of T lymphocytes. PD-L1 also interacts with B7-1 in addition to PD-1 [27]. However, the programmed death ligand 2 (PD-L2) expression was observed in the hematopoietic compartment, bone marrow-derived mast cells, activated DCs, peritoneal B1 cells, macrophages, helper T (Th) 2 cells, as well as intrapulmonary nonhematological cells. PD-1 exerts its action by inhibiting CD8 + T lymphocyte activation through TCR signal blockade while CD4 + T lymphocyte activation through IL-10 secretion. The expression of PD-L1 and PD-L2 ligands on tumor cells direct them for immunosurveillance escape mechanism [3,28,29]. PD-1 enhances the proliferation of the Treg cell population to exert immunosuppressive activity. PD-1 upon interaction with its ligands results in upregulation of p15 expression, thus reducing the transcription of S-phase kinase associated proetin 2 (SKP2), thereby averting the entry of T cells into the G1 phase subsequently inducing apoptosis in tumor-specific T cells, thus promoting Th cell differentiation into Treg cells [30,31], whereas PD-L2 performs its action by negative regulation of T cells establishing immune tolerance [32]. PD-L2 also enhances the response of Th1 lymphocytes through the action of IFN-γ. Both PD-L1 and PD-L2 ligands interact with PD-1 in a cross- competitive fashion and hence PD-1 inhibitors block the interaction of PD-L1 and PD-L2 with PD-1 simultaneously and antagonize PD-1/PD-L1 and PD-1/PD-L2 axes completely [6,33].

Pembrolizumab (Keytruda) and Nivolumab (Opdivo) are the two fully humanized PD-1 inhibitors (monoclonal antibodies) that got approval by the United States Food and Drug Administration (FDA) in March 2020 based on data obtained from clinical trials cohort 4 of CHECKMATE-040, (NCT01658878) in patients suffering from HCC and are intolerant to Sorafenib (http://www.fda.gov).

The monoclonal antibodies bind to corresponding domains in the epitopes of antagonist targets to attain stable conformation through molecular interactions. This results in conformational changes activating downstream signaling and suppressing physiological as well as pathological functions of the target molecule [34]. Pembrolizumab interacts with the C'D loop, whereas nivolumab binds to the N-terminal of PD-1, FG, and BC loop [35]. The binding of both these inhibitors is partially complementary; therefore, their simultaneous administration can be considered in the near future [31,35,36]. Further, Atezolizumab (Tecentriq), previously known as MPDL3280, is a mAb which is a fully humanized PD-L1 inhibitor that gained approval as a therapy for unresectable or metastatic HCC without prior systemic therapy by US FDA in May 2020 in combination with Bevacizumab (Avastin) based on IMbrave150 (NCT03434379) clinical trials data and it is engineered with Fc domain modification to eliminate cellular cytotoxicity in order to prevent PD-L1 expressing T cell depletion. This monoclonal antibody binds to the CC'FG antiparallel β sheet; BC, CC', C'C'' and FG loops present on PD-L1 to block its interaction with both PD-1 as well as B7-1 on tumor cells [31,37] (http://www.fda.gov).

Cytotoxic T-lymphocyte-associated antigen 4

Cytotoxic T-lymphocyte-associated antigen 4 (CTLA-4) is a molecule primarily expressed on membranes of activated T cells and also Treg cells. It is pivotal for the activation of CD4 + T lymphocytes to induce an immune response. It exhibits high affinity towards CD80 and CD86 molecules and competes with CD28 for binding to these receptors thus diminishing activation of T lymphocytes upon antigen presentation and also enhances the secretion of IL-10 an immunoregulatory cytokine. Along with transforming growth factor beta (TGF-β) and IL-10 signaling by activated TCR, Treg cells dampen the effector response of the immune system by reduction of IL-2 and secretion of adenosine, IL-10, or TGF-β to compete with costimulatory molecules CD28 through CTLA-4. Therefore, CTLA-4 prompts Treg cells to suppress activated T cells [38]. In tumors, CTLA-4 also upregulates IL-10 and Indoleamine 2,3-dioxygenase (IDO) in dendritic cells [39]. In March 2020, United States FDA permitted the treatment of Nivolumab (Opdivo) along with Ipilimumab (Yervoy) patients with HCC and underwent Sorafenib treatment based on cohort 4 of CHECKMATE-040, (NCT01658878) clinical trials. Another phase 3 clinical trial is in progress to assess the safety as well as the efficacy of combination therapy of Durvalumab and Tremelimumab in HCC patients without prior systemic therapy (NCT03298451).

T-cell immunoglobulin and mucin-domain containing-3

T-cell immunoglobulin and mucin-domain containing-3 (TIM-3) is a transmembrane protein principally expressed on CD4 + Th1 lymphocytes, CD8 + cytotoxic T lymphocytes (innate immune system and adaptive immune system) and display interactions with a variety of ligands such as galectin-9, phosphatidylserine (apoptotic cell membranes), etc. [40]. Galectin-9 is a protein expressed by the liver in a soluble form to regulate cellular differentiation, adhesion, and death. TIM-3 is a receptor on T cells with inhibitory action and interacts with galectin-9. Studies in animal models revealed that PD-1 coexpresses on CD8 + Tim-3 + T lymphocytes, resulting in aberrations in the progression of the cell cycle and production of cytokines such as IFN-γ, IL-2, and tumor necrosis factor (TNF). Therefore, in cancers, severe dysfunctional phenotypes can be observed regarding CD8 +

T lymphocytes due to synergistic effects of PD-1 and TIM-3 pathways [3,41,42]. A phase II clinical trial is underway to test the combined efficacy of TSR-042 (Dostarlimab, PD-1 binding antibody) and TSR-022 (Cobolimab, TIM-3 binding antibody) among patients with metastatic liver cancer (NCT03680508).

Lymphocyte activation gene 3

Lymphocyte activation gene 3 (LAG-3) is a protein bound to membranes and is closely associated with CD4, exhibiting high affinity towards MHC class II molecules functions by diminishing the costimulatory actions of DCs. It suppresses the activity of T lymphocytes and also the release of cytokines. Upon activation of T lymphocytes, upregulation of LAG-3 is observed which was absent in resting T cells. It is an exhausted T cell marker and functions along with PD-1 in a synergistic way to promote cancer [43,44]. In HCC patients, engineered LAG-3-binding therapy is already in the early phases of clinical trials and showed promising results in elevated CD8 + T lymphocytes infiltrating tumor [45]. However, tumor regression therapy by directing LAG-3 and PD-1 simultaneously has potential therapeutic applications in future [5].

Transforming growth factor-β

Transforming growth factor-β (TGF-β) is a membrane-associated molecule that functions along with Treg subsets to suppress CD4 + T lymphocyte responses in HCC [39]. Potential combination therapy is possible as PD-1 coexpresses on CD4 + CD69 + Treg cells. A phase I clinical trial towards parallel administration of NIS793, an anti-TGF-β mAb, and Spartalizumab, a PD-1 inhibitor to HCC patients is underway [5] (NCT02947165).

Immunotherapy using induced pluripotent stem cells

Induced pluripotent stem (iPS) cell-derived T lymphocytes are of significant value owing to their potential to eliminate effector T cell exhaustion and aging effects, facilitate gene modification, and are suitable for prolonged treatment at a low cost. A study conducted by Kaneko et al. successfully avoided reconstruction of TCRs in iPS cells derived from T cells by gene editing [46]. Development of TCR-iPS-T cell approach is under progress for the expression of TCR specific GPC3-peptide which can open new avenues for novel antitumor therapeutic strategies in the near future [10].

Advantages and disadvantages

The advantages associated with cancer immunotherapy include precision, targeted, safer compared to other conventional therapies. The use of small molecules as immunotherapeutic drugs has been recently approved by US FDA and are advantageous over biologics such as CAR-T cells, antibodies, etc. in a way that they selectively target intracellular pathways, ease in penetrating solid tumors, permitting oral administration of flexible doses, improve therapeutic index by inducing acute antitumor activities, and avoid systemic immunogenicity, suitable for long-term use and are cost-effective [47]. However, immunotherapeutic strategies are also associated with some drawbacks and limitations such as ineffective if tumors are immunosuppressive and immune exclusion type, immune checkpoint inhibitors may lead to autoimmune diseases by negative regulation and the patients may suffer from poor survival, uncertain prognosis associated with high costs and sometimes may end up in death [48].

Future direction and conclusion

The HCC is a challenging disease due to its high immunogenicity and inflammatory microenvironment resulting in pathogenicity either due to viral or nonviral processes. In addition, the mutational burden may prompt immunological responses to combat cancer. Though immunotherapies are exhibiting promising results they may be hampered by factors such as multifocal origin and heterogeneity of HCC. Therefore, it is the need of the hour to evaluate cell-based therapies like CAR-T cells, genome editing tools like clustered regularly interspaced short palindromic repeats-Cas 9 (CRISPR-Cas9), combination therapy strategies with different immunological approaches, or conventional therapies (radiotherapy, chemotherapy, etc.) to treat HCC effectively.

References

[1] Madduru D, et al. Systems challenges of hepatic carcinomas: a review. J Clin Exp Hepatol 2019;9(2):233–44. Available from: https://doi.org/10.1016/j.jceh.2018.05.002.

[2] Dal Bo M, et al. New insights into the pharmacological, immunological, and CAR-T-cell approaches in the treatment of hepatocellular carcinoma. Drug Resist Updat 2020;51:1–23. Available from: https://doi.org/10.1016/j.drup.2020.100702.

[3] Greten TF, Sangro B. Targets for immunotherapy of liver cancer. J Hepatol 2018;68.157–66. Available from. https://doi.org/10.1016/j.jhep.2017.09.007.

[4] Mizukoshi E, Kaneko S. Immune cell therapy for hepatocellular carcinoma. J Hematol Oncol 2019;12 (52):1–11. Available from: https://doi.org/10.1186/s13045-019-0742-5.

[5] Johnston MP, Khakoo SI. Immunotherapy for hepatocellular carcinoma: Current and future. World J Gastroenterol 2019;25(24):2977–89. Available from: 10.3748/wjg.v25.i24.2977.

[6] Medina PJ, Adams VR. PD-1 pathway inhibitors: immuno-oncology agents for restoring antitumor immune responses. Pharmacotherapy 2016;36:317–34. Available from: https://doi.org/10.1002/phar.1714.

[7] Morgan RA, et al. Cancer regression in patients after transfer of genetically engineered lymphocytes. Science 2006;314(5796):126–9. Available from: https://doi.org/10.1126/science.1129003.

[8] Johnson LA, et al. Gene therapy with human and mouse T-cell receptors mediates cancer regression and targets normal tissues expressing cognate antigen. Blood 2009;114(3):535–46. Available from: https://doi.org/10.1182/blood-2009-03-211714.

[9] Wu X, et al. Combined antitumor effects of sorafenib and GPC3-CAR T cells in mouse models of hepatocellular carcinoma. Mol Ther 2019;27(8):1483–94. Available from: https://doi.org/10.1016/j.ymthe.2019.04.020.

[10] Shimizu Y, et al. Next-generation cancer immunotherapy targeting glypican-3. Front Oncol 2019;9(248):1–10. Available from: https://doi.org/10.3389/fonc.2019.00248.

[11] Sawada Y, et al. Phase I trial of a glypican-3-derived peptide vaccine for advanced hepatocellular carcinoma: immunologic evidence and potential for improving overall survival. Clin Cancer Res 2012;18:3686–96. Available from: https://doi.org/10.1158/1078-0432.CCR-11-3044.

[12] Sun Z, et al. Status of and prospects for cancer vaccines against hepatocellular carcinoma in clinical trials. Bio Sci Trends 2016;10:85–91. Available from: https://doi.org/10.5582/bst.2015.01128.

[13] Nakatsura T, et al. Mouse homolog of a novel human oncofetal antigen, glypican-3, evokes T cell-mediated tumor rejection without autoimmune reactions in mice. Clin Cancer Res 2004;10:8630−40. Available from: https://doi.org/10.1158/1078-0432.CCR-04-1177.

[14] Komori H, et al. Identification of HLA-A2- or HLA-A24-restricted CTL epitopes possibly useful for glypican-3-specific immunotherapy of hepatocellular carcinoma. Clin Cancer Res 2006;12:2689−97. Available from: https://doi.org/10.1158/1078-0432.CCR-05-2267.

[15] Nobuoka D, et al. Peptide intra-tumor injection for cancer immunotherapy: enhancement of tumor cell antigenicity is a novel and attractive strategy. Hum Vaccin Immunother 2013;9:1234−6. Available from: https://doi.org/10.4161/hv.23990.

[16] Ishiguro T, et al. Anti-glypican 3 antibody as a potential antitumor agent for human liver cancer. Cancer Res 2008;68:9832−8. Available from: https://doi.org/10.1158/0008-5472.CAN-08-1973.

[17] Zhu AX, et al. First-in-man phase I study of GC33, a novel recombinant humanized antibody against glypican-3, in patients with advanced hepatocellular carcinoma. Clin Cancer Res 2013;19:920−8. Available from: https://doi.org/10.1158/1078-0432.CCR-12-2616.

[18] Abou-Alfa, et al. Randomized phase II placebo-controlled study of codrituzumab in previously treated patients with advanced hepatocellular carcinoma. J Hepatol 2016;65:289−95. Available from: https://doi.org/10.1016/j.jhep.2016.04.004.

[19] Abou-Alfa, et al. Phase Ib study of codrituzumab in combination with sorafenib in patients with non-curable advanced hepatocellular. Cancer Chemother Pharmacol 2017;79(2):421−9. Available from: https://doi.org/10.1007/s00280-017-3241-9.

[20] Ikeda M, et al. Japanese phase I study of GC33, a humanized antibody against glypican-3 for advanced hepatocellular carcinoma. Cancer Sci 2014;105:455−62. Available from: https://doi.org/10.1111/cas.12368.

[21] Ishiguro T, et al. An anti-glypican 3/CD3 bispecific T cell-redirecting antibody for treatment of solid tumors. Sci Transl Med 2017;9:eaal4291. Available from: https://doi.org/10.1126/scitranslmed.aal4291.

[22] Phung Y, et al. High-affinity monoclonal antibodies to cell surface tumor antigen glypican-3 generated through a combination of peptide immunization and flow cytometry screening. MAbs 2012;4(5):592−9. Available from: https://doi.org/10.4161/mabs.20933.

[23] Zhang YF, Ho M. Humanization of high-affinity antibodies targeting glypican-3 in hepatocellular carcinoma. Sci Rep 2016;6:33878. Available from: https://doi.org/10.1038/srep33878.

[24] Feng M, et al. Therapeutically targeting glypican-3 via a conformation-specific single-domain antibody in hepatocellular carcinoma. Proc Natl Acad Sci USA 2013;110:E1083−91. Available from: 10.1073/pnas.1217868110.

[25] Diaz Jr. LA, et al. A first in-human phase I study of MORAb-004, a monoclonal antibody to endosialin in patients with advanced solid tumors. Clin Cancer Res 2015;21:1281−8. Available from: https://doi.org/10.1158/1078-0432.CCR-14-1829.

[26] Doi T, et al. A phase I study of ontuxizumab, a humanized monoclonal antibody targeting endosialin, in Japanese patients with solid tumors. Invest New Drugs 2019;37:1061−74. Available from: https://doi.org/10.1007/s10637-018-0713-7.

[27] Li X, et al. Lessons learned from the blockade of immune checkpoints in cancer immunotherapy. J Hematol Oncol 2018;11(1):31. Available from: https://doi.org/10.1186/s13045-018-0578-4.

[28] Prieto J, Melero I, Sangro B. Immunological landscape and immunotherapy of hepatocellular carcinoma. Nat Rev Gastroenterol Hepatol 2015;12:681−700. Available from: https://doi.org/10.1038/nrgastro.2015.173.

[29] Le Mercier I, Lines JL, Noelle RJ. Beyond CTLA-4 and PD-1, the generation Z of negative checkpoint regulators. Front Immunol 2015;6:418. Available from: https://doi.org/10.3389/fimmu.2015.00418.

[30] Brown JA, et al. Blockade of programmed death-1 ligands on dendritic cells enhances T cell activation and cytokine production. J Immunol 2003;170:1257−66. Available from: https://doi.org/10.4049/jimmunol.170.3.1257.

[31] Zhang N, et al. Programmed cell death-1/programmed cell death ligand-1 checkpoint inhibitors: differences in mechanism of action. Immunotherapy 2019;11(5):429−41. Available from: https://doi.org/10.2217/imt-2018-0110.

[32] Zhang Y, et al. Regulation of T cell activation and tolerance by PDL2. Proc Natl Acad Sci USA 2006;103:11695−700. Available from: https://doi.org/10.1073/pnas.0601347103.

[33] Zheng P, Zhou Z. Human cancer immunotherapy with PD-1/PD-L1 blockade. Biomark Cancer 2015;7(2):15−18. Available from: https://doi.org/10.4137/BIC.S29325.

[34] Hamm HE, et al. Mechanism of action of monoclonal antibodies that block the light activation of the guanyl nucleotide-binding protein, transducin. J Biol Chem 1987;262:10831−8.

[35] Tan S, et al. An unexpected N-terminal loop in PD-1 dominates binding by nivolumab. Nat Commun 2017;8:14369. Available from: https://doi.org/10.1038/ncomms14369.

[36] Aldarouish M, Wang C. Trends and advances in tumor immunology and lung cancer immunotherapy. J Exp Clin Cancer Res 2016;35:157. Available from: https://doi.org/10.1186/s13046-016-0439-3.

[37] Akinleye A, Rasool Z. Immune checkpoint inhibitors of PD-L1 as cancer therapeutics. J Hematol Oncol 2019;12(92):1—13. Available from: https://doi.org/10.1186/s13045-019-0779-5.

[38] Wing K, et al. CTLA-4 control over Foxp3+ regulatory T cell function. Science 2008;322:271—5. Available from: https://doi.org/10.1126/science.1160062.

[39] Han Y, et al. Human CD14+ CTLA-4+ regulatory dendritic cells suppress T-cell response by cytotoxic T-lymphocyte antigen- 4-dependent IL-10 and indoleamine-2,3-dioxygenase production in hepatocellular carcinoma. Hepatology 2014;59:567—79. Available from: https://doi.org/10.1002/hep.26694.

[40] Monney L, et al. Th1-specific cell surface protein Tim-3 regulates macrophage activation and severity of an autoimmune disease. Nature 2002;415:536—41. Available from: https://doi.org/10.1038/415536a.

[41] Zarour HM. Upregulation of Tim-3 and PD-1 expression is associated with tumor antigen-specific CD8+ T cell dysfunction in melanoma patients. J Exp Med 2010;207:2175—86. Available from: https://doi.org/10.1084/jem.20100637.

[42] Anderson AC. Tim-3: An emerging target in the cancer immunotherapy landscape. Cancer Immunol Res 2014;2:393—8. Available from: https://doi.org/10.1158/2326-6066.CIR-14-0039.

[43] Nguyen LT, Ohashi PS. Clinical blockade of PD1 and LAG3—potential mechanisms of action. Nat Rev Immunol 2015;15:45—56. Available from: https://doi.org/10.1038/nri3790.

[44] Triebel F, et al. LAG-3, a novel lymphocyte activation gene closely related to CD4. J Exp Med 1990;17:1393—405. Available from: https://doi.org/10.1084/jem.171.5.1393.

[45] Li FJ, et al. Expression of LAG-3 is coincident with the impaired effector function of HBV-specific CD8(+) T cell in HCC patients. Immunol Lett 2013;150:116—22. Available from: https://doi.org/10.1016/j.imlet.2012.12.004.

[46] Minagawa A, et al. Enhancing T cell receptor stability in rejuvenated iPSC-derived T cells improves their use in cancer immunotherapy. Cell Stem Cell 2018;6:850—8. Available from: https://doi.org/10.1016/j.stem.2018.10.005.

[47] Liu M, Guo F. Recent updates on cancer immunotherapy. Precis Clin Med 2018;1(2):65—74. Available from: https://doi.org/10.1093/pcmedi/pby011.

[48] Tan S, Li D, Zhu X. Cancer immunotherapy: Pros, cons and beyond. Biomed Pharmacother 2020;124:109821. Available from: https://doi.org/10.1016/j.biopha.2020.109821.

Immunotherapy for hepatocellular cancer: a review of current status

James Yu[1], Vadim Zaytsev[2], Aimen Farooq[1], Anum Jalil[1], James Wert[1], Zohaib Ahmed[1] and Sarfraz Ahmad[3]

[1]Department of Internal Medicine, AdventHealth, Orlando, FL, United States [2]Department of Internal Medicine, Bridgeport Hospital, Bridgeport, CT, United States [3]AdventHealth Cancer Institute, FSU and UCF Colleges of Medicine, Orlando, FL, United States

Abstract

Hepatocellular carcinoma (HCC) is the most common liver cancer and the fourth common cause of malignancy-related death worldwide. Unfortunately, most patients with HCC are first diagnosed at advanced and metastatic stages which require systemic management including chemotherapy, molecularly targeted therapy, or immunotherapy (IT). HCC has been suggested as a relatively chemotherapy-refractory cancer so recent systemic therapy developments have been focused on targeted or IT. Recently, IT demonstrated promising anti-HCC effects in different settings of treatment. Also, multiple ongoing clinical trials are currently evaluating immune checkpoint inhibitors (ICIs) for HCC as monotherapy or combination therapy in different settings. This chapter reviews the current knowledge of IT for HCC with recently finished or ongoing clinical trials that may hold promise for better management and improved outcomes of patients with HCC.

Keywords: Hepatocellular cancer; immunotherapy; immune checkpoint inhibitors; combination therapy; clinical trials; survival outcomes; response rates; signaling pathways

Abbreviations

AEs	adverse events
CD	cluster differentiation
CI	confidence interval
CTLA	cytotoxic T-lymphocyte-associated protein
DC	dendritic cells
DCR	disease control rate
Deb	drug-eluting bead

Ganji Purnachandra Nagaraju, Sarfraz Ahmad (eds.)
Theranostics and Precision Medicine for the Management of Hepatocellular Carcinoma, Volume 3

245

FDA	Food and Drug Administration
FGFRs	fibroblast growth factor receptors
HCC	hepatocellular carcinoma
HR	Hazard ratio
ICI	immune checkpoint inhibitor
IL	interleukin
IT	immunotherapy
MDSCs	myeloid-derived suppressor cells
mo	months
NK	natural killer
ORR	objective response rate
OS	overall survival
PD-1	programmed cell death protein 1
PDGFR	platelet-derived growth factor receptor
PFS	progression-free survival
RECISTs	response evaluation criteria in solid tumors
SD	stable disease
TACE	transarterial chemoembolization
TKIs	tyrosine kinase inhibitors
TAAs	tumor-associated antigens
Tx	therapy
VEGF	vascular endothelial growth factor

Introduction

Hepatocellular carcinoma (HCC) is the most common primary liver malignancy and a leading cause of cancer-related mortality [1]. It is usually diagnosed late and the majority of patients present at an advanced and/or metastatic stages and have a poor prognosis with approximately 6–20 months median survival after diagnosis [2]. Although in early stage HCC may be treated by surgery or locoregional therapy, most patients are not eligible because of advanced stage or underlying liver dysfunction which leads to a limited number of approved therapeutic options for these patients. At this time, sorafenib and lenvatinib are the approved first-line treatments for unresectable HCC. Findings from the SHARP trial showed that sorafenib, an oral multityrosine kinase inhibitor (TKI), significantly prolonged survival by approximately 3 months compared to placebo [3]. Another multi-TKI, lenvatinib, was approved for first line when the REFLECT study revealed noninferiority of lenvatinib compared to sorafenib [4]. Resistance of HCC to a number or medications and liver dysfunction at the time of diagnosis impedes the development of prospective cytotoxic drugs. Recently there has been significant progress in systemic treatments, and regorafenib, ramucirumab, and cabozantinib have been recommended as second-line treatment options. IT has been a breakthrough in oncology, and given the limited numbers of systemic treatment options, immune system checkpoints, and target therapy agent exploration in HCC have dramatically changed treatment approaches.

Hepatocellular carcinoma immunology

The liver has a unique immune-regulatory environment because it needs to be responsive to gut pathogen exposure but also adapted to the nonpathogenic antigens which are delivered through the portal vein. This immunotolerant capacity explains the relatively low rates of allograft rejection [5]. The underlying inflammatory process associated with liver dysfunction and cirrhosis leads to cancer formation, and when HCC has developed there is an antitumor response from the immune system against tumor-associated antigens (TAAs). Often this reaction is dysfunctional, with a higher ratio of $CD4^+$ to $CD8^+$ cells with an increased number of $CD4^+$ $CD25^+$ regulatory cells playing a critical role in maintaining self-tolerance [6].

In addition, there are multiple other mechanisms to create an immunosuppressive environment, such as expansion of myeloid-derived suppressor cells (MDSCs) that can induce immunosuppressive $CD4^+$ T cells' interleukin 10 (IL-10) production by increasing activity of arginase [7], and a hypofunctionality of dendritic cells (DCs), and natural killer (NK) cells that cause a failure of TAA processing and presentation [8]. In addition, expression PD-L1 is the ligand for the receptor-programmed cell death-1 (PD-1), which causes $CD8^+$ T-cells apoptosis in HCC patients and inhibition of immune response [9]. Another checkpoint molecule, cytotoxic T-lymphocyte-associated protein 4 (CTLA-4), could be activated by tumor and decrease the immune response (Fig. 16.1).

Many different mechanisms may restrict TAA-specific T-cell reactions in HCC: abnormal TAA presentation and processing by DCs, production of the immunosuppressive IL-10, immune suppression by Tregs, and downregulation by PD-1/PD-L1 pathway (Fig. 16.1).

Immune checkpoint inhibitors

Multiple cancer medications that target the PD-L/-PD-1 and CTLA-4 pathways are being evaluated in HCC patients. These include antibodies against CTLA-4 on T cells such as ipilimumab and antibodies that target PD-1 and PD-L1 pathway such as pembrolizumab, nivolumab, durvalumab, and atezolizumab (Tables 16.1 and 16.2).

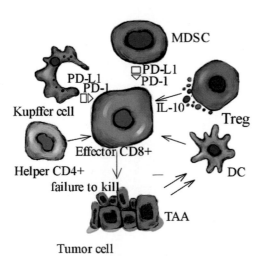

FIGURE 16.1 Immunobiology and molecular interactions in hepatocellular carcinoma.

TABLE 16.1 A summary of the results from selected key studies testing immune checkpoint inhibitors in hepatocellular carcinoma.

Study author/year (ref. no.)	Treatment (lines of therapy)	Target IT	Phase	Patient group (number of patients)	Outcomes				Clinical trial identifier
					ORR	DCR	PFS	OS	
AB El-Khoueiry 2017 [10]	Nivolumab (first and second line)	PD-1	1/2	Prior sorafenib Tx (182) Sorafenib naïve (80)	19% 23%	63% 63%	–	15.6 mo 28.6 mo	NCT01658878 (CheckMate 040)
J Edeline 2020 [11]	Nivolumab (first line)	PD-1	3	Advanced HCC (total 743) Nivolumab (371) vs sorafenib (372)	15% vs 7%	–	3.7 mo vs 3.8 mo	16.4 mo vs 14.7 mo	NCT02576509 (CheckMate 459)
AX Zhu 2018 [12]	Pembrolizumab (second line)	PD-1	2	Prior sorafenib Tx (104)	17%	62%	4.9 mo	12.9 mo	NCT02702414 (KEYNOTE224)
RS Finn 2020 [13]	Pembrolizumab (second line)	PD-1	3	Prior sorafenib Tx (total 413) Pembrolizumab (278) vs placebo (135)	18% vs 4%	62% vs 53%	3 mo vs 2.8 mo	13.9 mo vs 10.6 mo	NCT02702401 (KEYNOTE-240)
S Qin 2020 [14]	Camrelizumab (second line)	PD-1	2	Prior systemic Tx (217)	15%	44%	2.1 mo	13.8 mo	NCT02989922
ZA Wainberg 2017 [15]	Durvalumab (second line)	PD-L1	1/2	Advanced HCC (total 40, 37 prior sorafenib)	10%	33%	2.7 mo	13.2 mo	NCT01693562
A He 2020 [16]	Nivolumab + ipilimumab (second line)	PD-1 + CLTA4	1/2	Prior sorafenib Tx (148)	31%	49%	–	37% at 30 mo	NCT01658878 (CheckMate 040-Subgroup)
M Lee 2019 [17]	Atezolizumab + bevacizumab (first line)	PD-L1 + anti-VEGF	1b	Systemic naive unresectable HCC (60)	36%	71%	7.3 mo	–	NCT02715531
RS Finn 2020 [18]	Atezolizumab + bevacizumab (first line)	PD-L1 + anti-VEGF	3	Systemic naive unresectable HCC (total 501) Atezolizumab + bevacizumab (336) vs sorafenib (165)	27% vs 12%	74% vs 55%	6.8 mo vs 4.3 mo	67% vs 55% at 12 mo	NCT03434379 (IMbrave 150 trial)

| RS Finn 2020 [19] | Pembrolizumab + lenvatinib (first line) | PD-1 + multi-TKI | 1b | Systemic naive unresectable HCC (104) | 36% | 88% | 8.6 mo | 22 mo | NCT03006926 |
| J Xu 2020 [20] | Camrelizumab + apatinib (first and second line) | PD-1 + anti-VEGF | 2 | Advanced HCC (total 190); Treatment-naive (70) Refractory/intolerant to first-line Tx (120) | 34% 23% | – | 5.7 mo 5.5 mo | 74.7% 68.2% at 12 mo | NCT03463876 (RESCUE) |

IT, immunotherapy; ORR, objective response rate; DCR, disease control rate; PFS, progression-free survival; OS, overall survival; mo, months; Tx, therapy; HCC, hepatocellular carcinoma; PD-1, programmed cell death protein 1; PD-L1, programmed death-ligand 1; TKI, tyrosine kinase inhibitor; VEGF, vascular endothelial growth factor.

TABLE 16.2 Ongoing immune checkpoint inhibitors' trials in hepatocellular carcinoma (phase III).

Treatment (line of therapy) (Ref. No.)	Target IT	Patient group	Clinical trial identifier	Progression	Primary/projected completion dates
Pembrolizumab vs placebo (second line) [21]	PD-1	Prior systemically treated with advanced HCC, Asian population	NCT03062358 (KEYNOTE-394)	Active, not recruiting	April 17, 2021
Tislelizumab vs sorafenib (first line) [22]	PD-1	No prior systemic Tx with unresectable HCC	NCT03412773	Active, not recruiting	June 20, 2021
Durvalumab monotherapy vs durvalumab + tremelimumab vs sorafenib (first line) [23]	PD-L1PD-L1 + CTLA4	No prior systemic Tx with unresectable HCC	NCT03298451 (HIMALAYA)	Active, not recruiting	December 30, 2020
Nivolumab + ipilimumab vs sorafenib/lenvatinib (first line) [24]	PD-1 + CLTA4	Untreated advanced HCC	NCT04039607 (CheckMate 9DW)	Recruiting	March 27, 2023
Pembrolizumab + lenvatinib vs placebo + lenvatinib (first line) [25]	PD-1 + multi-TKI	No prior systemic Tx with unresectable HCC	NCT03713593	Active, not recruiting	May 13, 2022
Camrelizumab + apatinib vs sorafenib (first line) [26]	PD-1 + anti-VEGF	No prior systemic Tx with advanced HCC	NCT03764293	Recruiting	December, 2021
Nivolumab vs placebo (adjuvant) [27]	PD-1	HCC with complete radiological response after surgery or local ablation	NCT03383458 (CheckMate 9DX)	Recruiting	January 23, 2023
Pembrolizumab vs placebo (adjuvant) [28]	PD-1	HCC with complete radiological response after surgery or local ablation	NCT03867084 (KEYNOTE-937)	Recruiting	June 30, 2025

IT, immunotherapy; *Tx*, therapy; *HCC*, hepatocellular carcinoma; *PD-1*, programmed cell death protein 1; *PD-L1*, programmed death-ligand 1; *TKI*, tyrosine kinase inhibitor; *VEGF*, vascular endothelial growth factor; *CTLA4*, cytotoxic T-lymphocyte-associated protein 4.

Checkpoint inhibitors for hepatocellular carcinoma monotherapy

Nivolumab

This anti-PD-1 monoclonal antibody is one of the most investigated immunotherapies in HCC. Nivolumab has been investigated in HCC as a first-line therapy option. In 2017 the Checkmate 040 phase I/II, open-label, noncomparative trial with 262 patients, including 182 patients previously treated with sorafenib, nivolumab demonstrated an acceptable safety profile with promising efficacy. Objective response rates (ORRs) were 22.5% and 18.7% in sorafenib untreated and treated groups, respectively [10,29]. Based on these results, the Food and Drug Administration (FDA) approved nivolumab for the treatment of HCC patients pretreated with sorafenib [30]. Nivolumab is the first ICI approved by the FDA for HCC.

In succession, a phase III, randomized study (Checkpoint 459) compared sorafenib versus nivolumab as first-line treatment in advanced HCC population. An abstract for 743 patients, disclosed in February 2020, showed median overall survival (OS) was 16.4 months for nivolumab versus 14.7 months for sorafenib without statistical significance [hazard ratio (HR) 0.85 (95% CI 0.72–1.02); $P = .0752$]. However, the abstract reported nivolumab showed a superior quality of life with reduced side effects compared to sorafenib [11] At the time of this publication, the Checkpoint 459 trial's full article has not yet been released.

Pembrolizumab

This is another anti-PD-1 monoclonal antibody investigated as a second-line therapy after failing with initial sorafenib treatment. In 2018 the KEYNOTE-224 phase II, open-label, noncomparative trial with 104 advanced HCC patients who were refractory or intolerant to sorafenib received pembrolizumab. In this study, pembrolizumab revealed a safety profile with a promising efficacy of 17% ORR and 44% stable disease (SD) [12]. Based on these results, the FDA approved pembrolizumab for HCC previously treated with sorafenib in November 2019 [31].

In succession, a phase III, randomized study (KEYNOTE-240) compared pembrolizumab versus a placebo as a second-line treatment in advanced HCC previously treated with sorafenib in a 413-patient population. Pembrolizumab demonstrated improvement in OS and progression-free survival (PFS) compared to the placebo but was statistically not significant [OS: 13.9 vs 10.6 months, HR 0.78, (95% CI 0.61–1.00); $P = .0238$ / PFS: 3.0 vs 2.8 months, HR, 0.72, (95% CI, 0.57–0.90); $P = .0022$]. However, the ORR was higher for pembrolizumab versus placebo (18.3% vs 4.4%) [13]. Another phase III study, KEYNOTE-394, is underway with similar design to KEYNOTE-240 with Asian population [21].

Tislelizumab

Also known as BGB-A317, this is another anti-PD-1 antibody developed by BeiGene. A phase IA/B trial with multiple different advanced solid malignancies including 50 patients of HCC demonstrated tislelizumab monotherapy had an acceptable safety profile with antitumor activity [32]. A phase III, randomized, multicenter trial is ongoing to evaluate the efficacy and safety of tislelizumab compared to sorafenib in advanced HCC patients as a first-line treatment. This trial aims to verify the noninferiority of tislelizumab compared with sorafenib as the first line with OS as the primary endpoint (NCT03412773) [22,33]. At the time of publication, there are no available interim data.

Camrelizumab

Camrelizumab (SHR-1210) is an anti-PD-1 antibody developed by Jiangsu Hengrui Medicine Co. in China. A phase I trial with 58 advanced solid tumors including HCC demonstrated a safety profile with encoring antitumor efficacy [34]. A phase II trial was performed in 217 advanced HCC patients who were refractory or intolerant to prior systemic therapy [14]. The ORR was 14.7% and median OS was 13.8 months. Around 1% (2/217) had grade 5 treatment-related adverse events (AEs), which was judged an acceptable toxicity in pretreated advanced HCC patients by other experts [29].

Durvalumab

This is an anti-PD-L1 antibody. A phase I/II trial of durvalumab monotherapy for 40 advanced HCC patients with 93% previously treated by sorafenib demonstrated an acceptable safety of 20% grade 3−4 treatment-related adverse effects without grade 5 with promising antitumor activity of 10% response rate [15]. A phase III trial of durvalumab as a monotherapy or a combination treatment with tremelimumab as a first-line treatment is under evaluation (as described below in this chapter).

Tremelimumab

Tremelimumab is an anticytotoxic T-lymphocyte-associated protein 4 inhibitor (anti-CTLA-4 antibody). Tremelimumab monotherapy was investigated for 21 HCC patients with chronic hepatitis C infection. The treatment was well tolerated, with some patients having grade 3−4 toxicity with some promising antitumor activity of 17.6% objective response and 76.4% disease control rate [35]. A phase II trial of tremelimumab monotherapy compared to durvalumab monotherapy or a durvalumab-tremelimumab combination is underway [36].

Combination treatment

There have been some suggestions that anticancer effects of immune checkpoint inhibitors (ICIs) might be enhanced if these agents were combined with different treatments. This section introduces several combination treatments that are anticipated to show promising efficacy for HCC (Tables 16.1 and 16.2).

Combination between two different immune checkpoint inhibitors

Nivolumab (anti-PD-1 Ab) with ipilimumab (anti-CTLA4 Ab)

Ipilimumab is an anti-CTLA-4 antibody which has been evaluated as a combined therapy with nivolumab in HCC in different settings. This nivolumab with ipilimumab combined therapy demonstrated promising efficacy in phase III randomized studies in advanced melanoma and nonsmall cell lung cancer as a first-line treatment in 2018 and 2019, respectively [37,38]. This therapy targeting two different immune checkpoints is under investigation. The combination demonstrated a promising efficacy with an acceptable safety profile in subgroup investigation in the Checkmate 040 population with ORR of 31% and the 30-month OS rate of 37% [16,39]. In March 2020, the FDA approved this combination [40]. A phase III study (CheckMate 9DW) for nivolumab and ipilimumab combined treatment as a first-line in advanced HCC compared to sorafenib or lenvatinib is under investigation [24]. A phase II trial is underway to investigate ipilimumab and nivolumab combination as neoadjuvant therapy in HCC [41].

Durvalumab (anti-PD-L1 Ab) with tremelimumab (anti-CTLA4 Ab)

Tremelimumab is a cytotoxic T-lymphocyte-associated protein 4 inhibitor and a combination of tremelimumab and durvalumab has also been developed. In a study with 10 advanced HCC patients and 12 biliary tract carcinomas patients, this combination was well tolerated and revealed promising activity of a 20% response rate with a 60% disease control rate in the small cohort of 10 advanced HCC patients [42]. Currently, a phase II study for this combination regime in advanced HCC with either progressed/intolerant to or refused sorafenib or other TKI treatment is underway [36]. In addition, a phase III trial is now underway to evaluate the efficacy of both durvalumab plus tremelimumab combination therapy and durvalumab monotherapy as a first-line setting versus sorafenib in advanced HCC (HIMALAYA) [23,43].

Combination between immune checkpoint inhibitors with molecularly targeted agents

Atezolizumab + bevacizumab

Atezolizumab is another anti-PDL-1 antibody and a combination regime of atezolizumab with bevacizumab, an antivascular endothelial growth factor (VEGF) therapy, is under evaluation for other solid cancers, including advanced renal cell carcinoma, and has demonstrated promising antitumor activity [44]. Over-expression of VEGF has been suggested to be one of the key mechanisms of the development and progression of liver cancer, which makes this combination a reasonable target agent in HCC [45,46]. A phase Ib study investigated the bevacizumab and atezolizumab combined therapy in systemic therapy-naive unresectable HCC population. This combination demonstrated an acceptable safety profile with promising efficiency with an ORR of 36% and a median PFS of 7.3 months [17].

In succession, a phase III randomized trial (IMbrave 150) compared sorafenib to bevacizumab and atezolizumab combination as a first-line management in unresectable HCC. With 8.6 months of median follow-up, median OS of combined therapy was superior to that of sorafenib (HR for death 0.58, 95% CI 0.42–0.79, $P < .001$/survival at 12 months, 67% vs 55%), as well as PFS (6.8 vs 4.3 months, HR for death or disease progression 0.59, 95% CI 0.47–0.76, $P < .001$). The ORRs were also superior in the combination compared to sorafenib (27% vs 12%). The grade 3 or 4 AE rate was similar in each group (57% vs 55%) [18]. Based on the IMbrave 150 trial, the FDA approved this combination as a first-line treatment for unresectable or metastatic HCC with naive systemic therapy [47]. This combination was considered as a reasonable first-line alternative management option for a healthy population with no worse than Child-Turcotte-Pugh A cirrhosis [48].

Pembrolizumab + lenvatinib

Lenvatinib is a multi-TKI with various targets including *FGFR1–4, VEGFR1–3, c-Kit, RET*, and *PDGFRA*. A phase III randomized study in HCC population demonstrated that lenvatinib is noninferior compared to sorafenib as a first-line therapy in unresectable HCC [4]. In preclinical studies, the lenvatinib was shown to enhance anti-PD-1 antibodies anti-tumor activity, and clinical trials for this combination have been evaluated in various types of malignancies including HCC [49]. A phase Ib study was done in unresectable HCC for this combination. Sixty-seven percent of patients had grade 3 or higher treatment-related AEs with 3% experiencing grade 5. The most common grade 3 treatment-related AE was hypertension (17%), which was judged as acceptable safety. By response evaluation criteria in solid tumor (RECIST) criteria, ORR was 36.0% with 88% of disease control rates. Median PFS was 8.6 months by RECIST criteria and median OS was 22.0 months [19]. Currently, a phase III randomized study is underway to evaluate the lenvatinib plus pembrolizumab combination regime versus lenvatinib plus placebo as a first-line therapy in unresectable HCC [25].

Camrelizumab + apatinib

Recently, a phase 2 nonrandomized open-label trial evaluated a combination of camrelizumab plus apatinib (a VEGFR-2 TKI) in treatment-naive (70 patients) or refractory/intolerant to first-line targeted therapy (120 patients). This combination showed manageable safety with promising efficacy of ORR; 34.3% (24/70) in the first-line and 22.5% (27/120) in the second-line treatment cohort [20]. Currently, a phase III trial is underway to investigate survival benefit of this combination with sorafenib as a first-line systemic therapy [26]. No interim data are available for this phase III trial at the time of publication.

Combination between immune checkpoint inhibitors with local therapy

Nivolumab + transarterial chemoembolization

Combination therapy of nivolumab plus drug-eluting bead transarterial chemoembolization (deb-TACE) has started and a phase I trial of this therapy is under investigation. In this study, nivolumab is administered every 2 weeks at various times relative to deb-TACE in unresectable HCC patients. Interim data in July 2019 with nine patients revealed a safe and tolerable profile with no cases of dose-limiting toxicity, treatment-related liver failure, or grade 5 AEs. It also showed two (22%) partial remission and seven (78%) SD with 71% 12 months OS [50]. A phase II study (IMMUTACE) of this treatment with nivolumab administration 2—3 days after TACE is underway to evaluate the safety and efficacy with the response rate set as the primary endpoint [51]. In the phase III CheckMate 459 study, nivolumab revealed superior quality of life and favorable safety compared to sorafenib (grade 3 or AEs 4, 22% vs 49%). Based on this, anti-PD-1 antibodies were suggested to be ideal as adjuvant therapies [11,52]. Currently, a phase III randomized study (CheckMate 9DX) of nivolumab as an adjuvant setting versus placebo for HCC that underwent a curative resection or ablation is underway [27].

Pembrolizumab + TACE

The PETAL study is an ongoing phase I/II study evaluating pembrolizumab as an adjuvant setting after transarterial chemoembolization (TACE) [53]. Interim data on October 2019 revealed pembrolizumab following TACE showed a tolerable safety profile without any evidence of synergistic toxicity [54]. Pembrolizumab is also under investigation as an adjuvant. A phase III randomized trial (KEYNOTE-937) for pembrolizumab versus placebo in HCC with complete radiological response after local ablation or surgical resection is underway [28].

Conclusions and future perspective

HCC is the most common primary liver malignancy and the most common cause of cancer-related morbidity and death in chronic liver disease. Sorafenib and other molecular-targeted agents including lenvatinib have recently demonstrated survival benefits in advanced HCC. However, the prognosis of HCC patients is still quite poor, and further efforts to explore new treatment options are needed. IT is a promising frontier for HCC management and many novel strategies of mono or combination therapies are currently under development. As a monotherapy, ICIs including nivolumab and pembrolizumab demonstrated around 15%—20% response rate in phase III studies without significant benefit in relapse-free survival or OS [11,13]. However, very recently, the atezolizumab and bevacizumab combination regime showed significant improvement in response rate and OS and PFS as first-line therapy compared to sorafenib [18]. These results could mean that checkpoint blockade IT may be maximizing its efficacy in combination therapy. Currently, many phase III clinical trials are underway to investigate the efficacy of ICI in different settings, including as first- or second-line therapy, adjuvant with monotherapy or in combination with other ICI, TKI, or locoregional therapy. We anticipate that the accumulation of IT knowledge for HCC will continue to develop with these ongoing clinical trials.

References

[1] Bray F, Ferlay J, Soerjomataram I, Siegel RL, Torre LA, Jemal A. Global cancer statistics 2018: GLOBOCAN estimates of incidence and mortality worldwide for 36 cancers in 185 countries. CA Cancer J Clin 2018;68 (6):394—424. Available from: https://doi.org/10.3322/caac.21492.

[2] A new prognostic system for hepatocellular carcinoma: a retrospective study of 435 patients. 1998-Hepatology. Wiley Online Library, https://aasldpubs.onlinelibrary.wiley.com/doi/abs/10.1002/hep.510280322; 2020 [accessed 22.11.20].

[3] Llovet JM, Ricci S, Mazzaferro V, et al. Sorafenib in advanced hepatocellular carcinoma. N Engl J Med 2008;359(4):378–90. Available from: https://doi.org/10.1056/NEJMoa0708857.

[4] Kudo M, Finn RS, Qin S, et al. Lenvatinib vs sorafenib in first-line treatment of patients with unresectable hepatocellular carcinoma: a randomised phase 3 non-inferiority trial. Lancet 2018;391 (10126):1163–73. Available from: https://doi.org/10.1016/S0140-6736(18)30207-1.

[5] Takatsuki M, Uemoto S, Inomata Y, et al. Weaning of immunosuppression in living donor liver transplant recipients. Transplantation 2001;72(3):449–54. Available from: https://doi.org/10.1097/00007890-200108150-00016.

[6] Fu J, Xu D, Liu Z, et al. Increased regulatory T cells correlate with CD8 T-cell impairment and poor survival in hepatocellular carcinoma patients. Gastroenterology 2007;132(7):2328–39. Available from: https://doi.org/10.1053/j.gastro.2007.03.102.

[7] Hoechst B, Ormandy LA, Ballmaier M, et al. A new population of myeloid-derived suppressor cells in hepatocellular carcinoma patients induces CD4(+)CD25(+)Foxp3(+) T cells. Gastroenterology 2008;135 (1):234–43. Available from: https://doi.org/10.1053/j.gastro.2008.03.020.

[8] Ormandy LA, Färber A, Cantz T, et al. Direct ex vivo analysis of dendritic cells in patients with hepatocellular carcinoma. World J Gastroenterol WJG 2006;12(20):3275–82. Available from: https://doi.org/10.3748/wjg.v12.i20.3275.

[9] Shi F, Shi M, Zeng Z, et al. PD-1 and PD-L1 upregulation promotes CD8(+) T-cell apoptosis and postoperative recurrence in hepatocellular carcinoma patients. Int J Cancer 2011;128(4):887–96. Available from: https://doi.org/10.1002/ijc.25397.

[10] El-Khoueiry AB, Sangro B, Yau T, et al. Nivolumab in patients with advanced hepatocellular carcinoma (CheckMate 040): an open-label, non-comparative, phase 1/2 dose escalation and expansion trial. Lancet 2017;389(10088):2492–502. Available from: https://doi.org/10.1016/S0140-6736(17)31046-2.

[11] Edeline J, Yau T, Park J-W, et al. CheckMate 459: health-related quality of life (HRQoL) in a randomized, multicenter phase III study of nivolumab (NIVO) vs sorafenib (SOR) as first-line (1L) treatment in patients (pts) with advanced hepatocellular carcinoma (aHCC). J Clin Oncol 2020;38(4_suppl):483. Available from: https://doi.org/10.1200/JCO.2020.38.4_suppl.483.

[12] Zhu AX, Finn RS, Edeline J, et al. Pembrolizumab in patients with advanced hepatocellular carcinoma previously treated with sorafenib (KEYNOTE-224): a non-randomised, open-label phase 2 trial. Lancet Oncol 2018;19(7):940–52. Available from: https://doi.org/10.1016/S1470-2045(18)30351-6.

[13] Finn RS, Ryoo BY, Merle P, et al. Pembrolizumab as second-line therapy in patients with advanced hepatocellular carcinoma in KEYNOTE-240: a randomized, double-blind, phase III trial. J Clin Oncol 2020;38 (3):193–202. Available from: https://doi.org/10.1200/JCO.19.01307.

[14] Qin S, Ren Z, Meng Z, et al. Camrelizumab in patients with previously treated advanced hepatocellular carcinoma: a multicentre, open-label, parallel-group, randomised, phase 2 trial. Lancet Oncol 2020;21(4):571–80. Available from: https://doi.org/10.1016/S1470-2045(20)30011-5.

[15] Wainberg ZA, Segal NH, Jaeger D, et al. Safety and clinical activity of durvalumab monotherapy in patients with hepatocellular carcinoma (HCC). J Clin Oncol 2017;35(15_suppl):4071. Available from: https://doi.org/10.1200/JCO.2017.35.15_suppl.4071.

[16] He AR, Yau T, Hsu C, et al. Nivolumab (NIVO) + ipilimumab (IPI) combination therapy in patients (pts) with advanced hepatocellular carcinoma (aHCC): subgroup analyses from CheckMate 040. J Clin Oncol 2020;38(4_suppl):512. Available from: https://doi.org/10.1200/JCO.2020.38.4_suppl.512.

[17] Lee M, Ryoo B-Y, Hsu C-H, et al. LBA39 - randomised efficacy and safety results for atezolizumab (Atezo) + bevacizumab (Bev) in patients (pts) with previously untreated, unresectable hepatocellular carcinoma (HCC). Ann Oncol 2019;30:v875. Available from: https://doi.org/10.1093/annonc/mdz394.030.

[18] Finn RS, Qin S, Ikeda M, et al. Atezolizumab plus bevacizumab in unresectable hepatocellular carcinoma. N Engl J Med 2020;382(20):1894–905. Available from: https://doi.org/10.1056/NEJMoa1915745.

[19] Finn RS, Ikeda M, Zhu AX, et al. Phase Ib study of lenvatinib plus pembrolizumab in patients with unresectable hepatocellular carcinoma. J Clin Oncol 2020;38(26):2960–70. Available from: https://doi.org/10.1200/JCO.20.00808.

[20] Xu J, Shen J, Gu S, et al. Camrelizumab in combination with apatinib in patients with advanced hepatocellular carcinoma (RESCUE): a non-randomized, open-label, phase 2 trial. Clin Cancer Res 2020. Available from: https://doi.org/10.1158/1078-0432.CCR-20-2571.

[21] Sharp M, Corp D. A phase III randomized double-blind study of pembrolizumab plus best supportive care vs. placebo plus best supportive care as second-line therapy in Asian subjects with previously systemically treated advanced hepatocellular carcinoma (KEYNOTE-394). https://clinicaltrials.gov/ct2/show/NCT03062358; 2020 [accessed 11.11.20].

[22] Qin S, Finn RS, Kudo M, et al. A phase 3, randomized, open-label, multicenter study to compare the efficacy and safety of tislelizumab, an anti-PD-1 antibody, vs sorafenib as first-line treatment in patients with advanced hepatocellular carcinoma. J Clin Oncol 2018;36(15_suppl):TPS3110. Available from: https://doi.org/10.1200/JCO.2018.36.15_suppl.TPS3110.

[23] AstraZeneca. A randomized, open-label, multi-center phase III study of durvalumab and tremelimumab as first-line treatment in patients with advanced hepatocellular carcinoma. https://clinicaltrials.gov/ct2/show/NCT03298451; 2020 [accessed 16.11.20].

[24] Bristol-Myers Squibb. A randomized, multi-center, phase 3 study of Nivolumab in combination with Ipilimumab compared to sorafenib or lenvatinib as first-line treatment in participants with advanced hepatocellular carcinoma. https://clinicaltrials.gov/ct2/show/NCT04039607; 2020 [accessed 17.11.20].

[25] Safety and efficacy of lenvatinib (E7080/MK-7902) in combination with pembrolizumab (MK-3475) versus lenvatinib as first-line therapy in participants with advanced hepatocellular carcinoma (MK-7902-002/E7080-G000-311/LEAP-002). https://clinicaltrials.gov/ct2/show/NCT03713593; 2020 [accessed 19.11.20].

[26] Jiangsu HengRui Medicine Co., Ltd. A randomized, ppen-label, international, multi-center, phase 3 clinical study of PD-1 antibody SHR-1210 plus apatinib mesylate vs sorafenib as first-line therapy in patients with advanced hepatocellular carcinoma (HCC) who have not previously received systemic therapy. https://clinicaltrials.gov/ct2/show/NCT03764293; 2019 [accessed 12.11.20].

[27] A study of nivolumab in participants with hepatocellular carcinoma who are at high risk of recurrence after curative hepatic resection or ablation. https://clinicaltrials.gov/ct2/show/NCT03383458; 2020 [accessed 22.11.20].

[28] Merck Sharp & Dohme Corp. A phase 3 double-blinded, two-arm study to evaluate the safety and efficacy of pembrolizumab (MK-3475) vs placebo as adjuvant therapy in participants with hepatocellular carcinoma and complete radiological response after surgical resection or local ablation (KEYNOTE-937). https://clinicaltrials.gov/ct2/show/NCT03867084; 2020 [accessed 19.11.20].

[29] Ghavimi S, Apfel T, Azimi H, Persaud A, Pyrsopoulos NT. Management and treatment of hepatocellular carcinoma with immunotherapy: a review of current and future options. J Clin Transl Hepatol 2020;8(2):168−76. Available from: https://doi.org/10.14218/JCTH.2020.00001.

[30] Okusaka T, Ikeda M. Immunotherapy for hepatocellular carcinoma: current status and future perspectives. ESMO Open 2018;3(Suppl 1). Available from: https://doi.org/10.1136/esmoopen-2018-000455.

[31] Research C for DE and. FDA grants accelerated approval to pembrolizumab for hepatocellular carcinoma. https://www.fda.gov/drugs/fda-grants-accelerated-approval-pembrolizumab-hepatocellular-carcinoma + ; Published online December 20, 2019 [accessed 12.11.20].

[32] Desai J, Deva S, Lee JS, et al. Phase IA/IB study of single-agent tislelizumab, an investigational anti-PD-1 antibody, in solid tumors. J Immunother Cancer 2020;8(1). Available from: https://doi.org/10.1136/jitc-2019-000453.

[33] BeiGene. RATIONALE-301: a randomized, open-label, multicenter phase 3 study to compare the efficacy and safety of BGB-A317 vs sorafenib as first-line treatment in patients with unresectable hepatocellular carcinoma. https://clinicaltrials.gov/ct2/show/NCT03412773; 2020 [accessed 12.11.20].

[34] Huang J, Mo H, Wu D, et al. Phase I study of the anti-PD-1 antibody SHR-1210 in patients with advanced solid tumors. J Clin Oncol 2017;35(15_suppl):e15572. Available from: https://doi.org/10.1200/JCO.2017.35.15_suppl.e15572.

[35] Sangro B, Gomez-Martin C, de la Mata M, et al. A clinical trial of CTLA-4 blockade with tremelimumab in patients with hepatocellular carcinoma and chronic hepatitis C. J Hepatol 2013;59(1):81−8. Available from: https://doi.org/10.1016/j.jhep.2013.02.022.

[36] MedImmune L.L.C. A study of safety, tolerability, and clinical activity of durvalumab and tremelimumab administered as monotherapy, or durvalumab in combination with tremelimumab or bevacizumab in subjects with advanced hepatocellular carcinoma. https://clinicaltrials.gov/ct2/show/NCT02519348; 2020 [accessed 16.11.20].

[37] Hodi FS, Chiarion-Sileni V, Gonzalez R, et al. Nivolumab plus ipilimumab or nivolumab alone vs ipilimumab alone in advanced melanoma (CheckMate 067): 4-year outcomes of a multicentre, randomised, phase 3 trial. Lancet Oncol 2018;19(11):1480−92. Available from: https://doi.org/10.1016/S1470-2045(18)30700-9.

[38] Hellmann MD, Paz-Ares L, Caro RB, Zurawski B, Kim S-W, Costa EC, et al. Nivolumab plus ipilimumab in advanced non-small-cell lung cancer. N Engl J Med 2020;381:2020−31. Available from: https://www.nejm.org/doi/10.1056/NEJMoa1910231?url_ver = Z39.88-2003&rfr_id = ori:rid:crossref.org&rfr_dat = cr_pub%20%200pubmed.

[39] Tella SH, Mahipal A, Kommalapati A, Jin Z. Evaluating the safety and efficacy of nivolumab in patients with advanced hepatocellular carcinoma: evidence to date. OncoTargets Ther 2019;12:10335−42. Available from: https://doi.org/10.2147/OTT.S214870.

[40] Research C for DE and. FDA grants accelerated approval to nivolumab and ipilimumab combination for hepatocellular carcinoma. https://www.fda.gov/drugs/resources-information-approved-drugs/fda-grants-accelerated-approval-nivolumab-and-ipilimumab-combination-hepatocellular-carcinoma; Published online March 11, 2020 [accessed 12.11.20].

[41] Safety and bioactivity of ipilimumab and nivolumab combination prior to liver resection in hepatocellular carcinoma. https://clinicaltrials.gov/ct2/show/NCT03682276; 2020 [accessed 12.11.20].

[42] Floudas CS, Xie C, Brar G, et al. Combined immune checkpoint inhibition (ICI) with tremelimumab and durvalumab in patients with advanced hepatocellular carcinoma (HCC) or biliary tract carcinomas (BTC). J Clin Oncol 2019;37(4_suppl):336. Available from: https://doi.org/10.1200/JCO.2019.37.4_suppl.336.

[43] Abou-Alfa GK, Chan SL, Furuse J, et al. A randomized, multicenter phase 3 study of durvalumab (D) and tremelimumab (T) as first-line treatment in patients with unresectable hepatocellular carcinoma (HCC): HIMALAYA study. J Clin Oncol 2018;36(15_suppl):TPS4144. Available from: https://doi.org/10.1200/JCO.2018.36.15_suppl.TPS4144.

[44] Rini BI, Powles T, Atkins MB, et al. Atezolizumab plus bevacizumab vs sunitinib in patients with previously untreated metastatic renal cell carcinoma (IMmotion151): a multi-centre, open-label, phase 3, randomised controlled trial. Lancet. 2019;393(10189):2404−15. Available from: https://doi.org/10.1016/S0140-6736(19)30723-8.

[45] The Role of Angiogenesis in Hepatocellular Carcinoma | Clinical Cancer Research. https://clincancerres.aacrjournals.org/content/25/3/912.abstract [accessed 19.11.20].

[46] Zhu AX, Duda DG, Sahani DV, Jain RK. HCC and angiogenesis: possible targets and future directions. Nat Rev Clin Oncol 2011;8(5):292−301. Available from: https://doi.org/10.1038/nrclinonc.2011.30.

[47] Research C for DE and. FDA approves atezolizumab plus bevacizumab for unresectable hepatocellular carcinoma. https://www.fda.gov/drugs/drug-approvals-and-databases/fda-approves-atezolizumab-plus-bevacizumab-unresectable-hepatocellular-carcinoma; Published online June 1, 2020 [accessed 19.11.20].

[48] Systemic treatment for advanced hepatocellular carcinoma - UpToDate. https://www.uptodate.com/contents/systemic-treatment-for-advanced-hepatocellular-carcinoma?search = LBA39-%20Randomised%20efficacy%20and%20safety%20results%20for%20atezolizumab%20(Atezo)%20%2B%20bevacizumab%20(Bev)%20in%20patients%20(pts)%20with%20previously%20untreated,%20unresectable%20hepatocellular%20carcinoma&source = search_result&selectedTitle = 1~150&usage_type = default&display_rank = 1#H493158586 [accessed 19.11.20].

[49] Kato Y, Tabata K, Kimura T, et al. Lenvatinib plus anti-PD-1 antibody combination treatment activates CD8 + T cells through reduction of tumor-associated macrophage and activation of the interferon pathway. PLoS One 2019;14(2):e0212513. Available from: https://doi.org/10.1371/journal.pone.0212513.

[50] Harding JJ, Yarmohammadi H, Reiss KA, et al. Nivolumab (NIVO) and drug eluting bead transarterial chemoembolization (deb-TACE): preliminary results from a phase I study of patients (pts) with liver limited hepatocellular carcinoma (HCC). J Clin Oncol 2020;38(4_suppl):525. Available from: https://doi.org/10.1200/JCO.2020.38.4_suppl.525.

[51] Transarterial chemoembolization in combination with nivolumab performed for intermediate stage hepatocellular carcinoma. https://clinicaltrials.gov/ct2/show/NCT03572582 [accessed 12.11.20].

[52] Zhu X-D, Li K-S, Sun H-C. Adjuvant therapies after curative treatments for hepatocellular carcinoma: current status and prospects. Genes Dis 2020;7(3):359−69. Available from: https://doi.org/10.1016/j.gendis.2020.02.002.

[53] Study of pembrolizumab following TACE in primary liver carcinoma. https://clinicaltrials.gov/ct2/show/NCT03397654 [accessed 12.11.20].

[54] Pinato DJ, Cole T, Bengsch B, et al. A phase Ib study of pembrolizumab following trans-arterial chemoembolization (TACE) in hepatocellular carcinoma (HCC): PETAL. Ann Oncol 2019;30:v288. Available from: https://doi.org/10.1093/annonc/mdz247.076.

Updates on clinical trials for the management of hepatocellular carcinoma

Aimen Farooq[1], Zohaib Ahmed[1], James Wert[1], Anum Jalil[1], James Yu[1], Vadim Zaytsev[2] and Sarfraz Ahmad[3]

[1]Department of Internal Medicine, AdventHealth, Orlando, FL, United States
[2]Department of Internal Medicine, Bridgeport Hospital, Bridgeport, CT, United States
[3]AdventHealth Cancer Institute, FSU and UCF Colleges of Medicine, Orlando, FL, United States

Abstract

Hepatocellular carcinoma (HCC) is the most common primary liver cancer. It is the leading cause of death in patients with cirrhosis and the fourth most common cause of cancer-related mortality in the world. In the recent years, we have seen the emergence of promising therapies for the treatment of HCC. Locoregional therapies including surgical resection, liver transplant, Image-guided ablation, and chemoembolization have survival benefits in early disease limited to liver, however each modality has its own limitations. Unfortunately, most of the patients are diagnosed in advance stage of disease requiring systemic management. Sorafenib has been the mainstay of treatment for a decade until the introduction of lenvatinib, which is noninferior to sorafenib. Finally, survival benefit of regorafenib in HCC patients who progress on sorafenib has heralded a new era of second-line treatment, quickly followed by ramucirumab, cabozantinib, and immune checkpoint inhibitors (ICIs). Combination therapies with ICIs and targeted agents in conjunction with locoregional therapies have shown promise paving the way for further clinical trials. Effort is needed to develop additional novel therapies to potentially augment the current standard treatments as well as to understand the underlying drug resistance mechanisms and prognostic parameters in order to improve survival in patients with HCC.

Keywords: Hepatocellular cancer; chemoembolization; liver transplant; sorafenib; immunotherapy; hepatitis virus; cirrhosis; lenvatinib; clinical trials

Ganji Purnachandra Nagaraju, Sarfraz Ahmad (eds.)
Theranostics and Precision Medicine for the Management of Hepatocellular Carcinoma, Volume 3

259

DOI: https://doi.org/10.1016/B978-0-323-99283-1.00013-6

© 2022 Elsevier Inc. All rights reserved.

Abbreviations

BCLC system	Barcelona Clinic Liver Cancer staging system
CSPH	clinically significant pulmonary hypertension
DEB-TACE	drug-eluting bead transarterial chemoembolization
ECOG	Eastern Cooperative Oncology Group
HBV	hepatitis B virus
HCC	hepatocellular carcinoma
HCV	hepatitis C virus
ICI	immune checkpoint inhibitors
OS	overall survival
PFS	progression-free survival
RAF	rapidly accelerated fibrosarcoma
SBRT	stereotactic body radiation therapy
TACE	transarterial chemoembolization
TTP	time to progression

Introduction

Hepatocellular carcinoma (HCC) is a primary liver cancer that usually develops in the setting of chronic liver disease, peculiarly in patients with chronic hepatitis B virus (HBV) infection and cirrhosis. HCC is the most prevalent of the primary liver tumors and the sixth most frequently diagnosed cancer worldwide, with approximately 841,000 new cases reported in 2018 [1]. Furthermore, it is the fourth leading cause of cancer-related mortality worldwide with incidence rates and death rates increasing in many parts of the world [1–4]. However, the increase in mortality rate appears to be slowing compared with the prior time period (i.e., 3.2% increase in mortality during 2008–2013) [5]. In this chapter, we summarize the most updated treatment practices in the realm of HCC (see also Fig. 17.1).

Staging and prognosis in hepatocellular carcinoma

Prognostic assessment is an important step in the management of patients with HCC and is important to be discussed in order to understand indicated treatment for each stage.

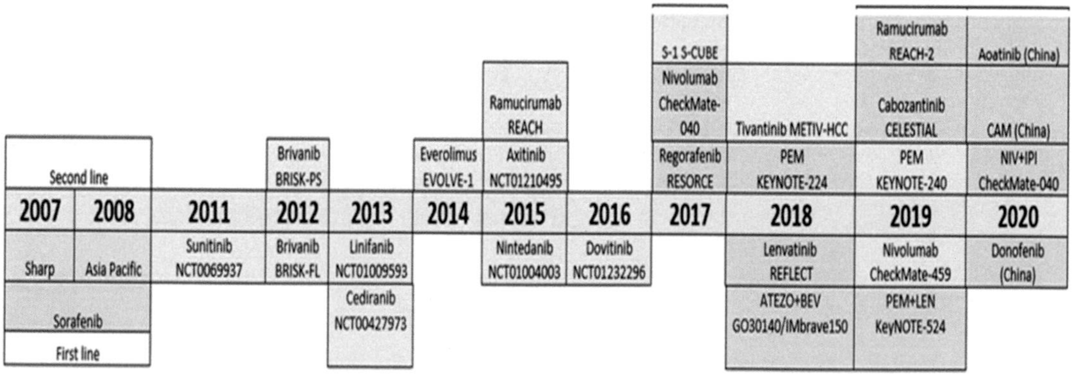

FIGURE 17.1   Timeline representation of the clinical trials for new therapies against hepatocellular carcinoma.

Most patients with HCC have an associated liver disease, therefore not only tumor stage, but the degree of liver function impairment should also be incorporated in prognostic evaluation along with presence or absence of symptoms due to its negative effect on survival. For a system to be clinically effective, treatment indications should always be incorporated with prognostic prediction [6]. The Barcelona Clinic Liver Cancer (BCLC) system [7] is the most widely used and extensively validated staging system that has been updated since its original publication to incorporate strong practice changing evidence.

Management of hepatocellular carcinoma

HCC is a complex disease and large number of potentially beneficial treatment options are available requiring careful selection of patient and expert application of treatment modalities by multidisciplinary teams in order to achieve the best therapeutic response (Fig. 17.2). Utmost importance should be given to examine the strength of scientific evidence for any treatment approach in order to select the most appropriate treatment option for each patient at each tumor stage.

Below is a brief discussion on the different modes of treatment for HCC in light of the results of most up-to-date clinical trials.

Locoregional treatments

Surgical resection

Resection is the treatment of choice for HCC in patients without cirrhosis. Careful evaluation should be undertaken for patients with compensated cirrhosis, to achieve long-term survival and avoid complications related to major hepatic resection (Table 17.1). Compared to open resection, laparoscopic surgery is a less invasive alternative with similar survival benefit and less perioperative morbidity [8]. Unfortunately, tumor recurrence is a common and unfortunate complication in 70% of cases at 5 years. The most effective treatment to prevent intrahepatic recurrence is liver transplantation.

Liver transplantation

Liver transplantation is the best theoretical treatment option since it might cure cancer and the underlying cirrhosis simultaneously (Table 17.2) [23]. The main limitation to the process is donor shortage, imposing a waiting time before transplantation, during which the possible progression of disease might impede transplantation or impair the effectiveness of the treatment [16]. Live donation is another valid strategy with limited applicability because of the scarcity of suitable donors and societal constraints. Implementation of policies to prioritize the sickest patients helps, but the only effective method to avoid waiting is to increase the number of available donors [16].

Image-guided tumor ablation

Tumor ablation is a well-known treatment choice for patients with early-stage HCC (Table 17.3). Tumor necrosis is induced either by temperature alteration using microwave,

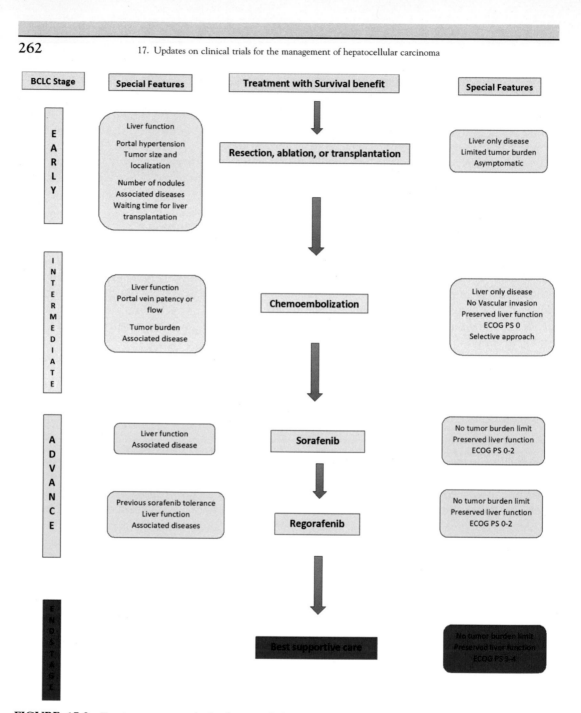

FIGURE 17.2 Treatment approach for hepatocellular carcinoma based on Barcelona Clinic Liver Cancer (BCLC) staging system and treatment stage migration based on individual patient's condition and/or untreatable progression.

TABLE 17.1 Results of studies on surgical resection alone or in combination with systemic therapy in hepatocellular carcinoma.

Locoregional treatments	Study design	Results	Limitations	Reference(s)
Surgical resection	Nonpopulation based/consecutive case series/*meta*-analysis	Increased survival	Presence of CSPH, multifocal tumors, malignant vascular invasion, tumor recurrence	[8−12]
Adjuvant immunotherapy, retinoids, vitamin k2, transarterial I-lipiodol, interferon therapies	Multicenter, randomized, controlled trials, phase II trial	Increased recurrence-free survival, progression-free survival, tumor response	Await validation, controversial results in increased overall survival	[12−14]
Adjuvant sorafenib	Randomized, controlled trial	Indirect surrogates including disease-free survival, progression-free survival, or tumor response	No increase in disease-free survival	[15]

TABLE 17.2 Results of studies on liver transplant in hepatocellular carcinoma.

Locoregional treatments	Study design	Results	Limitations	References
Liver transplantation	Nonpopulation based/consecutive case series/*meta*-analysis	Increased survival	Donor availability	[16−22]

TABLE 17.3 Results of the select studies on targeted ablation therapies in hepatocellular carcinoma.

Locoregional treatments	Study design	Results	Limitations	Reference(s)
Tumor ablation	Prospective, randomized trial	Increased survival	Tumor size	[24−30]
Radiofrequency ablation	Randomized controlled trial, *meta*-analysis	Increased survival	Tumor location, proximity to visceral organs	[24,31−36]
Microwave ablation	Phase III randomized, controlled trial	Noninferior to radiofrequency ablation in overall survival, fewer sessions required	Tumor size	[26]
Ethanol injection	Randomized controlled trial	No limitation to tumor location		[25]

radiofrequency, cryoablation, or laser, or injection of drugs, normally ethanol. Radiofrequency ablation is the first-line ablation technique due to better outcomes [24,25], especially in nodules greater than 2 cm in diameter, whereas the effectiveness and long-term results are very similar to ethanol injections for smaller lesions.

TABLE 17.4 Results of studies on chemoembolization and radiation strategies in hepatocellular carcinoma.

Locoregional treatments	Study design	Results	Limitations	Reference(s)
Chemoembolization (TACE)	Prospective, randomized trial	Increased survival	Poor tolerability in symptomatic patients, portal venous thrombosis	[24−30,37]
Internal radiation (^{131}I or ^{90}Y)	Nonblinded, randomized, controlled trial	Survival, treatment response		[32−36]

Transarterial chemoembolization

Image-guided transcatheter tumor therapies are based on the predominant arterial vascularization of HCC compared with the surrounding normal liver tissue and aim to induce tumor necrosis (Table 17.4). Polyvinyl alcohol provinces enable standardized vessel block with slow release of chemotherapy that helps to retain the efficacy with current median survival exceeding 30−40 months while reducing drug-related adverse events [38−40].

Transarterial chemoembolization (TACE) should be interrupted if substantial necrosis is not achieved in two rounds of treatment or when follow-up treatment fails to induce noticeable necrosis at progression sites after an initial tumor response (Table 17.5). TACE should also not be repeated on untreatable progression-extensive liver involvement, vascular invasion, or extrahepatic metastasis [45].

Systemic therapies

First-line systemic therapies: A summary of the key studies on first-line therapy for HCC is provided in Table 17.6. Below we describe some details to substantiate the impact and value of these therapies for HCC.

Sorafenib

Sorafenib works by inhibiting the activity of RAF kinase, vascular endothelial growth factor (VEGF) receptor and platelet-derived growth factor (PDGF) receptor. It is a multityrosine kinase inhibitor that was used as first-line treatment for HCC. Sorafenib was approved as first-line targeted therapy secondary to the results of the SHARP and Asia-Pacific trial [55,56]. Approved in 2007, it remained the only treatment available for more than 10 years. Its role as first-line therapy was further cemented after the SHARP trial demonstrated a median overall survival (OS) of 10.7 months with the follow-up trial CheckMate 459 showing even longer median OS of 14.7 months [48]. Unfortunately the combination of sorafenib and other chemotherapeutic agents has not been successful in phase III trials. Trials such as TACE 2 which compared TACE with sorafenib versus TACE alone failed to show an improvement in progression-free survival (PFS) [42]. In the SARAH trial yttrium-90 resin microspheres were compared against sorafenib in locally advanced and inoperable HHC and did not yield survival benefit [49]. The positive results from these trials have resulted in all other therapies being compared against sorafenib.

TABLE 17.5 Results of studies on combination therapies (locoregional treatment with targeted therapies and immune checkpoint inhibitors) in hepatocellular carcinoma (HCC).

Lines of therapy	Study	HCC stage	N	Primary endpoint	Results	P-value or hazard ratio	Reference(s)
DEB-TACE plus sorafenib	SPACE (2016) Randomized, controlled, phase II trial	Intermediate-stage multinodular HCC without (MVI) or (EHS)	Sorafenib (154) vs placebo (153)	TTP	Sorafenib plus DEB-TACE was technically feasible, but the combination did not improve TTP in a clinically meaningful manner compared with DEB-TACE alone.	169 vs 166 days respectively HR 0.79 $P = .072$	[41]
DEB-TACE plus sorafenib	TACE 2(2017) Randomized, controlled, phase III trial	Unresectable, liver-confined HCC	Sorafenib (157) vs placebo (156)	PFS	No improvement in PFS, no survival benefit in unresectable HCC	238 vs 235 days, respectively HR 0.99 $P = .94$	[42]
TACE plus SBRT		HCC with macrovascular invasion	TACE-SBRT (26) vs TACE-sorafenib (51)	Treatment response, OS, PFS	TACE plus SBRT could provide improved OS and PFS compared to TACE–sorafenib therapy in patients with HCC with macrovascular invasion	HR of OS to PFS 0.36, $P = .007$ and 0.35, $P < .001$, respectively	[43,44]

TABLE 17.6 Summary results of the key studies on first-line therapy in hepatocellular carcinoma (HCC).

Treatment (lines of therapy)	Study	HCC stage	N	Primary endpoint	Results	P-value or hazard ratio	Reference(s)
Sorafenib	SHARP 2008	Advanced HCC	Sorafenib (299) vs placebo (303)	Overall survival	10.7 months vs 7.9 months	Hazard ratio 0.69; P < .001	[46]
Sorafenib	Asia-Pacific 2008	Advanced HCC	Sorafenib (150) vs placebo (76)	Overall survival	6.5 months vs 4.2 months	Hazard ratio 0.68; P = .014	[47]
Sorafenib vs nivolumab	CheckMate 4592015	Advanced HCC	Sorafenib (372) vs nivolumab (371)	Overall survival	14.7 months vs 16.4 months	Hazard ratio 0.85; P = .0752	[48]
Sorafenib and TACE vs placebo and TACE	TACE-2 2016	Unresectable HCC	Sorafenib and TACE (157) vs placebo and TACE (156)	Progression-free survival	238 days vs 235 days	Hazard ratio .99; P = .94	[42]
Sorafenib vs selective internal radiotherapy with yttrium-90	SARAH	Inoperable HCC	Sorafenib (222) vs selective internal radiotherapy with yttrium-90 (459)	Overall survival	9.9 months vs 8.0 months	Hazard ratio 1.15; P = .18	[49]
Sorafenib vs sunitinib	SUN1170	HCC	Sorafenib (544) vs sunitinib (530)	Overall survival	10.2 months vs 7.9 months	Hazard ratio 1.30; P = .0014	[50]
Sorafenib vs brivanib	BRISK-FL	Advanced HCC	Sorafenib (578) vs brivanib (577)	Overall survival	9.9 months vs 9.5 months	Hazard ratio 1.06	[51]
Sorafenib vs linifanib	LIGHT	Advanced HCC	Sorafenib (521) vs linifanib (514)	Overall survival	9.8 months vs 9.1 months	Hazard ratio 1.046; P = .001	[52]
Sorafenib + erlotinib vs sorafenib	SEARCH	Advanced HCC	Sorafenib + erlotinib (362) vs sorafenib (358)	Overall survival	9.5 months vs 8.5 months	Hazard ratio 1.687; P = .001	[53]
Sorafenib + doxorubicin vs sorafenib	CALGB80802	Advanced HCC	Sorafenib + doxorubicin (180) vs sorafenib (176)	Overall survival	8.9 months vs 10.5 months	Hazard ratio 1.05	[54]
Sorafenib vs Y90	SIRveNIB	Unresectable HCC	Sorafenib (178) vs Y90 (182)	Overall survival	10.6 months vs 8.5 months	Hazard ratio 1.1; P = .36	[55]
Lenvatinib vs sorafenib	REFLECT 2017	Unresectable HCC	Lenvatinib (478) vs sorafenib (476)	Overall survival	13.6 months vs 12.3 months	Hazard ratio 0.92	[56]

Lenvatinib

More than 10 years later, the approval of lenvatinib brought about the second first line targeted therapy for HCC since sorafenib. Lenvatinib received approval after the results of the REFLECT trial which was a randomized phase III noninferiority trial studied in 2018 [57]. Results showed antitumor activity for greater than 4 years in unresectable HCC. In those patients with greater than seven tumors in whom TACE was not indicated, lenvatinib provided significantly better OS (37.9 vs 21.3 months) and PFS (16 vs 3 months). One important benefit is its improved cost effectiveness when compared to sorafenib. Unique to lenvatinib a tyrosine kinase inhibitor, thyroid function must be monitored.

Atezolizumab with bevacizumab

The GO 30140 study (NCT02715531) was the basis for the Food and Drug Administration (FDA) to approve atezolizumab and bevacizumab for the treatment of advanced or metastatic HCC [58]. As a follow-up the phase III trial IMbrave 150 study (NCT03434379) showed better OS and PFS with the combination atezolizumab and bevacizumab versus sorafenib in patients with unresectable HCC [59].

Second-line systemic therapies

The first-line therapy for HCC is not entirely perfect. In SHARP trial the median time to radiological progression was reported to be 5.5 months for the patients in sorafenib arm [46]. Recently, IMbrave 150 trial demonstrated the superiority of atezolizumab and bevacizumab combination to sorafenib [60]. However, even with this superior combination the median PFS is still 6.8 months. Therefore there is a growing need for second-line systemic agents in the management of HCC. The following text will focus on the agents which are currently the standard-of-care second-line therapies. Table 17.7 summarizes key phase III trials in second-line treatment for HCC.

Regorafenib

Regorafenib, a multikinase inhibitor, is approved as a second-line agent for the patients with HCC who had progressed on sorafenib. The approval was based on the results of a randomized, double-blind, placebo-controlled, and phase III trial (RESORCE trial) [64]. Moreover, regorafenib was also found to be safe and effective in setting of progression after the liver transplant [68].

Cabozantinib

Further in the search for second-line agents, cabozantinib was approved by the FDA in January 2019. The approval was based on results of the CELESTIAL trial that demonstrated median OS of 10.2 months compared with 8.0 months for the placebo group [57]. However, in true clinical setting it is less preferred as compared to regorafenib given the lack of cost effectiveness [69].

TABLE 17.7 Results of studies on second-line and newer systemic therapies in hepatocellular carcinoma (HCC).

Treatment (lines of therapy)	Study	HCC stage	N	Primary endpoint	Results (months)	P-value or hazard ratio	Reference(s)
Brivanib	BRISK-PS (2013)	Advanced HCC	Brivanib (263) placebo (132)	Overall survival	9.4 vs 8.2	Hazard ratio 0.89; $P = .33$	[61]
Everolimus	EVOLVE-1 (2014)	Advanced HCC	Everolimus (362) vs placebo (184)	Overall survival	7.6 vs 7.3	Hazard ratio 1.05; $P = .67$	[62]
Ramucirumab	REACH (2015)	Advanced HCC	Ramucirumab (283) vs placebo (282)	Overall survival	9.2 vs 7.6	Hazard ratio 0.87; $P = .14$	[63]
Regorafenib	RESORCE (2016)	HCC	Regorafenib (379) vs placebo (194)	Overall survival	10.6 vs 7.8	Hazard ratio 0.63; $P < .0001$	[64]
Tivantinib	METIV-HCC (2018)	Advanced HCC	Tivantinib (226) vs placebo (114)	Overall survival	8.4 vs 9.1	Hazard ratio 0.97; $P = .81$	[65]
ADI-PEG 20	ADI-PEG 20 (2018)	Advanced HCC	ADI-PEG 20 (424) vs placebo (211)	Overall survival	7.8 vs 7.4	Hazard ratio 1.02; $P = .88$	[66]
Cabozantinib	CELESTIAL (2018)	Advanced HCC	Cabozantinib (470) vs placebo (237)	Overall survival	10.2 vs 8	Hazard ratio 0.76; $P = .005$	[57]
Ramucirumab	REACH-2 (2019)	Advanced HCC	Ramucirumab (197) vs placebo (95)	Overall survival	8.5 vs 7.3	Hazard ratio 0.710; $P = .0199$	[67]

Ramucirumab

In contrast to regorafenib and cabozantinib, ramucirumab targets the VEGFR2. Ramucirumab was unable to meet its primary endpoint in the REACH trial [63]. However, subgroup analysis demonstrated improved survival with ramucirumab in patients with AFP of 400 ng/mL or higher. This observation was tested in REACH-2 trial with subsequent FDA approval of this drug in the second-line setting for treatment of advanced HCC [67].

Immune checkpoint inhibitors

Nivolumab

Nivolumab was the first immune checkpoint inhibitor (ICI) whose efficacy was evaluated in advance HCC and subsequently got accelerated FDA approval for HCC that was previously treated with sorafenib [70]. Recently, CheckMate 459, a multicenter phase III randomized trial that compared nivolumab with sorafenib in frontline setting, failed to meet its endpoints. Nonetheless, Nivolumab did prolong OS, demonstrated durable response, and had better safety profile regardless of PD-L1 (programmed death ligand 1) expression [71].

Pembrolizumab

Pembrolizumab is another immunotherapeutic that was found to be efficacious in advanced HCC. KEYNOTE-224, an open-labeled phase II, nonrandomized trial showed acceptable safety and efficacy of pembrolizumab in patients with advanced HCC that were either intolerant to or showed radiographic progression of their disease after sorafenib [72]. This resulted in accelerated FDA approval of Pembrolizumab as a second-line agent. However, subsequent phase III KEYNOTE-240 trail that compared pembrolizumab with placebo in second line setting, could not achieve statistical significance for overall survival and PFS [73]. An ongoing KEYNOTE-394 trial in the Asian population will further clarify the role of pembrolizumab in second-line setting (NCT03062358).

Camrelizumab

Camrelizumab, an anti-PD-1 (programmed death 1) antibody has been evaluated in second line setting for treatment of HCC in the Chinese population. The study provides evidence of the efficacy of anti-PD-1 in HBV-related HCC in the Chinese population [74].

Combination therapies with immune checkpoint inhibitors

The use of combination therapy, targeting different pathways in carcinogenesis, has shown promising efficacy and safety profile in different cancers. Therefore the ICIs are being investigated in HCC as dual ICI treatment or combination treatment of ICI with other targeted therapies. The success of nivolumab with ipilimumab combination in setting of advanced melanoma and advanced nonsmall cell lung cancer led the investigators to test this combination in HCC [75,76]. This combination got accelerated approval from the FDA in March 2020 for patients with HCC in second-line setting after sorafenib. The approval was based on successful results of CheckMate 040 cohort-4 trial [77]. The ongoing trails evaluating the role of immunotherapeutic agents in HCC will hopefully expand the spectrum of second-line agents for the management of advanced HCC.

Conclusions and future perspectives

Management of HCC has evolved enormously over the past decade, especially with the development of multiple treatment options at each stage of the disease. However, there are important areas that require improvement in order to achieve maximum survival benefit. The prevention of risk factors contributing to HCC is the best strategy to achieve a decrease in mortality. Promotion of a healthy lifestyle including decrease in alcohol use, clean and safe water usage, decrease in metabolic syndrome will have immense impact on the incidence of HCC. Elimination of chronic hepatitis C infection by high efficacy direct antivirals will also decrease the incidence of HCC but further information needs to be gathered about patients after the viral cure. Effective adjuvant therapies are urgently needed to cope with the recurrent tumors after ablation or chemoembolization. Another relevant issue is the radiological assessment of tumor response and its capacity to predict efficacy. Promising novel therapies such as immunotherapy are under investigation that needs further phase III trials to confirm survival benefits. Identification of new prognosis predictors through molecular profiling has become a ray of hope to identify new and precise therapeutic strategies, leading to further avenues of potential research in liver cancer.

References

[1] https://gco.iarc.fr/today/data/factsheets/cancers/11-Liver-fact-sheet.pdf. [accessed 26.06.21].

[2] Hashim D, Boffetta P, La Vecchia C, Rota M, Bertuccio P, Malvezzi M, et al. The global decrease in cancer mortality: trends and disparities. Ann Oncol 2016;27(5):926−33. Available from: https://doi.org/10.1093/annonc/mdw027.

[3] Tapper EB, Parikh ND. Mortality due to cirrhosis and liver cancer in the United States, 1999−2016: observational study. BMJ 2018;362:k2817. Available from: https://doi.org/10.1136/bmj.k2817.

[4] Siegel RL, Miller KD, Jemal A. Cancer statistics, 2020. CA Cancer J Clin 2020;70(1):7−30. Available from: https://doi.org/10.3322/caac.21590.

[5] Kulik L, El-Serag HB. Epidemiology and management of hepatocellular carcinoma. Gastroenterology 2019;156(2):477−491.e1. Available from: https://doi.org/10.1053/j.gastro.2018.08.065.

[6] Bruix J, Reig M, Sherman M. Evidence-based diagnosis, staging, and treatment of patients with hepatocellular carcinoma. Gastroenterology 2016;150:835−53.

[7] Llovet JM, Bru C, Bruix J. Prognosis of hepatocellular carcinoma: the BCLC staging classification. Semin Liver Dis 1999;19:329−38.

[8] Han H-S, Shehta A, Ahn S, Yoon Y-S, Cho JY, Choi Y. Laparoscopic vs open liver resection for hepatocellular carcinoma: case-matched study with propensity score matching. J Hepatol 2015;63:643−50.

[9] Roayaie S, Jibara G, Tabrizian P, et al. The role of hepatic resection in the treatment of hepatocellular cancer. Hepatology 2015;62:440−51.

[10] Berzigotti A, Reig M, Abraldes JG, Bosch J, Bruix J. Portal hypertension and the outcome of surgery for hepatocellular carcinoma in compensated cirrhosis: a systematic review and meta-analysis. Hepatology 2015;61:526−36.

[11] Ishizawa T, Hasegawa K, Aoki T, et al. Neither multiple tumors nor portal hypertension are surgical contraindications for hepatocellular carcinoma. Gastroenterology 2008;134:1908−16.

[12] Hasegawa K, Kokudo N, Makuuchi M, et al. Comparison of resection and ablation for hepatocellular carcinoma: a cohort study based on a Japanese nationwide survey. J Hepatol 2013;58:724−9.

[13] Lu L-C, Cheng A-L, Poon RTP. Recent advances in the prevention of hepatocellular carcinoma recurrence. Semin Liver Dis 2014;34:427−34.

[14] Lee JH, Lee J-H, Lim Y-S, et al. Adjuvant immunotherapy with autologous ctrokine-induced killer cells for hepatocellular carcinoma. Gastroenterology 2015;148:1383-91.e6.

[15] Bruix J, Takayama T, Mazzaferro V, et al. Adjuvant sorafenib for hepatocellular carcinoma after resection or ablation (STORM): a phase 3, randomised, double-blind, placebo-controlled trial. Lancet Oncol 2015;16:1344−54.

[16] Sapisochin G, Bruix J. Liver transplantation for hepatocellular carcinoma: outcomes and novel surgical approaches. Nat Rev Gastroenterol Hepatol 2017;14:203−21.

[17] Mazzaferro V, Llovet JM, Miceli R, et al. Predicting survival after liver transplantation in patients with hepatocellular carcinoma beyond the Milan criteria: a retrospective, exploratory analysis. Lancet Oncol 2009;10:35−43.

[18] Yao FY, Ferrell L, Bass NM, et al. Liver transplantation for hepatocellular carcinoma: expansion of the tumor size limits does not adversely impact survival. Hepatology 2001;33:1394−403.

[19] Herrero JI, Sangro B, Pardo F, et al. Liver transplantation in patients with hepatocellular carcinoma across Milan criteria. Liver Transpl 2008;14:272−8.

[20] Duvoux C, Roudot-Thoraval F, Decaens T, et al. Liver transplantation for hepatocellular carcinoma: a model including α-fetoprotein improves the performance of Milan criteria. Gastroenterology 2012;143:985−6.

[21] Toso C, Meeberg G, Hernandez-Alejandro R, et al. Total tumor volume and α-fetoprotein for selection of transplant candidates with hepatocellular carcinoma: a prospective validation. Hepatology 2015;62:158−65.

[22] Mazzaferro V. Squaring the circle of selection and allocation in liver transplantation for HCC: an adaptive approach. Hepatology 2016;63:1707−17.

[23] Mazzaferro V, Regalia E, Doci R, et al. Liver transplantation for the treatment of small hepatocellular carcinomas in patients with cirrhosis. N Engl J Med 1996;334:693−9.

[24] Breen DJ, Lencioni R. Image-guided ablation of primary liver and renal tumours. Nat Rev Clin Oncol 2015;12:175−86.

[25] Germani G, Pleguezuelo M, Gurusamy K, Meyer T, Isgro G, Burroughs AK. Clinical outcomes of radiofrequency ablation, percutaneous alcohol and acetic acid injection for hepatocelullar carcinoma: a *meta*-analysis. J Hepatol 2010;52:380—8.

[26] Yu J, Yu X, Han Z, et al. Percutaneous cooled-probe microwave vs radiofrequency ablation in early-stage hepatocellular carcinoma: a phase III randomised controlled trial. Gut 2017;66:1172—3.

[27] Chen MS, Li JQ, Zheng Y, et al. A prospective randomized trial comparing percutaneous local ablative therapy and partial hepatectomy for small hepatocellular carcinoma. Ann Surg 2006;243:321—8.

[28] Huang J, Yan L, Cheng Z, et al. A randomized trial comparing radiofrequency ablation and surgical resection for HCC conforming to the Milan criteria. Ann Surg 2010;252:903—12.

[29] Feng K, Yan J, Li X, et al. A randomized controlled trial of radiofrequency ablation and surgical resection in the treatment of small hepatocellular carcinoma. J Hepatol 2012;57:794—802.

[30] Cucchetti A, Piscaglia F, Cescon M, et al. Cost-effectiveness of hepatic resection vs percutaneous radiofrequency ablation for early hepatocellular carcinoma. J Hepatol 2013;59:300—7.

[31] Kalogeridi M-A, Zygogianni A, Kyrgias G, et al. Role of radiotherapy in the management of hepatocellular carcinoma: a systematic review. World J Hepatol 2015;7:101—12.

[32] Sangro B, Carpanese L, Cianni R, et al. Survival after yttrium-90 resin microsphere radioembolization of hepatocellular carcinoma across Barcelona clinic liver cancer stages: a European evaluation. Hepatology 2011;54:868—78.

[33] Mazzaferro V, Sposito C, Bhoori S, et al. Yttrium-90 radioembolization for intermediate-advanced hepatocellular carcinoma: a phase 2 study. Hepatology 2013;57:1826—37.

[34] Salem R, Gordon AC, Mouli S, et al. Y90 radioembolization significantly prolongs time to progression compared with chemoembolization in patients with hepatocellular carcinoma. Gastroenterology 2016;151:1155 63.e2.

[35] Vilgrain V, Pereira H, Assenat E, et al. Efficacy and safety of selective internal radiotherapy with yttrium-90 resin microspheres compared with sorafenib in locally advanced and inoperable hepatocellular carcinoma (SARAH): an open-label randomised controlled phase 3 trial. Lancet Oncol 2017;18:1624—36.

[36] Chow P, Gandhi M. Phase III multi-centre open-label randomized controlled trial of selective internal radiation therapy (SIRT) vs sorafenib in locally advanced hepatocellular carcinoma: the SIRveNIB study. Proc Am Soc Clin Oncol 2017;35:4002 (abstr).

[37] Brown KT, Do RK, Gonen M, et al. Randomized trial of hepatic artery embolization for hepatocellular carcinoma using doxorubicin-eluting microspheres compared with embolization with microspheres alone. J Clin Oncol 2016;34(17):2046—53.

[38] Varela M, Real MI, Burrel M, et al. Chemoembolization of hepatocellular carcinoma with drug eluting beads: efficacy and doxorubicin pharmacokinetics. J Hepatol 2007;46:474—81.

[39] Lammer J, Malagari K, Vogl T, et al. Prospective randomized study of doxorubicin-eluting-bead embolization in the treatment of hepatocellular carcinoma: results of the PRECISION V study. Cardiovasc Interv Radiol 2010;33:41—52.

[40] Golfieri R, Giampalma E, Renzulli M, et al. Randomised controlled trial of doxorubicin-eluting beads vs conventional chemoembolisation for hepatocellular carcinoma. Br J Cancer 2014;111:255—64.

[41] Lencioni R, et al. Sorafenib or placebo plus TACE with doxorubicin-eluting beads for intermediate stage HCC: the SPACE trial. J Hepatol 2016;64:1090—8.

[42] Meyer T, Fox R, Ma YT, Ross PJ, James MW, Sturgess R, et al. Sorafenib in combination with transarterial chemoembolisation in patients with unresectable hepatocellular carcinoma (TACE 2): a randomised placebo-controlled, double-blind, phase 3 trial. Lancet. Gastroenterol Hepatol 2017;2(8):565—75. Available from: https://doi.org/10.1016/S2468-1253(17)30156-5.

[43] Bettinger D, et al. Stereotactic body radiation therapy as an alternative treatment for patients with hepatocellular carcinoma compared to sorafenib: a propensity score analysis. Liver Cancer 2019;8:281—94.

[44] Shen L, et al. Combination therapy after TACE for hepatocellular carcinoma with macroscopic vascular invasion: stereotactic body radiotherapy vs sorafenib. Cancers. 2018;10:516.

[45] Forner A, Gilabert M, Bruix J, Raoul J-L. Treatment of intermediate-stage hepatocellular carcinoma. Nat Rev Clin Oncol 2014;11:525—35.

[46] Llovet JM, Ricci S, Mazzaferro V, Hilgard P, Gane E, Blanc J-F, et al. Sorafenib in advanced hepatocellular carcinoma. N Engl J Med 2008;359:378—90.

[47] Cheng AL, Kang YK, Chen Z, Tsao CJ, Qin S, Kim JS, et al. Efficacy and safety of sorafenib in patients in the Asia-Pacific region with advanced hepatocellular carcinoma: a phase III randomised, double-blind, placebo-controlled trial. Lancet Oncol 2009;10(1):25—34. Available from: https://doi.org/10.1016/S1470-2045(08)70285-7.

[48] Yau T, Park J-W, Finn RS, Cheng AL, Mathurin P, Edeline J, et al. LBA38_PR - CheckMate 459: a randomized, multi-center phase III study of nivolumab (NIVO) vs sorafenib (SOR) as first-line (1L) treatment in patients (pts) with advanced hepatocellular carcinoma (AHCC). Ann Oncol 2019;30:v874–5. Available from: https://doi.org/10.1093/annonc/mdz394.029.

[49] Vilgrain V, Pereira H, Assenat E, Guiu B, Ilonca AD, Pageaux GP, et al. SARAH Trial Group. Efficacy and safety of selective internal radiotherapy with yttrium-90 resin microspheres compared with sorafenib in locally advanced and inoperable hepatocellular carcinoma (SARAH): an open-label randomised controlled phase 3 trial. Lancet Oncol 2017;18(12):1624–36. Available from: https://doi.org/10.1016/S1470-2045(17)30683-6.

[50] Cheng AL, Kang YK, Lin DY, Park JW, Kudo M, Qin S, et al. Sunitinib vs sorafenib in advanced hepatocellular cancer: results of a randomized phase III trial. J Clin Oncol 2013;31(32):4067–75. Available from: https://doi.org/10.1200/JCO.2012.45.8372.

[51] Johnson PJ, Qin S, Park JW, Poon RT, Raoul JL, Philip PA, et al. Brivanib vs sorafenib as first-line therapy in patients with unresectable, advanced hepatocellular carcinoma: results from the randomized phase III BRISK-FL study. J Clin Oncol 2013;31(28):3517–24. Available from: https://doi.org/10.1200/JCO.2012.48.4410.

[52] Cainap C, Qin S, Huang WT, Chung IJ, Pan H, Cheng Y, et al. Linifanib vs sorafenib in patients with advanced hepatocellular carcinoma: results of a randomized phase III trial. J Clin Oncol 2015;33(2):172–9. Available from: https://doi.org/10.1200/JCO.2013.54.3298.

[53] Zhu AX, Rosmorduc O, Evans TR, Ross PJ, Santoro A, Carrilho FJ, et al. SEARCH: a phase III, randomized, double-blind, placebo-controlled trial of sorafenib plus erlotinib in patients with advanced hepatocellular carcinoma. J Clin Oncol 2015;33(6):559–66. Available from: https://doi.org/10.1200/JCO.2013.53.7746.

[54] Abou-Alfa GK, Shi Q, Knox JJ, Kaubisch A, Niedzwiecki D, Posey J, et al. Assessment of treatment with sorafenib plus doxorubicin vs sorafenib alone in patients with advanced hepatocellular carcinoma: phase 3 CALGB 80802 randomized clinical trial. JAMA Oncol 2019;5(11):1582–8. Available from: https://doi.org/10.1001/jamaoncol.2019.2792.

[55] Chow PKH, Gandhi M, Tan SB, Khin MW, Khasbazar A, Ong J, et al. Asia-Pacific Hepatocellular Carcinoma Trials Group. SIRveNIB: selective internal radiation therapy vs sorafenib in Asia-Pacific patients with hepatocellular carcinoma. J Clin Oncol 2018;36(19):1913–21. Available from: https://doi.org/10.1200/JCO.2017.76.0892.

[56] Personeni N, Pressiani T, Rimassa L. Lenvatinib for the treatment of unresectable hepatocellular carcinoma: evidence to date. J Hepatocell Carcinoma 2019;6:31–9. Available from: https://doi.org/10.2147/JHC.S168953.

[57] Abou-Alfa GK, et al. Cabozantinib in patients with advanced and progressing hepatocellular carcinoma. N Engl J Med 2018;379(1):54–63. Available from: https://doi.org/10.1056/NEJMoa1717002.

[58] Lee MS, Ryoo BY, Hsu CH, Numata K, Stein S, Verret W, et al. GO30140 investigators. Atezolizumab with or without bevacizumab in unresectable hepatocellular carcinoma (GO30140): an open-label, multicentre, phase 1b study. Lancet Oncol 2020;21(6):808–20. Available from: https://doi.org/10.1016/S1470-2045(20)30156-X Erratum in: Lancet Oncol 2020;21(7):e341.

[59] Finn RS, Qin S, Ikeda M, Galle PR, Ducreux M, Kim TY, et al. IMbrave150 Investigators. Atezolizumab plus bevacizumab in unresectable hepatocellular carcinoma. N Engl J Med 2020;382(20):1894–905. Available from: https://doi.org/10.1056/NEJMoa1915745.

[60] Finn R, et al. Atezolizumab plus bevacizumab in unresectable hepatocellular carcinoma. N Engl J Med 2020. Available from: https://doi.org/10.1056/NEJMoa1915745.

[61] Llovet J, et al. Brivanib in patients with advanced hepatocellular carcinoma who were intolerant to sorafenib or for whom sorafenib failed: results from the randomized phase III BRISK-PS study. J Clin Oncol 2013;31(28):3509–16. Available from: https://doi.org/10.1200/JCO.2012.47.3009.

[62] Zhu AX, et al. EVOLVE-1: phase 3 study of everolimus for advanced HCC that progressed during or after sorafenib. J Clin Oncol 2014;32(3_suppl):172. Available from: https://doi.org/10.1200/jco.2014.32.3_suppl.172.

[63] Zhu AX, et al. Ramucirumab vs placebo as second-line treatment in patients with advanced hepatocellular carcinoma following first-line therapy with sorafenib (REACH): a randomised, double-blind, multicentre, phase 3 trial. Lancet Oncol 2015;16(7):859–70. Available from: https://doi.org/10.1016/S1470-2045(15)00050-9.

[64] Bruix J, et al. Regorafenib for patients with hepatocellular carcinoma who progressed on sorafenib treatment (RESORCE): a randomised, double-blind, placebo-controlled, phase 3 trial. Lancet 2017;389(10064):56–66. Available from: https://doi.org/10.1016/S0140-6736(16)32453-9.

[65] Rimassa L, et al. Tivantinib for second-line treatment of MET-high, advanced hepatocellular carcinoma (METIV-HCC): a final analysis of a phase 3, randomised, placebo-controlled study. Lancet Oncol 2018;19(5):682–93. Available from: https://doi.org/10.1016/S1470-2045(18)30146-3.

[66] Abou-Alfa GK, et al. Phase III randomized study of second line ADI-PEG 20 plus best supportive care vs placebo plus best supportive care in patients with advanced hepatocellular carcinoma. Ann Oncol 2018;29 (6):1402−8. Available from: https://doi.org/10.1093/annonc/mdy101.

[67] Zhu AX, et al. Ramucirumab after sorafenib in patients with advanced hepatocellular carcinoma and increased α-fetoprotein concentrations (REACH-2): a randomised, double-blind, placebo-controlled, phase 3 trial. Lancet Oncol 2019;20(2):282−96. Available from: https://doi.org/10.1016/S1470-2045(18)30937-9.

[68] Iavarone M, et al. Preliminary experience on safety of regorafenib after sorafenib failure in recurrent hepatocellular carcinoma after liver transplantation. Am J Transpl 2019;19(11):3176−84. Available from: https://doi.org/10.1111/ajt.15551.

[69] Huang A, et al. Targeted therapy for hepatocellular carcinoma. Signal Transd Target Ther 2020;5. Available from: https://doi.org/10.1038/s41392-020-00264-x.

[70] El-Khoueiry AB, et al. Nivolumab in patients with advanced hepatocellular carcinoma (CheckMate 040): an open-label, non-comparative, phase 1/2 dose escalation and expansion trial. Lancet 2017;389 (10088):2492−502. Available from: https://doi.org/10.1016/S0140-6736(17)31046-2.

[71] Yau T, et al. CheckMate 459: a randomized, multi-center phase III study of nivolumab (NIVO) vs sorafenib (SOR) as first-line (1L) treatment in patients (pts) with advanced hepatocellular carcinoma (AHCC). Ann Oncol 2019;30:v874−5. Available from: https://doi.org/10.1093/annonc/mdz394.029.

[72] Zhu AX, et al. Pembrolizumab in patients with advanced hepatocellular carcinoma previously treated with sorafenib (KEYNOTE-224): a non-randomised, open-label phase 2 trial. Lancet Oncol 2018;19(7):940−52. Available from: https://doi.org/10.1016/S1470-2045(18)30351-6.

[73] Finn RS, et al. Pembrolizumab as second-line therapy in patients with advanced hepatocellular carcinoma in KEYNOTE-240: a randomized, double-blind, phase III trial. J Clin Oncol 2020;38(3):193−202. Available from: https://doi.org/10.1200/JCO.19.01307.

[74] Qin S, et al. Camrelizumab in patients with previously treated advanced hepatocellular carcinoma: a multicentre, open-label, parallel-group, randomised, phase 2 trial. Lancet Oncol 2020;21(4):571−80. Available from: https://doi.org/10.1016/S1470-2045(20)30011-5.

[75] Hodi FS, et al. Nivolumab plus ipilimumab or nivolumab alone vs ipilimumab alone in advanced melanoma (CheckMate 067): 4-year outcomes of a multicentre, randomised, phase 3 trial. Lancet Oncol 2018;19 (11):1480−92. Available from: https://doi.org/10.1016/S1470-2045(18)30700-9.

[76] Hellmann MD, et al. Nivolumab plus ipilimumab in advanced non−small-cell lung cancer. N Engl J Med 2019. Available from: https://doi.org/10.1056/NEJMoa1910231.

[77] Yau T, et al. Efficacy and safety of nivolumab plus ipilimumab in patients with advanced hepatocellular carcinoma previously treated with sorafenib: the CheckMate 040 randomized clinical trial. JAMA Oncol 2020. Available from: https://doi.org/10.1001/jamaoncol.2020.4564.

Theranostic and precision medicine for the diagnosis of hepatocellular carcinoma

Rafael Miret[1], Amir Riaz[1], Sikandar Khan[1] and Asad Ur Rahman[2]

[1]Department of Internal Medicine, Cleveland Clinic Florida, Weston, FL, United States
[2]Department of Gastroenterology and Hepatology, Cleveland Clinic Florida, Weston, FL, United States

Abstract

Hepatocellular carcinoma (HCC) is the most common primary liver malignancy in the world. Surveillance of HCC in high-risk populations is essential as the incidence of HCC in the United States continues to rapidly increase. Ultrasonography is a relatively simple and widely available imaging study used for the diagnosis of HCC in the United States and around the world. Tumor markers are often used in conjunction with available imaging modalities to increase the sensitivity. Guidelines for HCC surveillance have been issued by some of the major professional societies such as the American Association for the Study of Liver Diseases, the European Association for the Study of the Liver, and the Asian Pacific Association for the Study of Liver, which have been discussed here in perspective. This chapter also covers the cost-effectiveness of HCC pertaining to the diagnostic modalities and feasibility.

Keywords: Hepatocellular carcinoma; surveillance; diagnosis; therapy; risk factors; tumor markers; NAFLD; NASH; hepatitis

Abbreviations

AASLD	American Association for the Study of Liver Diseases
AFP	alpha-fetoprotein
APAS	Asian Pacific Association for the Study of Liver
CI	confidence interval
CT	computed tomography

© 2022 Elsevier Inc. All rights reserved.

DCP	des-γ-carboxyprothrombin
EASL	European Association for the Study of the Liver
GPC3	glypican-3
HBV	hepatitis B virus
HCC	hepatocellular carcinoma
HCV	hepatitis C virus
HDV	hepatitis D virus
LCA	lectin lens agglutinin
MRI	magnetic resonance Imaging
NAFLD	nonalcoholic fatty liver disease
NASH	nonalcoholic steatohepatitis
PAGE-B	platelets, age, GEnder B (score)
SCCA	squamous cell carcinoma antigen
US	ultrasonography

Epidemiology

Hepatocellular carcinoma (HCC) is the most common primary liver malignancy in the world [1]. It is one of the leading causes of cancer-related mortality, ranking second globally [2]. HCC usually affects individuals between the ages of 30 and 50 and is more common in males, with a male-to-female ratio of greater than 2 [3]. Risk factor and mortality rates vary depending on geographic locations, with higher disease burdens in areas endemic to HCC, such as East Asia and Sub-Saharan Africa, where incidence rates are as high as 20 per 100,000 individuals. Incidence rates are generally lower in western developed countries, with intermediate rates in nations such as France, Italy, and Spain (10–20 per 100,000) and lower (<5 per 100,000) in North and South America [4].

The vast majority of HCC cases occur in the background of cirrhosis [5], with the most common risk factor globally being chronic infection due to Hepatitis B virus (HBV) [3]. The majority of HBV infections are usually due to vertical or perinatal transmission. Other important risk factors include other hepatotropic viruses such as Hepatitis C virus (HCV) and Hepatitis D virus (HDV), with HCV being one of the leading risk factors for HCC in the United States and Japan [6]. Noninfectious risk factors for HCC include those which predispose individuals to the development of cirrhosis, such as alcohol abuse, nonalcoholic fatty liver disease (NAFLD), and nonalcoholic steatohepatitis (NASH) (Table 18.1).

In the western world, metabolic syndrome and increasing insulin resistance with NAFLD/NASH is thought to lead to chronic low-grade inflammation in hepatocytes, predisposing individuals to development of HCC. In the United States, there is a parallel rise between incidence of NAFLD and metabolic syndrome, which, in turn, has led to a rise in the incidence of HCC [8]. A population-based study between 2004 and 2009 found a 9% annual increase in the proportion of NAFLD-related HCC cases in the United States alone [9]. More studies are needed to further characterize and understand this epidemiological shift in the western world. In regions where aflatoxin-contaminated food products are consumed, such as Sub-Saharan Africa and Eastern Asia, there has been a high incidence of HCC with mutations of the *p53* tumor suppressor gene, thought to be caused by aflatoxins [10]. The global impact of HCC on societal health and economy is a major driving force behind the development of preventative measures for these major risk factors.

TABLE 18.1 Major risk factors and geographic predominance of hepatocellular carcinoma.

Major risk factors	Geographic predominance
HBV	Global: Eastern Asia (8% of population), Africa (6.1%), Eastern Mediterranean region (3.3%), Europe (1.6%), Americas (0.7%) [7]
HCV	Eastern Mediterranean Region (2.3%), Europe (1.5%), Americas (0.7%)
NAFLD / NASH	Americas, Europe, Middle East
Aflatoxin	Eastern Asia, Sub-Saharan Africa
Alcohol	Global
Other (genetic, smoking, medication-induced, etc.)	Variable

HBV, hepatitis B virus; *HCV*, hepatitis C virus; *NAFLD*, nonalcoholic fatty liver disease; *NASH*, nonalcoholic steatohepatitis.

Ultrasound

Ultrasonography is a relatively simple and widely available imaging study used for the diagnosis of HCC in the United States and around the world. Commonly, it is the initial study performed when evaluating liver disease, such as HCC. Ultrasonography helps aid in the diagnosis of HCC and is used for disease surveillance. Ultrasonography has become increasingly popular as it is inexpensive, noninvasive, limits radiation exposure, and delivers real-time information about liver pathology [11]. B-mode ultrasound is the most widely used modality of ultrasonography technique used to better characterize isolated liver lesions [12].

The typical HCC lesion seen on ultrasonography will be a hypoechoic or echogenic nodule, with the presence of a halo around the lesion. In lesions under 10 mm, the pattern will almost always be hypoechoic or isoechoic. As lesions progress in size ($\geq$10 mm), it will become hyperechoic due to the presence of fat infiltration in carcinogenic evolution [13]. For lesions $\geq$ 20 mm, the characteristics include a mosaic pattern, halo around the capsule, lateral shadow, and posterior echo enhancement, which when seen increase the ultrasonographic sensitivity to detect HCC [14]. Due to its easy accessibility and low cost, the American Association for the Study of Liver Diseases (AASLD-2017) recommends ultrasonography for routine screening for HCC in adults with cirrhosis. The initial screening is performed with ultrasonography with or without alpha-fetoprotein (AFP) every 6 months [15]. A recent *meta*-analysis looked at studies comparing the use of ultrasound with versus without AFP to detect early-stage HCC and showed a 63% sensitivity (95% confidence interval [CI] 48%−75%) and 45% sensitivity (95% CI 30%−62%), respectively (P = .002) [16].

In another *meta*-analysis, ultrasonographic technology detected HCC at any stage, with 84% sensitivity (95% CI 76%−92%); however, early-stage disease was detected with only 47% sensitivity (95% CI 33%−61%) [17]. Ultrasonography carries many benefits, yet there are limitations that may impede its utility, such as operator dependence, patient's body habitus, and advanced liver fibrosis [18]. Importantly, it has a very low sensitivity for HCC under <2 cm, which creates difficulties in early diagnosis of HCC and thus enhancing survival odds (Table 18.2).

TABLE 18.2   Sensitivities, advantages, and limitations of each study modality.

Study modality	Sensitivities (%)	Advantages	Limitations
Ultrasonography	47–84	Inexpensive, no ionizing radiation, noninvasive	Body habitus, operator skill dependent, low sensitivity for small lesions
Ultrasonography + AFP	63	Increased sensitivity for early HCC than ultrasonography alone, no ionizing radiation, noninvasive	Increased cost when compared to ultrasonography alone, body habitus, operator skill dependent; AFP shown in other chronic conditions
CT	62–87.5	Noninvasive, highly sensitive for lesions >2 cm	Ionizing radiation, low sensitivity for lesions <1 cm, contrast-induced nephropathy
MRI	50–96	No ionizing radiation, better structural characterization than CT	Cost, low sensitivity for lesions < 1 cm
Tumor markers	50–72	Inexpensive, noninvasive	Expressed in chronic liver conditions and in lung, gastric, squamous cancer

AFP, alpha-fetoprotein; *CT*, computed tomography; *HCC*, hepatocellular carcinoma; *MRI*, magnetic resonance imaging.

Computed tomography

As computed tomography (CT) scans have become more available to practicing clinicians, its use for the screening and diagnosis of HCC has increased. During the carcinogenesis of HCC, an alteration of the vascular supply to the liver parenchyma occurs. In a healthy liver, most of the vascular supply is provided by the portal vein (80%), with the remaining arterial supply being provided by the hepatic arteries (20%). As the angiogenesis of HCC nodules develops, the previously described vascular supply becomes abnormal with a disproportionate high arterial supply, derived from the tumor arteries [19].

The use of contrast agents in CT scans has granted the detection of this hypervascularity during the arterial phase and helps aid in screening for HCC at early stages [20]. Hence, hypervascularity in arterial phase washout, and hypoenhancement of HCC lesions due to unequal portal supply during the portal or delayed phase, has become a pathognomonic feature for the diagnosis of HCC using CT imaging with intravenous contrast agents. As described previously, compared to the ultrasonographic technique, CT has greater sensitivity in the detection of lesions above >2 cm. In any stage of HCC, CT demonstrates excellent sensitivity and specificity of 87.5% (95% CI, 50.8%–99.9%) and 87.5% (95% CI, 77.7%–93.5%), respectively [13]. However, in early-stage HCC, CT scan sensitivity is significantly decreased to 62.5% (95% CI, 30.4%–86.5%), although it does not differ significantly from that of ultrasonography [21].

In lesions ≤ 3 cm, a recent retrospective analysis in China reported the sensitivity of CT for the detection of HCC to be only 62.3%, with a specificity of 73.8% [22]. In a *meta*-analysis comparing the use of CT versus MRI for the detection of HCC, an overall sensitivity of CT to detect the disease was reported to be close to 68% (95% CI: 55%–80%), with a specificity of 93% (95% CI: 89%–96%) [23]. Although CT imaging is highly sensitive to the detection of

HCC, its use is also associated with ionizing radiation exposure and the possible development of contrast-induced nephropathy, after iodine contrast administration [24].

Magnetic resonance imaging

Similar to CT imaging, the use of magnetic resonance imaging (MRI) has also been employed in the diagnosis of HCC. Organizations, such as the United Network for Organ Sharing and the European Society for Organ Transplantation, now support the use of MRI in the diagnosis of HCC, in order to avoid obtaining liver tissue biopsies [25]. The clear advantage of MRI over CT imaging is the avoidance of ionizing radiation [26]. Another distinct advantage is the use of gadolinium contrast in MRI studies, as opposed to the use of iodinated contrast in CT. A study aimed to compare the degree of nephrotoxicity caused by gadolinium chelates versus iodinated contrast by trending the serum creatinine after exposure to these agents. It was concluded that of the 64 patients involved in the study, 11 patients who received iodinated contrast developed contrast-induced nephropathy. Furthermore, it was revealed that of the patients who received gadolinium, none developed contrast-induced renal failure [27].

Characteristic imaging findings of HCC in MRI studies are also dependent on the vascular pattern changes caused by the angiogenesis of the tumor. Typically, HCC displays a high-intensity signal on T2-weighted images, with hypointensity during the portal venous phase. This characteristic intense arterial phase enhancement is also present with variable degrees of intensity during T1-weighted images [28]. Additionally, another defining feature of HCC is the presence of a fibrous capsule that may be found surrounding various gross nodular subtypes. This capsule is described as a rim of hypointensity on T1-weighted images and an enhancing rim on the delayed phase images [29].

As described by the previous imaging studies, MRI continues to exhibit suboptimal sensitivity for lesions ≤2 cm, with sensitivities reported in some cases <50% [30]. In a single-center study, the sensitivity of MRI to the detection of HCC nodules, 2−4 cm in size, was reported to be 86%, with a specificity of 93% [30]. Furthermore, the sensitivity to nodules >4 cm reached 96%. In the detection of HCC nodules using MRI, another study placed the sensitivity closer to 96%; however, the parameter decreased to 30% with detecting nodules that are <2 cm [31].

Tumor markers

Even though the use of imaging studies to aid in the screening and diagnosis of HCC has become an exceptional tool in a modern clinician's arsenal, tumor markers are still used and are common in clinical practice. The use of AFP, a fetal-specific glycoprotein, which declines rapidly after birth, has been used to monitor the development and recurrence of hepatic cancer [32]. One of the shortcomings of using AFP to screen for HCC is that it may become elevated in the presence of chronic liver disease, as well as in gastric and lung cancer [33]. From previous studies, the use of AFP alone to detect HCC was reported to have a sensitivity of 39%−65%, specificity of 76%−94%, and a positive predictive value of 9%–50% [34]. The cut-off value for AFP to diagnose HCC is controversial; however, studies have shown that levels over >400 ng/mL are linked to advanced disease and poor survival [35]. Three different glycoforms of AFP have been discovered, (AFP-L1, AFP-L2, and AFP-L3), according to their ability to bind to the lectin lens agglutinin (LCA). Most specifically, AFP-L3 has only been found in the serum of patients with HCC with a sensitivity of up to 96.9% in detecting HCC [36].

Glypican-3 (GPC3), a cell-surface glycoprotein, has been shown to be expressed in 72% of HCC tissue [37]. In comparison to AFP, a distinct advantage of GPC3 is that it was not found in chronic liver disease or in healthy subjects. The use of both AFP and GPC3 combined to diagnose HCC was shown to increase overall sensitivity from 50% to 72% [38]. Squamous cell carcinoma antigen (SCCA), a serine protease inhibitor, has additionally been found to be elevated in the serum of HCC patients [39]. It has been shown to have a sensitivity of 84%, yet a low specificity of 49%, with a cut-off value of 0.37 ng/mL [39]. It has been hypothesized that combining several markers could help with the detection of HCC, though this has not been shown to be reliable in clinical practice.

An interesting molecule identified as Annexin A2, which is a phospholipid-binding protein found on cell surfaces, has also been used to screen for early HCC [40]. Annexin A2 is involved in cell cytoskeleton and endocytosis, with the hypothesis that it may play a role in HCC metastasis. A novel study conducted with mice aimed to compare the sensitivity of AFP versus Annexin A2 to detect early-stage HCC. The results from this study demonstrated a higher sensitivity of Annexin A2 (83.2%) when compared to AFP (67.5%), in the detection of early HCC tumors [41].

Lastly, des-γ-carboxyprothrombin (DCP) is a protein present in patients with vitamin K deficiency. Such deficiency is also present in HCC, affecting the normal function of liver cells and the vitamin K-dependent carboxylation system [42]. A recent *meta*-analysis demonstrated the superior sensitivity of AFP + DCP (82%) versus AFP (65%) alone to detection of HCC [43].

Guidelines for hepatocellular carcinoma surveillance

Surveillance of HCC in high-risk populations is essential as the incidence of HCC in the United States continues to increase rapidly. Screening in the United States remains suboptimal and requires improvement. Despite recommendations by international societies, only one out of five high-risk patients is screened [44]. Surveillance is essential because it allows for early tumor detection and exploiting the potential of curative therapies. Studies have shown that early diagnosis of HCC through surveillance programs improves prognosis and outcomes of curative treatments [45]. Prognosis of HCC depends on the stage, with remedial options available only for patients diagnosed at an early stage [46]. Therefore, surveillance in high-risk populations is vital as early diagnosis of HCC can lead to a better treatment and prognosis. As such, the awareness of management is paramount, and clinicians should work together to improve compliance.

It is vital to distinguish the potential harms and benefits of screening prior to enrolling a patient into a screening program. Although surveillance is important, it can potentially place the patient at risk for physical, financial, and psychological harm [45]. Harm may occur due to unnecessary imaging, biopsies, and procedures. Therefore, the benefits should be weighed and compared to the potential harms of false-positive or indeterminate surveillance results. Studies have shown that over one-fourth of patients with cirrhosis experience harm from false-positive or indeterminate surveillance tests [47]. The decision to enroll a patient into a surveillance program is ultimately made depending on the level of risk for HCC, while also considering factors such as the patient's age, functional status, overall health, willingness, and ability to comply with surveillance requirements [48].

Guidelines for HCC surveillance have been issued by the American Association for the Study of Liver Diseases (AASLD), the European Association for the Study of the Liver (EASL), and the Asian Pacific Association for the Study of Liver (APAS). These guidelines define high-risk populations and determine screening intervals, as well as provide recommendations regarding appropriate imaging modalities and biomarkers for HCC screening. The guidelines agree on recommendations for screening imaging modalities and screening intervals, though they differ in the definitions of "high-risk populations" and recommended screening biomarkers.

In light of the high annual risk (2%–4% annually) of HCC development in patients with cirrhosis, guidelines from all international professional societies state that every cirrhotic patient, regardless of etiology, should be screened for HCC [45]. Each of the societies has defined further recommendations as to which patients are considered high risk (Table 18.3).

All international guidelines have come to the consensus that ultrasound is the imaging modality of choice. The fact that it is inexpensive, noninvasive, readily available, fairly accurate, and well tolerated makes it ideal [45]. However, the sensitivity of ultrasonography is affected by the operator's experience. An experienced operator should ideally perform the ultrasonography to yield the highest sensitivity. In certain circumstances, CT and MRI may serve as viable imaging alternatives. However, these modalities are not considered cost-effective and, therefore, not regarded as first-line screening options.

Biomarkers such as AFP have been widely studied for the use of HCC surveillance. AFP levels are often used in conjunction with imaging modalities to increase the sensitivity. Obtaining AFP levels is inexpensive and easy to perform. However, not all the international guidelines agree with the use of AFP levels for screening. Others recommend leaving the decision to obtain AFP at the discretion of the clinician. Most international guidelines recommend screening patients every 6 months. The semiannual screening was initially recommended based on the tumor doubling time. Then, studies supported that semiannual screening was superior to annual screening in detecting HCC early and thus improving survival rates [49]. Early screening, such as 3-month instead of 6-month screening, has not been shown to detect HCC earlier, nor has it been shown to improve survival rates [49].

The AASLD defines noncirrhotic patients with hepatitis B virus (HBV) as high risk. Patients with chronic HBV are particularly at high risk. HBV has been shown to integrate with the host genome in the majority of patients with chronic HBV. Integration with the genome subsequently induces genetic damage and activates various pathways. Such damage has been noted in nontumor cells of patients with HCC even in the absence of liver cirrhosis. Thus this may suggest that those with chronic HBV are at a notable risk of developing HCC even in the absence of liver cirrhosis [50]. Studies show that a family history of HCC in patients with chronic HBV is associated with a significant risk of developing HCC as well [51].

TABLE 18.3   A summary of the key points of the "guidelines" from major international professional societies stating that every cirrhotic patient should be screened for hepatocellular carcinoma (HCC).

Guideline	American Association for the Study of Liver Diseases (AASLD)	European Association for the Study of the Liver (EASL)	Asian Pacific Association for the Study of Liver (APASL)
High-risk populations	Cirrhotic patients • Child–Pugh stage C awaiting liver transplant • Child–Pugh stages A and B Noncirrhotic patients with HBV	Cirrhotic patients • Child–Pugh stages A and B • Child–Pugh stage C awaiting liver transplant Noncirrhotic patients • With HBV and an intermediate or high risk of HCC • With chronic HCV and bridging fibrosis	Cirrhotic patients Noncirrhotic patients with HBV Noncirrhotic patients with HBV in addition to the following: females >50 years of age, Asian males >40 years of age, Africans >20 years of age, or those who have a family history of HCC
Screening intervals	Every 6 months	Every 6 months	Every 6 months
Imaging modality	Ultrasound	Ultrasound	Ultrasound
Biomarkers	At the discretion of physician	Not recommended	AFP

AFP, alpha-fetoprotein; *HCC*, hepatocellular carcinoma; *HBV*, hepatitis B virus; *HCV*, hepatitis C virus.

Preexisting cirrhosis, regardless of etiology, is considered a risk factor for the development of HCC [52]. Therefore, those diagnosed with the major symptoms of cirrhosis are also considered high risk for the development of HCC. These include patients with HBV, hepatitis C virus (HCV), and alcoholic and nonalcoholic fatty liver disease (NAFLD). There is also evidence that patients with HBV who consume alcohol and smoke heavily have a ninefold risk of developing HCC [53].

As per the AASLD, patients with cirrhosis who are Child–Pugh stages A and B or Child–Pugh stage C awaiting liver transplant are also considered as high risk. The AASLD is in concordance with the others as it also recommends screening these patients at 6-month intervals. The imaging modality of choice is ultrasound, with or without AFP levels. Like the AASLD guidelines, the European Association for the Study of the Liver (EASL) also defines high-risk populations as those with cirrhosis who are Child–Pugh stages A and B or Child–Pugh stage C awaiting a liver transplant. Also, the EASL defines high-risk patients as those without cirrhosis with HBV and at an intermediate or high risk of HCC [according to the PAGE-B (Platelets, Age, GEnder B) classes for Caucasian subjects] or those with chronic HCV and bridging fibrosis. Screening in such patients should occur at 6-month intervals with ultrasonography and without the need for concurrent measurement of biomarkers. However, the importance of having experienced personnel for sonographic imaging is emphasized. The APASL (Asian Pacific Association for the

Study of Liver) defines high-risk patients as those who have been diagnosed with cirrhosis. The noncirrhotic group includes patients who have HBV in addition to being female >50 years of age, Asian males >40 years of age, African >20 years of age, and those with a family history of HCC. Screening intervals are recommended every 6 month with both AFP levels and ultrasonography.

The guidelines provided by the aforementioned international professional societies aid clinicians in screening high-risk patients for HCC. These guidelines allow for early detection of HCC in high-risk populations and potential cures for those detected at an early stage. As the incidence rate of HCC in the United States continues to rise, it is imperative for clinicians to improve compliance and initiation of surveillance programs. Awareness of the current guidelines and application of these guidelines into clinical practice is vital. The recommendations from the individual societies may have slight differences; however, the collective aim is early detection of HCC and to ultimately improve prognosis.

Cost-effectiveness of hepatocellular carcinoma diagnostic modalities

Despite the many modalities available for the screening and diagnosis of HCC, clinicians must take into account the cost, both for the patient and for the healthcare system as a whole. In a 2012 retrospective study by Rugerri [54], the most cost-effective strategy was found to be ultrasonography and AFP, yielding the best incremental cost-to-effectiveness ratio in both the United States and Europe. In an earlier study by Saab et al. [55] in 2003, ultrasonography was found to be the most cost-effective imaging modality also when compared to CT. However, a more recent 2019 Canadian study by Lima et al. [56] found that CT for HCC surveillance and diagnosis and complete MRI for inadequate CT was the most cost-effective. Given the vast spread of HCC throughout different socioeconomic regions of the world, ultrasonography remains the most cost-effective imaging modality due to its low cost and high accessibility. Supplementing with tumor biomarkers remains at the discretion of the clinician based on the availability of resources and adequate compensation for testing.

Conflict of interest

None of the authors has any potential financial or commercial conflict of interest associated with this research work. The manuscript has been read by all the authors, who have diligently contributed to the writing and consented for its publication.

References

[1] Adami HO, Hunter DJ, Trichopoulos D, editors. Textbook of cancer epidemiology. Oxford University Press; 2008.
[2] IARC, International Agency for Research on Cancer, 2021.
[3] Parkin DM. The global health burden of infection-associated cancers in the year 2002. Int J Cancer 2006;118 (12):3030—44. Available from: https://doi.org/10.1002/ijc.21731.
[4] Mittal S, El-Serag HB. Epidemiology of HCC: consider the population. J Clin Gastroenterol 2013;47:S2.

[5] Zhang DY, Friedman SL. Fibrosis-dependent mechanisms of hepatocarcinogenesis. Hepatology 2012;56 (2):769–75.

[6] Ghouri YA, Mian I, Rowe JH. Review of hepatocellular carcinoma: epidemiology, etiology, and carcinogenesis. J Carcinog 2017;16:1. Available from: https://doi.org/10.4103/jcar.JCar_9_16.

[7] World Health Organization. Global Hepatitis Report 2017. WHO; 2017.

[8] Welzel TM, Graubard BI, Zeuzem S, El-Serag HB, Davila JA, McGlynn KA. Metabolic syndrome increases the risk of primary liver cancer in the United States: a study in the SEER-Medicare database. Hepatology 2011;54(2):463–71.

[9] Younossi ZM, Otgonsuren M, Henry L, Venkatesan C, Mishra A, Erario M, et al. Association of Nonalcoholic Fatty Liver Disease (NAFLD) with hepatocellular carcinoma (HCC) in the United States from 2004 to 2009. Hepatology 2015;62(6):1723–30.

[10] Bressac B, Kew M, Wands J, Ozturk M. Nature 1991;350:429–31.

[11] Tanaka H. Current role of ultrasound in the diagnosis of hepatocellular carcinoma. J Med Ultrason 2020;47 (2):239–55.

[12] Dong Y, Mao F, Cao J, Fan P, Wang WP. Characterization of focal liver lesions indistinctive on B mode ultrasound: benefits of contrast-enhanced ultrasound. BioMed Res Int 2017;2017:8970156. Available from: https://doi.org/10.1155/2017/8970156.

[13] Kutami R, Nakashima Y, Nakashima O, Shiota K, Kojiro M. Pathomorphologic study on the mechanism of fatty change in small hepatocellular carcinoma of humans. J Hepatol 2000;33(2):282–9.

[14] Higashi T, Tobe K, Asano KI, Ikeda H, Ohsawa T, Iwasaki Y, et al. Ultrasonographic characteristics of small hepatocellular carcinoma. Acta Medica Okayama 1988;42(3):151–7.

[15] Heimbach JK, Kulik LM, Finn RS, Sirlin CB, Abecassis MM, Roberts LR, et al. AASLD guidelines for the treatment of hepatocellular carcinoma. Hepatology 2018;67(1):358–80.

[16] Tzartzeva K, Obi J, Rich NE, Parikh ND, Marrero JA, Yopp A, et al. Surveillance imaging and alpha fetoprotein for early detection of hepatocellular carcinoma in patients with cirrhosis: a *meta*-analysis. Gastroenterology 2018;154(6):1706–18.

[17] Niu Y, Huang T, Lian F, Li F. Contrast-enhanced ultrasonography for the diagnosis of small hepatocellular carcinoma: a *meta*-analysis and *meta*-regression analysis. Tumor Biol 2013;34(6):3667–74.

[18] Bruix J, Sherman M. Management of hepatocellular carcinoma: an update. Hepatology 2011;53(3):1020.

[19] Cassinotto C, Aubé C, Dohan A. Diagnosis of hepatocellular carcinoma: an update on international guidelines. Diagnostic Interven Imaging 2017;98(5):379–91.

[20] Bruix J, Sherman M, Llovet JM, Beaugrand M, Lencioni R, Burroughs AK, et al. Clinical management of hepatocellular carcinoma. Conclusions of the Barcelona-2000 EASL Conference. J Hepatol 2001;35(3):421–30.

[21] Nault JC, Bioulac–Sage P, Zucman–Rossi J. Reviews in basic and clinical gastroenterology and hepatology. Gastroenterology 2013;144:888–902.

[22] Wang G, Zhu S, Li X. Comparison of values of CT and MRI imaging in the diagnosis of hepatocellular carcinoma and analysis of prognostic factors. Oncol Lett 2019;17(1):1184–8.

[23] Lee YJ, Lee JM, Lee JS, Lee HY, Park BH, Kim YH, et al. Hepatocellular carcinoma: diagnostic performance of multidetector CT and MR imaging - a systematic review and *meta*-analysis. Radiology 2015;275(1):97–109.

[24] Bruner A, Sutker W, Maxwell G. Minimizing patient exposure to ionizing radiation from computed tomography scans. Baylor University Medical Center proceedings, Vol. 22. Taylor & Francis; 2009. p. 119–23. No. 2.

[25] Compagnon P, Grandadam S, Lorho R, Turlin B, Camus C, Jianrong Y, et al. Liver transplantation for hepatocellular carcinoma without preoperative tumor biopsy. Transplantation 2008;86(8):1068–76.

[26] Attwa MH, El-Etreby SA. Guide for diagnosis and treatment of hepatocellular carcinoma. World J Hepatol 2015;7(12):1632.

[27] Prince MR, Arnoldus C, Frisoli JK. Nephrotoxicity of high-dose gadolinium compared with iodinated contrast. J Magn Reson Imaging 1996;6(1):162–6.

[28] Taouli B, Losada M, Holland A, Krinsky G. Magnetic resonance imaging of hepatocellular carcinoma. Gastroenterology 2004;127(5):S144–52.

[29] Onaya H, Itai Y. MR imaging of hepatocellular carcinoma. Magn Reson Imaging Clin North Am 2000;8(4):757–68.

[30] Nam CY, Chaudhari V, Raman SS, Lassman C, Tong MJ, Busuttil RW, et al. CT and MRI improve detection of hepatocellular carcinoma, compared with ultrasound alone, in patients with cirrhosis. Clin Gastroenterol Hepatol 2011;9(2):161–7.

[31] Ebara M, Ohto M, Watanabe Y, Kimura K, Saisho H, Tsuchiya Y, et al. Diagnosis of small hepatocellular carcinoma: correlation of MR imaging and tumor histologic studies. Radiology 1986;159(2):371–7.

[32] Gupta S, Bent S, Kohlwes J. Test characteristics of α-fetoprotein for detecting hepatocellular carcinoma in patients with hepatitis C: a systematic review and critical analysis. Ann Intern Med 2003;139(1):46−50.

[33] Gomaa AI, Khan SA, Leen EL, Waked I, Taylor-Robinson SD. Diagnosis of hepatocellular carcinoma. World J Gastroenterol WJG 2009;15(11):1301.

[34] Daniele B, Bencivenga A, Megna AS, Tinessa V. α-Fetoprotein and ultrasonography screening for hepatocellular carcinoma. Gastroenterology 2004;127(5):S108−12.

[35] Farinati F, Marino D, De Giorgio M, Baldan A, Cantarini M, Cursaro C, et al. Diagnostic and prognostic role of α-fetoprotein in hepatocellular carcinoma: both or neither? Am J Gastroenterol 2006;101(3):524−32.

[36] Singhal A, Jayaraman M, Dhanasekaran DN, Kohli V. Molecular and serum markers in hepatocellular carcinoma: predictive tools for prognosis and recurrence. Crit Rev Oncol/Hematol 2012;82(2):116−40.

[37] Capurro M, Wanless IR, Sherman M, Deboer G, Shi W, Miyoshi E, et al. Glypican-3: a novel serum and histochemical marker for hepatocellular carcinoma. Gastroenterology 2003;125(1):89−97.

[38] Zhou L, Liu J, Luo F. Serum tumor markers for detection of hepatocellular carcinoma. World J Gastroenterol 2006;12(8):1175.

[39] Giannelli G, Fransvea E, Trerotoli P, Beaugrand M, Marinosci F, Lupo L, et al. Clinical validation of combined serological biomarkers for improved hepatocellular carcinoma diagnosis in 961 patients. Clin Chim Acta 2007;383(1−2):147−52.

[40] Lokman NA, Ween MP, Oehler MK, Ricciardelli C. The role of annexin A2 in tumorigenesis and cancer progression. Cancer Microenviron 2011;4(2):199−208.

[41] Sun Y, Gao G, Cai J, Wang Y, Qu X, He L, et al. Annexin A2 is a discriminative serological candidate in early hepatocellular carcinoma. Carcinogenesis 2013;34(3):595−604.

[42] Naraki T, Kohno N, Saito H, Fujimoto Y, Ohhira M, Morita T, et al. γ-Carboxyglutamic acid content of hepatocellular carcinoma-associated des-γ-carboxy prothrombin. Biochim Biophys Acta Mol Basis Dis 2002;1586 (3):287−98.

[43] Chen H, Chen S, Li S, Chen Z, Zhu X, Dai M, et al. Combining des-gamma-carboxyprothrombin and alpha-fetoprotein for hepatocellular carcinoma diagnosing: an update *meta*-analysis and validation study. Oncotarget 2017;8(52):90390−401. Available from: https://doi.org/10.18632/oncotarget.20153.

[44] Singal AG, Yopp A, S Skinner C, Packer M, Lee WM, Tiro JA. Utilization of hepatocellular carcinoma surveillance among American patients: a systematic review. J Gen Intern Med 2012;27(7):861−7. Available from: https://doi.org/10.1007/s11606-011-1952-x.

[45] Frenette CT, Isaacson AJ, Bargellini I, Saab S, Singal AG. A practical guideline for hepatocellular carcinoma screening in patients at risk. Mayo Clin Proc Innov Qual Outcomes 2019;3(3):302−10. Available from: https://doi.org/10.1016/j.mayocpiqo.2019.04.005.

[46] Singal AG, Pillai A, Tiro J. Early detection, curative treatment, and survival rates for hepatocellular carcinoma surveillance in patients with cirrhosis: a *meta*-analysis. PLoS Med 2014;11(4):e1001624. Available from: https://doi.org/10.1371/journal.pmed.1001624.

[47] Atiq O, Tiro J, Yopp AC, Muffler A, Marrero JA, Parikh ND, et al. An assessment of benefits and harms of hepatocellular carcinoma surveillance in patients with cirrhosis. Hepatology 2017;65(4):1196−205. Available from: https://doi.org/10.1002/hep.28895.

[48] Marrero JA, Kulik LM, Sirlin CB, Zhu AX, Finn RS, Abecassis MM, et al. Diagnosis, staging, and management of hepatocellular carcinoma: 2018 Practice Guidance by the American Association for the Study of Liver Diseases. Hepatology 2018;68(2):723−50. Available from: https://doi.org/10.1002/hep.29913.

[49] Santi V, Trevisani F, Gramenzi A, Grignaschi A, Mirici-Cappa F, Del Poggio P, et al. Semiannual surveillance is superior to annual surveillance for the detection of early hepatocellular carcinoma and patient survival. J Hepatol 2010;53(2):291−7. Available from: https://doi.org/10.1016/j.jhep.2010.03.010.

[50] Ayub A, Ashfaq UA, Haque A. HBV induced HCC: major risk factors from genetic to molecular level. BioMed Res Int 2013;2013:810461. Available from: https://doi.org/10.1155/2013/810461.

[51] Loomba R, Liu J, Yang HI, Lee MH, Lu SN, Wang LY, et al. Synergistic effects of family history of hepatocellular carcinoma and hepatitis B virus infection on risk for incident hepatocellular carcinoma. Clin Gastroenterol Hepatol 2013;11(12):40−43. Available from: https://doi.org/10.1016/j.cgh.2013.04.043.

[52] Tarao K, Nozaki A, Ikeda T, Sato A, Komatsu H, Komatsu T, et al. Real impact of liver cirrhosis on the development of hepatocellular carcinoma in various liver diseases-*meta*-analytic assessment. Cancer Med 2019;8 (3):1054−65. Available from: https://doi.org/10.1002/cam4.1998.

[53] Kuper H, Tzonou A, Kaklamani E, Hsieh CC, Lagiou P, Adami HO, et al. Tobacco smoking, alcohol consumption and their interaction in the causation of hepatocellular carcinoma. Int J Cancer 2000;85(4):498—502.

[54] Ruggeri M. Hepatocellular carcinoma: cost-effectiveness of screening. A systematic review. Risk Manag Healthc Policy 2012;5:49—54. Available from: https://doi.org/10.2147/RMHP.S18677.

[55] Saab S, Ly D, Nieto J, Kanwal F, Lu D, Raman S, et al. Hepatocellular carcinoma screening in patients waiting for liver transplantation: a decision analytic model. Liver Transplant 2003;9(7):672—81. Available from: https://doi.org/10.1053/jlts.2003.50120.

[56] Lima PH, Fan B, Bérubé J, Cerny M, Olivié D, Giard JM, et al. Cost-utility analysis of imaging for surveillance and diagnosis of hepatocellular carcinoma. Am J Roentgenol 2019;213(1):17—25. Available from: https://doi.org/10.2214/AJR.18.20341.

Precision medicine approaches for treating hepatocellular carcinoma

Nadia Ahmed, Kevin Benny, Sohail Siraj, Hufsa Ali and Riyaz Basha

Texas College of Osteopathic Medicine, University of North Texas Health Science Center, Fort Worth, TX, United States

Abstract

Hepatocellular carcinoma (HCC) accounts for the majority of liver cancer diagnoses and deaths. Risk factors for HCC include viral infections, such as hepatitis B and C, heavy alcohol use, lifestyle choices, and certain inherited genetic disorders. The complex interheterogeneity and intraheterogeneity of HCC tumors requires a more individualized treatment approach. Precision medicine uses next-generation sequencing (NGS) to map a tumor's genome to identify molecular alterations that are targetable by small molecules and immunotherapies. Although the most common oncogenic drivers of HCC are currently nonactionable, precision medicine technology has been utilized to identify biomarkers capable of predicting treatment response or primary resistance to guide clinical decision-making. This chapter will discuss the current advancements and challenges of precision medicine in HCC.

Keywords: Hepatocellular carcinoma; precision medicine; biomarkers; therapeutic outcomes

Abbreviations

ABC	ATP-binding cassette
AFP	Alpha-fetoprotein
ARID	AT-rich interaction domain
BCLC	Barcelona Clinic Liver Cancer
CCND1	Cyclin D1
CD	Cell adhesion
CDKN2A	Cyclin-dependent kinase inhibitor 2A
CSF	Cerebrospinal fluid
CT	Computed tomography
CtDNA	Circulating tumor DNA

Ganji Purnachandra Nagaraju, Sarfraz Ahmad (eds.)
Theranostics and Precision Medicine for the Management of Hepatocellular Carcinoma, Volume 3

287

CTNNB1	β-Catenin
DEB	Drug eluting beads
EGFR	Epidermal growth factor receptor
EMT	Epithelial-mesenchymal transition
FGF19	Fibroblast growth factor 19
FGFR	FGF receptor
KEAP1	Kelch-like ECH-associated protein 1
KLF4	Kruppel-like factor 4
LI-RADS	Liver Reporting and Data System
MRI	Magnetic resonance imaging
MRPTs	Multidrug resistance protein transporters
NASH	Nonalcoholic steatohepatitis
NFE2L2	Nuclear factor, erythroid 2 like 2
NGS	Next-generation sequencing
PD-1	Programmed cell death protein 1
PDGFR	PDGF receptor
PD-L1	Programmed cell death 1 ligand 1
PI3K	Phosphoinositide 3-kinase
PTEN	Phosphatase and tensin homologue
RFA	Radiofrequency ablation
RPS6KA3	Ribosomal protein S6 kinase 90 kDa, polypeptide 3
TACE	Transarterial Chemoembolization
TARE	Transarterial Radioembolization
TERT	Telomerase reverse transcriptase
TGFβR1	TGFβ type 1 receptor
TP53	Tumor protein p53
US	Ultra sound
VEGFA	vascular endothelial growth factor A
VEGFR	VEGF receptor

General information on hepatocellular carcinoma

Liver cancer comprises a sizable share of the worldwide cancer burden with approximately 906,000 new cases and 830,000 deaths in 2020 [1]. It ranks as the sixth most frequently diagnosed cancer and the third leading cause of cancer death worldwide with both incidence and mortality being 2–3 times higher in men than women [1]. Due to the large reserve capacity of the liver, diagnosis is usually late in the disease course with overall median survival being 11 months following diagnosis [2].

Primary liver cancer can be classified into hepatocellular carcinoma (HCC) which comprises 75%–85% of cases, intrahepatic cholangiocarcinoma with 10%–15% of cases, and other rare types including angiosarcoma and hepatoblastoma. The incidence of HCC varies by geographic region with an estimated 72% of cases occurring in Asia, 10% in Europe, 8% in Africa, 5% in North America, and 4% in Latin America [1]. This disparity in geographical incidence is most likely due to regional differences in exposure to viral and environmental insults. Although the risk factors for HCC vary by geographical region, cirrhosis from any cause prevails as the most significant predictor of HCC [3]. At present, chronic infection with hepatitis B and hepatitis C virus stands as the most important global risk factor for the development of viral-associated HCC but that may change with the increasing rate of newborn vaccination against HBV and effective therapies for chronic

HBV and HCV. This gives way for the rising metabolic risk factors such as metabolic syndrome, type II diabetes, and nonalcoholic steatohepatitis (NASH) to take its place as the major cause of HCC worldwide [4].

Most patients with HCC exhibit no symptoms related to the tumor itself and those with advanced liver disease often present with signs and symptoms due to underlying cirrhosis rather than the primary liver tumor. The role of surveillance is the key in detecting early lesions especially in high-risk patients such as those with cirrhosis and chronic hepatitis B infection [5]. Surveillance is carried out via abdominal ultrasound at 6-month intervals and is focused on the liver with added studies of spleen for some cases [3]. Although alpha-fetoprotein (AFP) can be elevated in patients with HCC, serum levels are not used as a primary surveillance tool owing to its poor sensitivity and specificity [6].

The diagnostic approach to HCC is largely noninvasive and can be achieved through contrast-enhanced computed tomography (CT), magnetic resonance imaging (MRI), or ultrasound (US). Non-high-risk patients require a biopsy of the lesion to confirm the diagnosis, whereas imaging is sufficient to make the diagnosis in high-risk patients [7]. LI-RADS (Liver Reporting and Data System) is the standardized reporting tool used to characterize the relative likelihood of malignancy associated with HCC and details actions recommended at each category of lesion [7]. Treatment modality selection is informed by disease extent as well as the severity of underlying liver dysfunction. The Child-Turcotte-Pugh classification is a commonly used system to classify the level of cirrhosis according to prothrombin time, bilirubin, albumin, presence of ascites and/or encephalopathy. As per the Americas Hepato-Pancreato-Biliary Association and the American Join Committee on Cancer (AJCC) consensus conference in 2010, HCC staging should be achieved through multiple systems such as the TNM system, the Barcelona Clinic Liver Cancer (BCLC) system, as well as the Okuda and CLIP systems [8,9].

The general approach to selecting the most appropriate treatment modality relies on the combination of the above staging systems with consideration given to the severity of underlying liver disease (Fig. 19.1). The mainstay of treatment remains surgical resection or liver transplantation, but most patients are ineligible due to tumor burden or liver dysfunction [10].

Ablation

For nonsurgical early-stage cases of HCC, radiofrequency ablation (RFA) of the lesion is the preferred initial treatment modality. It is also used as "bridging" therapy in those awaiting liver transplants [11]. Percutaneous ablation using ethanol or acetic acid was widely used owing to its low cost and minimal need for equipment but has declined due to the increasing availability and efficacy of RFA [12]. Microwave ablation is a popular method of locoregional ablation used in China and Japan that is gaining increasing usage in the United States. It features the ability to perform multiple ablations simultaneously, an advantage over RFA [13]. For peripherally located lesions and lesions where thermal ablation is inappropriate, cryoablation may be more suitable.

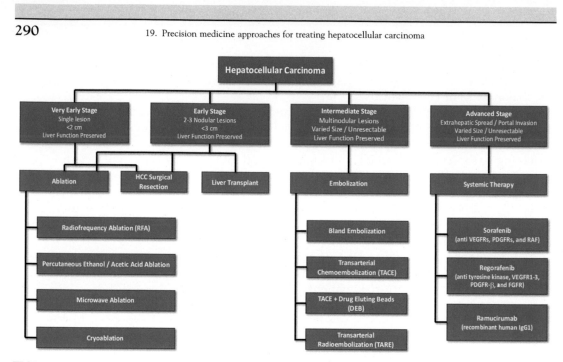

FIGURE 19.1 Overview of treatment options for hepatocellular carcinoma. This schematic outlines the most common modalities available for the treatment of hepatocellular carcinoma delineated by the prognostic stage at which each is typically utilized. The indications for each specific modality are not included but a summary of the criteria for each prognostic stage is included.

Embolization

Since the major blood supply for the liver is the hepatic artery, it follows that any HCC lesion developing within the hepatic capsule is susceptible to embolization. Although bland embolization, which utilizes particles to induce tumor ischemia has been utilized successfully in treatment of unresectable and recurrent HCC, numerous guidelines prefer transarterial chemoembolization (TACE) for intermediate-stage unresectable HCC [14]. Traditional TACE involves injection of a chemotherapy agent along with a procoagulant or lipiodol, an intratumor sequestrant, directly into the hepatic artery [15]. However, the most common form of TACE utilizes drug-eluting beads (DEB) which has been shown to cause less toxicity than using lipiodol. Transarterial radioembolization (TARE) uses intraarterial injection of 90-Y-labeled microspheres to trigger tumor ischemia but its high cost and questionable efficacy when compared to TACE has limited the utility of this treatment [16].

Precision medicine definition and use in cancers in general

As our understanding of the underlying biology behind cancer development improves, the conventional method of cancer classification and therapy selection based on tissue location and histology has been exposed as inadequate in certain cancers. An alternative approach, termed precision medicine, promises more personalized care by matching patients to therapies based on their tumor's genetics [17−19]. This is done using a process called next-generation sequencing (NGS), a large-scale DNA sequencing technology that allows for mapping of the tumor genome to search for clinically relevant molecular aberrations. Some of these aberrations are fundamental to cancer initiation and progression and are termed "actionable" if mechanism-based therapies such as small molecules or monoclonal antibodies are available to target them [20]. One of the earliest examples of using genetic information to guide cancer therapy was the use of trastuzumab in breast cancers that were identified to overexpress the *HER2/neu* gene, an important oncogenic driver of breast tumors [21,22]. The immunotherapeutic drug, trastuzumab, is a humanized monoclonal antibody made to target and binds the HER2 protein on the surface of cancer cells [23]. This causes internalization and degradation of the receptor, decreasing its downstream growth-promoting activity [24,25]. It also leads to accumulation of monoclonal antibodies on the cell surface, which serves as a signal for the immune system to then identify and kill cancerous cells [24,25]. Another actionable target is the V600E mutation on the BRAF gene, a mutation that causes overactivity of its protein product BRAF kinase leading to dysregulated cellular proliferation [26]. This mutation is most commonly associated with melanomas, but has also been identified in other neoplasms such as colorectal carcinomas and papillary thyroid carcinomas [27]. The small molecule inhibitor, vemurafenib, is used to selectively bind to and inhibit the mutated BRAF kinase protein to decrease its activity [28,29]. When using targeted therapies such as these, an important thing to consider is the presence of crosstalk between pathways, creating redundancies that cancerous cells may utilize to resist targeted treatment [30]. This obstacle led to low response rates with monotherapeutic precision medicine strategies and has inspired the idea for combination therapy, where multiple drugs work together to inhibit several steps of a molecular pathway (Fig. 19.2) [31−36]. Studies have shown increased disease control rates and overall survival in patients treated with multidrug regimens, making the use of combinatorial drug therapy likely in the future of precision medicine [37].

Significance for using precision medicine approaches for treating hepatocellular carcinoma

Due to significant intertumor and intratumor heterogeneity, HCC can be very complex and difficult to treat [38,39]. Future therapeutic strategies for HCC will likely make use of precision medicine to identify the specific oncogenic drivers and affected pathways involved. NGS technology has already revealed several of the driver genes commonly affected in HCC. These include the telomerase reverse transcriptase (TERT), β-catenin (CTNNB1), and tumor protein p53 (TP53) genes, none of which are actionable at present [40−44]. The targeted therapies currently being evaluated for use in HCC include tyrosine kinase inhibitors, antivascular endothelial growth factor receptor (VEGFR) antibodies, and immune checkpoint inhibitors. Response rates to these drugs have been low, indicating the need for predictive biomarkers to better guide clinical management [45−49]. Precision medicine and NGS technology are being used to identify these biomarkers, which not only

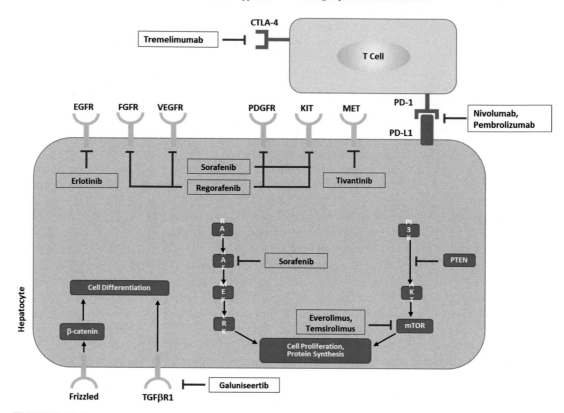

FIGURE 19.2   Examples of targeted therapies in hepatocellular carcinoma (HCC) and their mechanisms. Targeted therapies that are typically used in HCC are illustrated.

provides more information about which patients may benefit from treatment but also which patients may be resistant to certain targeted therapies.

The current first-line therapy, sorafenib, is a small molecule that inhibits tumor cell proliferation and angiogenesis by targeting VEGFRs, PDGFRs, and RAF [49]. Phase III studies have shown improved median overall survival (OS) and disease control rates (DCR) with the use of sorafenib in patients with advanced HCC [48,50]. Potential biomarkers predictive of sorafenib response include FGF3/FGF4 and VEGFA gene amplification, overexpression and increased activity of VEFGRs, and elevated MAPK14-ATF2 [51–54]. In contrast, presence of activating mutations in the PI3K/AKT/mTOR pathway is a predictor of primary resistance to sorafenib [55]. Biomarker investigations are also ongoing for regorafenib, the second-line multikinase inhibitor targeting tyrosine kinase, VEGFR1-3, PDGFR-β, and FGFR. Retrospective analysis of the RESORCE trial has identified 5 proteins and 9 miRNAs with the potential for regorafenib response prediction [56]. Further confirmation will be needed, however, prior to translation of these biomarker-guided therapies to clinical practice. The only phase III confirmed predictive biomarker translated to clinical practice exists for the recombinant human IgG1 monoclonal antibody, ramucirumab [45]. Elevated levels of serum α-fetoprotein ($\geq$400 ng/mL) were shown to have predictive value for ramucirumab response in the 2019 REACH-2 phase III trial [45]. When used outside of this context, the effectiveness of ramucirumab in HCC has been inconsistent, demonstrating the importance of these biomarkers in guiding clinical therapy [57—59].

Biomarkers may also be used to guide immunotherapy in HCC. For example, the immune checkpoint inhibitors nivolumab and pembrolizumab, which target programmed cell death protein 1 (PD-1), a protein on the surface of immune cells that downregulates cytotoxic activity when exposed to its ligand, PD-L1 [60]. One way that tumor cells can evade immune detection and destruction is by overexpressing PD-L1 [60—62]. By blocking the interaction of PD-1 with its ligand, immune checkpoint inhibitors can reactivate the ability for T cells to detect and lyse cancer cells [63]. Despite showing promise in phase II trials, both nivolumab and pembrolizumab did not reach their specified endpoints in phase III trials [64,65]. This inconsistency suggests that more information may be needed to identify the patient population most likely to benefit from these drugs. A new molecular classification of HCC, the "immune class," is currently being explored as a potential predictor of immunotherapy responsiveness. Tumors are grouped into this class based on the presence of PD-1 and/or PD-L1 overexpression, high amounts of tumor-infiltrating immune cells, and increased secretion of cytokines such as interferon-gamma on inflammatory gene expression profiles [66]. In contrast, HCCs with CTNNB1 mutations are considered to be "immune-excluded" and have been shown to be nonresponsive to immune checkpoint inhibitors [55,67]. With this new information provided by NGS data, therapeutic decision-making regarding the use of immunotherapy in advanced HCC will be much improved.

Chemo-resistive mechanisms in hepatocellular carcinoma

Despite the creation of novel drugs targeting tumor genetics, a looming issue relevant to past, present, and future therapies is drug resistance by tumor cells. The roadblock of chemo-resistance contributes to the refractory nature and poor outcomes in patients with inoperable HCC requiring classic or targeted chemotherapy. To date, the exact mechanisms behind this resistance are still largely unclear despite dozens of genes being identified as potentially synergistic contributors to this unwanted response. This section will shed light on some of the relevant chemo-resistive mechanisms of HCC to commonly used therapies [68].

First are the multidrug resistance protein transporters (MRPTs), most commonly ATP-binding cassette (ABC) proteins, which are cellular proteins participating in drug export. These MRPTs, particularly MRP2 and MRP3 are suspected to lend heavily to the multidrug-resistant phenotype of HCC as they were found to have increased expression in the vast majority of HCC samples. Furthermore, studies have demonstrated increased resistance to HCC-targeted therapies sorafenib, regorafenib, cabozantinib, and lenvatinib in patients with MRPT overexpression as well as increased plasma concentration of anti-HCC-targeted therapies upon inhibition of certain MRPTs. Most concerning are studies showing decreased median survival time in HCC patients expressing significantly high levels of certain MRPTs [69—73].

Second, are tumor adaptations to drug targets. The idea behind this mechanism is that overexpression, upregulation, or feedback loop interplay of certain pro-oncogenic factors may support the alteration or modification of therapy-targeted regulatory pathways, thus conferring resistance to common HCC therapies. One example of this is the positive feedback loop formed by epidermal growth factor receptor (EGFR) and Kruppel-like factor 4 (KLF4), found to contribute significantly to sorafenib resistance. EGFR and KLF4 were identified as notably overexpressed in sorafenib-resistant cells. The interplay between these two factors relies on the ability of each to induce transcription of the other, thus creating a loop that allows alternate survival of therapy-targeted pathways and resistance to sorafenib [70,74,75].

Lastly, is epithelial-mesenchymal transition (EMT), a process contributing to metastasis, poorer prognosis, and anti-HCC therapy resistance. The conversion to mesenchymal cells, a multipotent cell capable of differentiating into a variety of human cell types, involves both phenotypic and morphologic changes. These changes contribute to increased levels of biomarkers such as CD13, CD44, CD24, CD90, EpCAM, N-cadherin, keratin-19, and transcription factors that allow for resistance against anti-HCC therapies. The cell adhesion (CD) proteins (CD13, CD44, CD24, CD90) in particular were found to predict worse outcomes in patients treated with sorafenib, likely due to their overexpression causing tumor cell resistance to apoptosis induced by sorafenib [76,77].

One of the most difficult facets of chemo-resistance is the cellular and molecular interplay of these resistance mechanisms. This is the idea that pro-oncogenic adaptations leading to one pathway of chemo-resistance may simultaneously benefit the rise of a second pathway of chemo-resistance, thus complicating our molecular and clinical understanding of treatments as well as their capabilities and limitations. As mentioned previously, combination therapies targeting multiple pathways of tumor survival and proliferation are currently believed to be a potential method of accounting for these resistance mechanisms.

Liquid biopsy

Liquid biopsy (LB) is a rising alternative to classical tissue biopsy due to its noninvasiveness, accuracy, lack of dependency on proceduralists, and ease of integration in the clinical setting. This method relies on the detection of various tumor components such as fragments of tumor DNA known as circulating tumor DNA (ctDNA) and whole tumor cells. These novel biopsies are referred to as "liquid" as they can be extracted from nonsolid and nonmalignant body tissues, commonly from the blood. However, samples from cerebrospinal fluid (CSF), saliva, pleural fluid, ascites, stool, and urine can also contribute significant data depending on the origin of the malignancy. This section will examine the capabilities and advantages associated with LB [78].

HCC is a notoriously heterogenous malignancy which can predispose patients to drug resistance-inducing mutations and clonal tumor evolution. The issue of heterogeneity requires accurate assessment of tumor biology at many stages of the disease to determine the best individualized clinical management. LB offers a solution as its noninvasive nature allows for serial biopsy leading to superior genetic profiling of both the primary and any metastatic lesions as changes occur throughout the disease course. Another advantage of LB is its ability to monitor response to treatment as well as recurrence after tumor resection, which still remains the definitive treatment for HCC. Furthermore, studies have shown increased ctDNA levels to be negatively associated with overall survival as well as disease free survival showcasing the potential for the prognostic value of ctDNA in HCC [79–81].

Challenges facing LB in HCC include the need for a better understanding of the biology of ctDNA and verifying its origin. Analyses of methylation patterns show promise as they have helped us identify tissue-specific signatures of ctDNA. Other obstacles include the need for standardization as many studies have utilized diverse technologies for ctDNA detection and isolation leading to inconsistencies. Lastly, is the lack of conclusive evidence for using LB as a source of novel biomarkers in the clinical management of HCC. Despite these challenges LB remains a promising technique warranting significant attention in the field of cancer biology and HCC [82].

Summary and conclusions

HCC is among the most difficult to treat malignancies. Due to significant tumor heterogeneity, the previous "one-size-fits-all" treatment strategy may not be adequate in managing these cancers. The targeted nature of the precision medicine approach may be better suited to tackle the complex underlying biology of HCC. Using NGS technology, strides have been made in understanding the molecular aberrations involved. However, the successful implementation of precision medicine has been limited by the lack of actionability for the oncogenic drivers identified in HCC. The discovery of drugs targeting these mutations could revolutionize HCC treatment. Lastly, the continued identification of tumor biomarkers capable of predicting therapeutic response will significantly help guide clinical decision-making.

Future directions

Molecular profiling has led to the identification of the most frequent driver mutations and derailed regulatory pathways associated with HCC. However, there is still significant progress to be made in order to implement biomarker-guided therapy clinically. Currently, monotherapeutic management of HCC has led to acquired drug resistance. The combination of "omics" data, such as genomics, epigenomics, and metabolomics, will provide further insight into potential approaches for combination therapy in HCC [83]. One study has shown promise in resensitizing sorafenib-resistant tumors with the combined inhibition of TGF-β receptor kinase and PD-L1 [84,85]. These and other encouraging in vitro findings warrant future in vivo studies to validate and assess combinatorial precision therapies to clinical practice (Table 19.1).

TABLE 19.1 Commonly mutated genes in hepatocellular carcinoma [43,86−92].

Pathways	Genes	Function	Alteration effect	Frequency in HCC (%)
Telomere maintenance	TERT	Maintaining telomere length	Activating	44−59
Cell cycle control	TP53	Tumor suppressor	Loss of function	23−31
	CCND1	Cell proliferation	Loss of function	7
	CDKN2A	Cell cycle regulator	Loss of function	1−3
Wnt/β-catenin signaling	CTNNB1	Transcriptional regulator	Activating	23−36
	AXIN1	Signal transducer	Loss of function	5−10
Oxidative stress	NFE2L2	Transcriptional regulator	Activating	3−6
	KEAP1	Proteinase adaptor	Activating	2−5
Chromatin remodeling	ARID1A	Chromatin remodeling	Loss of function	4−12
	ARID2	Chromatin remodeling	Loss of function	3−10
AKT-mTOR-MAPK pathway	RPS6KA3	Kinase	Unclassified	3−6
	FGF19	Metabolic regulation factor	Focal amplification	5−6
	PI3KCA	Effector of PTEN-AKT pathway	Activating	1−4

Acknowledgments

RB is supported by grants from the National Institute on Minority Health and Health Disparities (#1S21MD012472-01;2U54 MD006882-06) and National Cancer Institute (#P20CA233355-01).

References

[1] Sung H, et al. Global cancer statistics 2020: GLOBOCAN estimates of incidence and mortality worldwide for 36 cancers in 185 countries. CA Cancer J Clin 2021;71(3):209−49.

[2] Greten TF, et al. Survival rate in patients with hepatocellular carcinoma: a retrospective analysis of 389 patients. Br J Cancer 2005;92(10):1862−8.

[3] Marrero JA, et al. Diagnosis, staging, and management of hepatocellular carcinoma: 2018 practice guidance by the American Association for the study of liver diseases. Hepatology 2018;68(2):723−50.

[4] McGlynn KA, Petrick JL, El-Serag HB. Epidemiology of hepatocellular carcinoma. Hepatology 2021;73(Suppl. 1):4−13.

[5] Kim DY, Han KH. Epidemiology and surveillance of hepatocellular carcinoma. Liver Cancer 2012;1(1):2−14.

[6] European Association for the Study of the Liver. EASL clinical practice guidelines: management of hepatocellular carcinoma. J Hepatol 2018;69(1):182−236.

[7] Tang A, et al. Evidence supporting LI-RADS major features for CT- and MR imaging-based diagnosis of hepatocellular carcinoma: a systematic review. Radiology 2018;286(1):29−48.

[8] Cho YK, et al. Comparison of 7 staging systems for patients with hepatocellular carcinoma undergoing transarterial chemoembolization. Cancer 2008;112(2):352−61.

[9] Vauthey JN, et al. Pretreatment assessment of hepatocellular carcinoma: expert consensus statement. HPB (Oxford) 2010;12(5):289−99.

[10] Raees A, et al. Updates on the diagnosis and management of hepatocellular carcinoma. Euroasian J Hepatogastroenterol 2021;11(1):32—40.

[11] Schwarz RE, et al. Nonoperative therapies for combined modality treatment of hepatocellular cancer: expert consensus statement. HPB (Oxford) 2010;12(5):313—20.

[12] Germani G, et al. Clinical outcomes of radiofrequency ablation, percutaneous alcohol and acetic acid injection for hepatocelullar carcinoma: a meta-analysis. J Hepatol 2010;52(3):380—8.

[13] Sastry AV, et al. A novel 3-dimensional electromagnetic guidance system increases intraoperative microwave antenna placement accuracy. HPB (Oxford) 2017;19(12):1066—73.

[14] Verslype C, et al. Hepatocellular carcinoma: ESMO-ESDO clinical practice guidelines for diagnosis, treatment and follow-up. Ann Oncol 2012;23(Suppl. 7):vii41—8.

[15] Marelli L, et al. Transarterial therapy for hepatocellular carcinoma: which technique is more effective? A systematic review of cohort and randomized studies. Cardiovasc Intervent Radiol 2007;30(1):6—25.

[16] Heimbach JK, et al. AASLD guidelines for the treatment of hepatocellular carcinoma. Hepatology 2018;67(1):358—80.

[17] Schwartzberg L, et al. Precision oncology: who, how, what, when, and when not? Am Soc Clin Oncol Educ Book 2017;37:160—9.

[18] Morash M, Mitchell H, Beltran H, Elemento O, Pathak J. The role of next-generation sequencing in precision medicine: a review of outcomes in oncology. J Pers Med 2018;8(3):30.

[19] Bode AM, Dong Z. Precision oncology - the future of personalized cancer medicine? NPJ Precis Oncol 2017;1(1):2.

[20] Zehir A, et al. Erratum: mutational landscape of metastatic cancer revealed from prospective clinical sequencing of 10,000 patients. Nat Med 2017;23(8):1004.

[21] Moasser MM. The oncogene HER2: its signaling and transforming functions and its role in human cancer pathogenesis. Oncogene 2007;26(45):6469—87.

[22] Goutsouliak K, et al. Towards personalized treatment for early stage HER2-positive breast cancer. Nat Rev Clin Oncol 2020;17(4):233—50.

[23] McKeage K, Perry CM. Trastuzumab: a review of its use in the treatment of metastatic breast cancer overexpressing HER2. Drugs 2002;62(1):209—43.

[24] Kreutzfeldt J, et al. The trastuzumab era: current and upcoming targeted HER2 + breast cancer therapies. Am J Cancer Res 2020;10(4):1045—67.

[25] Vu T, Claret FX. Trastuzumab: updated mechanisms of action and resistance in breast cancer. Front Oncol 2012;2:62.

[26] Ascierto PA, et al. The role of BRAF V600 mutation in melanoma. J Transl Med 2012;10:85.

[27] Loo E, et al. BRAF V600E mutation across multiple tumor types: correlation between DNA-based sequencing and mutation-specific immunohistochemistry. Appl Immunohistochem Mol Morphol 2018;26(10):709—13.

[28] Amaria RN, Lewis KD, Jimeno A. Vemurafenib: the road to personalized medicine in melanoma. Drugs Today (Barc) 2012;48(2):109—18.

[29] Cheng L, et al. Molecular testing for BRAF mutations to inform melanoma treatment decisions: a move toward precision medicine. Mod Pathol 2018;31(1):24—38.

[30] Nussinov R, et al. Review: precision medicine and driver mutations: computational methods, functional assays and conformational principles for interpreting cancer drivers. PLoS Comput Biol 2019;15(3):e1006658.

[31] Chen AP, et al. Feasibility of molecular profiling based assignment of cancer treatment (MPACT): a randomized NCI precision medicine study. J Clin Oncol 2016;34(15_Suppl.):2539.

[32] Wheler JJ, et al. Cancer therapy directed by comprehensive genomic profiling: a single center study. Cancer Res 2016;76(13):3690—701.

[33] Le Tourneau C, et al. Molecularly targeted therapy based on tumour molecular profiling vs conventional therapy for advanced cancer (SHIVA): a multicentre, open-label, proof-of-concept, randomised, controlled phase 2 trial. Lancet Oncol 2015;16(13):1324—34.

[34] Schwaederle M, et al. Precision oncology: the UC San Diego Moores Cancer Center PREDICT experience. Mol Cancer Ther 2016;15(4):743—52.

[35] Tsimberidou AM, et al. Personalized medicine in a phase I clinical trials program: the MD Anderson Cancer Center initiative. Clin Cancer Res 2012;18(22):6373—83.

[36] Von Hoff DD, et al. Pilot study using molecular profiling of patients' tumors to find potential targets and select treatments for their refractory cancers. J Clin Oncol 2010;28(33):4877—83.

[37] Sicklick JK, et al. Molecular profiling of cancer patients enables personalized combination therapy: the I-PREDICT study. Nat Med 2019;25(5):744–50.

[38] Friemel J, et al. Intratumor heterogeneity in hepatocellular carcinoma. Clin Cancer Res 2015;21(8):1951–61.

[39] Zhai W, et al. The spatial organization of intra-tumour heterogeneity and evolutionary trajectories of metastases in hepatocellular carcinoma. Nat Commun 2017;8:4565.

[40] Huang A, et al. Circumventing intratumoral heterogeneity to identify potential therapeutic targets in hepatocellular carcinoma. J Hepatol 2017;67(2):293–301.

[41] Martins-Filho SN, et al. A phenotypical map of disseminated hepatocellular carcinoma suggests clonal constraints in metastatic sites. Histopathology 2019;74(5):718–30.

[42] Torrecilla S, et al. Trunk mutational events present minimal intra- and inter-tumoral heterogeneity in hepatocellular carcinoma. J Hepatol 2017;67(6):1222–31.

[43] Schulze K, et al. Exome sequencing of hepatocellular carcinomas identifies new mutational signatures and potential therapeutic targets. Nat Genet 2015;47(5):505–11.

[44] Llovet JM, et al. Hepatocellular carcinoma. Nat Rev Dis Prim 2016;2(1):16018.

[45] Zhu AX, et al. Ramucirumab after sorafenib in patients with advanced hepatocellular carcinoma and increased alpha-fetoprotein concentrations (REACH-2): a randomised, double-blind, placebo-controlled, phase 3 trial. Lancet Oncol 2019;20(2):282–96.

[46] Abou-Alfa GK, et al. Cabozantinib in patients with advanced and progressing hepatocellular carcinoma. N Engl J Med 2018;379(1):54–63.

[47] Kudo M, et al. Lenvatinib vs sorafenib in first-line treatment of patients with unresectable hepatocellular carcinoma: a randomised phase 3 non-inferiority trial. Lancet 2018;391(10126):1163–73.

[48] Bruix J, et al. Regorafenib for patients with hepatocellular carcinoma who progressed on sorafenib treatment (RESORCE): a randomised, double-blind, placebo-controlled, phase 3 trial. Lancet 2017;389(10064):56–66.

[49] Llovet JM, et al. Sorafenib in advanced hepatocellular carcinoma. N Engl J Med 2008;359(4):378–90.

[50] Cheng AL, et al. Efficacy and safety of sorafenib in patients in the Asia-Pacific region with advanced hepatocellular carcinoma: a phase III randomised, double-blind, placebo-controlled trial. Lancet Oncol 2009;10(1):25–34.

[51] Rudalska R, et al. In vivo RNAi screening identifies a mechanism of sorafenib resistance in liver cancer. Nat Med 2014;20(10):1138–46.

[52] Peng S, et al. Autocrine vascular endothelial growth factor signaling promotes cell proliferation and modulates sorafenib treatment efficacy in hepatocellular carcinoma. Hepatology 2014;60(4):1264–77.

[53] Horwitz E, et al. Human and mouse VEGFA-amplified hepatocellular carcinomas are highly sensitive to sorafenib treatment. Cancer Discov 2014;4(6):730–43.

[54] Arao T, et al. FGF3/FGF4 amplification and multiple lung metastases in responders to sorafenib in hepatocellular carcinoma. Hepatology 2013;57(4):1407–15.

[55] Harding JJ, et al. Prospective genotyping of hepatocellular carcinoma: clinical implications of next-generation sequencing for matching patients to targeted and immune therapies. Clin Cancer Res 2019;25(7):2116–26.

[56] Teufel M, et al. Biomarkers associated with response to regorafenib in patients with hepatocellular carcinoma. Gastroenterology 2019;156(6):1731–41.

[57] Meguro M, et al. Prognostic roles of preoperative alpha-fetoprotein and des-gamma-carboxy prothrombin in hepatocellular carcinoma patients. World J Gastroenterol 2015;21(16):4933–45.

[58] Kudo M, et al. Ramucirumab as second-line treatment in patients with advanced hepatocellular carcinoma: Japanese subgroup analysis of the REACH trial. J Gastroenterol 2017;52(4):494–503.

[59] Zhu AX, et al. Ramucirumab vs placebo as second-line treatment in patients with advanced hepatocellular carcinoma following first-line therapy with sorafenib (REACH): a randomised, double-blind, multicentre, phase 3 trial. Lancet Oncol 2015;16(7):859–70.

[60] Syn NL, et al. De-novo and acquired resistance to immune checkpoint targeting. Lancet Oncol 2017;18(12):e731–41.

[61] Gandini S, Massi D, Mandala M. PD-L1 expression in cancer patients receiving anti PD-1/PD-L1 antibodies: a systematic review and meta-analysis. Crit Rev Oncol Hematol 2016;100:88–98.

[62] Wang X, et al. PD-L1 expression in human cancers and its association with clinical outcomes. Onco Targets Ther 2016;9:5023–39.

[63] Sliwkowski MX, Mellman I. Antibody therapeutics in cancer. Science 2013;341(6151):1192–8.

[64] Zhu AX, et al. Pembrolizumab in patients with advanced hepatocellular carcinoma previously treated with sorafenib (KEYNOTE-224): a non-randomised, open-label phase 2 trial. Lancet Oncol 2018;19(7):940—52.

[65] El-Khoueiry AB, et al. Nivolumab in patients with advanced hepatocellular carcinoma (CheckMate 040): an open-label, non-comparative, phase 1/2 dose escalation and expansion trial. Lancet 2017;389(10088):2492—502.

[66] Sangster B. Dangers of orphenadrine in psychiatric patients. Lancet 1985;2(8449):280.

[67] Ruiz de Galarreta M, et al. β-Catenin activation promotes immune escape and resistance to anti-PD-1 therapy in hepatocellular carcinoma. Cancer Discov 2019;9(8):1124—41.

[68] Marin JJG, et al. Molecular bases of drug resistance in hepatocellular carcinoma. Cancers (Basel) 2020;12(6).

[69] Beretta GL, et al. Overcoming ABC transporter-mediated multidrug resistance: the dual role of tyrosine kinase inhibitors as multitargeting agents. Eur J Med Chem 2017;142:271—89.

[70] Ozeki T, et al. Influence of CYP3A4/5 and ABC transporter polymorphisms on lenvatinib plasma trough concentrations in Japanese patients with thyroid cancer. Sci Rep 2019;9(1):5404.

[71] Tomonari T, et al. MRP3 as a novel resistance factor for sorafenib in hepatocellular carcinoma. Oncotarget 2016;7(6):7207—15.

[72] Ohya H, et al. Regorafenib is transported by the organic anion transporter 1B1 and the multidrug resistance protein 2. Biol Pharm Bull 2015;38(4):582—6.

[73] Hoffmann K, et al. Sorafenib modulates the gene expression of multi-drug resistance mediating ATP-binding cassette proteins in experimental hepatocellular carcinoma. Anticancer Res 2010;30(11):4503—8.

[74] Pang L, et al. Activation of EGFR-KLF4 positive feedback loop results in acquired resistance to sorafenib in hepatocellular carcinoma. Mol Carcinog 2019;58(11):2118—26.

[75] Gao L, et al. FGF19/FGFR4 signaling contributes to the resistance of hepatocellular carcinoma to sorafenib. J Exp Clin Cancer Res 2017;36(1):8.

[76] Scartozzi M, et al. VEGF and VEGFR genotyping in the prediction of clinical outcome for HCC patients receiving sorafenib: the ALICE-1 study. Int J Cancer 2014;135(5):1247—56.

[77] Agarwal S, et al. The role of the breast cancer resistance protein (ABCG2) in the distribution of sorafenib to the brain. J Pharmacol Exp Ther 2011;336(1):223—33.

[78] Ye Q, et al. Liquid biopsy in hepatocellular carcinoma: circulating tumor cells and circulating tumor DNA. Mol Cancer 2019;18(1):114.

[79] van de Stolpe A, et al. Circulating tumor cell isolation and diagnostics: toward routine clinical use. Cancer Res 2011;71(18):5955—60.

[80] Alix-Panabieres C, Pantel K. Clinical applications of circulating tumor cells and circulating tumor DNA as liquid biopsy. Cancer Discov 2016;6(5):479—91.

[81] Diaz Jr. LA, Bardelli A. Liquid biopsies: genotyping circulating tumor DNA. J Clin Oncol 2014;32(6):579—86.

[82] Crowley E, et al. Liquid biopsy: monitoring cancer-genetics in the blood. Nat Rev Clin Oncol 2013;10(8):472—84.

[83] Liu XN, et al. Multiple "Omics" data-based biomarker screening for hepatocellular carcinoma diagnosis. World J Gastroenterol 2019;25(30):4199—212.

[84] Shrestha R, et al. Combined inhibition of TGF-beta1-induced EMT and PD-L1 silencing re-sensitizes hepatocellular carcinoma to sorafenib treatment. J Clin Med 2021;10(9).

[85] Xu GL, et al. Upregulation of PD-L1 expression promotes epithelial-to-mesenchymal transition in sorafenib-resistant hepatocellular carcinoma cells. Gastroenterol Rep (Oxford) 2020;8(5):390—8.

[86] Chiang DY, et al. Focal gains of VEGFA and molecular classification of hepatocellular carcinoma. Cancer Res 2008;68(16):6779—88.

[87] Cleary SP, et al. Identification of driver genes in hepatocellular carcinoma by exome sequencing. Hepatology 2013;58(5):1693—702.

[88] Kan Z, et al. Whole-genome sequencing identifies recurrent mutations in hepatocellular carcinoma. Genome Res 2013;23(9):1422—33.

[89] Guichard C, et al. Integrated analysis of somatic mutations and focal copy-number changes identifies key genes and pathways in hepatocellular carcinoma. Nat Genet 2012;44(6):694—8.

[90] Llovet JM, et al. Advances in targeted therapies for hepatocellular carcinoma in the genomic era. Nat Rev Clin Oncol 2015;12(7):408—24.

[91] Boyault S, et al. Transcriptome classification of HCC is related to gene alterations and to new therapeutic targets. Hepatology 2007;45(1):42—52.

[92] Jhunjhunwala S, et al. Diverse modes of genomic alteration in hepatocellular carcinoma. Genome Biol 2014;15(8):436.

chapter 20

Decoding the functional role of extracellular vesicles in hepatocellular carcinoma: implications in clinical theranostics

Kalyani Patil[1], Said Dermime[2,3] and Shahab Uddin[1,4,5]

[1]Translational Research Institute, Academic Health System, Hamad Medical Corporation, Doha, Qatar [2]National Center for Cancer Care and Research, Hamad Medical Corporation, Doha, Qatar [3]Translational Cancer Research Facility and Clinical Trial Unit, Translational Research Institute, Hamad Medical Corporation, Doha, Qatar [4]Dermatology Institute, Academic Health System, Hamad Medical Corporation, Doha, Qatar [5]Laboratory Animal Research Center, Qatar University, Doha, Qatar

Abstract

Hepatocellular carcinoma (HCC) is the most common form of primary liver cancer in adults, the sixth most commonly diagnosed neoplasia, and the third leading cause of cancer-related deaths worldwide. Despite tangible mechanistic insights gained from clinical profiling data and experimental models, our knowledge on the molecular pathogenesis of HCC remains limited. Recent efforts directed toward reevaluating molecular pathways underlying HCC tumorigenesis and metastasis have been revolutionized by the discovery of extracellular vesicles (EVs) and their diverse pleiotropic roles in local and distant failures. In the past decade, EVs have emerged as versatile and critical intercellular cancer signalosomes that can induce malignant transformation and govern distant metastasis. New studies have begun to unravel the potential of EV-mediated regulatory mechanisms, coopted by tumor cells, in shaping favorable tumor microenvironments and defining the landscape of cancer metastasis-promoting systems. In this chapter, we outline the multifaceted roles of EVs in establishing fertile tumor milieu to promote the development and metastatic organotropism in HCC. Finally, we summarize current advancements in the application of EVs as clinical theranostic agents for subverting the development and progression of HCC.

Keywords: Extracellular vesicles; hepatocellular carcinoma; tumor progression; metastasis; theranostics

Ganji Purnachandra Nagaraju, Sarfraz Ahmad (eds.)
Theranostics and Precision Medicine for the Management of Hepatocellular Carcinoma, Volume 3

301

Abbreviations

ABCG2	ATP-binding cassette, subfamily G member 2
ADMSC	Adipose-derived mesenchymal stem cell
AFP	Alpha-fetoprotein
AKG	α-Ketoglutarate
AMPK	5′ Adenosine monophosphate-activated protein kinase
ANGPT	Angiopoietin
B4GALT3	β-1,4-galactosyltransferase
BAK1	Bcl-2 antagonist/killer 1
bFGF	Basic fibroblast growth factor
Breg	Regulatory B cells
CAAs	Cancer-associated adipocytes
CAF	Cancer-associated fibroblast
CCL	Chemokine (C−C motif) ligand
CDEs	Cancer-associated fibroblast-derived extracellular vesicles
CHB	Chronic hepatitis B
circRNA	Circular RNA
CLEC3B	C-type lectin domain family 3 member B
CLL	Chronic lymphocytic leukemia
COL1A1	Collagen type-I alpha 1 chain
COL3A1	Collagen type-III alpha 1 chain
COL4A1	Collagen type-IV alpha 1 chain
CSCs	Cancer stem cells
CSF-1	Colony-stimulating factor-1
CTGF	Connective tissue growth factor
CTLA-4	Cytotoxic T-lymphocyte-associated protein 4
CXCL	C−X−C motif chemokine ligand
CXCR	C−X−C chemokine receptor
CYLD	Cylindromatosis lysine 63 deubiquitinase
DAMP	Damage molecular pattern
DC	Dendritic cell
DLL4	Delta-like 4
DOX	Doxorubicin
DTC	Disseminated tumor cell
DVT	Deep vein thrombosis
E2F1	E2F transcription factor 1
EC	Endothelial cell
ECAR	Extracellular acidification rate
ECM	Extracellular matrix
eIF	Eukaryotic translation initiation factor
EMT	Epithelial-to-mesenchymal transition
ENO1	Alpha-enolase
eNOS	Endothelial nitric oxide synthase
EpCAM	Epithelial cell adhesion molecule
EPCs	Endothelial progenitor cells
ERG	Erythroblast transformation-specific-related gene
ERK	Extracellular-regulated protein kinase 1/2
EV	Extracellular vesicle
GC	Gastric cancer
GLUT	Glucose transporter
GSK3	Glycogen synthase kinase 3
GUCD1	Guanylyl cyclase domain containing 1

HBV	Hepatitis B virus
HCC	Hepatocellular carcinoma
HIF	Hypoxia-inducible factor
HK2	Hexokinase 2
HMGB1	High mobility group box 1
HPC	Hepatic progenitor compartment
HSC	Hepatic stellate cell
Hsp70	Heat shock protein 70
HSPG	Heparan sulfate proteoglycans
Ig	Immunoglobulin
IGF-1R	Insulin-like growth factor 1 receptor
ITG	Integrin
KC	Kupffer cell
LAG3	Lymphocyte activating 3
LEC	Lymphatic endothelial cell
Linc-ROR	Long intergenic noncoding RNA regulator of reprogramming
LN	Lymph node
lncRNA	Long noncoding RNA
LOXL4	Lysyl oxidase-like 4
LSAMP	Limbic system-associated membrane protein
LSEC	Liver sinusoidal endothelial cell
MAPK	Mitogen-activated protein kinase
MCP-1	Monocyte chemoattractant protein-1
MICA/B	Major histocompatibility complex class I chain-related protein A and B
miRNA/mir	MicroRNA
MMP	Matrix metalloproteinases
MSC	Mesenchymal stem cell
mTOR	Mechanistic target of rapamycin
NASH	Nonalcoholic steatohepatitis
ncRNA	Noncoding RNA
NDDS	Nanotechnology-based drug-delivery systems
NF-κB	Nuclear factor kappa-light-chain-enhancer of activated B cells
NID1	Nidogen 1
NK	Natural killer
NKG2D	Natural killer group 2-member D
NSCLC	Nonsmall cell lung carcinoma
OCR	Oxygen consumption rate
OS	Overall survival
OXPHOS	Oxidative phosphorylation
PBX3	Pre-B-cell leukemia homeobox 3
PD-1	Programmed cell death protein 1
PDGF	Platelet-derived growth factor
PDK1	3-Phosphoinositide-dependent protein kinase-1
PD-L1	Programmed death-ligand 1
PI3K	Phosphoinositide 3-kinase
PKM2	Pyruvate kinase M2
PLC	Primary liver cancer
POU5F1/Oct4	POU class 5 homeobox 1
PPP	Pentose-phosphate pathway
RAGE	Receptor for advanced glycation end products
RBBP4	Rb-binding protein 4
RTK	Receptor tyrosine kinase
S100A11	S100 calcium-binding protein A11

SALL4	Sal-like protein-4
SDF-1α	Stromal cell-derived factor-1α
siRNA	Small interfering RNA
STAT	Signal transducer and activator of transcription
TAAs	Tumor-associated antigens
TACE	Transarterial chemoembolization
TAK1	Transforming growth factor-beta-activated kinase 1
TAM	Tumor-associated macrophage
TAN	Tumor-associated neutrophils
TCA	Tricarboxylic acid
TF	Tissue factor
TGF-β	Transforming growth factor-beta
TIB	Tumor-infiltrating B cell
TIC	Tumor-initiating cell
TIM	T cell immunoglobulin and mucin domain-containing protein-3
TLS	Tertiary lymphoid structures
TME	Tumor microenvironment
TNFR1	Tumor necrosis factor receptor 1
TNM	Tumor-node-metastasis
Treg	Regulatory T-cell
TRM	Tissue-resident macrophage
TSP1	Thrombospondin-1
TTP	Tristetraprolin
USP7	Ubiquitin-specific protease 7
Vash1	Vasohibin 1
VE	Vascular endothelial
VEGF	Vascular endothelial growth factor
VEGFR	Vascular endothelial growth factor receptor
VHL	Von Hippel—Lindau
VM	Vasculogenic mimicry
VTE	Venous thromboembolism

Functional role of EVs in hepatocellular carcinoma: from angiogenesis to metastatic organotropism

Primary liver cancer (PLC) poses an important global health concern with an increasing trend of prevalence and mortality. According to the American Cancer Society statistics, the incidence rates of liver cancer have increased more than threefold, while the death rates have increased more than twofold since 1980 [1]. Hepatocellular carcinoma (HCC) is the most common form of PLC in adults, the sixth most commonly diagnosed neoplasia [2], and the third leading cause of cancer-related deaths worldwide [3]. HCC is one of the few malignancies where the major etiological factors have been decoded, including alcohol- and nonalcoholic steatohepatitis (NASH)-related cirrhosis, metabolic syndrome, sociodemographic factors, and infection by hepatitis B virus (HBV) or hepatitis C virus (HCV) [4]. Over the past few decades, tangible efforts have been undertaken to gain a comprehensive understanding of the molecular pathogenesis of this disease; however, like other solid malignant tumors, the unambiguous demonstration of tumor multifocality and heterogeneity, clinical variability, and genomic diversity has confounded the efforts to achieve diagnostic, prognostic, and therapeutic breakthroughs. The unreliability and lack of clinically validated diagnostic indicators, gaps in HCC armamentarium, high metastatic ability, and high rate of local/regional recurrence have prompted the need for a profound understanding of the molecular cascades underlying HCC formation, metastasis, and progression.

Since the formulation of Stephen Paget's classical "seed-and-soil" hypothesis [5], where disseminated tumor cells (DTCs; tumor cells that occupy permissive niches of secondary organs and engage in organ-specific metastatic colonization) and specific organ microenvironment are compared to the "seed" and "soil," respectively, mechanistic dissection of mechanisms underlying metastatic progression has focused on cooperative and dynamic host–tumor cell interactions. However, the temporal and spatial nature of such interactions, their precise hierarchy and functions in metastatic evolution are not well understood [6]. In recent years, the discovery of a new mode of intercellular communication, mediated by extracellular vesicles (EVs), has largely transformed our understanding of the dynamics of bidirectional tumor–host cell interactions and established new paradigms with a potential to guide future research on tumorigenesis and metastasis, as well as the development of novel diagnostic, predictive, and therapeutic approaches.

EVs are heterogeneous nano-sized membrane-enclosed vesicles that originate from various subcellular compartments and are released into the outer cellular milieu practically by all types of cells. These nanopackages mediate local and distant intercellular communication and arbitrate a repertoire of physiological and pathological functions (reflecting the wealth of data, there are excellent reviews [7–9] delineating the biology and function of EVs). This stance has dramatically expanded with the recognition of the "molecular signature" of EVs that consists of a complex but distinct mix of bioactive lipids, nucleic acids [DNA, mRNA, and noncoding RNAs (ncRNAs) such as microRNA (miRNA/miR), circular RNA (circRNA), and long ncRNA (lncRNA)], and proteins [receptors, enzymes, extracellular matrix (ECM) proteins, and transcription factors] [10]. The competence of EVs to orchestrate paracrine communication depends on the transfer of these bioactive molecules to target recipient cells either in close proximity or at distal anatomical locations [11].

Exosomes are a class of EVs that are defined as 30–150 nm diameter membrane nanovesicles and derived from the multivesicular endosome pathway. The term exosome is often used to designate a mixed population of small EVs isolated by various protocols without further analysis of their intracellular origin or biogenesis (endosome-derived vs plasma membrane-derived EVs). Also, most of the studies cannot be used to determine the precise functional specificity of the EVs analyzed, as the functions assigned to exosomes may either be distinct to exosomes or simply reflect generic EV activities. Due to these unresolved discrepancies, we, herein, choose to refer the secreted vesicles as "EVs," not necessarily indicating their endosomal or plasma membrane origin.

In the cancer setting, tumor cells employ EVs to architect local and distal microenvironments. The regulatory role of EVs in tumor formation and metastasis is distinct from other components of the tumor cell secretome [12]. In the tumor ecosystem, EV-derived molecular cargo and the associated extrinsic signaling cues orchestrate the establishment/remolding of the tumor microenvironment (TME) as well as participate in the initiation of metastasis, premetastatic niche preparation, cancer immunoediting and subversion, and organotropic metastasis [11,13] (Fig. 20.1).

A disease of multifactorial pathophysiology, HCC manifestations involve a complex interplay of various factors and biological mechanisms. These include polygenic

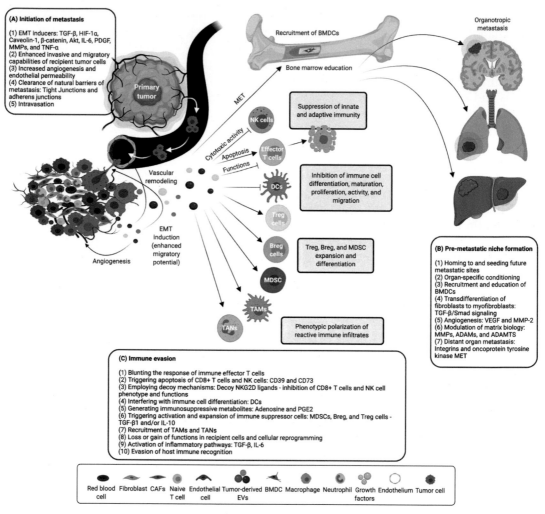

FIGURE 20.1   Role of extracellular vesicles (EVs) in invasion and metastasis. Tumor-derived EVs provide an array of signaling cues that contribute to the formation of a tumor-supportive ecosystem favorable for cancer progression and metastasis. The bioactive content of EVs has been implicated in initiating metastasis (A), premetastatic niche formation and organotropism (B), and modulation of immune responses (C). *DCs*, Dendritic cells; *MDSC*, myeloid-derived suppressor cells; *BMDC*, bone marrow-derived cells; *ADAM*, A disintegrin and metalloproteinases; *ADAMTS*, adamalysin metalloproteinases having disintegrin and thrombospondin domains (Figure inspired from [11]).

predisposition [14], reciprocal interactions between viral infections and nonviral etiological factors [15], the TME and its components, epithelial-to-mesenchymal transition (EMT), senescence bypass, cancer stem cells (CSCs), and the severity of the underlying cirrhosis/chronic liver disease [4,16]. Recent efforts in reanalyzing the molecular pathogenesis of HCC have revealed the multifarious role of EVs in controlling virtually all aspects of HCC pathobiology, including tumorigenesis, angiogenesis, immunology, progression, and metastasis. The discovery of EVs and their diverse tumorigenic functions have added new insights into the dynamic multifaceted interplay between heterogeneous HCC cells and the cells within the TME. While the EV-mediated bidirectional tumor—stromal cell interactions are ascertained, their involvement in the regulation of HCC progression and metastasis is still under scrutiny and has recently garnered immense attention.

HCC-derived EVs regulate the behavior of endothelial cells to induce angiogenesis

HCC is a typical hypervascular malignant liver tumor [17] characterized by marked vascular abnormalities, such as arteriogenesis and sinusoidal capillarization [18,19]. Several studies have demonstrated the presence of a dynamic angiogenic switch and delineated the roles of circulating pro- and antiangiogenic factors in multistep hepatic carcinogenesis, progression, and metastasis [20]. Beyond vascular endothelial growth factor (VEGF) and conventional signaling pathways, emerging evidence has uncovered the functional role of EVs in regulating proangiogenic stimuli in HCC. Since the discovery of miRNAs as abundant vesicular cargo [21,22] and the possibility that EV-associated miRNA reflects the miRNA signature of the parental tumor [23], emerging insights have implicated the direct miRNA-mediated effect on growth, migration, invasion, and chemosensitivity of HCC cells. In fact, tumor cells have been demonstrated to exert paracrine or autocrine effects through functional miRNAs acting as extracellular effectors of cell—cell communication [24]. Bioinformatics and functional assays have revealed the role of overexpressed miRNAs, secreted via EVs, in regulating endothelial cell (EC) behavior and thus, an active angiogenic process in HCC [25]. Investigations into the effects of HCC cell-derived vesicular miRNAs have substantiated the involvement of EV-associated miR-210 in promoting tumor angiogenesis by directly inhibiting the expression of SMAD family member 4 (SMAD4) and signal transducer and activator of transcription (STAT) 6 in EC cells [25]. In addition to miRNAs, proangiogenic and proinvasive roles of EV-associated circRNAs have been demonstrated in HCC progression and metastasis. In line with this, EV-associated circRNA-100,338, secreted by highly metastatic HCC cells, was shown to enhance the invasive and metastatic ability of HCC cells by regulating angiogenesis, permeability, and vasculogenic mimicry (VM) formation ability of recipient ECs [26]. Under hypoxic conditions, tumor cells undergo metabolic and molecular adaptations and help reorganize the TME suitable for their homeostasis and metastasis. Besides activation of target genes of hypoxia-inducible factor (HIF)-1, an oxygen-dependent transcriptional activator [27], hypoxic tumor cells release EVs that participate in intercellular communication and modulation of the TME to promote tumorigenesis via enhanced angiogenesis, cell proliferation/survival, and immunosuppression [28]. Specifically, hypoxic EVs mediate hypoxia-driven phenotypic and transcriptomic alterations in ECs and promote angiogenesis, tumor growth, and metastasis [29]. During hypoxia, HCC cell-derived EVs upregulate angiogenesis through miRNA-155-mediated network formation of HUVECs [30]. Clinical data have determined a clear association of higher miR-155 levels with a shorter 5-year overall survival (OS) and disease-free survival in HCC patients [31]. Through imaging, Yukawa et al. [32] reported VEGF receptor (VEGFR)-dependent stimulatory effects of HCC-derived EVs, expressing natural killer group 2 member D (NKG2D) and heat shock protein 70 (Hsp70), on the lumen formation of HUVECs and angiogenesis. Similarly, Li et al. [33] presented an in vitro evidence on the ability of HCC-derived EVs to mediate intercellular transfer of lysyl oxidase-like 4 (LOXL4) protein to HUVECs and induce angiogenesis and tube formation. LOXL4 belongs to the LOX family of ECM-remodeling enzymes and acts as a regulator of vascular ECM homeostasis as well as vascular pathologies associated with ECM remodeling and fibrosis [34]. Also, Wang et al. [35] documented the potential of adipocytes, educated by HCC-derived EVs, in stimulating tube formation in HUVECs and promoting angiogenesis of ECs both in vitro and in vivo through upregulation of proangiogenic genes angiopoietin (ANGPT) 1 and VEGFR2 (Flk1) and downregulation of antiangiogenic genes vasohibin 1 (Vash1) and thrombospondin-1 (TSP1).

Experimental and cross-sectional clinical studies have provided substantial evidence on the potential role of EVs in coagulation activation and cancer-associated venous thrombosis (venous thromboembolism, VTE). Tumor-derived EVs harbor coagulation-promoting tissue factor (TF) that potentially contributes to their prothrombotic effect linked to tumor metastasis, growth, and angiogenesis [36]. In the HCC setting, EV-associated cargoes influence the behavior of endothelial progenitor cells (EPCs) that are involved in thrombus repairment and resolution. For example, overexpressed miR-21 in HCC-derived EVs was shown to abrogate proliferation, migration, and invasion of EPCs by downregulating interleukin (IL)-6R expression, thus contributing to deep vein thrombosis (DVT) in cancer patients [37]. MiR-21 has also been found to affect hepatocellular carcinoma (HCC) angiogenesis and progression by mediating bidirectional communication between HCC cells and hepatic stellate cells (HSCs) in the tumor parenchyma. By downregulating PTEN expression and activating the 3-phosphoinositide-dependent protein kinase-1 (PDK1)/Akt signaling pathway, HCC EV-mediated transfer of miR-21 has been shown to potentiate the conversion of HSCs into cancer-associated fibroblasts. Consequently, these HCC cell-activated CAFs upregulate the expression levels of VEGF, matrix metalloproteinases (MMP)-2, MMP-9, basic fibroblast growth factor (bFGF), and transforming growth factor beta (TGF-β) that leads to angiogenesis and tumor progression [38]. Paracrine communications between HCC cells and EPCs have been demonstrated to remotely facilitate the differentiation and angiogenic activity of ECs, plausibly via EV-mediated signaling cascades. To this vein, Jamshidi-Parsian et al. [39] showed that HCC cells induce an "activated" phenotype of EPCs, typified by increased migration and angiogenic activity, through the EV-mediated transfer of ephrin-B2, and Notch ligand Delta-like 4 (DLL4). Both ephrin-B2 and DLL4/Notch signaling contribute to angiogenesis [40] by stimulating the arterial differentiation of ECs [41,42]. The ANGPT-Tie receptor tyrosine kinase pathway is an important regulator of developmental and pathological (tumor) angiogenesis and hence, represents an attractive target of antiangiogenic therapy [43]. Recently, Xie et al. [44] have described a novel (EV-mediated) pathway of tumor angiogenesis unlike the classic ANGPT2/Tie2 pathway involving free ANGPT2. Accordingly, the group showed that internalization of HCC cell-derived EVs, containing ANGPT2, into recipient HUVECs stimulate angiogenesis in a Tie2-independent manner, specifically, by activating Akt/endothelial nitric oxide synthase (eNOS) and Akt/β-catenin pathways [44]. In another study, the heparan sulfate proteoglycans (HSPGs)-mediated uptake of vasorin-containing HCC EVs enhanced the migration and proangiogenic activity of ECs [45].

The involvement of aberrant translational machinery/initiation in cancer development and progression is well accepted [46]. Of the 12 eukaryotic translation initiation factors (eIFs) that regulate the translation of oncogenic mRNAs and neoplastic transformation, eIF3 is the largest and most complex mammalian initiation factors composed of 13 subunits (eIF3a-m) that are assembled together to form eIF3 translational initiation complex [47–51]. Altered expression profiles of eIF3 subunits have been detected in several malignant tumors and correlated with tumor progression [52]. Upregulation of one such subunit, eIF3c has been associated with direct stimulation of cell proliferation and migration as well as secretion of EVs to accentuate angiogenesis and tumorigenic ability of HCC cells via increased expression of S100 family protein S100 calcium-binding protein A11 (S100A11). Notably, concomitant overexpression of eIF3c and S100A11 in tumor tissues has been found to correlate with poor survival in HCC patients [53].

In addition to the overexpressed cargo molecules, HCC-derived EVs harbor downregulated expression of certain protein and miRNA species that promote angiogenesis in tumor tissues. HCC cell-secreted EVs, with downregulated expression of a tumor suppressor protein C-type Lectin Domain Family 3 Member B (CLEC3B), were shown to promote metastasis and angiogenesis by suppressing the phosphorylation of 5′ adenosine monophosphate-activated protein kinase (AMPK), consequently, leading to an increased VEGF expression in both HCC cells and ECs [54]. Similarly, HCC cells generate and release EVs with low miR-200b-3p which drives angiogenesis in HCC tissues by augmenting erythroblast transformation-specific-related gene (ERG) expression in EC cells [55].

HCC-derived EVs target normal surrounding cells to regulate tumor progression

Irrespective of its nomenclature, one of the perplexing attributes of HCC is its precise cellular origin. The three potential cellular sources of HCC are namely hepatocytes, the liver progenitor cells (LPCs)/biliary compartment, and HSCs. Recent fate-tracing studies indicate that HCC predominantly originates from malignant/transformed hepatocytes that are endowed with a high degree of plasticity and capacity to expand the neighboring hepatic progenitor compartment (HPC) through the release of galectin-3 and α-ketoglutarate (AKG) [56,57]. Numerous lines of evidence have suggested a novel interplay between HCC cells and hepatocytes, in which tumor-derived EVs may facilitate hepatocyte malignant transformation and foster the fertile liver milieu to favor tumor metastasis.

He et al. [58] reported a novel finding that EVs, derived from highly metastatic HCC cells, can modulate the migratory and invasive behaviors of nonmotile immortalized hepatocytes. The authors found that EVs mediate the horizontal transfer of protumorigenic biomolecules, principally, MET proto-oncogene. Upon uptake, these cargo molecules elicit the activation of phosphoinositide 3-kinase (PI3K)/Akt and mitogen-activated protein kinase (MAPK) signaling pathways in the hepatocytes, leading to an increased secretion of MMP-2 and MMP-9. These results indicate that EV-mediated hepatocyte motility and degradation of the ECM may be one of the strategic approaches employed by HCC cells to enhance their protrusive activity through the liver parenchyma and metastasize [58].

Several studies have identified selective enrichment of ncRNAs in HCC cell-derived EVs and unveiled their potential to modulate gene expression and biologic behavior in target liver parenchyma cells. One study showed that HCC-secreted EVs, enriched with long intergenic noncoding RNA regulator of reprogramming (Linc-ROR) that helps to maintain stem cell pluripotency and EMT state [59], confer a stem cell-like phenotype in nontumorigenic hepatocytes through enhanced expression of stemness maintaining factors such as CD133, Nanog, Sox2, and Oct4 [60]. Another study reported that enrichment of miR-429 in epithelial cell adhesion molecule (EpCAM) + tumor-initiating cells (TICs), through HCC EV-mediated intercellular exchange, manipulates the characteristics of these liver TICs by targeting the Rb-binding protein 4 (RBBP4)/E2F transcription factor 1 (E2F1)/POU class 5 homeobox 1 (POU5F1/Oct4) axis. Additionally, the uptake of these miR-429-enriched EVs by recipient hepatocytes were shown to promote their self-renewal, tumorigenicity, chemoresistance ability, and malignant proliferation [61]. Likewise, HCC cells were demonstrated to epigenetically modulate target gene expression and stimulate cell signaling associated with anchorage-independent growth in recipient neighboring cells. This was found to be mediated through the secretion and release of miRNA-expressing EVs [24] that target TGF-beta-activated kinase 1 (TAK1), an essential regulator of cellular senescence programs in normal and tumor cells [62].

HCC cells have also been determined to induce malignant traits in surrounding normal cells through the EV-mediated transfer of circRNA Cdr1 [63]. The Cdr1/miR-1270/alpha-fetoprotein (AFP) regulatory loop is implicated in HCC progression, specifically, through its vital role in accelerating the migratory and invasive capabilities of HCC cells [63]. Similarly, EV-delivered circ-MMP2 (has_circ_0039411) was shown to change the biologic behavior of normal hepatic cells and promote HCC metastasis by sequestering miR-136-5p to enhance the expression of its host gene MMP-2 [64].

The potential of HCC-derived EVs in educating the surrounding adipocytes, differentiated from mesenchymal stem cells (MSCs), to create a cancer-permissive niche has also been demonstrated. Active incorporation of HCC-derived EVs by adipocytes was shown to cause significant transcriptomic alterations, activate phosphokinases [Akt, STAT5α, glycogen synthase kinase 3 (GSK3) α and β, p38α, and extracellular-regulated protein kinase (ERK)1/2] and nuclear factor kappa-light-chain-enhancer of activated B cells (NF-κB) signaling pathway, induce tumor-promoting properties, and confer inflammatory phenotype to adipocytes. In a mouse xenograft model, the EV-modified adipocytes appeared to aggravate tumor growth, promote cancer cell migration, enhance angiogenesis, and increase macrophage infiltration into tumors. These tumorigenic effects were ascribed to increased expression of proinflammatory adipokines such as IL-6, IL-8, and monocyte chemoattractant protein-1 (MCP-1, also known as CCl-2) [35]. The presence of such transformed adipocytes or the so-called cancer-associated adipocytes (CAAs) has been reported in several malignancies and found to modulate TME as well as tumor progression [65].

HCC-derived EVs target immune cells to evade immunosurveillance and generate immunosuppressive microenvironment

The liver hosts an immunoprivileged (the so-called immunotolerant) environment that is uniquely adapted to limit systemic immune responses against allo- and autoantigens

[66,67]. However, this hepatic immune-tolerogenic environment is coopted by HCC cells that lead to their poor immunogenicity and the generation of an immunosuppressive TME, resulting in the failure of immunotherapeutics [68]. HCC cells adopt multimodal strategies to reshape the immune landscape of the TME and modulate the anti-HCC immune responses, thus contributing to tumor proliferation and metastasis. Accumulating evidence has determined the multifarious role of tumor-derived EVs, with potent immunomodulatory properties, in modifying tumor immunity which involves modulating antigen presentation, immune suppression, immune activation, and immune recognition [69]. Recent studies have delineated the dynamics of EV-mediated interactions between HCC tumor and immune cells and their potential to mediate contextual cellular reprogramming which, in the TME, is heavily biased toward immune suppression.

Tumor-associated macrophages

Based on its etiology and pathologic/molecular features, HCC is a prototypical example of an inflammation-related cancer. The inflammatory immunosuppressive milieu is a characteristic feature of HCC tumors that facilitates HCC development and progression. This inflammatory environment is characterized by the continued but dysregulated expression of cytokines and the recruitment of immune cell infiltrates to the liver. Tumor-associated macrophages (TAMs) predominate the infiltrating leukocyte population in HCC tumors and critically regulate tumor growth, angiogenesis, invasion, metastasis, and immune tolerance by secreting cytokines, chemokines, and growth factors as well as by engaging in stromal/immune-tumor cell cross-talk [70].

Evidence suggests that the functional interplay between tumor cells and macrophages underscores the tumor cell-applied strategy to prime environmental myeloid cells to support tumor growth and progression. With this indication, HCC cells have been shown to recruit and induce phenotypic polarization (dynamic switching from classically activated/antitumor M1 subtype to alternatively activated/protumor immunosuppressive M2 subtype) in TAMs by secreting a plethora of chemoattractants, such as IL-4, IL-13, VEGF, platelet-derived growth factor (PDGF), connective tissue growth factor (CTGF), TGF-β, chemokine (C-C motif) ligand (CCL) 2, and colony-stimulating factor-1 (CSF-1) [70], thus facilitating tumor progression. EVs are known to shuttle important signaling cues required for macrophage polarization as well as participate in tumor-innate immune cell interactions. In agreement with this, Li et al. [71] identified lncRNA TUC339 as a novel signaling mediator, which when delivered to macrophages via HCC cell-derived EVs, induces activation and M1/M2 polarization by initiating cytokine-cytokine receptor signaling cascade and C-X-C chemokine receptor (CXCR) binding pathways. Under pharmacological or physiological endoplasmic reticulum (ER) stress, a known driver of inflammation, antitumor immunity, and tumor progression, cancer cells have been shown to condition macrophages to attain a proinflammatory phenotype through the toll-like receptor (TLR) 4-mediated transmission of ER stress and activation of ER stress-signaling pathways. This phenomenon, termed "transmissible" ER stress, represents one of the mechanisms by which tumor cells control the proinflammatory cytokine program in myeloid cells that are crucial for tumor growth and progression [72]. Besides the role of TLRs in sensing and potentiating transmissible ER stress, HCC cells have been demonstrated to communicate with infiltrated macrophages and transmit ER stress signals via miR-23a-3p-enriched EVs. This transmission inhibits PTEN, activates PI3K/Akt pathway, and increases programmed death-ligand 1 (PD-L1) expression on macrophages, consequently causing an impaired immune response of cytotoxic CD8$^+$ T cells and guarding tumor cells against immunologic toxicity [73]. Impairment of T-cell function by HCC EV-educated macrophages has also been established by Yin et al. [74]. The group showed that transcription factor Sal-like protein-4 (SALL4)-overexpressing HCC cells secrete miR-146a-5p-containing EVs, which when internalized by macrophages, remodel their cytokine profile, induce phenotypic transition into M2-polarized subtype, and impair T-cell-mediated antitumorigenic response [74].

TAMs are either derived directly from tissue-resident macrophages (TRMs) [75] or they differentiate from Ly6C + CCR2 + circulating monocytes that are recruited into the tumor tissues [76]. Therefore in the inflammatory tumor niche, the recruitment, survival, and differentiation of monocytes is essential for the continuous formation of TAMs. Monocytes undergo spontaneous caspase 3-dependent apoptosis [77] within 48 hours from entering into the blood circulation [78]. However, tumor-associated monocytes evade intrinsic apoptosis to enable constant generation of TAMs. Recent research has highlighted the central role of tumor-derived EVs in promoting and maintaining monocyte survival in the inflammatory TME before they can differentiate and generate sufficient TAMs. In HCC, EVs have been demonstrated to transfer functional receptor tyrosine kinases (RTKs) and confer survival-promoting properties to monocytes through the activation of the MAPK pathway [79].

The stimulatory effects of HCC-derived EVs on TAMs are well established, but the existence of TAM-derived EVs and their functions in tumor progression and metastasis remains elusive. Very recently, Wang et al. [80] found that tumor-associated macrophage-secreted extracellular vesicles (EVs) with low levels of miR-125a and miR-125b promote proliferation and bestow stem cell properties to HCC cells by upregulating stem cell marker CD90.

Natural killer cells

Several studies have reported perturbations in the phenotype and function of natural killer (NK) cells, the prime regulators of innate antitumor response, as well as in the NK cell receptor/ligand axes, majorly the NKG2D receptor-major histocompatibility complex class I chain-related protein A and B (MICA/B) axis in HCC [81]. HCC cells have been shown to induce NK cell dysfunction through the release of EVs and dampen NK cell cytotoxicity. For instance, HCC cells secrete both MICA- and MICB-harboring EVs [82] which are postulated to attenuate NK cell cytotoxicity by competitively inhibiting agonistic NKG2D receptor signaling [68]. The immune-activating receptor NKG2D and its cognate ligands (NKG2DL) constitute an efficient immune recognition system, essential for the stimulation of effector functions of NK cells and cytotoxic T cells. The central dogma suggests that the NKG2D-NKG2DL axis sensitizes malignant cells to cytotoxic lymphocyte-mediated recognition and elimination and provides an innate barrier against tumor development. However, a recent surge in research has appreciated the contribution of this recognition pathway to the development of autoimmunity and a decisive but paradoxical (inhibitory vs stimulatory) role in cancer immunosurveillance [83].

Additionally, HCC-derived vesicular circUHRF1 (hsa_circ_0048677) has been shown to inhibit NK cell function by degrading miR-449c-5p and upregulating miR-449c-5p target gene, T cell immunoglobulin and mucin domain-containing protein (TIM)-3, thus contributing to immune evasion and resistance to anti-PD1 immunotherapy [84]. TIM-3 is an immune checkpoint molecule that abrogates antitumor immunity by mediating effector T-cell exhaustion and apoptosis, enhancing regulatory T-cell (Treg) suppressor functions, and promoting M2 polarization of TAMs [85]. Cytokine-dependent upregulation of TIM-3 expression is generally associated with accelerated tumor growth and enhanced metastatic ability (via EMT) in HCC [86]. Similarly, EV-transfer of circUHRF1 was determined to inhibit NK cell secretion of TNF-α and IFN-γ as well as decrease the proportion and tumor infiltration of NK cells [84]. Furthermore, Nakano et al. [87] demonstrated the impact of circulating HCC-derived EVs, carrying miR-92b, on enhanced migratory abilities of tumor cells and decreased NK cell cytotoxicity via suppressed expression of a key activation marker, CD69. Recently, Yang et al. [88] appreciated the role of EVs in mediating HBV transmission to hepatocytes as well as to primary NK cells, suppressing their cytotoxic activity during chronic hepatitis B (CHB) infection. Considering the association of both HBV infection and NK cell dysfunction with HCC, it is plausible that EVs carrying hepatitis viral components underscore the link between chronic infection and HCC initiation.

Neutrophils

Neutrophils, the classic inflammatory cells, occupy a significant portion of tumor-infiltrating leukocytes and serve as a connecting link between inflammation and cancer [89,90]. Unlike TAMs, the roles of tumor-associated neutrophils (TANs) have been neglected due to their presumed short life span and metabolic incompetence [91]. However, advances in neutrophil biology research have unveiled distinct context-dependent roles of TANs in various TMEs [92]. In general, TANs influence tumor progression, cellular transformation, and tumor immunity [93] by secreting cytokines and chemokines endowed with TME-dependent pro- or antitumor functions [91,94]. In HCC, TANs modulate the TME, facilitate tumor progression, and confer drug resistance by mediating the migration and recruitment of macrophages and Tregs [92]. Zhou et al. [95] uncovered the existence of a positive feedback loop between TANs and HCC stem-like cells that is governed by a complex network involving miR-301b-3p, limbic system-associated membrane protein (LSAMP), cylindromatosis lysine 63 deubiquitinase (CYLD), NF-κB signaling, and C-X-C motif chemokine ligand (CXCL) 5. They further described the correlation of the feedback loop with HCC progression and poor patient outcomes. TANs have also been associated with T-cell dysfunction either via the release of Arginase I [96] or via programmed cell death protein 1 (PD-1)/PD-L1 interactions [97]. PD-L1 + TANs, derived from HCC patients, have been shown to inhibit the proliferation and activation of PD-1 + T cells via PD-1/PD-L1 interactions [97].

Recent studies have reported the capacity of tumor-derived EVs to promote the polarization of neutrophils into a protumor N2 phenotype [98]. For example, gastric cancer (GC) cell-derived EVs induce autophagy and N2 polarization of neutrophils via high mobility group box 1 (HMGB1)/TLR4/NF-κB signaling [98]. Li et al. [99] have demonstrated the functional significance of increased autophagy in sustaining prolonged survival and tumor-promoting effects of neutrophils in HCC. It is plausible that HCC cell-derived EVs may regulate neutrophil protumor phenotype and function through autophagic activation. Moreover, HCC cell-secreted EVs, enriched with TGF-β, have been shown to influence cell behavior and migration through the activation of the TGF-β/SMAD signaling pathway [100]. TGF-β signaling, in cooperation with Axl signaling, has recently been shown to participate in CXCL5-dependent attraction of neutrophils in HCC tumors [101]. It can be hypothesized that TGF-β HCC EVs may have similar effects on neutrophil infiltration and hence, tumor progression in HCC.

B cells

B cells are the central components of the adaptive humoral immune system whose principal function is to secrete antigen-specific immunoglobulins (Igs) [102]. Aside from their traditional role in humoral immunity, accumulating evidence suggests that B cells play an important role in cellular immunity, which is linked to the pathophysiology of autoimmunity and allograft rejection [102]. Moreover, with the discovery of tumor-infiltrating B cells (TIBs) and its subtypes and that of tertiary lymphoid structures (TLS) in peripheral tissues [sites of in situ immune response characterized by ectopic aggregation of lymphocytes and dendritic cells (DCs)], there has been an upsurge in studies investigating the complex association between B cells and tumors. Investigations have decoded the multifaceted dual role of TIBs in tumor immunity: TIBs positively regulate antitumor immune response through costimulation and cytokine secretion, antigen presentation, and antibody production, or negatively regulate antitumor immunity through differentiation into regulatory B cells (Breg) [102,103]. In the HCC setting, the role of TIBs remains contradictory. According to one report, the density of TIBs is closely related to the activation of CD8 + T and CD56 + NK cells in the TME and reduced tumor viability, which contributes to local antitumor immune response [104]. Other reports have identified enrichment of $CD19^+CD24^{high}CD38^{high}$ Breg phenotype in the TME and its association with accelerated HCC growth and invasiveness via the CD40/CD154 signaling pathway [105].

Ye and the team [106] established a novel mechanism by which protumorigenic TIM-1 + Breg subsets with $CD5^{high}CD24^-CD27^{-/+}CD38^{+/high}$ immunophenotype (unlike the conventional peripheral Breg cells) mediate immune evasion and progression in HCC: HCC-derived EVs, expressing membrane HMGB1, promote the production and expansion of TIM-1 + Breg cells via the TLR2/4-MAPK pathway and trigger their strong suppressive activity against CD8 + effector T cells. They also determined an association between TIM-1 + Breg cells with advanced disease stage and reduced survival in HCC patients. HMGB1 is a damage molecular pattern (DAMP) protein, which when released by tumor cells, engages with multiple surface receptors such as TLR2/4 and advanced glycation end products (RAGE) [107] that aid tumor cell invasion and metastasis [108].

T cells

The immunotolerant nature of the liver is largely attributed to its tolerogenic microenvironment characterized by T-cell dysfunction, including clonal deletion (elimination of high-affinity T-cell receptor-bearing self-reactive T-cell clones [109]), anergy (functional unresponsiveness in self-reactive lymphocytes [109]), deviation (gain of Th2 phenotype by naïve CD4 + T cells [66]), and exhaustion (disrupted immunodominance profile, altered transcriptomic signature, and impaired effector functions of T cells [110,111]) as well as the expansion of immunosuppressive Treg cells [66]. During HCC, this tolerogenic state suppresses the effective adaptive immune cell response against tumor cells.

The efficiency of tumor-derived EVs in inhibiting the antitumor response of effector T cells is well established: in HCC, secretion and uptake of 14-3-3 protein zeta (14-3-3ζ)-over-expressing EVs has been shown to impede the activity and functionality of tumor-infiltrating T lymphocytes (TILs; CD3 + T cells, CD4 + T cells, and CD8 + T cells) [112]. Overexpression of 14-3-3ζ protein is frequently detected in HCC [113] where it acts as a scaffold protein for Axl and mediates its stimulatory effects on HCC invasion and chemoresistance by inducing the prooncogenic functions of TGF-β [114]. By forming a complex with αB-crystallin, 14-3-3ζ has also been determined to foster HCC progression and drug resistance through the activation of ERK signaling cascade [115]. Specifically, EV-mediated transmission of 14-3-3ζ generates an exhaustive phenotype of CD8 + T cells (Tex cells), gauged from the upregulated expression of exhaustion markers [PD-1, TIM-3, lymphocyte activating 3 (LAG3), cytotoxic T-lymphocyte associated protein 4 (CTLA-4)] in the 14-3-3ζ^{high} subset in comparison to the 14-3-3ζ^{low} subset. Relative to the effector and memory CD8 + T cells, CD8 + Tex cells possess weak (but not absent) effector function and exhibit alterations in their differentiation patterns [116]. Similarly, overexpression of 14-3-3ζ significantly inhibits the function, proliferation, and activation of CD3 + and CD4 + T cells while directing their conversion into Treg cells. These results are well in accordance with the fact that tumor-derived EVs orchestrate a coordinated double insult to cellular immunity: EVs mediate the elimination of antitumor effector cells and, in parallel, support the expansion of Treg cells. In some studies, higher frequencies and suppressor functions of peripheral blood CD4^{+}CD25^{high} FOXP3^{+} Treg in cancer patients compared to normal controls have been linked to cancer progression and shorter survival [117,118]. Potentially, tumor-derived EVs induce Treg, promote Treg expansion, enhance Treg suppressor function, and confer Treg resistance to apoptosis [119].

HCC-derived EVs participate in metabolic reprogramming

The liver is a metabolically active organ that hosts an array of finely tuned metabolic processes that are tightly controlled by neuronal and hormonal systems [120,121]. The liver in general and hepatic glucose metabolism play an essential role in maintaining systemic glucose homeostasis [122]. The maintenance of blood glucose levels has important physiological outcomes and is regulated by multiple metabolic pathways, with a prominent role for hepatocytes. Net hepatic glucose metabolism primarily depends upon the systemic glucose fluxes from glycolysis, gluconeogenesis, glycogen metabolism, and other pathways in hepatocytes [123]. Acute regulation of these glucose fluxes relies on the availability of substrates, allosteric protein—metabolite interactions, transcriptional control, and redox states [124]. Hepatocyte-autonomous (direct) and hepatocyte-nonautonomous (indirect) mechanisms have also been implicated in regulating hepatic glucose metabolism [123].

HCC cells exhibit extensive reprogramming in a number of metabolic pathways to fulfill the increased bioenergetic and biosynthetic demands associated with rapid growth, proliferation, and metastasis [123]. These alterations have enabled the characterization and validation of numerous actionable metabolic vulnerabilities that can be targeted by metabolic inhibitors to effectively treat HCC. Genomic studies have revealed profound changes in gene expression signatures related to the metabolic network in HCC, with consistent upregulation of genes involved in glycolysis, pentose-phosphate pathway (PPP), nucleotide metabolism, tricarboxylic acid (TCA) cycle, mitochondrial oxidative phosphorylation (OXPHOS), proton transport, membrane lipid biochemistry, and glycan metabolism [125]. HCC tumors typically bear metabolomic signatures suggestive of dysregulated glycolysis-TCA cycle-OXPHOS axis and enhanced glucose metabolism [123]. In fact, HCC cells flaunt the most comprehensive glucose metabolism reprogramming of all cancer cells [126].

A growing body of evidence has uncovered the metabolism-centric regulatory role of EVs and their control over aerobic glycolysis ("Warburg effect") in recipient tumor and tumor-stroma cells [127]. In HCC, motile tumor cells have been shown to export proteins, via EVs, associated with sugar metabolism-related canonical pathways including glycolysis I, gluconeogenesis I, and PPP [128]. In addition to proteins, EV-mediated transfer of circ-ZNF652 to HCC cells has been found to positively regulate HCC progression by enhancing cell proliferation, migration, invasion, and glycolysis via the miR-29a-3p/guanylyl cyclase domain containing 1 (GUCD1) axis [129]. Both miR-29a-3p and its target gene GUCD1 are implicated in regulating HCC cell growth and tumorigenesis [130,131]. Another study recognized the role of vesicular circ-FBLIM1 in regulating HCC progression and glycolysis through the modulation of miR-338/low-density lipoprotein receptor-related protein 6 (LRP6) axis. The glycolytic phenotype in tumor cells was correlated to increased glucose consumption, increased lactic acid and ATP generation, an upregulated extracellular acidification rate (ECAR; manifesting overall glycolytic flux), and a downregulated oxygen consumption rate (OCR)/mitochondrial respiration [132].

Under hypoxic conditions, cancer cells gain a malignant phenotype by undergoing metabolic adaptations, achieved through enhanced stabilization and activity of HIF transcription factors [133]. During hypoxic stress, HCC cells secrete EVs containing hypoxia-responsive lncRNA linc-ROR, which modulates cellular responses in neighboring cells by sequestering miR-145 and thus increasing the expression of oncoprotein HIF-1α and its downstream target pyruvate dehydrogenase kinase isozyme 1 (PDK1) [134]. PDK1 has been identified as an important glycolytic enzyme that inhibits the entry of pyruvate into the TCA cycle, thereby suppressing OXPHOS and mitochondrial-dependent biosynthesis in hypoxia [135,136]. Irrespective of the contradictory data available on the regulatory role of PDKs in tumor metabolism and primary tumor growth [137], it is clear that hypoxia-induced metabolic rewiring via the miR-145/HIF-1α/PDK1 pathway modulates cellular responses in HCC through the glycolytic program [134].

In the context of liver fibrosis, EVs derived from activated HSCs and enriched with glycolytic proteins—glucose transporter (GLUT) 1, hexokinase 2 (HK2), and pyruvate kinase M2 (PKM2)—were shown to induce glycolysis in quiescent HSCs, Kupffer cells (KCs), and liver sinusoidal endothelial cells (LSECs) [138].

Stromal cell-derived EVs alter the biologic behavior of HCC cells to aid hepatocarcinogenesis and progression

It is well appreciated that dynamic interactions between the TME and cancer cells, governed by EV-mediated heterotypic signaling mechanisms, can confer and amplify crucial oncogenic functions in cancer cells beneficial for tumor progression, metastasis, and therapy-resistance (Table 20.1). In HCC, stromal/TME cell-secreted EVs pleiotropically regulate tumor development and progression through an array of bioactive cargo molecules capable of altering the behavior and functions of tumor cells, modulating the primary TME as well as favoring metastasis.

Normal hepatic cell-derived EVs

In comparison to HCC-derived EVs, the role of liver parenchyma cell-derived EVs in HCC tumorigenesis is far less understood. In this context, Chen et al. [161] recently identified the tumor-suppressive role of normal liver cell-derived EVs in HCC. HCC cells and their vesicular derivatives express low levels of circ-0051443, an ncRNA that regulates cell apoptosis and proliferation. However, normal hepatic cells and their EVs express significantly higher levels of circ-0051443. This EV-borne circ-0051443, when delivered to recipient HCC cells, was shown to alter the malignant phenotype of tumor cells by inducing apoptosis and cell cycle arrest. In vivo, it was demonstrated to inhibit tumor growth by sponging miR-331-3p and upregulating the expression of its target gene, Bcl-2 antagonist/killer 1 (BAK1) in HCC cells [161]. BAK1 essentially regulates apoptotic cell death and its dysregulation is often noted in multiple cancers, such as cervical cancer [162], nonsmall cell lung carcinoma (NSCLC) [163], pediatric germ cell tumors [164], and chronic lymphocytic leukemia (CLL) [165]. Similarly, Wang et al. [166] showed that vesicular transfer of normal cell-secreted lncRNA SENP3-EIF4A1 to HCC cells induces apoptosis and mitigates their invasive and migratory abilities. Also, like circ-0051443, the EV-associated SENP3-EIF4A1 was shown to inhibit xenograft tumor growth by sequestering miR-9-5p and enhancing the expression of its target gene, mRNA-binding protein tristetraprolin (TTP/ZFP36). Traditionally, TTP is a tumor suppressor, however, in HCC, it exhibits a dual role: tumor-promoting during HCC initiation and tumor-suppressive during HCC progression [167].

Adipocyte-derived EVs

Growing evidence has highlighted the protumorigenic roles of CAAs, especially in obesity-induced hepatocarcinogenesis, which is mediated through the paracrine communication network involving tumor cells. The key oncogenic events associated with the adipocyte-tumor cell cross-talk involve structural remodeling of the ECM, inflammation, metabolic alteration, angiogenesis, dedifferentiation into a fibroblast-like phenotype, immune evasion, EMT, and dysregulated production/release of hormones and adipokines [168–170].

As stated earlier, adipocytes, modified by tumor cell-derived EVs, participate in a "vicious cycle" to create a niche favorable for HCC tumor growth and progression. Recent research has provided novel mechanistic insights into the role of adipocyte-derived EVs in supporting a protumorigenic HCC microenvironment. Adipocytes provide bioactive substrates, through EV-mediated intercellular exchange, to HCC cells and thus govern signaling and HCC progression. For example, transfer of EV-borne miRNA-23a/b from adipocytes to HCC cells was shown to encourage HCC cell growth and migration as well as confer chemoresistance by targeting the tumor suppressor Von Hippel-Lindau (VHL)/HIF axis [171]. In addition, circ-deubiquitination (circ-DB,

TABLE 20.1 EV-mediated heterotypic signaling mechanisms in the TME.

Donor cells	Recipient cells	Mechanism of action	Effect	References
Influence of tumor-derived EVs on the functions of TME cells				
LLC or melanoma cells	Alveolar epithelial cells	• EV-associated RNA activates TLR3 in host epithelial cells, induces chemokine secretion, and promotes neutrophil recruitment to the lung microenvironment • Promotes metastasis progression by influencing NF-κB and MAPK pathways	• Induces TME inflammatory phenotype • Lung premetastatic niche formation • Induces antiinflammatory immunosuppressive microenvironment and promotes tumor progression	[139]
p53-mutant colon cancer cells	Macrophages	• EV-mediated transfer of miR-1246 induces reprogramming of macrophages into M2-polarized tumor-supportive and antiinflammatory macrophages • Increases secretion of VEGF, IL-10, CCL-2, and TGF-β by M2 macrophages • Decreases levels of IL-8 and TNF-α		[140]
CLL cells		• EV-associated noncoding Y RNA hY4 activates the TLR7 pathway in monocytes, induces the secretion of CCL2, CCL4, and IL-6, and elevates the expression of PD-L1	• Promotes inflammation and immune escape	[141]
LLC cells		• EV-mediated transfer of activated EGFR to macrophages inhibits IFN-β signaling via MEKK2-dependent phosphorylation of IRF3 at Ser_173	• Suppresses host innate immunity	[142]
LAC cells	Fibroblasts	• EV-mediated transfer of miR-142-3p confers tumor-associated phenotype to fibroblasts	• Malignant transformation of fibroblasts	[143]
GC cells		• EV-mediated transfer of miR-27a induces reprogramming of fibroblasts into CAFs		[144]
		• EV-mediated transfer of TGF-β into MSCs induces their differentiation into CAFs via activation of the TGF-β/SMAD pathway		[145]
PC cells	Adipocytes	• EVs carrying AM hormone bind to ADMR receptors on adipocytes, activates p38 and ERK1/2 MAPK pathways, and promotes phosphorylation of hormone-sensitive lipases	• Increases lipolysis in subcutaneous adipose tissue • Paraneoplastic effects: early onset of weight loss (cancer cachexia) in PC patients	[146]
LC cells		• Inhibits adipogenic differentiation of hAD-MSCs via TGF-β signaling pathway	• Adipose tissue loss associated with cancer cachexia	[147]
Influence of TME cell-derived EVs on the functions of tumor cells				
TAMs (M2 macrophages)	BCa cells	• EV-mediated delivery of oncogenic miR-223 promotes invasion of BCa cells via the Mef2c-β-catenin pathway	• Enhances invasive capabilities of BCa cells	[148]
	GC cells	• EV-mediated delivery of miR-21 activates PI3K/Akt pathway by downregulating PTEN	• Inhibits cancer cell apoptosis and confers drug resistance	[149]

Source	Target cell	Mechanism	Effect	Ref.
CAFs	Ovarian cancer cells	EV-associated TGF-β1 promotes EMT by activating the SMAD pathway	• Confers aggressive phenotype in tumor cells • Enhances tumor migration and invasion ability	[150]
	OSCC cells	EV-mediated transfer of miR-34a-5p activates Akt/GSK-3β/β-catenin/snail signaling pathway via miR-34a-5p/AXL axis Stimulates activation of MMP-2 and MMP-9	• Enhances proliferation and promotes EMT, tumor progression, and metastasis	[151]
Adipocytes	LLC cells	Promotes tumor cell metastasis through MMP-3/9 axis	• Enhances tumor cell invasion and metastasis	[152]
hBM-MSCs	BCa cells	EVs transport tumor supportive miRNA-21 and -34a and increase cell proliferation	• Enhances breast tumor growth	[153]
		EV-mediated transfer of miR-100 modulates mTOR/HIF-1α signaling axis in BCa cells and downregulates the expression and secretion of VEGF	• Inhibits angiogenesis	[154]
		EV-mediated transfer of miR-205 and miR-31 suppresses metastatic potential of tumor cells by targeting UBE2N/Ubc13 gene	• Suppresses angiogenesis and metastasis of nonorgan-committed BCa cells	[155]
		EVs mediate transfer of miR-222/223	• Confers quiescence and drug resistance	[156]
	GC cells	Increases VEGF and CXCR4 expression in tumor cells by activating the ERK1/2 pathway Stimulates Hedgehog signaling pathway	• Enhances angiogenesis and tumor growth	[157,158]
	Osteosarcoma cells	Stimulates Hedgehog signaling pathway	• Enhances tumor growth	[157]
	Colon cancer cells	Increases VEGF and CXCR4 expression in tumor cells by activating the ERK1/2 pathway	• Enhances angiogenesis and tumor incidence	[158]
MM BM-MSCs	MM cells	Increases expression of IL-6, CCL2, junction plakoglobin, and fibronectin in EVs Transfers low amount of tumor suppressor miR-15a	• MM growth, dissemination to bone marrow, and progression	[159]
GC tissue-derived MSCs	GC cells	EV-mediated delivery of miR-221	• Facilitates growth and migration of tumor cells	[160]

ADMR, adrenomedullin receptor; *AM*, adrenomedullin; *BCa*, breast cancer; *BM-MSCs*, bone marrow mesenchymal stem cells; *CCL2*, C-C motif chemokine ligand 2; *CLL*, chronic lymphocytic leukemia; *EV*, extracellular vesicle; *GSK-3β*, glycogen synthase kinase 3 beta; *hAD-MSCs*, human adipose-derived mesenchymal stem cells; *HCC*, hepatocellular carcinoma; *IFN-β*, interferon beta; *IRF3*, interferon regulatory transcription factor 3; *LAC*, lung adenocarcinoma; *LC*, lung cancer; *LLC*, Lewis lung carcinoma; *MEKK2*, mitogen-activated protein kinase kinase 2; *MM*, multiple myeloma; *OSCC*, oral squamous cell carcinoma; *PC*, pancreatic cancer; *PD-L1*, programmed death-ligand 1; *S100A*, S100 calcium-binding protein A; *TME*, tumor microenvironment; *UBE2N/Ubc13*, ubiquitin conjugating enzyme E2 N.

has_circ_0025129), highly expressed in adipocyte EVs, was determined to promote HCC proliferation and, in parallel, decrease DNA damage by absorbing miR-34a and activating the deubiquitinating enzyme ubiquitin-specific protease 7 (USP7)/Cyclin A2 signaling pathway [172].

Cancer-associated fibroblast-derived EVs

Studies focused on determining the metabolic influence of cancer-associated fibroblast (CAF)-derived EVs (CDEs) have shown their capacity to induce metabolic reprogramming and enhance the "Warburg effect" in tumor cells [173]. Research indicates that patient-derived CDEs participate in reprogramming of the metabolic machinery by inhibiting OXPHOS and providing de novo "off the shelf" metabolites such as acetate, lactate, TCA-cycle intermediates, amino acids, and lipids. Under nutrient-deprived conditions, such EV-supplied intact metabolites are utilized by recipient tumor cells for central carbon metabolism that promotes tumor growth. Moreover, CDE-mediated inhibition of OXPHOS leads to a compensatory increase in glycolysis and glutamine-dependent reductive carboxylation in tumor cells [173].

In HCC, CDEs, harboring circ-CCT3, regulate glucose metabolism by modulating the expression of high-affinity HK2 [174]. HK2 is a pleiotropic enzyme with significant roles in aerobic glycolysis [175], cell proliferation, and tumorigenesis [176]. During hepatocarcinogenesis, an isoform switch from HK4 or glucokinase (GCK) to HK2 occurs; this HK2 expression underlies the metabolically distinct nature of HCC cells when compared to normal hepatocytes [176]. The selective expression of HK2 in HCC cells has been exploited for targeted therapy in HCC.

Besides modulating tumor metabolism, CDEs are implicated in HCC tumor progression. To this vein, it was shown that CDEs, lacking antitumoral miRNAs—miR-320a [177] and miR-150-3p [178]—promote HCC progression by enhancing tumor cell proliferation, migration, invasion, and metastasis. MiR-320a is a tumor suppressor that inhibits the MAPK pathway in cancer cells by targeting pre-B-cell leukemia homeobox 3 (PBX3) gene implicated in cell cycle arrest and EMT [177].

HCC-derived EVs confer drug resistance

Significant technological advances and our ever-evolving knowledge of the molecular pathogenesis of HCC have added successful paradigms to its therapeutic landscape, aimed at targeting all evolutionary stages of HCC tumorigenesis. The past decade has witnessed an expansion in the HCC therapeutic armamentarium, owing to the substantial improvements in local ablation techniques, locoregional treatments, and systemic therapies, as well as the development of immunotherapies, other molecularly targeted therapies, and combinatorial regimens [179,180]. Because of its broad-spectrum antitumoral activity and good pharmacokinetic profile, sorafenib, a multikinase inhibitor, currently dominates the first-line systemic therapeutic strategy adopted for the management of advanced unresectable HCC [4,181]. Sorafenib has been linked to improved OS and time-to-tumor progression (TTP) in advanced-stage HCC cases (albeit, modest) [182], but not to improved clinical response in the adjuvant setting (after surgical resection or local ablation) [183] or in intermediate HCC cases [182]. Notably, HCC cells exhibit high refractoriness to sorafenib after long-term exposure, impacting the efficacy and tolerance to this first-line drug [184]. Several potential mechanisms defining the landscape of HCC therapeutic resistance have been outlined [184,185], including those mediated by EVs.

Qu et al. [186] presented both in vitro and in vivo evidence on the functional role of highly invasive HCC cell-derived EVs in regulating sorafenib-resistance in hepatoma cells by activating the HGF/c-Met/Akt signaling pathway and suppressing drug-induced apoptosis. Besides mediating hypoxia-induced metabolic reprogramming, enrichment of linc-ROR in HCC-released EVs has been determined to modulate pharmacological response to sorafenib or doxorubicin [DOX, an anthracycline commonly used in transarterial chemoembolization (TACE)] [187]. Enriched in response to TGF-β during chemotherapeutic stress, EV-associated linc-ROR was shown to confer survival advantage and inhibit drug-induced cell apoptosis in a p53-dependent manner. Also, linc-ROR was demonstrated to mediate the effects of TGF-β on the chemoresistant phenotype by enhancing stemness in CSCs [188]. Similarly, linc-VLDLR, upregulated in chemotherapeutic drug(s)-treated HCC cells as well as the secreted EVs, was shown to regulate the chemotherapy stress response by inhibiting apoptosis and upregulating ATP-binding cassette, subfamily G member 2 (ABCG2) in recipient cells [189]. ABCG2 is a member of the ABC superfamily of transporter proteins, which play a key role in the development of therapeutic resistance by facilitating anticancer drug extrusion and detoxification [190,191]. Another study demonstrated that the EV-mediated intercellular exchange of miR-32-5p between drug-resistant HCC cells and drug-sensitive HCC cells can bestow a multidrug-resistant phenotype in recipient cells by inhibiting PTEN, activating the PI3K/Akt pathway, and modulating both angiogenesis and the EMT program [192]. Furthermore, Wang et al. [193] determined the important role of EV-associated miR-744 in cell proliferation and chemoresistance in HCC. MiR-744, downregulated in EVs isolated from the serum of HCC patients as well as from sorafenib-resistant HCC cells, was found to effectively regulate paired box gene 2 (PAX2) and increase its expression in the surrounding tumor cells, thus promoting their proliferation and inhibiting the chemosensitivity to sorafenib.

HCC-derived EVs facilitate organotropic metastasis

Organotropic metastasis or metastasis organotropism is the disproportional and systematic distribution of distant metastasis to specific organs. Distant metastasis can be viewed as a multidimensional process whereby distant organ infiltration and colonization is one dimension of metastasis, the kinetics (time to relapse/recur) of metastatic progression is the second dimension, and the host organ loci in which these steps occur define the third dimension [194]. Innate properties of the cancer cells, genetic or epigenetic modifications, tissue affinities and circulation patterns, organ-specific microenvironment/niches, tumor-organ cross-talk, metabolic adaptations, tumor immune microenvironment, and EMT have been identified as critical factors that determine organ-specific metastatic behaviors and the efficiency of organotropic metastasis [195].

The specificity of metastasis in each host organ is largely dependent upon its unique microenvironmental and architectural features. For aggressive colonization, cancer cells gain adaptability or robust metastatic competence functions either through genetic/epigenetic programs or by interacting with the organ microenvironment [195]. Recent research has highlighted the role of EVs in mediating communication between cancer cells and the organ microenvironment (reviewed in Ref. [196,197]). Since EVs serve as critical mediators of intercellular and interorgan cross-talk, their involvement in organotropic metastasis is not surprising. Accumulating evidence indicates that selective organotropic integration of tumor-derived EVs, by the virtue of their affinity for specific resident cells in host organs, facilitates the preconditioning of the target organ niches that is essential for efficient metastatic organotropism. Fundamentally, this priming of the organ niches allows potent metastatic distribution of even those tumor cells that possess poor colonization capacity for that particular organ site.

The most preferential sites of extrahepatic metastatic HCC are the lungs, bones, peritoneum, spleen, brain, distant (abdominal) lymph nodes (LN), kidneys, and adrenal glands [198,199]. HCC patients exhibit a high propensity to develop lung metastasis, accounting for nearly 51%–54% of all extrahepatic metastatic cases [199,200]. Owing to its ideal physiology, the lungs provide a supportive microenvironment or niche, enabling the metastasis-initiating cells to gain a foothold, survive, and eventually grow in accordance with Paget's enduring "seed and soil" paradigm. Also, the lung is engaged in interorgan communication, dictating the complexity and dynamic nature of the lung tissue [201]. The extensive pulmonary capillary networks and a broad surface area (meant for efficient gas exchange) prove conducive to cancer cell attachment, invasion, and outgrowth [195,202]. However, the inter-EC tight junctions, essential for maintaining the integrity of the endothelial monolayer in the pulmonary vasculature, poses a structural barrier for the extravasation of tumor cells [195,202]. One of the mechanisms applied by metastatic primary tumor cells to traverse through this barrier and facilitate cell homing involves the formation of distinct foci of focal adhesion kinase (FAK)-dependent vascular hyperpermeability through the release of multiple secreted factors such as VEGF, TNF-α, TGF-β, and ANGPT-2 [203].

Several lines of evidence have demonstrated the imperative role of EVs in mediating lung microenvironmental modifications to support HCC growth. For instance, HCC cell-derived vesicular miR-103 was shown to increase vascular permeability and promote trans-endothelial invasion and metastatic dissemination of tumor cells to lungs by targeting multiple proteins involved in maintaining endothelial junction integrity, such as ZO-1, p120-catenin, and Vascular endothelial (VE)-cadherin [204]. Modulation of vascular permeability and stimulation of neoangiogenesis are important steps during the establishment of a premetastatic niche that favors initial extravasation and outgrowth of DTCs at secondary organs [205]. Perturbation of vascular cell barrier function through the modulation of EC activity represents one of the important prometastatic roles of tumor EVs [206]. In the lung premetastatic niche, miRNA-1247-3p-harboring HCC EVs were shown to target β-1,4-galactosyltransferase (B4GALT3) in normal fibroblasts and mediate their conversion into CAFs by activating β1-integrin (ITG)-NF-κB signaling. These EV-activated CAFs, with enhanced migratory and collagen contraction abilities, were then found to promote stemness, EMT, sorafenib resistance, and tumor progression via increased expression of proinflammatory genes, such as IL-6, IL-8, TGF-β, CXCL12, collagen type I alpha 1 chain (COL1A1), collagen type III alpha 1 chain (COL3A1), and collagen type IV alpha 1 chain (COL4A1). From the clinical perspective, high serum vesicular miR-1247-3p levels were linked to lung metastasis in HCC patients [207]. In addition, nidogen 1 (NID1), enriched in metastatic HCC cell-derived EVs, was demonstrated to activate pulmonary fibroblasts, stimulate tumor necrosis factor receptor 1 (TNFR1) secretion, and augment the motility and lung colonization capacity of HCC cells. The NID1-containing EVs were further shown to destabilize pulmonary vascular architecture and enhance angiogenesis, thereby facilitating the colonization of hepatoblasts in the lungs [208]. These studies validate the potential of EVs to abet a milieu of local cell types and prime the metastatic niche to enhance the adaptation of engrafted tumor cells to the radically different metastatic microenvironments.

Another study showed that HCC EV-mediated transfer of LOXL4 to parental HCC cells promotes invasion and metastasis by controlling the migratory and adhesion potential of tumor cells via the LOX catalytic activity-dependent activation of the FAK/Src pathway [33]. Evidence suggests that LOXL4, an oncogene endogenously overexpressed in HCC cells, fosters the development of intra- and extrahepatic metastasis in HCC in vivo, while the β1-ITG/FAK/Src signaling axis potently regulates cell survival and anoikis resistance [209] that are essential for both intrahepatic spreading and lung metastasis of HCC. Clinically, overexpressed LOXL4 was found to correlate with tumor differentiation, vascular invasion, tumor-node-metastasis (TNM) stage, and poor prognosis [33]. Likewise, the EV-induced activation of the FAK/Src-p38MAPK pathway and the concomitant HCC growth and lung metastasis was determined by Jiang et al. [210]. The group unveiled the capacity of EVs, derived from highly metastatic HCC cells, to deliver multifunctional protein alpha-enolase (ENO1) into low-metastatic HCC cells and promote tumor growth and metastasis by upregulating the expression of ITGα6β4 and activating its downstream signaling pathway via p38MAPK. The pioneering study by Prof. Layden and the team [211] have demonstrated that tumor-secreted EVs exhibit specific ITG expression profiles, distinct from tumor cells, that dictate their selective localization and organ-specific targeting to the lungs, brain, and LN. In particular, primary tumors, with a metastatic propensity to lung tissue, secrete EVs expressing ITGα6β4 and ITGα6β1 that mediate adhesion of tumor-derived EVs to lung-resident fibroblasts and epithelial cells and thus govern lung tropism. Moreover, EVs expressing ITGα6β4 and ITGα6β1 selectively adhere to laminin-rich lung microenvironments, whereby they activate proto-oncogene tyrosine-protein kinase Src and initiate promigratory and proinflammatory S100 gene upregulation in specific resident cells to promote migration and inflammation. Considering the functions of S100 proteins in lung tropism, Sun et al. [212] uncovered the potential of vesicular S100A4, derived from highly metastatic HCC cells, to encourage stemness, invasion, and lung metastasis formation ability of low metastatic HCC cells through the activation of STAT3 phosphorylation and increased osteopontin (OPN) expression. In addition to metastatic HCC cell-derived EVs, primary tumor-derived EVs have been shown to promote lung metastasis by regulating circulating HCC cell viability, proliferation, and adhesion to the pulmonary vasculature via the SMAD Family Member 3 (SMAD3)-ROS signaling pathway [213].

Besides lung metastasis, EVs secreted by highly metastatic HCC cells influence lymphangiogenesis and thus LN metastasis. Accordingly, horizontal transfer of CXCR4 from high LN metastatic HCC cells was shown to amplify the migratory potential and invasiveness of less metastatic HCC cells as well as enhance lymphangiogenesis by augmenting proliferation and tube formation capacity of lymphatic endothelial cells (LECs) via stromal cell-derived factor-1α (SDF-1α)/CXCR4 axis-mediated secretion of MMP-9, MMP-2, and

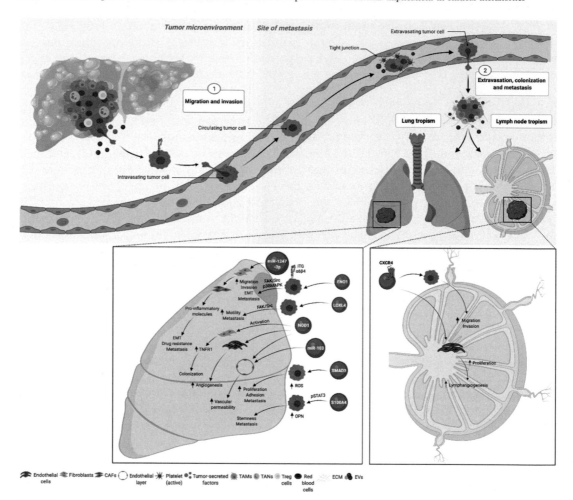

FIGURE 20.2 **Delineating extracellular vesicle (EV) mediated pathways in lung and lymph node metastasis in hepatocellular carcinoma (HCC).** HCC-derived EVs adopt numerous strategies and activate diverse signaling pathways to drive metastasis in the lungs and lymph nodes, including phenotypic differentiation of host stromal cells, increased angiogenesis, vascular remodeling, induction of epithelial-to-mesenchymal transition (EMT), and increased metastatic potential of low metastatic tumor cells.

VEGF-C [214] (Fig. 20.2). While the catalytic activity of MMPs is responsible for the processing of ECM and nonmatrix molecules that are necessary for the development of a premetastatic niche, multiple studies have highlighted their diverse cellular actions at all stages of the invasion-metastasis cascade. These include alteration of cell—cell and cell—ECM interactions, fibroblast switching and acquisition of mesenchymal state, migration, neoangiogenesis, distal metastatic dissemination, and metastatic organotropism [215—217].

Cumulatively, these results substantiate the functional role of EVs in pleiotropically regulating multistep tumor progression in HCC and serving as critical mediators of limitless events in a neoplastic system.

EVs in targeted therapeutic interventions in HCC

EVs as efficient drug delivery systems

In recent years, cancer nanomedicine, crafted using multifunctional theranostic nanoplatforms, has provided a compelling panacea for effective cancer diagnosis and treatment [218]. Several nanotechnology-based drug-delivery systems (NDDS) have been designed to achieve targeted delivery of systemically administered drugs, with a concomitant increase in tumor intracellular drug concentrations, improved biodistribution of drugs, enhanced antitumor activity, and low to no systemic toxicity [218]. Given their unique pharmacological and biological properties, similar to those of nanoparticles, EVs have emerged as a tantalizing source of nanoagents and nanocarriers in clinical theranostics. The utilization of EVs as effective drug delivery platforms has gained considerable interest, owing to their ability to deliver endogenous or exogenous therapeutic moieties, biocompatibility, barrier-avoiding capacities, lack of immunogenicity, low (systemic) toxicity, intrinsic cell-targeting and target-homing capabilities, and greater stability in circulation [219]. All these attributes reflect their potential as next-generation DDS in personalized medicine.

EVs have been assessed as efficient vectors of anticancer drugs, small RNAs, and antiinflammatory agents [220]. In order to harness the drug-delivery abilities of EVs and develop smart EV-based delivery systems, several endogenous drug-loading (where donor cells are "preloaded" with the desired drug which gets encapsulated in EVs and exocytosed into extracellular space) [221,222] or exogenous drug encapsulation (loading of drugs into isolated and purified EVs by electroporation or sonoporation) methods have been developed [223]. For example, Tang et al. [224] developed DOX-encapsulating EVs that were derived from HCC cells incubated with the same drug. These DOX-encapsulating EVs were shown to exhibit greater efficiency in delivering DOX directly to tumor cells and superior pharmacological efficacy (than direct treatment with DOX), as gauged from their potential to inhibit tumor growth in the murine HCC ascites model in lieu of any drug-associated side effects. Moreover, these drug-packaging EVs triggered the synthesis of a new generation of drug-packaging EVs as well as suppressed drug-efflux from tumor cells, thereby enhancing the cytotoxic effect and contributing to domino-like tumor cell killings [224]. Recently, Son and colleagues [225] employed EVs to transport sodium/iodide symporter (NIS) protein and enhance radioiodine avidity and cytotoxicity in HCC cells. As per the procedure, the authors constructed HCC (Huh7) cells expressing the NIS gene that successfully generated EVs enriched with the NIS protein. Treatment of Huh7 cells with these NIS-enriched EVs resulted in the transfer of functionally active NIS protein and enhanced the ^{125}I uptake into recipient cells. Furthermore, pre-treatment with EV-Huh7/NIS boosted the cytotoxicity of ^{131}I therapy against Huh7 cells by generating greater DNA damage. These results highlight the probable use of EVs in reverting radioiodine resistance to radioiodine sensitivity, especially in unresectable radiotherapy-refractory HCC.

Very recently, Yong et al. [226] developed a biomimetic nanoparticle delivery platform to efficiently deliver chemotherapeutic drugs to tumors. Taking inspiration from cell-mimicking nanoparticles that integrate unique chemistry of biological entities, such as membrane lipids and proteins and the engineering diversity/flexibility of synthetic materials [227], the authors developed biocompatible EV-sheathed DOX-loaded porous silicon nanoparticles (PSiNPs) (DOX@E-PSiNPs). These PSiNPs were derived from exocytosed by tumor cells incubated with DOX-loaded PSiNPs (DOX@PSiNPs). Upon intravenously injecting into H22 hepatocarcinoma tumor-bearing mice, the DOX@E-PSiNPs exhibited greater tumor accumulation and penetration into tumor parenchyma as well as strong cross-reactive cellular uptake and intracellular retention by bulk tumor cells and CSCs. By virtue of these enhanced features, DOX@E-PSiNPs contributed to increased in vivo DOX concentrations in total tumor cells and side population (a fraction of TICs with stem cell traits [228]), accounting for superior cytotoxicity in subcutaneous, orthotopic, and advanced metastatic tumor models.

Besides chemotherapy drugs, efforts have been made to engineer EVs to deliver heterologous nucleic acids such as therapeutic antitumor miRNAs. EVs provide an RNAse-free protective vesicle for the encapsulation and delivery of therapeutic miRNAs, thus guarding them against environmental/enzymatic degradation [229]. Pomatto et al. [230] demonstrated efficient miRNA encapsulation following electroporation into plasma-derived EVs for in vitro delivery. Electroporation represents an active loading technique that is used to pack nucleic acids into EVs and has been successfully employed to deliver exogenous small interfering RNA (siRNA) into monocytes and lymphocytes via engineered plasma EVs [231]. Plasma-derived EVs encapsulated with antitumor miRNAs—miR-31 and miR-451a—have been shown to effectively shuttle the loaded miRNAs into HepG2 HCC cells and induce apoptosis by silencing antiapoptotic genes [230].

Considering the chemoresistant nature of HCC tumors, the development of efficacious therapeutic systems to increase the chemosensitivity of tumor cells is of prime importance. EVs represent an advantageous therapeutic tool to overcome chemoresistance owing to their ability to evade drug efflux systems, profoundly accumulate in resistant tumor cells, increase drug intracellular trafficking, and deliver drug-sensitizing agents [232,233]. Benefiting from these attributes, Lou et al. [233] obtained EVs from miR-122-transfected adipose-derived mesenchymal stem cells (ADMSCs) and demonstratedtheir potential to sensitize HCC cells to chemotherapeutic agents, specifically sorafenib, by negatively regulating the expression of miR-122 target genes, causing apoptosis and cell cycle arrest. Evidence indicates that miR-122 contributes to sorafenib resistance through the activation of insulin-like growth factor 1 receptor (IGF-1R) and the downstream Ras/Raf/ERK signaling pathway [234]. Besides miR-122, the same group investigated the potential of ADMSC-derived EVs to deliver miR-199a-3p and boost the chemosensitivity of HCC tumors [235]. MiR-199a-3p is consistently downregulated in HCC tumors and correlates with poor prognosis [236] therefore, its restoration by miR-199a-3p-modified ADMSC-EVs enhances DOX sensitivity by inhibiting the expression of its direct target gene, mechanistic target of rapamycin (mTOR) [235,237]. Given these encouraging results, comprehensive research centered on EV-based DDS is a promising avenue for improving the efficacy of anticancer treatment regimens.

EVs as candidate immunotherapeutic agents in HCC

As inferred from the preceding sections, EVs play a multifarious role in virtually all facades of HCC pathobiology. Therefore, pharmacological strategies targeting EV biogenesis, packaging, trafficking, and internalization is an eminently exploitable facet that represents a new paradigm for clinically effective therapeutic modulation of HCC tumors. Intriguingly, EVs, which are strongly linked to immunosuppressive mechanisms, also possess immunostimulatory properties. This functional dichotomy makes them attractive immunotherapeutic agents in HCC. Extensive research is underway to develop EV-based strategies to tackle immunosuppression and enhance the antitumoral functions of cytotoxic cells.

In its immunotherapeutic facet of application, EVs are engaged as antigen carriers or tumor immunogenicity inducers to elicit potent antitumor immune responses. Researchers have explored the potential to modulate the immunoreactivity of endogenously derived EVs and reprogram them into artificial nanoscale controllers of antitumor immunity (termed "SMART-Exos") elicited through recruitment and activation of immune effector T cells [238]. Although open to manipulation, EVs also inherently express tumor-associated antigens (TAAs) that can be exploited to prime cytotoxic T cells and generate strong immune responses. For instance, HCC-derived EVs express strongly immunogenic TAAs, such as AFP and antigenic chaperones, such as Hsp70. Such competent TAA-carrying EVs were shown to mediate the targeted presentation of shared antigens to DCs, resulting in a DC-specific T-cell-dependent antitumor immune response in ectopic and orthotopic HCC tumor-bearing mice models [239]. Under chemotherapeutic drug-induced stress conditions, HCC cells secrete EVs enriched in Hsp60, Hsp70, and Hsp90 [240]. These Hsp-bearing EVs, specifically those released by HCC cell-resistant anticancer drugs (such as carboplatin and irinotecan hydrochloride)-treated tumor cells, employ decoy mechanisms to stimulate NK cell cytotoxic response and granzyme B production through enhanced expression of inhibitory receptor CD94 and downregulated expression of activating receptors CD69, NKG2D, and NKp44. Besides the EV-pulsed DCs, DC-derived EVs represent a new class of potent cell-free vaccines for HCC immunotherapy. Investigations into the immunomodulatory effects of EVs, isolated from AFP-expressing DCs, on HCC tumors with varying antigenic and pathological features have demonstrated their strong CD8 + T cell-dependent antitumor functions associated with tumor growth arrest, reshaping of the tumor immune microenvironment, and good survival rate [241]. In addition, EVs isolated from ADMSCs have been shown to promote NK cell-mediated tumor suppression in rats, resulting in low-grade tumor differentiation [242]. In light of these findings, the functionality and clinical implementation of EVs may be envisaged to broaden the therapeutic armamentarium of HCC.

Conclusion and future prospects

As we are approaching a "new era" of precision and personalized cancer medicine, a detailed understanding of the cell-biological processes involved in tumor onset, progression, and metastasis has become imperative. Nevertheless, research has made tangible progress in recent years and succeeded in adding new paradigms to the long-held traditional assumptions about the pathobiology of tumor progression and metastasis. With the discovery of EVs, our comprehension of the invasion-metastasis cascade has evolved into a detailed cellular and molecular circuitry endowed with EV-mediated functions.

Nevertheless, delineating the molecular underpinnings of EV-mediated tumor progression (i.e., assessing the complex interactions inherent to the fingerprint of EVs and the TME), especially in aggressive therapy-resistant cancers such as HCC, is critical to identifying candidate biomarkers and molecular targets amenable to anticancer targeting. Numerous studies have determined the prognostic value of HCC cell-derived EVs. Still, improvements in their sensitivity and validation as ex vivo biomarkers in predictive oncology is urgently needed. Moreover, standardization of EV isolation and characterization techniques, quality assessment, and careful clinical investigations are warranted to ensure effective therapeutic usage of EVs in clinics.

The physiological relevance of EV signaling in cancers is diverse and well-established in vitro, but their fate and signaling function in vivo is still debated. The majority of the mechanistic insights into the functional roles of tumor-derived EVs have been drawn either from in vitro studies using purified vesicles on cultured cells or under nonphysiological conditions in vivo. In comparison, the mechanisms governing tumor EV fate, dispersion, and uptake have been scarcely outlined in living organisms. Although many EV-tracking methods have been developed for live tracking of exogenous pathological EVs, they are inefficient at tracking tumor EVs shed from in vivo grown tumors. These shortcomings highlight the need to design appropriate in vivo experiments and develop suitable EV-imaging modalities for deciphering the real in vivo tumorigenic functions of EVs and applying the imaging-derived information for EV-based theranostics.

In the HCC setting, multiple molecular abnormalities and candidate therapeutic targets have been identified through integrative and comprehensive molecular and genetic screening. Furthermore, nearly every cargo species identified in HCC-derived EVs represents putative druggable targets that can be considered for novel molecularly guided therapeutic intervention modalities against HCC. Regardless, efficient translation of tumor-targeting to the clinic has still not been achieved. Undoubtedly, clinical translation can be accelerated by the development of suitable organotypic or experimental models that can fully recapitulate the HCC microenvironmental conditions and its natural history of clinical progression toward metastasis. Moreover, real-time analysis and targeted therapy against metastatic HCC tumors in preference to the primary tumors will provide an improved therapeutic window and help achieve effective management of patients with this dreadful disease.

Conflict of interest

The authors declare no conflict of interest.

Funding

The authors acknowledge support from a grant (MRC#16354/16) to SU from Medical Research Center, Hamad Medical Corporation, Doha, Qatar.

References

[1] American Cancer Society. Get Cancer Information Now; 2021. Available from: https://www.cancer.org/cancer/liver-cancer/about/what-is-key-statistics.html.

[2] Bray F, Ferlay J, Soerjomataram I, Siegel RL, Torre LA, Jemal A. Global cancer statistics 2018: GLOBOCAN estimates of incidence and mortality worldwide for 36 cancers in 185 countries. CA Cancer J Clin 2018;68 (6):394–424.

[3] The Global Cancer Observatory. The Global Cancer Observatory (GCO) is an interactive web-based platform presenting global cancer statistics to inform cancer control and research; 2021.

[4] Llovet JM, Kelley RK, Villanueva A, Singal AG, Pikarsky E, Roayaie S, et al. Hepatocellular carcinoma. Nat Rev Dis Prim 2021;7(1):6.

[5] Paget S. The distribution of secondary growths in cancer of the breast. 1889. Cancer Metastasis Rev 1989;8 (2):98–101.

[6] Labelle M, Hynes RO. The initial hours of metastasis: the importance of cooperative host-tumor cell interactions during hematogenous dissemination. Cancer Discov 2012;2(12):1091–9.

[7] van Niel G, D'Angelo G, Raposo G. Shedding light on the cell biology of extracellular vesicles. Nat Rev Mol Cell Biol 2018;19(4):213–28.

[8] Yanez-Mo M, Siljander PR, Andreu Z, Zavec AB, Borras FE, Buzas EI, et al. Biological properties of extracellular vesicles and their physiological functions. J Extracell Vesicles 2015;4:27066.

[9] van der Pol E, Boing AN, Harrison P, Sturk A, Nieuwland R. Classification, functions, and clinical relevance of extracellular vesicles. Pharmacol Rev 2012;64(3):676–705.

[10] Raposo G, Stoorvogel W. Extracellular vesicles: exosomes, microvesicles, and friends. J Cell Biol 2013;200 (4):373–83.

[11] Syn N, Wang L, Sethi G, Thiery JP, Goh BC. Exosome-mediated metastasis: from epithelial-mesenchymal transition to escape from immunosurveillance. Trends Pharmacol Sci 2016;37(7):606–17.

[12] Peinado H, Aleckovic M, Lavotshkin S, Matei I, Costa-Silva B, Moreno-Bueno G, et al. Melanoma exosomes educate bone marrow progenitor cells toward a pro-metastatic phenotype through MET. Nat Med 2012;18 (6):883–91.

[13] Guo Y, Ji X, Liu J, Fan D, Zhou Q, Chen C, et al. Effects of exosomes on pre-metastatic niche formation in tumors. Mol Cancer 2019;18(1):39.

[14] Feo F, De Miglio MR, Simile MM, Muroni MR, Calvisi DF, Frau M, et al. Hepatocellular carcinoma as a complex polygenic disease. Interpretive analysis of recent developments on genetic predisposition. Biochim Biophys Acta 2006;1765(2):126–47.

[15] Blonski W, Kotlyar DS, Forde KA. Non-viral causes of hepatocellular carcinoma. World J Gastroenterol 2010;16(29):3603–15.

[16] Ogunwobi OO, Harricharran T, Huaman J, Galuza A, Odumuwagun O, Tan Y, et al. Mechanisms of hepatocellular carcinoma progression. World J Gastroenterol 2019;25(19):2279–93.

[17] Murakami T, Tsurusaki M. Hypervascular benign and malignant liver tumors that require differentiation from hepatocellular carcinoma: key points of imaging diagnosis. Liver Cancer 2014;3(2):85–96.

[18] Muto J, Shirabe K, Sugimachi K, Maehara Y. Review of angiogenesis in hepatocellular carcinoma. Hepatol Res 2015;45(1):1–9.

[19] Yang ZF, Poon RT. Vascular changes in hepatocellular carcinoma. Anat Rec (Hoboken) 2008;291(6):721–34.

[20] Joo YY, Jang JW, Lee SW, Yoo SH, Kwon JH, Nam SW, et al. Circulating pro- and anti-angiogenic factors in multi-stage liver disease and hepatocellular carcinoma progression. Sci Rep 2019;9(1):9137.

[21] Graveel CR, Calderone HM, Westerhuis JJ, Winn ME, Sempere LF. Critical analysis of the potential for microRNA biomarkers in breast cancer management. Breast Cancer (Dove Med Press) 2015;7:59–79.

[22] Valadi H, Ekstrom K, Bossios A, Sjostrand M, Lee JJ, Lotvall JO. Exosome-mediated transfer of mRNAs and microRNAs is a novel mechanism of genetic exchange between cells. Nat Cell Biol 2007;9(6):654–9.

[23] Taylor DD, Gercel-Taylor C. MicroRNA signatures of tumor-derived exosomes as diagnostic biomarkers of ovarian cancer. Gynecol Oncol 2008;110(1):13–21.

[24] Kogure T, Lin WL, Yan IK, Braconi C, Patel T. Intercellular nanovesicle-mediated microRNA transfer: a mechanism of environmental modulation of hepatocellular cancer cell growth. Hepatology 2011;54(4):1237–48.

[25] Lin XJ, Fang JH, Yang XJ, Zhang C, Yuan Y, Zheng L, et al. Hepatocellular carcinoma cell-secreted exosomal microRNA-210 promotes angiogenesis in vitro and in vivo. Mol Ther Nucleic Acids 2018;11:243–52.

[26] Huang XY, Huang ZL, Huang J, Xu B, Huang XY, Xu YH, et al. Exosomal circRNA-100338 promotes hepatocellular carcinoma metastasis via enhancing invasiveness and angiogenesis. J Exp Clin Cancer Res 2020;39(1):20.

[27] Lee JW, Bae SH, Jeong JW, Kim SH, Kim KW. Hypoxia-inducible factor (HIF-1)alpha: its protein stability and biological functions. Exp Mol Med 2004;36(1):1−12.

[28] Jafari R, Rahbarghazi R, Ahmadi M, Hassanpour M, Rezaie J. Hypoxic exosomes orchestrate tumorigenesis: molecular mechanisms and therapeutic implications. J Transl Med 2020;18(1):474.

[29] Mao Y, Wang Y, Dong L, Zhang Y, Zhang Y, Wang C, et al. Hypoxic exosomes facilitate angiogenesis and metastasis in esophageal squamous cell carcinoma through altering the phenotype and transcriptome of endothelial cells. J Exp Clin Cancer Res 2019;38(1):389.

[30] Matsuura Y, Wada H, Eguchi H, Gotoh K, Kobayashi S, Kinoshita M, et al. Exosomal miR-155 derived from hepatocellular carcinoma cells under hypoxia promotes angiogenesis in endothelial cells. Dig Dis Sci 2019;64 (3):792−802.

[31] Zhang L, Wang W, Li X, He S, Yao J, Wang X, et al. MicroRNA-155 promotes tumor growth of human hepatocellular carcinoma by targeting ARID2. Int J Oncol 2016;48(6):2425−34.

[32] Yukawa H, Suzuki K, Aoki K, Arimoto T, Yasui T, Kaji N, et al. Imaging of angiogenesis of human umbilical vein endothelial cells by uptake of exosomes secreted from hepatocellular carcinoma cells. Sci Rep 2018;8 (1):6765.

[33] Li R, Wang Y, Zhang X, Feng M, Ma J, Li J, et al. Exosome-mediated secretion of LOXL4 promotes hepatocellular carcinoma cell invasion and metastasis. Mol Cancer 2019;18(1):18.

[34] Busnadiego O, Gonzalez-Santamaria J, Lagares D, Guinea-Viniegra J, Pichol-Thievend C, Muller L, et al. LOXL4 is induced by transforming growth factor beta1 through Smad and JunB/Fra2 and contributes to vascular matrix remodeling. Mol Cell Biol 2013;33(12):2388−401.

[35] Wang S, Xu M, Li X, Su X, Xiao X, Keating A, et al. Exosomes released by hepatocarcinoma cells endow adipocytes with tumor-promoting properties. J Hematol Oncol 2018;11(1):82.

[36] Gardiner C, Harrison P, Belting M, Boing A, Campello E, Carter BS, et al. Extracellular vesicles, tissue factor, cancer and thrombosis - discussion themes of the ISEV 2014 Educational Day. J Extracell Vesicles 2015;4: 26901.

[37] Wang W, Yuan X, Xu A, Zhu X, Zhan Y, Wang S, et al. Human cancer cells suppress behaviors of endothelial progenitor cells through miR-21 targeting IL6R. Microvasc Res 2018;120:21−8.

[38] Zhou Y, Ren H, Dai B, Li J, Shang L, Huang J, et al. Hepatocellular carcinoma-derived exosomal miRNA-21 contributes to tumor progression by converting hepatocyte stellate cells to cancer-associated fibroblasts. J Exp Clin Cancer Res 2018;37(1):324.

[39] Jamshidi-Parsian A, Griffin RJ, Kore RA, Todorova VK, Makhoul I. Tumor-endothelial cell interaction in an experimental model of human hepatocellular carcinoma. Exp Cell Res 2018;372(1):16−24.

[40] Ziyad S, Iruela-Arispe ML. Molecular mechanisms of tumor angiogenesis. Genes Cancer 2011;2(12):1085−96.

[41] Quillien A, Moore JC, Shin M, Siekmann AF, Smith T, Pan L, et al. Distinct Notch signaling outputs pattern the developing arterial system. Development 2014;141(7):1544−52.

[42] Salvucci O, Tosato G. Essential roles of EphB receptors and EphrinB ligands in endothelial cell function and angiogenesis. Adv Cancer Res 2012;114:21−57.

[43] Saharinen P, Eklund L, Alitalo K. Therapeutic targeting of the angiopoietin-TIE pathway. Nat Rev Drug Discov 2017;16(9):635−61.

[44] Xie JY, Wei JX, Lv LH, Han QF, Yang WB, Li GL, et al. Angiopoietin-2 induces angiogenesis via exosomes in human hepatocellular carcinoma. Cell Commun Signal 2020;18(1):46.

[45] Huang A, Dong J, Li S, Wang C, Ding H, Li H, et al. Exosomal transfer of vasorin expressed in hepatocellular carcinoma cells promotes migration of human umbilical vein endothelial cells. Int J Biol Sci 2015;11(8):961−9.

[46] Robichaud N, Sonenberg N. Translational control and the cancer cell response to stress. Curr Opin Cell Biol 2017;45:102−9.

[47] des Georges A, Dhote V, Kuhn L, Hellen CU, Pestova TV, Frank J, et al. Structure of mammalian eIF3 in the context of the 43S preinitiation complex. Nature 2015;525(7570):491−5.

[48] Valasek LS. 'Ribozoomin'−translation initiation from the perspective of the ribosome-bound eukaryotic initiation factors (eIFs). Curr Protein Pept Sci 2012;13(4):305−30.

[49] Jackson RJ, Hellen CU, Pestova TV. The mechanism of eukaryotic translation initiation and principles of its regulation. Nat Rev Mol Cell Biol 2010;11(2):113−27.

[50] Zhou M, Sandercock AM, Fraser CS, Ridlova G, Stephens E, Schenauer MR, et al. Mass spectrometry reveals modularity and a complete subunit interaction map of the eukaryotic translation factor eIF3. Proc Natl Acad Sci U S A 2008;105(47):18139—44.

[51] Pestova TV, Kolupaeva VG, Lomakin IB, Pilipenko EV, Shatsky IN, Agol VI, et al. Molecular mechanisms of translation initiation in eukaryotes. Proc Natl Acad Sci U S A 2001;98(13):7029—36.

[52] Dong Z, Zhang JT. Initiation factor eIF3 and regulation of mRNA translation, cell growth, and cancer. Crit Rev Oncol Hematol 2006;59(3):169—80.

[53] Lee HY, Chen CK, Ho CM, Lee SS, Chang CY, Chen KJ, et al. EIF3C-enhanced exosome secretion promotes angiogenesis and tumorigenesis of human hepatocellular carcinoma. Oncotarget 2018;9(17):13193—205.

[54] Dai W, Wang Y, Yang T, Wang J, Wu W, Gu J. Downregulation of exosomal CLEC3B in hepatocellular carcinoma promotes metastasis and angiogenesis via AMPK and VEGF signals. Cell Commun Signal 2019;17(1):113.

[55] Moh-Moh-Aung A, Fujisawa M, Ito S, Katayama H, Ohara T, Ota Y, et al. Decreased miR-200b-3p in cancer cells leads to angiogenesis in HCC by enhancing endothelial ERG expression. Sci Rep 2020;10(1):10418.

[56] Tummala KS, Brandt M, Teijeiro A, Grana O, Schwabe RF, Perna C, et al. Hepatocellular carcinomas originate predominantly from hepatocytes and benign lesions from hepatic progenitor cells. Cell Rep 2017; 19(3):584—600.

[57] Mu X, Espanol-Suner R, Mederacke I, Affo S, Manco R, Sempoux C, et al. Hepatocellular carcinoma originates from hepatocytes and not from the progenitor/biliary compartment. J Clin Invest 2015;125 (10):3891—903.

[58] He M, Qin H, Poon TC, Sze SC, Ding X, Co NN, et al. Hepatocellular carcinoma-derived exosomes promote motility of immortalized hepatocyte through transfer of oncogenic proteins and RNAs. Carcinogenesis 2015;36(9):1008—18.

[59] Chen W, Yang J, Fang H, Li L, Sun J. Relevance function of Linc-ROR in the pathogenesis of cancer. Front Cell Dev Biol 2020;8:696.

[60] He X, Yu J, Xiong L, Liu Y, Fan L, Li Y, et al. Exosomes derived from liver cancer cells reprogram biological behaviors of LO2 cells by transferring Linc-ROR. Gene 2019;719:144044.

[61] Li L, Tang J, Zhang B, Yang W, LiuGao M, Wang R, et al. Epigenetic modification of MiR-429 promotes liver tumour-initiating cell properties by targeting Rb binding protein 4. Gut 2015;64(1):156—67.

[62] Fujiki T, Miura T, Maura M, Shiraishi H, Nishimura S, Imada Y, et al. TAK1 represses transcription of the human telomerase reverse transcriptase gene. Oncogene 2007;26(36):5258—66.

[63] Su Y, Lv X, Yin W, Zhou L, Hu Y, Zhou A, et al. CircRNA Cdr1as functions as a competitive endogenous RNA to promote hepatocellular carcinoma progression. Aging (Albany NY) 2019;11(19):8183—203.

[64] Liu D, Kang H, Gao M, Jin L, Zhang F, Chen D, et al. Exosome-transmitted circ_MMP2 promotes hepatocellular carcinoma metastasis by upregulating MMP2. Mol Oncol 2020;14(6):1365—80.

[65] Dirat BA, Bochet L, Escourrou G, Valet P, Muller C. Unraveling the obesity and breast cancer links: a role for cancer-associated adipocytes? Endocr Dev 2010;19:45—52.

[66] Zheng M, Tian Z. Liver-mediated adaptive immune tolerance. Front Immunol 2019;10:2525.

[67] Simpson E. A historical perspective on immunological privilege. Immunol Rev 2006;213:12—22.

[68] Han Q, Zhao H, Jiang Y, Yin C, Zhang J. HCC-derived exosomes: critical player and target for cancer immune escape. Cells 2019;8(6).

[69] Greening DW, Gopal SK, Xu R, Simpson RJ, Chen W. Exosomes and their roles in immune regulation and cancer. Semin Cell Dev Biol 2015;40:72—81.

[70] Capece D, Fischietti M, Verzella D, Gaggiano A, Cicciarelli G, Tessitore A, et al. The inflammatory microenvironment in hepatocellular carcinoma: a pivotal role for tumor-associated macrophages. Biomed Res Int 2013;2013:187204.

[71] Li X, Lei Y, Wu M, Li N. Regulation of macrophage activation and polarization by HCC-derived exosomal lncRNA TUC339. Int J Mol Sci 2018;19(10).

[72] Mahadevan NR, Rodvold J, Sepulveda H, Rossi S, Drew AF, Zanetti M. Transmission of endoplasmic reticulum stress and pro-inflammation from tumor cells to myeloid cells. Proc Natl Acad Sci U S A 2011;108 (16):6561—6.

[73] Liu J, Fan L, Yu H, Zhang J, He Y, Feng D, et al. Endoplasmic reticulum stress causes liver cancer cells to release exosomal miR-23a-3p and up-regulate programmed death ligand 1 expression in macrophages. Hepatology 2019;70(1):241—58.

[74] Yin C, Han Q, Xu D, Zheng B, Zhao X, Zhang J. SALL4-mediated upregulation of exosomal miR-146a-5p drives T-cell exhaustion by M2 tumor-associated macrophages in HCC. Oncoimmunology 2019;8(7):1601479.

[75] Palaga T, Wongchana W, Kueanjinda P. Notch signaling in macrophages in the context of cancer immunity. Front Immunol 2018;9:652.

[76] Mantovani A, Bottazzi B, Colotta F, Sozzani S, Ruco L. The origin and function of tumor-associated macrophages. Immunol Today 1992;13(7):265−70.

[77] Fahy RJ, Doseff AI, Wewers MD. Spontaneous human monocyte apoptosis utilizes a caspase-3-dependent pathway that is blocked by endotoxin and is independent of caspase-1. J Immunol 1999;163(4):1755−62.

[78] Musson RA, Shafran H, Henson PM. Intracellular levels and stimulated release of lysosomal enzymes from human peripheral blood monocytes and monocyte-derived macrophages. J Reticuloendothel Soc 1980;28(3):249−64.

[79] Song X, Ding Y, Liu G, Yang X, Zhao R, Zhang Y, et al. Cancer cell-derived exosomes induce mitogen-activated protein kinase-dependent monocyte survival by transport of functional receptor tyrosine kinases. J Biol Chem 2016;291(16):8453−64.

[80] Wang Y, Wang B, Xiao S, Li Y, Chen Q. miR-125a/b inhibits tumor-associated macrophages mediated in cancer stem cells of hepatocellular carcinoma by targeting CD90. J Cell Biochem 2019;120(3):3046−55.

[81] Gladysh VV, Turbina NS. [Clinical aspects and diagnosis of refractory anemia with excess of blasts]. Klin Med (Mosk) 1990;68(11):84−7.

[82] Xiao W, Dong W, Zhang C, Saren G, Geng P, Zhao H, et al. Effects of the epigenetic drug MS-275 on the release and function of exosome-related immune molecules in hepatocellular carcinoma cells. Eur J Med Res 2013;18:61.

[83] Guerra N, Lanier LL. Editorial: emerging concepts on the NKG2D receptor-ligand axis in health and diseases. Front Immunol 2020;11:562.

[84] Zhang PF, Gao C, Huang XY, Lu JC, Guo XJ, Shi GM, et al. Cancer cell-derived exosomal circUHRF1 induces natural killer cell exhaustion and may cause resistance to anti-PD1 therapy in hepatocellular carcinoma. Mol Cancer 2020;19(1):110.

[85] Liu F, Liu Y, Chen Z. Tim-3 expression and its role in hepatocellular carcinoma. J Hematol Oncol 2018;11 (1):126.

[86] Ganjalikhani Hakemi M, Jafarinia M, Azizi M, Rezaeepoor M, Isayev O, Bazhin AV. The role of TIM-3 in hepatocellular carcinoma: a promising target for immunotherapy? Front Oncol 2020;10:601661.

[87] Nakano T, Chen IH, Wang CC, Chen PJ, Tseng HP, Huang KT, et al. Circulating exosomal miR-92b: Its role for cancer immunoediting and clinical value for prediction of posttransplant hepatocellular carcinoma recurrence. Am J Transpl 2019;19(12):3250−62.

[88] Yang Y, Han Q, Hou Z, Zhang C, Tian Z, Zhang J. Exosomes mediate hepatitis B virus (HBV) transmission and NK-cell dysfunction. Cell Mol Immunol 2017;14(5):465−75.

[89] Guan X, Lu Y, Zhu H, Yu S, Zhao W, Chi X, et al. The crosstalk between cancer cells and neutrophils enhances hepatocellular carcinoma metastasis via neutrophil extracellular traps-associated cathepsin G component: a potential therapeutic target. J Hepatocell Carcinoma 2021;8:451−65.

[90] Singel KL, Segal BH. Neutrophils in the tumor microenvironment: trying to heal the wound that cannot heal. Immunol Rev 2016;273(1):329−43.

[91] Mukaida N, Sasaki SI, Baba T. Two-faced roles of tumor-associated neutrophils in cancer development and progression. Int J Mol Sci 2020;21(10).

[92] Zhou SL, Zhou ZJ, Hu ZQ, Huang XW, Wang Z, Chen EB, et al. Tumor-associated neutrophils recruit macrophages and T-regulatory cells to promote progression of hepatocellular carcinoma and resistance to sorafenib. Gastroenterology 2016;150(7):1646−58 e17.

[93] Galdiero MR, Garlanda C, Jaillon S, Marone G, Mantovani A. Tumor associated macrophages and neutrophils in tumor progression. J Cell Physiol 2013;228(7):1404−12.

[94] Tecchio C, Scapini P, Pizzolo G, Cassatella MA. On the cytokines produced by human neutrophils in tumors. Semin Cancer Biol 2013;23(3):159−70.

[95] Zhou SL, Yin D, Hu ZQ, Luo CB, Zhou ZJ, Xin HY, et al. A positive feedback loop between cancer stem-like cells and tumor-associated neutrophils controls hepatocellular carcinoma progression. Hepatology 2019;70 (4):1214−30.

[96] Sippel TR, Shimizu T, Strnad F, Traystman RJ, Herson PS, Waziri A. Arginase I release from activated neutrophils induces peripheral immunosuppression in a murine model of stroke. J Cereb Blood Flow Metab 2015;35(10):1657−63.

[97] He G, Zhang H, Zhou J, Wang B, Chen Y, Kong Y, et al. Peritumoural neutrophils negatively regulate adaptive immunity via the PD-L1/PD-1 signalling pathway in hepatocellular carcinoma. J Exp Clin Cancer Res 2015;34:141.

[98] Zhang X, Shi H, Yuan X, Jiang P, Qian H, Xu W. Tumor-derived exosomes induce N2 polarization of neutrophils to promote gastric cancer cell migration. Mol Cancer 2018;17(1):146.

[99] Li XF, Chen DP, Ouyang FZ, Chen MM, Wu Y, Kuang DM, et al. Increased autophagy sustains the survival and pro-tumourigenic effects of neutrophils in human hepatocellular carcinoma. J Hepatol 2015;62 (1):131−9.

[100] Qu Z, Feng J, Pan H, Jiang Y, Duan Y, Fa Z. Exosomes derived from HCC cells with different invasion characteristics mediated EMT through TGF-beta/Smad signaling pathway. Onco Targets Ther 2019;12:6897−905.

[101] Haider C, Hnat J, Wagner R, Huber H, Timelthaler G, Grubinger M, et al. Transforming growth factor-beta and Axl induce CXCL5 and neutrophil recruitment in hepatocellular carcinoma. Hepatology 2019;69(1):222−36.

[102] Hoffman W, Lakkis FG, Chalasani G. B cells, antibodies, and more. Clin J Am Soc Nephrol 2016;11 (1):137−54.

[103] Guo FF, Cui JW. The role of tumor-infiltrating B cells in tumor immunity. J Oncol 2019;2019:2592419.

[104] Garnelo M, Tan A, Her Z, Yeong J, Lim CJ, Chen J, et al. Interaction between tumour-infiltrating B cells and T cells controls the progression of hepatocellular carcinoma. Gut 2017;66(2):342−51.

[105] Shao Y, Lo CM, Ling CC, Liu XB, Ng KT, Chu AC, et al. Regulatory B cells accelerate hepatocellular carcinoma progression via CD40/CD154 signaling pathway. Cancer Lett 2014;355(2):264−72.

[106] Ye L, Zhang Q, Cheng Y, Chen X, Wang G, Shi M, et al. Tumor-derived exosomal HMGB1 fosters hepatocellular carcinoma immune evasion by promoting TIM-1(+) regulatory B cell expansion. J Immunother Cancer 2018;6(1):145.

[107] Sims GP, Rowe DC, Rietdijk ST, Herbst R, Coyle AJ. HMGB1 and RAGE in inflammation and cancer. Annu Rev Immunol 2010;28:367−88.

[108] Yan W, Chang Y, Liang X, Cardinal JS, Huang H, Thorne SH, et al. High-mobility group box 1 activates caspase-1 and promotes hepatocellular carcinoma invasiveness and metastases. Hepatology 2012;55(6): 1863−75.

[109] Xing Y, Hogquist KA. T-cell tolerance: central and peripheral. Cold Spring Harb Perspect Biol 2012;4(6).

[110] Wherry EJ, Kurachi M. Molecular and cellular insights into T cell exhaustion. Nat Rev Immunol 2015;15 (8):486−99.

[111] Wherry EJ, Blattman JN, Murali-Krishna K, van der Most R, Ahmed R. Viral persistence alters CD8 T-cell immunodominance and tissue distribution and results in distinct stages of functional impairment. J Virol 2003;77(8):4911−27.

[112] Wang X, Shen H, Zhangyuan G, Huang R, Zhang W, He Q, et al. 14-3-3zeta delivered by hepatocellular carcinoma-derived exosomes impaired anti-tumor function of tumor-infiltrating T lymphocytes. Cell Death Dis 2018;9(2):159.

[113] Choi JE, Hur W, Jung CK, Piao LS, Lyoo K, Hong SW, et al. Silencing of 14-3-3zeta over-expression in hepatocellular carcinoma inhibits tumor growth and enhances chemosensitivity to cis-diammined dichloridoplatium. Cancer Lett 2011;303(2):99−107.

[114] Reichl P, Dengler M, van Zijl F, Huber H, Fuhrlinger G, Reichel C, et al. Axl activates autocrine transforming growth factor-beta signaling in hepatocellular carcinoma. Hepatology 2015;61(3):930−41.

[115] Huang XY, Ke AW, Shi GM, Zhang X, Zhang C, Shi YH, et al. αB-crystallin complexes with 14-3-3zeta to induce epithelial-mesenchymal transition and resistance to sorafenib in hepatocellular carcinoma. Hepatology 2013;57(6):2235−47.

[116] Huang AC, Postow MA, Orlowski RJ, Mick R, Bengsch B, Manne S, et al. T-cell invigoration to tumour burden ratio associated with anti-PD-1 response. Nature 2017;545(7652):60−5.

[117] Salama P, Phillips M, Grieu F, Morris M, Zeps N, Joseph D, et al. Tumor-infiltrating FOXP3+ T regulatory cells show strong prognostic significance in colorectal cancer. J Clin Oncol 2009;27(2):186−92.

[118] Curiel TJ, Coukos G, Zou L, Alvarez X, Cheng P, Mottram P, et al. Specific recruitment of regulatory T cells in ovarian carcinoma fosters immune privilege and predicts reduced survival. Nat Med 2004;10(9):942−9.

[119] Wieckowski EU, Visus C, Szajnik M, Szczepanski MJ, Storkus WJ, Whiteside TL. Tumor-derived microvesicles promote regulatory T cell expansion and induce apoptosis in tumor-reactive activated CD8+ T lymphocytes. J Immunol 2009;183(6):3720−30.

[120] Tenen DG, Chai L, Tan JL. Metabolic alterations and vulnerabilities in hepatocellular carcinoma. Gastroenterol Rep (Oxf) 2021;9(1):1–13.

[121] Rui L. Energy metabolism in the liver. Compr Physiol 2014;4(1):177–97.

[122] Moore MC, Coate KC, Winnick JJ, An Z, Cherrington AD. Regulation of hepatic glucose uptake and storage in vivo. Adv Nutr 2012;3(3):286–94.

[123] Petersen MC, Vatner DF, Shulman GI. Regulation of hepatic glucose metabolism in health and disease. Nat Rev Endocrinol 2017;13(10):572–87.

[124] Link H, Kochanowski K, Sauer U. Systematic identification of allosteric protein-metabolite interactions that control enzyme activity in vivo. Nat Biotechnol 2013;31(4):357–61.

[125] Nwosu ZC, Megger DA, Hammad S, Sitek B, Roessler S, Ebert MP, et al. Identification of the consistently altered metabolic targets in human hepatocellular carcinoma. Cell Mol Gastroenterol Hepatol 2017;4(2):303–23 e1.

[126] Hay N. Reprogramming glucose metabolism in cancer: can it be exploited for cancer therapy? Nat Rev Cancer 2016;16(10):635–49.

[127] Lucchetti D, Ricciardi Tenore C, Colella F, Sgambato A. Extracellular vesicles and cancer: a focus on metabolism, cytokines, and immunity. Cancers (Basel) 2020;12(1).

[128] Zhang J, Lu S, Zhou Y, Meng K, Chen Z, Cui Y, et al. Motile hepatocellular carcinoma cells preferentially secret sugar metabolism regulatory proteins via exosomes. Proteomics 2017;17:13–14.

[129] Li Y, Zang H, Zhang X, Huang G. Exosomal Circ-ZNF652 promotes cell proliferation, migration, invasion and glycolysis in hepatocellular carcinoma via miR-29a-3p/GUCD1 axis. Cancer Manag Res 2020;12: 7739–51.

[130] Xiao Z, Wang Y, Ding H. XPD suppresses cell proliferation and migration via miR-29a-3p-Mdm2/PDGF-B axis in HCC. Cell Biosci 2019;9:6.

[131] Bellet MM, Piobbico D, Bartoli D, Castelli M, Pieroni S, Brunacci C, et al. NEDD4 controls the expression of GUCD1, a protein upregulated in proliferating liver cells. Cell Cycle 2014;13(12):1902–11.

[132] Lai Z, Wei T, Li Q, Wang X, Zhang Y, Zhang S. Exosomal circFBLIM1 promotes hepatocellular carcinoma progression and glycolysis by regulating the miR-338/LRP6 axis. Cancer Biother Radiopharm 2020.

[133] Eales KL, Hollinshead KE, Tennant DA. Hypoxia and metabolic adaptation of cancer cells. Oncogenesis 2016;5:e190.

[134] Takahashi K, Yan IK, Haga H, Patel T. Modulation of hypoxia-signaling pathways by extracellular linc-RoR. J Cell Sci 2014;127(Pt 7):1585–94.

[135] Papandreou I, Cairns RA, Fontana L, Lim AL, Denko NC. HIF-1 mediates adaptation to hypoxia by actively downregulating mitochondrial oxygen consumption. Cell Metab 2006;3(3):187–97.

[136] Kim JW, Tchernyshyov I, Semenza GL, Dang CV. HIF-1-mediated expression of pyruvate dehydrogenase kinase: a metabolic switch required for cellular adaptation to hypoxia. Cell Metab 2006;3(3):177–85.

[137] Dupuy F, Tabaries S, Andrzejewski S, Dong Z, Blagih J, Annis MG, et al. PDK1-dependent metabolic reprogramming dictates metastatic potential in breast cancer. Cell Metab 2015;22(4):577–89.

[138] Wan L, Xia T, Du Y, Liu J, Xie Y, Zhang Y, et al. Exosomes from activated hepatic stellate cells contain GLUT1 and PKM2: a role for exosomes in metabolic switch of liver nonparenchymal cells. FASEB J 2019;33 (7):8530–42.

[139] Liu Y, Gu Y, Han Y, Zhang Q, Jiang Z, Zhang X, et al. Tumor exosomal RNAs promote lung pre-metastatic niche formation by activating alveolar epithelial TLR3 to recruit neutrophils. Cancer Cell 2016;30(2):243–56.

[140] Cooks T, Pateras IS, Jenkins LM, Patel KM, Robles AI, Morris J, et al. Mutant p53 cancers reprogram macrophages to tumor supporting macrophages via exosomal miR-1246. Nat Commun 2018;9(1):771.

[141] Haderk F, Schulz R, Iskar M, Cid LL, Worst T, Willmund KV, et al. Tumor-derived exosomes modulate PD-L1 expression in monocytes. Sci Immunol 2017;2(13).

[142] Gao L, Wang L, Dai T, Jin K, Zhang Z, Wang S, et al. Tumor-derived exosomes antagonize innate antiviral immunity. Nat Immunol 2018;19(3):233–45.

[143] Lawson J, Dickman C, Towle R, Jabalee J, Javer A, Garnis C. Extracellular vesicle secretion of miR-142-3p from lung adenocarcinoma cells induces tumor promoting changes in the stroma through cell-cell communication. Mol Carcinog 2019;58(3):376–87.

[144] Wang J, Guan X, Zhang Y, Ge S, Zhang L, Li H, et al. Exosomal miR-27a derived from gastric cancer cells regulates the transformation of fibroblasts into cancer-associated fibroblasts. Cell Physiol Biochem 2018;49 (3):869–83.

[145] Gu J, Qian H, Shen L, Zhang X, Zhu W, Huang L, et al. Gastric cancer exosomes trigger differentiation of umbilical cord derived mesenchymal stem cells to carcinoma-associated fibroblasts through TGF-beta/Smad pathway. PLoS One 2012;7(12):e52465.

[146] Sagar G, Sah RP, Javeed N, Dutta SK, Smyrk TC, Lau JS, et al. Pathogenesis of pancreatic cancer exosome-induced lipolysis in adipose tissue. Gut 2016;65(7):1165—74.

[147] Wang S, Li X, Xu M, Wang J, Zhao RC. Reduced adipogenesis after lung tumor exosomes priming in human mesenchymal stem cells via TGFbeta signaling pathway. Mol Cell Biochem 2017;435(1—2):59—66.

[148] Yang M, Chen J, Su F, Yu B, Su F, Lin L, et al. Microvesicles secreted by macrophages shuttle invasion-potentiating microRNAs into breast cancer cells. Mol Cancer 2011;10:117.

[149] Zheng P, Chen L, Yuan X, Luo Q, Liu Y, Xie G, et al. Exosomal transfer of tumor-associated macrophage-derived miR-21 confers cisplatin resistance in gastric cancer cells. J Exp Clin Cancer Res 2017;36(1):53.

[150] Li W, Zhang X, Wang J, Li M, Cao C, Tan J, et al. TGFbeta1 in fibroblasts-derived exosomes promotes epithelial-mesenchymal transition of ovarian cancer cells. Oncotarget 2017;8(56):96035—47.

[151] Li YY, Tao YW, Gao S, Li P, Zheng JM, Zhang SE, et al. Cancer-associated fibroblasts contribute to oral cancer cells proliferation and metastasis via exosome-mediated paracrine miR-34a-5p. EBioMedicine 2018; 36:209—20.

[152] Wang J, Wu Y, Guo J, Fei X, Yu L, Ma S. Adipocyte-derived exosomes promote lung cancer metastasis by increasing MMP9 activity via transferring MMP3 to lung cancer cells. Oncotarget 2017;8(47):81880—91.

[153] Vallabhaneni KC, Penfornis P, Dhule S, Guillonneau F, Adams KV, Mo YY, et al. Extracellular vesicles from bone marrow mesenchymal stem/stromal cells transport tumor regulatory microRNA, proteins, and metabolites. Oncotarget 2015;6(7):4953—67.

[154] Pakravan K, Babashah S, Sadeghizadeh M, Mowla SJ, Mossahebi-Mohammadi M, Ataei F, et al. MicroRNA-100 shuttled by mesenchymal stem cell-derived exosomes suppresses in vitro angiogenesis through modulating the mTOR/HIF-1alpha/VEGF signaling axis in breast cancer cells. Cell Oncol (Dordr) 2017;40 (5):457—70.

[155] Vallabhaneni KC, Penfornis P, Xing F, Hassler Y, Adams KV, Mo YY, et al. Stromal cell extracellular vesicular cargo mediated regulation of breast cancer cell metastasis via ubiquitin conjugating enzyme E2 N pathway. Oncotarget 2017;8(66):109861—76.

[156] Bliss SA, Sinha G, Sandiford OA, Williams LM, Engelberth DJ, Guiro K, et al. Mesenchymal stem cell-derived exosomes stimulate cycling quiescence and early breast cancer dormancy in bone marrow. Cancer Res 2016;76(19):5832—44.

[157] Qi J, Zhou Y, Jiao Z, Wang X, Zhao Y, Li Y, et al. Exosomes derived from human bone marrow mesenchymal stem cells promote tumor growth through hedgehog signaling pathway. Cell Physiol Biochem 2017;42 (6):2242—54.

[158] Zhu W, Huang L, Li Y, Zhang X, Gu J, Yan Y, et al. Exosomes derived from human bone marrow mesenchymal stem cells promote tumor growth in vivo. Cancer Lett 2012;315(1):28—37.

[159] Roccaro AM, Sacco A, Maiso P, Azab AK, Tai YT, Reagan M, et al. BM mesenchymal stromal cell-derived exosomes facilitate multiple myeloma progression. J Clin Invest 2013;123(4):1542—55.

[160] Wang M, Zhao C, Shi H, Zhang B, Zhang L, Zhang X, et al. Deregulated microRNAs in gastric cancer tissue-derived mesenchymal stem cells: novel biomarkers and a mechanism for gastric cancer. Br J Cancer 2014;110(5):1199—210.

[161] Chen W, Quan Y, Fan S, Wang H, Liang J, Huang L, et al. Exosome-transmitted circular RNA hsa_circ_0051443 suppresses hepatocellular carcinoma progression. Cancer Lett 2020;475:119—28.

[162] Wang YD, Cai N, Wu XL, Cao HZ, Xie LL, Zheng PS. OCT4 promotes tumorigenesis and inhibits apoptosis of cervical cancer cells by miR-125b/BAK1 pathway. Cell Death Dis 2013;4:e760.

[163] Gu XY, Wang J, Luo YZ, Du Q, Li RR, Shi H, et al. Down-regulation of miR-150 induces cell proliferation inhibition and apoptosis in non-small-cell lung cancer by targeting BAK1 in vitro. Tumour Biol 2014;35 (6):5287—93.

[164] Marcotte EL, Pankratz N, Amatruda JF, Frazier AL, Krailo M, Davies S, et al. Variants in BAK1, SPRY4, and GAB2 are associated with pediatric germ cell tumors: A report from the children's oncology group. Genes Chromosomes Cancer 2017;56(7):548—58.

[165] Slager SL, Skibola CF, Di Bernardo MC, Conde L, Broderick P, McDonnell SK, et al. Common variation at 6p21.31 (BAK1) influences the risk of chronic lymphocytic leukemia. Blood 2012;120(4):843—6.

[166] Wang J, Pu J, Zhang Y, Yao T, Luo Z, Li W, et al. Exosome-transmitted long non-coding RNA SENP3-EIF4A1 suppresses the progression of hepatocellular carcinoma. Aging (Albany NY) 2020;12(12):11550—67.

[167] Krohler T, Kessler SM, Hosseini K, List M, Barghash A, Patial S, et al. The mRNA-binding protein TTP/ZFP36 in hepatocarcinogenesis and hepatocellular carcinoma. Cancers (Basel) 2019;11(11).

[168] Rios-Colon L, Arthur E, Niture S, Qi Q, Moore JT, Kumar D. The role of exosomes in the crosstalk between adipocytes and liver cancer cells. Cells 2020;9(9).

[169] Baglieri J, Brenner DA, Kisseleva T. The role of fibrosis and liver-associated fibroblasts in the pathogenesis of hepatocellular carcinoma. Int J Mol Sci 2019;20(7).

[170] Duong MN, Geneste A, Fallone F, Li X, Dumontet C, Muller C. The fat and the bad: mature adipocytes, key actors in tumor progression and resistance. Oncotarget 2017;8(34):57622−41.

[171] Liu Y, Tan J, Ou S, Chen J, Chen L. Adipose-derived exosomes deliver miR-23a/b to regulate tumor growth in hepatocellular cancer by targeting the VHL/HIF axis. J Physiol Biochem 2019;75(3):391−401.

[172] Zhang H, Deng T, Ge S, Liu Y, Bai M, Zhu K, et al. Exosome circRNA secreted from adipocytes promotes the growth of hepatocellular carcinoma by targeting deubiquitination-related USP7. Oncogene 2019;38 (15):2844−59.

[173] Zhao H, Yang L, Baddour J, Achreja A, Bernard V, Moss T, et al. Tumor microenvironment derived exosomes pleiotropically modulate cancer cell metabolism. Elife 2016;5:e10250.

[174] Lv B, Zhu W, Feng C. Coptisine blocks secretion of exosomal circCCT3 from cancer-associated fibroblasts to reprogram glucose metabolism in hepatocellular carcinoma. DNA Cell Biol 2020.

[175] Gong L, Cui Z, Chen P, Han H, Peng J, Leng X. Reduced survival of patients with hepatocellular carcinoma expressing hexokinase II. Med Oncol 2012;29(2):909−14.

[176] DeWaal D, Nogueira V, Terry AR, Patra KC, Jeon SM, Guzman G, et al. Hexokinase-2 depletion inhibits glycolysis and induces oxidative phosphorylation in hepatocellular carcinoma and sensitizes to metformin. Nat Commun 2018;9(1):446.

[177] Zhang Z, Li X, Sun W, Yue S, Yang J, Li J, et al. Loss of exosomal miR-320a from cancer-associated fibroblasts contributes to HCC proliferation and metastasis. Cancer Lett 2017;397:33−42.

[178] Yugawa K, Yoshizumi T, Mano Y, Itoh S, Harada N, Ikegami T, et al. Cancer-associated fibroblasts promote hepatocellular carcinoma progression through downregulation of exosomal miR-150-3p. Eur J Surg Oncol 2021;47(2):384−93.

[179] Llovet JM, De Baere T, Kulik L, Haber PK, Greten TF, Meyer T, et al. Locoregional therapies in the era of molecular and immune treatments for hepatocellular carcinoma. Nat Rev Gastroenterol Hepatol 2021;18(5):293−313.

[180] Llovet JM, Montal R, Sia D, Finn RS. Molecular therapies and precision medicine for hepatocellular carcinoma. Nat Rev Clin Oncol 2018;15(10):599−616.

[181] Guo S, Xu X, Tang Y, Zhang C, Li J, Ouyang Y, et al. miR-15a inhibits cell proliferation and epithelial to mesenchymal transition in pancreatic ductal adenocarcinoma by down-regulating Bmi-1 expression. Cancer Lett 2014;344(1):40−6.

[182] Lencioni R, Llovet JM, Han G, Tak WY, Yang J, Guglielmi A, et al. Sorafenib or placebo plus TACE with doxorubicin-eluting beads for intermediate stage HCC: the SPACE trial. J Hepatol 2016;64(5):1090−8.

[183] Bruix J, Takayama T, Mazzaferro V, Chau GY, Yang J, Kudo M, et al. Adjuvant sorafenib for hepatocellular carcinoma after resection or ablation (STORM): a phase 3, randomised, double-blind, placebo-controlled trial. Lancet Oncol 2015;16(13):1344−54.

[184] Marin JJG, Macias RIR, Monte MJ, Romero MR, Asensio M, Sanchez-Martin A, et al. Molecular bases of drug resistance in hepatocellular carcinoma. Cancers (Basel) 2020;12(6).

[185] Dong J, Zhai B, Sun W, Hu F, Cheng H, Xu J. Activation of phosphatidylinositol 3-kinase/AKT/snail signaling pathway contributes to epithelial-mesenchymal transition-induced multi-drug resistance to sorafenib in hepatocellular carcinoma cells. PLoS One 2017;12(9):e0185088.

[186] Qu Z, Wu J, Wu J, Luo D, Jiang C, Ding Y. Exosomes derived from HCC cells induce sorafenib resistance in hepatocellular carcinoma both in vivo and in vitro. J Exp Clin Cancer Res 2016;35(1):159.

[187] Niessen C, Wiggermann P, Velandia C, Stroszczynski C, Pereira PL. Transarterial chemoembolization - status quo in Germany. Rofo 2013;185(11):1089−94.

[188] Takahashi K, Yan IK, Kogure T, Haga H, Patel T. Extracellular vesicle-mediated transfer of long non-coding RNA ROR modulates chemosensitivity in human hepatocellular cancer. FEBS Open Bio 2014;4:458−67.

[189] Takahashi K, Yan IK, Wood J, Haga H, Patel T. Involvement of extracellular vesicle long noncoding RNA (linc-VLDLR) in tumor cell responses to chemotherapy. Mol Cancer Res 2014;12(10):1377−87.

[190] Quinonero F, Mesas C, Doello K, Cabeza L, Perazzoli G, Jimenez-Luna C, et al. The challenge of drug resistance in pancreatic ductal adenocarcinoma: a current overview. Cancer Biol Med 2019;16(4):688–99.

[191] Leslie EM, Deeley RG, Cole SP. Multidrug resistance proteins: role of P-glycoprotein, MRP1, MRP2, and BCRP (ABCG2) in tissue defense. Toxicol Appl Pharmacol 2005;204(3):216–37.

[192] Fu X, Liu M, Qu S, Ma J, Zhang Y, Shi T, et al. Exosomal microRNA-32-5p induces multidrug resistance in hepatocellular carcinoma via the PI3K/Akt pathway. J Exp Clin Cancer Res 2018;37(1):52.

[193] Wang G, Zhao W, Wang H, Qiu G, Jiang Z, Wei G, et al. Exosomal MiR-744 inhibits proliferation and sorafenib chemoresistance in hepatocellular carcinoma by targeting PAX2. Med Sci Monit 2019;25:7209–17.

[194] Nguyen DX, Bos PD, Massague J. Metastasis: from dissemination to organ-specific colonization. Nat Rev Cancer 2009;9(4):274–84.

[195] Gao Y, Bado I, Wang H, Zhang W, Rosen JM, Zhang XH. Metastasis organotropism: redefining the congenial soil. Dev Cell 2019;49(3):375–91.

[196] Patil KC, Soekmadji C. Extracellular vesicle-mediated bone remodeling and bone metastasis: implications in prostate cancer. Subcell Biochem 2021;97:297–361.

[197] Urabe F, Patil K, Ramm GA, Ochiya T, Soekmadji C. Extracellular vesicles in the development of organ-specific metastasis. J Extracell Vesicles 2021;10(9):e12125. Available from: https://doi.org/10.1002/jev2.12125.

[198] Abbas A, Medvedev S, Shores N, Bazzano L, Dehal A, Hutchings J, et al. Epidemiology of metastatic hepatocellular carcinoma, a nationwide perspective. Dig Dis Sci 2014;59(11):2813–20.

[199] Katyal S, Oliver 3rd JH, Peterson MS, Ferris JV, Carr BS, Baron RL. Extrahepatic metastases of hepatocellular carcinoma. Radiology 2000;216(3):698–703.

[200] Natsuizaka M, Omura T, Akaike T, Kuwata Y, Yamazaki K, Sato T, et al. Clinical features of hepatocellular carcinoma with extrahepatic metastases. J Gastroenterol Hepatol 2005;20(11):1781–7.

[201] Doi K, Ishizu T, Fujita T, Noiri E. Lung injury following acute kidney injury: kidney-lung crosstalk. Clin Exp Nephrol 2011;15(4):464–70.

[202] Townsley MI. Structure and composition of pulmonary arteries, capillaries, and veins. Compr Physiol 2012;2(1):675–709.

[203] Hiratsuka S, Goel S, Kamoun WS, Maru Y, Fukumura D, Duda DG, et al. Endothelial focal adhesion kinase mediates cancer cell homing to discrete regions of the lungs via E-selectin up-regulation. Proc Natl Acad Sci U S A 2011;108(9):3725–30.

[204] Fang JH, Zhang ZJ, Shang LR, Luo YW, Lin YF, Yuan Y, et al. Hepatoma cell-secreted exosomal microRNA-103 increases vascular permeability and promotes metastasis by targeting junction proteins. Hepatology 2018;68(4):1459–75.

[205] Sceneay J, Smyth MJ, Moller A. The pre-metastatic niche: finding common ground. Cancer Metastasis Rev 2013;32(3–4):449–64.

[206] Lobb RJ, Lima LG, Moller A. Exosomes: Key mediators of metastasis and pre-metastatic niche formation. Semin Cell Dev Biol 2017;67:3–10.

[207] Fang T, Lv H, Lv G, Li T, Wang C, Han Q, et al. Tumor-derived exosomal miR-1247-3p induces cancer-associated fibroblast activation to foster lung metastasis of liver cancer. Nat Commun 2018;9(1):191.

[208] Mao X, Tey SK, Yeung CLS, Kwong EML, Fung YME, Chung CYS, et al. Nidogen 1-enriched extracellular vesicles facilitate extrahepatic metastasis of liver cancer by activating pulmonary fibroblasts to secrete tumor necrosis factor receptor 1. Adv Sci (Weinh) 2020;7(21):2002157.

[209] Beausejour M, Noel D, Thibodeau S, Bouchard V, Harnois C, Beaulieu JF, et al. Integrin/Fak/Src-mediated regulation of cell survival and anoikis in human intestinal epithelial crypt cells: selective engagement and roles of PI3-K isoform complexes. Apoptosis 2012;17(6):566–78.

[210] Jiang K, Dong C, Yin Z, Li R, Mao J, Wang C, et al. Exosome-derived ENO1 regulates integrin alpha6beta4 expression and promotes hepatocellular carcinoma growth and metastasis. Cell Death Dis 2020;11(11):972.

[211] Hoshino A, Costa-Silva B, Shen TL, Rodrigues G, Hashimoto A, Tesic Mark M, et al. Tumour exosome integrins determine organotropic metastasis. Nature 2015;527(7578):329–35.

[212] Sun H, Wang C, Hu B, Gao X, Zou T, Luo Q, et al. Exosomal S100A4 derived from highly metastatic hepatocellular carcinoma cells promotes metastasis by activating STAT3. Signal Transduct Target Ther 2021;6(1):187.

[213] Fu Q, Zhang Q, Lou Y, Yang J, Nie G, Chen Q, et al. Primary tumor-derived exosomes facilitate metastasis by regulating adhesion of circulating tumor cells via SMAD3 in liver cancer. Oncogene 2018;37(47):6105–18.

[214] Li M, Lu Y, Xu Y, Wang J, Zhang C, Du Y, et al. Horizontal transfer of exosomal CXCR4 promotes murine hepatocarcinoma cell migration, invasion and lymphangiogenesis. Gene 2018;676:101−9.

[215] Nawaz M, Shah N, Zanetti BR, Maugeri M, Silvestre RN, Fatima F, et al. Extracellular vesicles and matrix remodeling enzymes: the emerging roles in extracellular matrix remodeling, progression of diseases and tissue repair. Cells 2018;7(10).

[216] Shay G, Lynch CC, Fingleton B. Moving targets: emerging roles for MMPs in cancer progression and metastasis. Matrix Biol 2015;44−46:200−6.

[217] Gialeli C, Theocharis AD, Karamanos NK. Roles of matrix metalloproteinases in cancer progression and their pharmacological targeting. FEBS J 2011;278(1):16−27.

[218] Patil KCYJ. Nanotechnology for cancer therapy: invading the mechanics of cancer. In: Applications of nanobiomaterials. In: Gromezsescu A, editor. Nanobiomaterials in cancer therapy. Elsevier; 2016. p. 395−470.

[219] Vader P, Mol EA, Pasterkamp G, Schiffelers RM. Extracellular vesicles for drug delivery. Adv Drug Deliv Rev 2016;106(Pt A):148−56.

[220] Soekmadji C, Li B, Huang Y, Wang H, An T, Liu C, et al. The future of extracellular vesicles as theranostics - an ISEV meeting report. J Extracell Vesicles 2020;9(1):1809766.

[221] Ohno S, Takanashi M, Sudo K, Ueda S, Ishikawa A, Matsuyama N, et al. Systemically injected exosomes targeted to EGFR deliver antitumor microRNA to breast cancer cells. Mol Ther 2013;21(1):185−91.

[222] Akao Y, Iio A, Itoh T, Noguchi S, Itoh Y, Ohtsuki Y, et al. Microvesicle-mediated RNA molecule delivery system using monocytes/macrophages. Mol Ther 2011;19(2):395−9.

[223] Alvarez-Erviti L, Seow Y, Yin H, Betts C, Lakhal S, Wood MJ. Delivery of siRNA to the mouse brain by systemic injection of targeted exosomes. Nat Biotechnol 2011;29(4):341−5.

[224] Tang K, Zhang Y, Zhang H, Xu P, Liu J, Ma J, et al. Delivery of chemotherapeutic drugs in tumour cell-derived microparticles. Nat Commun 2012;3:1282.

[225] Son SH, Gangadaran P, Ahn BC. A novel strategy of transferring NIS protein to cells using extracellular vesicles leads to increase in iodine uptake and cytotoxicity. Int J Nanomed 2019;14:1779−87.

[226] Yong T, Zhang X, Bie N, Zhang H, Zhang X, Li F, et al. Tumor exosome-based nanoparticles are efficient drug carriers for chemotherapy. Nat Commun 2019;10(1):3838.

[227] Hu CM, Zhang L, Aryal S, Cheung C, Fang RH, Zhang L. Erythrocyte membrane-camouflaged polymeric nanoparticles as a biomimetic delivery platform. Proc Natl Acad Sci U S A 2011;108(27):10980−5.

[228] Ho MM, Ng AV, Lam S, Hung JY. Side population in human lung cancer cell lines and tumors is enriched with stem-like cancer cells. Cancer Res 2007;67(10):4827−33.

[229] Cheng L, Sharples RA, Scicluna BJ, Hill AF. Exosomes provide a protective and enriched source of miRNA for biomarker profiling compared to intracellular and cell-free blood. J Extracell Vesicles 2014;3.

[230] Pomatto MAC, Bussolati B, D'Antico S, Ghiotto S, Tetta C, Brizzi MF, et al. Improved loading of plasma-derived extracellular vesicles to encapsulate antitumor miRNAs. Mol Ther Methods Clin Dev 2019;13:133−44.

[231] Wahlgren J, De LKT, Brisslert M, Vaziri Sani F, Telemo E, Sunnerhagen P, et al. Plasma exosomes can deliver exogenous short interfering RNA to monocytes and lymphocytes. Nucleic Acids Res 2012;40(17):e130.

[232] Kim MS, Haney MJ, Zhao Y, Mahajan V, Deygen I, Klyachko NL, et al. Development of exosome-encapsulated paclitaxel to overcome MDR in cancer cells. Nanomedicine 2016;12(3):655−64.

[233] Lou G, Song X, Yang F, Wu S, Wang J, Chen Z, et al. Exosomes derived from miR-122-modified adipose tissue-derived MSCs increase chemosensitivity of hepatocellular carcinoma. J Hematol Oncol 2015;8:122.

[234] Xu Y, Huang J, Ma L, Shan J, Shen J, Yang Z, et al. MicroRNA-122 confers sorafenib resistance to hepatocellular carcinoma cells by targeting IGF-1R to regulate RAS/RAF/ERK signaling pathways. Cancer Lett 2016;371(2):171−81.

[235] Lou G, Chen L, Xia C, Wang W, Qi J, Li A, et al. MiR-199a-modified exosomes from adipose tissue-derived mesenchymal stem cells improve hepatocellular carcinoma chemosensitivity through mTOR pathway. J Exp Clin Cancer Res 2020;39(1):4.

[236] Hou J, Lin L, Zhou W, Wang Z, Ding G, Dong Q, et al. Identification of miRNomes in human liver and hepatocellular carcinoma reveals miR-199a/b-3p as therapeutic target for hepatocellular carcinoma. Cancer Cell 2011;19(2):232−43.

[237] Callegari E, D'Abundo L, Guerriero P, Simioni C, Elamin BK, Russo M, et al. miR-199a-3p modulates MTOR and PAK4 pathways and inhibits tumor growth in a hepatocellular carcinoma transgenic mouse model. Mol Ther Nucleic Acids 2018;11:485−93.

[238] Cheng Q, Shi X, Han M, Smbatyan G, Lenz HJ, Zhang Y. Reprogramming exosomes as nanoscale controllers of cellular immunity. J Am Chem Soc 2018;140(48):16413–17.

[239] Rao Q, Zuo B, Lu Z, Gao X, You A, Wu C, et al. Tumor-derived exosomes elicit tumor suppression in murine hepatocellular carcinoma models and humans in vitro. Hepatology 2016;64(2):456–72.

[240] Lv LH, Wan YL, Lin Y, Zhang W, Yang M, Li GL, et al. Anticancer drugs cause release of exosomes with heat shock proteins from human hepatocellular carcinoma cells that elicit effective natural killer cell antitumor responses in vitro. J Biol Chem 2012;287(19):15874–85.

[241] Lu Z, Zuo B, Jing R, Gao X, Rao Q, Liu Z, et al. Dendritic cell-derived exosomes elicit tumor regression in autochthonous hepatocellular carcinoma mouse models. J Hepatol 2017;67(4):739–48.

[242] Ko SF, Yip HK, Zhen YY, Lee CC, Lee CC, Huang CC, et al. Adipose-derived mesenchymal stem cell exosomes suppress hepatocellular carcinoma growth in a rat model: apparent diffusion coefficient, natural killer T-cell responses, and histopathological features. Stem Cell Int 2015;2015:853506.

Cathepsin B: structure, function, tumorigenesis, and prognostic value in hepatocellular carcinoma

Baha Aldeen Bani Fawwaz[1], Aimen Farooq[1], Mengni Guo[1], Gurdeep Singh[1] and Sarfraz Ahmad[2]

[1]Department of Internal Medicine, AdventHealth, Orlando, FL, United States [2]AdventHealth Cancer Institute, FSU and UCF Colleges of Medicine, Orlando, FL, United States

Abstract

Hepatocellular carcinoma (HCC) is the most common primary liver malignancy, and it is one of the leading causes of cancer-related mortality in the United States and around the world. A variety of biomarkers are currently being studied to evaluate the connection between those markers and the prognosis of patients with HCC, and one of those promising markers are cathepsin B. Cathepsin B is an intracellular lysosomal enzyme that participates in various physiological processes inside and outside the cells. Dysregulation of this enzyme play multiple roles in the formation, invasion, and spread of multiple types of cancers. Moreover, this enzyme interacts with multiple biological pathways sharing the same outcome, which is tumorigenesis. Multiple studies have investigated the role of this enzyme in HCC as well as other cancers. Some of those studies have been experimental/preclinical (in animal models) and some were clinical (in humans). These studies have focused on linking this marker with the prognosis and clinical outcomes of HCC. Recognizing the fact that reliable prognostic biomarkers help in the decision-making process and formulating treatment plans for those patients with cancer, particularly HCC, therefore in this chapter we put spotlight on the structure–function relationship of cathepsin B and its impact on tumorigenesis and potential prognostic value for HCC.

Keywords: Cathepsin B; structure; function; hepatocellular carcinoma; liver cancer; tumorigenesis; prognosis

Abbreviations

AFP	alpha-fetoprotein
Akt	protein kinase A

Ganji Purnachandra Nagaraju, Sarfraz Ahmad (eds.)
Theranostics and Precision Medicine for the Management of Hepatocellular Carcinoma, Volume 3

341

Avβ3   alpha-V beta-3
BSG   besigin
CD147   cluster of differentiation 147
E-box   enhancer box
EBS   extracellular binding site
ECM   extracellular matrix
Ets   E-twenty-six
HCC   hepatocellular carcinoma
HR   hazard ratio
IGF-1   insulin-like growth factor - 1
kD   kilodalton
MMP   matrix metalloproteinase
PI3K   phosphoinositide 3-kinase
PTEN   phosphatase and tensin homolog
Sp1   specificity protein 1

Introduction

Liver cancer is ranked globally among the top 10 most common malignancies and the fourth in terms of cancer-related mortality. Hepatocellular carcinoma (HCC) accounts for about 90% of the primary liver malignancies [1]. Risk factors of HCC includes, but not limited to, viral hepatitis, alcohol abuse, and obesity [2]. It is believed that those risk factors provoke the molecular pathogenesis pathways that end up with the formation of malignant cells. This pathway starts with the overexpression of oncogenes and/or underexpression of tumor suppressor genes. The phosphoinositide 3-kinase (PI3K) pathway is one of the most important signaling pathways involved in the oncogenesis of cancer. This pathway is regulated by multiple enzymes, and some of those enzymes act as antagonist, such as phosphatase and tensin homolog (PTEN). Others act as agonist, such as protein kinase A (Akt) [3]. Cathepsin B is one of the lysosomal proteinase enzymes that plays multiple roles in activating and degrading proteins, enzymes, and hormones [4,5]. It was found that cathepsin B can activate PI3K pathway through Akt, which leads to proliferation of HCC cells [6]. In this chapter, we sought to discuss the structure, function, metastatic roles, and prognostic value of cathepsin B in relation to HCC.

Structure-function properties of cathepsin B

Structure of cathepsin B

Cathepsin B has a molecular weight of approximately 31 kD. It is a bi-lobal protein with two distinct domains, with a 25–26 kD heavy-chain and a 5 kD light-chain [7]. Fig. 21.1 shows the ribbon structure of cathepsin B (as widely available on public domain). Extensive reports have covered about the purification and physiochemical properties of cathepsin B from various mammalian organs/sources [4,5], including buffalo liver cathepsin B [8]. The amino acid sequences of rat liver [9] and human liver [10] cathepsin B have also been worked out. All these sequences show close similarities among each other, and also with papain and actinidin [11]. The catalytic triad of the enzyme is comprised of the

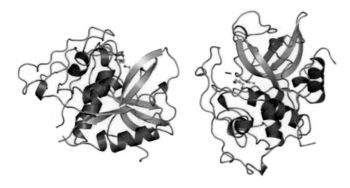

FIGURE 21.1 Cartoon illustration of ribbon structure of cathepsin B. Source: *Adapted from Wikimedia Commons (http:// www.ebi.ac.uk/pdbe-srv/view/images/entry/ 1csb600.png), by Jawahar Swaminathan and MSD staff at the European Bioinformatics Institute, as displayed on Public Domain.*

amino acid aspartic acid, cysteine, and histidine. Its catalytic site is located at the interface between its two lobes with histidine on the right lobe and cysteine on the left lobe [12].

Normal function of cathepsin B

The cathepsins are a group of lysosomal proteases that are structurally somewhat similar to the papaya enzyme, papain [12]. The name of "cathepsin" is derived from the Greek word "kathepsin," which means "to digest," initially for the acidic protease activity found in aqueous extracts of mammalian tissues [13]. These enzymes are the most abundant lysosomal proteases, which exist in many organisms including viruses, bacteria, plants, and animals [14]. According to the catalytic domains, human cathepsins are grouped into three classes: aspartic, cysteine, and serine proteases. The cysteine proteinases comprise of the largest cathepsin family, including cathepsins B, C, F, H, K, L, V, O, S, W, and Z [15].

Cathepsin B is considered as a housekeeping enzyme and is ubiquitously expressed in human tissues [15]. It is unique among the cathepsins due to its endopeptidase and exopeptidase activities, which is modulated by a flexible occluding loop [14]. The displacement of the occluding loop is pH dependent. At acidic pH, the occluding loop blocks the active site, allowing cathepsin B to act as an exopeptidase. At neutral and alkaline pH, cathepsin B acts as an endopeptidase due to the displacement of the occluding loop away from the active site [13].

Active cathepsin B is mainly found in endosomal/lysosomal compartment under the normal physiological conditions. The primary role for cathepsin B is bulk turnover of intracellular and extracellular proteins, maintaining intracellular homeostasis. It is also involved in the pro-hormone and pro-enzyme activation, tissue remodeling, wound healing, bone resorption, antigen processing, inflammatory responses against antigens, and apoptosis [16–18]. Using the growth hormone-deficient Ames dwarf mouse model and proteomic analysis with bioinformatics-driven approaches, a recent study has indicated that cathepsin B regulates very low-density lipoprotein secretion and free fatty acid uptake via cleavage of liver fatty acid-binding protein that occurs in response to oleic acid exposure [19]. It is also found in cytoplasm, nucleus, and in the extracellular milieu [20]. It plays an essential role in the remodeling of extracellular matrix (ECM) by degrading structural components of the ECM.

Tumorigenesis and metastatic role of cathepsin B in cancers with emphasis on hepatocellular carcinoma

Cathepsin B role in cancer and regulation

Proteases, including cathepsin B, play a crucial role(s) in various cellular activities such as ovulation, cellular migration, and apoptosis [21,22]. It also affects the ECM remodeling, which is a crucial process for homeostasis at tissue level. It is hypothesized that the unregulated release of those proteases mediates the local invasion and distant metastasis of cancer cells mainly by the degradation of the ECM as illustrated in Fig. 21.2 [23,24]. Moreover, a correlation was found between the protein lytic activity of catheterization and serum alpha-fetoprotein (AFP), which is known marker for HCC [25]. Also, a correlation between the ratio of "cathepsin B to stefin A" and "cathepsin B to stefin B" proteins and the metastasis of HCC was illustrated by Lin et al. [26].

Cathepsin B protease has multiple regulatory mechanisms at different cellular levels that control its activation and/or inhibition. Increased expression of cathepsin B has been described in different types of cancers such as breast, esophageal, glioblastoma, gastric, and hepatic malignancies [27]. At the transcriptional level, *cathepsin B* gene is located on chromosome 8 and has multiple promoters. One of the promoter regions (Fig. 21.3) has different binding sites for different regulatory proteins. It includes four binding sites for E-twenty-six (Ets) transcription factors, six binding sites for specificity protein 1 (Sp1), and one enhancer box (E-box) binding site [28]. The Sp1 and Ets1 proteins increase the transcription of cathepsin B. Ets1 is a proto-oncogene that has been linked with invasiveness of malignant cells and considered as a poor prognostic indicator [12]. The E-box binding site (Fig. 21.3) interacts with

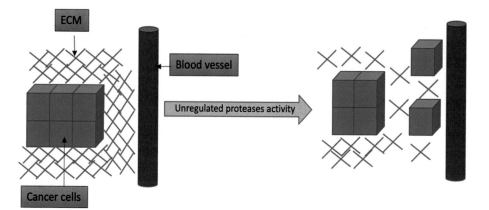

FIGURE 21.2   Schematic representation showing the effects of unregulated proteases on extracellular matrix, which aids cancer cells in local invasion as well as distant metastasis.

FIGURE 21.3   Schematic illustration of cathepsin B promoter region with 11 binding sites. *SP1*, specificity protein 1; *EBS*, extracellular binding site; *E-box*, enhancer box.

multiple upstream stimulatory factors to regulate cathepsin B transcription, some of those factors increase the expression of cathepsin B while others can repress it [29]. Increased levels of some of those proteins, and of cathepsin B levels as well, have been described in various carcinomas [30]. Below we focus on the role of cathepsin B protein in HCC.

Cathepsin B role in fibrogenesis and cirrhosis

Most cases of HCC are preceded by fibrosis and liver cirrhosis [31]. Fibrosis occurs as a result of injury to the liver parenchyma. Several etiologies for liver injury have been identified in the peer-reviewed literature, including infections, like hepatitis B and C, alcohol use, autoimmune processes as well as genetic factors. Hepatic stellate cells play a major role in responding to those obnoxious factors. Those cells are activated in response to liver injury and differentiate into myofibroblast cells, which initiate the fibrogenesis process [32]. Studies have shown that cathepsin B plays role(s) in the activation and differentiation of hepatic stellate cell into myofibroblasts, mainly through the phosphorylation of Akt (Fig. 21.4), and that with inhibition of cathepsin B there was a decrease in the proliferation and activation of the stellate cells in both human and mouse cells [33]. Another study showed that serum levels of cathepsin B was elevated in patients with HCC and liver cirrhosis as compared to the control subjects, and rather more interestingly, a significant relationship was found between cathepsin B levels and severity of cirrhosis [34].

Cathepsin B role in modulating growth, invasion, and metastasis of hepatocellular carcinoma

Cathepsin B mediates growth and spread of HCC throughout various molecular pathways and mechanisms (Table 21.1), and some of those mechanisms arise from proteolytic

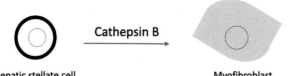

Hepatic stellate cell   Myofibroblast

FIGURE 21.4 Schematic representation of simplified pathway where cathepsin B activates/differentiates hepatic satellite cells into myofibroblast.

TABLE 21.1 Molecular pathways involvement in promoting hepatocellular carcinoma through cathepsin B modulation.

Molecule/pathway	Relation to cathepsin B	End results
Insulin-like growth factor-1 (IGF-1)	Delays the degradation of cathepsin B	Promoting growth, invasiveness, and metastasis of hepatocellular carcinoma
Cluster of differentiation 147 (CD147)	Activates cathepsin B	
Phosphoinositide 3-kinase (PI3K)/protein kinase A (Akt) pathway	Cathepsin B activates this pathway	

activity of the enzyme. On the other hand, cathepsin B can also promote tumor growth through signal transduction pathways [35–37].

Insulin-like growth factor-1 (IGF-1) was found to play role(s) in proliferation of multiple malignancies including HCC [38]. A recent study has shown that IGF-1 promotes growth of HCC by delaying the degradation of cathepsin B [35]. In this study, HCC cells of diabetic mice, which contain higher levels of IGF-1, proliferated more and was associated with more metastatic nodules compared to the nondiabetic mice [35].

Cluster of differentiation 147 (CD147), also known as besigin (BSG), is another molecule that was found to have tumor invasion and metastasis promoting factors. It is a transmembrane glycoprotein that induces secretion of matrix metalloproteinases (MMPs) which participate in the ECM remodeling; thus facilitating the invasion and spread of tumors [39]. It was also found that CD147 can activate other proteases, like cathepsin B. The CD147 and cathepsin B expressions correlates positively in HCC cells, increased expression of these macromolecules, especially at marginal cells of HCC, is hypothesized to be associated with more invasive HCC [37] (Table 21.1).

Another mechanism in which cathepsin B mediates HCC invasion is through PI3K/Akt signaling pathway (Table 21.1). This pathway was found to promote proliferation of HCC. It is suggested that cathepsin B activates this pathway through integrin αvβ3, and when integrin αvβ3 levels are low, PI3K/Akt activation will be prevented resulting in a decrease of HCC cells proliferation and progression. Therefore cathepsin B/integrin αvβ3/PI3K/Akt pathway plays an important role in promoting HCC [36].

Prognostic values of cathepsin B in hepatocellular carcinoma

In recent years, cathepsin B has emerged as a potential biomarker for many cancers [40–47]. Studies into the utility of cathepsin B in the prognosis of HCC are although relatively scarce; but have provided mixed results to date. It has been established that cathepsin B facilitates tumor migration and metastasis through protease-mediated degradation of the ECM as well as upregulation of matrix metalloproteases in HCC [37,48]. The study suggested that HCC subtypes positive for cathepsin B should portend a more unfavorable prognosis. Lee et al. [49] developed a classifier model to distinguish HCC from nonmalignant tissues as well as to predict tumor cells progression. This model is composed of six biomarkers, and one of those biomarkers is cathepsin B [49].

This sentiment was echoed by Ruan et al. [50] through Western blotting, where the authors determined that increased cathepsin B levels were exhibited in cancerous tissues compared to the noncancerous tissues. Increased expression of cathepsin B in cell lines engineered to have higher metastatic potential compared to the nonmetastatic cell lines was also noted. In a univariate analysis, a positive correlation was established between cathepsin B expression and tumor stage, recurrence, and differentiation [50]. The authors also examined the correlation of cathepsin B expression with 2- and 5-year survival rates in 168 patients and discovered that the cohort exhibiting lower cathepsin B expression had a significantly higher overall survival rate at 5 years as compared to the patients with higher cathepsin B expression (43.4% vs 19.3%, $P = .001$) [50]. Multivariate analysis through a Cox proportional-hazard model demonstrated that cathepsin B expression had a significant correlation with poor prognosis and as an independent factor [hazard ratio (HR) = 5.132, P = .000] [50].

Qin et al. [6] also sought to evaluate the prognostic utility of cathepsin B in patients with HCC; however, their findings were in stark contrast to those reported by Ruan et al. [50]. Using immunohistochemistry, Qin et al. [6] identified lower levels of expressions of cathepsin B mRNA and protein in HCC tissues as compared to para-carcinoma or healthy tissues. The authors also discovered that downexpression of cathepsin B was significantly associated with survival (P = .001) and tumor grade (P = .007). A 60.6% survival rate over 6 years was noted in the group expressing high cathepsin B levels compared to only 39.4% in the lower cathepsin B group, revealing that the lower expression of cathepsin B was found to be correlated with overall worse survival [6]. Upon review of 90 patients with HCC that were followed for 5 years after hepatectomy, 55 patients were found to be negative for cathepsin B whereas 35 patients were positive demonstrating a higher overall survival rate in the cohort positive for cathepsin B (P = .005). A multivariate analysis revealed that cathepsin B expression to be an independent prognostic factor in the overall survival of patients with HCC after curative resection (HR = 0.514, P = .031) [6].

Conclusions and future perspective

HCC accounts for majority of the primary liver malignancies. The major risk factors for HCC include viral hepatitis, alcohol abuse, and obesity, etc., which provoke cellular/molecular pathogenesis resulting in malignant cells formation. Cathepsin B is one of the lysosomal proteinase enzymes that plays multiple roles in activating/degrading proteins, enzymes, and hormones through multiple pathways, including PI3K, Akt, IGF-1, and CD147, etc. There is a growing interest and expanding role of cathepsin B in HCC; however, presently it remains difficult to make any discrete conclusions on the prognostic value of cathepsin B expression in patients with HCC. Thus further studies are required to discern the role of cathepsin B as a prognostic tool in patients with HCC.

Conflict of interest

All the authors declare that there are no conflicts of interest associated with this research manuscript (chapter) and have reviewed and approved its publication.

References

[1] Bray F, Ferlay J, Soerjomataram I, Siegel RL, Torre LA, Jemal A. Global cancer statistics 2018: GLOBOCAN estimates of incidence and mortality worldwide for 36 cancers in 185 countries. CA Cancer J Clin 2018;68:394−424. Available from: https://doi.org/10.3322/caac.21492.

[2] Yang JD, Hainaut P, Gores GJ, Amadou A, Plymoth A, Roberts LR. A global view of hepatocellular carcinoma: trends, risk, prevention, and management. Nat Rev Gastroenterol Hepatol 2019;16(10):589−604. Available from: https://doi.org/10.1038/s41575-019-0186-y.

[3] Liu P, Cheng H, Roberts TM, Zhao JJ. Targeting the phosphoinositide 3-kinase pathway in cancer. Nat Rev Drug Discov 2009;8(8):627−44. Available from: https://doi.org/10.1038/nrd2926.

[4] Ahmad S, Agarwal SK, Khan MY. Purification and some properties of buffalo spleen cathepsin B. J Biosci 1989;14:261—8.

[5] Agarwal S.K., Singh S., Sharma S. Structural and functional dynamics of lysosomal cysteine proteases with particular reference to cathepsin B and cathepsin H. In: Frontiers in protein structure, function, and dynamics. Singh D.B., Tripathi T. (Eds.); Springer Nature, Singapore, 2020; pp. 391—424.<https://doi.org/10.1007/978-981-15-5530-5_16>.

[6] Qin L, Chen J, Wang J, Ye J, Tan H, Xu L. Expression of cathepsin B in human hepatocellular carcinoma and its prognostic significance. Int J Clin Exp Pathol 2016;9(2):1343—50.

[7] Klose A, Wilbrand-Hennes A, Zigrino P, Weber E, Krieg T, Mauch C, et al. Contact of high-invasive, but not low-invasive, melanoma cells to native collagen I induces the release of mature cathepsin B. Int J Cancer 2006;118(11):2735—43. Available from: https://doi.org/10.1002/ijc.21700.

[8] Fazili KM, Qasim MA. Purification and some properties of buffalo liver cathepsin B. J Biochem 1986;100 (2):293—9. Available from: https://doi.org/10.1093/oxfordjournals.jbchem.a121715.

[9] Takio K, Towatari T, Katunuma N, Teller DC, Titani K. Homology of amino acid sequences of rat liver cathepsins B and H with that of papain. Proc Natl Acad Sci USA 1983;80(12):3666—70. Available from: https://doi.org/10.1073/pnas.80.12.3666.

[10] Ritonja A, Popovic T, Turk V, Wiedenmann K, Machleidt W. Amino acid sequence of human liver cathepsin B. FEBS Lett 1985;181(1):169—72. Available from: https://doi.org/10.1016/0014-5793(85)81136-4.

[11] Dufour E. Sequence homologies, hydrophobic profiles and secondary structures of cathepsins B, H and L: comparison with papain and actinidin. Biochimie 1988;70(10):1335—42. Available from: https://doi.org/10.1016/0300-9084(88)90004-1.

[12] Aggarwal N, Sloane BF. Cathepsin B: multiple roles in cancer. Proteomic Clin Appl 2014;8(5—6):427—37. Available from: https://doi.org/10.1002/prca.201300105.

[13] Cavallo-Medved D, Moin K, Sloane B. Cathepsin B: basis sequence: mouse. AFCS Nat Mol 2011;2011: A000508.

[14] Li YY, Fang J, Ao GZ. Cathepsin B and L inhibitors: a patent review (2010-present). Expert Opin Ther Pat 2017;27(6):643—56. Available from: https://doi.org/10.1080/13543776.2017.1272572.

[15] Araujo TF, Cordeiro AV, Vasconcelos DAA, Vitzel KF, Silva VRR. The role of cathepsin B in autophagy during obesity: a systematic review. Life Sci 2018;209:274—81. Available from: https://doi.org/10.1016/j.lfs.2018.08.024.

[16] Li C, Chen L, Wang J, Zhang L, Tang P, Zhai S, et al. Expression and clinical significance of cathepsin B and stefin A in laryngeal cancer. Oncol Rep 2011;26(4):869—75. Available from: https://doi.org/10.3892/or.2011.1344.

[17] Mijanović O, Branković A, Panin AN, Savchuk S, Timashev P, Ulasov I, et al. Cathepsin B: a sellsword of cancer progression. Cancer Lett 2019;449:207—14. Available from: https://doi.org/10.1016/j.canlet.2019.02.035.

[18] Kim EK, Song MJ, Jang HH, Chung YS. Clinicopathologic analysis of cathepsin B as a prognostic marker of thyroid cancer. Int J Mol Sci 2020;21(24):9537. Available from: https://doi.org/10.3390/ijms21249537.

[19] Thibeaux S, Siddiqi S, Zhelyabovska O, Moinuddin F, Masternak MM, Siddiqi SA. Cathepsin B regulates hepatic lipid metabolism by cleaving liver fatty acid-binding protein. J Biol Chem 2018;293(6):1910—23. Available from: https://doi.org/10.1074/jbc.M117.778365.

[20] Vizovišek M, Fonović M, Turk B. Cysteine cathepsins in extracellular matrix remodeling: extracellular matrix degradation and beyond. Matrix Biol 2019;75:141—59. Available from: https://doi.org/10.1016/j.matbio.2018.01.024.

[21] Barbolina MV, Stack MS. Membrane type 1-matrix metalloproteinase: substrate diversity in pericellular proteolysis. Semin Cell Dev Biol 2008;19(1):24—33. Available from: https://doi.org/10.1016/j.semcdb.2007.06.008.

[22] Malla RR, Gopinath S, Gondi CS, Alapati K, Dinh DH, Tsung AJ, et al. uPAR and cathepsin B downregulation induces apoptosis by targeting calcineurin A to BAD via Bcl-2 in glioma [Retracted in. J Neurooncol 2021;152(2):417. Available from: https://doi.org/10.1007/s11060-011-0727-x J Neurooncol 2012;107(1):69—80.

[23] Duffy MJ. The urokinase plasminogen activator system: role in malignancy. Curr Pharm Des 2004;10 (1):39—49. Available from: https://doi.org/10.2174/1381612043453559.

[24] Terada T, Ohta T, Minato H, Nakanuma Y. Expression of pancreatic trypsinogen/trypsin and cathepsin B in human cholangiocarcinomas and hepatocellular carcinomas. Hum Pathol 1995;26(7):746—52. Available from: https://doi.org/10.1016/0046-8177(95)90222-8.

[25] Niewczas M, Paczek L, Krawczyk M, Pawlak J, Bartłomiejczyk I, Górnicka B. Enzymatic activity of cathepsin B, cathepsin B and L, plasmin, trypsin and collagenase in hepatocellular carcinoma. Pol Arch Med Wewn 2002;108(1):653−62 PMID: 12412410.

[26] Lin YY, Chen ZW, Lin ZP, Lin LB, Yang XM, Xu LY, et al. Tissue levels of stefin A and stefin B in hepatocellular carcinoma. Anat Rec (Hoboken) 2016;299(4):428−38. Available from: https://doi.org/10.1002/ar.23311.

[27] Herszényi L, István G, Cardin R, Paoli MD, Plebani M, Tulassay Z, et al. Serum cathepsin B and plasma urokinase-type plasminogen activator levels in gastrointestinal tract cancers. Eur J Cancer Prev 2008;17 (5):438−45. Available from: https://doi.org/10.1097/CEJ.0b013e328305a130.

[28] Berquin IM, Sloane BF. Cathepsin B expression in human tumors. Adv Exp Med Biol 1996;389:281−94. Available from: https://doi.org/10.1007/978-1-4613-0335-0_35.

[29] Yan S, Sloane BF. Isolation of a novel USF2 isoform: repressor of cathepsin B expression. Gene 2004;337:199−206. Available from: https://doi.org/10.1016/j.gene.2004.05.005.

[30] Li L, Davie JR. The role of Sp1 and Sp3 in normal and cancer cell biology. Ann Anat 2010;192(5):275−83. Available from: https://doi.org/10.1016/j.aanat.2010.07.010.

[31] Friedman SL. Hepatic stellate cells: protean, multifunctional, and enigmatic cells of the liver. Physiol Rev 2008;88(1):125−72. Available from: https://doi.org/10.1152/physrev.00013.2007.

[32] Bataller R, Brenner DA. Liver fibrosis. J Clin Invest 2005;115(2):209−18. Available from: https://doi.org/10.1172/JCI24282.

[33] Moles A, Tarrats N, Fernández-Checa JC, Marí M. Cathepsins B and D drive hepatic stellate cell proliferation and promote their fibrogenic potential. Hepatology 2009;49(4):1297−307. Available from: https://doi.org/10.1002/hep.22753.

[34] Leto G, Tumminello FM, Pizzolanti G, Montalto G, Soresi M, Gebbia N. Lysosomal cathepsins B and L and stefin A blood levels in patients with hepatocellular carcinoma and/or liver cirrhosis: potential clinical implications. Oncology 1997;54(1):79−83. Available from: https://doi.org/10.1159/000227666.

[35] Lei T, Ling X. IGF-1 promotes the growth and metastasis of hepatocellular carcinoma via the inhibition of proteasome-mediated cathepsin B degradation. World J Gastroenterol 2015;21(35):10137−49. Available from: https://doi.org/10.3748/wjg.v21.i35.10137.

[36] Xu ZZ, Xiu P, Lv JW, Wang F-H, Dong X-F, Liu F, et al. Integrin $\alpha v \beta 3$ is required for cathepsin B-induced hepatocellular carcinoma progression. Mol Med Rep 2015;11(5):3499−504. Available from: https://doi.org/10.3892/mmr.2014.3140.

[37] Wang SJ, Chao D, Wei W, Nan G, Li J-Y, Liu F-L, et al. CD147 promotes collective invasion through cathepsin B in hepatocellular carcinoma. J Exp Clin Cancer Res 2020;39(1):145. Available from: https://doi.org/10.1186/s13046-020-01647-2.

[38] Shan J, Shen J, Liu L, Xia F, Xu C, Duan G, et al. Nanog regulates self-renewal of cancer stem cells through the insulin-like growth factor pathway in human hepatocellular carcinoma. Hepatology 2012;56(3):1004−14. Available from: https://doi.org/10.1002/hep.25745.

[39] Landras A, Reger de Moura C, Jouenne F, Lebbe C, Menashi S, Mourah S. CD147 is a promising target of tumor progression and a prognostic biomarker. Cancers (Basel) 2019;11(11):1803. Available from: https://doi.org/10.3390/cancers11111803.

[40] Nouh MA, Mohamed MM, El-Shinawi M, Shaalan MA, Cavallo-Medved D, Khaled HM, et al. Cathepsin B: a potential prognostic marker for inflammatory breast cancer. J Transl Med 2011;9:1. Available from: https://doi.org/10.1186/1479-5876-9-1.

[41] Zhang H, Fu T, McGettigan S, Kumar S, Liu S, Speicher D, et al. IL-8 and cathepsin B as melanoma serum biomarkers. Int J Mol Sci 2011;12(3):1505−18. Available from: https://doi.org/10.3390/ijms12031505.

[42] Kotaska K, Dusek P, Prusa R, Vesely S, Babjuk M. Urine and serum cathepsin B concentrations in the transitional cell carcinoma of the bladder. J Clin Lab Anal 2012;26(2):61−5. Available from: https://doi.org/10.1002/jcla.21483.

[43] Wu D, Wang H, Li Z, Wang L, Zheng F, Jiang J, et al. Cathepsin B may be a potential biomarker in cervical cancer. Histol Histopathol 2012;27(1):79−87. Available from: https://doi.org/10.14670/HH-27.79.

[44] Gong F, Peng X, Luo C, Shen G, Zhao C, Zou L, et al. Cathepsin B as a potential prognostic and therapeutic marker for human lung squamous cell carcinoma. Mol Cancer 2013;12(1):125. Available from: https://doi.org/10.1186/1476-4598-12-125.

[45] Chen T, Yang S, Lin C, Lee H, Tsai C, Weng C. A4383C and C76G SNP in cathepsin B is respectively associated with the high risk and tumor size of hepatocarcinoma. Tumour Biol 2014;35(11):11193−8. Available from: https://doi.org/10.1007/s13277-014-2004-z.

[46] Monsouvanh A, Proungvitaya T, Limpaiboon T, Wongkham C, Wongkham S, Luvira V, et al. Serum cathepsin B to cystatin C ratio as a potential marker for the diagnosis of cholangiocarcinoma. Asian Pac J Cancer Prev 2014;15(21):9511–15. Available from: https://doi.org/10.7314/apjcp.2014.15.21.9511.

[47] Bian B, Mongrain S, Cagnol S, Langlois M-J, Boulanger J, Bernatchez G, et al. Cathepsin B promotes colorectal tumorigenesis, cell invasion, and metastasis. Mol Carcinog 2016;55(5):671–87. Available from: https://doi.org/10.1002/mc.22312.

[48] Tumminello FM, Leto G, Pizzolanti G, Candiloro V, Crescimanno M, Crosta L, et al. Cathepsins D, B and L circulating levels as prognostic markers of malignant progression. Anticancer Res 1996;16(4B):2315–19 [Erratum in: Anticancer Res 1996;16(6C):4003]. PMID: 8694562.

[49] Lee NP, Chen L, Lin MC, Tsang FH, Yeung C, Poon RT, et al. Proteomic expression signature distinguishes cancerous and nonmalignant tissues in hepatocellular carcinoma. J Proteome Res 2009;8(3):1293–303. Available from: https://doi.org/10.1021/pr800637z.

[50] Ruan J, Zheng H, Rong X, Rong X, Zhang J, Fang W, et al. Over-expression of cathepsin B in hepatocellular carcinomas predicts poor prognosis of HCC patients. Mol Cancer 2016;15:17. Available from: https://doi.org/10.1186/s12943-016-0503-9.

Chemotherapy for hepatocellular carcinoma—an updated review

Sarojamma Vemula[1], Jeelan Basha Shaik[2], Amooru G. Damu[2] and Ramakrishna Vadde[3]

[1]Department of Microbiology, Government Medical College, Anantapur, India [2]Department of Chemistry, Biotechnology and Bioinformatics, Yogi Vemana University, Kadapa, India [3]Department of Biotechnology & Bioinformatics, Yogi Vemana University, Kadapa, India

Abstract

Hepatocellular carcinoma (HCC) is the leading liver cancer with high morbidity and mortality globally. The etiological factors involved in HCC comprises of hepatitis B and C virus infection, genetic factors, smoking, obesity, alcohol abuse, environmental carcinogens, and microbial toxins. Despite its widespread incidence, the treatment is still a hard challenge due to lack of therapeutic choices at disease advanced stage. HCC can be cured if it is diagnosed at an early stage. Drug development in past few years against HCC is getting increased due to overall survival in HCC treatment. So far no approved first-line and second-line systemic treatments are available for advanced liver cancer treatment, and only sorafenib, regorafenib, and nivolumab are used. There is a paucity of information available on treatment of HCC. Several chemotherapeutic drugs have been developed particularly against HCC-related therapeutic targets. In the present chapter, a brief overview is provided on the HCC and its prevention through chemotherapeutic drugs.

Keywords: Hepatocellular carcinoma; risk factors; pathology; therapy; chemotherapeutics; drugs

Abbreviations

ABCB1	multidrug resistance gene, MDR1
ABCC1	multidrug resistance-associated protein 1; MRP1
ALDH	Aldehyde Dehydrogenase
BCLC	Barcelona-Clínic Liver Cancer
CTLA4	cytotoxic T lymphocyte-associated antigen
Dr5	death receptor
ECM	extracellular matrix

Ganji Purnachandra Nagaraju, Sarfraz Ahmad (eds.)
Theranostics and Precision Medicine for the Management of Hepatocellular Carcinoma, Volume 3

351

EGFR	epidermal growth factor receptor
FGFR	fibroblast growth factor receptors
HBV	hepatitis B virus
HCC	hepatocellular carcinoma
HCV	hepatitis C virus
HDAC	Histone deacetylase
HER	human epidermal growth factor receptor
IFN	interferons
mTOR	mammalian target of rapamycin
MET	Mesenchymal—epithelial transition factor
NAFLD	nonalcoholic fatty liver disease
NASH	nonalcoholic steatohepatitis
PDGFR-β	platelet-derived growth factor receptor-beta
RFA	radiofrequency ablation
TACE	transarterial chemoembolization
TME	tumor microenvironment
TNF	tumor necrosis factor
VEGFR	vascular endothelial growth factor receptors

Introduction

Globally cancer is classified as a foremost cause of death and a hurdle to increasing life expectations. It is estimated that new cancer cases of 19.3 million and cancer deaths of 10 million occurred in 2020 [1]. According to WHO reports in 2019, cancer is the first or second leading cause of death in 112 among 183 countries and ranks third or fourth in a further 23 countries [2]. Liver cancer is the sixth most commonly diagnosed cancer and is assessed as third leading cause of cancer death after lung, colorectal, and stomach cancer worldwide. Incidence rates of both occurrence and deaths are two to three times higher in men as compared to women in many countries [3]. Of primary liver cancer cases, hepatocellular carcinoma (HCC) accounts for >90% and constitutes a major health problem worldwide and is the fifth highest general cause of cancer and third most conventional cause of death worldwide, reporting for approximately 10% of cancer fatalities worldwide [4]. Often HCCs exhibit the multifactorial pathogenesis, different factors like ecological, contagious, metabolic, nutritional, and endocrine promote hepatic carcinogenesis. The individual factors differ geographically relying on ecological and socioeconomic changes. Various risk factors associated with HCC are hepatitis B or C, or D virus infection, chronic alcoholism, obesity and diabetes, smoking, cirrhosis, and use of oral contraceptives.

Risk factors and pathogenesis of hepatocellular carcinoma

The pathogenesis of HCC is mainly studied as sequences causing liver injury, redevelopment, cirrhosis, fibrosis, dysplasia, and cancer. HCC cases majorly occur in setting of chronic liver diseases, with cirrhosis being an important risk factor [5]. Hepatitis is connected with liver cell swelling, regeneration, fibrosis, and necrosis, which may further proceed to cirrhosis. After liver cell necrosis, inactive hepatocytes start to multiply. The repetitive cycles of necrosis and regeneration are the major causes for prolonged hepatitis, which further facilitate genomic alterations that evade the repair mechanisms and take the lead for the development of HCC, as a result of monoclonal expansion. In small number of cases, HCC also appears even in liver cirrhosis absence [6]. In recent days it has been shown that regeneration of hepatocytes in irregular ways became an important factor for liver cancer and even for noncirrhotic livers. Development of HCC is caused by some of the fundamental aspects like genetic mutations both hereditary and acquired and other risk factors like hepatotropic viruses B, C, and D, alcohol, and smoking. It is widely accepted that both the factors play a pivotal role in HCC development. Carcinogenic changes by cirrhosis are observed in 90% of patients identified with HCC, whereas in 10% noncirrhotic mechanisms are participating in carcinogenesis more responsible for the fatal disease. Hepatitis B virus (HBV) is a DNA virus, the widespread source for HCC and estimated 54% of cause of all liver cancers in the world [7]. HBV causes 33% deaths in worldwide, tracked by alcohol (30%), hepatitis C virus (HCV) (21%), and other causes (16%). Universally, 2 billion individuals have been exposed to HBV among 250–350 million were consider to be chronic carriers. The risk of HCC with HBV patients varies from 10% to 25% [7].

The high risk of developing HCC with hepatitis C is almost similar to hepatitis B. HCV is a RNA virus and it is the second most common cause for HCC. In developed countries HCV is most common causative agent [8] and globally it is about 10%–25% of HCC cases are HCV related. About 20–30-fold risk HCC development was attained with chronic HCV infection as compared to uninfected individuals. The development of HCC with HCV infection is mainly connected with fibrosis and the viral copy number [9]. HCC development through HCV occurs in a step-by-step fashion, normally extends over decades. All cases of HCC occur with the mutations in hepatocytes within a cirrhotic environment, and the year wise prevalence of HCC in persons with HCV-related cirrhosis extends from 0.5% to 10%. HCV proteins have also been involved in the promotion of cellular proliferation, transformation, and tumor growth which altogether causes the higher risk of developing HCC.

The intake of excessive alcohol is the highest reason for liver cirrhosis and the third most cause for HCC. The risk of developing HCC was observed in individuals who consumed alcohol more than 60 g/day [10]. Alcohol also synergistically works with hepatotropic viruses to enhance the risk of developing HCC. HBV patients with chronic consumption of alcohol increase the risk of cause for HCC by almost three times; however, alcohol can separately cause HCC independent of the presence of viral hepatitis. This might be due to variations in aldehyde dehydrogenase (ALDH) activity or expected to stronger connection between alcohol consumption and cirrhosis [11]. Recent studies suggest that excessive alcohol intake results in production of CYP2E1 in liver cells and precedes inflammation and sequentially necrosis and regeneration of hepatocyte with oxidative stress, which may further proceed to cirrhosis. Modern epidemiologic case-control studies propose that besides alcohol, tobacco consumption is also a relevant cofactor for tumor growth. In disparity, several studies revealed a protective effect of coffee on the advancement of liver cirrhosis and HCC [12].

Certain conditions such as abdominal obesity, insulin resistance, hypertension, and atherogenic dyslipidemia increase the risk of HCC. It is probable that metabolic syndrome which is linked with the above-mentioned conditions has showed an 81% increased risk of developing HCC. Type 2 diabetes causes twofold to threefold increased HCC risk, and drastically showed larger risk among men than women [13]. Suffering lengthier with diabetes being combined with an increase in risk of HCC, moreover, the connection between diabetes severity and HCC risk is not yet clear.

Nonalcoholic fatty liver disease (NAFLD) is a cause of chronic liver disease extending from simple steatosis to nonalcoholic steatohepatitis (NASH), which may ultimately lead to cirrhosis. Studies have demonstrated that NAFLD or NASH promotes oxidative stress, and altered endocrine or adipokine signaling specifically leads to HCC induction [14]. It is considered that unusual deposition of iron in the liver is most common in NASH. Moreover, deposition of iron and hyperinsulinaemia are the key risk factors for the development of NASH and further involve in insulin resistance and HCC. The developing risk of HCC in 5 years with NASH group is 11.7% whereas in chronic HCV infection group it is 30.4%. The risk of death is same in both the groups after the development of HCC. Curiously, NASH patients short of cirrhosis have no risk of HCC expansion [15].

Aflatoxins and mycotoxins are other significant risk factors for HCC produced by fungi of the *Aspergillus* species. The toxins of the fungus pollute a range of foodstuffs, most remarkably, ground nuts, tree nuts, and maize, and further enter into food chain and affect population. Aflatoxins are particularly carcinogenic after they coappear along with chronic HBV infections; this combination of both factors has a collaborative impact on developing the HCC risk. Aflatoxins and HBV infections increase the HCC risk by 6 and 11 times, respectively, whereas the two factors synergistically increases the risk of HCC by 54-fold [16].

Finally, the genetic factors particularly the mutations in the genes for hemochromatosis (HFE), glycogen storage diseases (SLC37A4, G6PC), alpha 1-antitrypsin deficiency (SERPINA1), porphyrias (UROD, HMBS), Wilson's disease (ATP7B), and tyrosinemia (FAH) enhance the sensitivity toward HCC development [17].

TME (tumor microenvironment) is a complex system organized primarily by the inflammatory cells mainly comprising stromal cells, cancer cells, and extracellular matrix (ECM) where the cancer cells experience an optimal environment for its growth, proliferation, and development. The TME provides the requisite signals that activate transcription factors, which in turn allows the stromal cells to infect the distantly present tissues and create a new environment for the survival of the cancer cells. Additionally, as compared to normal cells, HCC cells experience a decrease of pH along with oxygen intake [18]. In the present chapter, the authors make an effort to understand the HCC-associated TME components and how they modulate to the formation of HCC.

Chemotherapy for hepatocellular carcinoma

Unfortunately, the diagnosis of HCC can be analyzed only when patients become symptomatic with improved disease with severe liver impairment. At later stages no efficient treatment is available for improvisation of survival. Few studies claimed that in many cases screening was done properly, among 0.7 million patients one case is claimed for NAFLD/NASH/HCV. Over one-fourth of HCC diagnosed/screened cases have shown no symptoms of liver disease [19]. At present, there are a number of treatment options available, showing positive impact on the survival; these are surgical and nonsurgical treatments. Irrespective of the single-treatment approach, for better outcome the selection of treatment approach should be in multidisciplinary pattern. For this a team typically consists of a medical oncologist, a hepatologist, a pathologist, a transplant surgeon, a radiologist, an interventional radiologist, and a hepatobiliary surgeon. Surgery and liver transplantation are considered as only essential treatments for HCC disease, but it is not sufficient for the advanced stage of the disease or substantial hepatic dysfunction. Specifically, according to the classification of Barcelona-Clínic Liver Cancer (BCLC), surgery is the best choice in HCC early stage, that is, in stage 0, while liver transplantation is possible in the early stage of HCC (stage A) [20]. In advanced diseased conditions, radiofrequency ablation (RFA) and transarterial chemoembolization (TACE) are used in treatment. RFA treatment is used in early stage (stage A) and TACE in midway stage (stage B) of the disease, and nonsurgical approaches like ethanol injection, transarterial radiation, and microwave ablation are uncommonly used in clinical practices as they show limited or meager encouraging results [20]. The special concern is the method with TACE, it is purely therapeutic indication, which showed the utility for its capability in downstaging the disease and for its neo-adjuvant effect. In the case of less liver function stage (advanced stage C), or TACE resistance HCC stage, it is suggested to use systemic chemotherapy.

Sorafenib—a first-line chemotherapeutic agent

Among systemic chemotherapy treatments, sorafenib is a standard drug for HCC in advanced stage. Many efforts are in way to improvise the use of sorafenib in HCC treatment, and further to optimize the chemotherapy against HCC, small molecules are being used in prevention of malignancies [21]. With this consideration, this chapter aims to review the chemotherapeutic options available for the treatment of advanced HCC along with other possible strategies concerning HCC systemic therapy.

Before use of sorafenib in therapy, the hormonal therapies or cytotoxic agents, or in combination used as systemic chemotherapeutic approaches in HCC advanced stage, but these treatments are not improve the overall survival as single treatment gives 0%—20% and combination exhibited little higher survival rates [21]. Later studies show that doxorubicin significantly increases patients' survival with advanced HCC as compared to earlier best supportive care [22]. In this treatment they observed the sepsis and cardiac toxicities due to adverse events of doxorubicin, and finally not considered for HCC treatment. Later in randomized phase III trial, treatment was done with doxorubicin alone, and in combination of IFNα-2b, 5-FU, and cisplatin, the results showed no significant disparity in survival rates between above treatments [22]. Conflicting results were seen in various clinical trials in HCC patients. In summary, no standard therapy was established for advanced HCC in the pre-sorafenib era; further the randomized controlled trials with cytotoxic regimens, hormonal, interferon therapies, and *meta*-analyses failed to confirm the overall survival in HCC patients.

The sorafenib targets the tumor growth and angiogenesis. It is a multikinase inhibitor involved in serine-threonine kinases inhibition. Sorafenib is also involved in MEK/RAF/ERK pathway, and act on RET, FLT-3, the receptor tyrosine kinase activity of PDGFR-β and VEGFRs 1, 2, and 3 [23]. In the two pivotal placebo-controlled phase III studies, it was shown that sorafenib drastically enhances overall survival time in advanced stage of HCC.

With these results, sorafenib was approved as a standard drug in advanced HCC therapy [23]. In a STORM trial, the testing was performed with double-blind, placebo-controlled randomized methods, and it further showed the sorafenib efficacy after the resection, but no change in survival rates noticed [24]. It is also evaluated that sorafenib was used as a second-line therapy agent after the fluoropyrimidine and the platinum-based chemotherapy [25]. Nowadays in search of markers in resistance to sorafenib, new systemic therapeutic options are used for advanced HCC by doing many clinical trials with the aim of personalized therapeutic approach for individual patients.

There are several other first-line therapeutic agents considered worldwide in clinical trials in patients suffering from HCC either in single treatment or in combination with sorafenib.

Sunitinib

Sunitinib is a small-molecule inhibitor of multikinases, which targets VEGFR1, 2, 3; PDGFR-α, β; c-KIT, and other tyrosine kinases, involved in antiangiogenic and antitumor events. In a phase III trial of sunitinib versus sorafenib (SUN1170 trial) [26], this drug was used as a first-line treatment.

Brivanib

Brivanib is a small-molecule playing a vital role as tyrosine kinase inhibitor (TKI) of FGFR and VEGFR. The quantity of 800 mg once on a daily basis was administrated orally and was primarily assessed for the first-line treatment compared to sorafenib. In BRISK-FL trial, the drug brivanib found to be not suitable in predefining noninferiority boundary for overall survival, even though the overall survival, progression time, response rate toward the objective, and control of minimizing the disease rate are similar in brivanib plus sorafenib and single therapy of sorafenib [27]. Ultimately, the drug brivanib, the same as sorafenib, was tested in a double-blind randomized, placebo-controlled trial [28] as an accessary treatment after the TACE in association with the placebo, and the results showed that brivanib did not improve overall survival rate in HCC patients. A placebo-controlled randomized, double-blind trial conducted in HCC patients with sorafenib plus brivanib and brivanib [29], and the results obtained revealed that brivanib significantly delayed progression time and no effect on overall survival.

Linifanib

Linifanib is an ATP-competitive inhibitor targeting PDGFR and VEGFR. This drug showed substantial action against cytosolic tyrosine/serine/threonine kinases. In LIGHT trial (phase III) [30] linifanib showed as the first-line treatment as compared to sorafenib. This drug showed overall survival similar to sorafenib.

Erlotinib

Erlotinib is a potent selective and orally available reversible inhibitor of EGFR/HER1 tyrosine kinase. The tyrosine kinase inhibition avoids the HER1/EGFR phosphorylation, and prevents associated downstream signaling incidents, further stopping the process of tumorigenesis facilitated by the inappropriate HER1/EGFR signaling. In phase III SEARCH trial [31], the results in both groups of HCC with sorafenib plus erlotinib versus sorafenib plus placebo demonstrated similar results of survival and progression.

Vandetanib

Vandetanib is a small molecule used for prevention of solid tumors. It is involved in the cancer signaling pathways by inhibiting VEGFR-dependent tumor angiogenesis along with tumor cell proliferation and survival. A randomized phase II trial conducted [32] with vandetanib and evaluated the tumor stabilization rate in unresectable HCC patients and results revealed vandetanib did not enhance tumor stabilization, even though improved survival rate.

Nintedanib

Nintedanib is an angiokinase inhibitor, which prevents the pro-angiogenic receptor tyrosine kinases including PDGFR, FGFR, and VEGFR1/2/3. This drug shows lower activity against RET, Flt-3, and Src. For the treatment of HCC, nintedanib is being used for safety and efficacy in HCC prevention [33].

Dovitinib

The small-molecule dovitinib acts as an inhibitor of multiple RTK, including FGFR, c-KIT, VEGFR, and FMS-like tyrosine kinase 3. The dovitinib showed a potential tumor growth inhibition in animal models. A trial of dovitinib versus sorafenib in phase II was performed for safety and efficacy of dovitinib with sorafenib as a first-line treatment in adult patients with advanced HCC. Further it revealed no significant benefit compared to sorafenib observed either in the survival or progression [34,35].

Doxorubicin

Doxorubicin is a commonly used drug showing intercalation with DNA, and inhibits topoisomerase II activity, and is further involved in the generation of ROS, inducing apoptosis [36]. Doxorubicin is primarily connected with the expression of ABC transporters such as ABCB1 or ABCC1 [37]. In a randomized phase II trial with sorafenib plus doxorubicin versus doxorubicin alone in HCC patients and Child-Pugh class A, the results revealed that the sorafenib plus doxorubicin treatment showed greater progression and survival, as compared to doxorubicin [38].

Along with the first-line chemotherapeutic agents (sorafenib and its combination with all above first-line therapeutic agents), the HCC is treated with second-line chemotherapeutic agents as discussed in the following. The drug agents, such as brivanib, everolimus, axitinib, tigatuzumab, etc., versus placebo were performed in patients with advanced HCC intolerance to sorafenib.

Everolimus

Everolimus performs as an inhibitor against mTOR pathway. A randomized, double-blind, phase III study conducted in patients with Child-Pugh A and stage B or C of HCC, who are intolerant of sorafenib [39]. The results revealed no considerable disparities in overall survival among both the treatment groups. Moreover, median time to progression was nearly identical in both the everolimus and placebo.

Axitinib

Axitinib is a potential inhibitor of VEGFR and is approved for advanced renal cell carcinoma as a second-line therapeutic drug; moreover it has shown nonclinical activity in animal models of HCC and provided evidence for its therapeutic potential. In a study evaluated for efficiency and safety of axitinib in a randomized placebo-controlled phase II trial [40], the results showed safety of axitinib in combination and it was observed that there was no improvement in survival in HCC patients.

Tigatuzumab

Tigatuzumab, a humanized monoclonal antibody, acts as a Dr5 agonist and participates in TNF-associated apoptosis. In a phase II randomized trial conducted with tigatuzumab plus sorafenib versus sorafenib alone in HCC patients [41], it was observed that the median time to progression was identical in tigatuzumab plus sorafenib versus sorafenib alone group. Combination of tigatuzumab and sorafenib did not have effect on progression and survival as compared to sorafenib monotherapy.

Presently, the following new novel drug agents are used in first-line setting (lenvatinib and resminostat) and in second-line setting (regorafenib and cabozantinib) for the HCC treatment. A few more drugs like tivantinib and ramucirumab also have been involved in establishing superior efficiency in the biomarker-enriched population as compared to whole population.

Lenvatinib

Lenvatinib is a tyrosine kinase inhibitor of FGFR1−4, VEGFR1−3, PDFGRα, KIT, and RET. It is approved for the treatment of thyroid cancer. Lenvatinib dose-dependently stifles the tumor growth, blood vessels, and micro vessel density and increases the rate of necrosis with no observation of apoptosis. Lenvatinib could ruin the formation of tumors by preventing angiogenesis, and cause antiproliferative effect in some liver cancer cells.

Resminostat

Resminostat is a novel histone deacetylase (HDAC) inhibitor involving in the inhibition of classes I, IIb, and IV of HDACs. It also inhibits the phosphorylation of 4E-BP1 and p70S6k, and affects Akt signaling pathway. During the phase I study in patients with advanced solid tumors the recommended dose and safety of resminostat were evaluated and confirmed in a group of Japanese patients [42]. Use of sorafenib in association with resminostat shows more overall survival than that of single-use resminostat.

Regorafenib

Regorafenib is a multikinase inhibitor targeting angiogenesis kinases VEGFR1—3, c-KIT or Ret, and TME with PDGFR or FGFR, and oncogenesis. Regorafenib was accepted for treatment of patients having colorectal cancer and advanced gastrointestinal stromal tumors.

Cabozantinib

Cabozantinib is a small-molecule multikinase inhibitor that targets receptor tyrosine kinases including c-Mesenchymal—epithelial transition factor (MET), AXL, VEGFR2, and c-KIT. c-MET plays a role in HCC development. Overexpression of this protein is observed in 20%—48% in HCC samples. In that cabozantinib promotes cell survival, HCC proliferation, invasiveness, and angiogenesis along with the resistance toward chemotherapy and radiotherapy. Cabozantinib targets receptor tyrosine kinases including c-MET and plays a major role in the treatment of progressed HCC [43].

Ramucirumab

Ramucirumab is a human IgG1 monoclonal antibody that blocks VEGFR2 interaction and further inhibits endothelial cell proliferation and migration. The ramucirumab binds to VEGFR2 with the highest affinity. Ramucirumab treatment significantly improves the overall survival rate as compared to the placebo studies.

Tivantinib

Tivantinib is a non-ATP-competitive inhibitor of c-MET, and acts as an antimitotic agent. This drug favorably inhibits cell growth, and induces apoptosis in human tumor cell lines expressing MET. Besides its role in tumor growth, c-MET is also linked with metastasis [44]. In placebo studies, tivantinib is treated in single agent prolonged progression in patients suffering from advanced HCC [45].

In summary, it is identified that the sorafenib is the best and standard first-line chemotherapeutic agent for HCC. It is actively involved in delaying progression time and prolonging the survival time. Even though other novel drugs were discovered after sorafenib, none of the drugs exhibited an effective survival rate in HCC as compared to sorafenib with first-line or second-line placebo setting with novel drugs single or in combination.

Immunotherapeutic agents

Tumor immunotherapy is an encouraging, upcoming strategy in medication that may have an advantage in the improvement of treatment-associated outcomes. Recently, several immunotherapeutic agents have been developed, some of the immune checkpoint inhibitors are PD-1, PDL-1, and CTLA4, and B-7 [46]. These agents have offered a promising outcome and proven efficacy in HCC patients.

Tremelimumab

Tremelimumab is a fully humanized IgG2 monoclonal antibody developed against CTLA4. This CTLA4 is an extracellular receptor with CD28 homolog expressed in T cells. CTLA4 inhibitors enable immune-mediated antitumor response, leading to direct activation and expansion of effector T cells to target cancer antigens [47]. CTLA4 is an immune checkpoint receptor expressed in Tregs cells and naïve T cells. Tremelimumab suppresses the CTLA4 expression, and enhances T-cell activation and cell proliferation.

Nivolumab

It is a human IgG4 PD-1 immune-checkpoint-inhibitor that interacts with PD-1 and PD-L1/PD-L2 and is involved in the process of remaking of the T-cell antitumor immunity and finally targets tumor cells [48].

Immunotherapeutic agents are potentially useful agents in the HCC systemic treatment after sorafenib. Clinical trials of various anticancer agents like tremelimumab plus PD-L1 antibody, nivolumab plus TGF-β inhibitor, MEDI4736, and galunisertib are being planned, and positive results are expected in the future.

Conclusion

Even today, the treatment concerning to HCC has become a major surgical and medical challenge. Further it has become truer with respect to advanced HCC, which can be treated with systemic therapy. Nowadays sorafenib is an excellent systemic treatment drug for HCC treatment, though it contains a few unsolved issues. In recent years molecular therapeutics plays a vital role and significant part in the prevention of HCC. In connection, numerous drugs are in progress and under further evaluation; moreover, a well-known drug under the category is regorafenib, which exhibits substantial positive outcomes and is considered a future drug for HCC. It is also noticed the increase in cancer weaknesses with available drugs. Currently, the cytotoxic drugs and immunotherapeutic drugs are doing promising contest to sorafenib, and acting in different directions for prevention of HCC. The potential accessibility of different possibilities with superior mechanisms certainly creates much positive hope in advanced HCC treatment particularly through personalized therapy.

Conflict of interest

None

References

[1] Bray F, Laversanne M, Weiderpass E, Soerjomataram I. The ever-increasing importance of cancer as a leading cause of premature death worldwide. Cancer. 2021;127(16):3029−30.

[2] World Health Organization. Projections of mortality and causes of death, 2016 to 2060. Geneva: World Health Organization, Switzerland, 2020.

[3] Sung H, Ferlay J, Siegel RL, Laversanne M, Soerjomataram I, Jemal A, et al. Global cancer statistics 2020: GLOBOCAN estimates of incidence and mortality worldwide for 36 cancers in 185 countries. CA Cancer J Clin 2021;71(3):209−49. Available from: https://doi.org/10.3322/caac.21660.

[4] Villanueva A. Hepatocellular carcinoma. N Engl J Med 2019;380:1450−62.

[5] Thorgeirsson SS, Grisham JW. Molecular pathogenesis of human hepatocellular carcinoma. Nat Genet 2002;31:339−46.

[6] van Meer S, van Erpecum KJ, Sprengers D, Coenraad MJ, Klümpen HJ, Jansen PL, et al. Hepatocellular carcinoma in cirrhotic vs noncirrhotic livers: results from a large cohort in the Netherlands. Eur J Gastroenterol Hepatol 2016;28(3):352−9.

[7] Llovet JM, Kelley RK, Villanueva A, Singal AG, Pikarsky E, Roayaie S, et al. Hepatocellular carcinoma. Nat Rev Dis Primers 2021;7(1):6.

[8] El-Serag HB, Rudolph KL. Hepatocellular carcinoma: epidemiology and molecular carcinogenesis. Gastroenterology 2007;132:2557−76.

[9] Hoshida Y, Fuchs BC, Bardeesy N, Baumert TF, Chung RT. Pathogenesis and prevention of hepatitis C virus-induced hepatocellular carcinoma. J Hepatol 2014;61(1 Suppl):S79−90.

[10] Hutchinson SJ, Bird SM, Goldberg DJ. Influence of alcohol on the progression of hepatitis C virus infection: a meta-analysis. Clin Gastroenterol Hepatol 2005;3:1150−9.

[11] Lin CW, Lin CC, Mo LR, Chang CY, Perng DS, Hsu CC, et al. Heavy alcohol consumption increases the incidence of hepatocellular carcinoma in hepatitis B virus-related cirrhosis. J Hepatol 2013;58(4):730−5.

[12] Bravi F, Bosetti C, Tavani A, Gallus S, La Vecchia C. Coffee reduces risk for hepatocellular carcinoma: an updated meta-analysis. Clin Gastroenterol Hepatol 2013;11(11):1413−21.

[13] Ohkuma T, Peters SAE, Woodward M. Sex differences in the association between diabetes and cancer: a systematic review and meta-analysis of 121 cohorts including 20 million individuals and one million events. Diabetologia 2018;61:2140−54.

[14] Sutti S, Albano E. Adaptive immunity: an emerging player in the progression of NAFLD. Nat Rev Gastroenterol Hepatol 2020;17:81−92.

[15] Pietrangelo A. Iron in NASH, chronic liver diseases and HCC: how much iron is too much? J Hepatol 2009;50:249−51.

[16] Liu Y, Chang CC, Marsh GM, Wu F. Population attributable risk of aflatoxin-related liver cancer: systematic review and meta-analysis. Eur J Cancer 2012;48(14):2125−36.

[17] McGlynn KA, Petrick JL, El-Serag HB. Epidemiology of hepatocellular carcinoma. Hepatology 2021;73:4−13.

[18] Nishida N, Kudo M. Oncogenic signal and tumor microenvironment in hepatocellular carcinoma. Oncology 2017;93(1):160−4.

[19] Sanyal A, Poklepovic A, Moyneur E, Barghout V. Population-based risk factors and resource utilization for HCC: US perspective. Curr Med Res Opin 2010;26(9):2183−91.

[20] Belghiti J, Fuks D. Liver resection and transplantation in hepatocellular carcinoma. Liver Cancer 2012;1:71−82.

[21] Schwartz M, Roayaie S, Konstadoulakis M. Strategies for the management of hepatocellular carcinoma. Nat Clin Pract Oncol 2007;4:424−32.

[22] Yeo W, Mok TS, Zee B, Leung TW, Lai PB, Lau WY, et al. A randomized phase III study of doxorubicin vs cisplatin/interferon alpha-2b/doxorubicin/fluorouracil (PIAF) combination chemotherapy for unresectable hepatocellular carcinoma. J Natl Cancer Inst 2005;97(20):1532−8.

[23] Wilhelm SM, Adnane L, Newell P, Villanueva A, Llovet JM, Lynch M. Preclinical overview of sorafenib, a multikinase inhibitor that targets both Raf and VEGF and PDGF receptor tyrosine kinase signaling. Mol Cancer Ther 2008;7(10):3129–40.

[24] Bruix J, Takayama T, Mazzaferro V, Chau GY, Yang J, Kudo M, et al. STORM investigators. Adjuvant sorafenib for hepatocellular carcinoma after resection or ablation (STORM): a phase 3, randomised, double-blind, placebo-controlled trial. Lancet Oncol 2015;16(13):1344–54.

[25] Kim JW, Lee JO, Han SW, Oh DY, Im SA, Kim TY, et al. Clinical outcomes of sorafenib treatment in patients with metastatic hepatocellular carcinoma who had been previously treated with fluoropyrimidine plus platinum-based chemotherapy. Am J Clin Oncol 2011;34(2):125–9.

[26] Cheng AL, Kang YK, Lin DY, Park JW, Kudo M, Qin S, et al. Sunitinib vs sorafenib in advanced hepatocellular cancer: results of a randomized phase III trial. J Clin Oncol 2013;31(32):4067–75.

[27] Johnson PJ, Qin S, Park JW, Poon RT, Raoul JL, Philip PA, et al. Brivanib vs sorafenib as first-line therapy in patients with unresectable, advanced hepatocellular carcinoma: results from the randomized phase III BRISK-FL study. J Clin Oncol 2013;31(28):3517–24.

[28] Kudo M, Han G, Finn RS, Poon RT, Blanc JF, Yan L, et al. Brivanib as adjuvant therapy to transarterial chemoembolization in patients with hepatocellular carcinoma: a randomized phase III trial. Hepatology. 2014;60(5):1697–707.

[29] Llovet JM, Decaens T, Raoul JL, Boucher E, Kudo M, Chang C, et al. Brivanib in patients with advanced hepatocellular carcinoma who were intolerant to sorafenib or for whom sorafenib failed: results from the randomized phase III BRISK-PS study. J Clin Oncol 2013;31(28):3509–16.

[30] Cainap C, Qin S, Huang WT, Chung IJ, Pan H, Cheng Y, et al. Linifanib vs Sorafenib in patients with advanced hepatocellular carcinoma: results of a randomized phase III trial. J Clin Oncol 2015;33(2):172–9.

[31] Zhu AX, Rosmorduc O, Evans TR, Ross PJ, Santoro A, Carrilho FJ, et al. SEARCH: a phase III, randomized, double-blind, placebo-controlled trial of sorafenib plus erlotinib in patients with advanced hepatocellular carcinoma. J Clin Oncol 2015;33(6):559–66.

[32] Hsu C, Yang TS, Huo TI, Hsieh RK, Yu CW, Hwang WS, et al. Vandetanib in patients with inoperable hepatocellular carcinoma: a phase II, randomized, double-blind, placebo-controlled study. J Hepatol 2012;56(5):1097–103.

[33] Hilberg F, Roth GJ, Krssak M, Kautschitsch S, Sommergruber W, Tontsch-Grunt U, et al. BIBF 1120: triple angiokinase inhibitor with sustained receptor blockade and good antitumor efficacy. Cancer Res 2008;68(12):4774–82.

[34] Dey JH, Bianchi F, Voshol J, Bonenfant D, Oakeley EJ, Hynes NE. Targeting fibroblast growth factor receptors blocks PI3K/AKT signaling, induces apoptosis, and impairs mammary tumor outgrowth and metastasis. Cancer Res 2010;70(10):4151–62.

[35] Cheng Ann-Lii, Thongprasert Sumitra, Lim Ho Yeong, Sukeepaisarnjaroen Wattana, Yang Tsai-Sheng, Wu Cheng-Chung, et al. Phase II study of front-line dovitinib (TKI258) vs sorafenib in patients (Pts) with advanced hepatocellular carcinoma (HCC). J Clin Oncol 2015;33(Suppl):S3.

[36] Tacar O, Sriamornsak P, Dass CR. Doxorubicin: an update on anticancer molecular action, toxicity and novel drug delivery systems. J Pharm Pharmacol 2013;65:157–70.

[37] Li G, Chen X, Wang Q, Xu Z, Zhang W, Ye L. The roles of four multi-drug resistance proteins in hepatocellular carcinoma multidrug resistance. J Huazhong Univ Sci Technol Med Sci 2007;27(2):173–5.

[38] Abou-Alfa GK, Johnson P, Knox JJ, Capanu M, Davidenko I, Lacava J, et al. Doxorubicin plus sorafenib vs doxorubicin alone in patients with advanced hepatocellular carcinoma: a randomized trial. JAMA. 2010;304(19):2154–60.

[39] Zhu AX, Kudo M, Assenat E, Cattan S, Kang YK, Lim HY, et al. Effect of everolimus on survival in advanced hepatocellular carcinoma after failure of sorafenib: the EVOLVE-1 randomized clinical trial. JAMA. 2014;312(1):57–67.

[40] Kang YK, Yau T, Park JW, Lim HY, Lee TY, Obi S, et al. Randomized phase II study of axitinib vs placebo plus best supportive care in second-line treatment of advanced hepatocellular carcinoma. Ann Oncol 2015;26(12):2457–63.

[41] Cheng AL, Kang YK, He AR, Lim HY, Ryoo BY, Hung CH, et al. Investigators' Study Group. Safety and efficacy of tigatuzumab plus sorafenib as first-line therapy in subjects with advanced hepatocellular carcinoma: a phase 2 randomized study. J Hepatol 2015;63(4):896–904.

[42] Kitazono S, Fujiwara Y, Nakamichi S, Mizugaki H, Nokihara H, Yamamoto N, et al. A phase I study of resminostat in Japanese patients with advanced solid tumors. Cancer Chemother Pharmacol 2015;75(6):1155—61.

[43] herardi E, Birchmeier W, Birchmeier C, Vande Woude G. Targeting MET in cancer: rationale and progress. Nat Rev Cancer 2012;12(2):89—103. Available from: https://doi.org/10.1038/nrc3205 Erratum in: Nat Rev Cancer. 2012 Sep;12(9):637.

[44] Engelman JA, Zejnullahu K, Mitsudomi T, Song Y, Hyland C, Park JO, et al. MET amplification leads to gefitinib resistance in lung cancer by activating ERBB3 signaling. Science. 2007;316(5827):1039—43.

[45] Santoro A, Rimassa L, Borbath I, Daniele B, Salvagni S, Van Laethem JL, et al. Tivantinib for second-line treatment of advanced hepatocellular carcinoma: a randomised, placebo-controlled phase 2 study. Lancet Oncol 2013;14(1):55—63.

[46] El Dika I, Khalil DN, Abou-Alfa GK. Immune checkpoint inhibitors for hepatocellular carcinoma. Cancer 2019;125:3312—19.

[47] Chambers CA, Kuhns MS, Egen JG, Allison JP. CTLA-4-mediated inhibition in regulation of T cell responses: mechanisms and manipulation in tumor immunotherapy. Annu Rev Immunol 2001;19:565—94.

[48] Larkin J, Chiarion-Sileni V, Gonzalez R, Grob JJ, Cowey CL, Lao CD, et al. Combined nivolumab and ipilimumab or monotherapy in untreated melanoma. N Engl J Med 2015;373(1):23—34.

Recent advances in medical treatment of hepatocellular cancer

Ahmet Sümbül Taner and Ali Ayberk Beşen

Başkent Üniversitesi Tıp Fakültesi Tıbbi Onkoloji BD, Adana, Turkey

Abstract

Hepatocellular carcinoma (HCC) is a malignant tumor that typically develops in patients with chronic liver disease and cirrhosis. Advanced HCC patients have a dismal prognosis. The therapeutic paradigm for HCC has changed dramatically during the last two decades. In 2007 the SHARP study demonstrated sorafenib had a survival advantage over placebo. Phase III results of the REFLECT trial demonstrated that the efficacy of lenvatinib was comparable to sorafenib in terms of overall survivability in the first-line setting. Three agents (viz., regorafenib, cabozantinib, and ramucirumab) revealed improved survival over placebo in patients who progressed on sorafenib and were approved as a second-line option for patients with advanced HCC. Recently, the immune checkpoint inhibitors nivolumab and pembrolizumab have also emerged as second-line option for HCC after sorafenib with a distinct toxicity profile. According to the results of the IMbrave 150 trial, the atezolizumab and bevacizumab combination was found to be superior to sorafenib as a first-line treatment for advanced HCC, and this combination is suggested by consensus guidelines. In view of the above, this chapter summarizes the recent advances in newer medical treatment of HCC focusing on patents quality-of-life with clinical outcomes.

Keywords: Hepatocellular carcinoma; medical treatment; systemic treatment; clinical trials; clinical outcomes; outcome measures; quality-of-life

Abbreviations

AE	Adverse event
AFP	α-Fetoprotein
ALT	Alanine aminotransferase
AST	Aspartate transaminase
CD	Cluster differentiation
CI	Confidence interval
CTLA	Cytotoxic T-lymphocyte-associated protein
DCR	Disease control rate
ECOG-PS	Eastern Cooperative Oncology Group—Performance Status

Ganji Purnachandra Nagaraju, Sarfraz Ahmad (eds.)
Theranostics and Precision Medicine for the Management of Hepatocellular Carcinoma, Volume 3

365

EGD	Esophagogastroduodenoscopy
EGF	Epidermal growth factor
EMA	The European Medicines Agency
FDA	Food and Drug Administration (United States)
FGFR	Fibroblast growth factor receptors
FLT 3	fms-like tyrosine kinase 3
HBV	Hepatitis B virus
HCC	Hepatocellular carcinoma
HCV	Hepatitis C virus
HR	Hazard ratio
HFSR	Hand-foot skin reaction
ICIs	Immune checkpoint inhibitors
mRECIST	Modified response evaluation criteria in solid tumors
N/A	Not applicable (or not available)
ORR	Objective response rate
OR	Odds ratio
OS	Overall survival
PD-1	Programmed cell death protein 1
PD-L1	Programmed death-ligand 1
PDGFR	Platelet-derived growth factor receptor
PFS	Progression-free survival
RECIST	Response evaluation criteria in solid tumors
SD	Stable disease
TACE	Transarterial chemoembolization
TIE	Tyrosine kinase with immunoglobulin-like and EGF-like domains
TKI	Tyrosine kinase inhibitors
TTP	Time to progression
VEGF	Vascular endothelial growth factor

Introduction

Hepatocellular carcinoma (HCC) accounts for a majority of nonmetastatic tumors occurring in the liver and is the fourth most common cause of cancer-associated deaths [1,2]. HCC occurrence is often associated with various risk factors, such as chronic infections with hepatitis B virus (HBV) or hepatitis C virus (HCV), metabolic syndrome, and alcohol abuse. The projected 5-year survival rate for HCC patients is nearly 18% [3,4]. Current treatment methods for HCC patients are surgery, liver transplantation, ablative therapies, transarterial chemoembolization (TACE), hepatic arterial infusion chemotherapy, novel drugs, and their combinations [3–6].

In systemic treatments, all treatment pathways target vascular endothelial growth factor (VEGF) [7]. In 2007 sorafenib, one of the first multikinase inhibitors, showed a survival advantage over placebo in the SHARP study. Later, there was no significant improvement in studies conducted with many agents until the last 5 years. In the advances since 2017, four drugs had positive results, of which lenvatinib was approved in first-line, and regorafenib, ramucirumab, and cabozantinib were approved in the second-line treatment approaches [8–11]. Immunotherapies, one of the popular treatment modalities during the last 10 years have not shown effective results on their own, but with VEGF-based combination therapies, it has taken a place among the new treatment options in the first step, thus providing the survival advantage expected for many years in the first step [12]. Below we summarize some of the most relevant and advanced medical treatments for HCC.

Lenvatinib

After a 10-year failure period in newer treatment options of HCC, the phase III REFLECT study, it is the second agent to show efficacy in the first line. Lenvatinib inhibits tumor angiogenesis and malignant transformation by blocking VEGFR1−2−3, FGFR1−2−3−4, PDGFR-alfa, KIT, and RET receptors. In a single-arm phase II study, lenvatinib provided an outcome of 7.4 months in time to progression (TTP) and 18.7 months in overall survival (OS) [13].

The REFLECT is designed as a noninferiority study. Patients were randomized 1:1 to lenvatinib versus sorafenib. Patients diagnosed with hepatitis C-associated HCC were more in the sorafenib group (27% vs 19%), whereas patients with hepatitis B-associated HCC were more in the lenvatinib group (53% vs 48%). The lenvatinib patient group with α-fetoprotein (AFP) levels > 200 ng/mL was higher (46% vs 39%). The primary endpoint of the study was OS was found to be 13.6 months in the lenvatinib group and 12.3 months in the sorafenib group [8]. The other endpoints of the study were found to be better in the lenvatinib arm presented as: progression-free survival (PFS) (7.4 vs 3.7 months), TTP (8.9 vs 3.7 months), and objective response rate (ORR) (24.1% vs 9.2%) [odds ratio (OR) = 3.13; 95% CI, 2.15−4.56, $P < .0001$]. Since the objective response per mRECIST criteria predicts better survivability, lenvatinib proved to be more effective with patients diagnosed with advanced HCC [8]. As illustrated by the ORR per independent imaging review using mRECIST criteria, tumor shrinkage/necrotic effects were notably better in the levantinib arm (40.6% vs 12.4%) (OR = 5.01; 95% CI: 3.59−7.01; $P < .0001$) [13−15].

In the REFLECT study, patients were not stratified according to their AFP level [8]. The number of patients with AFP >200 ng/mL was higher in the lenvatinib arm. In regard to the OS, lenvatinib was statistically superior to sorafenib (HR = 0.856; 95% CI: 0.736−0.995; $P = .0342$) [8]. Thus if patients were stratified by the AFP level assessments, this trial could have demonstrated superiority as well [16].

Patients, when treated with lenvatinib, with high baseline AFP values (≥200 ng/mL) a poor prognostic marker, yielded a longer OS as illustrated by an HR of 0.78 (95% CI: 0.63−0.98). The treatment duration was found to be longer in the lenvatinib arm (5.7 months) than the sorafenib arm (3.7 months). Lenvatinib and sorafenib showed different safety profiles in terms of adverse events. Hand-foot skin reactions (HFSRs) and diarrhea were seen lower in lenvatinib arm. However, systemic therapy effects which are rarely seen in patients with tumor occupancy ≥50%, main portal vein invasion, and biliary tract invasion, were not included in this study. In the REFLECT study, it is demonstrated that lenvatinib is not inferior to sorafenib regarding the endpoints such as OS, PFS, TTP, and ORR. Based on these results, lenvatinib was approved by the US Food and Drug Administration (FDA) as a reliable option of many first-line drugs for unresectable HCC.

Regorafenib

Regorafenib is another multikinase inhibitor, affecting *VEGFR1−2−3*, tyrosine kinase with immunoglobulin-like and EGF-like domains 2 (*TIE2*), *PDGFRβ*, FGFR, *KIT, RET, RAF-1*, and *BRAF* [17] receptors. It is separated from sorafenib with a fluorine bond in the structure. In the

RESORCE study [10], it was used against placebo in second-line therapy for patients who progressed under sorafenib. The primary endpoint of this study was OS, and the regorafenib arm was found to be significantly better compared to the placebo (10.6 vs 7.8 months, respectively) (HR = 0.63; 95% CI: 0.50−0.79; $P < .0001$) [9]. The PFS and TTP were also significantly better.

In 2017 regorafenib was indicated for use in cases that progressed after sorafenib. During the design of the RESORCE study, patients who progressed due to side effects or intolerance of sorafenib and patients who did not use an effective dose of sorafenib were excluded from the study. A balanced distribution was achieved between the study and placebo arms in terms of poor risk factors and prognostic factors such as AFP. Based on the findings of RESORCE trial, the median OS on regorafenib was found to be 10.6 months (placebo: 7.8 months; HR = 0.63; $P < .0001$). In addition, in this study, it was observed that survival was better in the patient group who started sorafenib early after an ineffective TACE and switched to regorafenib in progression. In this study, although the relatively long duration of sorafenib use in the first step (7.8 months) raised a question mark in terms of efficacy in rapidly progressing patients, it was demonstrated in the following reports that similar efficacy was observed in patients with early progress [18]. Furthermore, in the subgroup analyses, regorafenib sequential therapy after sorafenib was observed to achieve survival at a similar degree to survival after TACE in mid-stage HCC with a survival period of 26 months from the start of sorafenib treatment compared to the 19.2 months survival period for the placebo group [18,19].

After the results of this study, regorafenib was approved by the US FDA and the European Medicines Agency (EMA) as second-line treatment after sorafenib failure in patients with advanced HCC. Due to exclusion of specific patient groups such as patients with significant comorbidities Child-Pugh B, cirrhosis, or sorafenib users from the RESORCE trial, we do not recommend moving forward with the utilization of rgorafenib in these patients [17,20].

Cabozantinib

Cabozantinib is a novel oral multikinase inhibitor targeting VEGF, c-MET, RET, TIE2, FLT3, and the TAM family of receptor kinases (TYRO-3, AXL, and MER). The CELESTIAL trial was designed to test cabozantinib as a second-line drug in patients who progressed or intolerant under sorafenib treatment and it prolonged survival (compared with placebo) [10,21]. The trial was a placebo controlled and a total of 707 patients with unresectable HCC were included in a 2:1 ratio. Primary endpoint of the CELESTIAL trial was PFS, and it was found as 5.2 versus 1.9 months for cabozantinib versus placebo arm, respectively (HR = 0.44; 95% CI: 0.36−0.52; $P < .001$). Also, the other endpoint median OS was significantly longer in the cabozantinib arm than in the placebo arm, respectively ($n = 470$; 10.2 months; 95% CI: 9.1−12.0) versus (8.0 months; 95% CI: 6.8−9.4) (HR = 0.76; 95% CI: 0.63−0.92; $P < .001$) [11]. The ORR was found to be 4% in the cabozantinib arm and <1% in the placebo arm ($P = .009$) [11]. In the subgroup of patients whose previous systemic therapy was only sorafenib ($n = 486$, 69%), the median OS was found to be as 11.3 months for cabozantinib arm and 7.2 months for placebo arm (HR = 0.70; 95% CI: 0.55−0.88), and the median PFS was found to be as 5.5 months for cabozantinib arm and 1.9 months for placebo arm (HR = 0.40; 95% CI: 0.32−0.50).

When we consider the safety for cabozantinib, grade 3 or 4 AEs occurred in 68% of patients using the study drug arm and in 36% of the placebo arm. The most common seen high-grade AEs were similar with other areas such as hand-foot skin syndrome (17% vs 0%), hypertension (16% vs 2%), increased aspartate transaminase (AST) level (12% vs 7%), fatigue (10% vs 4%), and diarrhea (10% vs 2%), respectively.

Representing of elderly patients in HCC trials is a real debate and in the subgroup analysis of the CELESTIAL trial [10,22], outcomes of PFS and OS were found to be better in the cabozantinib arm than that in the placebo arm [PFS in elderly patients ($\geq$65 years) 5.4 vs 2.0 months; HR = 0.46; 95% CI: 0.35−0.59, in nonelderly patients (< 65 years) (5.0 vs 1.9 months; HR = 0.45; 95% CI: 0.35−0.57), OS ($\geq$65 years) (11.1 vs 8.3 months; HR = 0.74; 95% CI: 0.56−0.97)] [22,23]. In addition, cabozantib showed main class adverse effects of tyrosine kinase inhibitors (TKIs) and the main grade 3/4 AEs were HFSR (17%) and hypertension (16%).

Ramucirumab

As a known antitumor effect of anti-VEGFs, ramucirumab is another recombinant human immunoglobulin G1 monoclonal antibody of this drug class, primarily targeting VEGFR-2. By this it prevents binding to VEGF-A, VEGF-C, and VEGF-D and results as a cascade inhibition of tumor angiogenesis, endothelial proliferation, migration, and survival.

From this standpoint, the REACH trial was designed and ramucurumab was given to sorafenib refractory or intolerant HCC patients as second-line setting; the results were disappointing for primary endpoints [24]. However, subanalysis of the REACH trial revealed that survival is improved if patients are stratified by AFP values, which is a strong poor prognostic factor. AFP levels $\geq$ 400 ng/mL group has statistically significant and better outcomes than the placebo group [25]. After this finding, investigators planned a new study to investigate this situation. The REACH-2 trial design was similar as the original REACH trial but only patients with AFP levels $\geq$ 400 ng/mL were recruited to the trial and stratified by gross vascular invasion. Results of this study were positive, median OS, which primary endpoint of this study, in the ramucirumab arm was longer than that in the placebo arm (8.5 vs 7.3 months, respectively; HR = 0.710; P = .0199) [11,23]. After these encouraging results, ramucirumab was approved by the FDA in sorafenib refractory or intolerant HCC patients whom AFP levels $\geq$ 400 ng/mL.

In the REACH trials, it was showed that tolerability of ramucurumab is better than TKIs and a 98% dose intensity is achieved [8,9,11,26−28]. Also, the investigators pooled the REACH (baseline AFP $\geq$ 400 ng/mL) and REACH-2 trials to investigate the effect of drug in subgroups. The authors showed that ramucirumab prolonged the OS over placebo in all patients' groups (<65 years, $\geq$65 to <75 years, and $\geq$75 years) [28]. Furthermore, the PFS and TTP advantages were observed in all the age groups [29]. Notably, the safety profile of the drug was similar in all the three groups.

Bevacizumab plus atezolizumab

The efficacy of atezolizumab (anti-PD-L1 monoclonal antibody) plus bevacizumab [a vascular endothelial growth factor (VEGF) inhibitor] was firstly questioned in phase Ib trial

(GO30140) in unresectable HCC. This phase Ib analysis on patients with advanced HCC who had not undergone prior systemic therapy found that the combination of atezolizumab and bevacizumab was efficacious and had a tolerable safety profile. The patients who received atezolizumab plus bevacizumab had a 36% and 71% OR and DCR, respectively [30].

The promising antitumor activity and safety of VEGF and ICI (immune checkpoint inhibitor) combination proceed this therapy to a phase III trial. IMbrave 150 is a phase III, prospective multicenter trial that assessed the safety profile and effectiveness of atezolizumab with bevacizumab versus sorafenib in patients with advanced-stage HCC who had not previously received systemic therapy. In the IMbrave 150 trial, 501 patients with unresectable HCC who had Child-Pugh A chronic liver disease were randomly assigned to receive either atezolizumab plus bevacizumab (336 patients) or sorafenib (165 patients). The study's primary objectives were the OS and PFS, while the ORR, the duration of response, and quality-of-life measures were secondary endpoints. The estimated survival rate of 12 months was 67.2% (95% CI, 61.3–73.1) in the atezolizumab plus bevacizumab group and 54.6% (95% CI, 45.2–64.0) in the sorafenib group, and was considerably longer in combination. As compared to sorafenib, the PFS was significantly prolonged with atezolizumab plus bevacizumab, 6.8 months (95% CI, 5.7 to 8.3) versus 4.3 months (95% CI, 4.0–5.6).

The ORRs were 27.3% (95% CI, 22.5–32.5) and 11.9% (95% CI, 7.4–18.0) with atezolizumab plus bevacizumab and sorafenib, respectively, according to RECIST 1.1 ($P < .001$). The ORRs were higher for both groups according to the HCC-specific mRECIST criteria, 33.2% (95% CI, 28.1–38.6) for atezolizumab plus bevacizumab and 13.3% (95% CI, 8.4–19.6) with sorafenib ($P < .001$). Eighteen patients (5.5%) in the atezolizumab–bevacizumab arm had a complete response, compared to none in the sorafenib treatment arm.

Grade 3 or grade 4 AEs were in similar proportions of participants in each group (57% vs 55%), with the notable exception of hypertension (15.2%), transaminase elevation (7%, AST), and proteinuria (3%), which were more common with atezolizumab plus bevacizumab. Participants in this trial were required to have undergone esophagogastroduodenoscopy (EGD) within 6 months of starting treatment. Upper gastrointestinal hemorrhage was detected at a higher rate in the atezolizumab plus bevacizumab arm (7%) than in the sorafenib arm (4.5%). Regarding the encouraging results of the IMbrave 150 trial, atezolizumab with bevacizumab emerged as the most appropriate first-line treatment option for individuals with advanced HCC [12].

Nivolumab and nivolumab plus ipilimumab

Nivolumab

Nivolumab is a fully human monoclonal antibody that blocs programmed cell death protein-1 (PD-1) immune checkpoint signaling by inhibiting the immune checkpoint interaction between PD-1 and programmed death-ligand 1 (PD-L1) [31]. In patients with unresectable HCC, the safety and efficacy of nivolumab were evaluated in a phase I/II dose escalation and expansion trial. Patients with Child-Pugh A or Child-Pugh B7 were eligible for the dose-escalation cohort (37 individuals), and patients with Child-Pugh A were eligible for the dose-expansion cohort (214 individuals). The primary aim was to establish the safety and tolerability of nivolumab during the dosage escalation phase as well as to evaluate the ORR during the dose-expansion phase (with RECIST criteria version 1.1). In the dose-escalation phase, patients received intravenous nivolumab monotherapy dosing ranged from 0.1 to 10 mg/kg every 2 weeks. This phase included 23 individuals without viral hepatitis, 15 with HBV infection, and 10 with HCV infection.

A dose of 3 mg/kg of nivolumab was chosen for the dose-expansion phase of this trial. Of the 214 individuals with advanced HCC in this phase, 56 cases had no viral hepatitis (HBV or HCV) and had not previously received sorafenib or were intolerant, 57 cases had progressed on sorafenib, 50 cases were infected with HCV, and 51 cases were infected with HBV. The objective response was seen in 20% of the patients (95% CI, 15–26) in the dose-expansion phase of the trial who administered nivolumab 3 mg/kg every 2 weeks. Three of the 42 responses were complete, with the remaining 39 being partial. In the expansion phase of the trial, the median duration of response was 9.9 months, and 74% of patients were still alive at 9 months follow-up.

Adverse events in more than 10% were documented in 10 patients (21%) with an increase in AST, 7 (15%) with an increase in alanine aminotransferase (ALT), 10 (21%) with a rise in lipase, and 9 (19%) in a rise in amylase. In 12 (25%) of 48 patients in the dose-escalation cohort, grade 3 or 4 treatment-related AEs occurred including adrenal insufficiency ($n = 1$), diarrhea ($n = 1$), hepatitis ($n = 2$), infusion hypersensitivity ($n = 1$), and acute kidney injury ($n = 1$). Safety outcomes of the dose-expansion cohort were similar to the safety findings of patients in dose-escalation cohort. These results led the FDA to extend the indications for nivolumab, at a dose of 240 mg every 2 weeks, to cover the management of patients with HCC who previously received sorafenib [29].

Nivolumab plus ipilimumab

Ipilimumab is a recombinant human IgG1 monoclonal antibody that specifically targets cytotoxic T-lymphocyte-associated antigen 4 (CTLA-4). CTLA-4 downregulates T-cell activation pathways. Blocking CTLA-4 promotes T-cell activation and proliferation. Clinical trial results show that the combination of nivolumab and ipilimumab is effective in treating different tumor types such as advanced renal cell carcinoma, malignant melanoma, and nonsmall cell lung cancer [32–34]. In an open-label, phase I/II randomized clinical trial, CheckMate 040, evaluated the therapeutic outcomes of combining ipilimumab and nivolumab in subjects with advanced-stage HCC who had previously been treated with sorafenib. In total, 144 of 148 patients (98%) received prior sorafenib therapy, with 86% discontinuing sorafenib because of progressive disease and 14% for toxicity.

In this study, 148 patients were assigned randomly to one of three arms. Nivolumab 1 mg/kg in combination with ipilimumab 3 mg/kg was administered every 3 weeks for four doses, followed by nivolumab 240 mg every 2 weeks in arm A. The arm B got nivolumab 3 mg/kg in combination with ipilimumab 1 mg/kg every 3 weeks for four doses, followed by nivolumab 240 mg every 2 weeks, whereas the arm C received nivolumab 3 mg/kg in combination with ipilimumab 1 mg/kg every 6 weeks. The primary objective of the study was to evaluate ORR, duration of response, and the safety and tolerability of combined therapy. The ORRs in arms A, B, and C were 32%, 27%, and 29%, respectively, while the median duration of response was not reached, 15.2 months, and 21.7 months, respectively. Of the 16 objective responses (32%) among the 50 patients in arm A, 4 of them were with complete responses (8%). The median OS in arm A was 22.8 months (95% CI: 9.4—not reached), compared to 12.5 months (95% CI: 7.6—16.4) in arm B and 12.7 months (95% CI: 7.4—33.0) in arm C. The median duration of response was 17.5, 22.2, and 16.6 months, and the disease control rates were comparable among the three groups (54%, 43%, and 49%, respectively).

More treatment-related AEs were found in arm A (94%) compared to arm B (71%) and arm C (79%). Though the risk of treatment-related AEs was higher for arm A, the types of AEs were comparable, and no new safety signals were identified. Grade 3—4 immune-mediated AEs requiring immune-modulating medication were also higher in arm A including rash in 6%, adrenal insufficiency in 4%, diarrhea/colitis in 6%, and pneumonitis in 6%. Among the entire cohort, high-dose glucocorticoids were administered to 70% of patients (median 14 days), and complete resolution occurred in 70% of them. Based on the outcomes of this trial, the FDA has accepted the combination of nivolumab 1 mg/kg with ipilimumab 3 mg/kg, given every 3 weeks (then nivolumab 240 mg every 2 weeks or 480 mg every 4 weeks) for second-line treatment of HCC in the United States [35].

Pembrolizumab

After the encouraging antitumor efficacy and safety of nivolumab was demonstrated in patients with advanced HCC, another anti-PD-1 monoclonal antibody, pembrolizumab, was tested in a nonrandomized, KEYNOTE-224 trial in this population. Patients who had pathologically proven HCC and who had previously received sorafenib were eligible. Eighteen (17%; 95% CI 11—26) of 104 patients had an objective response to treatment [one (1%) complete, and 17 (16%) partial responses] [36]. Based on these findings, randomized, double-blind, phase III KEYNOTE-240 trial was performed in this population. Patients were scheduled to either receive 200 mg of pembrolizumab or placebo through an intravenous infusion every 3 weeks. The primary objectives were OS and PFS according to RECIST (1.1). A total of 413 patients were allocated randomly to receive pembrolizumab ($n = 278$) or placebo ($n = 135$). The median OS in the pembrolizumab and placebo groups was 13.9 months (95% CI, 11.6—16.0 months) and 10.6 months (95% CI, 8.3—13.5 months), respectively (HR, 0.781; 95% CI, 0.611—0.998; $P = .0238$). Pembrolizumab had a median PFS of 3 months (95% CI: 2.8—4.1 months) while placebo had a median PFS of 2.8 months (95% CI: 1.6—3 months) (HR = 0.718; 95% CI: 0.570—0.904; $P = .0022$).

Pembrolizumab provided a better ORR (18.3% vs 4.4%), and six pembrolizumab patients demonstrated a complete response (vs none with control), and responses were durable (median duration of response 13.8 months, range 1.5—23.6 + months). In the pembrolizumab and placebo groups, grade 3 or greater AEs happened in 147 (52.7%) and 62 (46.3%) patients, respectively. Forty-eight (17.2%) patients in the pembrolizumab arm and 12 (9%) patients in the placebo arm discontinued treatment due to adverse events. The KEYNOTE-240 trial failed to reach its prespecified endpoints of improving the PFS and OS with pembrolizumab in subjects with advanced HCC treated as a second-line treatment [37]. In November 2018, the FDA eventually approved pembrolizumab monotherapy for the management of patients with HCC who had previously been treated with sorafenib.

Sequencing systemic in advanced hepatocellular carcinoma

In a recently published phase III IMbrave 150 trial, the atezolizumab and bevacizumab combination demonstrated a superiority advantage over sorafenib in first-line advanced HCC [12]. Largely based on this trial, we recommend atezolizumab plus bevacizumab over sorafenib monotherapy for fit patients with no worse than Child-Pugh class A cirrhosis.

For patients who are not candidates for atezolizumab with bevacizumab, sorafenib, and lenvatinib are feasible first-line alternatives (e.g., where immunotherapy is contraindicated or associated with an increased toxicity, such as in patients with autoimmune diseases or organ transplantation or increased bleeding risk due to bevacizumab).

There are several second-line therapeutic options for patients with sufficient liver function, including regorafenib, cabozantinib, and ramucirumab. Nivolumab, pembrolizumab, combined nivolumab plus ipilimumab and lenvatinib (if it was not administered for first-line therapy) are other alternatives.

Conclusions and future perspectives

Multiple therapeutic options for advanced HCC are currently available in the first-line and later settings. Although the combination of ICI (e.g., atezolizumab) and VEGF inhibitor (e.g., bevacizumab) is considered as the standard-of-care in the first-line setting, the sequence of therapy is not established yet. Newer studies are desirable for superior therapeutic combinations with better toxicity profiles for patients with HCC.

References

[1] Villanueva A. Hepatocellular carcinoma. N Engl J Med 2019;380:1450−62.

[2] Ervik M, Lam F, Ferlay J, et al. Cancer today. Lyon, France: International Agency for Research on Cancer; 2016Available from. Available from: http://gco.iarc.fr/today.

[3] Altekruse SF, McGlynn KA, Dickie LA, Kleiner DE. Hepatocellular carcinoma confirmation, treatment, and survival in surveillance, epidemiology, and end results registries, 1992−2008. Hepatology 2012;55(2):476−82.

[4] European Association for the Study of the Liver. EASL clinical practice guidelines. Management of hepatocellular carcinoma. J Hepatol 2018;69:182−236.

[5] Marrero JA, Kulik LM, Sirlin CB, Zhu AX, Finn RS, Abecassis MM, et al. Diagnosis, staging, and management of hepatocellular carcinoma: 2018 practice guidance by the American Association for the Study of Liver Diseases. Hepatology. 2018;68(2):723−50.

[6] Kokudo N, Takemura N, Hasegawa K, Takayama T, Kubo S, Shimada M, et al. Clinical practice guidelines for hepatocellular carcinoma: the Japan Society of Hepatology 2017 (4th JSH-HCC guidelines) a 2019 update. Hepatol Res 2019;49(10):1109−13.

[7] Llovet JM, Ricci S, Mazzaferro V, Hilgard P, Gane E, Blanc JF, et al. SHARP Investigators Study Group. Sorafenib in advanced hepatocellular carcinoma. N Engl J Med 2008;359(4):378−90.

[8] Kudo M, Finn RS, Qin S, Han K-H, Ikeda K, Piscaglia F, et al. Lenvatinib vs sorafenib in first-line treatment of patients with unresectable hepatocellular carcinoma: a randomised phase 3 non-inferiority trial. Lancet. 2018;391(10126):1163−73.

[9] Bruix J, Qin S, Merle P, Granito A, Huang YH, Bodoky G, et al. Regorafenib for patients with hepatocellular carcinoma who progressed on sorafenib treatment (RESORCE): a randomised, double-blind, placebo-controlled, phase 3 trial. Lancet. 2017;389(10064):56−66.

[10] Abou-Alfa GK, Meyer T, Cheng AL, El-Khoueiry AB, Rimassa L, Ryoo BY, et al. Cabozantinib in patients with advanced and progressing hepatocellular carcinoma. N Engl J Med 2018;379(1):54−63.

[11] Zhu AX, Kang YK, Yen CJ, Finn RS, Galle PR, Llovet JM, et al. Ramucirumab after sorafenib in patients with advanced hepatocellular carcinoma and increased alpha-fetoprotein concentrations (REACH-2): a randomised, double-blind, placebo-controlled, phase 3 trial. Lancet Oncol 2019;20:282−96.

[12] Finn RS, Qin S, Ikeda M, et al. IMbrave150 investigators. Atezolizumab plus bevacizumab in unresectable hepatocellular carcinoma. N Engl J Med 2020;382(20):1894−905.

[13] Ikeda K, Kudo M, Kawazoe S, Osaki Y, Ikeda M, Okusaka T, et al. Phase 2 study of lenvatinib in patients with advanced hepatocellular carcinoma. J Gastroenterol 2017;52(4):512−19.

[14] Kudo M. Objective response by mRECIST is an independent prognostic factor of overall survival in systemic therapy for hepatocellular carcinoma. Liver Cancer 2019;8:73−7.

[15] Kudo M. Extremely high objective response rate of lenvatinib: its clinical relevance and changing the treatment paradigm in hepatocellular carcinoma. Liver Cancer 2018;7(3):215−24.

[16] Kudo M. Lenvatinib may drastically change the treatment landscape of hepatocellular carcinoma. Liver Cancer 2018;7:1−19.

[17] Cainap C, Qin S, Huang WT, Chung IJ, Pan H, Cheng Y, et al. Linifanib vs sorafenib in patients with advanced hepatocellular carcinoma: results of a randomized phase III trial. J Clin Oncol 2015;33(2):172−9.

[18] Wilhelm SM, Dumas J, Adnane L, Lynch M, Carter CA, Schütz G, et al. Regorafenib (BAY 73−4506): a new oral multi-kinase inhibitor of angiogenic, stromal and oncogenic receptor tyrosine kinases with potent preclinical antitumor activity. Int J Cancer 2011;129(1):245−55.

[19] Finn RS, Merle P, Granito A, Huang YH, Bodoky G, Pracht M, et al. Outcomes of sequential treatment with sorafenib followed by regorafenib for HCC: additional analyses from the phase III RESORCE trial. J Hepatol 2018;69(2):353−8.

[20] Kudo M, Cheng A-L, Park J-W, Park JH, Liang P-C, Hidaka H, et al. Orantinib vs placebo combined with transcatheter arterial chemo-embolisation in patients with unresectable hepatocellular carcinoma (ORIENTAL): a randomised, double-blind, placebo-controlled, multicentre, phase 3 study. Lancet Gastroenterol Hepatol 2018;3(1):37−46.

[21] Kudo M. Cabozantinib as a second-line agent in advanced hepatocellular carcinoma. Liver Cancer 2018;7(2):123−33.

[22] Rimassa L, Blanc JF, Klumpen HJ, Zagonel V, Tran A, Kim SC, et al. Outcomes based on age in the phase 3 CELESTIAL trial of cabozantinib vs placebo in patients with advanced hepatocellular carcinoma. J Clin Oncol 2018;36(15_suppl):4090.

[23] Kudo M. Ramucirumab as second-line systemic therapy in hepatocellular carcinoma. Liver Cancer 2018;7 (4):305−11.

[24] Zhu AX, Park JO, Ryoo BY, Yen CJ, Poon R, Pastorelli D, et al. Ramucirumab vs placebo as second-line treatment in patients with advanced hepatocellular carcinoma following first-line therapy with sorafenib (REACH): a randomised, double-blind, multicentre, phase 3 trial. Lancet Oncol 2015;16(7):859−70.

[25] Galle PR, Foerster F, Kudo M, Chan SL, Llovet JM, Qin S, et al. Issue cover. Liver Int 2019;39(12):2214−29.

[26] Kudo M, Okusaka T, Motomura K, Ohno I, Morimoto M, Seo S, et al. Ramucirumab after prior sorafenib in patients with advanced hepatocellular carcinoma and elevated alpha-fetoprotein: Japanese subgroup analysis of the REACH-2 trial. J Gastroenterol 2020;55(6):627−39.

[27] Yamashita T, Kudo M, Ikeda K, Izumi N, Tateishi R, Ikeda M, et al. REFLECT-a phase 3 trial comparing efficacy and safety of lenvatinib to sorafenib for the treatment of unresectable hepatocellular carcinoma: an analysis of Japanese subset. J Gastroenterol 2020;55(1):113−22.

[28] Kudo M, Galle PR, Llovet JM, Finn RS, Vogel A, Motomura K, et al. Ramucirumab in elderly patients with hepatocellular carcinoma and elevated alpha-fetoprotein after sorafenib in REACH and REACH-2. Liver Int 2020. Available from: https://doi.org/10.1111/liv.14462.

[29] FDA grants accelerated approval to nivolumab for HCC previously treated with sorafenib. https://www. fda.gov/drugs/informationondrugs/approveddrugs/ucm577166.htm [accessed 30.06.21].

[30] Lee MS, Ryoo B-Y, Hsu C-H, Numata K, Stein S, et al. Atezolizumab with or without bevacizumab in unresectable hepatocellular carcinoma (GO30140): an open-label, multicentre, phase 1b study. Lancet Oncol 2020;21(6):808−20.

[31] Whiteside TL, Demaria S, Rodriguez-Ruiz ME, et al. Emerging opportunities and challenges in cancer immunotherapy. Clin Cancer Res 2016;22:1845−55.

[32] Motzer RJ, Tannir NM, McDermott DF, et al. CheckMate 214 investigators. Nivolumab plus ipilimumab vs sunitinib in advanced renal-cell carcinoma. N Engl J Med 2018;378(14):1277−90.

[33] Wolchok JD, Kluger H, Callahan MK, et al. Nivolumab plus ipilimumab in advanced melanoma. N Engl J Med 2013;369(2):122−33.

[34] Hellmann MD, Rizvi NA, Goldman JW, et al. Nivolumab plus ipilimumab as first-line treatment for advanced non−small-cell lung cancer (CheckMate 012): results of an open-label, phase 1, multicohortstudy. Lancet Oncol 2017;18(1):31−41.

[35] Yau T, Kang Y-K, Kim T-Y, El-Khoueiry AB, Santoro A, Sangro B, et al. Efficacy and safety of nivolumab plus ipilimumab in patients with advanced hepatocellular carcinoma previously treated with sorafenib: the CheckMate 040 randomized clinical trial. JAMA Oncol 2020;6(11):e204564. Available from: https://doi.org/10.1001/jamaoncol.2020.4564.

[36] Zhu AX, Finn RS, Edeline J, et al. Pembrolizumab in patients with advanced hepatocellular carcinoma previously treated with sorafenib (KEYNOTE-224): a non- randomised, open-labelphase 2 trial. Lancet Oncol 2018;19:940−52.

[37] Finn RS, Ryoo BY, Merle P, et al. Pembrolizumab as second-line therapy in patients with advanced hepatocellular carcinoma in KEYNOTE-240: a randomized, double-blind, phase III trial. J Clin Oncol 2020;38(3):193−202.

CHAPTER

24

Recent perspectives on therapeutic significance of microRNAs in hepatocellular carcinoma

Madelyn Miller and Shadab A. Siddiqi

Burnett School of Biomedical Sciences, College of Medicine, University of Central Florida, Orlando, FL, United States

Abstract

Despite prudent efforts and many scientific breakthroughs, hepatocellular carcinoma (HCC) continues to be one of the deadliest cancers with high mortality and low survival rate. The low survival rate is attributed to poor prognosis of HCC and limited treatment options and, therefore, underscores the significance of developing new efficient diagnostic markers and novel therapeutic approaches. Among various putative diagnostic and therapeutic targets, microRNAs (miRNAs) are receiving great attention as biomarkers for early detection and therapeutic agents to curtail HCC. miRNAs are small molecules which have been demonstrated to be involved in the development and progression of HCC. A number of miRNAs have been identified as potent biomarkers and have shown promising results in early detection of HCC. In this chapter, we will discuss the recent research advancements made to explore miRNAs as robust biomarkers for early detection and potent therapy for HCC.

Keywords: Hepatocellular carcinoma; hepatic steatosis; nonalcoholic fatty liver disease; microRNA; exosomes; exosomal miRNA

Abbreviations

AFLD	Alcoholic fatty liver disease
AFP	Alpha fetoprotein
ALD	Alcohol-related liver disease
CD8 + T cell	Cluster of differentiation 8 T cell
CDKs	Cyclin dependent kinases
circRNA	CircularRNA
DNA	Deoxyribonucleic acid
DGCR8	DiGeorge Syndrome Critical Region 8

Ganji Purnachandra Nagaraju, Sarfraz Ahmad (eds.)
Theranostics and Precision Medicine for the Management of Hepatocellular Carcinoma, Volume 3
DOI: https://doi.org/10.1016/B978-0-323-99283-1.00008-2

© 2022 Elsevier Inc. All rights reserved.

ERα	Estrogen receptor α
EMT	Epithelial–mesenchymal transition
EV	Extracellular vesicle
GTP	Guanosine-5′-triphosphate
HBx	HBV-encoded X antigen
HBeAg	Hepatitis B e-antigen
HCC	Hepatocellular carcinoma
HPC	HCC progenitor cell
HAV	Hepatitis A virus
HBV	Hepatitis B virus
HCV	Hepatitis C virus
HMOX1	Heme oxygenase decycling 1
ILV	Intraluminal vesicle
JNK	c-Jun N-terminal kinase
JAK2	Janus kinase 2
lncRNA	Long noncoding RNA
mRNA	Messenger RNA
MAPK	Microtubule associated protein kinase
MRI	Magnetic resonance imaging
mTOR	Mammalian target of rapamycin
MVBs	Multivesicular bodies
NASH	Nonalcoholic steatohepatitis
NAFLD	Nonalcoholic fatty liver disease
ncRNA	Noncoding RNA
NSF	N-ethylmaleimide sensitive factor
PI3K	Phosphoinositide 3-kinase
pre-miRNA	Precursor RNA
RNA	Ribonucleic acid
RISC	RNA-induced silencing complex
miRNA	Micro-RNA
ROCK	Rho-associated protein kinase
ROS	Reactive oxygen species
SMAD7	Mothers against Dpp homolog 8
snRNA	Small nuclear RNA
snoRNA	Small nucleolar RNA
SNAP	Soluble NSF attachment protein
SNARE	SNAP receptor
STAT3	Signal transducer and activator of transcription 3
TGF-β1	Transforming growth factor beta 1
TNFα	Tumor necrosis factor alpha
UTR	Untranslated region
VEGF	Vascular endothelial growth factor

Introduction

Hepatocellular carcinoma (HCC) is the most common form of primary liver cancers with the highest mortality rate and a very low 5-year survival rate [1]. With rapidly increasing numbers of new cases and associated deaths worldwide, HCC is currently considered the second most common cause of primary cancer-related mortalities [2]. In general, the pathogenesis of HCC is a complex and multistep process, which can arise from chronic or even acute liver injury caused by various factors such as viral infections, metabolic dysregulation, accumulation of toxic materials, and genetic susceptibility [3].

Generally, a slow and constant progression of liver injury over a period of several years or even decades leads to the development of fibrosis and cirrhosis, which are the initial indicators of HCC-development. Even though eastern Asia and Africa have the majority of the HCC cases because of higher tendency of viral infections, an increasing incidence of HCC-associated mortality has been noticed in the western countries in recent years [3]. In the United States alone, more than 20,000 new HCC cases are identified every year and almost 18,000 people die from the HCC each year [4].

Hepatitis B and hepatitis C infections are the major factors that prominently contribute to either chronic or acute liver damage in most of the Asian and African countries. Hepatitis B infection predisposes individuals to develop HCC 100-times more than the uninfected individuals [5]. Endemic hepatitis and high malignancy rate due to HCC demonstrate the lack of appropriate vaccination programs in these countries. Another causative factor that is often considered to be accountable for the pathogenesis of liver fibrosis and cirrhosis and eventually leading to the development of HCC is the prolonged heavy consumption of alcohol. However, a direct role of alcohol consumption in cancer development remains to be studied [6]. Many potent hepato-carcinogens have been identified that cause DNA damage, such as aflatoxin. Aflatoxin is thought to potentiate the pathogenesis of hepatic malignancies in hepatitis B and hepatitis C patients [6].

Even though viral infections leading to liver cirrhosis are the major contributors of HCC development, several other factors such as genetics, obesity, type 2 diabetes, nonalcoholic fatty liver disease (NAFLD), and nonalcoholic steatohepatitis (NASH) have been associated with the pathogenesis of HCC [7–11]. Recently, genetics has been shown to play a role in the development of HCC and many genetic correlations have been established [12]. Several studies have demonstrated that both obesity and diabetes can cause abnormal lipid accumulation that results in hepatic lipotoxicity and eventually leading to the pathogenesis of hepatic steatosis, NAFLD, and NASH [7,9,13,14]. NASH and NAFLD cause apoptosis of hepatocytes and several studies indicate that the steady apoptosis is responsible for hepatocytic mitogenesis resulting in an incessant cell turnover leading to tumor formation [14,15]. It has been suggested that excess lipid deposition causes oxidative stress and inflammation in liver, which contribute to the development of NASH and liver cirrhosis, a major risk factor for HCC [9,15–17]. Leptin is one of the many hormones that have increased expression in obese individuals which has been associated with carcinogenesis and NAFLD development. Leptin has been shown to trigger the activation of JAK2/STAT3 and PI3K/Akt pathways, which cause hepatic inflammation leading to liver cirrhosis and then HCC [13,18–22]. Adiponectin, which antagonizes the adverse effects of leptin, is downregulated in obese individuals suggesting an increasing role of obesity in the advancement of liver cirrhosis and HCC [13,18–22].

Early detection of any type of cancer is the key for a positive prognosis; however, HCC remains asymptomatic and the tumor grows slowly in the early stages that results in diagnosis at the advanced stage of the disease [23]. Consequently, most HCC patients at the time of diagnosis have poor prognosis. The pathogenesis of HCC is highly variable among different individuals and therefore treatment of HCC depends upon patient's condition and cancer progression. Patients in the early stages of HCC have limited options and can undergo surgical resection followed by chemotherapy and liver transplantation; however, patients in late stages are not candidates for surgical cytoreduction and have limited treatment options leading to very low survival rate [24–26]. This emphasizes the importance of early diagnosis of the HCC which can improve the survival rate, and hence identification of robust molecular markers associated with HCC pathogenesis are of high significance.

The pathogenesis of all cancers is highly variable and complicated, which involves numerous molecular aberrations yielding altered gene expressions that eventually leads to altered protein compositions and abnormal expression of specific proteins. These aberrations or alterations—associated with the structures or expression of genes and proteins—can be detected utilizing the classical tumor biopsies and body fluid analyses and these findings can be sued as potential biomarkers for a particular kind of cancer. A number of biomarkers specific to various cancers or in particular HCC have been discovered during last several years. The identification of these biomarkers has proved to be very important in early detection of various cancers and has significantly increased the survival rate because early detection allowed to monitor tumor size, metastasis, tumor progression, which can be used to decide the treatment approaches [27].

Generally, patients with liver cancer do not have any symptoms until the end stages of the disease; however, if liver dysfunction is suspected during regular examination, then blood tests are recommended to assess liver function and serum biomarkers, such as α-fetoprotein (AFP). Because of complicated and poor diagnosis of HCC in early stages, imaging tests are often recommended to ascertain hepatic cancer. One of the most common imaging techniques used to detect hepatic lesions is ultrasonography. However, there are several limitations associated with ultrasonography such as the specificity of data analysis and insufficient sensitivity of this technique to detect small hepatic lesions [28]. Current advances made in the direction of discovering novel diagnostic biomarkers for the early detection of HCC will be discussed in this review.

Currently, treatment modalities for HCC vary among patients and are often dictated by different stages of the disease at the time of diagnosis. Different stages of HCC are classified as 0, A, B, C, and D; 0 being the very early stage whereas D is the end stage of the HCC. In general, widely accepted treatment modalities for HCC depend upon the different stages of the disease and include surgical resection, liver transplantation, radiofrequency ablation, microwave therapy, percutaneous ethanol injection, cryoablation, chemoembolization, and radioembolization [29,30]. Most of the time, patients with advanced stage of HCC such as with portal invasion have poor prognosis and undergo aggressive treatment approaches such as hepatectomy followed by chemotherapy regimen whereas patients with HBV/HCV infection-derived HCC are primarily treated with interferon therapy in combination with nucleotide analogs [31,32]. Other commonly used treatment options for HCC patients include chemotherapeutics such as Cisplatin, Oxaplatin, Doxorubicin, and Gemcitabine. Recent advances in the development of molecular target-based therapies have shown promising outcomes during clinical trials of HCC. HCC causes changes in a number of signaling pathways and triggers epigenetic or mutational alterations in liver. Additionally, HCC is characterized by dense vasculature with significantly increased micro-vessels in tumors. Tyrosine kinase inhibitors are common drugs used as targeted therapies to modulate angiogenesis-related signaling pathways. Sorafenib, Lenvatinib, and Regorafenib are commonly used tyrosine kinase inhibitors. Sorafenib and regorafenib in combination with some conventional chemotherapeutic drugs have demonstrated promising results in HCC treatment [33].

Despite of many efforts been made to develop robust treatment options for HCC, currently available treatment options have not proven to be sufficient to treat HCC successfully [34–44]. This is due to the heterogeneity of HCC cell lines and the lack of prudent biomarkers for early detection [34–44]. Because of increasing incidence and poor prognosis of HCC, the discovery of novel biomarkers for early diagnosis and development of potent therapeutic approaches are warranted. To this end, microRNAs (miRNAs) are receiving great attention as biomarkers for early diagnosis and potent therapeutic agents against various types of cancer including HCC. miRNAs are small molecules and play a number of important roles in controlling the pathogenesis of HCC. A number of miRNAs have been identified as potent biomarkers and have shown promising results in early detection of HCC. In this review, we will discuss the recent developments made in the direction of miRNAs as potent biomarkers for early diagnosis and therapeutic agents for HCC.

Biogenesis of microRNAs

Human genome comprises approximately 20,000 genes; however, less than 2% of these genes encode proteins suggesting the majority of these genes are noncoding. These noncoding transcripts of human genome are characterized as noncoding RNA (ncRNA). Based on their physical properties such as length and shape, these ncRNA are divided into several types: small noncoding RNAs (microRNAs or miRNAs) long noncoding RNAs (lncRNAs), small nuclear RNAs (snRNAs), small nucleolar RNAs (snoRNAs), and circularRNAs (circRNAs).

miRNAs were discovered in 1993 by the Ambros and Ruvkun groups in *Caenorhabditis elegans*. Their groups found that *lin-4* was a nonprotein coding small RNA which downregulated the *lin-14* gene through the 3′ untranslated region (UTR) [45–48]. Since then, many miRNAs have been discovered and their role in gene expression is highly recognized. miRNAs are found in prokaryotic cells, eukaryotes, and viruses [49]. They are nonprotein-coding genes, partially complementary to messenger RNA (mRNA), and are involved in regulation of gene expression [50]. When mature, miRNAs are single-stranded and about 21–23 nucleotides in length. Mature miRNA regulates gene expression at a transcriptional or posttranscriptional level through RNA interference (RNAi) in both the nucleus and the cytoplasm [50].

Most miRNAs are transcribed from DNA into primary miRNA (pri-miRNA) and eventually are processed into precursor RNA (pre-miRNA) and finally mature miRNA [51]. To suppress gene expression, miRNAs typically interact with the 3′ UTR of the target mRNA [52]. miRNAs have also been shown to activate or suppress gene expression under other conditions, either by interacting with the 5′ UTR, promoter regions, or coding sequences of genes [53,54]. The biogenesis of miRNA begins with RNA polymerase II or III transcript processing either posttranslationally or cotranslationally [52]. Approximately, half of currently identified miRNAs are processed from introns and a few exons from DNA sequences or miRNA genes [55,56]. The rest of the miRNAs are transcribed independently of a host gene and are regulated by their own promoters [55]. In addition, some miRNAs are transcribed as a long transcript called miRNA clusters or families [57,58]. Currently, miRNA has been described as undergoing biogenesis through either a canonical or a noncanonical pathway.

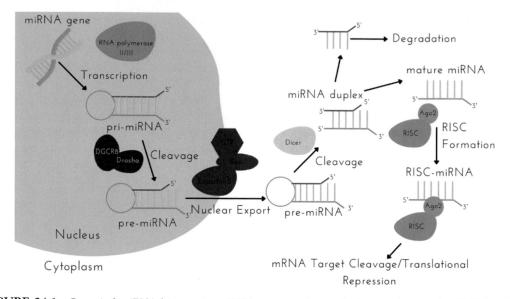

FIGURE 24.1 Canonical miRNA biogenesis. miRNA genes are transcribed into primary microRNA by RNA polymerase II. The hairpin pri-miRNA is recognized by DiGeorge Syndrome Critical Region 8 (DGCR8) in the microprocessor complex, and acts as a substrate for Drosha. Drosha cleaves the pri-miRNA into pre-miRNA, which is exported from the nucleus by Exportin-5 to reach the cytosol in a GTP-dependent manner with Ran-GTPase. In the cytoplasm, the terminal loop of the hairpin pre-miRNA is cleaved by Dicer. Then, the mature miRNA duplex is formed. The active/guide strain of miRNA is able to bind to the RNA-induced silencing complex (RISC) via interaction with the Ago2 protein of the RISC complex. The other, passenger strand, of miRNA is degraded. Mature miRNA bound to the RISC targets mRNA and regulates gene expression through translational inhibition, mRNA cleavage, or by reducing mRNA stability.

Canonical microRNA biogenesis

The primary pathway in which miRNAs are processed is the canonical pathway (Fig. 24.1). In the canonical pathway, pri-RNAs are transcribed from DNA by RNA polymerase II [59]. From there, pri-miRNAs fold into hairpins, which are substrates for members for Drosha and Dicer, RNAse III enzymes family members [60]. Pri-miRNA is recognized by the microprocessor complex with two multiprotein units. The first unit is a large unit including RNA-associated proteins, dsRNA binding proteins, ribonucleoproteins, and more proteins. The other unit is smaller and includes Drosha and the RNA-binding protein DiGeorge Syndrome Critical Region 8 (DGCR8) [61]. The microprocessor is able to recognize pri-RNA through DGCR8 dimers recognizing the pri-miRNA stem through the double-stranded RNA-binding domains [62]. Pri-miRNA is cleaved by Drosha in the nucleus, cleaving the stem-loop, resulting in pre-miRNAs, which are 70 nucleotides in length and also are stem-loop structures [62]. The binding of hemes to the microprocessor unit promotes its activity by promoting interaction between the DGCR8 dimer and the pri-miRNA [63,64].

Once cleaved by the microprocessor, the newly created pre-miRNA has a 5′-monophophshate and a 3′-2-nt overhang [65]. Exportin-5 and Ran-GTPase bind to pre-miRNAs to export the pre-miRNA from the nucleus to cytosol [66]. Once in the cytoplasm, pre-miRNA's terminal loop is cleaved by Dicer [67]. From here, miRNA duplexes are loaded onto the RNA-induced silencing complex (RISC), a large, multiprotein complex [68]. The catalytic component of RISC, Ago2, cleaves one strand of the miRNA duplex [69]. One strand of the mature miRNA will remain on the RISC, stay active, and become the guide strand of the miRNA, while the other strand, the passenger strand, will be degraded [70,71].

Mature miRNA bound to RISC targets the 3′ UTR of target mRNA to regulate gene expression posttranslationally by inducing translational inhibition, or through mRNA cleavage, or by affecting target mRNA stability [72,73]. Typically, miRNA bound to RISC can bind to target mRNA through base complementarity [74]. Research suggests that translation blocking occurs through miRNA-mediated gene silencing on the rough endoplasmic reticulum membrane, leading to mRNA degradation and decay on the endosome [75,76]. DNA methylation, histone modification, and other forms of epigenetic control may affect miRNA gene regulation [77].

Noncanonical microRNA biogenesis

There are various alternative pathways which have been shown to generate miRNAs (Fig. 24.2) [78]. The two main noncanonical pathways are Drosha-DGCR8-independent or Dicer-independent [79]. In the first pathway, the step with Drosha is bypassed and mRNA splicing is used to create a small RNA precursor from miRtrons, forming a stem-loop structure that is similar to pre-miRNA (Fig. 24.2A) [80]. This type of pre-miRNA can be

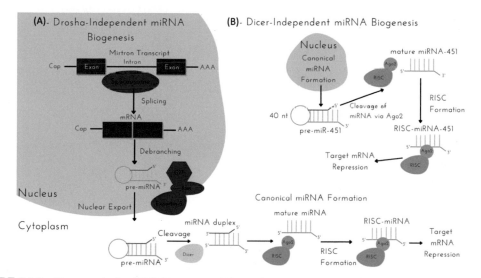

FIGURE 24.2   Noncanonical miRNA biogenesis. (A) Drosha-Independent miRNA biogenesis. In this pathway, Drosha cleavage is bypassed and mRNA splicing is used to create a small RNA precursor from a miRtron. Debranching occurs forming a stem-loop structure similar to pre-miRNA. This type of pre-miRNA is structurally different from canonical pre-miRNA. From here, pre-miRNA is exported from the nucleus and processed as in the canonical pathway, eventually leading to target mRNA suppression. (B) Dicer-independent miRNA biogenesis. In this pathway, pre-miRNA for miR-451 is generated as in the canonical pathway in the nucleus. However, pre-miRNA-451 is only approximately 40 nucleotides in length and is too small to be recognized by dicer. It has been shown that Ago2 is sufficient to recognize and cleave pre-miR-451 to produce mature miR-451, and load it into the RNA-induced silencing complex (RISC), leading to target mRNA suppression.

differentiated from canonical miRNA due to bulges in the stem region, as well as differences in the hairpin length and free energy, and guanine content [81]. In an example of a Dicer-independent pathway, pre-miR-451 is processed by Drosha to free pre-miRNA as in the canonical pathway, where it is transferred to the cytoplasm in a similar manner (Fig. 24.2B). However, once in the cytoplasm, pre-miR-451 is not processed by Dicer and is loaded to Ago2 in the RISC complex instead. This occurs because pre-miR-451 is too short to be recognized by DICER, and Ago2 is sufficient for RISC loading and RNAi to occur [82–84].

MicroRNA involvement in development of hepatocellular carcinoma

miRNAs are involved in the development of HCC by regulating responses to various risk factors (such as HCC-associated virus infection, carcinogen exposure, cirrhosis, and NASH) [85]. Hepatitis B virus (HBV) or HCV infection can increase the chance of HCC development, with 70% of HCC patients presenting with chronic infection of these viruses [86] (Fig. 24.3).

Cellular miRNAs can regulate HBV infection, and subsequent development of HCC. For instance, miR-18a targets the ERS1 gene, encoding for estrogen receptor α (ERα) protein in hepatocytes, which could turn off the protective effect of estrogens in female HBV patients by blocking suppression of HBV transcription. Interestingly, miR-18a is highly

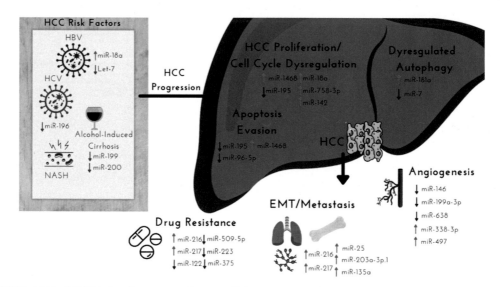

FIGURE 24.3 MiRNA involvement in hepatocellular carcinoma (HCC). miRNA is upregulated (green) or downregulated (red) in the context of HCC. miRNAs can be dysregulated in response to risk factors for HCC, such as nonalcoholic steatohepatitis (NASH), alcohol-induced chirrhosis, hepatitis C virus (HCV), and hepatitis B virus (HBV), leading to increased HCC susceptibility and progression. miRNAs are dysregulated in HCC, leading to increased proliferation due to abberant signaling or cell cycle progression, evasion of apoptosis, or dysregulation of autophagy. All of these factors lead to further progression of HCC. miRNAs in HCC can also lead to increased chemotherapy resistance, increased epithelial to mesenchymal transition and subsequent metastasis, and may be involved in angiogenesis as well. Thus miRNAs play a substantial role in the progression and development of HCC.

overexpressed in female HCC tissue [87]. This may elucidate why HCC affects men at much higher rates ($2-4 \times$ more likely) than females, and provides further evidence for the protective role of estrogen in HCC [65,88].

Furthermore, miRNAs can be influenced by HBV infection. In one elegant study, Wang and colleagues demonstrated differential induction/downregulation of various miRNAs in response to HBx protein in HepG2 cells. Expression of the let-7 family miRNAs were significantly downregulated in response to HBx [89]. Let-7 was the first miRNA identified in humans and targets a variety of cellular oncogenes such as MYC [90], RAS [91], and HMGA2 [92], and has been shown to be downregulated in a variety of cancers such as thyroid, breast, lung, prostate, and liver cancer [93]. Wang and colleagues also identified an additional target of let-7 in response to HBx protein, STAT3, a member of the JAK/STAT pathway [89]. STAT3 is involved in metastasis, angiogenesis, and immune suppression, leading to tumor formation and progression [94,95].

In addition to HBV infection, HCV infection has been shown to be a risk factor for HCC. miRNA has been implicated in the induction of HCC through HCV infection. For instance, miR-196 has been shown to protect against HCC by upregulating heme oxygenase decycling 1 (HMOX1) expression and thus HCV transcription in HCV infection [96].

A variety of other risk factors are associated with the development of HCC, including alcohol-induced cirrhosis, NASH, and carcinogen exposure, and miRNAs have been shown to be regulated in the context of these factors. For instance, miR-199 and 200 are downregulated in HCC, and were also shown to be downregulated in a mouse model of alcohol-induced cirrhosis, where mice were fed an ethanol-containing diet [97].

Proliferation and apoptosis

Cell growth, proliferation, and apoptosis are important for balancing cell functions and maintaining homeostasis [98]. Cyclin-dependent kinases (CDKs) function in regulating the cell cycle and proliferation of cells [99]. In cancer, CDKs can be dysregulated leading to an aberrant cell cycle and proliferation, and eventually tumor formation. On the other hand, apoptosis, or programmed cell death, is also dysregulated in the setting of tumorigenesis [100,101]. Dysregulated proliferation and apoptosis play a large role in the development of HCC. miRNAs involved in apoptosis and proliferation have been shown to be aberrantly expressed in HCC [102].

miRNAs can control the cell cycle, proliferation, and apoptosis in HCC, likely through the binding of target genes which control these processes. For example, miRNA-1468 overexpression led to cell cycle transition from G1 to S phase, while leading to apoptosis resistance as well [103]. miRNA-195 overexpression led to G1 phase cell cycle arrest and promotion of apoptosis in HCC through the Wnt3 signaling pathway [104]. miRNA-1299 was able to inhibit the HCC cell cycle from going to the S phase by regulating CDK6 [105]. In addition, miRNA can inhibit cell proliferation and apoptosis in HCC. For example, miR-96-5p can target the apoptosis pathway protein, caspase-9, and inhibit apoptosis in HCC [106].

The mammalian target of rapamycin (mTOR) pathway is another pathway which regulates cell growth and survival. mTOR is aberrantly activated in up to 50% of HCC cases, downstream of growth factor signaling cascades [107]. Some tumor suppressor miRNAs can activate the mTOR pathway in HCC, including miR-758-3p, miR-142, and others

[108,109]. The Wnt signaling pathway and MAPK cascade have also been shown to be upregulated or overactivated in the context of HCC, leading to increased cell proliferation. These pathways have also been shown to be regulated by miRNAs in the context of HCC [110]. Thus miRNAs may regulate signaling pathways involved in apoptosis and proliferation through gene targeting, and aberrant expression of these miRNAs are highly linked to HCC tumorigenesis.

Metastasis

Metastasis is a complex process by which tumors migrate locally, infiltrate or invade the vasculature, survive in the bloodstream, implant into distant organs, and finally lead to secondary tumor growth [111]. The EMT, or epithelial to mesenchymal transition is important for metastasis to occur as it gives tumor cells invasive properties [112]. When cancer reaches metastasis, it becomes a large risk factor for death [113]. miRNAs can regulate the EMT, promote or inhibit invasion, and control metastasis in HCC. They can also contribute to activation of normal fibroblasts into cancer-associated fibroblasts, enhancing the EMT [114]. Overexpression of miR-25, miR-203a-3p.1, and miR-135a lead to increased EMT, migration, and metastasis in HCC [115−117]. In an interesting study, miR-216 and 217 overexpression led to increased TGF-β signaling pathway activation, resulting in an EMT phenotype that is typically associated with chemotherapy resistance [118]. This shows how miRNAs can regulate various processes associated with HCC.

Drug resistance

Since 2007 the mainstay molecular biologic for advanced HCC has been sorafenib, a multikinase inhibitor which targets Raf-kinase and several tyrosine kinase receptors. In HCC, sorafenib can induce apoptosis through downregulation of Mcl-1 and also target angiogenesis through various tyrosine kinase receptor pathways [119,120]. Though sorafenib has been useful in treating advanced HCC, its effectiveness is still less than optimal, due to acquired resistance [121,122]. miRNAs play a role in regulating resistance to sorafenib through their involvement with canonical drug-resistance pathways [120].

One of the main pathways to sorafenib resistance is drug elimination through the ATP-binding cassette transporters, which are found in abundance in hepatocytes (Fig. 24.4) [123]. ABC members are overexpressed in HCC and work to pump exogenous drugs out of cells [124]. miR-122 is downregulated in HCC, and overexpression of miR-122 leads to apoptosis, increased cell cycle arrest, as well as downregulation of multidrug resistant genes and ABC family members [125−127]. MiR-509-5p, miR-122, miR-223, and miR-375 have been shown to be able to downregulate multidrug resistance genes and re-sensitize cells to chemotherapy treatment [128−131]. Taken together, this shows how miRNAs are involved in chemotherapy resistance in HCC and how miRNA therapy coupled with chemotherapy may help prevent drug resistance in HCC.

Autophagy

Autophagy is a catabolism process which uses lysosomes to degrade and recycle organelles and proteins via self-digestion [132]. Autophagy is an important regulator for cell survival, the cell cycle, and cell death, and it has been shown to be linked to regulation in HCC [133,134]. Autophagy is assumed to have a protective role in cancer by preventing

ABC Transporters in HCC

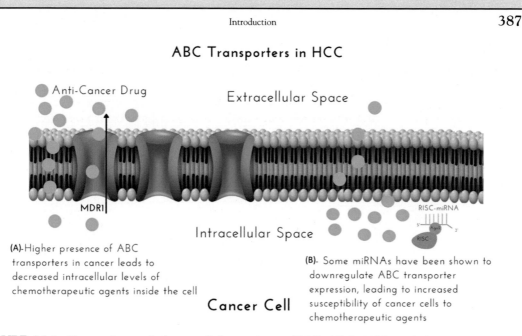

(A) Higher presence of ABC transporters in cancer leads to decreased intracellular levels of chemotherapeutic agents inside the cell

(B) Some miRNAs have been shown to downregulate ABC transporter expression, leading to increased susceptibility of cancer cells to chemotherapeutic agents

FIGURE 24.4 Drug resistance in hepatocellular carcinoma (HCC), (A) In HCC multidrug resistant genes (MDR) code for ABC transporters such as MDR1. This leads to increased pumping of anticancer drugs from the intracellular to extracellular space, and the drug resistance seen in many types of cancer, including HCC. (B) Some miRNAs have been shown to downregulate ABC transporter expression and MDR genes leading to less drug resistance. In HCC cells, overexpression of specific miRNA can reduce ABC transporter expression leading to increased susceptibility of cancer cells to chemotherapy drugs.

neoplasms by removing damaged cells that are exposed to stress and oncogenic conditions. Conversely, in cancer cells, autophagy may protect cancer cells which are stressed [135,136]. miRNAs may regulate HCC development through autophagy. For instance, miR-181a can repress the pro-autophagy protein Atg5, reducing apoptosis of HCC cells and inducing tumor growth [137]. miR-7 overexpression could help increase autophagy in HCC cells and lead to decreased tumor proliferation through targeting of the mTOR pathway [138]. miRNAs regulating autophagy may also play a role in preventing or promoting resistance to chemotherapy through this homeostatic pathway [139]. Thus miRNA plays a role in HCC tumorigenesis through autophagy.

Angiogenesis

Angiogenesis, or formation of blood vessels providing tumor nutrition, is an important step in metastasis and tumor growth [140]. HCC is a solid tumor which is characterized by deformed blood vessel tissue and angiogenesis [141]. Angiogenesis is highly regulated by vascular endothelial growth factors (VEGF), and high levels of VEGF in circulating blood correlate with invasion and metastasis [142,143]. A variety of miRNAs, including miR-146, 199a-3p, and miR-638, have been shown to repress angiogenesis through VEGF downregulation [144–146]. Conversely, miRNA-338-3p and miR-497 were shown to promote angiogenesis through inhibition of VEGF [147,148]. miRNAs are important for the HCC development and angiogenesis regulation in HCC.

MicroRNA as diagnostic biomarker in hepatocellular carcinoma

HCC is currently diagnosed in late stages, due to low accuracy of individual biomarkers such as AFP [149]. Thus it is important to find noninvasive biomarkers with specificity for early-stage HCC diagnoses. Various miRNAs are dysregulated in human HCC tissue compared to healthy tissue, and among these are miRNAs which have been identified as differentially expressed in more than one study, making these more likely involved in tumorigenesis (Table 24.1) [150–159]. These include miR-18 (upregulated in HCC), 21 (up), 221 (up), 222 (up), 224 (up), 122 (down), 125 (down), 125b-1 (down), 130a (down), 150 (down), 199 (down), and 200 (down) [159]. Interestingly, a few of these miRNAs are upregulated in other forms of cancer, such as colon, pancreas, stomach, breast, and lung carcinomas.

TABLE 24.1   Diagnostic and prognostic microRNA biomarkers in hepatocellular carcinoma.

miRNA biomarkers for HCC

miRNA	Dysregulation	miRNA associated with exosomes in HCC?
miR-18	Upregulated	Yes
miR-21	Upregulated	
miR-221	Upregulated	Yes
miR-222	Upregulated	Yes
miR-224	Upregulated	Yes
miR-122	Downregulated	Yes
miR-125	Downregulated	
miR-125b-1	Downregulated	Yes
miR-130a	Downregulated	
miR-150	Downregulated	
miR-199	Downregulated	
miR-200	Downregulated	
miR-1972	Upregulated	
miR-193a-5p	Upregulated	
miR-214-3p	Upregulated	
miR-365-3p	Upregulated	
miR-665	Upregulated	Yes
miR-368	Downregulated	Yes

miRNAs can serve as diagnostic or prognostic biomarkers for HCC. The table shows identified serum diagnostic and prognostic miRNA biomarkers for HCC and if they are upregulated or downregulated. Some miRNAs are shown to be upregulated in HCC but not in cirrhosis or hepatitis including miR-1972, miR-193a-5p, miR-214-3p, and miR-365-3p. Some miRNAs can be found to be dysregulated in serum exosomes of HCC, and exosomal biomarkers may serve as better biomarkers than regular serum biomarkers.

The targets of these miRNAs include genes involved in tumorigenesis, the cell cycle, and cell death [160]. It is also possible that aberrant miRNA expression in HCC may be protective against stress stimuli, as some miRNAs upregulated in HCC are upregulated in hypoxic conditions [160]. More recently, additional circulating plasma miRNA biomarkers for HCC compared to other liver pathologies such as hepatitis and cirrhosis have been identified as diagnostic and prognostic biomarkers, including miRNA-1972, miR-193a-5p, miR-214-3p, and miR-365a-3p [161]. The mechanism of action of these miRNAs remains to be elucidated.

miRNAs could also be used to classify HCC and served as prognosis biomarkers. Clinically, HCC is a heterogeneous disease with tumor status, liver function indicators, and portal hypertension presence being different in patients [162,163]. Various miRNA expression patterns have been identified which correlated with clinical and pathological parameters. For example, miRNA-221 has been shown to be associated with shorter time to reoccurrence as well as response to treatments, likely through regulation of the p53 pathway [164]. miRNA-21 is overexpressed in increased invasion and cancer cell migration in HCC, and correlates with poorer prognosis in clinical cases [165–168]. This is likely because miRNA-21 targets tumor suppressors including phosphatase and tensin homolog and programmed cell death-4 [169,170]. Thus miRNA expression patterns may be useful as biomarkers for HCC classification and prognosis. In addition, exosomal miRNAs, which will be discussed later in this chapter, can also serve as excellent biomarkers for HCC prognosis and diagnosis.

MicroRNA as therapeutic targets in hepatocellular carcinoma

As miRNA has been shown to modulate HCC signaling pathways, using miRNA as a cancer treatment could be effective in HCC prevention. Replacement with miRNA helps suppress cell proliferation or can induce apoptosis in HCC cell lines [171]. However, miRNA administration alone results in poor gene knockdown, as cell permeability is poor, miRNA can be degraded easily by RNAses. miRNA oligomers, cholesterol-bound oligonucleotides, or LNA-modified oligonucleotides (LNA anti-MiRNA) and other technologies have been used to modulate miRNAs, by suppressing or increasing miRNA activity (Fig. 24.5) [172,173]. In addition, vectors can be utilized for the transfer of miRNAs [174,175]. For example, adeno-associated virus (AAV) vectors can be utilized for delivery of miRNA inhibitors or precursors. For example, miR-26a, which is downregulated in HCC compared to normal liver, can suppress HCC development when delivered via AAV vectors [176]. Other potential miRNA replacement targets include miR-122 and 124 [177,178]. Inhibition of miRNA-221 may help with survival in HCC [164,179]. Little toxicity is noted in animal models using miRNA as therapies. In addition, miRNA therapies target the liver, which makes them a good candidate for treatment of HCC [160]. In addition, miRNAs can influence the sensitivity of cancer to various anticancer treatments. For example, miR-21 and miR-181b can induce chemoresistance to doxorubicin and IFN-5-fluorouracil therapy in HCC [180,181]. Other techniques for miRNA delivery are used as well, such as exosomal delivery, which will be discussed below. Exosomes are excellent candidates for delivery of miRNA as they protect miRNA from degradation and do not have toxic effects. The potential for miRNA therapies for HCC is great due to the safety, efficacy, and targeting of the liver directly through hepatic artery branches.

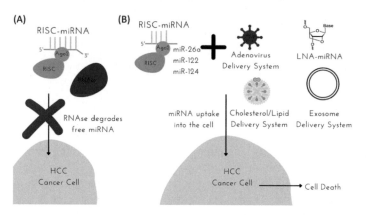

FIGURE 24.5   miRNA delivery for hepatocellular carcinoma (HCC) therapy. (A) Without an efficient delivery system, miRNA is not easily taken up by cells and can be degraded by RNAses. Thus free delivery of miRNAs alone may not be an efficient method of drug delivery for HCC treatment. (B) Several miRNAs have been shown to be effective at reducing HCC proliferation, metastasis, and drug resistance, while enhancing apoptosis, including miR-26a, miR-122, and miR-124. Combined with drug delivery systems such as LNA, cholesterol, liposomes, adenoviruses, and exosomes, these microRNAs can more efficiently be taken up by cancer cells and increase HCC cell death. These drug delivery systems increase miRNA stability, reduce miRNA exposure to RNAses, and increase cell uptake by cancer cells.

Exosomal microRNA in hepatocellular carcinoma

The exosome is an extracellular vesicle (EV) of endosomal origin that ranges from 40 to 160 nm in size and is released from many cell types into the extracellular space [182]. The membranes of the exosome are composed of lipids and proteins, mainly, and the cargo of the exosomal lumen includes proteins, mRNAs, miRNAs, and noncoding RNAs [183]. Exosomes are formed via double invagination of the plasma membrane, early endosome formation, formation of the late sorting endosome, and eventually the formation of multivesicular bodies (MVBs) which contain intraluminal vesicles (ILVs). The MVB will fuse with the plasma membrane, releasing ILVs into the extracellular space, releasing ILVs, or exosomes (Fig. 24.6) [182]. First, the plasma membrane is invaginated, forming a cup-like structure which includes both cell surface and extracellular soluble proteins. The ER and Golgi apparatus can also contribute to the formation of this early sorting endosome that is formed [184]. These early sorting vesicles are matured into late-sorting endosomes, which mature to MVBs. The ILVs inside the MVBs are future exosomes. MVBs can be degraded by fusing with lysosomes or autophagosomes, or fuse with the plasma membrane to release ILVs as exosomes [185]. Exosome trafficking and release is mediated by the RAS GTPase, Rab, as well as other proteins such as Sytenin-1 and SNARE proteins, however, the mechanism of action of these proteins remains to be elucidated [186]. Incorporation of secreted macrophages into the recipient cell is mediated by a variety of mechanisms, including phagocytosis, endocytosis, micropinocytosis, or cell surface protein—receptor interactions [187,188].

Exosomes are highly heterogenic in regard to their size, content, and function [182]. While exosomes often contain protein, lipids, and other metabolites, they also can contain nucleic acids such as miRNA. Exosomes have different amounts of protein and nucleic

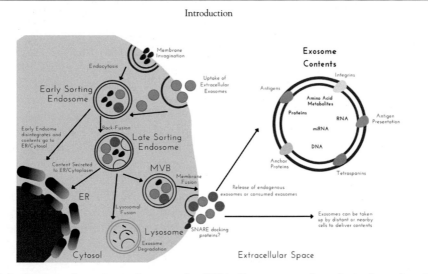

FIGURE 24.6 Exosome formation and exosomal miRNA. Exosomes are formed via the endocytic pathway. Extracellular exosomes can be taken up by the cell and sorted into the early sorting endosome. Double membrane invagination occurs in the endocytic pathway leading to formation of the early sorting endosome. The early sorting endosome can disintegrate and empty its content into the endoplasmic reticulum (ER) or cytoplasm. The late sorting endosome undergoes back-fusion to create intravesicular bodies, which will form the basis for endogenous exosomes. The late sorting endosome may be degraded via fusion with the lysosomes, leading to degradation of exosomes. The late sorting endosome can become a multivesicular body (MVB), with exogenous endosomes, intravesicular bodies (endogenous endosomes), and other protein, nucleic acid, and amino acid metabolites inside of it. The MVB will fuse with the plasma membrane, likely using SNARE proteins for docking mechanisms. This will lead to the release of exosomes that were created endogenously or exogenous exosomes. Exosomes have a variety of proteins associated with their membranes, but also have contents such as proteins, DNA, RNA, amino acid metabolites, and miRNA. Exosomes can be taken up by distant or nearby cells to deliver their contents. In the context of HCC, exosomes can deliver miRNA leading to increased tumor formation in nearby cells but may also contribute to metastasis in this manner.

acid depending on cell type, disease, pathological and physiological conditions, and tissue type [189,190]. The lipids in exosomes not only aid in biological processes but also help maintain stability of exosomes in extracellular fluids [191]. Exosomal miRNAs and long-noncoding RNAs (ncRNAs) can be taken up by recipient cells and then modulate gene expression between cells [192]. Among small RNAs, miRNAs are higher in proportion in exosomes than in parent cells [193]. In addition, miRNA that is sorted into exosomes have specific signal sequences which preferentially sort them into their exosomes and proteins and enzymes may assist with this process [192].

Tumor cells secrete at least 10 times more exosomes than normal cells, and exosomes from tumors can use miRNAs to facilitate this cell−cell communication [194,195]. Exosomal miRNAs can act as tumor suppressors and promoters, by enhancing cell proliferation, metastasis, angiogenesis, and the epithelial-to-mesenchymal transition [195]. One way in which exosomal miRNA may regulate cancer progression is through conversion of normal fibroblasts to cancer-associated fibroblasts. For example, exosomal miRNA-1247-3p is secreted by metastatic HCC cells to activate normal fibroblasts into cancer-associated fibroblasts, promoting metastasis of HCC to the lung [114]. Cancer-associated fibroblasts promote invasion and growth of tumor cells by producing growth factors and inflammatory cytokines, such as IL-8 and IL-6, which activate the extracellular matrix, inducing cancer growth [196]. miRNA-122, a liver-specific miRNA, can inhibit HCC cell growth and is transferred through exosomes between cells [197,198]. Interestingly, when HepG2 cells and Huh7 cells are cocultured, miRNA-122 can be released by exosomes and taken up by miR-122-deficient HepG2 cells, inhibiting growth and promoting HepG2 senescence [199]. These studies show how miRNAs delivered via exosomes may play a role in the promotion/inhibition of tumor metastasis and growth in HCC. Exosomal miRNAs play a role in tumor angiogenesis, metastasis, development, and immune invasion in other forms of cancer, pointing to the importance of furthering our understanding of exosomal miRNAs in HCC development [200].

Exosomal miRNA can also serve as an important biomarker for prognosis, diagnosis, and recurrence in HCC (Table 24.1). The use of exosomal miRNA as a potential biomarker is appealing since exosomes prevent the degradation from RNAse activity, making exosomal miRNA relatively stable [201]. Exosomal miRNAs can be upregulated and downregulated in the context of HCC and a variety of potential diagnostic and prognostic exosomal miRNA biomarkers have been identified. Interestingly, it has been demonstrated that HCC patients have significantly higher serum exosomal miRNA levels than healthy subjects. In this study, serum exosomal miRNA-665 was found to be directly correlated to tumor progression and HCC prognosis [202]. Another miRNA, miR-368 is negatively associated with HCC prognosis [203]. Additionally, exosomal miRNA has been shown to be better at distinguishing HCC from chronic hepatitis B and liver cirrhosis than serum miRNA, with exosomal miR-18a, miR-222, miR-221, and miR-224 dramatically higher than in individuals with cirrhosis and hepatitis [204]. In terms of recurrence, exosome miR-718 has been shown to be lower in serum of patients with recurrence after liver transplantation, which suggests that it may be beneficial to select patients with higher miR-718 for transplantation [205]. Patients with lower exosomal miR-125b also have lower recurrence and better survival in HCC cases [206]. Thus exosomal miRNAs can help with the diagnosis and prognosis of HCC while predicting recurrence as well.

Furthermore, exosomal miRNAs could serve as a tool against HCC as exosomes have the potential to reduce adverse side effects. Exosomes may be used as shuttles to deliver therapeutic miRNAs. Some groups have produced exosomes from adipose tissue-derived mesenchymal stem cells and delivered miRNAs via these delivery systems to inhibit proliferation of tumor cells as well as enhance chemosensitivity in mice [207–209]. Further investigation of the safety and efficacy of therapeutic miRNA delivery via exosomes is undergoing.

Conclusions

HCC is a complex liver disease with high mortality rate, and multiple cellular and molecular factors contribute to its pathogenesis and progression. Asymptomatic nature combined with slow progression in the beginning makes early detection of HCC implausible, emphasizing the requirement of robust diagnostic tools and novel therapies. Recent studies demonstrate that miRNAs are the key regulators in pathogenesis and progression of HCC and represent novel targets for early detection and treatment of HCC. Differential expression of several miRNAs in HCC patients, as authenticated by multiple studies (Table 24.1), make them attractive diagnostic targets. The ability of various miRNA to modulate the signaling pathways in HCC patients as discussed earlier indicate their role in HCC treatment; however, their toxicity, delivery to specific targets, and their interference with other HCC therapies pose a major challenge that require further studies. Importantly, recent data demonstrate exosomal miRNA represent excellent diagnostic as well as therapeutic targets that are less toxic and can be delivered to target organ with high specificity.

Acknowledgment

Authors were supported by NIH's R01-DK1255596 (to SAS) from the National Institute of Diabetes and Digestive and Kidney Diseases and by the UCF Reach for the Stars Award (to SAS). The content is solely the responsibility of the authors and does not necessarily represent the official views of the National Institute of Diabetes and Digestive and Kidney Diseases or the National Institutes of Health.

References

[1] He G, Karin M. NF-κB and STAT3 — key players in liver inflammation and cancer. Cell Res 2011;21:159—68.

[2] Ferlay J, Soerjomataram I, Dikshit R, Eser S, Mathers C, Rebelo M, et al. Cancer incidence and mortality worldwide: sources, methods and major patterns in GLOBOCAN 2012. Int J Cancer 2015;136:E359—86.

[3] Newell P, Villanueva A, Friedman SL, Koike K, Llovet JM. Experimental models of hepatocellular carcinoma. J Hepatol 2008;48:858—79.

[4] Neumann II, Longo D, Fauci A, Kasper D, Hauser S, Jameson J, et al. Harrison's principles of internal medicine; 2011. CDC. Available from: https://www.cdc.gov/cancer/liver/index.htm.

[5] Gavilán JC, Ojeda G, Arnedo R, Puerta S. Predictive factors of risk of hepatocellular carcinoma in chronic hepatitis C. Eur J Intern Med 2013;24:846—51.

[6] El-Serang HB, Rudolph KL. Hepatocellular carcinoma: epidemiology and molecular carcinogenesis. Gastroenterology 2007;132:2557—76.

[7] Idilman IS, Ozdeniz I, Karcaaltincaba M. Hepatic steatosis: etiology, patterns, and quantification. Semin Ultrasound CT MRI 2016;37(6):501—10.

[8] Moore JB. From sugar to liver fat and public health: systems biology driven studies in understanding non-alcoholic fatty liver disease pathogenesis. Proc Nutr Soc 2019;78:290—304.

[9] Marengo A, Rosso C, Bugianesi E. Liver cancer: connections with obesity, fatty liver, and cirrhosis. Annu Rev Med 2016;67:103—17.

[10] Peng S, Chen Y, Gong Y, Li Z, Xie R, Lin Y, et al. Predictive value of intratumour inflammatory cytokine mRNA levels of hepatocellular carcinoma patients and activation of two distinct pathways govern IL-8 induced epithelial-mesenchymal transition in human hepatic cancer cell lines. Cytokine 2019;119:81—9.

[11] Jena P, Sheng L, Liu HX, Kalanetra KM, Mirsoian A, Murphy W, et al. Western diet-Induced dysbiosis in farnesoid X receptor knockout mice causes persistent hepatic inflammation after antibiotic treatment. Am J Pathol 2017;187(8):1800—13.

[12] Mani SKK, Andrisani O. Hepatitis B virus-associated hepatocellular carcinoma and hepatic cancer stem cells. Genes 2018;9(3):137.

[13] Shoelson SE, Herrero L, Naaz A. Obesity, inflammation and insulin resistance. Gastroenterology 2007;132:2169—80.

[14] Caldwell SH, Crespo DM, Kang HS, Al-Osaimi AM. Gastroenterology 2004;127:97—103.

[15] Marchesini G, Moscatiello S, Di Domizio S, Forlani G. Obesity-associated liver disease. J Clin Endocrinol Metab 2008;93:74—80.

[16] Yatsuji S, Hashimoto E, Tobari M. Clinical features and outcomes of cirrhosis due to nonalcoholic steatohepatitis compared with cirrhosis caused by chronic hepatitis C. J Gastroenterol Hepatol 2009;24:248—54.

[17] Sanyal AJ, Banas C, Sargeant C. Similarities and differences in outcomes of cirrhosis due to nonalcoholic steatohepatitis and hepatitis C. Hepatology 2006;43:682—9.

[18] Hirosumi J, Tuncman G, Chang L, et al. A central role for JNK in obesity and insulin resistance. Nature 2002;420:333—6.

[19] Hodge DR, Hurt EM, Farrar WL. The role of IL-6 and STAT3 in inflammation and cancer. Eur J Cancer 2005;41:2502−12.

[20] Jiang N, Sun R, Sun Q. Leptin signaling molecular actions and drug target in hepatocellular carcinoma. Drug Des Dev Ther 2014;8:2295−302.

[21] Villanueva A, Chiang DY, Newell P, et al. Pivotal role of mTOR signaling in hepatocellular carcinoma. Gastroenterology 2008;135:1972−83.

[22] Sharma D, Wang J, Fu PP, et al. Adiponectin antagonizes the oncogenic actions of leptin in hepatocellular carcinogenesis. Hepatology 2010;52:1713−22.

[23] Yang N, Ekanem NR, Sakyi CA, Ray SD. Hepatocellular carcinoma and microRNA: new perspectives on therapeutics and diagnostics. Adv Drug Deliv Rev 2015;81:62−74.

[24] Altekruse SF, McGlynn KA, Reichman ME. J Clin Oncol 2009;27:1485−91.

[25] Chen L, Ho DW, Lee NP, Sun S, Lam B, Wong KF, et al. Enhanced detection of early hepatocellular carcinoma by serum SELDI-TOF proteomic signature combined with alpha-fetoprotein marker. Ann Surg Oncol 2010;17:2518−25.

[26] Forner A, Reig ME, de Lope CR, Bruix J. Current strategy for staging and treatment: the BCLC update and future prospects. Seminars in liver disease. Thieme Medical Publishers; 2010. p. 61−74.

[27] Sidransky D. Emerging molecular markers of cancer. Nat Rev Cancer 2002;2:210−19.

[28] Daniele B, Bencivenga A, Megna AS, Tinessa V. Alpha-fetoprotein and ultrasonography screening for hepatocellular carcinoma. Gastroenterology 2004;127:108−12.

[29] Gish RG, Marrero JA, Benson AB. A multidisciplinary approach to the management of hepatocellular carcinoma. Gastroenterol Hepatol 2010;6:1−16.

[30] Liu JG, Wang YJ, Du Z. Radiofrequency ablation in the treatment of small hepatocellular carcinoma: A meta analysis. World J Gastroenterol 2010;16:3450−6.

[31] Ota H, Nagano H, Sakon M, Eguchi H, Kondo M, Yamamoto T, et al. Treatment of hepatocellular carcinoma with major portal vein thrombosis by combined therapy with subcutaneous interferon-α and intra-arterial 5-fluorouracil; role of type 1 interferon receptor expression. Br J Cancer 2005;93:557−64.

[32] Yu LH, Li N, Cheng SQ. The Role of Antiviral Therapy for HBV-Related Hepatocellular Carcinoma. Int J Hepatol 2011;2011:416459.

[33] Hsu CH, Yang TS, Hsu C, Toh HC, Epstein RJ, Hsiao LT, et al. Efficacy and tolerability of bevacizumab plus capecitabine as first-line therapy in patients with advanced hepatocellular carcinoma. Br J Cancer 2010;102:981−6.

[34] Chan LH, Luk ST, Ma S. Turning hepatic cancer stem cells inside out − a deeper understanding through multiple perspectives. Mol Cell 2015;38(3):202−9.

[35] Haraguchi N, Ishii H, Mimori K, Tanaka F, Ohkuma M, Kim HM, et al. CD13 is a therapeutic target in human liver cancer stem cells. J Clin Invest 2010;120:3326−39.

[36] Ma S, Chan KW, Hu L, Lee TK, Wo JY, Ng IO, et al. Identification and characterization of tumorigenic liver cancer stem/progenitor cells. Gastroenterology 2007;132:2542−56.

[37] Llovet JM, Bru C, Bruix J. Prognosis of hepatocellular carcinoma: the BCLC staging classification. Semin Liver Dis 1999;19:329−38.

[38] Bruix J, Sherman M. Management of hepatocellular carcinoma: an update. Hepatology 2011;53:1020−2.

[39] Haznadar M, Diehl CM, Parker AL, Krausz KW, Bowman ED, Rabibhadana S, et al. Urinary metabolites diagnostic and prognostic of intrahepatic cholangiocarcinoma. Cancer Epidemiol Biomarkers Prev 2019;28:1704−11.

[40] DePeralta DK, Wei L, Ghoshal S, Schmidt D, Lauwers G, Lanuti M, et al. Metformin prevents hepatocellular carcinoma development by suppressing hepatic progenitor cell activation in a rat model of cirrhosis. Cancer 2016;122(8):1216−27.

[41] Kubo N, Araki K, Kuwano H, Shirabe K. Cancer-associated fibroblasts in hepatocellular carcinoma. World J Gastroenterol 2016;22:6841−50.

[42] McDonald GB, Freston JW, Boyer JL, DeLeve LD. Liver complications following treatment of hematologic malignancy with anti-CD22-calicheamicin (inotuzumab ozogamicin). Hepatology 2019;69:831−44.

[43] Oh J, Hlatky L, Jeong YS, Kim D. Therapeutic effectiveness of anticancer phytochemicals on cancer stem cells. Toxins 2016;8:199.

[44] Li S, Yang F, Ren X. Immunotherapy for hepatocellular carcinoma. Drug Discov Ther 2015;9:363−71.

[45] Lee RC, Feinbaum RL, Ambros V. The *C. elegans* heterochronic gene lin-4 encodes small RNAs with antisense complementarity to lin-14. Cell 1993;75:843—54.

[46] Wightman B, Ha I, Ruvkun G. Posttranscriptional regulation of the heterochronic gene lin-14 by lin-4 mediates temporal pattern formation in *C. elegans*. Cell 1993;75:855—62.

[47] Lee R, Feinbaum R, Ambros V. A short history of a short RNA. Cell 2004;116(2 Suppl.):S89—92.

[48] Almeida MI, Reis RM, Calin GA. MicroRNA history: discovery, recent applications, and next frontiers. Mutat Res 2011;717:1—8.

[49] Annese T, et al. MicroRNAs biogenesis, functions and role in tumor angiogenesis. Frontiers Oncol 2020;10:581007.

[50] Farazi TA, Juranek SA, Tuschl T. The growing catalog of small RNAs and their association with distinct Argonaute/Piwi family members. Development 2008;135:1201—14.

[51] O'Brien J, et al. Overview of microRNA biogenesis, mechanisms of actions, and circulation. Front Endocrinol 2018;9:402.

[52] Ha M, Kim VN. Regulation of microRNA biogenesis. Nat Rev Mol Cell Biol 2014;15:509—24.

[53] Broughton JP, Lovci MT, Huang JL, Yeo GW, Pasquinelli AE. Pairing beyond the seed supports microRNA targeting specificity. Mol Cell 2016;64:320—33.

[54] Vasudevan S. Posttranscriptional upregulation by microRNAs. Wiley Interdiscip Rev RNA 2012;3:311—30.

[55] Kim YK, Kim VN. Processing of intronic microRNAs. EMBO J 2007;26(3):775—83.

[56] Olena AF, Patton JG. Genomic organization of microRNAs. J Cell Physiol 2010;222(3):540—5.

[57] Rodriguez A, et al. Identification of mammalian microRNA host genes and transcription units. Genome Res 2004;14(10A):1902—10.

[58] Tanzer A, Stadler PF. Molecular evolution of a microRNA cluster. J Mol Biol 2004;339:327—35. Available from: https://doi.org/10.1016/j.jmb.2004.03.065.

[59] Krol J, et al. The widespread regulation of microRNA biogenesis, function and decay. Nat Rev Genet 2010;11:597—610.

[60] Michlewski G, Caceres JF. Post-transcriptional control of miRNA biogenesis. RNA 2019;25:1—16.

[61] Gregory RI, Yan KP, Amuthan G, Chendrimada T, Doratotaj B, Cooch N, et al. The microprocessor complex mediates the genesis of microRNAs. Nature 2004;432:235—40.

[62] Nguyen TA, Jo MH, Choi YG, Park J, Kwon SC, Hohng S, et al. Functional anatomy of the human microprocessor. Cell 2015;161:1374—87.

[63] Cleveland Q, Jacob JP, Weitz SH, Shoffner G, Senturia R, Guo F. The DGCR8 RNA-binding heme domain recognizes primary microRNAs by clamping the hairpin. Cell Rep 2014;7:1994—2005.

[64] Nguyen TA, Park J, Dang TL, Choi YG, Kim VN. Microprocessor depends on hemin to recognize the apical loop of primary microRNA. Nucleic Acids Res 2018;46:5726—36.

[65] Liu P, et al. Age-specific sex difference in the incidence of hepatocellular carcinoma in the United States. Oncotarget 2017;8(40):68131—7.

[66] Okada C, et al. A high-resolution structure of the pre-microRNA nuclear export machinery. Science 2009;326 (5957):1275—9.

[67] Cullen BR. Transcription and processing of human microRNA precursors. Mol Cell 2004;16(6):861—5.

[68] Noland CL, Doudna JA. Multiple sensors ensure guide strand selection in human RNAi pathways. RNA 2013;19:639—48.

[69] Liu J, et al. Argonaute2 is the catalytic engine of mammalian RNAi. Science 2004;305(5689):1437—41.

[70] Kobayashi H, Tomari Y. RISC assembly: coordination between small RNAs and Argonaute proteins. Biochim Biophys Acta 2016;1859:71—81.

[71] Siomi H, Siomi MC. On the road to reading the RNA-interference code. Nature 2009;457(7228):396—404.

[72] Kanellopoulou C, Monticelli S. A role for microRNAs in the development of the immune system and in the pathogenesis of cancer. Semin Cancer Biol 2008;18(2):79—88.

[73] Filipowicz W, et al. Mechanisms of post-transcriptional regulation by microRNAs: are the answers in sight? Nat Rev Genet 2008;9(2):102—14.

[74] Seok H, et al. MicroRNA target recognition: insights from transcriptome-wide non-canonical interactions. Mol Cell 2016;39(5):375—81.

[75] Bose M, et al. Spatiotemporal uncoupling of microRNA-mediated translational repression and target RNA degradation controls microRNP recycling in mammalian cells. Mol Cell Biol 2017;37(4):e00464 16.

[76] Stalder L, et al. The rough endoplasmic reticulum is a central nucleation site of siRNA-mediated RNA silencing. EMBO J 2013;32(8):1115—27.

[77] Davis-Dusenbery BN, Hata A. Mechanisms of control of microRNA biogenesis. J Biochem 2010;148:381—92.

[78] Yang JS, Lai EC. Alternative miRNA biogenesis pathways and the interpretation of core miRNA pathway mutants. Mol Cell 2011;43:892–903.

[79] Felekkis K, Touvana E, Stefanou C, Deltas C. MicroRNAs: a newly described class of encoded molecules that play a role in health and disease. Hippokratia 2010;14:236–40.

[80] Ruby JG, et al. Intronic microRNA precursors that bypass Drosha processing. Nature 2007;448:83–6.

[81] Rorbach G, et al. Distinguishing mirtrons from canonical miRNAs with data exploration and machine learning methods. Sci Rep 2018;8(1):7560.

[82] Cheloufi S, et al. A dicer-independent miRNA biogenesis pathway that requires Ago catalysis. Nature 2010;465(7298):584–9.

[83] Herrera-Carrillo E, Berkhout B. Dicer-independent processing of small RNA duplexes: mechanistic insights and applications. Nucleic Acids Res 2017;45(18):10369–79.

[84] Harwig A, Kruize Z, Yang Z, Restle T, Berkhout B. Analysis of AgoshRNA maturation and loading into Ago2. PLoS One 2017;12(8):e0183269.

[85] Sun J. MicroRNAs in hepatocellular carinoma: regulation, function and clinical implications. Sci World J 2013;924206.

[86] El-Serag HB. Epidemiology of viral hepatitis and hepatocellular carcinoma. Gastroenterology 2012;142:1264–73.

[87] Liu WH, Yeh SH, Lu CC, Yu SL, Chen HY, Lin CY, et al. MicroRNA-18a prevents estrogen receptor-alpha expression, promoting proliferation of hepatocellular carcinoma cells. Gastroenterology 2009;136:683–93.

[88] Jemal A, et al. Global cancer statistics. CA: Cancer J Clinicians 2011;61(2):69–90.

[89] Wang Y, et al. Lethal-7 is down-regulated by the hepatitis B virus x protein and targets signal transducer and activator of transcription 3. J Hepatol 2007;53(1):57–66.

[90] Sampson VB, et al. MicroRNA let-7a down-regulates MYC and reverts MYC-induced growth in Burkitt lymphoma cells. Cancer Res 2007;67:9762–70.

[91] Johnson SM, et al. RAS is regulated by the let-7 microRNA family. Cell 2005;120:635–47.

[92] Lee YS, Dutta A. The tumor suppressor microRNA let-7 represses the HMGA2 oncogene. Genes Dev 2007;21:1025–30.

[93] Wang Y, Lee CG. MicroRNA and cancer-focus on apoptosis. J Cell Mol Med 2009;13:12–23.

[94] Huynh J, et al. Therapeutically exploiting STAT3 activity in cancer-using tissue repair as a roadmap. Nat Rev Cancer 2019;19:82–96.

[95] Al Zaid Siddiquee K, Turkson J. STAT3 as a target for inducing apoptosis in solid and hematological tumors. Cell Res 2008;18:254–67.

[96] Hou W, et al. MicroRNA-196 represses Bach1 protein and hepatitis C virus gene expression in human hepatoma cells expressing hepatitis C viral proteins. Hepatology 2010;51(5):1494–504.

[97] Dolganiuc A, et al. MicroRNA expression profile in lieber-decarli diet-induced alcoholic and methionine choline deficient diet-induced nonalcoholic steatohepatitis models in mice. Alcoholism Clin Exp Res 2009;33(10):1704–10.

[98] Li J, et al. Long noncoding RNAs regulate cell growth, proliferation, and apoptosis. DNA Cell Biol 2016;35(9):459–70.

[99] Ruijtenberg S, van den Heuvel S. Coordinating cell proliferation and differentiation: antagonism between cell cycle regulators and cell type-specific gene expression. Cell Cycle 2016;15:196–212.

[100] Matsuura K, et al. Metabolic regulation of apoptosis in cancer. Int Rev Cell Mol Biol 2016;327:43–87.

[101] Mohamed MS, et al. Inhibitors of apoptosis: clinical implications in cancer. Apoptosis 2017;22(12):1487–509.

[102] Xu X, et al. The role of microRNAs in hepatocellular carcinoma. J Cancer 2018;9(19):3557–69.

[103] Liu Z, Wang Y, Dou C, Sun L, Li Q, Wang L, et al. MicroRNA-1468 promotes tumor progression by activating PPAR-gamma-mediated AKT signaling in human hepatocellular carcinoma. J Exp Clin Cancer Res 2018;37:49.

[104] Yang Y, Li M, Chang S, Wang L, Song T, Gao L, et al. MicroRNA-195 acts as a tumor suppressor by directly targeting Wnt3a in HepG2 hepatocellular carcinoma cells. Mol Med Rep 2014;10:2643–8.

[105] Zhu H, Wang G, Zhou X, Song X, Gao H, Ma C, et al. miR-1299 suppresses cell proliferation of hepatocellular carcinoma (HCC) by targeting CDK6. Biomed Pharmacother 2016;83:792–7.

[106] Iwai N, Yasui K, Tomie A, Gen Y, Terasaki K, Kitaichi T, et al. Oncogenic miR-96-5p inhibits apoptosis by targeting the caspase-9 gene in hepatocellular carcinoma. Int J Oncol 2018;53(1):237–45.

[107] Villanueva A, et al. Pivotal role of mTOR signaling in hepatocellular carcinoma. Gastroenterology 2008;135 (6):1972–83.

[108] Jiang D, et al. MiR-758-3p suppresses proliferation, migration and invasion of hepatocellular carcinoma cells via targeting MDM2 and mTOR. Biomed Pharmacother 2017;96:535–44.

[109] Yu Q, et al. Loss-of-function of miR-142 by hypermethylation promotes TGF-β-mediated tumour growth and metastasis in hepatocellular carcinoma. Cell Prolif 2017;50(6).

[110] Vasuri F, et al. Role of microRNAs in the main molecular pathways of hepatocellular carcinoma. World J Gasteroenterol 2018;24(25):2647–60.

[111] Valastyan S, Weinberg RA. Tumor metastasis: molecular insights and evolving paradigms. Cell 2011;147 (2):275–92.

[112] Zaravinos A. The regulatory role of microRNAs in EMT and cancer. J Oncol 2015;865816.

[113] Jiang C, Li X, Zhao H, Liu H. Long non-coding RNAs: potential new biomarkers for predicting tumor invasion and metastasis. Mol Cancer 2016;15(1):62.

[114] Fang T, et al. Tumor-derived exosomal miR-1247-3p induces cancer-associated fibroblast activation to foster lung metastasis of liver cancer. Nat Commun 2018;9:191.

[115] Wang C, Wang X, Su Z, Fei H, Liu X, Pan Q. miR-25 promotes hepatocellular carcinoma cell growth, migration and invasion by inhibiting RhoGDI1. Oncotarget 2015;6:36231–44.

[116] Zeng YB, Liang XH, Zhang GX, Jiang N, Zhang T, Huang JY, et al. miRNA-135a promotes hepatocellular carcinoma cell migration and invasion by targeting forkhead box O1. Cancer Cell Int 2016;16:63.

[117] Lou W, et al. MicroRNAs in cancer metastasis and angiogenesis. Oncotarget 2017;8(70):115787–802.

[118] Xia H, Ooi LLPJ, Hui KM. MicroRNA-216a/217-induced epithelial-mesenchymal transition targets PTEN and SMAD7 to promote drug resistance and recurrence of liver cancer. Hepatology 2013;58:629–41. Available from: https://doi.org/10.1002/hep.26369.

[119] Liu X, et al. MicroRNAs: biogenesis and molecular functions. Brain Pathol 2008;18(1):113–21.

[120] Zhu YJ, Zheng B, Wang HY, Chen L. New knowledge of the mechanisms of sorafenib resistance in liver cancer. Acta Pharmacol Sin 2017;38(5):614–22.

[121] Le Grazie M, Biagini MR, Tarocchi M, Polvani S, Galli A. Chemotherapy for hepatocellular carcinoma: the present and the future. World J Hepatol 2017;9(21):907–20.

[122] Chen KF, Chen HL, Tai WT, Feng WC, Hsu CH, Chen PJ, et al. Activation of phosphatidylinositol 3-kinase/Akt signaling pathway mediates acquired resistance to sorafenib in hepatocellular carcinoma cells. J Pharmacol Exp Ther 2011;337(1):155–61.

[123] Cox J, Weinman S. Mechanisms of doxorubicin resistance in hepatocellular carcinoma. Hepat Oncol 2016;3 (1):57–9.

[124] Vasiliou V, Vasiliou K, Nebert DW. Human ATP-binding cassette (ABC) transporter family. Hum Genomics 2009;3(3):281–90.

[125] Wen DY, Huang JC, Wang JY, Pan WY, Zeng JH, Pang YY, et al. Potential clinical value and putative biological function of miR-122-5p in hepatocellular carcinoma: a comprehensive study using microarray and RNA sequencing data. Oncol Lett 2018;16(6):6918–29.

[126] Yahya SMM, Fathy SA, El-Khayat ZA, et al. Possible role of microRNA-122 in modulating multidrug resistance of hepatocellular carcinoma. Indian J Clin Biochem 2018;33:21–30. Available from: https://doi.org/10.1007/s12291-017-0651-8.

[127] Xu Y, Xia F, Ma L, Shan J, Shen J, Yang Z, et al. MicroRNA-122 sensitizes HCC cancer cells to adriamycin and vincristine through modulating expression of MDR and inducing cell cycle arrest. Cancer Lett 2011;310 (2):160–9.

[128] Yang T, Zheng ZM, Li XN, et al. miR-223 modulates multidrug resistance via downregulation of ABCB1 in hepatocellular carcinoma cells. Exp Biol Med 2013;238:1024–32. Available from: https://doi.org/10.1177/1535370213497321.

[129] Pan C, Wang X, Shi K, et al. miR-122 reverses the doxorubicin-resistance in hepatocellular carcinoma cells through regulating the tumor metabolism. PLoS One 2016;11:e0152090. Available from: https://doi.org/10.1371/journal.pone.0152090.

[130] Fan YP, Liao JZ, Lu YQ, Tian DA, Ye F, Zhao PX, et al. MiR-375 and doxorubicin co-delivered by liposomes for combination therapy of hepatocellular carcinoma. Mol Ther Nucleic Acids 2017;7:181–9.

[131] Chen M, Wu L, Tu J, Zhao Z, Fan X, Mao J, et al. miR-590-5p suppresses hepatocellular carcinoma chemoresistance by targeting YAP1 expression. EBioMedicine 2018;35:142–54.

[132] Aredia F, Scovassi AI. A new function for miRNAs as regulators of autophagy. Future Med Chem 2017;9 (1):25–36.

[133] Chen L, Zhou Y, Sun Q, Zhou J, Pan H, Sui X. Regulation of autophagy by miRNAs and their emerging roles in tumorigenesis and cancer treatment. Int Rev Cell Mol Biol 2017;334:1–26.

[134] Lee YJ, Jang BK. The role of autophagy in hepatocellular carcinoma. Int J Mol Sci 2015;16(11):26629–43.

[135] Sui X, Chen R, Wang Z, Huang Z, Kong N, Zhang M, et al. Autophagy and chemotherapy resistance: a promising therapeutic target for cancer treatment. Cell Death Dis 2013;4:e838.

[136] White E, DiPaola RS. The double-edged sword of autophagy modulation in cancer. Clin Cancer Res 2009;15 (17):5308–16.

[137] Yang J, He Y, Zhai N, Ding S, Li JP, Peng Z. MicroRNA-181a inhibits autophagy by targeting Atg5 in hepatocellular carcinoma. Front Biosci 2018;23:388–96.

[138] Wang Y, Wang Q, Song J. Inhibition of autophagy potentiates the proliferation inhibition activity of microRNA-7 in human hepatocellular carcinoma cells. Oncol Lett 2017;14(3):3566–72.

[139] Pratama MY, et al. The role of microRNA in the resistance to treatment of hepatocellular carcinoma. Ann Transl Med 2019;7(20):577.

[140] Yao H, Liu N, Lin MC, Zheng J. Positive feedback loop between cancer stem cells and angiogenesis in hepatocellular carcinoma. Cancer Lett 2016;379(2):213–19.

[141] Terry K, Copur MS. Molecular targeted therapy of hepatocellular carcinoma. J Cancer Ther 2013;4:426–39.

[142] Liu K, Min XL, Peng J, Yang K, Yang L, Zhang XM. The changes of HIF-1α and VEGF expression after TACE in patients with hepatocellular carcinoma. J Clin Med Res 2016;8(4):297–302.

[143] Zhu AX, Duda DG, Sahani DV, Jain RK. HCC and angiogenesis: possible targets and future directions. Nat Rev Clin Oncol 2011;8(5):292–301.

[144] Zhang Z, Zhang Y, Sun XX, Ma X, Chen ZN. microRNA-146a inhibits cancer metastasis by downregulating VEGF through dual pathways in hepatocellular carcinoma. Mol Cancer 2015;14:5.

[145] Ghosh A, Dasgupta D, Ghosh A, Roychoudhury S, Kumar D, Gorain M, et al. MiRNA199a-3p suppresses tumor growth, migration, invasion and angiogenesis in hepatocellular carcinoma by targeting VEGFA, VEGFR1, VEGFR2, HGF and MMP2. Cell Death Dis 2017;8:e2706.

[146] Cheng J, Chen Y, Zhao P, Liu X, Dong J, Li J, et al. Downregulation of miRNA-638 promotes angiogenesis and growth of hepatocellular carcinoma by targeting VEGF. Oncotarget 2016;7:30702–11.

[147] Zhang T, Liu W, Zeng XC, Jiang N, Fu BS, Guo Y, et al. Down-regulation of microRNA-338-3p promoted angiogenesis in hepatocellular carcinoma. Biomed Pharmacother 2016;84:583–91.

[148] Yan JJ, Zhang YN, Liao JZ, Ke KP, Chang Y, Li PY, et al. MiR-497 suppresses angiogenesis and metastasis of hepatocellular carcinoma by inhibiting VEGFA and AEG-1. Oncotarget 2015;6:29517–42.

[149] Bertino G, et al. Diagnostic and prognostic value of alpha-fetoprotein, des-gamma-carboxy prothrombin and squamous cell carcinoma antigen immunoglobulin M complexes in hepatocellular carcinoma. Minerva Med 2011;102(5):363–71.

[150] Braconi C, Patel T. MicroRNA expression profiling: a molecular tool for defining the phenotype of hepatocellular tumors. Hepatology 2008;47:1807–9.

[151] Huang YS, Dai Y, Yu XF, Bao SY, Yin YB, Tang M, et al. Microarray analysis of microRNA expression in hepatocellular carcinoma and non-tumorous tissues without viral hepatitis. J Gastroenterol Hepatol 2008;23:87–94.

[152] Ladeiro Y, Couchy G, Balabaud C, Bioulac-Sage P, Pelletier L, Rebouissou S, et al. MicroRNA profiling in hepatocellular tumors is associated with clinical features and oncogene/tumor suppressor gene mutations. Hepatology 2008;47:1955–63.

[153] Varnholt H, Drebber U, Schulze F, Wedemeyer I, Schirmacher P, Dienes HP, et al. MicroRNA gene expression profile of hepatitis C virus-associated hepatocellular carcinoma. Hepatology 2008;47:1223–32.

[154] Wang Y, Lee AT, Ma JZ, Wang J, Ren J, Yang Y, et al. Profiling microRNA expression in hepatocellular carcinoma reveals microRNA-224 up-regulation and apoptosis inhibitor-5 as a microRNA-224-specific target. J Biol Chem 2008;283:13205–15.

[155] Wong QW, Lung RW, Law PT, Lai PB, Chan KY, To KF, et al. MicroRNA-223 is commonly repressed in hepatocellular carcinoma and potentiates expression of Stathmin1. Gastroenterology 2008;135:257–69.

[156] Murakami Y, Yasuda T, Saigo K, Urashima T, Toyoda H, Okanoue T, et al. Comprehensive analysis of microRNA expression patterns in hepatocellular carcinoma and non-tumorous tissues. Oncogene 2006;25:2537–45.

[157] Kutay H, Bai S, Datta J, Motiwala T, Pogribny I, Frankel W, et al. Downregulation of miR-122 in the rodent and human hepatocellular carcinomas. J Cell Biochem 2006;99:671—8.

[158] Budhu A, Jia HL, Forgues M, Liu CG, Goldstein D, Lam A, et al. Identification of metastasis-related microRNAs in hepatocellular carcinoma. Hepatology 2008;47:897—907.

[159] Gramantieri L, Ferracin M, Fornari F, Veronese A, Sabbioni S, Liu CG, et al. Cyclin G1 is a target of miR-122a, a microRNA frequently down-regulated in human hepatocellular carcinoma. Cancer Res 2007;67:6092—9.

[160] Gramantieri L, et al. MicroRNA involvement in hepatocellular carcinoma. J Cell Mol Med 2008;12 (6a):2189—204.

[161] Jin Y, et al. Circulating microRNAs as potential diagnostic and prognostic biomarkers in hepatocellular carcinoma. Sci Rep 2019;9:10464.

[162] Barbara L, et al. Natural history of small untreated hepatocellular carcinoma in cirrhosis: a multivariate analysis of prognostic factors of tumor growth rate and patient survival. Hepatology 1992;16:132—7.

[163] Bruix J, Boix L, Sala M, Llovet JM. Focus on hepatocellular carcinoma. Cancer Cell 2004;5:215—19.

[164] Callegari E, et al. Liver tumorigenicity promoted by microRNA-221 in a mouse transgenic model. Hepatology 2012;56:1025—33.

[165] Liu C, Yu J, Yu S, et al. MicroRNA-21 acts as an oncomir through multiple targets in human hepatocellular carcinoma. J Hepatol 2010;53:98—107.

[166] Meng F, Henson R, Wehbe-Janek H, Ghoshal K, Jacob ST, Patel T. MicroRNA-21 regulates expression of the PTEN tumor suppressor gene in human hepatocellular cancer. Gastroenterology 2007;133:647—58.

[167] Tomimaru Y, Eguchi H, Nagano H, et al. Circulating microRNA-21 as a novel biomarker for hepatocellular carcinoma. J Hepatol 2012;56:167—75.

[168] Tomimaru Y, Eguchi H, Nagano H, et al. MicroRNA-21 induces resistance to the anti-tumour effect of interferon-alpha/5-fluorouracil in hepatocellular carcinoma cells. Br J Cancer 2010;103:1617—26.

[169] Bao L, Yan Y, Xu C, et al. MicroRNA-21 suppresses PTEN and hSulf-1 expression and promotes hepatocellular carcinoma progression through AKT/ERK pathways. Cancer Lett 2013;337:226—36.

[170] Zhu Q, Wang Z, Hu Y, et al. miR-21 promotes migration and invasion by the miR-21-PDCD4-AP-1 feedback loop in human hepatocellular carcinoma. Oncol Rep 2012;27:1660—8.

[171] Chung HJ, et al. miR-29b attenuates tumorigenicity and stemness maintenance in human glioblastoma multiforme by directly targeting BCL2L2. Oncotarget 2015;6:18429—44.

[172] Krutzfeldt J, Rajewsky N, Braich R, Rajeev KG, Tuschl T, Manoharan M, et al. Silencing of microRNAs in vivo with 'antagomirs'. Nature 2005;438:685—9.

[173] Elmen J, Lindow M, Schutz S, Lawrence M, Petri A, Obad S, et al. LNA-mediated microRNA silencing in non-human primates. Nature 2008;452:896—9.

[174] Amodeo V, et al. Effects of anti-miR-182 on TSP-1 expression in human colon cancer cells: there is a sense in antisense? Expert Opin Ther Targets 2013;17:1249—61.

[175] Nedaeinia R, et al. Locked nucleic acid anti-miR-21 inhibits cell growth and invasive behaviors of a colorectal adenocarcinoma cell line: LNA-anti-miR as a novel approach. Cancer Gene Ther 2016;23:246—53.

[176] Kota J, et al. Therapeutic microRNA delivery suppresses tumorigenesis in a murine liver cancer model. Cell 2009;137:1005—17.

[177] Lang Q, et al. MiR-124 suppresses cell proliferation in hepatocellular carcinoma by targeting PIK3CA. Biochem Biophys Res Commun 2012;426:247—52.

[178] Tsai WC, et al. MicroRNA-122, a tumor suppressor microRNA that regulates intrahepatic metastasis of hepatocellular carcinoma. Hepatology 2009;49:1571—82.

[179] Park JK, et al. miR-221 silencing blocks hepatocellular carcinoma and promotes survival. Cancer Res 2011;71:7608—16.

[180] Scisciani C, et al. Transcriptional regulation of miR-224 upregulated in human HCCs by NFB inflammatory pathways. J Hepatol 2012;56:855—61.

[181] Wang B, et al. TGF-mediated upregulation of hepatic miR-181b promotes hepatocarcinogenesis by targeting TIMP3. Oncogene 2010;29:1787—97.

[182] Kalluri R, LeBlue VS. The biology, function, and biomedical applications of exosomes. Science 2020;367: eaau6977.

[183] Mathivanan S, et al. Exosomes: extracellular organelles important in intercellular communication. J Proteom 2010;73:1907—20.

[184] Kalluri R. The biology and function of exosomes in cancer. J Clin Investigation 2016;126:1208–15.

[185] Van Niel G, et al. Shedding light on the cell biology of extracellular vesicles. Nat Rev Mol Cell Biol 2018;19:213–28.

[186] Mathieu M, et al. Specificities of secretion and uptake of exosomes and other extracellular vesicles for cell-to-cell communication. Nat Cell Biol 2019;21:9–17.

[187] Hessvik NP, Llorente A. Current knowledge on exosome biogenesis and release. Cell Mol Life Sci 2018;75(2):193–208.

[188] McKelvey KJ, et al. Exosomes: mechanisms of uptake. J Circ Biomark 2015;4(7).

[189] Kogure T, Lin WL, Yan IK, Braconi C, Patel T. Intercellular nanovesicle-mediated microRNA transfer: a mechanism of environmental modulation of hepatocellular cancer cell growth. Hepatology 2011;54:1237–48.

[190] Yang N, Li S, Li G, Zhang S, Tang X, Ni S, et al. The role of extracellular vesicles in mediating progression, metastasis and potential treatment of hepatocellular carcinoma. Oncotarget 2017;8:3683–95.

[191] Yuyama K, Sun H, Mitsutake S, Igarashi Y. Sphingolipid-modulated exosome secretion promotes clearance of amyloid-β by microglia. J Biol Chem 2012;287:10977–89.

[192] Zhang J, et al. Exosome and exosomal microRNA: trafficking, sorting and function. Genom Proteom Bioinform 2015;13(1):17–24.

[193] Goldie BJ, et al. Activity-associated miRNA are packaged in Map1b-enriched exosomes released from depolarized neurons. Nucleic Acids Res 2014;42:9195–208.

[194] Akers JC, et al. Biogenesis of extracellular vesicles (EV): exosomes, microvesicles, retrovirus-like vesicles, and apoptotic bodies. J Neuro-Oncol 2013;113:1–11.

[195] Mao L, et al. Serum exosomes contain ECRG4 mRNA that suppresses tumor growth via inhibition of genes involved in inflammation, cell proliferation, and angiogenesis. Cancer Gene Ther 2018;25:248–59.

[196] Du YE, et al. MiR-205/YAP1 in activated fibroblasts of breast tumor promotes VEGF-independent angiogenesis through STAT3 signaling. Theranostics 2017;7:3972–88.

[197] Hsu SH, et al. Essential metabolic, anti-inflammatory, and anti-tumorigenic functions of miR-122 in liver. J Clin Invest 2012;122(8):2871–83.

[198] Zeisel MB, Pfeffer S, Baumert TF. miR-122 acts as a tumor suppressor in hepatocarcinogenesis in vivo. J Hepatol 2013;58(4):821–3.

[199] Basu S, Bhattacharyya SN. Insulin-like growth factor-1 prevents miR-122 production in neighbouring cells to curtail its intercellular transfer to ensure proliferation of human hepatoma cells. Nucleic Acids Res 2014;42(11):7170–85.

[200] Sun S, et al. Effect of exosomal miRNA on cancer biology and clinical applications. Mol Cancer 2018;17:147.

[201] Chen X, et al. Characterization of microRNAs in serum: a novel class of biomarkers for diagnosis of cancer and other diseases. Cell Res 2008;18(10):997–1006.

[202] Qu Z, et al. Exosomal miR-665 as a novel minimally invasive biomarker for hepatocellular carcinoma diagnosis and prognosis. Oncotarget. 2017;8(46):80666–78.

[203] Shi M, et al. Decreased levels of serum exosomal miR-638 predict poor prognosis in hepatocellular carcinoma. J Cell Biochem 2017;119(6):4711–16.

[204] Sohn W, et al. Serum exosomal microRNAs as novel biomarkers for hepatocellular carcinoma. Exp Mol Med 2015;47:e184.

[205] Sugimachi K, et al. Identification of a bona fide microRNA biomarker in serum exosomes that predicts hepatocellular carcinoma recurrence after liver transplantation. Br J Cancer 2015;112(3):532–8.

[206] Liu W, et al. Serum exosomal miR-125b is a novel prognostic marker for hepatocellular carcinoma. Onco Targets Ther 2017;10:3843–51.

[207] Yeo RW, et al. Mesenchymal stem cell: an efficient mass producer of exosomes for drug delivery. Adv Drug Deliv Rev 2013;65(3):336–41.

[208] Lou G, et al. Exosomes derived from miR-122-modified adipose tissue-derived MSCs increase chemosensitivity of hepatocellular carcinoma. J Hematol Oncol 2015;8:122.

[209] Tsai WC, et al. MicroRNA-122 plays a critical role in liver homeostasis and hepatocarcinogenesis. J Clin Invest 2012;122(8):2884–97.

Pharmacogenomics and outcomes for hepatocellular cancer treatment

Mohan Krishna Ghanta[1], Mohammad Faiz Hussain[2], Asmita Karnalkar[3], Sirpu Natesh Nagabhishek[4], Poojith Nuthalapati[5] and L.V.K.S. Bhaskar[6]

[1]Department of Pharmacology, MVJ Medical College and Research Hospital, Bangalore, India
[2]Department of General Surgery, Apollo Institute of Medical Sciences and Research, General Hospital, Hyderabad, India [3]Department of Anaesthesia, BKL Rural Medical College & Hospital, Ratnagiri, India [4]Cancer Biology Lab, Molecular and Nanomedicine Research Unit, Sathyabama Institute of Science and Technology, Chennai, India [5]PJ Biousys, Irving, TX, United States [6]Department of Zoology, Guru Ghasidas Vishwavidyalaya, Bilaspur, India

Abstract

Pharmacogenomics by name implies pharmacotherapeutics in relation to human genome. Currently pharmacogenomics is expanding its scope from single-gene screening to multiple genes, to enhance efficacy, safety and reduce the economic burden on healthcare system. Hepatocellular carcinoma (HCC) is a growing worldwide problem which is caused by several risk factors such as viral infections, food habits, and alcohol. The risk factors predominantly result in genetic mutations leading to HCC. These genetic abnormalities differ geographically which may decide the effectiveness of systemic treatments in HCC. In light of this, the current chapter discusses the geographical prevalence of genetic variants linked to HCC or HCC recurrence, as well as potential targets for systemic therapy efficacy.

Keywords: Liver cancer; systemic treatment; pharmacogenetics

Abbreviations

AKT	protein kinase B
APC	adenomatous polyposis coli
ARID2	AT-rich interactive domain 2
CDK4/6	cyclin-dependent kinase

CK1α1	casein kinase1α1
DC	ductular cells
ECOG	Eastern Cooperative Oncology Group
EMT	epithelial-mesenchymal transition
ERK	extracellular-regulated kinase
GSK3-β	glycogen synthase kinase 3-β
HBV	hepatitis B virus
HCC	hepatocellular carcinoma
HCV	hepatitis C virus
HH pathway	hedgehog pathway
Hhip	HH-interacting proteins
HPC	hepatic progenitor cells
LEF	lymphoid-enhancer-binding factor
MAPK	mitogen-activated protein kinase
OS	overall survival
PBAF	polybromo-associated factor complex
PI3K	phosphoinositide 3-kinase
PIK3CA	phosphoinositide-3-kinase-catalytic-alpha
PIP2	phosphatidylinositol 4,5-bisphosphate
PIP3	phosphoinositide 3-kinase
ptch1	protein-patched homolog
PTEN	phosphatase and tensin homolog
Raf	rapidly accelerated fibrosarcoma
Ras	protooncogene-derived protein
SHH	sonic HH
SMO	smoothened protein
Sufu	suppressor of fused homolog
TCF	T-cell-specific transcription factor
Wnt	wingless/int-1

Introction

    Hepatocellular carcinoma (HCC) is the most prevalent form of liver cancer. HCC is the fourth leading cause of cancer-related death globally. By 2030, the global burden of HCC mortality is expected to surpass 1 million deaths per year [1,2]. The HCC is more prevalent in developing countries such as Africa, Japan, and China. The principal etiology of HCC includes viral hepatitis, alcoholism, and aflatoxin exposure [2]. Other risk factors include smoking, obesity, and type 2 diabetes [3]. Viral hepatitis causing HCC includes hepatitis B virus (HBV) and hepatitis C virus (HCV) types. Latest WHO estimates revealed that 350 million population are affected with HBV and 177 million with HCV globally [4,5]. The regional prevalence of HBV and HCV is detailed in Table 25.1. The principal factors predisposing HCC vary by region. Aflatoxin and HBV are the major factors in Eastern Africa and China. In Japan and Egypt, HCV is the predominant factor. The HCC incidence in Mongolia is large and significantly related to HBV, HCV, or both diseases, as well as alcohol consumption [10]. Obesity is one of the risk factors of HCC and is associated with greater mortality in HCC patients [11].

TABLE 25.1 Regional incidence of hepatocellular carcinoma (HCC).

Region	HBV infection per total population	HCV infection per total population	HCC incidence	Reference
South-east Asia	100 million	10 million	27.6/lakh population	[6]
Africa	6.1%	18 million	>20/lakh population	[6]
Eastern Mediterranean Region	3.3%	0.8 million	>20	[7]
India	1.46%	0.5%−1.5%	0.9−9.7/lakh population	[8]
Egypt	14.5 million	7.8 million	33.5/lakh population	[9]
Europe	1.4 million	9 million	8.7−14/lakh population	[6]
Western Pacific Region	115 million	60 million	93.7/lakh population	[6]
America	0.7%	7−9 million	9.3−13.5/lakh population	[6]

HBV, hepatitis B virus; *HCV*, hepatitis B virus.

Pathophysiological aspects

Liver parenchymal cells constitute hepatocytes and ductular cells (DCs). These DCs represent hepatic progenitor cells (HPCs) [12]. Hepatocytes perform various physiological functions based upon their location such as high perfusion periportal region zone I to low perfusion centrilobular zone III. Cellular oxidative processes take place in hepatocytes of zone I and detoxification, biotransformation of drugs takes place in centrilobular zone hepatocytes [13]. The "space of Disse" located between the basolateral membrane of hepatocytes and sinusoidal lumen comprises Kupffer/macrophage cells and Ito/stellate cells. Stellate cells help in mechanisms of liver injury, fibrosis, and regeneration as well [14]. The HPCs stimulated by acute or chronic liver injury regenerate hepatocytes and cholangiocytes [15]. These HPC, upon persistent stimulation may cause early hepatic tumorigenesis and progress to HCC [16].

Chronic inflammation accompanied with fibrosis evidenced in liver cirrhosis principally ascends to HCC [17,18]. Cirrhotic events are inclined to dysplasia and liver malignancies. HCC pathogenesis includes genetic/epigenetic mutations of multiple signaling pathways leading to array of known clinical manifestations and biological events [19−21]. These pathways are discussed below and illustrated in Fig. 25.1.

p53 gene pathways

p53 gene central codons bind to deoxyribonucleic acid (100−293 amino acids) and initiate transcription of genes which are responsible for apoptosis and downregulation of angiogenesis. Nuclear import and export of *p53* was related to the antitumorigenesis action [22]. Derailment of these activities of *p53* in HCC and mutations at exon-7 was reported by many studies [23−28]. Mutation of *p53* also reduced sensitivity to chemotherapy and radiotherapy in recurrent HCC treatment [29,30].

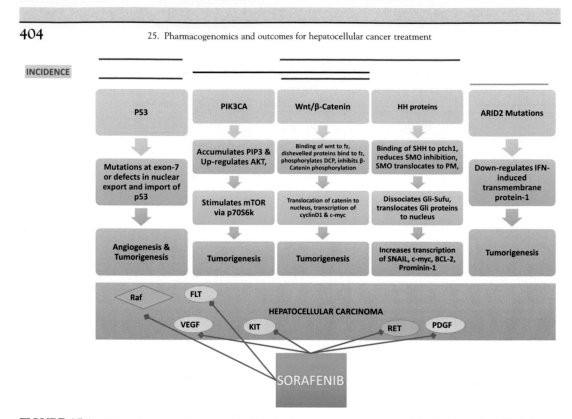

FIGURE 25.1   Illustration of pathways and their incidence in various geographical regions. *Red, black, brown,* and *green* lines represent China, Korea, Europe, and America, respectively.

Incidence of *p53* mutation in HCC patients was 48% in China [31], 41% in Egypt [32], 35.1% in Africa, 31.6% in Asia, 25.2% in Europe, 11.4% in America [33], 17.39% in Western Kenya [34], and 14.28% in India [35]. The incidence of p53 mutation in other type of cancer was 50%−70% in Western Europe, 50%−60% in Iran, 41% in Thailand and 34.8% in Brazil. Recurrence of HCC after resection treatment in patients with p53 mutation was in an average of 7.8 months. But in patients without p53 mutation showed recurrence of HCC in an average of 16.4 months [35−38].

Phosphoinositide-3-kinase-catalytic-alpha gene

Phosphoinositide-3-kinase-catalytic-alpha (PIK3CA) is an effector protein kinase of PTEN-AKT pathway. This protein is said to have inhibitory property of focal cell adhesion formation, cell motility, and initiation of MAPK signaling through growth factors. PI3K is involved in conversion of PIP2 to PIP3. The available PIP3 is utilized for activation of Akt. This promotes the activation of mTOR which may be tumorigenic acting through p70S6K or directly enhancing cell cycle progression by Akt through CyclinD1. Conversely, PTEN is involved in conversion of PIP3 to PIP2 and inactivates the Akt due to unavailability of PIP3.

PIK3CA gene encoded in PI3K catalytic site. Its mutations are responsible for upregulated activity of Akt [39,40]. Simultaneously, mutation identified at *intron4* gene of PTEN in HCC downregulated the dephosphorylation of PIP3 which may further increase the activity of Akt [41]. Many studies revealed beneficial effects of PTEN-targeted therapies in HCC.

Incidence of PIK3CA mutations in HCC patients was 35.6% in Korea, 3.5% in France, 4% in Switzerland, 1.11% in China [42]. A study has reported zero incidence of PIK3CA mutations in Japanese HCC patients during 2006 [43].

Wingless/int-1 (Wnt)/β-catenin pathway

Wnts are glycoproteins that bind to frizzled receptors (Fz) which are 7-transmembrane-span proteins homologous to G-coupled receptors [44,45]. Wnts regulate various cellular processes through canonical and noncanonical pathways. Canonical pathways are β-catenin dependent and, noncanonical pathways are β-catenin independent including Wnt/Ca + 2 pathway and Wnt/Planar Cell Polarity pathway [46]. The incidence of aberrant Wnt/β-catenin pathway is high in HCC and related to early carcinogenesis [47].

In absence of Wnts, the cytoplasmic destruction complex which includes axin, glycogen synthase kinase 3-β (GSK3-β), adenomatous polyposis coli (APC), and casein kinase1α1 (CK1α1) [48]. This destruction complex proteins phosphorylate β-catenin followed by ubiquitination which is catalyzed by E3-ubiquitin ligase [49,50]. As a result, the cytoplasmic β-catenin is degraded and kept at a minimal threshold level so that it is not translocated to nucleus [51]. In absence of β-catenin in nucleus, T-cell-specific transcription factor (TCF) and lymphoid-enhancer-binding factor (LEF) bind to Groucho proteins or transducin-like enhancer proteins and this complex targets histone deacetylases to silence the transcription [52,53].

Binding of Wnts to Fz receptor or low-density lipoprotein-receptor-related protein 5 and 6 activates the Wnt/β-catenin pathway [54–56], initiates binding of disheveled proteins to intracellular regions of Wnt-interacted receptors followed by phosphorylation of LRP6 and translocate destruction complex proteins [54,55,57–59]. This inhibits phosphorylation of β-catenin and increases cytoplasmic levels of β-catenin. This accumulation of unphosphorylated β-catenin is translocated to nucleus where it interacts with TCF and LEF resulting in initiation of transcription of cyclinD1, *c-myc*, etc. [60,61]. This action of β-catenin results in cell proliferations and tumorigenesis. Apart from Wnt overexpression, activating mutations of β-catenin and inactivating mutations of axin1, GSK3-β have been identified in HCC [62–65].

Incidence of β-catenin overexpression in HCC patients of China was 43.29% during 2008 [66], 39.53%–40.12% during 2009 [67,68], 43.5% during 2010 [69], 55.55% during 2011 [70], 68.04%–68.23% during 2012 [71,72]. 32.58%, 80.46% incidence was seen in the United States and Korea, respectively, during 2014 [73,74]. But the incidence was 32.6% during 2005 in Korea [75]. In Japan, the incidence was 78.5% (2000), 35.29% (2002), 46.87% (2005), and 12.8% (2008) [76–79]. In European countries, 34.04% (2013) incidence was seen in Netherland [80], 58.64% (2010) in Austria [81], 80% (2003) in Germany [82]. A study in African HCC patients revealed absolutely no incidence of β-catenin overexpression either in cytoplasm or nucleus [83]. In India, the incidence was 53% among

HCC patients [84]. Significant HCC recurrence was observed in patients with β-catenin pathway dysregulation [78,84].

Hedgehog pathway

In the adult liver, Hedgehog (HH) signaling has no function; in fact, normal hepatocytes have minimal concentrations of HH signaling proteins and no obvious HH pathway action. The hepatic endothelial and stellate cells produce HH-interacting proteins (Hhip) which antagonize HH-soluble ligands and inhibit the HH pathway. Sonic HH (SHH) ligand is the most commonly related to HCC. In absence of SHH, protein-patched homolog (ptch1) impede smoothened protein (SMO), but when SHH interacts with ptch1, SMO inhibition is reduced and subsequently activates Gli proteins (Gli 1,2,3) which regulates the transcription process. The SMO, upon activation translocate to plasma membrane from cytoplasm and also dissociates Gli-suppressor of fused homolog (Sufu) complex. This enables translocation of Gli proteins to nucleus where it interacts with Gli-binding consensus sequence and increases the transcription of *SNAIL, c-MYC, BCL-2*, and *Prominin-1*.

A study revealed 84% of incidence of HH pathway aberration in HCC patients in China [85]. A pilot study including 21 patients of HCC with liver transplantation in the United States, demonstrated HH pathway aberrations in all patients [86].

AT-rich interactive domain 2 (ARID2) pathway

Recently inactivating mutations of ARID2 gene is being investigated in HCC. The exact pathway mechanism is not completely elucidated. It is a component of polybromo-associated factor complex (PBAF) which is related SWI/SNF-chromatin-remodeling complex [87]. Inactivation of ARID2 causes downregulation of interferon-induced transmembrane protein 1 which are essential in IFN-induced antiproliferative activity [88].

Increasing ARID2 mutations was observed in US and European population (14% incidence), comparatively it was noticed in 2% Chinese HCC patients. These mutations had an association with viral infections [89].

Guidelines for treatment of hepatocellular carcinoma

Hepatocellular cancer treatment is based on the severity of disease categorized based on staging systems. Different countries follow different staging systems. EASL guidelines for HCC management recommend modified BCLC and AASLD guidelines endorse TNM (8th TNM edition) staging systems. The use of staging systems in management of HCC predicts the prognosis of the disease linked to treatment indication, and treatment outcomes. Both the guidelines suggest cirrhotic patients, noncirrhotic HBV/HCV patients and stage 3 fibrosis patients as target population for surveillance. These guidelines recommend systemic therapy for HCC patients who underwent resection or radiofrequency ablation, patients with cirrhosis plus advanced HCC. Sorafenib, regorafenib, lenvatinib, cabozantinib, and novolumab were the approved drugs for systemic therapy.

Challenges in treatment of hepatocellular carcinoma

The systemic treatments in advanced HCC included sorafenib as first-line drug. Other drugs are regorafenib, lenvatinib, cabozantinib, and novolumab. The main issues with systemic treatments are development of drug resistance and inability to completely cure or increase the HCC recurrence free survival.

Sorafenib acts through inhibition of multiple kinases such as raf kinase, and other kinases regulating various growth factors such as vascular endothelial growth factor, and platelet-derived growth factors [90]. These actions of sorafenib have shown proven benefits through attenuation of tumor angiogenesis, tumor cell proliferation, and accentuation of apoptosis [91,92].

The median overall survival (OS) has improved with sorafenib treatment in HCC patients. But this median OS differed in various studies. A study including 602 HCC patients from various sites of Europe, North America, South America, and Australia demonstrated a median OS of 10.7 months with sorafenib treatment [93]. A median OS of 6.5 months was seen with sorafenib treatment in 271 HCC patients of China, South Korea, and Taiwan [94]. Median OS of 12.3 months with sorafenib was reported by a study which recruited 1492 HCC patients from Asia, Europe, and North America [95]. 467 HCC patients treated with sorafenib in France had a median OS of 9.9 months [96]. A study including 360 HCC patients from Asia alone had a median OS of 10 months with sorafenib treatment [97]. HCC patients ($n = 206$) of Japan had a median OS of 11.5 months with sorafenib treatment [98]. One study has reported 53% disease progression and 15% toxicity in sorafenib treatment group resulting in discontinuation from the study, which included HCC patients ($n = 1155$) from Asia (65%), Europe (23%), and America (13%) [99].

Regorafenib is another second-line drug in treatment of HCC. It acts through inhibition of kinases as similar to sorafenib. But regorafenib profile differs with sorafenib in inhibition of KIT tyrosine-protein kinase and tyrosine-protein kinase receptor Tie-2 resulting in stronger inhibition of angiogenesis [100]. In the randomized phase III RESORCE trial, regorafenib, an oral multikinase antagonist of numerous carcinogenic pathways, increased OS in HCC patients who had tumor progression after developing resistance to sorafenib [101]. The median OS for HCC patients in the Child-Pugh A class and stage 0 of the Eastern Cooperative Oncology Group (ECOG) was 11.08 months when regorafenib was included as second-line therapy. This conclusion is reassuring in a situation where effective therapy alternatives are limited, and it is comparable to the median OS reported in the SHARP trial using a first-line drug, sorafenib [93].

5-Fluorouracil (5-FU), an anticancer drug, stops cells from progressing into the S-phase and increases p53 expression [102]. Drug resistance to 5-FU is a problem for many malignancies, including liver tumors. HCC cells induce defensive autophagy against the drug utilizing noncoding RNAs [103]. Using 5-FU with other chemotherapy drugs can improve its effectiveness. Compared to patients who receive 5-FU alone (median OS 5.2 months), hepatic-arterial infusion of 5-FU in combination with cisplatin-enhanced survival (median OS 14 months) in HCC patients [104]. Recently a trial (NTC02967887) has been initiated to evaluate the efficacy of 5-FU combined with cisplatin in HCC patients with sorafenib resistance.

Pharmacogenomic considerations for hepatocellular carcinoma treatments

Sorafenib inhibits the Raf/MAPK pathway but subsequently activates the PI3K/AKT signaling, implying a connection between the MAPK/ERK as well as the PI3K/AKT mechanisms. The PI3K/AKT pathway's putative compensation mechanism may result in sorafenib failure in HCC patients [105,106]. As a result, a combination therapy may yield a better survival outcome by inhibiting several therapeutic targets in HCC. In HCC cells and sorafenib-resistant HCC cells, copanlisib-arrested cell cycle by disrupting the cyclinD1/CDK4/6 mechanisms, which significantly reduced cell activity and impeded the colony-formation process. Copanlisib also upregulated the AKT phosphorylation in both sorafenib treated and sorafenib-resistant HCC cell cultures. This potential benefit for late-stage HCC may be due to combination of sorafenib with copanlisib [107].

Palbociclib and ribociclib, two recent CDK4/6 antagonists, exhibited anticancer activity in SR HCC Cell lines and were synergistic with sorafenib. Both drugs caused cell-cycle arrest in Rb-expressing HCC cells [108,109]. Combining sorafenib, which modulates PI3K/AKT/mTOR signaling, with PKI-587, which predominantly acts on Ras/Raf/MAPK pathway, was found to be more effective than single-agent therapy [110]. But combination of full-dose sorafenib with 5 mg everolimus increased adverse effects when compared to sorafenib alone [111].

Sorafenib resistance is induced in HepG2 cells after prolonged treatment, along with increased epithelial-mesenchymal transition and invasive potency [112]. The epithelial-mesenchymal transition (EMT) is a sign for invasion and metastasis, and it is triggered by a variety of effectors, of the Wnt/β-catenin, and HH pathways [113–118]. E-cadherin was found responsible for upregulation of proteins-related SNAIL/slug pathway and β-catenin which causes metastasis and tumor recurrence [119–121].

ERK and AKT activation may be considered as marker for poor prognosis in HCC as it augments disease progression [122]. Sorafenib acts on ERK pathway but not on AKT pathway, but regorafenib acts on both the pathways. However, on prolonged exposure of regorafenib to HuH7 cells exhibited resistance with increased CD24, CD133 expression, and TGF-β activity [123].

To summarize, this chapter discussed geographical incidences of genetic mutations. China has higher incidence of p53, β-catenin, HH pathway mutations. Korea has higher incidences of PIK3CA and β-catenin mutations. Some regions of Europe showed incidences of p53 and β-catenin mutations. ARID2 mutations were seen in American population. This information of incidences may guide to effective treatments such as, sorafenib which is the mainstay of systemic therapy in advanced HCC may develop resistance due to influence of p53 mutations in Chinese population and European population, similarly PI3K/AKT pathway aberrations may impact HCC treatments in Korean population, β-catenin mutations, HH pathway aberrations in Chinese HCC patients. With these genetic variations influencing HCC treatments, there is further need to consider for improvements in HCC treatments regimens with respect to population of different regions and to discover new therapeutic targets that overcome these challenges which may increase the OS of the HCC patients or completely cure HCC. Understanding the significance of pharmacogenomics in the treatment of hepatocellular malignancies aids in the development of new successful targeted treatments.

References

[1] Anstee QM, Reeves HL, Kotsiliti E, Govaere O, Heikenwalder M. From NASH to HCC: current concepts and future challenges Nat Rev Gastroenterol Hepatol 2019;16(7):411–28Available from. Available from: http://www.nature.com/articles/s41575-019-0145-7.

[2] Akinyemiju T, Abera S, Ahmed M, Alam N, Alemayohu MA, Allen C, et al. The burden of primary liver cancer and underlying etiologies from 1990 to 2015 at the global, regional, and national level JAMA Oncol 2017;3(12):1683Available from. Available from: http://oncology.jamanetwork.com/article.aspx?doi = 10.1001/jamaoncol.2017.3055.

[3] McGlynn KA, Petrick JL, El-Serag HB. Epidemiology of hepatocellular carcinoma. Hepatology 2021;73(1):4–13.

[4] Custer B, Sullivan SD, Hazlet TK, Iloeje U, Veenstra DL, Kowdley KV. Global epidemiology of hepatitis B virus J Clin Gastroenterol 2004;(10):38Available from. Available from: https://journals.lww.com/jcge/Fulltext/2004/11003/Global_Epidemiology_of_Hepatitis_B_Virus.8.aspx.

[5] Petruzziello A, Marigliano S, Loquercio G, Cozzolino A, Cacciapuoti C. Global epidemiology of hepatitis C virus infection: an up-date of the distribution and circulation of hepatitis C virus genotypes. World J Gastroenterol 2016;22(34):7824–40.

[6] Bray F, Ferlay J, Soerjomataram I, Siegel RL, Torre LA, Jemal A. Global cancer statistics 2018: GLOBOCAN estimates of incidence and mortality worldwide for 36 cancers in 185 countries CA Cancer J Clin 2018;68(6):394–424Available from. Available from: https://acsjournals.onlinelibrary.wiley.com/doi/abs/10.3322/caac.21492.

[7] Sabzalizadeh-Ardabili S, Alizadeh-Navaei R, Hedaytizadeh-Omran A, Janbabaei G. Cancer incidence and mortality pattern in Eastern Mediterranean Regional Office Countries and its association with the human development index Clin Cancer Investig J 2019;8(1):15. Available from. Available from: http://www.ccij-online.org/text.asp?2019/8/1/15/255446.

[8] Chavda HJ. Hepatocellular carcinoma in India. Indian J Surg 2021. Available from: https://doi.org/10.1007/s12262-021-02762-w. Available from.

[9] Ma W, Soliman AS, Anwar WA, Hablas A, El Din TB, Ramadan M, et al. Forecasted impacts of a sofosbuvir-based national hepatitis C treatment programme on Egypt's hepatocellular cancer epidemic: simulation of alternatives BMJ Glob Heal 2018;3(2):e000572Available from. Available from: http://gh.bmj.com/content/3/2/e000572.abstract.

[10] Chimed T, Sandagdorj T, Znaor A, Laversanne M, Tseveen B, Genden P, et al. Cancer incidence and cancer control in Mongolia: results from the National Cancer Registry 2008-12. Int J cancer 2017;140(2):302–9.

[11] Gupta A, Das A, Majumder K, Arora N, Mayo HG, Singh PP. Obesity is Independently Associated With Increased Risk of Hepatocellular Cancer-related Mortality: A Systematic Review and Meta-Analysis. Am J Clin Oncol 2018;41(9):874–81.

[12] He G, Dhar D, Nakagawa H, Font-Burgada J, Ogata H, Jiang Y, et al. Identification of liver cancer progenitors whose malignant progression depends on autocrine IL-6 signaling. Cell. 2013;155(2):384–96.

[13] Saxena R, Theise ND, Crawford JM. Microanatomy of the human liver-exploring the hidden interfaces. Hepatology. 1999;30(6):1339–46.

[14] Si-Tayeb K, Lemaigre FP, Duncan SA. Organogenesis and development of the liver. Dev Cell 2010;18(2):175–89.

[15] Malato Y, Naqvi S, Schürmann N, Ng R, Wang B, Zape J, et al. Fate tracing of mature hepatocytes in mouse liver homeostasis and regeneration. J Clin Invest 2011;121(12):4850–60.

[16] Tummala KS, Brandt M, Teijeiro A, Graña O, Schwabe RF, Perna C, et al. Hepatocellular carcinomas originate predominantly from hepatocytes and benign lesions from hepatic progenitor cells. Cell Rep 2017;19(3):584–600.

[17] Block TM, Mehta AS, Fimmel CJ, Jordan R. Molecular viral oncology of hepatocellular carcinoma. Oncogene. 2003;22(33):5093–107.

[18] Lu H, Ouyang W, Huang C. Inflammation, a key event in cancer development. Mol Cancer Res 2006;4(4):221–33.

[19] Bruix J. Usefulness of the molecular profile in the diagnosis, prognosis and treatment of hepatocellular carcinoma. Gastroenterol Hepatol 2014;37(2):81–9.

[20] Luca A, Caruso S, Milazzo M, Mamone G, Marrone G, Miraglia R, et al. Multidetector-row computed tomography (MDCT) for the diagnosis of hepatocellular carcinoma in cirrhotic candidates for liver transplantation: prevalence of radiological vascular patterns and histological correlation with liver explants. Eur Radiol 2010;20(4):898–907.

[21] McKillop IH, Moran DM, Jin X, Koniaris LG. Molecular pathogenesis of hepatocellular carcinoma. J Surg Res 2006;136(1):125–35.

[22] Stewart ZA, Pietenpol JA. p53 signaling and cell cycle checkpoints. Chem Res Toxicol 2001;14(3):243–63.

[23] Yu MW, Yang SY, Chiu YH, Chiang YC, Liaw YF, Chen CJ. A p53 genetic polymorphism as a modulator of hepatocellular carcinoma risk in relation to chronic liver disease, familial tendency, and cigarette smoking in hepatitis B carriers. Hepatology. 1999;29(3):697–702.

[24] Lee YI, Lee S, Das GC, Park US, Park SM, Lee YI. Activation of the insulin-like growth factor II transcription by aflatoxin B1 induced p53 mutant 249 is caused by activation of transcription complexes; implications for a gain-of-function during the formation of hepatocellular carcinoma. Oncogene. 2000;19(33):3717–26.

[25] Heinze T, Jonas S, Kärsten A, Neuhaus P. Determination of the oncogenes p53 and C-erb B2 in the tumour cytosols of advanced hepatocellular carcinoma (HCC) and correlation to survival time. Anticancer Res 1999;19(4A):2501–3.

[26] Honda K, Sbisà E, Tullo A, Papeo PA, Saccone C, Poole S, et al. p53 mutation is a poor prognostic indicator for survival in patients with hepatocellular carcinoma undergoing surgical tumour ablation. Br J Cancer 1998;77(5):776–82.

[27] Katiyar S, Dash BC, Thakur V, Guptan RC, Sarin SK, Das BC. P53 tumor suppressor gene mutations in hepatocellular carcinoma patients in India. Cancer. 2000;88(7):1565–73.

[28] Jeng KS, Sheen IS, Chen BF, Wu JY. Is the p53 gene mutation of prognostic value in hepatocellular carcinoma after resection? Arch Surg 2000;135(11):1329–33.

[29] Matsuzoe D, Hideshima T, Kimura A, Inada K, Watanabe K, Akita Y, et al. p53 mutations predict non-small cell lung carcinoma response to radiotherapy. Cancer Lett 1999;135(2):189–94.

[30] Blandino G, Levine AJ, Oren M. Mutant p53 gain of function: differential effects of different p53 mutants on resistance of cultured cells to chemotherapy. Oncogene. 1999;18(2):477–85.

[31] Chen GG, Merchant JL, Lai PBS, Ho RLK, Hu X, Okada M, et al. Mutation of p53 in recurrent hepatocellular carcinoma and its association with the expression of ZBP-89. Am J Pathol 2003;162(6):1823–9.

[32] El-Kafrawy SA, Abdel-Hamid M, El-Daly M, Nada O, Ismail A, Ezzat S, et al. P53 mutations in hepatocellular carcinoma patients in Egypt. Int J Hyg Env Health 2005;208(4):263–70.

[33] Tornesello ML, Buonaguro L, Tatangelo F, Botti G, Izzo F, Buonaguro FM. Mutations in TP53, CTNNB1 and PIK3CA genes in hepatocellular carcinoma associated with hepatitis B and hepatitis C virus infections Genomics 2013;102(2):74–83Available from. Available from: https://www.sciencedirect.com/science/article/pii/S0888754313000633.

[34] Odumo CO, Ondigo BN, Kimotho JH. Codon 249 P53 gene mutation among hepatocellular carcinoma patients in Western Kenya Open Access J Biomed Sci 2020;(4):1Available from. Available from: https://biomedscis.com/fulltext/codon-249-p53-gene-mutation-among-hepatocellular-carcinoma-patients-in-western-kenya.ID.000136.php.

[35] Lowe SW, Bodis S, McClatchey A, Remington L, Ruley HE, Fisher DE, et al. p53 status and the efficacy of cancer therapy in vivo. Science. 1994;266(5186):807–10.

[36] Easson EC. General principles of radiotherapy The radiotherapy of malignant disease. London: Springer London; 1991. p. 111–29Available from. Available from: http://link.springer.com/10.1007/978-1-4471-3168-7_5.

[37] Chao C, Goldberg M, Hoffman JP. Surgical salvage therapy: abdominoperineal resection for recurrent anal carcinoma, metastasectomy of recurrent colorectal cancer, and esophagectomy after combined chemoradiation. Curr Opin Oncol 2000;12(4):353–6.

[38] Law GL, Itoh H, Law DJ, Mize GJ, Merchant JL, Morris DR. Transcription factor ZBP-89 regulates the activity of the ornithine decarboxylase promoter. J Biol Chem 1998;273(32):19955–64.

[39] Kang S, Bader AG, Vogt PK. Phosphatidylinositol 3-kinase mutations identified in human cancer are oncogenic. Proc Natl Acad Sci U S A 2005;102(3):802–7.

[40] Link W, Rosado A, Fominaya J, Thomas JE, Carnero A. Membrane localization of all class I PI 3-kinase isoforms suppresses c-Myc-induced apoptosis in Rat1 fibroblasts via Akt. J Cell Biochem 2005;95(5):979–89.

[41] Wang L, Wang W-L, Zhang Y, Guo S-P, Zhang J, Li Q-L. Epigenetic and genetic alterations of PTEN in hepatocellular carcinoma. Hepatol Res 2007;37(5):389–96.

[42] Li X, Zhang Q, He W, Meng W, Yan J, Zhang L, et al. Low frequency of PIK3CA gene mutations in hepatocellular carcinoma in Chinese population. Pathol Oncol Res 2012;18(1):57–60.

[43] Tanaka Y, Kanai F, Tada M, Asaoka Y, Guleng B, Jazag A, et al. Absence of PIK3CA hotspot mutations in hepatocellular carcinoma in Japanese patients. Oncogene. 2006;25(20):2950–2.

[44] Schulte G, Bryja V. The Frizzled family of unconventional G-protein-coupled receptors. Trends Pharmacol Sci 2007;28(10):518—25.

[45] He X, Semenov M, Tamai K, Zeng X. LDL receptor-related proteins 5 and 6 in Wnt/beta-catenin signaling: arrows point the way. Development. 2004;131(8):1663—77.

[46] Habas R, Dawid IB. Dishevelled and Wnt signaling: is the nucleus the final frontier? J Biol 2005;4(1):2.

[47] Whittaker S, Marais R, Zhu AX. The role of signaling pathways in the development and treatment of hepatocellular carcinoma. Oncogene. 2010;29(36):4989—5005.

[48] Kimelman D, Xu W. beta-catenin destruction complex: insights and questions from a structural perspective. Oncogene. 2006;25(57):7482—91.

[49] Behrens J, Jerchow BA, Würtele M, Grimm J, Asbrand C, Wirtz R, et al. Functional interaction of an axin homolog, conductin, with beta-catenin, APC, and GSK3beta. Science. 1998;280(5363):596—9.

[50] Amit S, Hatzubai A, Birman Y, Andersen JS, Ben-Shushan E, Mann M, et al. Axin-mediated CKI phosphorylation of beta-catenin at Ser 45: a molecular switch for the Wnt pathway. Genes Dev 2002;16(9):1066—76.

[51] Aberle H, Bauer A, Stappert J, Kispert A, Kemler R. Beta-catenin is a target for the ubiquitin-proteasome pathway. EMBO J 1997;16(13):3797—804.

[52] Jennings BH, Ish-Horowicz D. The Groucho/TLE/Grg family of transcriptional co-repressors. Genome Biol 2008;9(1):205.

[53] Chen G, Fernandez J, Mische S, Courey AJ. A functional interaction between the histone deacetylase Rpd3 and the corepressor groucho in Drosophila development. Genes Dev 1999;13(17):2218—30.

[54] Kikuchi A, Yamamoto H, Kishida S. Multiplicity of the interactions of Wnt proteins and their receptors. Cell Signal 2007;19(4):659—71.

[55] Gordon MD, Nusse R. Wnt signaling: multiple pathways, multiple receptors, and multiple transcription factors. J Biol Chem 2006;281(32):22429—33.

[56] Wang H, Liu T, Malbon CC. Structure-function analysis of Frizzleds. Cell Signal 2006;18(7):934—41.

[57] Kikuchi A, Yamamoto H, Sato A. Selective activation mechanisms of Wnt signaling pathways. Trends Cell Biol 2009;19(3):119—29.

[58] Schwarz-Romond T, Fiedler M, Shibata N, Butler PJG, Kikuchi A, Higuchi Y, et al. The DIX domain of dishevelled confers Wnt signaling by dynamic polymerization. Nat Struct Mol Biol 2007;14(6):484—92.

[59] Schwarz-Romond T, Metcalfe C, Bienz M. Dynamic recruitment of axin by dishevelled protein assemblies. J Cell Sci 2007;120(14):2402—12.

[60] Schmitt-Graeff A, Ertelt-Heitzmann V, Allgaier H-P, Olschewski M, Nitschke R, Haxelmans S, et al. Coordinated expression of cyclin D1 and LEF-1/TCF transcription factor is restricted to a subset of hepatocellular carcinoma. Liver Int. 2005;25(4):839—47.

[61] Kawate S, Fukusato T, Ohwada S, Watanuki A, Morishita Y. Amplification of c-myc in hepatocellular carcinoma: correlation with clinicopathologic features, proliferative activity and p53 overexpression. Oncology. 1999;57(2):157—63.

[62] Merle P, de la Monte S, Kim M, Herrmann M, Tanaka S, Von Dem Bussche A, et al. Functional consequences of frizzled-7 receptor overexpression in human hepatocellular carcinoma. Gastroenterology 2004;127(4):1110—22.

[63] de La Coste A, Romagnolo B, Billuart P, Renard CA, Buendia MA, Soubrane O, et al. Somatic mutations of the beta-catenin gene are frequent in mouse and human hepatocellular carcinomas. Proc Natl Acad Sci U S A 1998;95(15):8847—51.

[64] Miyoshi Y, Iwao K, Nagasawa Y, Aihara T, Sasaki Y, Imaoka S, et al. Activation of the beta-catenin gene in primary hepatocellular carcinomas by somatic alterations involving exon 3. Cancer Res 1998;58(12):2524—7.

[65] Audard V, Grimber G, Elie C, Radenen B, Audebourg A, Letourneur F, et al. Cholestasis is a marker for hepatocellular carcinomas displaying beta-catenin mutations. J Pathol 2007;212(3):345—52.

[66] Zhai B, Yan H-X, Liu S-Q, Chen L, Wu M-C, Wang H-Y. Reduced expression of E-cadherin/catenin complex in hepatocellular carcinomas. World J Gastroenterol 2008;14(37):5665—73.

[67] Du G-S, Wang J-M, Lu J-X, Li Q, Ma C-Q, Du J-T, et al. Expression of P-aPKC-iota, E-cadherin, and beta-catenin related to invasion and metastasis in hepatocellular carcinoma. Ann Surg Oncol 2009;16(6):1578—86.

[68] Yu B, Yang X, Xu Y, Yao G, Shu H, Lin B, et al. Elevated expression of DKK1 is associated with cytoplasmic/nuclear beta-catenin accumulation and poor prognosis in hepatocellular carcinoma. J Hepatol 2009;50(5):948—57.

[69] Liu L, Zhu X-D, Wang W-Q, Shen Y, Qin Y, Ren Z-G, et al. Activation of beta-catenin by hypoxia in hepatocellular carcinoma contributes to enhanced metastatic potential and poor prognosis. Clin Cancer Res 2010;16 (10):2740—50.

[70] Feng Z, Fan X, Jiao Y, Ban K. Mammalian target of rapamycin regulates expression of β-catenin in hepatocellular carcinoma. Hum Pathol 2011;42(5):659−68.

[71] Zhao N, Sun B, Zhao X, Liu Z, Sun T, Qiu Z, et al. Coexpression of Bcl-2 with epithelial-mesenchymal transition regulators is a prognostic indicator in hepatocellular carcinoma. Med Oncol 2012;29(4):2780−92.

[72] Geng M, Cao Y-C, Chen Y-J, Jiang H, Bi L-Q, Liu X-H. Loss of Wnt5a and Ror2 protein in hepatocellular carcinoma associated with poor prognosis. World J Gastroenterol 2012;18(12):1328−38.

[73] Jin J, Jung HY, Wang Y, Xie J, Yeom YI, Jang J-J, et al. Nuclear expression of phosphorylated TRAF2- and NCK-interacting kinase in hepatocellular carcinoma is associated with poor prognosis. Pathol Res Pract 2014;210(10):621−7.

[74] Lee JM, Yang J, Newell P, Singh S, Parwani A, Friedman SL, et al. β-Catenin signaling in hepatocellular cancer: implications in inflammation, fibrosis, and proliferation. Cancer Lett 2014;343(1):90−7.

[75] Park JY, Park WS, Nam SW, Kim SY, Lee SH, Yoo NJ, et al. Mutations of beta-catenin and AXIN I genes are a late event in human hepatocellular carcinogenesis. Liver Int 2005;25(1):70−6.

[76] Korita PV, Wakai T, Shirai Y, Matsuda Y, Sakata J, Cui X, et al. Overexpression of osteopontin independently correlates with vascular invasion and poor prognosis in patients with hepatocellular carcinoma. Hum Pathol 2008;39(12):1777−83.

[77] Tien LT, Ito M, Nakao M, Niino D, Serik M, Nakashima M, et al. Expression of beta-catenin in hepatocellular carcinoma. World J Gastroenterol 2005;11(16):2398−401.

[78] Inagawa S, Itabashi M, Adachi S, Kawamoto T, Hori M, Shimazaki J, et al. Expression and prognostic roles of beta-catenin in hepatocellular carcinoma: correlation with tumor progression and postoperative survival. Clin Cancer Res an J Am Assoc Cancer Res 2002;8(2):450−6.

[79] Endo K, Ueda T, Ueyama J, Ohta T, Terada T. Immunoreactive E-cadherin, alpha-catenin, beta-catenin, and gamma-catenin proteins in hepatocellular carcinoma: relationships with tumor grade, clinicopathologic parameters, and patients' survival. Hum Pathol 2000;31(5):558−65.

[80] Witjes CDM, Ten Kate FJW, Verhoef C, De Man RA, IJzermans JNM. Immunohistochemical characteristics of hepatocellular carcinoma in non-cirrhotic livers. J Clin Pathol 2013;66(8):687−91.

[81] Zulehner G, Mikula M, Schneller D, van Zijl F, Huber H, Sieghart W, et al. Nuclear beta-catenin induces an early liver progenitor phenotype in hepatocellular carcinoma and promotes tumor recurrence. Am J Pathol 2010;176(1):472−81.

[82] Schmitt-Gräff A, Ertelt V, Allgaier H-P, Koelble K, Olschewski M, Nitschke R, et al. Cellular retinol-binding protein-1 in hepatocellular carcinoma correlates with beta-catenin, Ki-67 index, and patient survival. Hepatology. 2003;38(2):470−80.

[83] Elmileik H, Paterson AC, Kew MC. Beta-catenin mutations and expression, 249serine p53 tumor suppressor gene mutation, and hepatitis B virus infection in southern African Blacks with hepatocellular carcinoma. J Surg Oncol 2005;91(4):258−63.

[84] Verma A, Bal M, Ramadwar M, Deodhar K, Patil P, Goel M. Clinicopathologic characteristics of Wnt/β-catenin-deregulated hepatocellular carcinoma. Indian J Cancer 2017;54(4):634−9.

[85] Lin M, Guo LM, Liu H, Du J, Yang J, Zhang LJ, et al. Nuclear accumulation of glioma-associated oncogene 2 protein and enhanced expression of forkhead-box transcription factor M1 protein in human hepatocellular carcinoma. Histol Histopathol 2010;25(10):1269−75.

[86] Dugum M, Hanouneh I, McIntyre T, Pai R, Aucejo F, Eghtesad B, et al. Sonic Hedgehog signaling in hepatocellular carcinoma: a pilot study. Mol Clin Oncol 2016;4(3):369−74.

[87] Yan Z, Cui K, Murray DM, Ling C, Xue Y, Gerstein A, et al. PBAF chromatin-remodeling complex requires a novel specificity subunit, BAF200, to regulate expression of selective interferon-responsive genes. Genes Dev 2005;19(14):1662−7.

[88] Yang G, Xu Y, Chen X, Hu G. IFITM1 plays an essential role in the antiproliferative action of interferon-gamma. Oncogene. 2007;26(4):594−603.

[89] Satoh S, Daigo Y, Furukawa Y, Kato T, Miwa N, Nishiwaki T, et al. AXIN1 mutations in hepatocellular carcinomas, and growth suppression in cancer cells by virus-mediated transfer of AXIN1. Nat Genet 2000;24(3):245−50.

[90] Roberts PJ, Der CJ. Targeting the Raf-MEK-ERK mitogen-activated protein kinase cascade for the treatment of cancer. Oncogene. 2007;26(22):3291−310.

[91] Liu Y, Poon RT, Li Q, Kok TW, Lau C, Fan ST. Both antiangiogenesis- and angiogenesis-independent effects are responsible for hepatocellular carcinoma growth arrest by tyrosine kinase inhibitor PTK787/ZK222584. Cancer Res 2005;65(9):3691–9.

[92] Wiesenauer CA, Yip-Schneider MT, Wang Y, Schmidt CM. Multiple anticancer effects of blocking MEK-ERK signaling in hepatocellular carcinoma. J Am Coll Surg 2004;198(3):410–21.

[93] Llovet JM, Ricci S, Mazzaferro V, Hilgard P, Gane E, Blanc J-F, et al. Sorafenib in advanced hepatocellular carcinoma. N Engl J Med 2008;359(4):378–90.

[94] Cheng A-L, Kang Y-K, Chen Z, Tsao C-J, Qin S, Kim JS, et al. Efficacy and safety of sorafenib in patients in the Asia-Pacific region with advanced hepatocellular carcinoma: a phase III randomised, double-blind, placebo-controlled trial. Lancet Oncol 2009;10(1):25–34.

[95] Kudo M, Finn RS, Qin S, Han K-H, Ikeda K, Piscaglia F, et al. Lenvatinib vs sorafenib in first-line treatment of patients with unresectable hepatocellular carcinoma: a randomised phase 3 non-inferiority trial. Lancet 2018;391(10126):1163–73.

[96] Vilgrain V, Pereira H, Assenat E, Guiu B, Ilonca AD, Pageaux G-P, et al. Efficacy and safety of selective internal radiotherapy with yttrium-90 resin microspheres compared with sorafenib in locally advanced and inoperable hepatocellular carcinoma (SARAH): an open-label randomised controlled phase 3 trial. Lancet Oncol 2017;18(12):1624–36.

[97] Chow PKH, Gandhi M, Tan S-B, Khin MW, Khasbazar A, Ong J, et al. SIRveNIB: selective internal radiation therapy vs sorafenib in Asia-Pacific patients with hepatocellular carcinoma. J Clin Oncol 2018;36(19):1913–21.

[98] Kudo M, Ueshima K, Yokosuka O, Ogasawara S, Obi S, Izumi N, et al. Sorafenib plus low-dose cisplatin and fluorouracil hepatic arterial infusion chemotherapy vs sorafenib alone in patients with advanced hepatocellular carcinoma (SILIUS): a randomised, open label, phase 3 trial. Lancet Gastroenterol Hepatol 2018;3 (6):424–32.

[99] Cheng A-L, Kang Y-K, Lin D-Y, Park J-W, Kudo M, Qin S, et al. Sunitinib vs sorafenib in advanced hepatocellular cancer: results of a randomized phase III trial. J Clin Oncol 2013;31(32):4067–75.

[100] Frenette CT. The role of regorafenib in hepatocellular carcinoma. Gastroenterol Hepatol 2017;13(2):122–4.

[101] Bruix J, Qin S, Merle P, Granito A, Huang Y-H, Bodoky G, et al. Regorafenib for patients with hepatocellular carcinoma who progressed on sorafenib treatment (RESORCE): a randomised, double-blind, placebo-controlled, phase 3 trial. Lancet 2017;389(10064):56–66.

[102] Luo L-J, Zhang L-P, Duan C-Y, Wang B, He N-N, Abulimiti P, et al. The inhibition role of miR-22 in hepatocellular carcinoma cell migration and invasion via targeting CD147. Cancer Cell Int 2017;17(1):17. Available from: https://doi.org/10.1186/s12935-016-0380-8. Available from.

[103] Huo X, Han S, Wu G, Latchoumanin O, Zhou G, Hebbard L, et al. Dysregulated long noncoding RNAs (lncRNAs) in hepatocellular carcinoma: implications for tumorigenesis, disease progression, and liver cancer stem cells. Mol Cancer 2017;16(1):165.

[104] Nouso K, Miyahara K, Uchida D, Kuwaki K, Izumi N, Omata M, et al. Effect of hepatic arterial infusion chemotherapy of 5-fluorouracil and cisplatin for advanced hepatocellular carcinoma in the Nationwide Survey of Primary Liver Cancer in Japan. Br J Cancer 2013;109(7):1904–7.

[105] Zhang H, Wang Q, Liu J, Cao H. Inhibition of the PI3K/Akt signaling pathway reverses sorafenib-derived chemo-resistance in hepatocellular carcinoma. Oncol Lett 2018;15(6):9377–84.

[106] Zhu Y, Zheng B, Wang H, Chen L. New knowledge of the mechanisms of sorafenib resistance in liver cancer. Acta Pharmacol Sin 2017;38(5):614–22. Available from: https://doi.org/10.1038/aps.2017.5. Available from.

[107] Ye L, Mayerle J, Ziesch A, Reiter FP, Gerbes AL, De Toni EN. The PI3K inhibitor copanlisib synergizes with sorafenib to induce cell death in hepatocellular carcinoma. Cell Death Discov 2019;5(1):86. Available from: https://doi.org/10.1038/s41420-019-0165-7. Available from.

[108] Reiter FP, Denk G, Ziesch A, Ofner A, Wimmer R, Hohenester S, et al. Predictors of ribociclib-mediated antitumour effects in native and sorafenib-resistant human hepatocellular carcinoma cells. Cell Oncol 2019;42(5):705–15.

[109] Bollard J, Miguela V, Ruiz de Galarreta M, Venkatesh A, Bian CB, Roberto MP, et al. Palbociclib (PD-0332991), a selective CDK4/6 inhibitor, restricts tumour growth in preclinical models of hepatocellular carcinoma. Gut. 2017;66(7):1286–96.

[110] Gedaly R, Angulo P, Hundley J, Daily MF, Chen C, Evers BM. PKI-587 and sorafenib targeting PI3K/AKT/mTOR and Ras/Raf/MAPK pathways synergistically inhibit HCC cell proliferation. J Surg Res 2012;176(2):542–8.

[111] Koeberle D, Dufour J-F, Demeter G, Li Q, Ribi K, Samaras P, et al. Sorafenib with or without everolimus in patients with advanced hepatocellular carcinoma (HCC): a randomized multicenter, multinational phase II trial (SAKK 77/08 and SASL 29). Ann Oncol 2016;27(5):856−61.

[112] van Malenstein H, Dekervel J, Verslype C, Van Cutsem E, Windmolders P, Nevens F, et al. Long-term exposure to sorafenib of liver cancer cells induces resistance with epithelial-to-mesenchymal transition, increased invasion and risk of rebound growth. Cancer Lett 2013;329(1):74−83.

[113] Xu J, Lamouille S, Derynck R. TGF-beta-induced epithelial to mesenchymal transition. Cell Res 2009;19 (2):156−72.

[114] Ogunwobi OO, Liu C. Hepatocyte growth factor upregulation promotes carcinogenesis and epithelial-mesenchymal transition in hepatocellular carcinoma via Akt and COX-2 pathways. Clin Exp Metastasis 2011;28(8):721−31.

[115] Lee JM, Dedhar S, Kalluri R, Thompson EW. The epithelial-mesenchymal transition: new insights in signaling, development, and disease. J Cell Biol 2006;172(7):973−81.

[116] Wu Y, Zhou BP. New insights of epithelial-mesenchymal transition in cancer metastasis. Acta Biochim Biophys Sin 2008;40(7):643−50.

[117] Singh A, Settleman J. EMT, cancer stem cells and drug resistance: an emerging axis of evil in the war on cancer. Oncogene. 2010;29(34):4741−51.

[118] Larue L, Bellacosa A. Epithelial−mesenchymal transition in development and cancer: role of phosphatidylinositol 3' kinase−AKT pathways. Oncogene 2005;24(50):7443−54. Available from: https://doi.org/10.1038/sj.onc.1209091. Available from.

[119] Yao X, Wang X, Wang Z, Dai L, Zhang G, Yan Q, et al. Clinicopathological and prognostic significance of epithelial mesenchymal transition-related protein expression in intrahepatic cholangiocarcinoma. Onco Targets Ther 2012;5:255−61.

[120] Masugi Y, Yamazaki K, Hibi T, Aiura K, Kitagawa Y, Sakamoto M. Solitary cell infiltration is a novel indicator of poor prognosis and epithelial-mesenchymal transition in pancreatic cancer. Hum Pathol 2010;41 (8):1061−8.

[121] Kim MA, Lee HS, Lee HE, Kim JH, Yang H-K, Kim WH. Prognostic importance of epithelial-mesenchymal transition-related protein expression in gastric carcinoma. Histopathology. 2009;54(4):442−51.

[122] Schmitz KJ, Wohlschlaeger J, Lang H, Sotiropoulos GC, Malago M, Steveling K, et al. Activation of the ERK and AKT signalling pathway predicts poor prognosis in hepatocellular carcinoma and ERK activation in cancer tissue is associated with hepatitis C virus infection. J Hepatol 2008;48(1):83−90.

[123] Karabicici M, Azbazdar Y, Ozhan G, Senturk S, Firtina Karagonlar Z, Erdal E. Changes in Wnt and TGF-β signaling mediate the development of regorafenib resistance in hepatocellular carcinoma cell line HuH7 Front Cell Dev Biol 2021;2015Available from. Available from: https://www.frontiersin.org/article/10.3389/fcell.2021.639779.

C H A P T E R

26

Epigenetic biomarkers in diagnosis, prognosis, and treatment of hepatocellular carcinoma

Eka Kvaratskhelia, Ketevani Kankava, Sandro Surmava and Elene Abzianidze

Department of Molecular and Medical Genetics, Tbilisi State Medical University, Tbilisi, Georgia

Abstract

Hepatocellular carcinoma (HCC) is one of the most commonly occurring solid cancers worldwide and is the second cause of death due to malignancy. Infection by hepatitis B and hepatitis C viruses, alcohol abuse, and various metabolic syndromes, including type 2 diabetes and nonalcoholic steatohepatitis (NASH) are the main risk factors for HCC development. Over the past decade, advances in genomic and epigenomic technologies have increased our knowledge of molecular pathogenesis in HCC. However, the exact molecular mechanisms underlying the development of HCC or the malignant transformation of chronic liver injury are still not fully understood. Cancers, including HCC, develop due to the accumulation of both genetic and epigenetic events. Epigenetics is defined as heritable changes in gene expression that are not accompanied by changes in DNA sequence. Epigenetic mechanisms include DNA methylation, histone variants, histone modifications, and noncoding RNAs (ncRNAs). In this chapter, relationships between epimutations and development and/or progression of HCC have been studied from relevant peer-reviewed literature.

Keywords: DNA methylation; histone methylation; histone acetylation; HCC; HAT; HDAC

Abbreviations

BSP	Bisulfite-assisted sequencing PCR
COBRA	Combined bisulfite restriction analysis
CpG	Cytosine-guanine dinucleotide
CTLs	Cytotoxic T cells
DEGs	Differentially expressed genes
DMRs	Differentially methylated regions

© 2022 Elsevier Inc. All rights reserved.

DNMTs	DNA methyltransferases
HATs	Histone acetyltransferases
HBHC	Hepatitis B positive HCC
HCB	Hepatitis B viruses
HCC	Hepatocellular carcinoma
HCV	Hepatitis C virus
HDACs	Histone deacetylases
HDMs	Histone demethylases
HMTs	Histone methyltransferases
LINEs	Long interspersed nuclear elements
MeDEGs	Methylation-regulated differentially expressed genes
MeDIP	Methylated DNA immunoprecipitation microarray
MIRA	Methylated-CpG island recovery assay
miRNAs	MicroRNAs
MSP	Methylation-specific PCR
ncRNAs	Noncoding RNAs
SAM	s-adenosyl-L-methionine
TSGs	Tumor suppressor genes

Introduction

The initiation and progression of hepatocellular carcinoma (HCC) is complex and multifaceted with variable clinical outcomes and molecular features [1,2]. Although HCC's variety is attributed to genetic events such as mutations in cancer-associated genes or a loss of heterozygosity (LOH), epigenetic deregulation also plays a role in its carcinogenesis which may occur due to consistent risk factor exposure, cirrhosis, lifestyle, and environmental cues [3–5].

Epigenetics is defined as heritable changes in gene expression that are not accompanied by changes in DNA sequence. Epigenetic mechanisms include DNA methylation, histone variants, histone modifications, and noncoding RNAs (ncRNAs) [6]. The elements involved in different modification patterns can be divided into three groups by their roles, "writer," "reader," and "eraser." Epigenetic "writers" and "erasers" catalyze the addition or removal of chemical groups to or from DNA or histones, respectively. These modifications are known as epigenetic marks [7,8].

DNA methylation, the most extensively studied heritable epigenetic mark, is the chemical reaction catalyzed by the DNA methyltransferases (DNMTs) class of enzymes which results in the covalent transfer of a methyl group from s-adenosyl-L-methionine (SAM) to a cytosine residue in CpG dinucleotides. The CpG dinucleotides, known as CpG islands, are preferentially located in the proximal promoter end of approximately 60% of genes in the human genome. The net effect of this reaction is gene silencing by either preventing or promoting the recruitment of regulatory proteins to DNA. DNA methylation is a reversible, enzymatically controlled mechanism of gene expression involved, among other processes, in normal embryogenesis, tissue differentiation, and chromosome stability [9,10]. The global hypomethylation, especially, at long-interspersed nuclear element (LINEs) regions as well as site-specific hypermethylation is a common epigenetic alteration in cancer [11].

A covalent posttranslational modification of histone proteins includes but is not limited methylation, acetylation, phosphorylation, ubiquitination, sumoylation of histone proteins. A wide variety of histone-modifying enzymes have been described, such as histone acetyltransferases (HATs), histone deacetylases (HDACs), histone methyltransferases (HMTs), and histone demethylases (HDMs) [12]. These modifications can control gene expression by altering the chromatin structure [13]. The attachment of methyl groups to histone proteins occurs predominantly at specific lysine (K) or arginine (A) residues on histones H3 and H4 that influences the recruitment and binding of different regulatory proteins [14]. H3K9, H3K27, and H4K20 are well-known as repressive marks, while the methylation of H3K4 and H3K36 are considered to be "activation" marks [15]. Histone acetylation involves the addition of an acetyl group to lysine residues in the protruding histone tails. It is usually associated with transcriptional activation [16,17].

MicroRNAs (miRNAs) are a class of small, noncoding RNAs of approximately 19−24 nt that can modify gene expression [18]. A very small number of miRNAs base-pair to mRNAs with nearly perfect complementarity and trigger mRNA cleavage. In general, miRNAs and their target mRNAs are only partially complementary and inhibit gene expression [19]. Abnormal miRNA expression has been documented in many types of cancers, including HCC [4,5]. Altered epigenetic modifications of cancer in the context of various cellular responses are shown in Fig. 26.1.

In this chapter we briefly discuss the current discoveries related to epigenetic alterations involved in the pathogenesis of HCC focusing on DNA methylation, histone acetylation, and histone methylation.

DNA methylation in hepatocellular carcinoma

Human cancers, including HCC, develop due to the accumulation of genetic mutations and epigenetic aberrations, which lead to changes to the tissue microenvironment. While the genetic abnormalities are associated with irreversible changes in DNA sequence, the epigenetic events modify the activation of certain genes that occur through alterations in the chromosome rather than in the DNA sequence. Specific patterns of alterations are associated with exposure to environmental factors. After a normal cell lineage acquires protumorigenic genetic mutations or epimutations, they are positively selected for the microenvironment. The microenvironment surrounding the mutant cells may also be altered by the "cancerized field." Crosstalk between the tumor cells and their microenvironment might be a promising therapeutic and/or preventive target [20−22].

The most frequent mutations in HCC affect the TERT promoter (60%), associated with an increased telomerase expression. TP53 and CTNNB1 are the next most prevalent mutations, affecting 25%−30% of HCC patients [23]. Mutations in these genes, on the other hand, are associated with epigenetic dysregulation. It has been reported that, the presence of TP53 mutation is associated with genome-wide hypomethylation and a high degree of chromosomal alteration, whereas CTNNB1 mutation is more frequently observed in HCC with advanced regional hypermethylation in known TSGs [24,25].

It is now becoming increasingly clear that epigenetic dysregulation and genome instability play a key role in a hepatocarcinogenesis [26−28]. Changes in DNA methylation considered to be the early events in carcinogenesis [6]. Aberrant DNA methylation patterns, such as global hypomethylation and site-specific hypo- or hypermethylation, lead to genome instability and inappropriate expression of genes, for example, activation of oncogenes and silencing of tumor suppressor genes (TSGs) [29,30].

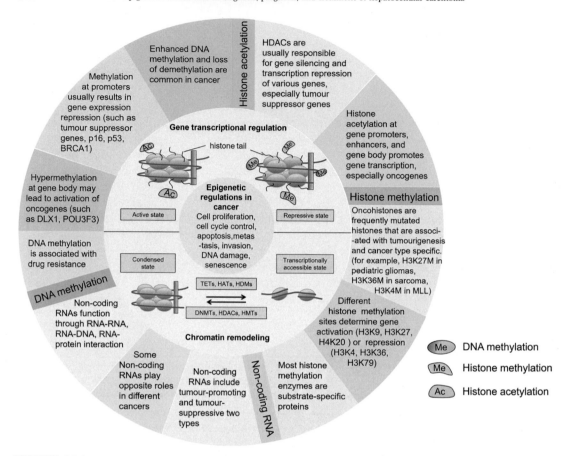

FIGURE 26.1 Epigenetic regulations in cancer. Alterations in epigenetic modifications in cancer regulate various cellular responses, including cell proliferation, apoptosis, invasion, and senescence. Through DNA methylation, histone modification, chromatin remodeling, and noncoding RNA regulation, epigenetics play an important role in tumorigenesis. These main aspects of epigenetics present reversible effects on gene silencing and activation via epigenetic enzymes and related proteins. *DNMTs*, DNA methyltransferases; *TETs*, ten-eleven translocation enzymes; *HATs*, histone acetylases; *HDACs*, histone deacetylases; *HMTs*, histone methyltransferases; *HDMs*, histone-demethylating enzymes. *MLL*, biphenotypic (mixed lineage) leukemia. *Source: Cheng Y, He C, Wang M, Ma X, Mo F, Yang S, et al. Targeting epigenetic regulators for cancer therapy: mechanisms and advances in clinical trials. Signal Transduct Target Ther 2019;4(1):1−39. https://doi.org/10.1038/s41392-019-0095-0*

A number of powerful technologies have been developed and utilized in past decades to profile methylation in HCC, including COBRA (combined bisulfite restriction analysis) [31], BSP (bisulfite-assisted sequencing PCR) [32], MSP (methylation-specific PCR) [33] to detect methylation at a single locus or a gene, and microarray-based approaches such as a whole-genome assay [methylated-CpG island recovery assay (MIRA), the methylated DNA immunoprecipitation microarray (MeDIP) chip or bead arrays] to identify genome-scale methylation profiles (Table 26.1) [34].

In the context of patients diagnosed with HCC, 12-gene methylation biomarkers detected through the optimized liquid hybridization capture-based bisulfite sequencing

TABLE 26.1 Different method in genome-wide methylation profiling [34].

	Platform	Features	Number of regions analyzed per sample	Methylation information on site-specific CpG loci	Methylation information on non-CpG loci	Advantages	Disadvantages
Microarray based	Methylated CpG island amplification and microarray (MCAM-chip)	Enzyme-based techniques that rely on restriction enzymes (SmaI and XmaI) followed by profiling on promoter array	~25,000 human promoters (depends on array density)	No	No	Do not require bisulfite conversion, good coverage on region with low CpG density.	Require substantial quantities of input genomic DNA, low sample throughput, do not report methylation status at single nucleotide level, bias may occur due to genomic distribution of CpG loci, limited to mostly promoter regions.
	Differential methylation hybridization and microarray (DMH-chip)	Enzyme-based techniques that rely on restriction enzymes (MseI and BstUI) followed by profiling on promoter array					
	Methylated DNA immunoprecipitation and microarray (MeDIP-chip)	Immunoprecipitation of methylated DNA with a monoclonal antibody followed by profiling on promoter array					
Beadarray based	GoldenGate	Bisulfite conversion of DNA followed by microbead-based microarray	~1,500 CpG sites	Yes	No	Require minimum input genomic DNA, high sample throughput, provide methylation status at CpG loci, fairly accurate and reproducible.	Bisulfite treatment may not be complete, bisulfite treatment caused DNA degradation, limited to mostly promoter regions.

(Continued)

TABLE 26.1 (Continued)

Platform	Features	Number of regions analyzed per sample	Methylation information on site-specific CpG loci	Methylation information on non-CpG loci	Advantages	Disadvantages
Infinium 27 K	~27,000 CpG sites					
Infinium 450 K	~450,000 CpG sites					
High throughput sequencing	Bisulfite conversion of DNA followed by capture and high throughput sequencing	Whole genome	Yes	Yes	High-resolution mapping of methylation status at single nucleotide level, no cross hybridization bias.	Bisulfite treatment may not be complete, bisulfite treatment caused DNA degradation, low sample throughput, expensive, complex bioinformatic analysis.

(LHC-BS) platform. This is the effective and cost-efficient technique that captures differentially methylated regions (DMRs). These 12 DMR-associated genes were identified by linking the DMRs in promoters to the differentially expressed genes (DEGs). In addition, seven genes showed either promoter hypermethylation (SMAD6, IFITM1, LRRC4, CHST4, and TBX15) or hypomethylation (CCL20 and NQO1) in HCC [35].

Genome-wide methylation microarray analysis in primary HCC revealed that there were 2670 CpG sites that significantly differed in regard to the methylation level between the tumor and nontumor liver tissues. The study showed that, in addition to three known TSGs (APC, CDKN2A, and GSTP1), eight genes (AKR1B1, GRASP, MAP9, NXPE3, RSPH9, SPINT2, STEAP4, and ZNF154) were significantly hypermethylated and silenced in the HCC tumors compared to the nontumor liver tissues [36].

Nine upregulated and 72 downregulated methylation-regulated differentially expressed genes (MeDEGs) were identified in the study conducted by Liang Yu et al. Using RNA expression profiles, Illumina Human Methylation 450 K BeadChip data, clinical information, and pathological features, authors showed that the methylation status of four MeDEGs (CTF1, FZD8, PDK4, and ZNF334) were negatively associated with overall survival. Moreover, the methylation status of CDF1 and PDK4 was identified as an independent prognostic factor [27]. In addition, in a similar study, three public genome-wide DNA methylation data sets of HCCs (all detected by Illumina Infinium HumanMethylation450 Beadchip) with ∼800 clinical samples and the corresponding gene expression data sets were analyzed. The study identified 222 candidate epigenetic driver genes whose expressions were strongly negatively regulated by promoter methylations. Several high-confidence candidates, including SFN, SPP1, and TKT, were significantly associated with overall survivals of HCC patients [28].

The power of epigenetic biomarkers in a diagnosis and prognosis of HCC is illustrated in a review article from *JHEP Reports*. Fernández-Barrena et al. also summarized the potential drugs that target epigenetic mechanisms for HCC treatment. The authors focus on the epigenetic changes, such as DNA methylation and histone modifications and discuss epigenetic alterations during the progression from chronic hepatic injury to HCC (Fig. 26.2) [8].

It has been observed that aberrant DNA methylation markedly increase during the progression from liver cirrhosis to HCC. In addition, a study of the relationship between multiple etiologic factors driving HCC and DNA methylation pattern revealed that (1) HCV infection has a greater impact on DNA methylation during cirrhosis than other etiologies, (2) chronic alcoholism has a greater effect on the DNA methylation landscape than HCV infection in advanced liver disease (HCC), (3) rare cirrhosis etiologies had relatively few epigenetic changes, while methylation changes in cryptogenic HCC substantially overlapped with HCC-HCV and HCC-EtOH, (4) a substantially hypomethylated genome with large DMRs were identified in HCC regardless of etiology, and (5) methylation changes observed in cirrhosis-HCV and conserved though HCC are associated with tumorigenic pathways [37].

A specific subset of eight TSGs (HIC1, GSTP1, SOCS1, RASSF1, CDKN2A, APC, RUNX3, and PRDM2) that showed significantly higher methylation levels in the early HCCs were identified in HCC individuals. Moreover, in the chronic hepatitis C (CHC) patients, methylation frequencies in these TSGs were associated with shorter time to HCC occurrence and number of methylated genes was an independent risk factor for HCC [38].

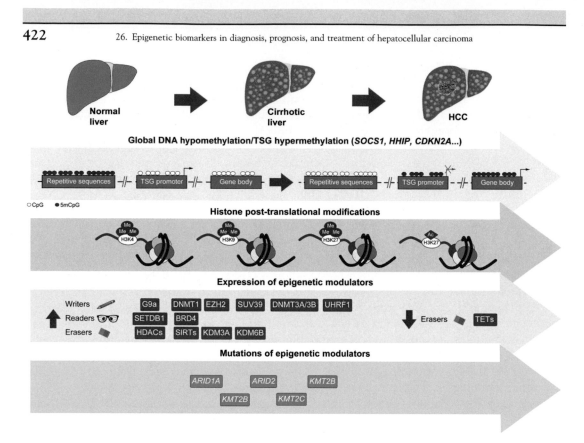

FIGURE 26.2 Alterations in epigenetic mechanisms during hepatocarcinogenesis. *Ac*, acetylation; *HCC*, hepatocellular carcinoma; *Me*, methylation; *TETs*, ten-eleven translocation enzymes; *TSG*, tumor suppressor gene.

In another quantitative methylation study, significant methylation was found in five CpG island loci—APC, RASSF1A, SOCS1, p16, and COX2 [39]. In addition, seven significantly methylated genes (EMILIN2, WNK2, TM6SF1, TLX3, HIST1H4F, TRIM58, and GRASP) were identified in hepatitis B positive HCC (HBHC) [40].

Given its relative ease of measurement, DNA methylation has a great potential to be used as a prognostic epigenetic biomarker. A methylation-based risk signature has been developed for HCC to predict the prognosis of HCC patients [41]. In addition, using a methylation microarray, Qiu et al. generated and validated a methylation signature for early-stage HCC to predict recurrence based on three CpG methylations [42].

Numerous studies have shown the relationship between DNA methylation and antitumor immune response [43,44]. The immune cells infiltrate into the tumor microenvironment (TME) and modulate carcinogenesis [45]. Remarkable advances have been achieved in cancer immunotherapies that have revolutionized the field of oncology [46,47].

Circulating and liver-infiltrating $CD4^+$ cytotoxic T cells (CTLs) were found to be significantly increased in HCC patients during the early stages of the disease but decreased in progressive stages of HCC. In addition, the progressive deficit in CD4 (+) CTLs induced by increased FoxP3 (+) regulatory T cells was correlated with poor survival and high recurrence rates in HCC patients [48]. A two-gene risk prognostic signature (LRRC41 and

KIAA1429) was generated by Xu et al. with significant prognostic predictive accuracy in HCC samples and the risk score was correlated with the tumor immune microenvironment and immune checkpoint blockade-related genes [49].

In the last several years, a new approach has emerged utilizing circulating tumor DNA (cfDNA) methylation for the early detection, monitoring, and the evaluation of treatment response [50]. A large cohort study on cfDNAm in HCC showed that detection of the methylation of multiple genes might improve the diagnosis, surveillance, and prognosis of HCC [51].

In conclusion, these current findings emphasize the potential utility of DNA methylation-based techniques for the early detection of HCC. The identification of the genome-wide and site-specific methylation changes might improve diagnostic and prognostic efficiency.

Histone modifications in hepatocellular carcinoma

Another epigenetic mechanism investigated in HCC is related to chromatin modifications. Chromatin represents a complex structure of DNA and proteins, which serve a key role in DNA conservation and regulation of its activity. Major proteins in the chromatin structure are histones H2A, H2B, H3, H4, and H1. Main types of histone modifications that affect DNA expression are related to covalent binding of different chemical groups to histone molecules. Modifications of histone proteins include methylation, acetylation, phosphorylation, ubiquitination, sumoylation, biotinylation, citrullination, poly-ATP ribosylation, N-glycosylation, and others [8,52–54] (Table 26.2). All of these changes are reversible by intrinsic enzymatic pathways, and therefore most of them could potentially be targeted by therapeutic approaches. Best studied out of histone modifications are acetylation and methylation.

Histone acetylation is managed by two types of enzymes: HATs and HDACs. There are three major families of HATs known: GNAT, MYST, and CBP/p300. During acetylation, an acetyl group from acetyl coenzyme A is transferred to an amino group of lysine residues [55,56]. This results in the neutralization of positive charge of lysine residues and allows a higher rate of transcription in a given area of chromatin [52,57], whereas HDAC action results in an opposite effect. At least four classes of HDAC have been identified [55] and changes in HDAC1, HDAC2, and HDAC3 have all been described to induce HCC development [58,59].

Methylation of histones occurs at lysine or arginine residues and both can be mono-, di-, or trimethylated. Methyltransferases involved in this process are also different: the SET-domain-containing HMTs, the non-SET-domain-containing HMTs and the protein arginine methyltransferases. HDMs belong to one of two families—LSD or JARID demethylases [8].

Histones might be phosphorylated at serine, threonine, and tyrosine residues. Serine-threonine kinases, as well as tyrosine kinases, are subdivided into a number of families, each of them mediating complex influences on chromatin remodeling [60]. There is increasing evidence that a phosphorylated state also alters the effects of other histone modifiers (such as methylators or acetylators) [61].

Different histone modifications may act in coordination with other epigenetic mechanisms, most commonly DNA methylation, and regulate many cellular processes including DNA replication, DNA repair, and DNA transcription.

TABLE 26.2   List of epigenetic modifiers of chromatin structure [8].

Epigenetic modifiers	Major modified/recognized site	Family	Examples
Histone methyltransferases (HMTs): lysine (KMTs)	H3 K4/K9/K27/K36/K79 (Met) H4 K20 (Met)	SUV39 SET1/2 EZH PRDMs	G9a/KMT1C MLL1/ KMT2A SETD1A EZH2/ KMT6
Histone methyltransferases (HMTs): protein arginine (PRMTs)	H3 R2/R8/R17 (Met) H4 R3 (Met)	PRMT	PRMT1 PRMT4/CARM1
Histone demethylases (HDMs/ KDMs)	H3 K4/K9/K27/K36/K79 H4 K20	LSD/KDM1A-B JARID/KDM2−8	KDM1A/LSD1 KDM4/ JMJD2 KDM5/RBP2
Histone acetyltransferases (HATs)	H3 K9/K14/K56 (Ac) H4 K5/ K8/K16 (Ac) H2A K5 (Ac)	GNAT MYST CBP/p300	GCN5 TIP60 CBP/P300
Histone deacetylases (HDACs)	H3 K9/K14 H4 K5/K8/K12	HDAC I-IV	HDAC1 Sirtuin
Serine-threonine and tyrosine kinases	Ser (P) Thr (P) Tyr (P)		Haspin MSK CKII
Chromo domain-containing proteins	Methylated H3 K4/K9/K27/ K36		CHD1 HP1
Tudor domain-containing proteins	Methylated H3 K4/K9/K20/ K36		UHRF1
MBT-containing proteins	Methylated H3 K4/K9/K27/ K36		SFMBT1 MBTD1
PHD-containing proteins	Acetylated H3 K14 methylated H3 K4/K9		TFIID KMT2D
Bromodomain (BRD)-containing proteins	Acetylated H3 K14 acetylated H4 K5/K8/K16		GCN5 BRD4 PCAF (HAT)
Yeats domain-containing proteins	Acetylated H3 K9		AF9

Histone modifications are usually (but not strictly) associated with gene silencing and this drives carcinogenesis in some tumors [62].

Well-studied histone modifications in HCC are related to histone 3 (H3). High levels of trimethylation at lysine 4 residue (H3K4) as well as H3 acetylation are found in HCC [63]. H3K4 hypertrimethylation has also been associated with poor prognosis of HCC [64].

Low levels of H3K4 dimethylation has also been described in hepatocellular tumors [65]. Alterations of H3K4 dimethylation appear to be a well-investigated marker in other tumors as well including prostate cancer and other gastrointestinal carcinomas [65,66]. This process is associated with expression of several oncogenes, some of which are related to a well-known tumor-promoting gene MYC [65].

Controversial results exist on the effects of another modification in histone proteins— H3K27 trimethylation appears to be lower at a certain region in a study by Li et al. [63], inducing a complex loop of protein expression changes. On the other hand, Cao et al. [62]

consider H3K27 trimethylation to be involved in silencing of TSGs. H2A monoubiquitination (H2Aub) is thought to be related with H3K27 trimethylation [67]. H2A monoubiquitination promotes H3K27 trimethylation on H2Aub-containing nucleosomes and can therefore be associated with HCC. A study on animal models demonstrated that H2A ubiquitination was decreased in HCC [68] and this effect was reversible with HDAC inhibitor treatment. In some HCC cases, H3K27 can be simultaneously acetylated and trimethylated and these tumors are thought to have a more aggressive phenotype. It was even suggested that modifications in H3K27 can predict the 5-year survival rate of HCC [69]. Interestingly these two modifications have opposite effects on DNA activation [70] and they were found in different regions (central euchromatin vs peripheral heterochromatin regions) [71]. This could correlate with the genes, which are responsible for mediating the correlation of histone modifications and tumor characteristics.

Hypertrimethylation of H3K4 and hyperacetylation of H3 and H4 have been described in the promoter of fatty acid synthase (FASN), which in turn leads to insulin resistance of HCC cells [72]. H3 acetylation at lysin 9 (K9) leads to a lowering of nucleosome density and this might be associated with tumorigenesis [73].

Phosphorylation of H2B and H3 is crucial for DNA repair, gene regulation, and cell division [65]. In HCV-associated HCC H2AX, phosphorylation causes inhibition of PRMT1 (protein arginine methyltransferase 1), leading to abnormalities in DNA repair [74]. Hyperphosphorylation has also been seen in viral hepatitis facilitating its progression to cancer [75].

Data on other histone modifications are rather limited. There is some evidence that sumoylation (small ubiquitin-like modification) is altered in HCC—the enzyme-mediating sumoylation, UBC9, is downregulated and it probably has some effect on cell cycle, cell growth and function, as UBC9 was found to regulate Bcl-2 expression [76].

Poly-ADP ribosylation has also been found to be increased in HCC cells compared to normal hepatocytes [77] and is thought to contribute to carcinogenesis in HBV-related tumors [78].

Histone acetylation has been described to regulate a number of genes. RIZ1 (retinoblastoma-interacting zinc finger gene) is one of them [63]. Interestingly, both DNA methylation and a low level of H3K9 acetylation contribute to this process [79].

The mechanisms causing histone modifications at certain sites in certain conditions are yet unknown, but the interaction with some environmental, as well as genetic changes have been described (Table 26.3) [52]. For example, integration of a hepatitis virus into the human genome might alter activity of methyltransferases [80]. In addition, histone modifications caused by somatic mutations in enzymes responsible for this process have also been described [81].

For some histone modifications, investigations have already identified the genes, whose expression is altered to mediate the effects of those changes on hepatocyte function or effects of HCC-causing viral injury. It has been shown that histone modifications determine alterations in hTERT transcription, which regulates telomerase activity, increasing the risk of HCC [82]. Reduction in levels of acetyltransferases lead to inactivation of apoptotic genes, resulting in a sustainable growth of hepatocytes [83–85]. Low levels of H3K4 dimethylation, already described above, seem to be a result of low levels of methylating and demethylating enzyme activity [65].

TABLE 26.3   Histone modification effects of hepatocellular carcinoma (HCC) risk factors [52].

HCC risk factor	Effects of histone modifications
HBV infection	Altered expression of critical cellular genes (hTERT, IGFBP-3 interleukin-4 receptor and metallothionein-1F and CDH6)
HCV infection	Increased histone deacetylation activity regulates iron metabolism through affecting hepcidin expression. Overexpression of protein phosphatase 2 A (PP2Ac), affecting the H4 acetylation and methylation and histone H2AX phosphorylation.
Alcoholism	CYP2E1 downregulation results in decreased mitochondrial oxidative stress and apoptotic potential. Adh, GST-yc2 are upregulated, while Lsdh, cytP4502c11 are downregulated.

HBV, hepatitis B virus; *HCV*, hepatitis C virus.

A very interesting link has been found between HCV infection and the pattern of histone modifications [75,83,86,87]. HCV infection inhibits activity of protein arginine methyltransferase 1 (PRMT1). This results in low levels of H4 methylation at arginine 3 and preserved phosphorylation of H2AX. These histone modifications change the expression of genes involved in HCC pathogenesis. Different mechanisms are thought to guide carcinogenesis in an alcohol-damaged liver—CYP enzymes are reported to be downregulated due to the altered histone structure [88,89].

Recent studies have identified that mutations in genes regulating epigenetic modifications (including histone changes) are important contributors to HCC development and progression. Mutations have been described in ARID1A and ARID2, which are parts of chromatin remodeling complex SWI/SNF as well as in histone-modifying enzymes [81,90—93].

Increased EZH2 (a member of HMT family) expression has been found in HCC and it's thought to correlate with tumor aggressiveness [94]. Its depletion reduces growth of tumor in vivo [95]. High levels of some demethylases have been found to correlate with tumor progression [96]. Activation of other HMTs (through mutations or other influences) has also been described in HCC cells [55]. It has even been proposed that mutated TP53 can alter HTM activity and, while the latter can be pharmacologically targeted, this could be discussed as a promising tool to treat TP53-mutated HCCs [97].

All the above listed modifications, studied in correlations with HCC provide just some isolated, often nonbound associations. Significant additional investigations are needed to understand the complex mechanism of how these epigenetic mechanisms interact with each other, genetic or environmental factors to contribute to hepatocellular carcinogenesis.

Some attempts have already been made to target histone modifications for treatment of HCC. Their reversible nature makes this approach even more attractive, especially given the fact that some HDAC inhibitors have already been well tested and approved by FDA for treatment of different disorders. One class of the medications being tested are HDAC inhibitors. Trichostatin A (TSA) is one of them. Bhattacharya et al. showed that it can restore H2A ubiquitination level, which is diminished in HCC [68]. TSA raises the levels of mRNA of deubiquitinase CYLD [98]. Investigations on cell lines have shown that TSA in combination with other medications (including sorafenib) has a promising effect on HCC therapy [99]. Resminostat, another HDACi, has also shown to improve sorafenib effect on HCC, by inducing change of cell phenotype (from mesenchymal to epithelial) and making them more sensitive to sorafenib [100]. Panobinostat is a potent HDACi, affecting proliferation, apoptosis, and cell reprogramming in HCC [101].

Therapeutic inhibition of HMTs and HDMs is also being tested for HCC treatment. Conflicting evidence exists on the effectiveness of a KMT6/EZH2 inhibitor GSK126 on HCC cells—Bugide et al. reported that this molecule improves cell-mediated immune response facilitating eradication of HCC cells [102], while on the other hand the same drug was seen to cause impaired T-cell response and increased growth of HCC [103].

Attempts have been made to use HMT inhibitors for HCC treatment. For example, deazaneplanocin A is an EZH2 inhibitor, which represses HCC cell proliferation in mouse models [104]. Another small molecule, AMI-1 decreases HCC cell survival and migration by inhibiting PRMTs [105]. Clinical trials on some of the drugs affecting histone modifications in HCC are currently running and hopefully will end up in significant improvement of HCC treatment results (Table 26.4) [8,101].

Considering all above-described progress in understanding histone modifications, they can be considered promising not only in studying the pathogenesis of HCC, but also for development of cancer treatment and approaches to more precise determination of prognosis and treatment sensitivity.

Conclusion

Accumulation of epigenetic alterations and genetic changes play a critical role in the cancer initiation and progression. Unlike genetic mutations, which are relatively rare events with permanent consequences on genes, epigenetic changes are reversible and responsive to environmental influences [106]. Epigenetic markers such as alterations in DNA methylation, histone modifications, and epigenetic reprogramming are known to occur during carcinogenesis [107], including HCC. In this chapter we summarized recent findings related to abnormal DNA methylation and histone modifications in HCC. Current progress in genome-wide methylation techniques allow researchers to identify distinct methylation profile of HCC, as well as its association with different etiological factors such as HBV infection and alcohol consumption [34].

We, also, highlight the potential of epigenetic drugs for the treatment of HCC. Epigenome-targeted therapies which aim to reprogram neoplastic cells have emerged in recent years. Histone deacetylase inhibitors and DNA methylation inhibitors are FDA-approved therapeutics that successfully applied in clinics for the treatment of hematological malignancies. In addition, many studies have proven the usefulness of combined epigenetic drugs. Moreover, epigenetic therapy can be combined with the chemo- and radiotherapies to provide certain treatments of the drug-resistant tumors [99,104].

In summary, although the major challenge remains early diagnoses of HCC due to silence progression, specific epigenetic marks could be used as biomarkers to diagnose or predict HCC. In addition, a better understanding of tumor genetics and epigenetics might help in development of novel therapies, including combination therapies that will effectively target molecular pathway of HCC.

TABLE 26.4   A selection of drugs affecting histone modifications currently being tested for hepatocellular carcinoma (HCC) treatment [8,101].

Drug	Disease	Phase	Reference/ Clinical trial number	Effect
DNMTi				
Decitabine + chemo- or immunotherapy	HCC	Phase I/II	NCT01799083	Resensitize tumor cells to sorafenib; effective and safe at low doses alone and in combination with chemo- or adoptive immunotherapy
Guadecitabine (SGI-110) + sorafenib + oxaliplatin	HCC	Phase II	NCT01752933	Suppress tumor growth and progression, induce reexpression of silenced TSGs, alone or in combination with sorafenib; pretreatment potentiates antitumor effects of oxaliplatin
Guadecitabine (SGI-110) + durvalumab	HCC and biliopancreatic tumors	Phase I	NCT03257761	Stable disease in 45% of patients; HR23B identified as response biomarker
TdCyd (4′-thio-2′-deoxycytidine)	Advanced solid tumors	Phase I	NCT02423057	
HDACi				
Belinostat (PXD-101)	HCC	Phase I/II	NCT00321594	
Resminostat + sorafenib	HCC	Phase I/II	NCT00943449	
HMTi				
MAK683	DLBCL, NPC, and other advanced solid tumors	Phase I/II	NCT02900651	
HDMi				
INCB059872	Advanced solid tumors and hematologic malignancies	Phase I/II	NCT02712905	
BETi				
BMS-986158	Advanced solid tumors and hematologic malignancies	Phase I/II	NCT02419417	
GS-5829	Solid tumors, lymphoma	Phase I	NCT02392611	
INCB057643	Advanced solid tumors and hematologic malignancies	Phase I/II	NCT02711137	

Conflict of interest

No potential conflicts of interest were disclosed.

References

[1] Ally A, Balasundaram M, Carlsen R, Chuah E, Clarke A, Dhalla N, et al. Comprehensive and integrative genomic characterization of hepatocellular carcinoma. Cell 2017;169(7):1327−41.

[2] Amaddeo G, Cao Q, Ladeiro Y, Imbeaud S, Nault JC, Jaoui D, et al. Integration of tumour and viral genomic characterisations in HBV-related hepatocellular carcinomas. Gut 2015;64(5):820−9.

[3] Herceg Z, Paliwal A. Epigenetic mechanisms in hepatocellular carcinoma: how environmental factors influence the epigenome. Mutat Res/Reviews Mutat Research 2011;727(3):55−61.

[4] Wiemer EA. The role of microRNAs in cancer: no small matter. Eur J Cancer 2007;43(10):1529−44.

[5] Murakami Y, Yasuda T, Saigo K, Urashima T, Toyoda H, Okanoue T, et al. Comprehensive analysis of microRNA expression patterns in hepatocellular carcinoma and non-tumorous tissues. Oncogene 2006;25 (17):2537−45.

[6] Jones PA, Baylin SB. The epigenomics of cancer. Cell 2007;128(4):683−92.

[7] Cheng Y, He C, Wang M, Ma X, Mo F, Yang S, et al. Targeting epigenetic regulators for cancer therapy: mechanisms and advances in clinical trials. Signal Transduct Target Ther 2019;4(1):1−39.

[8] Fernández-Barrena MG, Arechederra M, Colyn L, Berasain C, Avila MA. Epigenetics in hepatocellular carcinoma development and therapy: the tip of a big iceberg. JHEP Reports 2020;2(6):100167.

[9] Jaenisch R, Bird A. Epigenetic regulation of gene expression: how the genome integrates intrinsic and environmental signals. Nat Genet 2003;33(3):245−54.

[10] Sharma S, Kelly TK, Jones PA. Epigenetics in cancer. Carcinogenesis 2010;31(1):27−36.

[11] Kankava K, Kvaratskhelia E, Burkadze G, Kokhreidze I, Gogokhia N, Abzianidze E. LINE-1 methylation in blood and tissues of patients with breast cancer Georgian Med N 2018;(276):107−12PMID. Available from: 29697392.

[12] Bártová E, Krejčí J, Harničarová A, Galiová G, Kozubek S. Histone modifications and nuclear architecture: a review. J Histochem Cytochem 2008;56(8):711−21.

[13] Rice JC, Allis CD. Histone methylation vs histone acetylation: new insights into epigenetic regulation. Curr OpCell Biol 2001;13(3):263−73.

[14] Kaniskan HU, Martini ML, Jin J. Inhibitors of protein methyltransferases and demethylases. Chem Rev 2018;118(3):989−1068.

[15] Mellor J, Dudek P, Clynes D. A glimpse into the epigenetic landscape of gene regulation. Curr Opin Genet Dev 2008;18(2):116−22.

[16] Bannister AJ, Kouzarides T. Regulation of chromatin by histone modifications. Cell Res 2011;21(3):381−95.

[17] Gujral P, Mahajan V, Lissaman AC, Ponnampalam AP. Histone acetylation and the role of histone deacetylases in normal cyclic endometrium. Reprod Biol Endocrinol 2020;18(1):1−11.

[18] Ruvkun G. Glimpses of a tiny RNA world. Science 2001;294(5543):797−9.

[19] Bartel DP. MicroRNAs: target recognition and regulatory functions. Cell 2009;136(2):215−33.

[20] Takeshima H, Ushijima T. Accumulation of genetic and epigenetic alterations in normal cells and cancer risk. NPJ Precis Oncol 2019;3(1):1−8.

[21] Castven D, Fischer M, Becker D, Heinrich S, Andersen JB, Strand D, et al. Adverse genomic alterations and stemness features are induced by field cancerization in the microenvironment of hepatocellular carcinomas. Oncotarget 2017;8(30):48688.

[22] Curtius K, Wright NA, Graham TA. An evolutionary perspective on field cancerization. Nat Rev Cancer 2018;18(1):19−32.

[23] Zucman-Rossi J, Villanueva A, Nault JC, Llovet JM. Genetic landscape and biomarkers of hepatocellular carcinoma. Gastroenterology 2015;149(5):1226−39.

[24] Nishida N, Nishimura T, Nagasaka T, Ikai I, Ajay G, Boland CR. Extensive methylation is associated with β-catenin mutations in hepatocellular carcinoma: evidence for two distinct pathways of human hepatocarcinogenesis. Cancer Res 2007;67(10):4586−94.

[25] Nishida N, Kudo M, Nishimura T, Arizumi T, Takita M, Kitai S, et al. Unique association between global DNA hypomethylation and chromosomal alterations in human hepatocellular carcinoma. PLoS One 2013;8 (9):e72312.

[26] Lee S, Lee HJ, Kim JH, Lee HS, Jang JJ, Kang GH. Aberrant CpG island hypermethylation along multistep hepatocarcinogenesis. Am J Pathol 2003;163(4):1371—8.

[27] Liang Y, Ma B, Jiang P, Yang HM. Identification of methylation-regulated differentially expressed genes and related pathways in hepatocellular carcinoma: a study based on TCGA database and bioinformatics analysis. Front Oncol 2021;11:2040.

[28] Zheng Y, Huang Q, Ding Z, Liu T, Xue C, Sang X, Gu J, et al. Genome-wide DNA methylation analysis identifies candidate epigenetic markers and drivers of hepatocellular carcinoma. Brief Bioinforma 2018;19 (1):101—8.

[29] Alvarez H, Opalinska J, Zhou L, Sohal D, Fazzari MJ, Yu Y, et al. Widespread hypomethylation occurs early and synergizes with gene amplification during esophageal carcinogenesis. PLoS Genet 2011;7(3):e1001356.

[30] Feber A, Dhami P, Dong L, de Winter P, Tan WS, Martínez-Fernández M, et al. UroMark—a urinary biomarker assay for the detection of bladder cancer. Clin epigenetics 2017;9(1):1—10.

[31] Tangkijvanich P, Hourpai N, Rattanatanyong P, Wisedopas N, Mahachai V, Mutirangura A. Serum LINE-1 hypomethylation as a potential prognostic marker for hepatocellular carcinoma. Clin Chim Acta 2007;379 (1—2):127—33.

[32] Zheng X, Wu Q, Wu H, Leung KS, Wong MH, Liu X, Cheng L, et al. Evaluating the consistency of gene methylation in liver cancer using bisulfite sequencing data. Front Cell Dev Biol 2021;9:671302.

[33] Yang B, Guo M, Herman JG, Clark DP. Aberrant promoter methylation profiles of tumor suppressor genes in hepatocellular carcinoma. Am J Pathol 2003;163(3):1101—7.

[34] Mah WC, Lee CG. DNA methylation: potential biomarker in Hepatocellular Carcinoma. Biomarker Res 2014;2(1):1—13.

[35] Gao F, Liang H, Lu H, Wang J, Xia M, Yuan Z, et al. Global analysis of DNA methylation in hepatocellular carcinoma by a liquid hybridization capture-based bisulfite sequencing approach. Clin Epigenetics 2015;7(1):1—11.

[36] Yamada N, Yasui K, Dohi O, Gen Y, Tomie A, Kitaichi T, et al. Genome-wide DNA methylation analysis in hepatocellular carcinoma. Oncol Rep 2016;35(4):2228—36.

[37] Hlady RA, Tiedemann RL, Puszyk W, Zendejas I, Roberts LR, Choi JH, et al. Epigenetic signatures of alcohol abuse and hepatitis infection during human hepatocarcinogenesis. Oncotarget 2014;5(19):9425.

[38] Nishida N, Kudo M, Nagasaka T, Ikai I, Goel A. Characteristic patterns of altered DNA methylation predict emergence of human hepatocellular carcinoma. Hepatology 2012;56(3):994—1003.

[39] Um TH, Kim H, Oh BK, Kim MS, Kim KS, Jung G, Park YN, et al. Aberrant CpG island hypermethylation in dysplastic nodules and early HCC of hepatitis B virus-related human multistep hepatocarcinogenesis. J Hepatol 2011;54(5):939—47.

[40] Tao R, Li J, Xin J, Wu J, Guo J, Zhang L, et al. Methylation profile of single hepatocytes derived from hepatitis B virus-related hepatocellular carcinoma. PLoS One 2011;6(5):e19862.

[41] Villanueva A, Portela A, Sayols S, Battiston C, Hoshida Y, Méndez-González JHEPTROMIC Consortium. DNA methylation-based prognosis and epidrivers in hepatocellular carcinoma. Hepatology 2015;61 (6):1945—56.

[42] Qiu J, Peng B, Tang Y, Qian Y, Guo P, Li M, et al. CpG methylation signature predicts recurrence in early-stage hepatocellular carcinoma: results from a multicenter study. J Clin Oncol 2017;35(7):734—42.

[43] Chang C, Kong W, Mou X, Wang S. Investigating the correlation between DNA methylation and immune-associated genes of lung adenocarcinoma based on a competing endogenous RNA network. Mol Med Rep 2020;22(4):3173—82.

[44] Jung H, Kim HS, Kim JY, Sun JM, Ahn JS, Ahn MJ, et al. DNA methylation loss promotes immune evasion of tumours with high mutation and copy number load. Nat Commun 2019;10(1):1—12.

[45] Seager RJ, Hajal C, Spill F, Kamm RD, Zaman MH. Dynamic interplay between tumour, stroma and immune system can drive or prevent tumour progression. Convergent Sci Phys Oncol 2017;3(3):034002.

[46] Hoos A, Britten CM. The immuno-oncology framework: enabling a new era of cancer therapy. Oncoimmunology 2012;1(3):334—9.

[47] Tchekmedyian N, Gray JE, Creelan BC, Chiappori AA, Beg AA, Soliman H, et al. Propelling immunotherapy combinations into the clinic. Oncology 2015;29(12) 990-990.

[48] Fu J, Zhang Z, Zhou L, Qi Z, Xing S, Lv J, et al. Impairment of CD4 + cytotoxic T cells predicts poor survival and high recurrence rates in patients with hepatocellular carcinoma. Hepatology 2013;58(1):139–49.

[49] Xu Q, Hu Y, Chen S, Zhu Y, Li S, Shen F, et al. Immunological significance of prognostic DNA methylation sites in hepatocellular carcinoma. Front Mol Biosci 2021;8:448.

[50] Li W, Zhou XJ. Methylation extends the reach of liquid biopsy in cancer detection. Nat Rev Clin Oncol 2020;17(11):655–6.

[51] Xu RH, Wei W, Krawczyk M, Wang W, Luo H, Flagg K, et al. Circulating tumour DNA methylation markers for diagnosis and prognosis of hepatocellular carcinoma. Nat Mater 2017;16(11):1155–61.

[52] Yousef MH, El-Fawal HA, Abdelnaser A. Hepigenetics: a review of epigenetic modulators and potential therapies in hepatocellular carcinoma. BioMed Res Int 2020;2020.

[53] Peterson CL, Laniel MA. Histones and histone modifications. Curr Biol 2004;14(14):R546–51.

[54] Fu W, Gao L, Huang C, Yao J, Lin Y, Bai B, et al. Mechanisms and importance of histone modification enzymes in targeted therapy for hepatobiliary cancers. Discovery Med 2019;28(151):17–28.

[55] Marmorstein R, Zhou MM. Writers and readers of histone acetylation: structure, mechanism, and inhibition. Cold Spring Harb Perspect Biol 2014;6(7):a018762.

[56] Zhao Z, Shilatifard A. Epigenetic modifications of histones in cancer. Genome Biol 2019;20(1):1–16.

[57] Proietti G, Wang Y, Rainone G, Mecinović J. Effect of lysine side chain length on histone lysine acetyltransferase catalysis. Sci Rep 2020;10:13046.

[58] Ler SY, LEuNG CHW, Khin LW, Lu GD, Salto-Tellez M, Hartman M, et al. HDAC1 and HDAC2 independently predict mortality in hepatocellular carcinoma by a competing risk regression model in a Southeast Asian population. Oncol Rep 2015;34(5):2238–50.

[59] Wu H, Yang TY, Li Y, Ye WL, Liu F, He XS, et al. Tumor necrosis factor receptor–associated factor 6 promotes hepatocarcinogenesis by interacting with histone deacetylase 3 to enhance c-myc gene expression and protein stability. Hepatology 2020;71(1):148–63.

[60] Kumar R, Deivendran S, Santhoshkumar TR, Pillai MR. Signaling coupled epigenomic regulation of gene expression. Oncogene 2017;36(43):5917–26.

[61] Sabbattini P, Sjoberg M, Nikic S, Frangini A, Holmqvist PH, Kunowska N, et al. An H3K9/S10 methyl-phospho switch modulates Polycomb and Pol II binding at repressed genes during differentiation. Mol Biol Cell 2014;25(6):904–15.

[62] Cao R, Zhang Y. The functions of E (Z)/EZH2-mediated methylation of lysine 27 in histone H3. Curr Opin Genet Dev 2004;14(2):155–64.

[63] Li D, Zeng Z. Epigenetic regulation of histone H3 in the process of hepatocellular tumorigenesis. Biosci Rep 2019;39(8) BSR20191815.

[64] He C, Xu J, Zhang J, Xie D, Ye H, Xiao Z, et al. High expression of trimethylated histone H3 lysine 4 is associated with poor prognosis in hepatocellular carcinoma. Hum Pathol 2012;43(9):1425–35.

[65] Magerl C, Ellinger J, Braunschweig T, Kremmer E, Koch LK, Höller T, et al. H3K4 dimethylation in hepatocellular carcinoma is rare compared with other hepatobiliary and gastrointestinal carcinomas and correlates with expression of the methylase Ash2 and the demethylase LSD1. Hum Pathol 2010;41(2):181–9.

[66] Seligson DB, Horvath S, Shi T, Yu H, Tze S, Grunstein M, Kurdistani SK, et al. Global histone modification patterns predict risk of prostate cancer recurrence. Nature 2005;435(7046):1262–6.

[67] Kalb R, Latwiel S, Baymaz HI, Jansen PW, Müller CW, Vermeulen M, Müller J, et al. Histone H2A monoubiquitination promotes histone H3 methylation in Polycomb repression. Nat Struct Mol Biol 2014;21(6):569–71.

[68] Bhattacharya S, Reddy D, Ingle A, Khade B, Gupta S. Brief communication: featured article: histone H2A mono-ubiquitination and cellular transformation are inversely related in N-nitrosodiethylamine-induced hepatocellular carcinoma. Exp Biol Med 2016;241(16):1739–44.

[69] Hayashi A, Yamauchi N, Shibahara J, Kimura H, Morikawa T, Ishikawa S, et al. Concurrent activation of acetylation and tri-methylation of H3K27 in a subset of hepatocellular carcinoma with aggressive behavior. PLoS One 2014;9(3):e91330.

[70] Ong CT, Corces VG. Enhancer function: new insights into the regulation of tissue-specific gene expression. Nat Rev Genet 2011;12(4):283–93.

[71] Littau VC, Allfrey VG, Frenster JH, Mirsky AE. Active and inactive regions of nuclear chromatin as revealed by electron microscope autoradiography. Proc Natl Acad Sci USA 1964;52(1):93.

432 26. Epigenetic biomarkers in diagnosis, prognosis, and treatment of hepatocellular carcinoma

[72] Du X, Cai C, Yao J, Zhou Y, Yu H, Shen W. Histone modifications in FASN modulated by sterol regulatory element-binding protein 1c and carbohydrate responsive-element binding protein under insulin stimulation are related to NAFLD. Biochem Biophys Res Commun 2017;483(1):409—17.

[73] Nishida H, Suzuki T, Kondo S, Miura H, Fujimura YI, Hayashizaki Y. Histone H3 acetylated at lysine 9 in promoter is associated with low nucleosome density in the vicinity of transcription start site in human cell. Chromosome Res 2006;14(2):203—11.

[74] Thompson LL, Guppy BJ, Sawchuk L, Davie JR, McManus KJ. Regulation of chromatin structure via histone post-translational modification and the link to carcinogenesis. Cancer Metastasis Rev 2013;32(3):363—76.

[75] Duong FH, Christen V, Lin S, Heim MH. Hepatitis C virus—induced up-regulation of protein phosphatase 2A inhibits histone modification and DNA damage repair. Hepatology 2010;51(3):741—51.

[76] Fang S, Qiu J, Wu Z, Bai T, Guo W. Down-regulation of UBC9 increases the sensitivity of hepatocellular carcinoma to doxorubicin. Oncotarget 2017;8(30):49783.

[77] Nomura F, Yaguchi M, Togawa A, Miyazaki M, Isobe K, Miyake M, et al. Enhancement of poly-adenosine diphosphate-ribosylation in human hepatocellular carcinoma. J Gastroenterol Hepatol 2000;15(5):529—35.

[78] Na TY, Ka NL, Rhee H, Kyeong D, Kim MH, Seong JK, et al. Interaction of hepatitis B virus X protein with PARP1 results in inhibition of DNA repair in hepatocellular carcinoma. Oncogene 2016;35(41):5435—45.

[79] Zhang C, Li H, Wang Y, Liu W, Zhang Q, Zhang T, et al. Epigenetic inactivation of the tumor suppressor gene RIZ1 in hepatocellular carcinoma involves both DNA methylation and histone modifications. J Hepatol 2010;53(5):889—95.

[80] Sung WK, Zheng H, Li S, Chen R, Liu X, Li Y, et al. Genome-wide survey of recurrent HBV integration in hepatocellular carcinoma. Nat Genet 2012;44(7):765—9.

[81] Schulze K, Imbeaud S, Letouzé E, Alexandrov LB, Calderaro J, Rebouissou S, et al. Exome sequencing of hepatocellular carcinomas identifies new mutational signatures and potential therapeutic targets. Nat Genet 2015;47(5):505—11.

[82] Horikawa I, Barrett JC. Transcriptional regulation of the telomerase hTERT gene as a target for cellular and viral oncogenic mechanisms. Carcinogenesis 2003;24(7):1167—76.

[83] Domovitz T, Gal-Tanamy M. Tracking down the epigenetic footprint of HCV-induced hepatocarcinogenesis. J Clin Med 2021;10:551.

[84] Shon JK, Shon BH, Park IY, Lee SU, Fa L, Chang KY, et al. Hepatitis B virus-X protein recruits histone deacetylase 1 to repress insulin-like growth factor binding protein 3 transcription. Virus Res 2009;139(1):14—21.

[85] Zheng DL, Zhang L, Cheng N, Xu X, Deng Q, Teng XM, et al. Epigenetic modification induced by hepatitis B virus X protein via interaction with de novo DNA methyltransferase DNMT3A. J Hepatol 2009;50(2):377—87.

[86] Sawan C, Vaissière T, Murr R, Herceg Z. Epigenetic drivers and genetic passengers on the road to cancer. Mutat Res 2008;642(1—2):1—13.

[87] Huang J. Current progress in epigenetic research for hepatocarcinomagenesis. Sci China C Life Sci 2009;52(1):31—42.

[88] Yang H, Nie Y, Li Y, Wan YJY. Histone modification-mediated CYP2E1 gene expression and apoptosis of HepG2 cells. Exp Biol Med 2010;235(1):32—9.

[89] Pal-Bhadra M, Bhadra U, Jackson DE, Mamatha L, Park PH, Shukla SD. Distinct methylation patterns in histone H3 at Lys-4 and Lys-9 correlate with up-& down-regulation of genes by ethanol in hepatocytes. Life Sci 2007;81(12):979—87.

[90] Fujimoto A, Totoki Y, Abe T, Boroevich KA, Hosoda F, Nguyen HH, et al. Whole-genome sequencing of liver cancers identifies etiological influences on mutation patterns and recurrent mutations in chromatin regulators. Nat Genet 2012;44(7):760—4.

[91] Li M, Zhao H, Zhang X, Wood LD, Anders RA, Choti MA, et al. Inactivating mutations of the chromatin remodeling gene ARID2 in hepatocellular carcinoma. Nat Genet 2011;43(9):828—9.

[92] Totoki Y, Tatsuno K, Covington KR, Ueda H, Creighton CJ, Kato M, et al. Trans-ancestry mutational landscape of hepatocellular carcinoma genomes. Nat Genet 2014;46(12):1267—73.

[93] Kan Z, Zheng H, Liu X, Li S, Barber TD, Gong Z, et al. Whole-genome sequencing identifies recurrent mutations in hepatocellular carcinoma. Genome Res 2013;23(9):1422—33.

[94] Au SLK, Ng IOL, Wong CM. Epigenetic dysregulation in hepatocellular carcinoma: focus on polycomb group proteins. Front Med 2013;7(2):231—41.

[95] Chen Y, Lin MC, Yao H, Wang H, Zhang AQ, Yu J, et al. Lentivirus-mediated RNA interference targeting enhancer of zeste homolog 2 inhibits hepatocellular carcinoma growth through down-regulation of stathmin. Hepatology 2007;46(1):200–8.

[96] Yamada D, Kobayashi S, Yamamoto H, Tomimaru Y, Noda T, Uemura M, et al. Role of the hypoxia-related gene, JMJD1A, in hepatocellular carcinoma: clinical impact on recurrence after hepatic resection. Ann Surg Oncol 2012;19(3):355–64.

[97] Ding X, He M, Chan AW, Song QX, Sze SC, Chen H, et al. Genomic and epigenomic features of primary and recurrent hepatocellular carcinomas. Gastroenterology 2019;157(6):1630–45.

[98] Kotantaki P, Mosialos G. The expression of tumor suppressor gene Cyld is upregulated by histone deacetylace inhibitors in human hepatocellular carcinoma cell lines. Cell Biochem Funct 2016;34(7):465–8.

[99] Chen JCH, Chuang HY, Liao YJ, Hsu FT, Chen YC, Wang WH, Hwang JJ, et al. Enhanced cytotoxicity of human hepatocellular carcinoma cells following pretreatment with sorafenib combined with trichostatin A. Oncol Lett 2019;17(1):638–45.

[100] Soukupova J, Bertran E, Peñuelas-Haro I, Urdiroz-Urricelqui U, Borgman M, Kohlhof H, Fabregat I, et al. Resminostat induces changes in epithelial plasticity of hepatocellular carcinoma cells and sensitizes them to sorafenib-induced apoptosis. Oncotarget 2017;8(66):110367.

[101] Toh TB, Lim JJ, Chow EKH. Epigenetics of hepatocellular carcinoma. Clin Transl Med 2019;8(1):13.

[102] Bugide S, Green MR, Wajapeyee N. Inhibition of enhancer of zeste homolog 2 (EZH2) induces natural killer cell-mediated eradication of hepatocellular carcinoma cells. Proc Natl Acad Sci 2018;115(15):E3509–18.

[103] Wei Y, Lao XM, Xiao X, Wang XY, Wu ZJ, Zeng QH, et al. Plasma cell polarization to the immunoglobulin G phenotype in hepatocellular carcinomas involves epigenetic alterations and promotes hepatoma progression in mice. Gastroenterology 2019;156(6):1890–904.

[104] Chiba T, Suzuki E, Negishi M, Saraya A, Miyagi S, Konuma T, et al. 3-Deazaneplanocin A is a promising therapeutic agent for the eradication of tumor-initiating hepatocellular carcinoma cells. Int J Cancer 2012;130(11):2557–67.

[105] Zhang B, Dong S, Li Z, Lu L, Zhang S, Chen X, et al. Targeting protein arginine methyltransferase 5 inhibits human hepatocellular carcinoma growth via the downregulation of beta-catenin. J Transl Med 2015;13(1):1–10.

[106] Baylin SB, Jones PA. Epigenetic determinants of cancer. Cold Spring Harb Perspect Biol 2016;8(9):a019505.

[107] Miranda-Furtado CL, Dos Santos Luciano MC, Silva Santos RD, Furtado GP, Moraes MO, Pessoa C. Epidrugs: targeting epigenetic marks in cancer treatment. Epigenetics. 2019;14(12):1164–76.

Index

Note: Page numbers followed by "*f*" and "*t*" refer to figures and tables, respectively.

Printed in the United States
by Baker & Taylor Publisher Services